M000205145

The Architecture of Sharpe, Paley and Austin

Research for this book has been aided by a grant from the Paul Mellon Centre for Studies in British Art, and photography has been assisted by a Dorothy Stroud Bursary from the Society of Architectural Historians of Great Britain. This generous assistance is gratefully acknowledged.

The Architecture of Sharpe, Paley and Austin

Geoff Brandwood

with Tim Austin, John Hughes and James Price and photographs by Mark Watson

Published by English Heritage, The Engine House, Fire Fly Avenue, Swindon SN2 2EH
www.english-heritage.org.uk

English Heritage is the Government's statutory adviser on all aspects of the historic environment.

First published 2012

ISBN 978 1 84802 049 8
Product code 51526

British Library Cataloguing in Publication data
A CIP catalogue record for this book is available from the British Library.

Brought to publication by Jess Ward, Publishing, English Heritage

Typeset in Charter 9.25pt on 11.75pt

Edited by Wendy Toole
Indexed by Geoff Brandwood
Page layout by Anthony Cohen

Printed in UK by Butler Tanner and Dennis

CONTENTS

Preface and acknowledgments vi

Note on geography and measurements viii

Abbreviations ix

The Sharpe, Paley and Austin families and their connections x

Introduction: a practice like no other 1

1 Edmund Sharpe: architect and scholar 7

2 Developing the practice: Edward Graham Paley 48

3 Paley & Austin, 1868–1886 80

4 Paley, Austin & Paley/Austin & Paley, 1886–1915 134

5 The last years of the practice: Harry Paley 178

Appendix 1 Edmund Sharpe: engineer, businessman and reformer 188

Appendix 2 Pupils and others associated with the office 198

Appendix 3 Contractors and craftsmen 202

Appendix 4 Distant commissions and their origins 207

Appendix 5 Catalogue of works and projects 210

Notes 260

Bibliography 272

Index 274

PREFACE AND ACKNOWLEDGEMENTS

This book has been a long time in gestation and thanks are due to a great many people who have helped make it possible. My interest in the architects at its centre began in the late 1980s after I had completed my PhD research into 19th-century church-building and restoration in Leicestershire. I was acutely aware that I knew much less about church architecture in the late Victorian and Edwardian periods than I should have liked. Part of the remedy for this deficiency was extensive visits to many of the finer churches built after about 1870. My particular hero was Temple Moore for the sheer beauty of his buildings and masterly handling of space, and this enthusiasm led on to writing a book about him and his work, which was published in 1997. Much of Moore's best work lies in the North, in Yorkshire, and for me the other great discovery was also in the North, but on the other side of the Pennines. Here I was immensely impressed by the work of another great architectural practice – Paley & Austin (and Austin & Paley). I claim no originality for this realisation since the architectural press, competition assessors and clients all recognised the sheer quality of the firm's work in its own day. During the past half-century it has attracted many enthusiastic admirers.

After the Great War, however, Victorian architecture became a subject for excoriation, if not mirth, among those of a modernist disposition, but in the late 1950s there began a reaction against such views. Many will have first noticed buildings by the practice thanks to entries in Peter Fleetwood-Hesketh's *Murray's Lancashire* of 1955, a gazetteer-style volume which was part of an aborted series covering English counties. The campaign to save the Euston 'Arch' in the late 1950s provoked a furious response, which led to the formation of the Victorian Society and signalled a growing appreciation of all things from this hitherto disdained past. It was about this time that serious study of the architects in this book began. The founder of the practice, the multi-faceted Edmund Sharpe, was the subject of an excellent MA thesis for Liverpool University by Robert Jolley in 1966. At the same time (1965), David McLaughlin, then a pupil at Rossall School, had his eyes opened to architecture by Paley's work there and developed a life-long interest in the practice. He gained an RIBA research award to study the post-Sharpe years and wrote the admirable descriptions of the firm's churches in the *The Faber Guide to Victorian Churches* (1989). He contributed information to Nikolaus Pevsner's immensely influential Buildings of England series, which in 1969 described the buildings of the historic county of Lancashire in two volumes. Pevsner was most enthusiastic about the firm's work during its most productive years when Hubert Austin was a partner, and made many references to its diversity and invention. From the late 1960s, Philip Browning, Assistant City Planning Officer for Liverpool, also studied the Paley & Austin/Austin & Paley years and did much to enthuse others about the work of the practice.

Both Robert Jolley and Geoffrey Beard were involved in setting up a small exhibition in 1977 at the University of Lancaster Visual Arts Centre to mark the centenary of Sharpe's death, and Jolley produced a small booklet to accompany it. Paley & Austin's churches were the subject of a perceptive Sheffield University BA thesis by John Fidler in 1974 (a copy of which he kindly supplied to me). From 1996 and building on the work of Robert Jolley, John Hughes embarked on a further exploration of the life and career of the remarkable Edmund Sharpe, which unearthed much new material and in 2010 culminated in a three-volume, privately printed work which brought all of this together. A further study has been Mark D Pearce's Architectural Association diploma thesis of 2006 about the development of the ecclesiastical work of the firm. James Price's interest in the firm went back much further, to the start of the 1970s. This resulted in the first published study of the practice as a whole in 1994. Any intentions on my part around this time to produce a larger work were halted by Jim's more substantial volume about the practice published in 1998. But it became apparent that a still wider-ranging, fully illustrated study was needed, and so the idea of the present book took shape. This was kick-started on the steps of the Esplanade Hotel in Llandudno at the Victorian Society's AGM weekend in 2006 when Mark Watson offered to take photographs for such a book for me. The idea of publication was enthusiastically adopted by English Heritage and for this I would like to thank John Hudson, Head of Publishing, and Robin Taylor, Managing Editor: John Minnis kindly reviewed the text in its early stages, and the excellent maps and charts were drawn up by Philip Sinton and Anthony Cohen respectively. I am grateful to Wendy Toole for her expert copy-editing and many useful suggestions, and would especially thank Jess Ward who steered the whole project to a successful conclusion.

The book has been made possible through the collaboration of four individuals. Mark Watson, already mentioned, was responsible for most of the photography, and accompanying him on many excursions provided both a pleasure and a photographic education. Tim Austin, great-grandson of

Hubert, has been an amazing source of information and his meticulous, skilful researches into the manifold families involved with the practice, their contacts and the patronage of the firm has brought to light much entirely new information. Without his help the book would be immeasurably poorer and it would lack the family photographs which add an extra dimension to it. John Hughes has been very generous in sharing the data he gathered since becoming interested in the extraordinary, multi-talented Edmund Sharpe in the 1990s; the material on Sharpe presented here is very largely my distillation of John's achievement. The maps of Sharpe's travels in Europe in 1832–5 are based on reconstructions of his route compiled by Robert Jolley and John Hughes from letters written by Sharpe to William Whewell, now in the Whewell archive at Trinity College, Cambridge. The fourth colleague, James Price, is the real pioneer of Sharpe, Paley and Austin publication, and he has placed his extensive knowledge and records at the disposal of the project, drafted various sections of the text, and teased out documentation about large numbers of buildings. He also undertook the great labour of mapping the firm's commissions, and this work has been expertly drawn up by Philip Sinton. Tim, John and Jim have all read drafts of the book and it benefits from their numerous helpful suggestions.

I would also like to acknowledge the help provided by the staff at record offices in Lancashire, Cumbria and Cheshire, and am especially grateful for the personal assistance of Aidan Jones (Barrow) and his successor Michael Stephens, and Alex Miller (Leigh). David McLaughlin gave access to his records about the firm and provided historic photographs. Colin Stansfield has also been of great assistance in supplying much helpful documentary information on Lancaster buildings drawn from his many years of research: numerous minor works by the firm would otherwise have gone undetected. Others to whom I am grateful are, in various ways, and in alphabetical order, Michael Andrews, Tim Ashworth, Neil Barrow, Martin Baxendale, John Beckett, Marion Blackburn, Steven Brindle, Alan Brooks, Clare Brown (Lambeth Palace Library), Lord Cavendish (permission to photograph within Holker Hall), Martin Cherry (Library and Museum of Freemasonry), Neil Darlington, Ken Davies (Lancashire Sites & Monuments Record), Jean Fryer, Stephen Gardner (Conservation Officer for Lancaster), Les Gilpin, Clare Hartwell, Paul Hatch, Sir Bernard de Hoghton, Matthew Hyde, Katy Iliffe (Archivist at Sedbergh School), Tony Jackson (for loan of Paley sketchbooks and Hatch photo album), Alwyne Loyd, Andrew Martindale, Peter Mason, Paula Moorhouse (Manchester Local Studies Library), Peter Robinson (Furness Railway archival material), Joseph Sharples and Christopher Webster.

My colleagues would also like to acknowledge their own debts. Tim Austin wishes to thank his cousin Fanny Mitchell who first drew him into family history; his cousin Francis Sandison who first gave him family trees and who loaned family photograph albums; John Hughes for help in liberating the Austin Langshaw Archive, now placed in Lancaster University; Madeline Goold for telling him about the Austin Paley Archive in Lancaster Museum; and, in particular, Ian, Gill and Ella Cutts, for their support in many ways over many years, without which he would probably not have participated in this work. John Hughes would like to thank Barrie Bullen (Reading University), Fiona Colbert (St John's College, Cambridge), Robert Cornish, Roger Fawthrop, Valerie Fox, Elspeth Griffiths (formerly Librarian and Archivist at Sedbergh School), Ray Jackson, Robert Jolley, and the late Joan Leach (historian of Knutsford). James Price expresses his thanks for assistance in various ways from John Champness, Stephen Gardner, Caroline Hull, Lois Louden, Mark Pearce, Peter Robinson, Colin Stansfield, Jenny Suggitt and Madgie Vintin. Both John and Jim gratefully acknowledge the help they both received from Jenny Loveridge, formerly Senior Reference Librarian at Lancaster Reference Library.

The practice worked for a little over a century and was immensely prolific. I am only too well aware that there is so much more that could be said and illustrated. Many fine buildings are inevitably relegated to brief mentions or references in the Catalogue (*see* Appendix 5), while there are several subjects that could benefit from fuller discussion, such as church restorations, furnishings and fittings, and the firm's involvement with stained glass makers. However, research can extend interminably, which, sad to say, can easily result in no publication at all. Whatever the failings of the present work may be, I take full responsibility for them.

During its most creative years, the firm's work stands comparison with that by any of the great names of Victorian and Edwardian architecture. It is very much valued in its heartland of the north-west, and I hope that this book will help to spread knowledge and appreciation of it more widely.

Geoff Brandwood
Richmond-on-Thames
December 2011

NOTE ON GEOGRAPHY

So much of the work covered by this book was in the ancient county of Lancashire. This stretched north from the Mersey, took in the great cities of Liverpool and Manchester and extended as far as a wide and deep tract of country on the north side of Morecambe Bay. The latter could only be reached over land by passing through the south-west tip of Westmorland where it embraced the estuary of the River Kent or, as was the normal practice until Victorian times, by sea or at low tide over the treacherous but then well-understood sands of the bay. English local government presents shifting sands too, in this case in terms of locating places for readers. The ruling principle adopted is the use of modern ceremonial counties as established since 1974. All places mentioned (apart from a few well-known towns and cities) are in the ceremonial county of Lancashire unless otherwise stated. With Cumbria, which in 1974 was the amalgam of two counties plus the inclusion of parts of two others, it seems advisable to indicate the previous county where places lay.

Abbreviations for non-Lancashire places are given as follows:

Ch	Cheshire
D	County Durham
CuC	Cumbria (formerly Cumberland)
CuL	Cumbria (formerly Lancashire)
CuW	Cumbria (formerly Westmorland)
CuWY	Cumbria (formerly West Riding of Yorkshire)
EY	East Yorkshire
GM	Greater Manchester
Me	Merseyside
NY	North Yorkshire
St	Staffordshire
WY	West Yorkshire

NOTE ON MEASUREMENTS

Imperial measurements are used throughout the text; please see the conversion table right, for details of metric equivalents.

Conversion Table

1ft = 304.8mm
1 yard = 0.914m
1 mile = 1.6km
1 acre = 0.4 hectares

ABBREVIATIONS

AF Austin family
ALA Austin Langshaw Archive, Rare Books and Archives, Lancaster University
A&P Austin & Paley
APA Austin Paley Archive, Lancaster Museum, MS LM 86/129.
B *The Builder*
BA *British Architect*
BarrN *Barrow News*
BE The Buildings of England series, latest edition as at 2011 for the appropriate county (unless extra clarification is required)
BH *Barrow Herald*
BN *Building News*
BS *Blackburn Standard*
BW The Buildings of Wales series latest edition (then as BE)
C(C) contractor(s)
CALS Cheshire Archives & Local Studies
CBC Church Building Commissioners
CCT Churches Conservation Trust
ChBldr *Church Builder*
CHLLD Community History Library, Lancaster District
CRO(B) Cumbria Record Office (Barrow)
CRO(K) Cumbria Record Office (Kendal)
CRO(W) Cumbria Record Office (Whitehaven)
CS Colin Stansfield
CW Clerk of Works
DM David McLaughlin
Eccl *The Ecclesiologist*
EGP Edward Graham Paley
ERYAO East Riding of Yorkshire Archive Office
ES Edmund Sharpe
ex info information from
FR Furness Railway Company
FS foundation stone
GB Geoff Brandwood
HAP Henry Anderson Paley
HJA Hubert James Austin
ICBS Incorporated Church Building Society papers, Lambeth Palace Library (file no)
IT invitation to tender
JB/JP Notes by John Brassington ex info James Price
JMH John Michael Hughes
JP James Price: in the context of references, *see* Price, 1998 (*see* bibliography)
JTD James Tate junior's diaries, 1844–61 (8 vols), Tate Archive, Peter Wenham Memorial Trust, Richmondshire Museum, Richmond
JWW John William Whittaker
K *Kelly's Directory of …* [appropriate county (Lancashire unless otherwise stated)]
KCN *Kendal & County News*
LBS English Heritage, Listed Building System (reference no). Descriptions viewable on www.imagesofengland.co.uk
LGaz *Lancaster Gazette*
LGuar *Lancaster Guardian*
LL Lancaster Library
LL 1, 2 or 3 volumes of drawings by 'Austin & Paley', numbered 1 to 3 formerly in Lancaster Library but now transferred to the LRO and renumbered in their archives as DDX 2743 acc 10980 vols 1, 2 and 3 respectively.
LM Lancaster Museum
LMerc *Leeds Mercury*
LRO Lancashire Record Office, Preston
LSMR Lancashire Sites & Monuments Record
LStd *Lancaster Standard*
MALS Manchester Archive and Local Studies
MRO Manchester Record Office
NADFAS National Association of Decorative and Fine Arts Societies (report, year)
NS National Society for Promoting Religious Knowledge records in the Church of England Record Centre, London
PA&P Paley, Austin & Paley
P&A Paley & Austin
PG *Preston Guardian*
RIBA RIBA, Drawings & Archives collection, V&A Museum
S&P Sharpe & Paley
SSGM Sedbergh School, Governors' Minutes
SUA *Soulby's Ulverston Advertiser*
TBA Timothy Bowes Austin
UM *Ulverston Mirror & Furness Reflector*
VCH *Victoria County History: Lancashire*
WAS Wigan Archive Services

THE SHARPE, PALEY AND AUSTIN FAMILIES AND THEIR CONNECTIONS

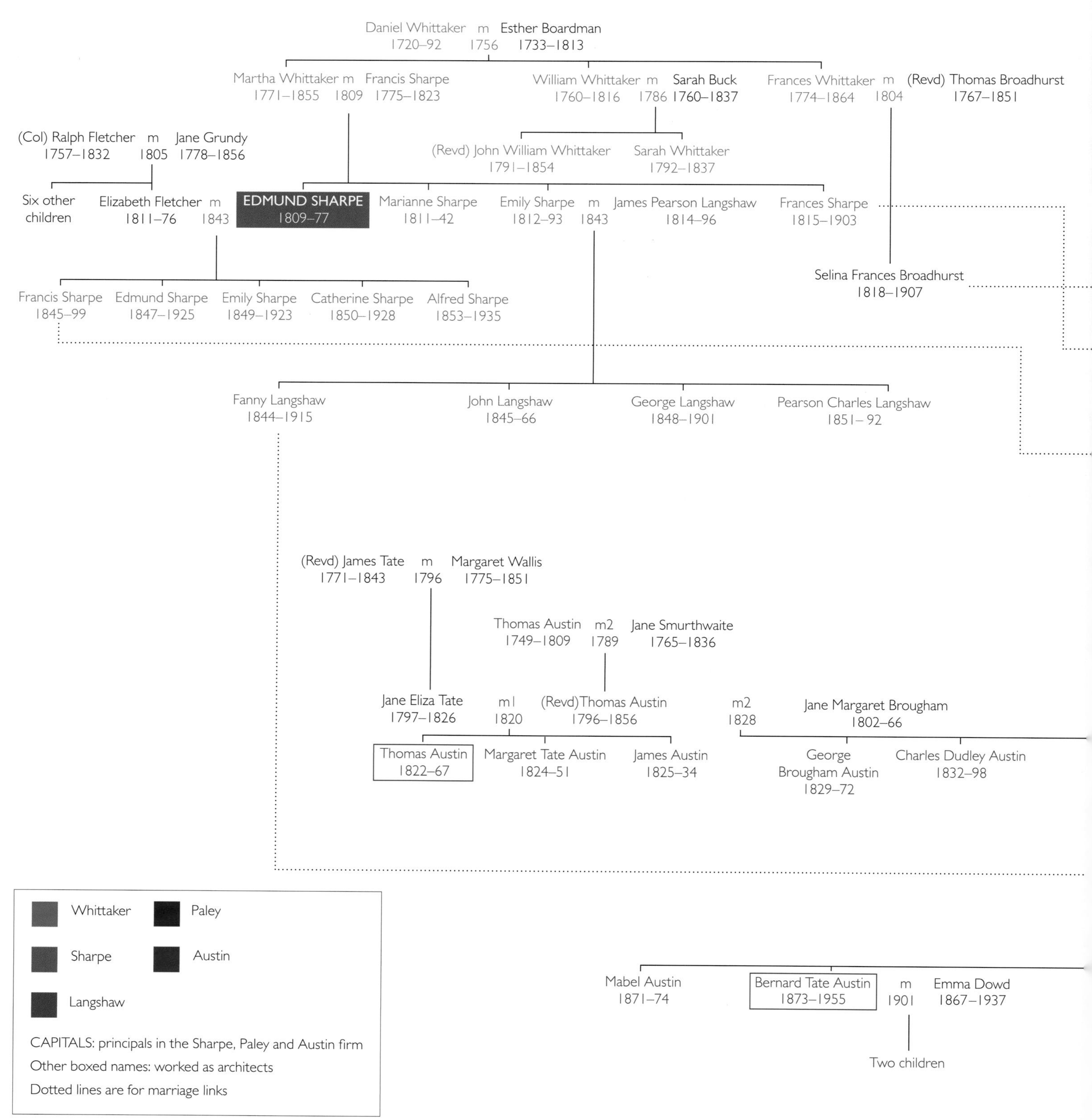

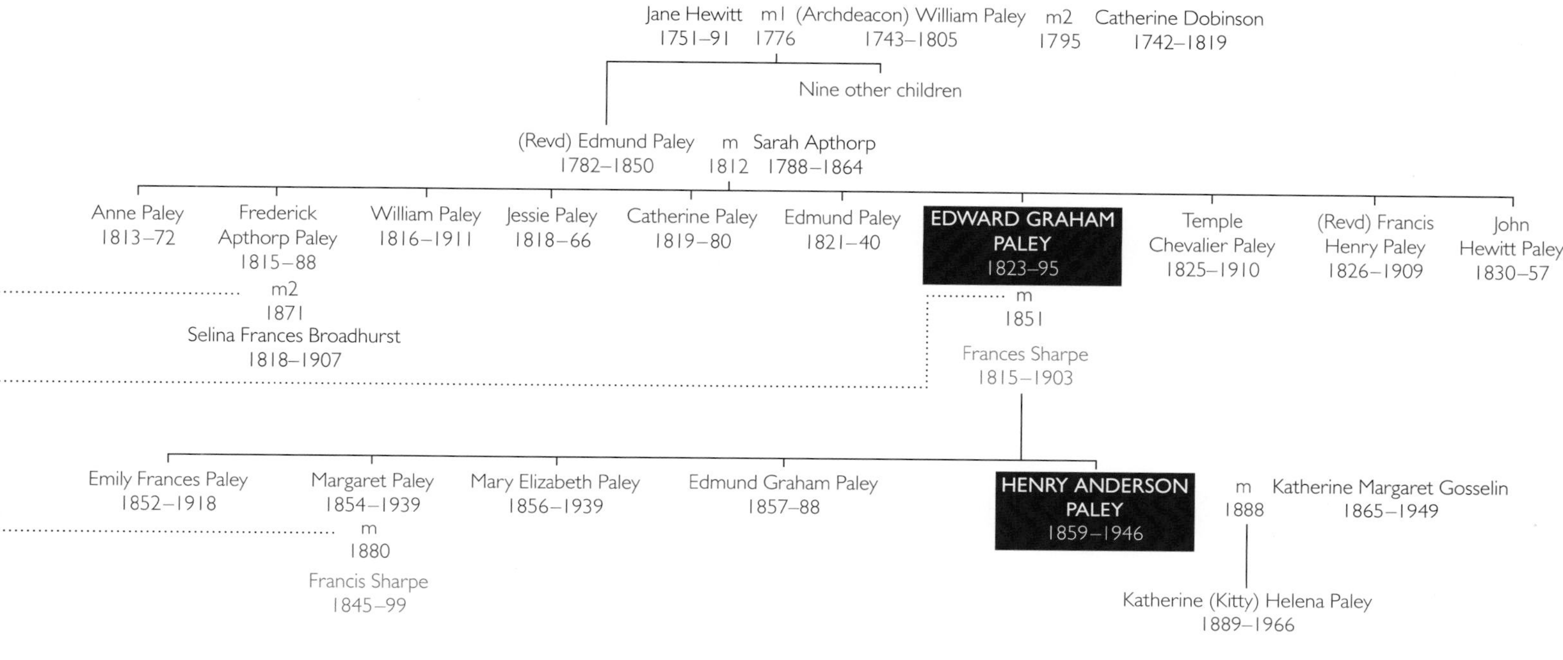

Jane Hewitt 1751–91
m1 1776
(Archdeacon) William Paley 1743–1805
m2 1795
Catherine Dobinson 1742–1819
Nine other children
(Revd) Edmund Paley 1782–1850
m 1812
Sarah Apthorp 1788–1864
Anne Paley 1813–72
Frederick Apthorp Paley 1815–88
m2 1871
Selina Frances Broadhurst 1818–1907
William Paley 1816–1911
Jessie Paley 1818–66
Catherine Paley 1819–80
Edmund Paley 1821–40
EDWARD GRAHAM PALEY 1823–95
m 1851
Frances Sharpe 1815–1903
Temple Chevalier Paley 1825–1910
(Revd) Francis Henry Paley 1826–1909
John Hewitt Paley 1830–57
Emily Frances Paley 1852–1918
Margaret Paley 1854–1939
m 1880
Francis Sharpe 1845–99
Mary Elizabeth Paley 1856–1939
Edmund Graham Paley 1857–88
HENRY ANDERSON PALEY 1859–1946
m 1888
Katherine Margaret Gosselin 1865–1949
Katherine (Kitty) Helena Paley 1889–1966

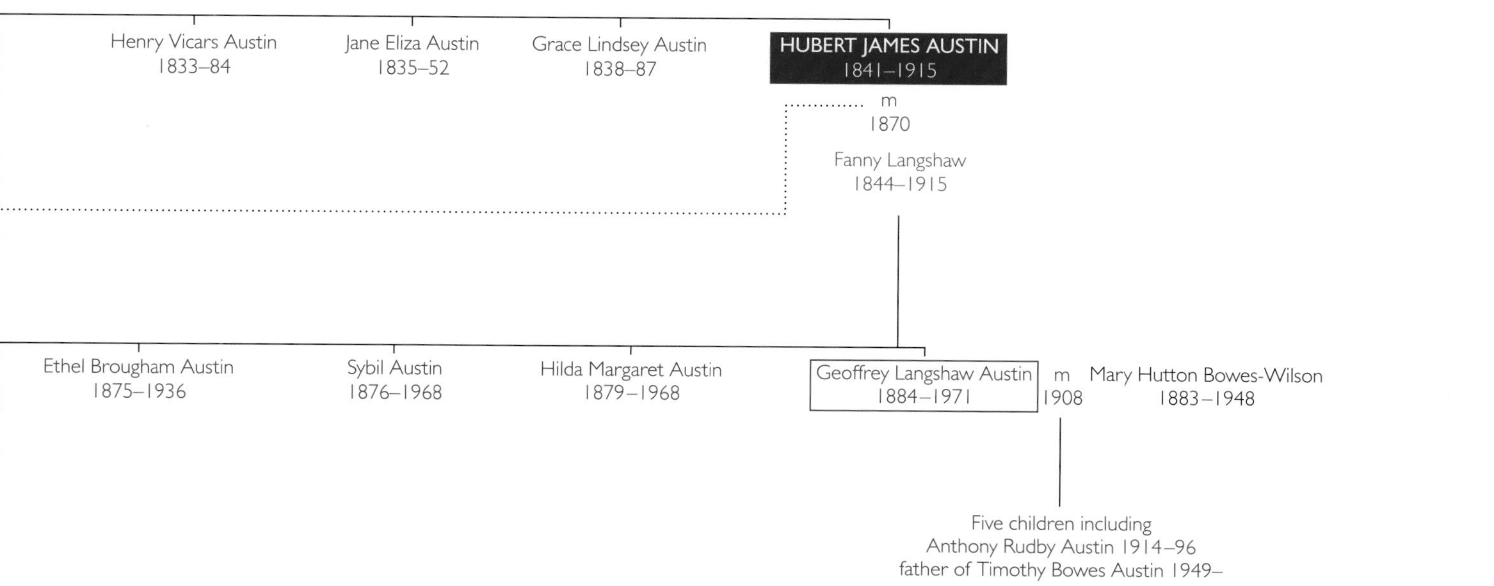

Henry Vicars Austin 1833–84
Jane Eliza Austin 1835–52
Grace Lindsey Austin 1838–87
HUBERT JAMES AUSTIN 1841–1915
m 1870
Fanny Langshaw 1844–1915
Ethel Brougham Austin 1875–1936
Sybil Austin 1876–1968
Hilda Margaret Austin 1879–1968
Geoffrey Langshaw Austin 1884–1971
m 1908
Mary Hutton Bowes-Wilson 1883–1948
Five children including
Anthony Rudby Austin 1914–96
father of Timothy Bowes Austin 1949–

Introduction

A practice like no other

For just over a hundred years – from the start of Queen Victoria's reign until the end of the Second World War – Lancaster was home to one of England's most remarkable architectural practices. It had four principals during its lifetime – Edmund Sharpe, Edward Graham Paley, Paley's son Harry and Hubert Austin – and the name of the practice varied accordingly through time (Fig 0.1). The firm's reputation rests chiefly upon its achievements from about 1870 to 1910, when it is linked inextricably with a wealth of fine churches and the work of Austin. The high quality of this output was recognised in its own time by clients and patrons, within the architectural profession, and in Hermann Muthesius's pioneering study of English church-building in 1901. In more recent times, when assessing a range of the firm's late Victorian churches in his *South Lancashire* of 1969, Pevsner considered these to be 'of the highest European standard of their years'.[1] He was admiring of many late 19th-century churches by north-western architects, but added that 'of all these Lancashire men only one had genius: Austin'.[2] Among today's architectural historians and enthusiasts for Victorian buildings, the firm's reputation stands in high regard – an unusual thing for a provincial practice.[3]

Of the north and in the North

The development of the practice is bound up with a wide and complex network of personal and educational links which are explored in this book, and it is family reasons which explain how it came to be established in Lancaster in the first place. The town was the adopted home of Edmund Sharpe's family because his mother, Martha, and her family of four settled here in 1824 following the death of her husband the previous year. This choice had been determined by the fact that her sister, Esther, was living in Lancaster with her husband, Benjamin Satterthwaite, a prosperous wine merchant. So it was here that Martha's eldest child, Edmund, university-educated, talented and ambitious, returned in late 1835 after a three-year architectural study tour on the continent and set himself up as an architect.

Lancaster, although the county town, was not large, being then home to some 13,500 people, and a long distance from the larger, burgeoning industrial centres further south which, by 1831, had turned Lancashire into England's most populous county.[4] Lancaster was past its trading heyday of the 18th century, yet it was not such an unpromising base for the aspiring young architect. There were no other practitioners there to capitalise on its local building opportunities at a time when industrial expansion and the consequent growth in population and wealth were starting to create an unprecedented demand for buildings of many different kinds. Family connections were crucial in enabling the young Sharpe to make a rapid and brilliantly successful entry into practice. His uncle, Benjamin Satterthwaite, was a prominent figure in Lancaster and district while his cousin, the Revd Dr J W Whittaker, vicar of Blackburn, promoted his career through a series of connections which even went to the top of the established church and had links into the aristocracy. Sharpe prospered and became an important figure in the affairs of the town. His business interests ranged beyond architecture and, from the late 1840s, led him away from its practice, although he later returned to the field as a distinguished writer. He had, however, taken on assistants, including Edward Graham Paley who became not only his partner and successor but also his brother-in-law. Paley, in turn, would join forces with Hubert Austin, after

Natland (CuW), St Mark, 1909–11, a late village church by Austin & Paley. It exemplifies the restrained but beautiful architecture and furnishings the firm brought to its churches. It is a memorial church to William Dillworth Crewdson (1838–1908), a Kendal banker whose family was distantly related to Edmund Sharpe, and thus the Paleys and the Austins. (Mark Watson)

Fig 0.1
The Sharpe, Paley and Austin architectural practice: summary of dates and titles.

which the firm entered its golden years up to the First World War. Thereafter the practice would be run for its last quarter-century by Paley's son, Harry.

All four principals in the Sharpe, Paley and Austin firm were northerners and none of them, apart from Hubert Austin, who spent three years in Gilbert Scott's office in the early 1860s, ever worked in London. Even for Austin the London experience was but a stepping stone between serving his articles in Newcastle upon Tyne under his elder half-brother Tom and being attracted to Lancaster by connections of family and friendship, and the prospect of a partnership with Paley. Nor did the practice carry out a single commission in the capital. The nearest it ever got was the building of a big, northern-style Perpendicular church at Hertford in the 1890s. The firm's activity was very much concentrated in the north-west of England in an area extending some 60 miles or so from the southern valleys of the Lake District to the Lancashire coalfield and with some forays into Cheshire (Fig 0.2). The success of the practice in its heartland was such that its principals never felt the need to locate elsewhere.

The firm, then, was based in a relatively small town some distance from major industrial cities and was clearly a provincial architectural practice. This carried with it considerable implications for the range and scale of the work it undertook.[5] The word 'provincial' has pejorative associations while the term 'provincial architects' may convey an expectation of uninteresting, routine work by men who never gained entry to the elite of their profession. The vast majority of those who did achieve this were Londoners, if not by origin, like Butterfield, Burges or Lutyens, then by training and subsequent careers, as with Scott, Bodley or Pearson. Some who became leaders in the profession, such as William White, J D Sedding or Alfred Waterhouse, started out in the provinces but, sooner or later, and under different circumstances, established offices in London. For those at, or aspiring to, the top of the architectural profession, London was a powerful magnet whose attraction derived from a stimulating cultural environment, opportunities for architectural discourse and education, and contacts with peers and many influential clients. From early in the Victorian period the railway system radiated from the capital, allowing easy travel to most parts of the country. In addition, there were on-the-spot opportunities to get one's work drawn by the best draughtsmen, and to get it noticed at exhibitions and published in various journals. By the time of the 1881 census, in England and Wales 30 per cent of those describing themselves as architects were resident in London at a time when it contained but 15 per cent of the population.

Buildings great and small

Although the firm did achieve national recognition, especially at the end of the 19th century and in particular for its churches, it still displayed characteristics typical of a provincial practice. When one thinks of the best-known leaders of the Victorian architectural profession, one associates them with the 'polite' end of the market. The idea of G E Street designing a branch line station or Lutyens the extension to a local shop seems both improbable and slightly absurd.[6] Yet such modest buildings were (and are) the bread and butter of unsung and unknown practices, whether provincial or London-based – nearly 2,570 practices in England and Wales in 1883, according to a list published in the *British Architect*.[7]

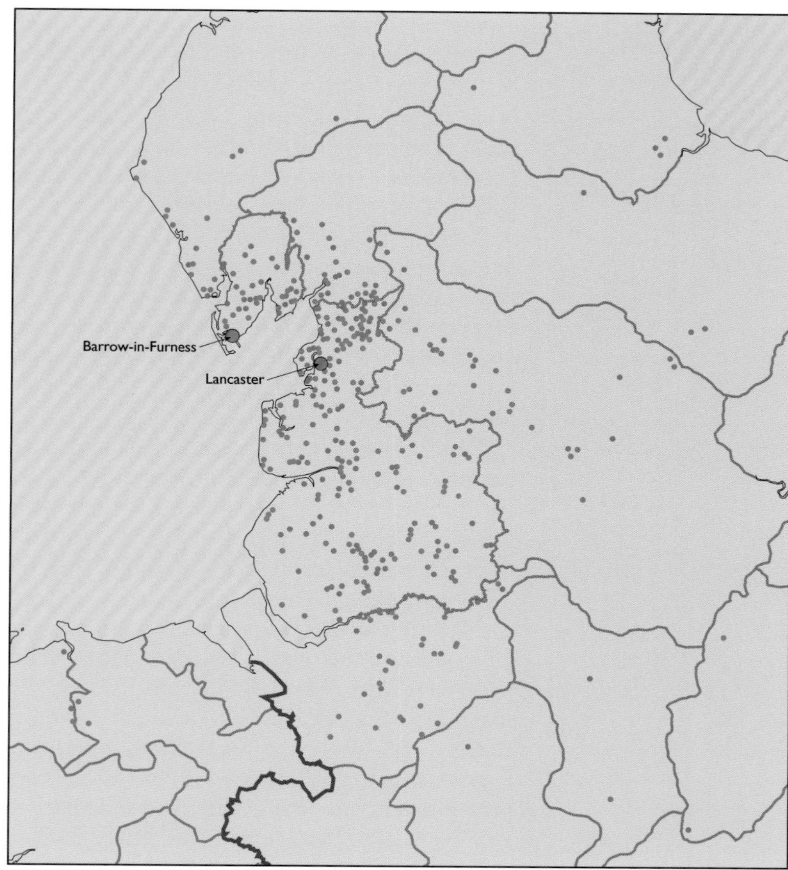

Fig 0.2
Location of works and projects by the practice, 1836–1944. This map clearly shows the concentration of activity in the north-west stretching up from Cheshire, through Lancashire and into the southern parts of Cumberland and Westmorland. The counties are shown as they were when the practice was at work. A small number of commissions were carried out further afield and these are mostly mentioned in Appendix 4.

From its earliest days under Edmund Sharpe, the practice developed a specialism in churches which lasted for its entire life and it was therefore particularly associated with the Gothic Revival. With churches came the related building types of parsonages and schools and also country house work, in all of which Gothic was deployed until the stylistic watershed of about 1870 when medieval credentials were called into question for secular work. As an architect, Sharpe was expected to turn his hand to other things as well – bridges for railways and over rivers, various routine works as architect to the Lancaster county lunatic asylum, and other building projects around the town. When the practice passed to E G Paley he continued to carry out large numbers of church commissions, becoming best remembered for them, but he also inherited the wide spectrum of work expected from provincial architectural practices. Even at the end of the 19th century, when a national reputation had been firmly established, this diversity is still very evident. In the 1890s the firm was responsible for the building of Austin's St George, Stockport, one of the greatest masterpieces of 19th- and early 20th-century church architecture. Yet while it was being built, the firm was also running up a red-brick mission church for £250 at Sunderland Point, a remote spot cut off at high tide on the Lune estuary. There were new classrooms and a gym at Casterton School (CuW), a village cross at Bootle (CuC), three shops and houses for the Lancaster businessman William Blades, and a large number of minor schemes for church fittings and extensions. It was even advising the governors of Sedbergh School (CuWY), whom the firm served for over 60 years, on minor matters of repair and maintenance.

The firm carried out substantial commissions across a wide range of building types right up to its demise. Country house work begins with Edmund Sharpe's recasting of Capernwray Hall in north Lancashire in 1844–8, ranges through the remodelling of Hornby Castle in 1847–8 and the building of Wennington Hall in 1855–6, and culminates in the rebuilding of the magnificent state wing at Holker Hall (CuL) in 1871–5. Furthermore although the firm's work at Thurland Castle in the 1880s is truly excellent, so is that at Hoghton Tower in the later 1870s.[8] Significant public works are represented by hospitals in Barrow (CuL), 1882–7, and Lancaster, 1893–6, and the firm's largest commission of all, the mighty Royal Albert Asylum in Lancaster of 1867–73; there are also the Storey Institute in Lancaster, 1887–91, cemetery buildings in Barrow and Lancaster, 1855, and a market hall in Barrow. There were factories in Lancaster and Barrow, hotels in Morecambe, Grange-over-Sands and Barrow; industrial housing, again in Barrow; shops in Lancaster; and for over 20 years the practice was, it seems, designing most of the buildings for the Furness Railway Company. Schools provided the firm with a steady stream of work, and the important establishments at Giggleswick (NY), Rossall and Sedbergh (CuWY) each provided commissions over many decades. In addition, there were many other town and village schools, mostly spread over an area from the Fylde northwards. This distribution is significant. All the examples mentioned in this paragraph are north of the Fylde and indicate the total dominance of the practice over the more significant architectural projects in this area for much of its life. To the south secular commissions are much less common, indeed almost absent, and here it is churches – the firm's speciality – with which it achieved its greatest success.

Churches and churchmanship

Churches underpinned what the practice did and this was the case from the outset. Edmund Sharpe was fortunate to be able to tap into the vast amount of church-building, rebuilding and restoration which grew prodigiously from precisely the time he began his career. The vast majority of the commissions were from the Anglican Church, but not exclusively so. Rarely did architects who excelled in church-building cross denominational lines. Pugin, of course, was an exception in working for both Anglicans and Roman Catholics, although far more for the latter than the former. Other Roman Catholic architects, such as J A Hansom and Leonard Stokes, seem to have worked almost exclusively for their co-religionists. Nonconformists, too, had their specialists – the Baineses for Methodists and James Tait for Congregationalists. Among Anglicans, leading architects were often divided by the fractured planes of churchmanship. We therefore associate Butterfield, Bodley and Street with the Anglo-Catholic wing, G G Scott and A W Blomfield with the Broad Church, and E B Lamb and S S Teulon with the Low. All the principals of the Sharpe, Paley and Austin firm were devout Anglicans, yet from the 1850s Paley was building for north Lancashire's Roman Catholic community, starting with convent schools in Lancaster in 1851 and Yealand Conyers church the following year. At the end of the decade came the fine church of St Peter's in Lancaster, whose spire is as prominent a feature in that town as Hansom's St Walburge's is in Preston. The Austin & Paley firm remained responsible for work at this church (a cathedral from 1924) until the late 1920s. Other Roman Catholic work included a church, presbytery and schools at Garstang in 1857–8 and Nazareth House for 'waifs and strays' in Lancaster between 1898 and 1902. Work for Congregationalists involved a Sunday school at Lancaster in 1856 and a church at Morecambe, 1862–3. For Presbyterians there was a chapel at Barrow-in-Furness in 1874–5 and the remodelling of another in Lancaster in 1874. No other Victorian practice which achieved such eminence in church-building worked across so wide a denominational spectrum.

The story of the great revival of church-building in Victorian times is often filtered through Anglican High Church developments – Tractarianism, the Cambridge Camden Society, Anglo-Catholicism, ritualism, and sympathetic architects like Butterfield, Street, Bodley, Scott junior and Moore. But Lancastrian Anglicanism was not inclined in this direction. A good statistical indicator of this is the relative absence of churches offering daily services in Lancashire. In proportion to population size, only Cheshire had fewer among all the English counties.[9] This bias is usually seen as a Protestant reaction away from Roman Catholicism which had maintained a strong, continuous presence in the county through penal times. The first bishop of Manchester from 1848, James Prince Lee, had no time for Tractarianism, while his successor from 1870, James Fraser, though probably of a somewhat more ecumenical disposition, famously refused to veto the prosecution of the Revd Sidney Green of Miles Platting under the Public Worship Regulation Act of 1874. As a consequence, Green languished for 20 months in the gaol at Lancaster Castle, just across the road from Paley & Austin's offices, for his Anglo-Catholic practices. When consecrating P&A's imposing new church of St Thomas, Bolton, Bishop Fraser claimed in 1875 that there were 'probably no more than three or four cases' in his diocese where 'extreme and extravagant ideas' were to be found and even these could be handled 'rationally and charitably ... as they arose'.[10]

Consequently and unusually for a firm in the top flight of church architects, the firm was building very largely for middle-of-the-road or Low Church patrons. Sharpe had firmly Low Church sympathies himself, indeed becoming a committee member of the newly formed local branch of the Protestant Association in April 1840. Towards the end of his life he designed a church for his own community, Scotforth in the southern suburbs of Lancaster, built in 1874–5. Here an extreme precaution against processions is said to explain the filling of the nave with benches (hence no central alley) to discourage such popish pomp and ceremony. As individuals, neither Paley nor Austin (both of whom were sons of clergymen) is believed to have entertained anything other than moderate churchmanship. Austin is thought to have been a particularly committed churchman and was vicar's warden for a number of years at Lancaster's principal church, St Mary's, where he and his wife built the south porch in 1902–3 as a memorial to the latter's parents. The trappings of Anglo-Catholicism are absent from the churches by Paley & Austin, yet they have a dignity and beauty that is to be expected from the finest Victorian church architects. Indeed, some even show that strongly Evangelical clients were willing to pay for architectural magnificence, even (and, indeed, especially) in what was sometimes referred to as the 'Geneva of the North' – Bolton (GM).

The great period of church-building by the firm was between the late 1860s and the end of the Edwardian period, a time which coincides with Austin's partnership, along with unprecedented prosperity in a time of faith. Money was thus available to express that faith in tangible form and, although many buildings and restorations were funded from broadly based donations, some of the greatest churches were paid for outright by individuals who had accumulated (or sometimes inherited) their wealth from cotton-spinning, coal-mining, commerce or banking. But, as discussed earlier, fine churches were but part – albeit the pinnacle – of the firm's achievement at this time, and it can be argued that, for sheer range of output and its quantity and quality, there was no comparable architectural practice in the country.

The firm: information, organisation and people

In common with most other major 19th-century architectural practices, there is no comprehensive archive for the Sharpe, Paley and Austin firm. When the business closed down towards the end of the Second World War and the end of Harry Paley's life, the office records and drawings were destroyed. Seventy years on, such material would now be a cherished resource but at the time a combination of lack of interest in (or indeed hatred of) Victorian architecture and the exigencies of wartime sealed their fate. The chief exception is three volumes of specifications, correspondence and other material from the 1920s onwards which survive among the papers of Shrigley & Hunt, the firm of stained-glass makers who occupied premises just down the hill from Austin & Paley's offices.[11] They provide much otherwise unknown information about the late work of the firm and probably were passed over to Shrigley & Hunt as being of potential use, since they had worked at many A&P buildings. There are also three bound volumes of miscellaneous drawings, formerly in the Lancaster reference library and now in the Lancashire Record Office. These take the form of scrapbooks and we do not know how they came into being but, again, they contain valuable if often tantalising examples – mostly of details – of work by the firm in the mid- to late 19th century. There is also a handful of sketchbooks by Paley recording various travels but they shed no real light on his output. For Edmund Sharpe there is a good deal of private correspondence which tells much about his early years and also gives extensive information about his non-architectural activities, but no body of papers about his career as an architect. The consequence is that knowledge of the firm and its work has to be built up from a multiplicity of sources – newspapers, parish documents, building control records, private papers and so on. In compiling the Catalogue of works and projects (*see* Appendix 5) every effort has been made to use primary sources, but the vast volume and range of work by the firm has sometimes meant this has not been possible and in such cases secondary sources have been relied on.

The result is that we know very little about the office, and how it was organised. Something can be deduced from various sources about the character of the principals. Sharpe emerges as a man of multifarious talents, with business ability, active in local affairs and politics, and with an outgoing, engaging personality. Paley too seems to have been an attractive individual, popular and a leading figure in the life of Lancaster. Austin, though active in St Mary's church, was more retiring and lived primarily for his work and family. He and Paley seem to have been rather different personalities and we have no idea about their personal interaction. But they stayed together as partners for over a quarter of a century, building up an immensely respected practice. Paley, as the older (and more out-going) partner, tended to 'front' many of the dealings of the firm, and it is easy to picture him as being at ease when calling on the duke of Devonshire in 1871 to discuss the rebuilding of Holker Hall after a disastrous fire.[12] After the First World War, when Harry Paley was in charge, the practice slimmed down, partly because of there being less work available, and also, being comfortably well off, he could afford to make architecture just one of his interests. Like his father, he played an important part in the life of Lancaster and district and was an active sportsman.

What has been discovered about pupils and assistants is summarised in Appendix 2, but there may well have been others. At the peak of the practice we might envisage the office on Castle Hill having a couple of articled pupils and perhaps half a dozen or so assistants and clerks. However, Hubert Austin's son, Geoffrey, recalled: 'There were certainly no pupils in my father's lifetime because, as he said, he would not be able to give them sufficient of the personal attention to which they would be entitled.'[13] This cannot be literally true since, as Appendix 2 shows, pupils were taken on in the period before E G Paley's death, but the statement seems to hold good for the period after it. Hubert Austin seems to have been a rather private individual unlikely to be interested in the burden of having to deal with pupils. His sons Bernard and Geoffrey spent brief periods with the firm, but Bernard's future was to be outside it and he developed a fairly successful architectural career of his own. Geoffrey, although briefly a partner, pursued a bursarial career after the war. In any case, the limited opportunities for architects after 1918 meant that there was little scope for more than one principal. This was Harry Paley, who was loyally supported by long-serving figures in the office. With the closure of the firm at the end of the Second World War and Harry's death in 1946, there came to an end one of England's most effective and successful architectural practices of the 19th and early 20th centuries.

1

Edmund Sharpe: architect and scholar

Edmund Sharpe, who laid the foundations of the practice, was a man of many talents (Fig 1.1). His career as a practising architect was quite brief, spanning little more than a decade, and into his busy life he also packed a host of other achievements – businessman, railway builder, local politician and reformer, musician, and major contributor to the social and cultural life of Lancaster. Besides all this he was an architectural historian of some note, and it was for his publications that he was honoured in 1875 with the RIBA Royal Gold Medal, the highest award the English profession could bestow.

His career and interests were so diverse that it is unwise to try to compress them into a single chapter and a straightforward chronological story. This chapter therefore concentrates on those aspects of his life and work which are relevant to an understanding of the man and his architectural achievements, both as a historian and as a practitioner. His other, mostly entrepreneurial and political activities, which tell of Victorian drive and progress, have been grouped separately in Appendix 1.

Fig 1.1
Edmund Sharpe in 1863 when he was busy with tram and railway ventures in Switzerland and France.
Carte de visite, *studio of Alphonse Legros, Palais Royal, Paris.*
(Austin Family collection)

Family background

Sharpe was the eldest of four children born to Francis and Martha Sharpe of Knutsford, Cheshire. Theirs was a prosperous middle-class household, Francis being a peripatetic music teacher from Stamford in Lincolnshire who had settled in the town by 1800 and was, towards the end of his life, earning almost £1,000 a year.[1] Martha (Fig 1.2) was the 11th child of Daniel and Esther Whittaker of Manchester,[2] and at the time of her marriage taught at Belvedere House in Bath, a boarding and finishing school for young ladies superintended by her youngest sister, Frances.[3] Another sister, Mary, had married (as his second wife) Knutsford's leading doctor, Peter Holland. Mary and Martha were married within two weeks of each other at St Swithin, Walcot, Bath, in early 1809, and almost immediately both were pregnant.[4] It was Martha's child, Edmund, who arrived first, on 31 October, as a premature baby.

Early 19th-century Knutsford, where Edmund Sharpe grew up, was a quiet market town of fewer than 3,000 people, and a total contrast to Manchester, the first great city of the Industrial Revolution, just 15 miles away. Most of what we know about Sharpe's life in Knutsford and that of his relatives and neighbours comes from an extraordinary collection of correspondence amassed over nearly 30 years by the Revd John

Fig 1.2 (right)
Martha Sharpe: portrait by the Liverpool miniaturist Thomas Carlyle, 1839. It is a companion piece to that of her son (see Fig 1.13). The location of the original is now unknown and this illustration is from a photographic copy. (Manchester Libraries and Information Service, Local Studies; Tim Austin)

Fig 1.3 (far right)
The Revd John William Whittaker, vicar of Blackburn, who played a key role in the upbringing of his cousin Edmund Sharpe, and helped his early career as an aspiring architect. (Ray Jackson collection)

William Whittaker DD (1791–1854), who was Sharpe's first cousin and played a crucial role in his early life and subsequent architectural career (Fig 1.3).[5] Educated at Bradford Grammar School and briefly at Sedbergh School, Whittaker took advantage of the latter's scholarships to St John's College, Cambridge, which he entered in 1810. His book of 1819 on the interpretation of the Hebrew scriptures attracted the attention of the Archbishop of Canterbury, Charles Manners-Sutton, who in 1820 made him his examining chaplain. In 1822, Whittaker was appointed as vicar to the large and lucrative living of Blackburn where he remained until his death.[6] He had wide interests, encompassing geology, astronomy and philology, and was an early fellow of the Royal Astronomical Society. He knew many leading intellectuals of the day such as the astronomer John Herschel and, importantly for our story, the great Cambridge polymath William Whewell. Whittaker's marriage in 1825 to Mary Feilden would provide a family link, some years later, to Sharpe's first architectural commission.

One letter to Whittaker in 1815 from Sharpe's aunt Catherine noted how the boy (affectionately known as Teb) had broken his arm having been tipped out of a cart while playing at the Hollands'.[7] A playmate on this occasion was 'a little niece of Mrs Lumbs' who, although not named, was Elizabeth Stevenson, cousin of the Holland children, and the future Mrs Gaskell (1810–65).[8] Later in life she recalled, with evident nostalgia, blissful childhood days in Knutsford, portrayed in her novel *Cranford*. In a letter of 1838 she recalled that 'the Sharpes' (probably Edmund's two youngest sisters, Emily and Frances) had been singing duets together.[9] She established a lifelong friendship with Emily Sharpe, who was to marry the Lancaster surgeon James Pearson Langshaw and become the mother-in-law of Hubert Austin.

In 1812 the Sharpes moved to a farm on the west side of Knutsford (Fig 1.4) which, on top of his teaching activities, must have kept Francis Sharpe a busy man (he was also teaching part-time at a school near Runcorn). The family were well respected in Knutsford – energetic, generous, and much given to hospitality, regularly making and receiving visits from relatives and friends.

Early education

Edmund Sharpe's education began early, under the tutelage of his mother, the former schoolteacher, and his father, the music master. Every aspect of his development was eagerly recorded by Whittaker's frequent correspondents. In 1815, we glimpse, perhaps, something of a precocious feeling for architecture: Aunt Catherine told Whittaker of a letter from Edmund's mother about the family's journey from Bath when

> Edmund ... was highly delighted with Gloucester Cathedral & the Abbey at Bath & Martha says he pointed out every part most striking in the former & stepped on his toes as if afraid to disturb the dead – & when he was examining the latter place he said it was not so fine & grand a place as the Cathedral of Gloucester.[10]

By 1818 Sharpe was attending a school in Knutsford and learning Latin. Two years later he was a pupil in Runcorn, presumably at the school his father visited so regularly. He was then sent to Greenwich, to the distinguished private academy run since 1813 by Dr Charles Parr Burney, where many naval and military officers were educated.[11] Sharpe arrived there on 7 August 1821 and soon impressed Burney, whose comments were relayed to Whittaker by the delighted Martha Sharpe: 'He is a very nice fellow, & steady, quite teachable, amiable & regular, nor will his six Months progress bring discredit on himself or his Master.'[12]

By 1823 Sharpe was a senior pupil at Burney's school, but that year brought tragedy. In the spring Francis Sharpe's health had given cause for concern, Aunt Catherine informing her nephew that his uncle had a bout of influenza and had contracted a cough and a fever.[13] For a time it seemed that he had recovered, but on 8 November he died, aged just 48.

The move to Lancaster

Martha Sharpe soon decided to move to Lancaster, which had strong family attractions. It was home, from October 1823, to both Sarah Whittaker, Martha's widowed sister-in-law, and her daughter, also Sarah, who rented a house on Castle Hill (the top part was renamed Castle Park in 1824), the street where Paley would later establish the office that would serve the firm till the end of its days. Furthermore, Martha's elder sister Esther was married to a successful wine merchant in the town, Benjamin Satterthwaite, who had long taken an interest in young Edmund's development and was well connected within Lancaster's commercial elite. The extent of the influence of his uncle Benjamin's patronage on Sharpe's later career will probably never be known. Martha Sharpe moved to Penny Street in April 1824 with her four 'bantlings' (as she called her children), and so it was, that Edmund, then aged 14, came to the town where much of his later life would be spent.

Fig 1.4
Heathside, a farm on the west side of Knutsford (Ch), which was home to Sharpe from 1812. Drawing by his sister Marianne, 1830. (Austin Paley Archive, Lancaster City Museums, MS LM 86/129; Tim Austin)

Sharpe returned to Dr Burney's school early in 1824 and continued to make his mark. By the autumn of 1826 he told Whittaker that he expected to become head boy, which indeed he did, some two weeks before his 17th birthday.[14] He was a good intermediary between the masters and the boys, and his mother was pleased to report to Whittaker that Burney considered him 'worthy of his post'.[15]

Sedbergh School

On 8 August 1827 Sharpe became a boarder at Sedbergh School, an ancient grammar school then enjoying a revival under the Revd Henry Wilkinson, its headmaster since 1819. It was still small, and many boys, Sharpe included, lodged with Wilkinson and his family. Sharpe's letters show that this was a very happy time, and he won the headmaster's approval, just as he had at Greenwich. In his last years Sharpe became a governor at Sedbergh, while the firm he founded carried out architectural work there for well over half a century.

Sedbergh plays an important part in Sharpe's story, with significant links to other pupils (Fig 1.5). J W Whittaker, for example, attended briefly in 1809–10 and went on to St John's, Cambridge, with Wilkinson. It was at Sedbergh that Sharpe became friends with Thomas Paley (1810–99), then at Ripon but born in Halifax, who is almost certainly the family link through whom Edward Graham Paley later came to join Sharpe.[16] Their families knew one another, and Sharpe and Thomas Paley attended St John's College, Cambridge, together. Sedbergh endowed two fellowships and eight scholarships there, which enabled Sharpe to be admitted as a pensioner on 15 December 1828.[17]

University

Sharpe took up residence at St John's on 15 October 1829. He kept 10 terms and achieved, in 1833, a respectable but far from outstanding degree, ranking 47th out of 125. By this time, however, his architectural interests had been developing, influenced and assisted by friendship with the great William Whewell (1794–1866) of Trinity College, one of the finest minds of the time (Fig 1.6). Whewell came from Lancaster, one of seven children of a master carpenter, and his talents won him an exhibition to Trinity College, Cambridge, in 1812. In the small world of early 19th-century Lancaster, he became known to the Sharpe family through their relatives, the Satterthwaites.[18] Through them, no doubt, Whewell also became friends with J W Whittaker. Correspondence suggests that Edmund Sharpe probably first met Whewell on 12 August 1824 at a party in Lancaster to celebrate J W Whittaker's engagement to Mary Haughton Feilden.[19] Shortly after, Martha Sharpe noted with pleasure that 'Mr. Whewell was much pleased with him [Edmund] ... and speaking of him as a very intelligent, fine genteel boy likely to get on'.[20] For his part, Edmund Sharpe thought of Whewell with great affection and respect. In a letter from Greenwich to

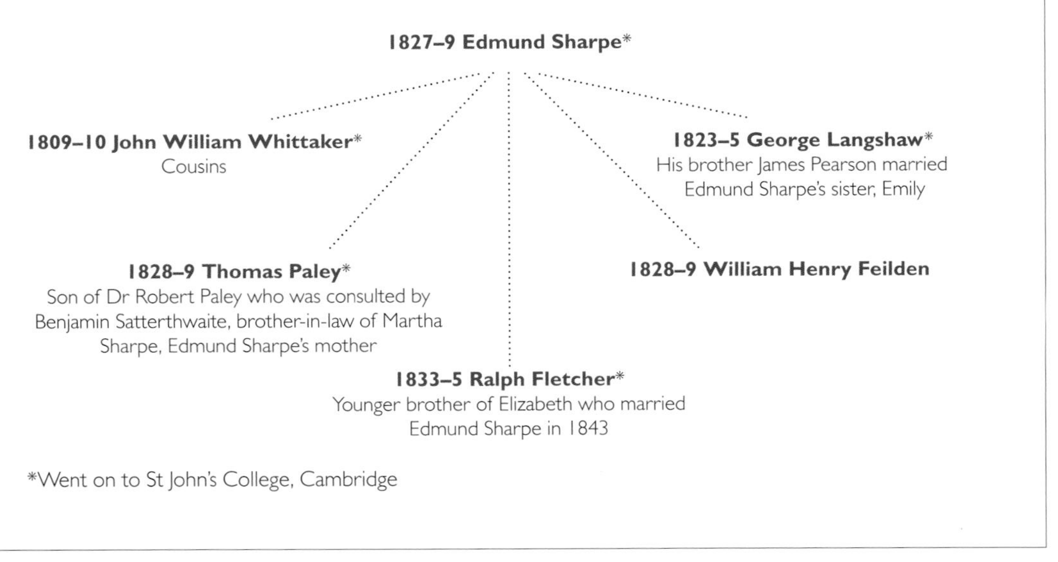

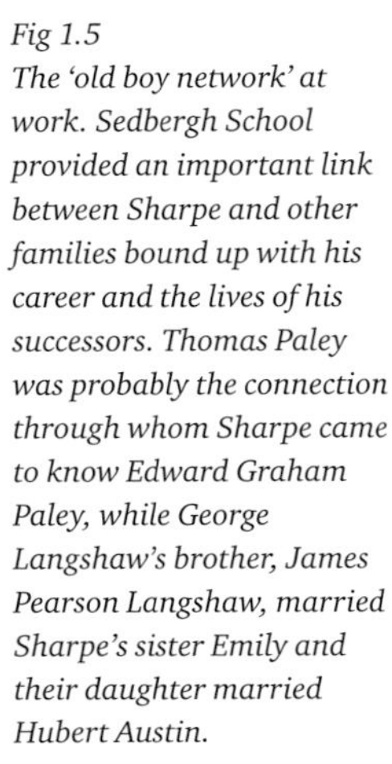
Fig 1.5
The 'old boy network' at work. Sedbergh School provided an important link between Sharpe and other families bound up with his career and the lives of his successors. Thomas Paley was probably the connection through whom Sharpe came to know Edward Graham Paley, while George Langshaw's brother, James Pearson Langshaw, married Sharpe's sister Emily and their daughter married Hubert Austin.

Fig 1.6
William Whewell, a key influence on Sharpe, by James Lonsdale, c 1825. Later he became Master of Trinity and Vice-Chancellor of Cambridge University. (The Master & Fellows of Trinity College, Cambridge)

Whittaker at the end of that month, he wrote: 'Pray have you heard anything of Mr. Whewell lately? You know he is a great favourite of mine, remember me to him the next time you see him.'[21]

Whewell distinguished himself in many fields – mathematics, geology, theology, poetry, philosophy, economics and in what he is best known for today, the history and philosophy of science (he coined the terms 'scientist' and 'physicist'). This extraordinary polymath took an interest in architecture from his childhood and produced accomplished drawings of buildings. He made tours to France in 1819 and Switzerland in 1822,[22] and in 1823 he was in Picardy and Normandy looking at buildings with his student Kenelm Digby, the romantic medievalist.[23] In 1829–31 he visited northern France, Holland and Germany, and in 1830 published, anonymously, *Architectural Notes on German Churches with Remarks on the Origin of Gothic Architecture*.[24] He was a friend of the architect Thomas Rickman (1776–1841), 18 years his senior (Fig 1.7). Like Whewell, Rickman had a deep interest in methodical classification, which resulted in his enduring book, *An Attempt to Discriminate the Styles of English Architecture from the Conquest to the Reformation*, which first appeared in 1817 and popularised the terms 'Early English' and 'Decorated' and coined that of 'Perpendicular'.

Rickman was already also known to Whittaker, who had purchased the *Attempt* in 1817, and struck up a friendship with its author.[25] Whewell may have met Rickman when he came to Cambridge to design the New Court at St John's, although he does not actually appear in Rickman's diaries until 1829, when he dined at Trinity College with Whewell, the geologist Adam Sedgwick, and others on 1 November. Supported no doubt by Whewell, in 1832 Sharpe gained a Worts Travelling Bachelorship, two of which were awarded annually under a bequest of 1709 by William Worts. Sharpe used this to undertake a three-year study of early medieval architecture in Germany and France – a subject of intense interest for Whewell and Rickman, to whom Sharpe might almost be described as a research assistant.

It was through Whewell or Whittaker (or both) that Sharpe came into contact with Rickman. He stayed with Rickman in Birmingham for a few days (presumably in preparation for his tour) on his way back to Cambridge for his last term. The architect wrote delightedly in his diary for 6 October how

> this morning Edmund Sharpe, Dr Whittaker's Cousin came & I find him a very pleasant intelligent young man. [H]e has worked hard & is disposed to work harder still. [H]e has some Method & has made good use of his Eyes in England so I hope he will abroad. [H]e has begun examining & copying from my books & has shewn me [a] variety of his sketches in different parts.[26]

Fig 1.7
Thomas Rickman (and lofty assistant, Henry Hutchinson) by his friend Charles Barber, c 1820, entitled A view near the Exchange.
(Liverpool Athenaeum Club Library)

The next day Rickman wrote to Whewell that Sharpe 'will be a valuable addition to our Hunters as he appears to have a pretty good discrimination of the English styles and therefore I trust will hunt well in other countries'.[27] The pleasure was evidently mutual because, towards the end of his life, when receiving the RIBA Royal Gold Medal in 1875, Sharpe recalled: 'I had the pleasure of his [Rickman's] acquaintance when a young man, and of staying some time in his house; and knowing much of the manner in which he amassed that extraordinary amount of knowledge which he possessed ... I have the greatest respect and veneration for his name.'[28]

Worts Bachelors were supposed to write a monthly account of their studies, in Latin, to the university vice chancellor. How assiduously Sharpe did this is unclear since only three such letters survive in the university records.[29] However, there are nine letters in Whewell's massive archive – two of them in fact written to Rickman, and forwarded to Whewell. This correspondence, written in a dense longhand script (though on two occasions, strangely, by an unknown amanuensis), contains detailed and graphic descriptions of Sharpe's continental travels, first in Germany and then through France.

Two years in Germany

Sharpe's European tour lasted from late 1832 until late 1835. His comments on what he saw and experienced are of some significance since the understanding of medieval architecture was still in its relative infancy. The origins of the pointed arch were still being debated, and the historical precedence of France over Germany as the cradle of Gothic would not be settled finally for another 10 years.[30] It is not surprising that the focus of Sharpe's tour was on early medieval architecture – Romanesque work and the intriguing transition to Gothic, with Cistercian abbeys holding a particular fascination for him. The itinerary, at least its first stages, was probably suggested by Whewell and Rickman,[31] and Sharpe was provided with introductions to some of the key figures in the small but widely connected world of architectural studies. The first phase of his tour (Fig 1.8) may have been conditioned by the fact that they – Rickman and Whewell – had planned a trip up the Rhine that year but were prevented by quarantine restrictions, and settled for a month-long visit in August to Normandy and Picardy instead. Sharpe was in Cologne before Christmas, busy visiting churches, and marvels

Fig 1.8
Sharpe's tour of Germany, 1832–5.

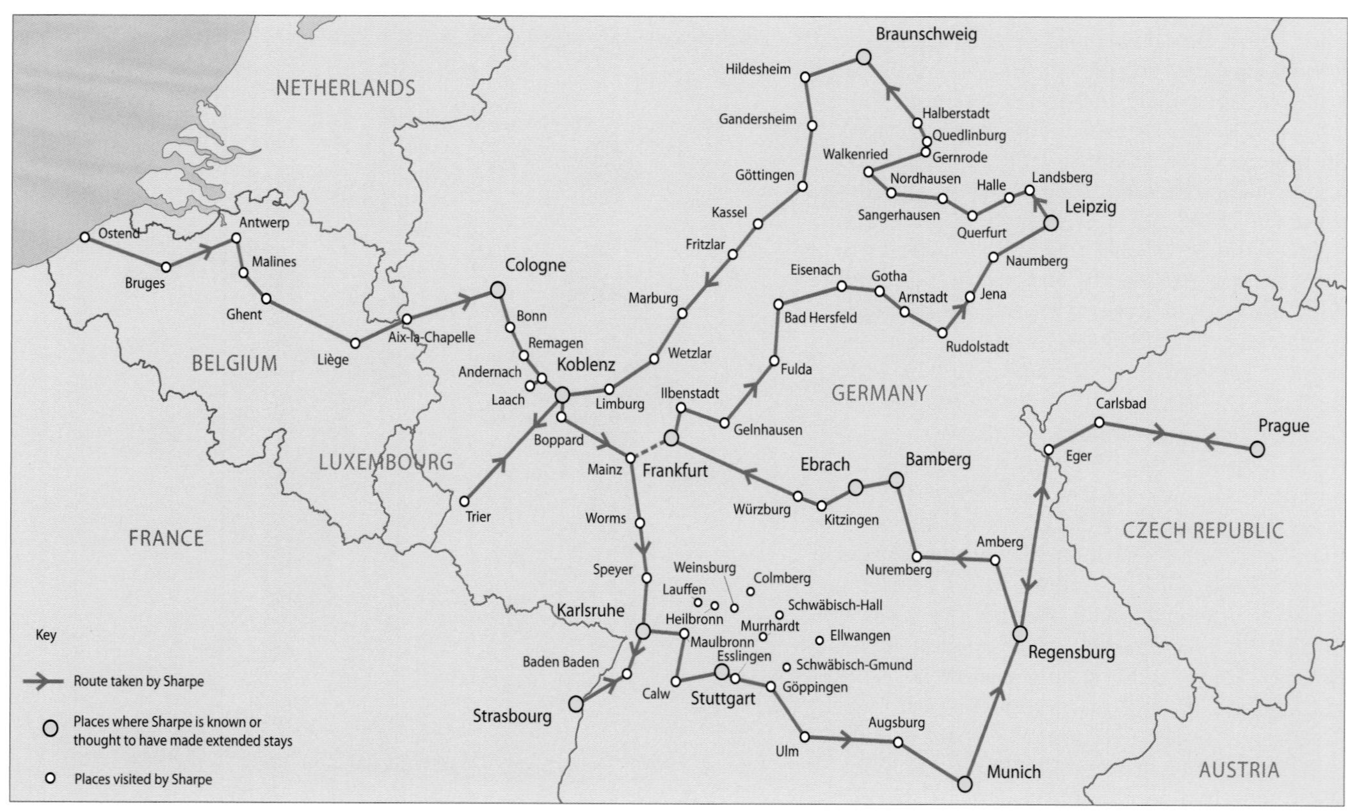

were soon revealing themselves (Fig 1.9). Over three decades later he recalled how, before the end of 1832, he had visited the Cistercian abbey at Altenberg where he found 'the most beautiful stained glass that I ever beheld'.[32]

Sharpe's first letter to Whewell, on 2 July 1833 (a surprisingly long time after he set off), summarised his travels thus far.[33] It was written from Koblenz, where he became friendly with Johann Claudius von Lassaulx (1781–1848), the Prussian official architect and building inspector for the Rhineland province. Lassaulx's buildings of the 1820s and 1830s 'were among Germany's most distinctive and portentous architectural achievements of the time'.[34] He made much use of round-arched architecture, drawing inspiration from the Rhenish Romanesque which Sharpe was studying. His knowledge of early medieval churches was immense, and he was very generous in sharing this with the young Sharpe, together with his books and drawings. At the time Lassaulx was preparing a German translation of Whewell's book on German churches, and Whewell had enquired about progress. Sharpe could only report the all-too-familiar story: 'He cannot at present determine when it will be ready for the press'!

Sharpe's letter continued by outlining his journey thus far. It had taken him through Ostend, Bruges, Antwerp, Malines, Louvain, Liège and Aix-la-Chapelle to Cologne. His eyes had been opened by 'a great deal of very interesting work in Flanders, and of a style perfectly strange to me', in addition to which his enthusiasm for music was evident in his having 'a pretty complete account of all the organs in that part of the country'. In Cologne Sharpe met Sulpiz Boisserée (1773–1854) at the latter's country seat at St Apollinarisberg. Like Lassaulx, Boisserée was a key figure in reviving interest in early medieval architecture, and between 1823 and 1831 had produced lavish studies of Cologne Cathedral. Sharpe was impressed by his enthusiasm and his recent book on Rhenish churches, *Denkmäler der Baukunst vom 7ten bis 13ten Jahrhundert* (1833), and offered to procure a copy for the university library at Cambridge. In a later letter Sharpe refers to him familiarly as 'My old friend Mr. Boisserée'.[35]

Sharpe's second letter to Whewell, headed 'Munich Decr. 1833. No 11, Promenade Platz', notes his meeting with Georg Moller (1784–1852), yet another major figure in the study of German architecture.[36] He was, from 1810, the Director of Architecture in the Grand Duchy of Hesse-Darmstadt, and author of *Denkmähler der deutschen Baukunst,* published between 1815 and 1821 and available in English in 1824.[37] It was Moller who, with Boisserée, had recovered a late 13th-century drawing for the west end of Cologne Cathedral which was to be a vital document in the great project to complete that building. By now Sharpe was increasing his knowledge and felt confident enough to write, 'I received from Moller some very useful information, tho' I found he deceived me much with respect to the style and character of some of the buildings I afterwards visited.' Clearly the general state of knowledge was not what Sharpe might have wished, for he added, 'Indeed most of the German architects with whom I have conversed I found possessed of but very vague and indefinite notions with respect to the distinction of styles.' His hero, in fact, was Lassaulx, of whom he says, 'No one did I find in this respect equal to De Lassaulx.'

It had taken Sharpe a full year to travel from Cologne to Munich, including detours to Trier and Strasbourg. Language seems to have presented no problems. He told Whewell, 'I am picking up a little Italian: German goes on swimmingly.' From Koblenz he had travelled south, sometimes on foot but mostly by public transport. However, he does mention that he 'bought a young 5 year old in the neighbourhood of Rastadt, and a light trotschke [gig] in Carlsruhe, and both have proved a capital

Fig 1.9
The late Romanesque church of St Peter, Sinzig, Rheinland-Pfalz, a building that Sharpe probably took in on his journey up the Rhine. The Romanesque style and Germanic elements found expression in Sharpe's first churches, see Figure 1.15.
(Wolfgang Dietz)

bargain; the convenience and advantages of this method of travelling for one engaged in a pursuit like mine are not to be told, and the expence [*sic*] barely exceeds that of the ordinary method.' After Koblenz the journey to Munich had taken him up the Rhine to Mainz, 'examining all the churches on both sides of the river', through Karlsruhe to Stuttgart, from where he made forays to several towns to the north and east. By October he had reached Ulm, an area of architectural disappointment apart from the tower of the minster.

Sharpe then explained to Whewell that he had attached himself 'to the atelier of a celebrated architectural painter' and was improving his drawing style. He added that this painter had 'almost entered into a definite compact to join me in my travels, and to proceed with me into Italy next autumn'.[38] Nothing appears to have come of this – certainly not a trip to Italy. His main travelling companion seems to have been his dog, Tartar, for which he was obliged to purchase 'residence permits' when passing from one German state to another![39]

He passed the winter of 1833–4 in Munich, visiting the galleries, museums and, especially, the Royal Library, whose many manuscripts held a particular fascination. He also seems to have enjoyed an active social life. He wrote that 'here I meet all the literaries of Munich; – I have not hitherto gone much into Society, but intend doing so when the Carnival commences.' He explored the triangle between Munich, Augsburg and Regensburg (Ratisbon) and was staying in the latter in May 1834 when he wrote a long letter to Rickman.[40] Evidently he had become friendly with Bernhard Grüber (1807–82), the recently appointed (1833) professor of architecture at the Polytechnicum.[41] Sharpe explained that he and Grüber were thinking of publishing in England a work on the Benedictine Abbey of St Jakob (Fig 1.10). Its appeal for British readers lay in the fact that it had been founded by Hiberno-Scottish missionaries and was in the hands of first Irish, then Scottish monks.[42] The two men also thought about travelling together in the south of France, again with publishing in mind. Sharpe asked Rickman to advise on such a venture, but nothing came of these ideas.

At Regensburg, Sharpe came across the architect Carl Alexander von Heideloff (1789–1865).[43] He evidently admired Whewell, whom (Sharpe said) he had 'lionised' in Nuremberg where he was the city architect from 1818.

Fig 1.10
The great north portal at St Jakob's, the Benedictine 'Scottish Church', at Regensburg. Sharpe and Professor Bernhard Grüber contemplated a joint publication on the building. Etching by Ernst Rauch after Ludwig Lange, c *1850.*

Heideloff was busy restoring Regensburg Cathedral, of which he was preparing 'a series of superb drawings'. Once again publication in England was mooted, this time with Sharpe translating the German's text. The two men even got down to details of numbers of plates, what return Heideloff would expect, and the fact that he thought he could drum up 300 subscribers in Germany. Sharpe told Whewell: 'I intend to write to Longman for advice.' But again, the grand intentions came to naught! The restoration work at Regensburg Cathedral was, like many other projects, spurred on by King Ludwig of Bavaria and his devotion to the German Middle Ages. Sharpe waxed enthusiastic:

> We have to thank the King ... for this [work] as well as numerous other benefits to the architectural world: & too much cannot be said of his care in this particular, & woe betide the unfortunate 'Landrichter' [country judge] who suffers a stone of an ancient building to fall out of its place, without paying attention to it – More than one functionary of this kind will have been removed from their offices, for allowing even proprietors of ancient buildings to alter or destroy any part of them, & empty convent buildings when any part of them are sold have always the condition attached to them that no stone shall be replaced or the parts in any way damaged.

From Regensburg, Sharpe travelled through Nuremberg and on to Bamberg from where he wrote to Whewell in August 1834. He was particularly enthused by the Cistercian abbey at Ebrach, whose buildings he dated to 1200–85. They suggested to him that 'it is in the Cistercian buildings we are to look for those principles upon w^{h}. we are to form our laws respecting the transition of the Rom^{que} arch^{re} into Gothic'. Perhaps this was owing to standard building practices observed throughout the order. He commented:

> I am led to this belief from the striking coincidences, w^{h}. I have met with in many of the Abbeys of this order. … I am in great hopes of finding some prescriptions of this kind in a work with the Title of w^{h}. I am alone acquainted, called 'Menologium Cisterciense': – reputedly containing all the regulations & ordinances of the order, for w^{h}. I have in vain searched hitherto in the Libraries I have lately met with.

Sharpe then explained how unexpected circumstances had led him to make a detour. His horse had sprained its shoulder at Regensburg, so while it recuperated he determined to see the castle at Cheb and to visit Prague. Prague turned out to lack those things he was most seeking, and he confided to Whewell that it had 'not a vestige of Romanesque, & very little Gothic'. On the return journey he got a soaking and then fell ill 'with a violent sore throat & inflammation on the chest'; and 'To add to [his] perplexities' his horse was still not fit and he was obliged to change it, 'of course, much to my disadvantage, & having a tolerable doctors bill to pay'. In consequence, he dispensed with the services of a young man called Haindl who, we now learn, had travelled with Sharpe for some four and a half months to make architectural drawings with an eye on publication. He told Whewell that with 40 guineas from the Society of Antiquaries he could

> give a complete history of the rise & progress of Romanesque architecture,/$^{its\ decline}$, and formation & origin of the Gothic to the beginning of the 13th. Cent. over/$^{the\ whole\ of}$ Germany, exclusive of the Austrian territories & Polish Prussia. … I have the most distinct & complete notices of all the buildings in Thuringia, Saxony & Westphalia. I have besides the dates of foundation& erection, of nearly the whole.

From Regensberg Sharpe made his way through Bamberg and Würzburg back towards the Rhine, where he planned to part company with Haindl. There he intended to leave his (no doubt voluminous) drawings and effects with Lassaulx, whom he found restoring the Romanesque castle at Reineck, near Andernach.[44] He left Lassaulx on 5 September 1834, made for Frankfurt, and thence embarked on a trip to Leipzig. Here he had an introduction to Dr Ludwig Puttrich (1783–1856), a lawyer and historian who was then working on his monumental, eventually four-volume *Denkmale der Baukunst des Mittelalters in Sachsen* (1835–50). Sharpe was pleased to discover that Puttrich had a 'devoted attachment to the Romanesque' and a large collection of drawings. As president of what Sharpe described as the 'Society of Antiquaries of Germany', Puttrich proposed Sharpe for membership, which he duly accepted.[45]

Sharpe journeyed next through the Harz mountains with Brunswick as his destination, and then on to Hildesheim where he was impressed by the Romanesque work – despite its being hard to make out in the 'Jesuitified Cathedral'. With winter closing in, and beset by cold and ill health, he was forced to abandon a proposed detour to Westphalian towns such as Osnabrück, Münster and Paderborn, and so returned to Koblenz via Göttingen, Kassel, Marburg and Limburg. His choice of Koblenz, where he stayed over Christmas, was doubtless due to his friendship with Lassaulx, with whom Sharpe seems to have been the regular go-between for a proposed joint publication with Whewell.[46]

On to France

Sharpe now proceeded to France where, unfortunately, his travels are less well documented (Fig 1.11). There is a gap of about five months in his correspondence with Whewell, the next letter being from Lyon on 6 May 1835.[47] His journey had taken him through Strasbourg, where he met Professor Jean Geoffroy Schweighaeuser (1771–1844), yet another pioneer of the study of early architecture, whose *Notice sur les anciens chateaux et autres monuments de la partie méridionale du départment du Bas-Rhin* had been published in 1824. He possessed, Sharpe noted, 'a most valuable & interesting collection of drawings of all the remarkable churches of lower Alsace'. Despite being truly comprehensive, he reflected ruefully but for unstated reasons, 'they do not however stand much chance of publication, I fear'.

The harsh winter months took their toll on Sharpe's health, and he abandoned a projected trip through Switzerland. Having disposed of his horse and gig at Basle, he headed south by

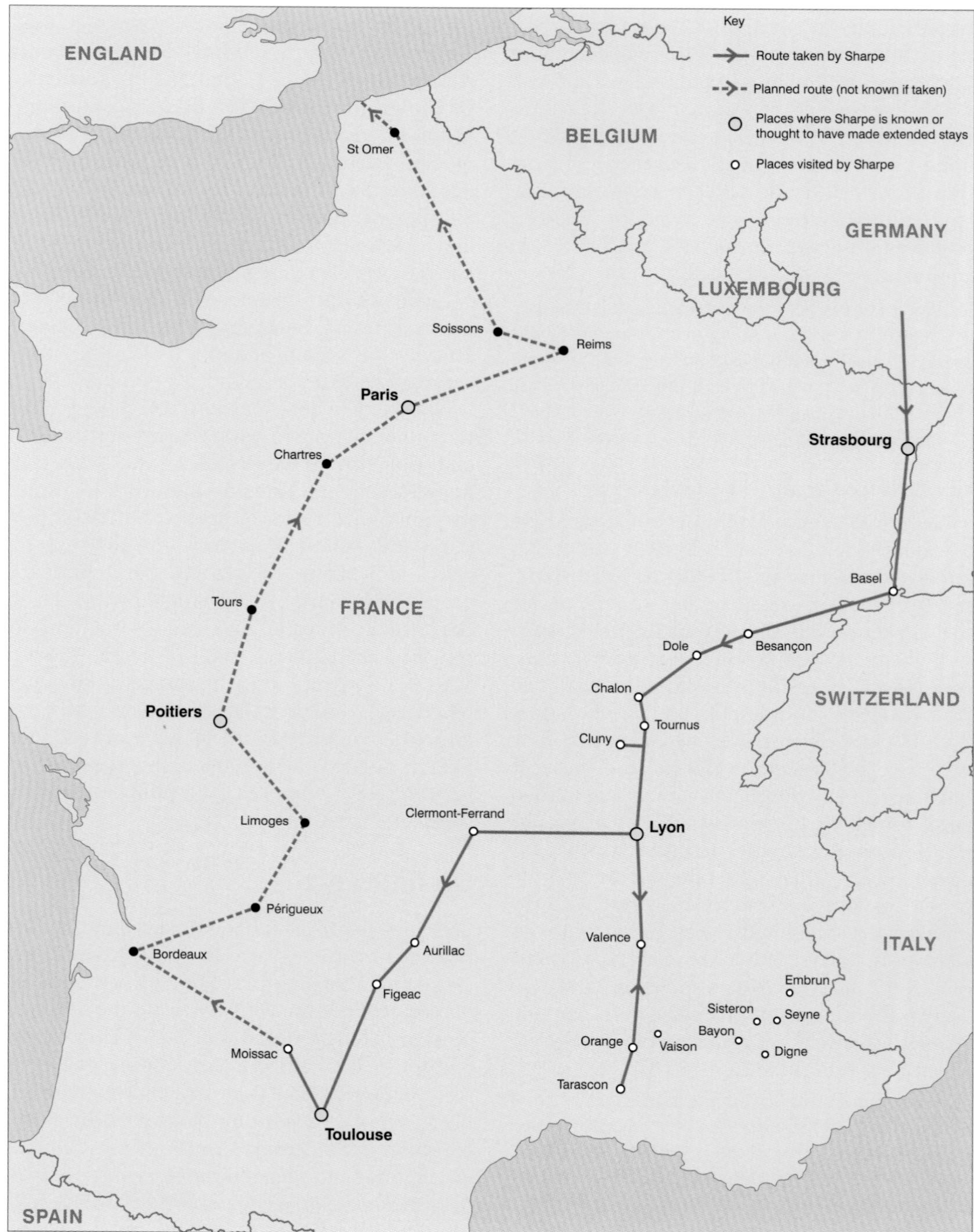

Fig 1.11
Sharpe's tour of France, 1835.

boat to Lyon, where he arrived at the start of February 1835 and set about detailed library research. In the spring he proceeded further south and was intrigued by the architecture in the Hautes and Basses Alpes, which 'exemplifies the influence which the vaulting has [on?] the other members & arrangements of a church: & is a particularly forcible illustration of the causes which if they did not call the pointed arch into existence, contributed certainly to its universal employment in certain parts of buildings'. In Provence he found that 'almost all the churches are of a peculiar Transitional character' but discovered little reliable information about them. Yet another revelation was

> the influence … Roman Architecture continued to exert over that of the South of France even at a very advanced period … The egg moulding, the modil-

lions, the leaves of the acanthus and plane tree are found consistently on monuments of the latter end of the 12th Century ... And a door-way of a church in Lyon which I had always regarded as Roman Work ... I recognised ... as the work of the same period.

Sharpe was thrilled by the prospect of future discoveries in France: 'I look forward to this period', he told Whewell (expecting to return home in July), 'with the childish longing of a school boy.' He wondered at the ruins of Cluny 'destroyed by the barbarians of the 18th Century'; visited the 10th-century abbey at Tournus; saw the churches of the Auvergne; and made his way down to Toulouse where he marvelled at the great church of Saint-Saturnin. His last letter to Whewell from the continent was from Toulouse in June 1835, by which time his plans for returning to England were being put on hold.[48] He proceeded first to Moissac, where 'the details were of decided Romanesque character ... [but] the pointed arch prevailed throughout'. Then he planned to proceed west to Bordeaux and up to Paris by way of Périgueux, Limoges, Poitiers, Tours and Chartres.

Medievalism and the understanding of medieval architecture

Sharpe's infrequent correspondence from France has few details of his movements, but it does give illuminating insights into a rising tide of medievalism there in the mid-1830s, akin to that taking place in England and Germany. His letter to Whewell from Toulouse describes how 'within the few last years people have begun to manifest a wonderful affection for the Middle Ages.' He noted the initiative of François Guizot (1787–1874), Minister of Public Instruction from 1832, 'to collect, decipher, & publish all hitherto unpublished remains of the Litterature [*sic*] of these times possessing interest preserved in the different Archives of the Kingdom'. Medievalism even seemed to invade fashionable life, with Sharpe observing:

Moreover it has become the Rage at Paris to affect in furniture, ornaments, trinkets, & even in dress, & tonsure, the modes of the Middle Ages. – Witness your apartments 'meubles à la Gothique', your stained windows, the 'Boisseries' – Vessels, – Crucifixes – & relics of all kinds, (I speak from report) daily exhibited in the Broker's shops. Witness the peaked Hats, embroidered collars, long hair, & beards of your modern dandies of the Middle Ages. – and above all the multitude of architectural Lithographs, which are daily published & with which the windows of the Booksellers shop are inundated: – scraps of ruins, windows, etc.: – the greater part it is true are imaginary, & all simply picturesque: without any architectural merit, or ulterior design: but they serve to shew the turn of the popular passion.

Allied to such feelings, interest in ancient monuments gained early government support in France through an earlier creation of Guizot's, the Commission des Monuments historiques of 1830, headed first by Ludovic Vitet, then from 1834, by Prosper Merimée. It is undoubtedly that body which Sharpe calls the 'Société Française pour la Conservation & Description des Monuments Historiques' and about the work of which he writes admiringly:

This society publishes Bulletins or Periodical accounts of all the churches in the different Departments; it is establishing branch Societies & Commissions in all parts of the Kingdom: in each Department there is an Inspector General for that Department, whose business it is to communicate to the Society details of the existence, peculiarities, state of preservation etc. of e[h]. remarkable monument in his District: – together with any historical Notices & local traditions, which he may collect, these details are published in the Periodical Bulletins above mentioned. The Society is superintended & regulated by a Travelling Director, whose expenses are paid by the general fund. – It has obtained promises of assistance & support from the government & is already intrusted [*sic*] with considerable prohibitory Powers as regards the Demolition or alteration of any Public Building of antiquity. – And I have just read a circular issued by the Minister & addressed to the Prefects in accordance with this promise.

It is a matter of the greatest regret that in England Sharpe never published the fruits of his continental tour. No doubt his immediate and highly successful plunge into architectural practice, together with other business ventures later on, squeezed out any such good intentions. He had met many experts on his travels, had done primary research in museums, galleries and libraries, had studied and drawn a multitude of important buildings and was undoubtedly in a position to advance the knowledge of European architecture of the 12th and 13th centuries and the rise of Gothic. In the mid-1830s there was a widespread and longstanding belief that Gothic was a German style. After all, had not Vasari in the mid-16th century referred to northern architecture as being in the *maniera tedesca*? Among Sharpe's contacts,

Boisserée remained a defender of the Germanness of Gothic, and as late as 1841 even Grüber, who befriended Sharpe in Regensburg, still regarded the pinnacle of Gothic achievement as Cologne Cathedral.[49]

Sharpe distilled some of his thinking in 1834 for Thomas Rickman, at the end of his two-year tour through Germany.[50] While Romanesque features survived into the early 13th century, he said, transitional work dated from 1200 to 1250, and was similar to, but also different from, that in England. He considered that the new style was introduced by the Cistercians, who were responsible for the earliest work in the new style in Germany, but that it had originated elsewhere. He suggested to Rickman that 'it appears in the highest degree possible, in consequence of the sudden appearance, – short duration – & paucity of examples in this style, – that Germany was not the land of its birth; and as it never took root & flourished in this soil, we are strongly entitled to suppose that it was a plant of foreign growth.' At this point France and its early medieval buildings still awaited Sharpe's exploration, but he felt the answer lay in the work of the Cistercians. As he told Rickman excitedly, 'I am burning with curiosity to see what the Cistercian Buildings of France exhibit, where there/were so many hundreds founded: at the close & in the middle of the 12 Century.'

Six months later, in June 1835, Sharpe's letter to Whewell from Lyon set out his conclusions on the matter of the pointed arch. As to when it was introduced, he admitted, 'I must confess myself just at present more than ever involved in doubt and contradiction.' However, he was certain that Germany had to yield to France in terms of historical precedence, and he had this to say:

> 1. That no example of a pointed arch can be adduced of which the Date is historically and satisfactorily fixed as anterior the XIIIth. Cent. – (Tho' there be grounds for conjecturing that it may have been employed somewhat sooner.)
> 2. That numerous examples may be pointed out of Buildings down to the very commencement of the XIIIth. Cent. in wh. no trace of a ∧[pointed arch] exists. But as regards France, the former axiom is certainly not tenable; for I have/testimony as full & plain as it is possible, which proves the existence of this form as early as the first part of the latter half of the XIIth. Cent. [1150–1175] – if indeed a still earlier date be not admissible. – 2.ly I have not yet found an example capable of supporting the latter axiom.

Eventually Sharpe arrived in Paris, exhausted and in the grip of a fever, as a fellow Lancastrian, who met him there, later recalled.[51] The details of his final months in France are unclear, but he was certainly in Paris in August and October 1835, before returning to Lancaster to begin his career as an architect.[52]

Lancaster in 1835

In 1835 Lancaster was a relatively small county town of about 13,000 inhabitants (Fig 1.12).[53] It had long been outstripped by the burgeoning industrial and commercial centres further south. It was still a port, but much affected by the silting up of the Lune and no longer participating in the lucrative triangular trade of manufactured goods, slaves and sugar: the last slave ship had left in 1792.[54] After 1815 the West Indies trade went into a final slump, unemployment soared and the poor rates reached record levels. The town's two private banks both failed in the 1820s (Benjamin Satterthwaite had lost heavily in the collapse of Worswick's in 1822), and even Lancaster's historic cabinet-making industry suffered.

For a while textile manufacture took the place of trade in Lancaster's economy, but with mixed success. Several former merchants bought or built mills for cotton- or silk-spinning in Lancaster and the surrounding area. Taking pride of place among these was probably the purpose-built steam-powered Canal Side Mill of Thomas Mason, later known as White Cross, which was supplied with cotton and coal via Glasson Dock and the Lancaster Canal. Considerable impetus came from the involvement of the Greg family of Styal, near Wilmslow (Ch). In 1817 Samuel Greg acquired Low Mill at Caton, four miles up the Lune Valley, and proceeded to combine it with a former sailcloth factory in Moor Lane for production, respectively, of cotton warp and weft, weaving the finished velveteen cloth in Lancaster. By 1832 it was the largest operation both in the Gregs' extensive empire and in Lancaster itself, where it employed 560 workers.[55] Other newcomers were James Williamson (1813–79), who arrived from Keswick in 1827 to found a successful oilcloth and linoleum business, and the Storey brothers, who came from Bardsea on the other side of Morecambe Bay in 1835 and built up an important oilcloth- and baize-manufacturing business. The Sharpe, Paley and Storey families would be linked by marriage as the century wore on.

Establishing home and office

On returning to Lancaster in late 1835, Edmund Sharpe started his architectural practice at his mother's house in Penny Street, moving to Sun Street in 1838.[56] In 1839 he moved both home and practice to St Leonard's Gate, and a building large enough to accommodate his promising new pupil, E G Paley, who joined him in October the previous year.[57] In June 1841 the two of them were using it as both home and office.

In 1843 Sharpe moved his home to 11 Fenton Street.[58] In May that year (before marrying in July) he bought a plot of land on the south-west corner of Fenton Street, then at the edge of open country.[59] Here he built another house, number 14 (very much later called 'Fenton House'), as both home and office. It is not clear exactly when it was constructed, very possibly as early as 1844, but seemingly it was complete by November 1847 when his second son, Edmund, was said to have been born there.[60] The offices in St Leonard's Gate appear to have been retained until 1860, when Paley moved them to the slopes of Castle Hill, opposite Lancaster Castle, where they remained until the very end of the practice.[61]

Architecture: a meteoric beginning and Sharpe's Romanesque churches

At the end of 1835 Sharpe had written to Whewell about becoming an architect and explained that he was 'already busily employed in collecting all the information connected with the practical part of it'.[62] He had every reason for doing so, as he explained excitedly:

> My decision has been rather hastened by concurrent circumstances which afforded opportunities of making such commencement of the profession as few young architects can boast of. The plans for my first church were projected executed, & lodged in the / Incorporated [Church Building] Society's hands, within a fortnight of my determination to adopt the Profession, and I am already in treaty about another, to be built at Bamber Bridge, near Preston. I have also been mentioned favourably to Ld. Derby who is about to build a ch. at Knowsley, so that I have lost no time.

Few architects of his generation can have got off to such a flourishing start, and it was churches that underpinned his early success. Sharpe (Fig 1.13) had every advantage – well-educated, his head full of architecture from his foreign travels, in practice in a town with no

Fig 1.12
Lancaster from the south at the time that Sharpe began his architectural career, as drawn by his sister Emily, 9 September 1837.
(Austin Paley Archive, Lancaster City Museums, MS LM 86/129; Tim Austin)

Fig 1.13
Edmund Sharpe painted in 1839 by Thomas Carlyle: a companion piece to the picture of his mother (see Fig 1.2). As a copy of the missing original, this picture is indistinct but in the bottom left-hand corner a representation can be made out of Sharpe's first church, St Mark's, Witton – a clear sign that this commission was of great importance to him. (Manchester Libraries and Information Service, Local Studies; Tim Austin)

other architects and, above all, well connected. The pivotal figure in this early success was his cousin, the Revd J W Whittaker of Blackburn, who had in fact designed a small Perpendicular-style church nearby at Feniscowles, consecrated in 1836. Whittaker was only too happy to promote his talented young cousin. A glimpse of such patronage at work survives in a letter of 22 December 1835, from a Henry Hargreaves of Blackburn to a Henry Hoyle of New Whalley, who appears to have had church-building in mind: 'Dr. Whittaker ... has a Relation of the Name of Sharpe who has made a plan for the intended Church at Witton whom he sho[d] recommend to make your Plan. – His Plans he says are cheap and handsome, and his Charge wo[d] be trifling.'[63]

The first church for which Sharpe was responsible and to which he referred in the letter quoted above was at Witton on the outskirts of Blackburn (Figs 1.14, 1.15, 1.16 and 1.17), and was surely an example of Whittaker's influence. In 1825 Whittaker had married Mary Haughton Feilden, daughter of Sir William Feilden of Feniscowles Hall, and it was Joseph Feilden, from the senior branch of the family at Witton Park, who commissioned the new church. A Feilden link may help explain Sharpe's hopes of work from the 13th Earl of Derby. In 1817 Joseph Feilden married Frances Mary Master, and it was her brother, the Revd Robert Mosley Master, the incumbent at St Peter's in Burnley since 1826, who in 1827 had been appointed chaplain to the 12th earl. Another strong possibility is the continuing influence of his late godfather, Edmund Yates (1770–1835) of Ince Hall, who had died in April 1835 and whose niece's parents-in-law were both closely related to the 13th earl.[64]

Despite the speed with which Sharpe gained the commission for St Mark, Witton,

Fig 1.14
Blackburn, St Mark, Witton, 1836–8, in a suburban area of Blackburn, early Victorian view before the addition of a south transept. The building to the right is a school. (© Blackburn with Darwen Library and Information Services)

Fig 1.15 (far left)
St Mark, Witton, showing the tower placed between the nave and the east end, and the church having a decidedly Germanic detailing (see also *St Peter's, Sinzig, Fig 1.9).*

Fig 1.16 (left)
Preston, St Thomas, 1837–9, by the local architect, John Lathom. Although rather more English in appearance, this church has the same odd plan as St Mark's. It is hard to believe that Lathom was not aware of Sharpe's Witton church.
(Mark Watson)

the foundation stone was not laid until a year later, on 10 October 1836, three months later than that of his next commission, St Saviour, Bamber Bridge, near Preston. The delay was presumably due to fund-raising. When the big day came, the ceremony was a grand affair with over a thousand people taking part in a mile-long procession to the site where J W Whittaker officiated: Sharpe, of course, was present, to see Joseph Feilden lay the foundation stone.[65] Furthermore, the consecration of St Mark's by Bishop Sumner of Chester did not take place until 10 June 1838, eight months after that of St Saviour's. Even then, according to the local newspaper, it was 'by no means in a state of completion'.[66] Both churches are Romanesque in style, a natural choice for Sharpe in the light of his recent studies on the Continent. It also had the advantage of cheapness, as Sharpe explained to Whewell in connection with St Mark's: 'no style can be worked so cheap as the Romanesque,

Fig 1.17 (below)
St Mark, Witton. The yellow seats are free, the pink ones appropriated. The gallery held 208 seats, 164 of them for children. Within the north wall of the tower is a recess for a fireplace.
(Lambeth Palace Library, ICBS 01933)

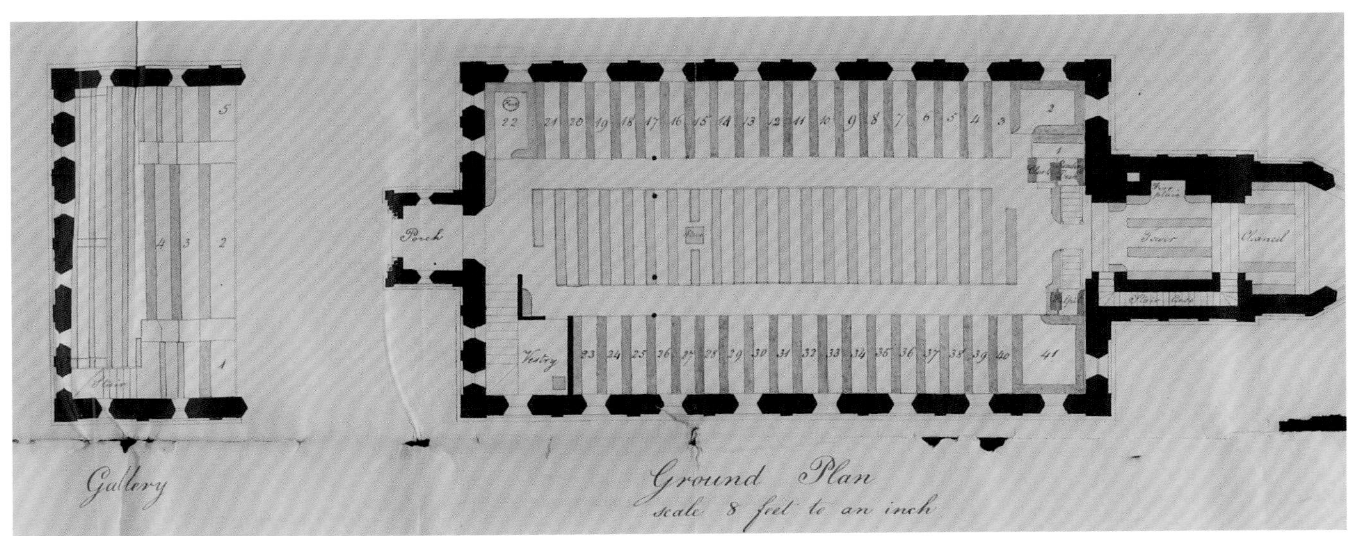

that is the plain romanesque of Northern Germany'. The same reasoning was given in the printed appeal leaflet for St Mark's (with wording probably suggested by Sharpe): 'The style of the building which it is proposed to adopt is that which generally prevailed on the Continent of Europe, in the tenth and eleventh centuries, for ecclesiastical buildings, in which the entire absence of expensive decorations ensures moderation of expenditure.'[67]

St Mark's is a curious building, clearly Germanic in inspiration. The tower and spire are placed just beyond the east wall of the nave and, even allowing for the fact that chancels in Anglican churches had not yet acquired their later Victorian importance, the tower with its narrow passage through to the east end is an obstructive and ungainly internal feature. It is as though all that mattered was the external appearance. The west end presents a stern façade to the road, with two storeys plus a gable, quite small windows, and Lombard bands at the top of each tier – all features which are carried through on to the side elevations of the broad, aisleless nave (no doubt there were galleries).

St Saviour, Bamber Bridge (Fig 1.18) (now much extended), is a simpler and rather cheaper church which shares motifs with St Mark's – a tower (in this case at the west end) turning from square to octagonal, Lombard banding, single-light, round-arched windows, and an aisleless nave with, originally, a small, pre-ecclesiological projection for the communion table. Across the road from the church is a school which continues the Romanesque theme (Fig 1.19); although there is no documentary proof that this is by Sharpe, the stylistic similarity and the

Fig 1.18 (above)
Bamber Bridge, St Saviour, 1836–7, with Lombardic band details, and an octagonal top to the tower. (Mark Watson)

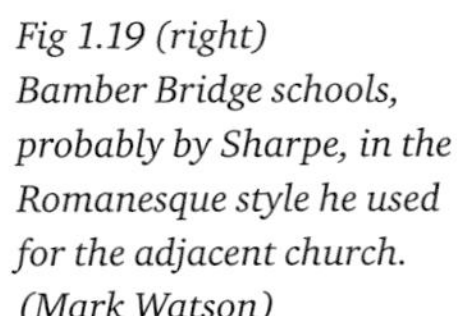

Fig 1.19 (right)
Bamber Bridge schools, probably by Sharpe, in the Romanesque style he used for the adjacent church. (Mark Watson)

NEW CHURCH.

TO BUILDERS AND OTHERS.

PERSONS desirous of Contracting for the Execution of the MASON'S and FLAGGER'S WORK, the CARPENTER'S and JOINER'S WORK, the PLASTERER'S and SLATER'S WORK, or the PLUMBER'S, GLAZIER'S, and PAINTER'S WORK of a NEW CHURCH about to be erected at LANCASTER, can see the Plans and Specifications at the Office of EDMUND SHARPE, Architect, St. Leonard-gate, Lancaster, where they will remain for inspection from MONDAY, JANUARY 13th, until THURSDAY, JANUARY 23rd, and where the conditions of Tender and further particulars can be ascertained.

Lancaster, Dec. 27, 1839.

Fig 1.20 (above left) Farington, St Paul, 1839–40, again in the Romanesque style, and, unusually, built of brick. (Mark Watson)

Fig 1.21 (above) Invitation to tender in the Lancaster Guardian, *1839, for the building of St Thomas' church in Lancaster. Rather than a single tender, bids from four separate trades are being sought.* (Lancaster Guardian *28 December 1839)*

fact that it is seemingly co-eval with the church makes it highly probable.[68]

Sharpe's two earliest churches were both in his beloved Romanesque, and others followed before he gave it up in the early 1840s as the tide of taste shifted powerfully in favour of Gothic. His other round-arched essays were at Chatburn in 1837–8, a fairly modest design with a west tower and decidedly un-Romanesque broach spire; Marthall (Ch) in 1839, a small, red-brick building with four round-arched windows on each side (its rounded apse is later); and Farington (Fig 1.20) in 1839–40, an unusual building, also of red brick, but with contrasted stone pilaster strips and, on the tower, Lombard friezes.

The Catalogue in this book notes building contractors when known (*see* Appendix 5). It is apparent that, especially in Edmund Sharpe's day, contracts were usually divided up into separate trades, with one man being responsible for, say, masonry, another for carpentry and joinery, another for plumbing and glazing, and so on. Contracting 'by the great' – to use an 18th-century term – whereby a single, main contractor took responsibility for the whole scope, seems to have be fairly unusual, at least in this area at this time. In the invitation to tender shown in Figure 1.21, Edmund Sharpe clearly expected to get bids for four separate scopes of work. This way of working meant that no margins and contingencies would be added by a main contractor, thus securing a lower overall price. The subject is discussed more fully in Appendix 3.

On to Gothic

Although Sharpe had praised the cheapness of the Romanesque style, the same could be said in favour of the most basic kind of Gothic, used again and again during the church-building boom of the late 1830s and early 1840s. Tall, single lancet windows with buttresses between, a west tower (when there was money available, and a bell-cote when it wasn't); a short eastern projection for the communion table probably with a triple lancet east window; transepts or aisles for the larger churches; a western gallery in smaller churches and on three sides in more substantial ones – these are the familiar stock-in-trade features of late 1830s churches.

Sharpe designed a number of such churches. The first were a pair of simple, aisleless chapels of 1837–8 at Cowgill and Howgill (both CuWY) in the Sedbergh area (Fig 1.22). The foundation stone for the former was laid by the great geologist Adam Sedgwick, a close friend of William Whewell who no doubt put his young friend and architectural protégé forward for the commission.[69] The Howgill job must have come Sharpe's way through Sedbergh School and church links, although Stephen Sedgwick, who gave the site, was from a different branch of the family.[70] Then came a similar building at Bickerton in Cheshire in 1838–9. In 1839–41 there was the church of St Catherine, Scholes, an inner suburb of Wigan (GM). Once again Sharpe introduced an octagonal form in the belfry stage that carries a crown of gablets behind which sprouts the spire. It is a rather awkward composition, but the main interest at St Catherine's lies in the fact that it has the only Sharpe interior largely untouched since his day (Fig 1.23). Sharpe's favourite square-turning-to-octagonal tower device recurs yet again at St James the Great, Briercliffe, near Burnley (Figs 1.24 and 1.25), where it has more of a German flavour. Like the Scholes church, it has conventional double lancets to the side elevations.

Fig 1.22
A pair of small, cheap lancet chapels at Cowgill (top) and Howgill (bottom) for the isolated, hilly country in the north-west tip of what was the West Riding of Yorkshire (now Cumbria).
(Mark Watson)

Fig 1.23
Wigan (GM), St Catherine, Scholes, 1839–41, where the box-pews, galleries, tiny chancel and factory-like roof show Sharpe so far untouched by ecclesiological principles.
(Mark Watson)

This commission seems to have come Sharpe's way through his Whittaker/Feilden/Mosley connections. Although the church was refitted in 1881, unusually the three galleries survive, as at Scholes. Holy Trinity, Wray (Fig 1.26), of 1839–40, has graded lancets in the side walls and a large western bell-cote under a bold single gable. A simple lancet design was executed at Glasson at exactly the same time but with a single bell-cote. Christ Church, Barnton (Ch), of 1841–2, attributed to Sharpe, offers conventional single lancets in the side walls and a rather inadequate west end with a double-gabled, double bell-cote perched above three tall lancets. In 1839–40 two remarkably similar churches were built at Bretherton (Fig 1.27) and Mawsdesley (Fig 1.28) in mid-Lancashire. Both have west towers with thin recessed spires and openings in the ground-floor stage (now filled in at Mawdesley), and square-headed windows replace Sharpe's hitherto customary lancet style. Sharpe's employment for these two last churches came possibly through the Revd William Yates, rector of nearby Eccleston, and brother of Sharpe's godfather Edmund Yates,

Fig 1.24
Briercliffe, St James, 1840–1. Sharpe again turns his square tower base into an octagon below the spire. From an original watercolour by Lester Whittaker (date unknown).

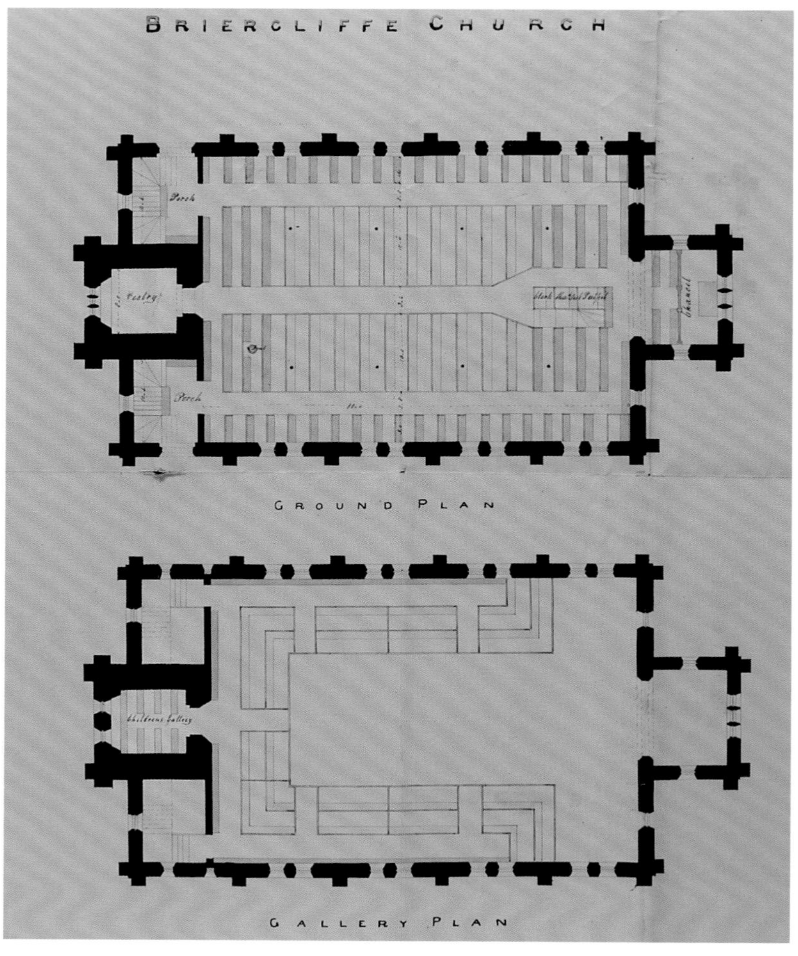

Fig 1.25
Briercliffe, plan, c 1841, with pre-ecclesiological arrangements of a three-decker pulpit in front of a tiny chancel and gallery. (Lambeth Palace Library, ICBS 02312)

or more likely through the Revd Streynsham Master, rector of Croston and father of the Revd Robert Mosley Master, whom we have met as the brother-in-law of Joseph Feilden.

Personal recommendation also lay behind Sharpe's first substantial aisled church, Christ Church, Walmsley, just outside Bolton, of 1837–9 (Figs 1.29 and 1.30). In January 1837 he was invited to discuss the project by its future incumbent, who was then the master at Bolton Grammar School.[71] Sharpe had been mentioned by two leading citizens. One was a solicitor, Edmund Langshaw, brother of Pearson, whose father, John, lived in Lancaster where he was organist at the parish church. The second was probably John Fletcher, who was owner of the Ladyshore Colliery. The Langshaws and the Fletchers were cousins, while Edmund Sharpe would have known the Langshaws from 1829 as he would have met the brilliant George Langshaw (brother of Edmund and Pearson) when he went up to St John's College, Cambridge (Fig 1.31).[72] The links between the Fletchers and Sharpes would be tied when Edmund married John Fletcher's sister Elizabeth in 1843. The church at Walmsley is a four-square essay in typical late 1830s Early English, with paired lancets in the aisles and graded, triple lancets in the clerestory and top stage of the tower. A spire, proposed initially, was abandoned on cost grounds. What is extraordinary, however, is the use of monolithic piers, some 16 feet high and without bases, for the six-bay arcades.[73] Transepts and a full chancel were added in 1867 and reordering took place in the later 20th century.

Soon after Christ Church came Sharpe's largest, grandest church, Holy Trinity, Blackburn (Figs 1.32 and 1.33). The instigator was the vicar of Blackburn, J W Whittaker, and unsurprisingly the commission went to his architect cousin. The foundation stone was laid in October 1837, but economic distress in the town delayed progress. The church was not opened until June 1845 (finally consecrated July 1846). The church could seat over 1,600 people, half of them in free seats, and the size of the building is a clear indication of how substantial new Anglican accommodation was needed in early Victorian Blackburn. The church cost just over £5,000, of which the Church Building Commissioners contributed £1,519. It is very tall, and has massive transepts as high as the nave and some most impressive, soaring fenestration. At the east end and in the ends of the transepts Sharpe used a very beautiful divided arrangement of 2–3–2 lights. Such a design is not an English medieval feature. It occurs once in Scot-

Fig 1.26
Wray, Holy Trinity, 1839–40. The porch is no doubt later.

land, at Dunblane Cathedral (1–4–1), but is more common in Germany where Sharpe probably met with it in his reading and his travels, although he failed to get to Paderborn where it occurs at the cathedral; it is also found at the church of St Marien auf dem Berge at Herford. It was these churches, both in North Rhine-Westphalia, which may have inspired Gilbert Scott to use a 1–3–1 configuration at St Mary Abbots, Kensington, of 1868–72.[74] But this was 30 years after Sharpe's masterly design. The tower at Holy Trinity had to wait for completion until 1853, and the spire was never built. At the east end, schools were placed under a series of four gables, an idea which Sharpe possibly took from the famous Lady Chapel at the east end of Holy Trinity, Long Melford, in Suffolk. A notable feature of the interior is the ceiling with its 88 panels decorated with armorial bearings and underlining, in what was a major church extension project around 1840, the linkage between important families and the established church. As well as royal arms stretching back to Edward the Confessor there are the arms of serving bishops and other leading clergymen (including J W Whittaker), the Feildens, Pudsey Dawson (High Sheriff of Lancashire in 1845, and a friend and client of Sharpe's) and William Whewell. Whittaker had canvassed Whewell in November 1844: 'The contribution from each party will not exceed three guineas. As we consider you one of y^e luminaries of y^e Palatinate, you are by no means to be omitted.'[75] And, indeed, he was not.

Fig 1.27 (above) Bretherton, St John the Baptist, 1839–40. The porte cochère/steeple is very similar to that at Mawdesely. (Mark Watson)

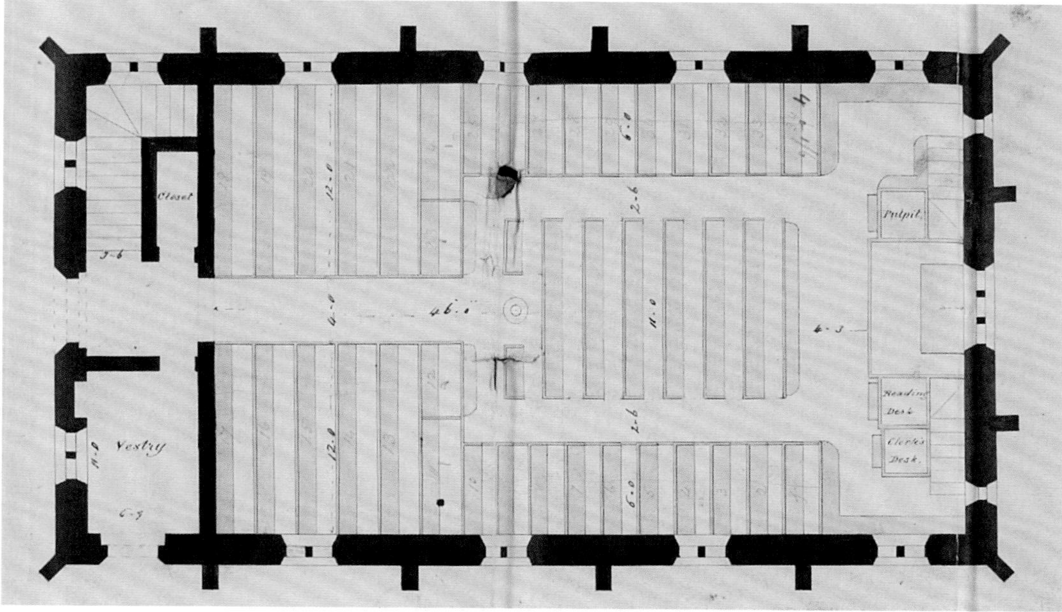

Fig 1.28 (left) Mawdesley, St Peter, 1839–40. Another set of pre-ecclesiological arrangements. The stairs at the north-west corner lead to a (surviving) gallery. Curiously the plan omits the tower. (Lambeth Palace Library, ICBS 02359)

Multiple successes in Cheshire

Sharpe secured an impressive tally of eight or nine church commissions in Cheshire between 1837 and 1845. He had quickly come to the notice of the bishop of Chester, John Bird Sumner. In February 1837 Sharpe proudly explained to his prospective clients at Walmsley church (GM) that he had a letter from Sumner appointing him as architect for a new church at Stalybridge (Ch, now GM) (Fig 1.34): to be paid for largely by the Church Building Commissioners of whom Sumner was one.[76] How had this important contact come about? Until the creation of Manchester diocese in 1848, the Bishop of Chester's vast territory also took in Lancashire, and Sumner very probably knew of Sharpe through J W Whittaker, one of his most important and dynamic clergymen. It is also worth noting that Sumner was an Evangelical, and so Sharpe's own Low Church leanings can have done him no harm in this staunchly Protestant diocese.

Fig 1.29 (right) Walmsley (Bolton, GM), Christ Church, 1837–9. (Mark Watson)

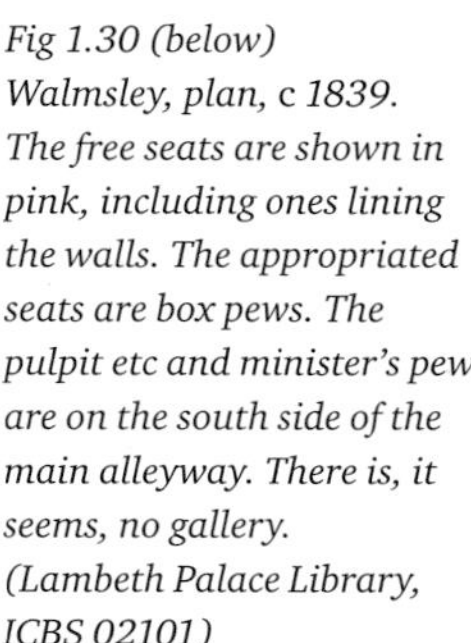

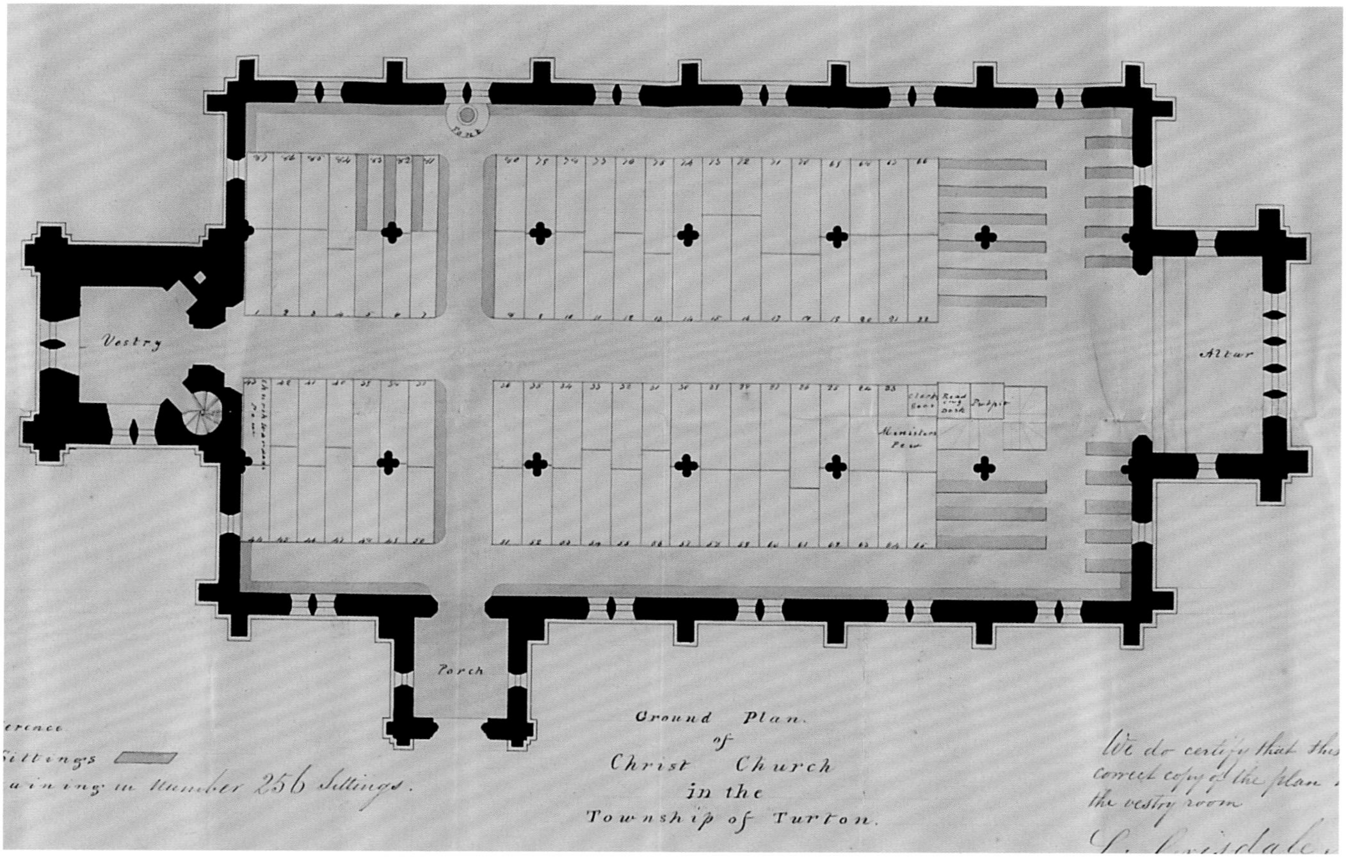

Fig 1.30 (below) Walmsley, plan, c 1839. The free seats are shown in pink, including ones lining the walls. The appropriated seats are box pews. The pulpit etc and minister's pew are on the south side of the main alleyway. There is, it seems, no gallery. (Lambeth Palace Library, ICBS 02101)

But there were other links too. The Sharpe family maintained links with its Cheshire roots, especially after Edmund's eldest sister Marianne (1811–42) returned to live in Knutsford on marrying in 1832. An important influence also seems to have been the Revd Richard Greenall (1806–67).[77] He was curate from 1829 to 1831 to the Revd James John Hornby of Winwick (then Lancashire), who was related to Sharpe's godfather, Edmund Yates of Ince Hall,

Fig 1.31 (above left) George Langshaw (1806–43), c 1825–9, whom Edmund Sharpe would have met in 1829 on going to Cambridge. The Sharpe, Paley, Austin and Langshaw families would become closely interlinked. The portrait appears to have been added to a stock-in-trade figure. (Austin Paley Archive, Lancaster City Museums, MS LM 86/129; Tim Austin)

Fig 1.32 (above) Blackburn, Holy Trinity, Sharpe's finest church, begun in 1837 and initiated by his cousin, the Revd J W Whittaker, whose parish church can be seen bottom left. (Churches Conservation Trust)

and also to the 12th and 13th Earls of Derby.[78] In 1831 he was appointed by Bishop Sumner to the living of St Matthew, Stretton, and in 1839 became rural dean of Frodsham, again nominated by Sumner. Any links between the Greenalls and Sharpes were strengthened from 1836 when Edmund Yates's daughter moved into Ince Hall with her husband, the Revd William W Park.[79] His family, already well known to the Sharpes, were on friendly terms with the Greenalls. Richard Greenall was a trustee of the Weaver Navigation,[80] and was no doubt instrumental in helping Sharpe secure three church commissions from it, two of which were within the Frodsham deanery.

Sharpe's career in Cheshire began with a flourish on 3 September 1838, which saw the laying not only of the foundation stone of St George, Stalybridge, but also that of another Sharpe church, St John the Evangelist, Dukinfield (Ch, now also GM), just over a mile away across a valley.[81] Again it was largely paid for by the church Commissioners. Both churches have west towers, and aisles and nave under a common roof, but the fenestration is very different. Dukinfield has pairs of plain lancets whereas Stalybridge has Geometrical windows of 'two lights and an uncusped circle – which', as Pevsner remarked, 'before 1840 is entirely unexpected'.[82]

In the early 1840s Sharpe was engaged upon three churches for the trustees of the Weaver Navigation to minister to watermen and others connected with traffic on the river. This had recently been improved to increase its capacity for moving salt from the Cheshire saltfields to the coast. The need for churches had to an extent been brought about by the trustees themselves who, in 1839, passed a by-law forbidding movement on the navigation on Sundays. Christ Church, Weston Point, near Runcorn, completed in 1841, has a broach spire, transepts and Geometrical detailing. The other two churches, Holy Trinity, Northwich (1841–2) (Fig 1.35), and Christ Church, Over at Winsford (1843–4; demolished 1881), were both bigger and were given broach spires and Geometrical detail but lack transepts. Sharpe's other Cheshire churches

Fig 1.33
Blackburn, Holy Trinity. The spacious interior has fine vistas and makes pioneering use of a 'divided' east window, an idea Sharpe may have picked up on his German travels. Some of its numerous painted heraldic panels can be seen on the nave and crossing roofs. (Mark Watson)

were at Bickerton (1838); Marthall (*c* 1839), over which a slight uncertainty exists; Davenham (1842–4, rebuilt); and probably Barnton (1845), which was commissioned by the Revd Richard Greenall.

Fig 1.34
Stalybridge (GM), St George, 1838–40, departs from the usual lancet detailing of the time with the use of Geometrical tracery. (Mark Watson)

The evolving practice and marriages

Sharpe's early success obliged him to obtain assistance. In October 1838 he took on a pupil, Edward Graham Paley,[83] who from 1845 would become his partner and from 1851 his brother-in-law. Paley's background and how he came to join Sharpe are considered in the next chapter. In 1841 Sharpe accepted another pupil, Thomas (Tom) Austin (1822–67), half-brother of Hubert, who was born earlier that same year. Tom left in 1852 for Newcastle upon Tyne, where he set up in practice for himself. Both Tom Austin's and Paley's names appear as having prepared some of the lithography for illustrations in Sharpe's *Architectural Parallels* and *Decorated Windows*, as does that of Robert Jewell Withers (1824–94), who went on to become a well-respected church architect. How he came to be involved with Sharpe remains a mystery, since he had been articled to the busy Isle of Wight architect Thomas Hellyer from 1839. However, he was in Lancaster by September 1842, accompanying the practice's trip to Furness Abbey.

In the mid- or late 1840s the practice was also joined by another pupil, John Douglas (1830–1911), who continued to work under Paley as his chief assistant, leaving, probably some time before his marriage in January 1860, to set up in practice in Chester. Thereafter he designed many fine buildings, both ecclesiastical and secular, during a long and immensely successful career. The connection may have come about through Douglas' father who came from Sandiway, Cheshire, and made his living as a builder.

In 1843 Edmund Sharpe married Elizabeth Fletcher (1811–76) (Fig 1.36). She was the third daughter of Lt-Col Ralph Fletcher and his wife Jane, and the younger sister of John Fletcher whom we have met in connection with Christ Church, Walmsley. He was owner of the Ladyshore Colliery, 2½ miles south-east of Bolton, and the prime mover behind Sharpe's innovative terracotta church discussed on pp 34–6. Edmund and Elizabeth were married on 27 July at Bolton parish church (later rebuilt by Paley), and were to have five children – three boys (Francis, Edmund and Alfred) and two girls (Emily and Kate).[84] The 1840s saw marriage connections made not only between the Sharpe and Fletcher families but also involving the Langshaws and Sharpes, which had an impact on the architectural practice and its commissions. These marriages were the result of family links going back decades. The closeness of all the families is shown by the fact that at the wedding in 1840 of the youngest Langshaw, Catherine, to Charles Merriman in Lancaster, George Langshaw was the officiating minister and recorded witnesses included Edmund Sharpe, Elizabeth Fletcher and Ralph Fletcher.[85] The links are shown diagrammatically in Figure 1.37.

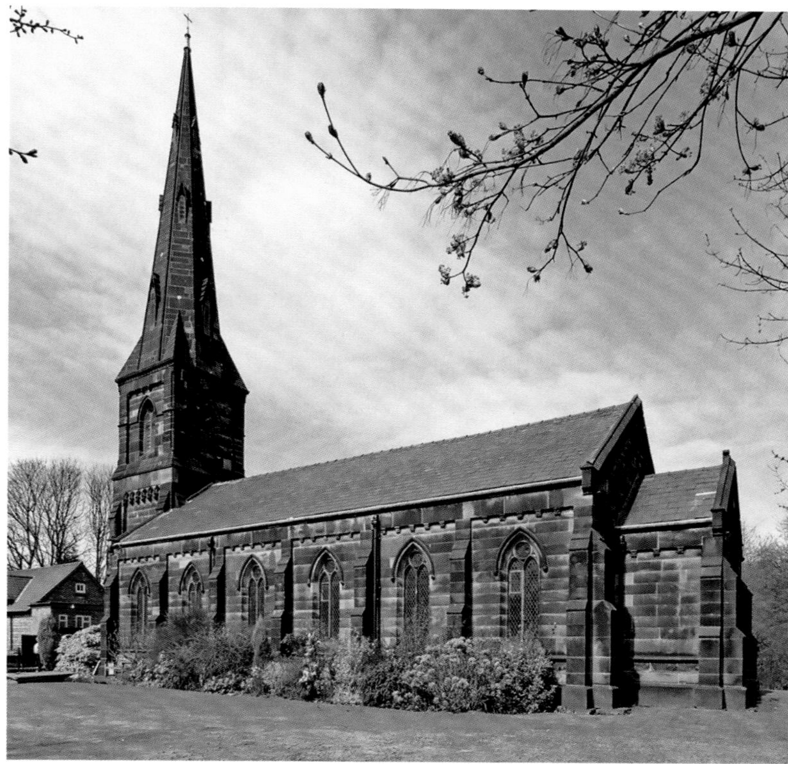

Fig 1.35
Northwich (Ch), Holy Trinity, 1841–2. One of the churches provided by the trustees of the Weaver Navigation for those who depended on the waterway. (Mark Watson)

Fig 1.36
Sharpe's wife Elizabeth (née Fletcher) photographed in Geneva in 1863. (Austin Family collection)

Sharpe and Ecclesiology

On 7 April 1842 Edmund Sharpe penned a letter to William Whewell in Cambridge.[86] 'I am happy', he wrote, 'to be able to answer your kind enquiries after my practical progress in architecture satisfactorily. – I am now engaged in my 31st. Church'[87] – a truly remarkable tally for a 33-year-old with a career of less than six years behind him. By 1841 even the prolific Gilbert Scott had only been involved with 13 new churches.[88] Sharpe was very conscious about the place of his work in a rapidly changing world in which the tenets of Ecclesiology and the High Church stance they represented were rapidly gaining ascendancy, along with the belief that Gothic was the only proper style for churches. He decided to join this new movement and was elected as a member of the Cambridge Camden Society on 8 November 1841. Like Gilbert Scott, who, in his *Recollections*, famously charted his conversion to the new movement and became aware of his 'errors' hitherto,[89] Sharpe confided to Whewell:

> I am sorry to say that but few of them [my churches] have been such as would satisfy the demands of Ecclesiologists of the present day; and I have been unfortunately guilty of carrying [into] effect the suggestions of Mr. Petit, even before they were made – if I may be allowed to use an Irishism; – in the four Romanesque Churches I have built in this Diocese.

The reference here is to a long review in the fifth number of *The Ecclesiologist* to J L Petit's two-volume *Remarks on Church Architecture*, which had appeared the previous year.[90] Petit's failings were to regard church-building with 'a merely utilitarian view of the subject', taking an excessive interest in foreign examples, and not approaching his subject from sufficiently 'exalted principles'. Sharpe evidently felt for Petit, remarking, 'I cannot help thinking that the Camden Society have treated Mr. Petit's Book rather hardly.' Indeed, the criticism was perhaps rather close to home for a man who had spent three years studying medieval churches on the Continent, incorporating some continental ideas into his own churches, was Low Church, and had often used simple, utilitarian designs. Furthermore, Sharpe was expecting to collaborate with Professor Robert Willis[91] and the excoriated Petit on a book on the churches of Sussex, though, like Sharpe's other publishing projects of the 1830s and early 1840s, this came to nothing.[92] Yet paradoxically Sharpe had actually won praise in the second number of *The Ecclesiologist* in November 1841 for an etching of an Early English church design which was 'dedicated to the Cambridge Camden and Oxford Architectural Societies':[93] 'the design is so chaste, elegant, and correct', it continued, '... and so greatly superior in all its details to the wretched modern imitations of that glorious style'. A year later Sharpe was commended 'for a Chancel somewhat longer than usual' at his new church at Calder Bridge (CuC) built in 1841–2, although that is where the praise stopped.[94]

In January 1843 *The Ecclesiologist* gave a whole-page review of Sharpe's designs for Lord Derby's church at Knowsley (Me) (Fig 1.38).[95] This is a well-proportioned Early English aisled church in local red sandstone, much added to later. *The Ecclesiologist* thought that 'as a whole it may safely be pronounced a most successful example of modern church building ... a good Chancel ... no galleries, a well-defined Clerestory, supported by beautiful clustered piers and arches'. There were various faults to be found, the most serious being 'no central passage to the Altar' as the space was taken up with seats for the children. Nonetheless, Sharpe had acquitted himself well in the journal's eyes.

The third volume of *The Ecclesiologist* (1844) is notorious for its index listing 'Architects approved' and 'Architects condemned'. It is sometimes assumed that global judgements were being passed on the architects concerned, but in fact they are reactions to specific works. Sharpe achieved two appearances as 'approved', and found himself in the exalted

Fig 1.37 (opposite)
Four families closely linked by marriage, friendship and business connections. George Langshaw may be regarded as the pivotal figure.

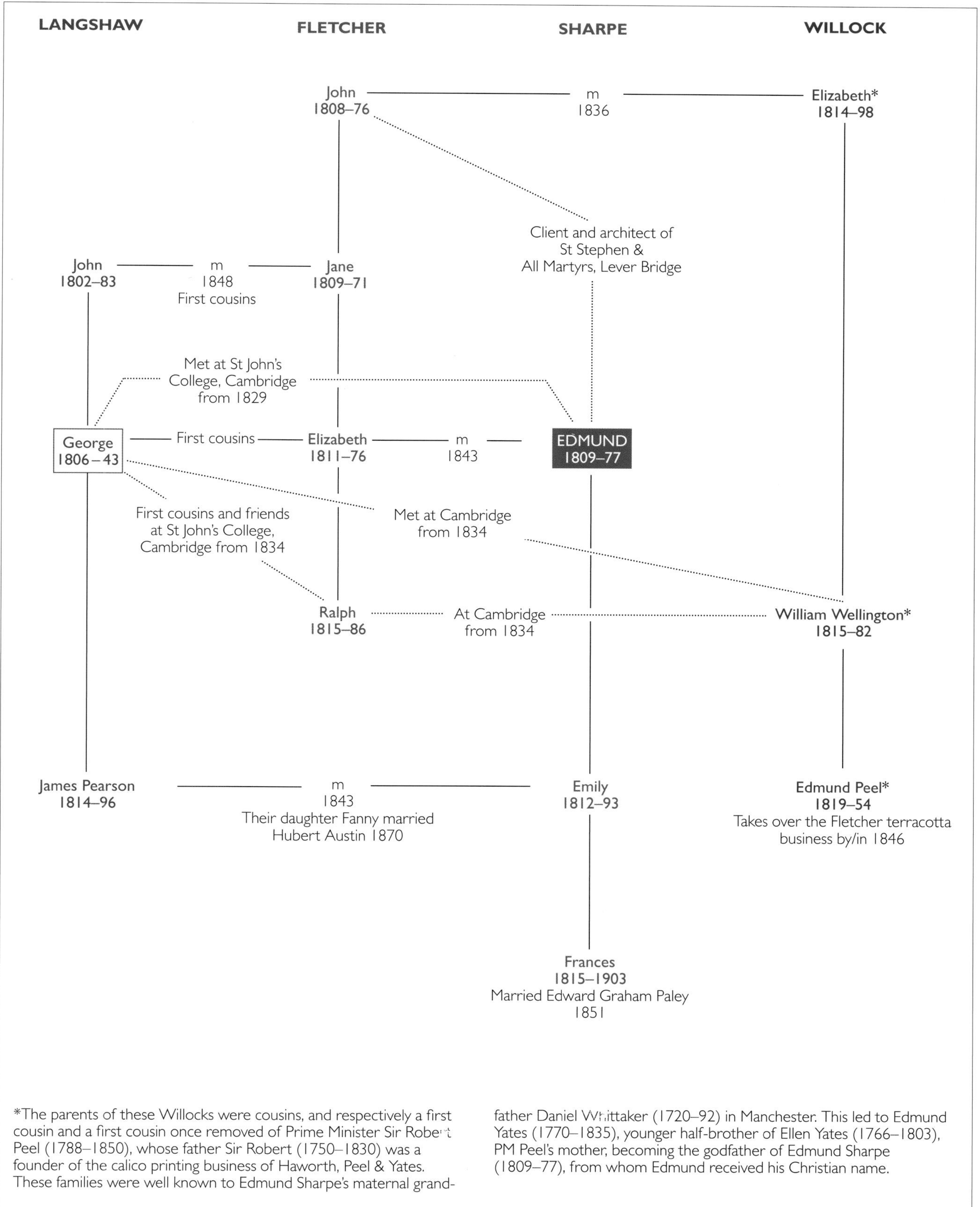

*The parents of these Willocks were cousins, and respectively a first cousin and a first cousin once removed of Prime Minister Sir Robert Peel (1788–1850), whose father Sir Robert (1750–1830) was a founder of the calico printing business of Haworth, Peel & Yates. These families were well known to Edmund Sharpe's maternal grandfather Daniel Whittaker (1720–92) in Manchester. This led to Edmund Yates (1770–1835), younger half-brother of Ellen Yates (1766–1803), PM Peel's mother, becoming the godfather of Edmund Sharpe (1809–77), from whom Edmund received his Christian name.

Fig 1.38
Knowsley (Me), St Mary, 1843–4, for the 13th Earl of Derby whose principal seat was at Knowsley Hall. Photograph taken after the addition of transepts by Paley in 1860 and before Paley, Austin & Paley enlarged the vestry and made a new east window in 1892–3.
(St Mary's Parochial Church Council)

company of Butterfield, Carpenter and Ferrey. The first of these notices was for his steeple at Kirkham (Fig 1.39), which Pevsner suggested enthusiastically as 'perhaps the finest work of Edmund Sharpe',[96] a judgement which rather downplays the fine internal spaces at Holy Trinity, Blackburn, or his second terracotta

Fig 1.39
Kirkham, St Michael, steeple of 1843–4, added to a nave of 1822: a fine composition closely following early 14th-century precedents.
(Mark Watson)

church in Manchester, which will be considered shortly. The steeple is, noted the hard-to-please *Ecclesiologist*, 'beautiful and correct, and conceived quite in the spirit of ancient composition'.[97] The second Sharpe entrant in the 1844 *Ecclesiologist* was St Stephen & All Martyrs, Lever Bridge (GM), which secured a full-page review in February, the month in which the church opened.[98] This is Sharpe's most famous and remarkable building, being built entirely of terracotta, and needs to be considered in some detail. It is strange that this building did not get Sharpe into the 'condemned' list since the journal could hardly find a good word to say about it.

The 'pot' churches

In 1876 Sharpe planned to give a lecture at the RIBA describing his pioneering experiments with terracotta for church-building. In the event this did not take place, but his paper was printed in both *The Builder* and the *Building News*.[99] Here Sharpe explained that the idea for his first 'pot' church (to use his own affectionate term) came from John Fletcher (1808–76), owner of the Ladyshore Colliery and, from 1843, his brother-in-law (Fig 1.40). This was St Stephen & All Martyrs at Lever Bridge (Fig 1.41).

Associated with Fletcher's coal seams were layers of clay which he had been using to make refractory bricks for furnaces.[100] Sharpe claimed that this was the only use to which terracotta had hitherto been put. One possible ecclesiastical challenger is its use by Thomas Penson of Oswestry for details at Christ Church, Welshpool, Montgomeryshire, of 1839–44.[101] Terracotta was even envisaged for vaulting in the competition designs (1841 or 1842) for Gilbert Scott's famous church of St Giles, Camberwell.[102] Nevertheless, Sharpe's church is distinctively different because the *entire* structure, apart from the foundations and rubble infill of the walls, is of terracotta. It remains a remarkable building, and originally was even more so, when its tower was crowned by an openwork spire modelled on the medieval example at Freiburg Cathedral in Baden-Würtemberg (Fig 1.42), which Sharpe probably visited on his way to France in 1834. Furthermore, many of the fittings, which would normally be of wood, were made out of terracotta (Figs 1.43 and 1.44).

The intention was evidently to provide a showcase for Fletcher's fireclay and Ladyshore terracotta. Edmund Sharpe, ever the entrepreneur looking for new challenges, seems to have relished the opportunity. The design was drawn up in 1841 and the church was built between 1842 and 1844, although the consecration was not until 26 June 1845. In his paper of 1876 Sharpe recalled the various difficulties encountered with the new material, which revolved around the three interrelated issues of warping, shrinkage and the calculation of how long each piece should be fired. When 'first built the church was a ruddy buff', Sharpe said, but the colour soon deepened in smoky mid-Victorian Bolton.

In 1876 Sharpe claimed the cost had been £2,600 (for 350 seats) and that, in stone, the spire alone would have cost more than this. But prototypes are never cheap, and it seems questionable that this was the true figure: Fletcher could well have ignored the costs of experimentation in the interests of promoting his new product. Certainly *The Ecclesiologist* was not convinced by the cost argument (but it wouldn't wish to be!): 'Such a material is not even *cheap,*

Fig 1.40
John Fletcher, owner of the Ladyshore Colliery, promoter of St Stephen's church and, from 1843, Sharpe's brother-in-law. Photograph taken at Fletcher's home from 1871, 'Croft', Ambleside (CuW). (Austin Family collection)

Fig 1.41
Lever Bridge (Bolton, GM), St Stephen & All Martyrs, 1842–4. Edmund Sharpe's first terracotta church. The steeple is crowned by an openwork spire, modelled on ones he would have encountered on his European travels. Below it, the composition, in which the square tower is capped by gables and then turns octagonal and has a crown of gablets, is a much refined version of the steeple at Scholes, Wigan. The spire was demolished in 1936, the octagonal and top of the tower in 1966. Mid-19th-century photograph. (Copyright Bolton Council from the Bolton Museum & Archive Service collection, LS01676)

except as a device of repeating parts and details which', it pointed out in a pre-Ruskinian gibe at industrial production, 'is entirely subversive of the variety and originality necessary for true art.' Yet it seems to have harboured a little surreptitious admiration for 'the ingenuity which has made an ambitious church out of so few moulds'. Words like 'showy', 'very meagre … Chancel', 'pretence and affected decoration' were invoked to disparage the church, while the gabled stage at the top of the tower (as used at St Mark, Witton) was, regrettably, 'quite un-English'.

Fig 1.42
Freiburg-im-Breisgau Münster, in the south-west corner of Germany. Sharpe would almost certainly have seen its early 14th-century openwork spire (claimed to be the earliest of its kind). Early 20th-century photograph.
(E Kreise; Geoff Brandwood collection)

Fig 1.43
Lever Bridge, terracotta bench ends and pierced seat backs, bare terracotta blocks in the wall and ornamented details in the frieze and window jambs.
(Mark Watson)

Edmund Sharpe's second 'pot church' was Holy Trinity, Rusholme in Manchester (Figs 1.45 and 1.46), paid for entirely by the wealthy bachelor-owner of nearby Platt Hall, Thomas Carill-Worsley (1792–1848). Seeking a suitable architect, he asked the advice of the archdeacon of Manchester, Dr John Rushton, who recommended Sharpe.[103] In a letter to Bishop Sumner of Chester on 28 September 1844, Rushton wrote: 'I enclose Mr. Sharpe's letter. It is rather encouraging. He married the sister of Mr. Fletcher, to whom the Terra cotta works belong.'[104] And so it was that the church was conceived as a terracotta building. Worsley also had strong Evangelical leanings, so he and his architect were well matched.

As Sharpe recalled in 1876, the experience gained at Lever Bridge 'much lessened our difficulties' at the second terracotta church.[105] The construction differed markedly from Lever Bridge: both were faced with coursed, five-inch blocks but now the inner walls were of brick and were plastered. Its design, Sharpe said was 'a genuine example of the true Lincolnshire type of the fourteenth century, without stint as to the nature of the moulded and carved work with which its main features should be clothed'.[106] 'The whole work', he added, 'has been treated … as a work in masonry, and I believe very few of those who live in the populous neighbourhood in which it stands are aware that it is not so.' The cost for such a rich building was indeed quite modest – about £4,000 for 650 seats. Work began in March 1845 and the consecration took place just 15 months later on 26 June 1846 (but with the steeple incomplete until 1850). *The Builder* reviewed the church during construction: undulations in the window sills, parts of the mullions out of perpendicular, scoring of the blocks to imitate tooling, and the 'remarkably slender piers' were all reasons for finding fault.[107] The reviewer simply hated the material, condemning the constructional blocks as 'nothing more than pots'. Despite approval of the 'good effect in capitals and buttresses' and the 'lofty arch' from the tower to the aisle, the church did not bear close scrutiny, with the writer concluding that it 'may please the traveller, from his post-chaise, but will not satisfy those, whose praise the architect is most desirous of receiving, that of his brother artists, of

Fig 1.44
Lever Bridge, interior. The terrazzo flooring post-dates Sharpe's work but the church retains its exposed terracotta blocks in the walls, the original hammerbeam roof and many fittings made of terracotta.
(Mark Watson)

men of education and refinement of taste'. *The Ecclesiologist* finally produced a review of the church in October 1848.[108] Despite the use of 'Middle Pointed' Gothic, it too savaged the building, but in a grudging comment, reminiscent of *The Builder*, it said: 'at a distance there is something attractive about its general appearance'. In the final analysis, despite the general appearance and some of the details, it committed that most cardinal of ecclesiological sins: it was a 'sham' – terracotta masquerading as stone.

Manufacture of the terracotta for the Lever Bridge and Rusholme churches was undertaken by John Fletcher, but from 1846 a new name appears. Ten years earlier, in October 1836, Fletcher had married Elizabeth (1814–98), the sister of Edmund Peel Willock (1819–54), who appears to have taken over the terracotta business. As part of Sharpe & Paley's restoration of Bridlington Priory (EY), six terracotta angels

Fig 1.45
Manchester, Holy Trinity, Rusholme, 1845–6, Sharpe's second terracotta church; illustrated in The Builder, *1876. As so often with such drawings, the smallness of the figures overemphasises the size of the building.*
*(*The Builder *34, 1876, 641)*

Fig 1.46
Holy Trinity, Rusholme. The bench ends, while not as elaborate as at Lever Bridge, are remarkable in having terracotta ornamentation applied to the sunk panels. (Mark Watson)

were used to embellish the new roof at the west end of the nave (Fig 1.47). The accounts in 1846 show that these were supplied by 'Messrs Willocks & Co Terra Cotta Works', near Manchester, at a cost totalling £11 14s 0d.[109] By 1850 the firm had a showroom in Manchester's prestigious Exchange Arcade, and at the Great Exhibition the following year E P Willock & Co actually displayed a 'Model of a decorated Gothic Church at Lever Bridge, Bolton, Lancashire; designed by E. Sharpe'.[110]

By 1851 Sharpe had withdrawn from architecture, leaving Edward Graham Paley to practise alone. However, he did return to architecture one last time in the 1870s for his final 'pot church', St Paul, Scotforth, built in 1874–5 (Figs 1.48, 1.49 and 1.50). This was a very personal project for Sharpe; it was built 300 yards south of his home, and he was one of the chief promoters and subscribers. In 1876 he declared the aim had been to realise an idea conceived 30 years earlier – 'to produce a structure of greater comeliness and ecclesiastical character than we could expect to accomplish were we to use exclusively the grit-stone of the neighbourhood'. This was done by using terracotta detailing made by Cliff & Son of Wortley, Leeds. Sharpe must have relished working again with a material, the use of which he had pioneered as a young man and which was starting to find its way into widespread architectural currency. There must also have been some nostalgia involved: as he drew up the tower, placed in the French manner over the choir, he no doubt recalled buildings he visited as a young travelling scholar. The building was also the embodiment of the robust Protestantism for which Sharpe stood: the placing of seats right across the nave was a deliberate statement that processions would not be taking place in *this* church. The downward slope of the floor towards the east may well have had similar intent.

Secular works

Churches formed by far the largest part of Edmund Sharpe's architectural output; yet, as the only architect practising from Lancaster in the late 1830s, he was the natural choice for other work, including a steady stream for the county authorities. By the start of 1837 he had been appointed Bridgemaster for the South Lonsdale Hundred, reporting on the condition of its bridges and roads in the area of north Lancashire east of Morecambe Bay. In consequence, Sharpe built new bridges at Fournessford, near Wray (Fig 1.51), in 1840 and near Abbeystead in 1847. By autumn 1838 he had been appointed architect to the County Lunatic Asylum on Lancaster Moor, where he dealt first with its water supply and then, between 1839 and 1845, with a string of six extension wings and a chapel. He also designed additions to the Lancaster Workhouse (1840–1), heating and ventilating facilities at Lancaster Castle (1841), and other sundry work. In 1843 the Annual Session of magistrates in Preston learned that he was being paid a salary £52 10s a year as architect to the Asylum, but this (although charged to the Asylum) also covered his supervision of Lancaster Castle and the Judges' Lodgings nearby: in all, it was revealed, Sharpe received no less than £674 in 1842–3 from the county authorities.[111] For his native Knutsford he designed a new house for the prison governor in 1844 and a new (unexecuted) chapel for the gaol.

Country house commissions played an intermittent part in the work of the practice down to the 1890s, some of them of considerable significance. Sharpe's biggest was the remodelling of Capernwray Hall in 1844–8 for George Marton (1801–67), MP for Lancaster from 1837 to 1847 (Figs 1.52, 1.53, 1.54, 1.55 and

Fig 1.47
Bridlington Priory (EY). The hammerbeam roof at the west end is by Sharpe & Paley (far left). The angel figures are of terracotta and made by Willock & Co, who were paid £11 14s for them in 1846 (left).
(Mark Watson)

Fig 1.48 (below)
Scotforth, St Paul, 1874–5, designed by Sharpe late in life for the area where he lived. It makes much use of terracotta dressings. The top of the tower is of buff brick. The west end with the transept is an addition by Paley, Austin & Paley, 1891.
(Mark Watson)

1.56). Sharpe had already designed the chapel of 1840 for Marton's father, a promoter of the Lancaster–Preston railway which Sharpe helped to build. Marton junior and Sharpe must have known each other well: both men were Conservatives, and shared sporting and social interests through the Lancaster Regatta and John O'Gaunt Bowmen.[112] Marton succeeded in 1843 and promptly called in Sharpe for an ambitious enlargement of the existing house of 1805. This comprised a rectangular block aligned roughly north–south, with a service wing leading off to the north-east. Sharpe more than doubled the size of the building by adding large drawing and dining rooms, and a tower. This tower, modelled on others in the area (both ancient and modern), had a water cistern at the top, fed from a nearby hill, and provided the novel convenience of running water throughout the house.[113] Sharpe clothed the extensions in late Perpendicular dress, having large bay windows with panel tracery to the two main rooms, and smaller, simpler fenestration for the less showy parts. In the centre of the house is a large, full-height staircase-hall covered by a cambered tie beam roof with king posts and Gothic arcading. The eastern parts were transformed by the building of new stables, a gateway with a tower above, a brew-

Fig 1.49
Scotforth, terracotta detailing on the apse at St Paul's.

house and other service buildings. This tower bears the date 1848, by which time E G Paley seems to have been in charge of the project.

The next major country house commission was the remodelling of Hornby Castle (Fig 1.57), on a hilltop overlooking the River Wenning, for which Sharpe & Paley were called in 1846 as work at Capernwray was progressing. The client was Pudsey Dawson, who inherited the estate in 1840: he was from a Liverpool mercantile and banking family, and was High Sheriff of Lancashire for 1845 and Deputy Lord Lieutenant in 1846. He would have known Sharpe well as the two men were, respectively, chairman and secretary of the 'Little' North Western Railway which had just been started. Who was responsible for what work at Hornby Castle is unclear, and it seems likely that Sharpe was probably involved early on but handed control over to his new partner as work progressed. Paley's obituary in the *JRIBA* says 'the entire superintendence of the improvement to the frontage of Hornby Castle' was entrusted to him.[114] Clare Hartwell notes: 'They designed an almost symmetrical frontage, large and more imposing than Capernwray. ... There are some similarities, e.g. the choice of Perp, dictated partly no doubt by the existing Perp remains.'[115] 'The entrance', she adds, 'leads via a vaulted vestibule through a timber Gothic screen to the hall. Here there is a Gothic fireplace and Gothic doorcases. ... [There is] a large staircase hall to the rear ... lit by a large churchy Perp window similar to the one at Capernwray.'

Contemporary with the work at Hornby Castle was another substantial remodelling, the creation of the Furness Abbey Hotel in 1847–8. The ruins of the great Cistercian abbey were one of Sharpe's favourite sites to which he often took visitors, for example in 1850 when he led a party there from the Manchester meeting of the British Archaeological Association, of which he was a vice president. The tourist potential it offered suggested to the Furness Railway Company, which had recently laid its tracks alongside the abbey and built a station there, that a hotel would be a good investment. Sharpe & Paley were thus the architects for the resulting conversion and enlargement of a disused manor house on the site of the abbey's main gatehouse. This commission formed the springboard from

Fig 1.50
Scotforth, interior with its terracotta detailing and by then unfashionable Romanesque style. The seats filling the width of the nave are a strongly Protestant gesture in line with Sharpe's Low Church beliefs.
(Mark Watson)

which the firm went on to become, in effect, in-house architects to the railway company. To create a suitably antiquarian atmosphere for the guests, the entrance hall had stained glass windows, an inglenook fireplace and a roof modelled on that at Bury St Edmunds Abbey. The reading and sitting room on the first floor was known as the Abbots' Room and displayed stained glass monastic figures.

A few other non-church commissions down to 1851 are worth mentioning. Sharpe provided a large new vicarage at Cockerham in 1843 for the Revd John Dodson. After inheriting land and property from his father, a Lancaster businessman, he built Littledale Hall, south of Brookhouse, near Lancaster in 1849. It is an asymmetrical Jacobethan essay, and Sharpe's known involvement at Cockerham and the stylistic similarity with other domestic work by Paley suggest that the firm may have been responsible. Another parsonage was rebuilt in 1845 at Redmarshall, Co Durham, for the Revd Thomas Austin, father of Sharpe's assistant, Thomas, and Paley's future partner Hubert. There seems every reason to suppose that Tom Austin was closely involved, if not fully responsible for this project.

Other secular works included a large hotel in 1847–8 at Morecambe, the North Western, to service this burgeoning resort at the end of the newly built 'Little' North Western Railway; extensions to Ince Hall (Me) (Fig 1.58) in 1847–9 for Eliza Jane Park, the widowed younger daughter of Edmund Yates, Sharpe's godfather; and a new building at Giggleswick School (NY) in 1850–1.

Fig 1.51 (above)
Bridge at Fournessford, near Wray, 1840, a commission arising from Sharpe's role as Bridgemaster for the South Lonsdale Hundred.

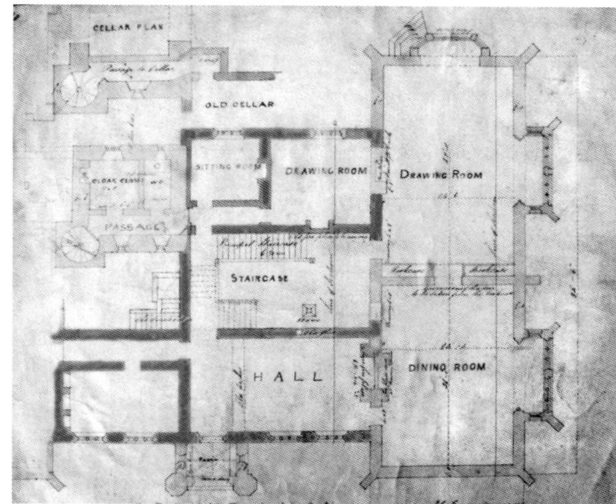

Fig 1.52 (left)
Capernwray Hall, plan, c 1844. The structure of the old house (darker shading) was retained but remodelled; a large drawing room, dining room and tower added. (Capernwray Archive; Geoff Brandwood)

Fig 1.53
Capernwray Hall, design for entrance front, c 1844, for George Marton MP. (Capernwray Archive; Geoff Brandwood)

Fig 1.54 (above) Capernwray Hall, garden front from the remodelling of 1844–8. Dining room left, drawing room right, added to the existing house with the tower behind. (Mark Watson)

Fig 1.55 (right) Capernwray Hall, the staircase hall. (Mark Watson)

Fig 1.56 (far right) Capernwray Hall, stained glass in the hall. The maker is unknown.

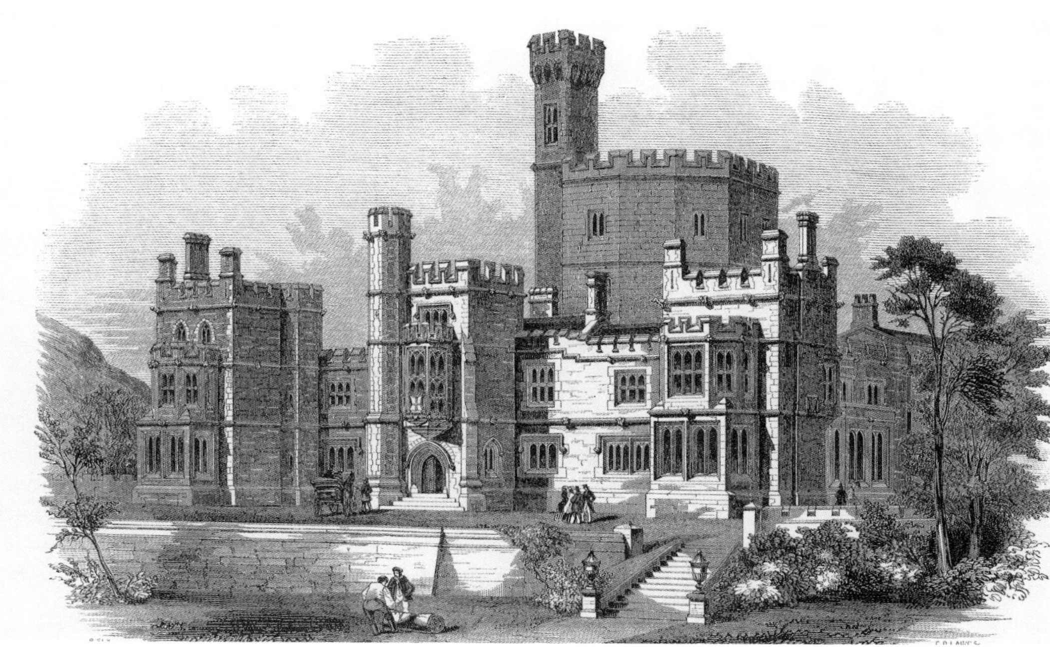

Fig 1.57
Hornby Castle, as remodelled by Sharpe & Paley, 1847–8.
*(*The Builder *8, 1850, 402)*

Fig 1.58
Ince Hall (Me), 1847–9 (demolished), front entrance.

Over the coming decades this would provide the practice with another six commissions down to the 1920s, a pattern which was repeated at two other important boarding schools in the north-west, Rossall and Sedbergh (CuWY).

Architectural writer

Publication about medieval architecture was never far from Sharpe's mind. However, the good intentions expressed as a travelling scholar came to nothing – sadly, as there is little doubt he could have made a contribution to the knowledge of continental 12th- and 13th-century architecture, which he loved so much. In due course he found the time and energy to produce a number of publications by subscription. The first, published by John Van Voorst, was *Architectural Parallels* (Figs 1.59, 1.60 and 1.61), issued in 12 parts at irregular intervals between 1845 and 1847 and prepared with the assistance of Paley, R J Withers and Tom Austin. It traced the progress of ecclesiastical architecture in England in the 12th and 13th centuries through 15 abbey churches 'so selected', said the publisher's note, 'as to present parallel instances of the manner in which the same feature was treated by the builders of different ages'.[116] The

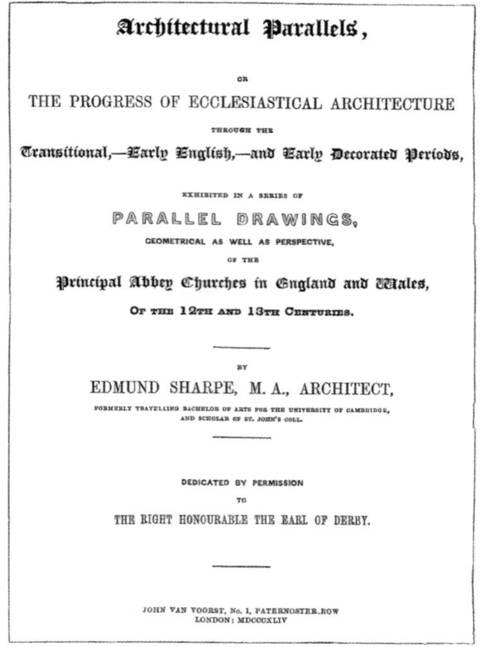

Architectural Parallels,

or

THE PROGRESS OF ECCLESIASTICAL ARCHITECTURE

through the

Transitional,—Early English,—and Early Decorated Periods,

exhibited in a series of

PARALLEL DRAWINGS,

geometrical as well as perspective,

of the

Principal Abbey Churches in England and Wales,

of the 12th and 13th Centuries.

by

EDMUND SHARPE, M. A., ARCHITECT,

formerly travelling bachelor of arts for the university of cambridge, and scholar of st. john's coll.

DEDICATED BY PERMISSION

TO

THE RIGHT HONOURABLE THE EARL OF DERBY.

JOHN VAN VOORST, No. 1, PATERNOSTER ROW
LONDON: MDCCCXLIV

Fig 1.59
Front page of an advertising leaflet for Architectural Parallels, *bearing the dedication of the work to Sharpe's most illustrious patron, the 13th Earl of Derby.*
(Christopher Webster collection)

first part, consisting of 10 prints, was warmly welcomed by *The Ecclesiologist* but as time went on its usual crabbiness crept in, so that of part 6 we read: 'We see very little use in thus cutting up a church like Rievaulx; a plan such as that which Mr. Sharpe gives, can have no ritual, and comparatively little architectural value.'[117] The review ends with a patronising: 'The lithographs are extremely creditable specimens of provincial art.' Sir Gilbert Scott, when presenting Sharpe with the RIBA Royal Gold Medal in 1875, was more generous, referring to its importance in raising awareness about ruined abbeys. The plates were collected together and published without a text in 1848. Sharpe planned to supply one in due course, comprising a full survey of English and Welsh architecture from 1130 to 1300, but this never materialised.

At the same time as *Architectural Parallels*, Sharpe was also issuing illustrations of Decorated tracery, again published by Van Voorst and using material prepared by Paley, Withers and Austin. The material was collected into the two-volume *Decorated Windows* of 1849, a work which was welcomed by John Ruskin in his widely read and immensely influential *The Stones of Venice*: 'Of works of this kind, by far the best I have met … containing a clear and masterly enunciation of the general principles by which the design of tracery has been regulated.'[118] Sharpe must have felt pleased.

His next venture, in 1851, was *The Seven Periods of English Architecture*, a slim volume of no more than 50 pages, published by George Bell, and including 12 illustrations by Tom Austin. It was intended as a modification of the scheme put forward by his former mentor,

Fig 1.60 (right)
Kirkstall Abbey (WY), drawn by Sharpe and published in Architectural Parallels.

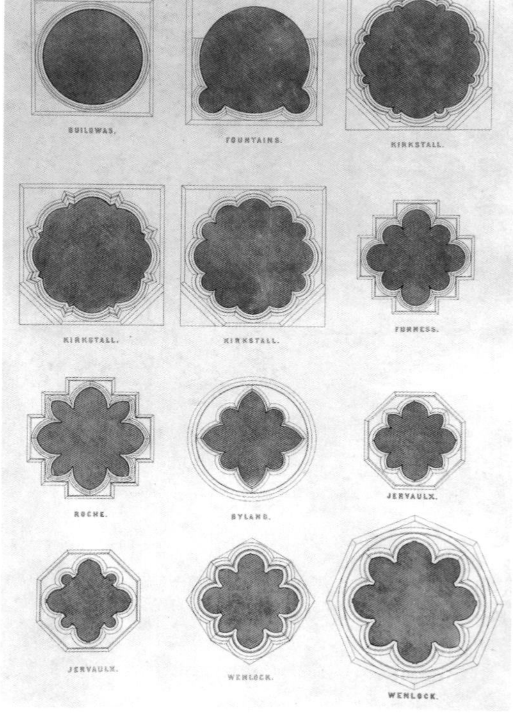

Fig 1.61 (far right)
Comparative pier sections at English abbeys from Architectural Parallels, *lithographed by R J Withers.*

Thomas Rickman. Sharpe sought to divide medieval architecture into Saxon to 1066; Norman to 1145; transitional to 1190; Lancet to 1245; Geometrical to 1315; Curvilinear to 1360; and Rectilinear to 1550. But he was too late. Rickman's book was already in its fifth edition and had, effectively, established the briefer, simpler nomenclature comprising Norman, Early English, Decorated and Perpendicular which is still in use today. Sharpe read a paper to the RIBA on the subject in 1851, which was published in *The Builder* for 7 June 1851. This provoked a furious war of words over the next six months about the merits of the case. First to the fray was 'F.S.A.', an anonymous correspondent who eventually turned out (as Sharpe suspected) to be J H Parker of Oxford, antiquarian, author, and publisher of Rickman's classification! Even Gilbert Scott entered the arena, appealing for calm debate and rebuking Sharpe for his pugnacious stance, yet finding merits in his case.[119] The correspondence rumbled on and became so acrimonious and personal that the editor, George Godwin, was obliged to stop it.

Further scholarly work had to wait another 20 years or more for publication, although Sharpe did read a paper entitled 'The Architectural History of St. Mary's Church, New Shoreham' to the Archaeological Institute's annual meeting at Chichester in 1853 (not published until 1861). A subsequent publication was entitled *Supplemental Sketch of the Collective Architectural History of Chichester Cathedral, Boxgrove Priory, and St. Mary's Church, New Shoreham, as indicated by their Mouldings*, with contributions from Professor Willis (Chichester) and J L Petit (Boxgrove). In 1853 Sharpe visited all but two of the noteworthy Sussex churches with a view to publication in the latter volume, but he 'had not leisure enough at [his] disposal to complete the task'.[120] This is not exactly surprising given the range and depth of his other activities.

Back to Lancaster: architectural excursions

In 1856 Sharpe and his family left Lancaster to live in North Wales, where he built the railway from Conwy to Llanrwst. They then moved to the Continent, taken there by Sharpe's successful building of tramways in Geneva and then very unsuccessful construction of a railway in the south of France. Sometime in 1866, probably quite early, they returned to take up residence in the Higher Greaves area of Scotforth on the southern fringes of Lancaster. They moved into a block of three separate houses erected about 1852 to a gaunt design by J A Hansom. Sharpe knocked two of these into one and laid out the adjoining grounds. The third house was occupied from 1873 by Sharpe's second son, Edmund, following his marriage to Alice, third daughter of his employer from February 1866, William Storey of Storey Brothers.[121]

In November 1869 Edmund Sharpe found a new outlet for his architectural energies. He joined the Architectural Association and offered to organise annual excursions for members. Between 1870 and 1875 four were made in England, followed by two in France. The first was to Lincoln, Sleaford and Spalding in August 1870, lasting for several days and subsequently written up for *The Builder* by Sharpe himself.[122] The 1871 tour went to Ely, King's Lynn and Boston; that in 1872 to Stamford, Oundle, Wellingborough and Northampton.[123] The 1873 excursion also focused on the Midlands and eastern England, taking in Grantham, Newark, Southwell, Ashbourne, Lichfield and Nottingham.

According to a letter to the RIBA Secretary in 1869 declining an invitation to join its council, Sharpe gave his reason as spending six months of each year in France, for which he had great affection.[124] His vast knowledge of the country's medieval architecture was put to good use on two AA tours and subsequent lectures and publications. In 1874 Sharpe and the AA ventured over to northern France. He took with him some 50 students and they ranged round Paris taking in Soissons, Laon, Rheims and Chartres, but no report was ever published. The excursion the following year to the Charente district of southwest France, including Angoulême, lasted a fortnight. Sharpe himself gave a masterly account of this last excursion to a large London audience in June 1876, when 160 of the 662 illustrations made on the tour were displayed (Fig 1.62). The paper was printed in *The Builder* for 1 July, which recorded the accolade from T Roger Smith: 'Mr. Sharpe had in some sense, but in a different sphere, filled the void occasioned by the death of the late Professor Willis.' The tour was recorded in a memorial volume published in 1882 by the Architectural Association as a tribute to Sharpe, entitled *A Visit to the Domed Churches of the Charente in 1875*. This handsome, leather-bound volume

Fig 1.62
*'Angouleme Cathedral West Front illustrating Mr Sharpe's Lecture "Architecture of La Charente"', from (*Building News* 30 June 1876)*

Fig 1.63
Portrait of Sharpe in the Architectural Association's memorial volume, A Visit to the Domed Churches of the Charente *(1882).*

begins with a five-page 'Memoir' about Sharpe (Fig 1.63), and includes a list of his many publications, comprising 13 major works and 9 pamphlets, plus papers presented to different meetings and societies, 7 papers read before the Architectural Association and 13 articles or letters published in the professional press: without allowing for overlap and repetition, a total of some 55 items.

The RIBA Royal Gold Medal

Shortly before setting out for Charente, Sharpe was honoured with the RIBA's Royal Gold Medal for 1875. It was presented on 7 June by the president, Sir Gilbert Scott, who explained that the award was for Sharpe's published achievements.[125] He referred particularly to *Architectural Parallels*, which belonged to the early group of Sharpe's works. This may even have been a possible model for Scott's own *Spring Gardens Sketchbook*, which started to appear 20 years later with help from the young Hubert Austin. Scott's address went on to refer to Sharpe's later works, which are separated from the earlier ones by some 20 years. He drew particular attention to Sharpe's recent two-volume *The Architecture of the Cistercians.*[126] This was almost his last work of substance, and perhaps his best, dealing with a subject which had been close to his heart for over 40 years. Scott then praised Sharpe's lecturing and guiding skills 'at archaeological gatherings in different parts of the country' and spoke with admiration of Sharpe's lecture at Fountains Abbey, which he had heard the previous year.

Last days

In early 1877 Sharpe wrote to the RIBA asking if it 'knew of one or two young men who might accompany him to Tuscany to help make measured drawings of 25 12th-century churches in Pisa, Pistoia and Lucca'.[127] In the event he went to northern Italy in early March, accompanied by his two daughters, Emily and Kate, his youngest son Alfred (who had just qualified as a solicitor) and three research assistants, W Talbot Brown (who went on to a busy and successful architectural career in Northamptonshire), Gill and Deane – 'a visit made specially to collect material for dealing with developments in his favourite Transitional period'.[128] Two months later he suddenly became seriously unwell, starting with a cold which brought on a severe sore throat and inflammation of the left lung. Back in Lancaster the rest of his family received a telegram on the morning of 8 May to say that he was dangerously ill, followed by another within two hours announcing his death in Milan. His body was brought back to Lancaster and interred on 19 May in a simple ceremony at the cemetery to the east of the town, alongside his wife, Elizabeth, who had died on 15 March the previous year.[129]

Conclusion

Edmund Sharpe is remembered now largely by architectural historians who see him as the founder of a long-lived and important architectural practice; who may refer to his books on historic architecture; and who are intrigued by his strikingly innovative terracotta churches. However, he achieved a great deal more in his energetic and varied life. Every day thousands travel on the railways he helped to build, although his success as a railway engineer was qualified. He had an independent spirit, always ready to fight for what he believed was right. He had well-developed oratorical and political skills, which he used to put Lancaster's sanitation and water supply on a sound footing. He played a key part in developing the industrial, cultural, social and sporting life of the town.

Sharpe's activity as an architectural writer spanned three decades but, as a designer of buildings, his years in practice were brief. His career took off quite spectacularly after his return from France at the end of 1835, aided by influential family connections, but after 1845 he probably designed little. He withdrew entirely in 1851, apart from designing the unusual and very personal St Paul's, Scotforth, a short distance from his home, which was a symbol of his own Evangelical sympathies. His 'pot' churches continue to fascinate, but they were an ambitious experiment which produced no direct issue. It is a great tragedy that his steeple at Lever Bridge is lost to us, but his Manchester church is a fine building which deserved a better welcome than *The Ecclesiologist* gave it. The Buildings of England has been more generous with its praise for Holy Trinity, Blackburn, which has an interior of some grandeur, and for the lovely Decorated steeple at Kirkham. However, much of Sharpe's early work is modest and often repetitive, and by no reckoning can he be numbered among the top flight of Victorian architects. By the mid-1840s perhaps Sharpe may have sensed this himself, as rising Gothic stars such as Butterfield, Scott, Pearson and, shortly, Street seized the architectural high ground. Whether or not this was the case, he sought other challenges. His involvement with architectural history as a tour leader, lecturer and writer in two phases during his life won him great acclaim, symbolised by the award of the RIBA Royal Gold Medal in 1875. Other winners in the 1870s included James Fergusson, G E Street and Alfred Waterhouse: distinguished company indeed.

2

Developing the practice: Edward Graham Paley

In June 1851 Edward Graham Paley (Fig 2.1) married Frances (Fanny) Sharpe (1815–1903), youngest sister of Edmund, his former master and partner from 1845.[1] The couple were to have five children, the last of whom, Henry (Harry) Anderson, born in 1859, would carry on the practice almost to the middle of the 20th century. From 1847 Sharpe largely handed over responsibility for design work, and Paley's marriage was probably the right moment for him to terminate the partnership, leaving Paley as sole principal. Yet until 1856, when Sharpe left Lancaster, commissions continued to be carried out under the banner of 'Sharpe & Paley', presumably because Sharpe's name still lent gravitas to the practice. Paley continued as sole principal until 1868, when he made Hubert Austin his partner.

Fig 2.1
Edward Graham Paley poses for the camera in 1861. (Austin Family collection)

Paley maintained the range of activity established so effectively during the previous decade: that is, focused geographically on central and north Lancashire, church building and restoration work predominating, together with associated parsonages and schools. Some country house work was also undertaken, as well as a few public buildings, a large factory and patronage from the Furness Railway Company.

But first we should take a look at Paley's family history and background; explain how he came to enter into architecture by joining Sharpe in Lancaster; and say something about Paley the man.

Family history

Edward Graham Paley was a Yorkshireman from a clerical background. His ancestors originated from the large parish of Giggleswick in the Craven district, where by the early 16th century they were established in the small village of Langcliffe.[2] They owned a property known as Paley's Farm, now the Old Vicarage, which remained in the family until 1962. Other local place names include Paley's Puddle, High Paley and Low Paley Green.

Paley's ancestry can be traced with a high degree of certainty to a John Paley (1632–1717), who in 1672 married his neighbour Isobel Lawson, a descendant of a prominent Craven yeoman family. John prospered, and the family fortunes increased further under his son Thomas (1675–1740), whose son William (1711–99) would be educated at Giggleswick School and then at Christ's College, Cambridge.[3] Eventually William became a minor canon of Peterborough Cathedral, before being appointed headmaster at Giggleswick School in 1745. Here he remained for half a century until his death in 1799, and made many improvements. William was colourfully described by his grandson Edmund as 'a cheerful, jocose man, a great wit, and an enlivening companion; in his days of activity, fond of field sports, and more fond of company than was relished at home ... esteemed a good and even a popular preacher ... a conscientious clergyman ... rather coarse, but strong and significant in his language'.[4]

In 1742 Headmaster William married Elizabeth Clapham. They had four children, the eldest of whom, another William (1743–1805), achieved national fame as a theologian (Fig 2.2). Like his father, he was educated first at Giggleswick, then at Christ's College. After graduating in 1763 he taught at Bracken's Academy at Greenwich, the school later attended on a different site by the young Edmund Sharpe, and in 1766 he became a fellow of Christ's. He later achieved great fame with his writings. His *Principles of Moral and Political Philosophy* (1785) became a standard textbook, outlining a system of Utilitarian ethics largely identical to that of Jeremy Bentham, although conceived independently. *A View of the Evidences of Christianity* (1795) also became required reading for undergraduates, and owed its huge popularity not so much to original arguments as to its lucid presentation. His last book, *Natural Theology* (1802), sought to demonstrate the existence and attributes of God from the appearances of Nature, and it is here that the famous idea of 'Paley's watch' appears.[5] In his lifetime Paley held many ecclesiastical posts, including those of Archdeacon of Carlisle from 1782 (a role united in 1785 with that of Chancellor), prebend of St Paul's, London, and sub-dean of Lincoln, and from 1795 he spent the last 10 years of his life as rector of Bishopwearmouth, Co Durham.

Parents, brother and education

Archdeacon Paley had 10 children by his first wife, Jane Hewitt of Carlisle (d 1791, aged 40).[6] His second son, Edmund, born in October 1782, would become the father of our architect, Edward Graham Paley.[7] After education in Carlisle, Edmund was admitted to Jesus College, Cambridge, but before taking up residence there he made the unusual move of matriculating at Queen's College, Oxford.[8] In 1808 he was ordained deacon and priest, becoming vicar at Cawthorne, near Barnsley, until his appointment as vicar of Easingwold, some 12 miles north-north-west of York, in 1812.[9] In the same year he married, at Cambridge, Sarah Apthorp, whose half-sister Harriet's husband was Samuel

Fig 2.2
Archdeacon William Paley by George Romney.
(© National Portrait Gallery, London NPG 3659)

Butler (1774–1839), headmaster of Shrewsbury School, which he raised to be a public school of the first rank. Edmund and Sarah, like Archdeacon Paley, had 10 children, in whom Butler would take a keen interest, including financing the education of Edmund's eldest son Frederick Apthorp (1815–88) at Shrewsbury.[10] F A Paley was to play an important part in the burgeoning ecclesiological movement of the early 1840s, joining the Cambridge Camden Society by mid-1840, and becoming one of its secretaries from 1841 until 1845. The following year he seceded to Rome and was thus obliged to leave Cambridge where he had been a tutor in classics. He was the author of several architectural works including the *Manual of Gothic Mouldings*, first published in 1845. This was widely read and, in the fifth reprint nearly half a century later in 1891, the editor quoted a letter received from E G Paley who described how he had stimulated his elder brother's interest in the subject through Thomas Rickman's celebrated book, *An Attempt to Discriminate the Styles of Architecture in England*.[11]

Edward Graham Paley was born at Easingwold on 3 September 1823, the seventh child and fourth son of Edmund and Sarah. After being educated at home and possibly at a dame school, he followed in the footsteps of his elder brother Edmund when he entered Christ's Hospital School, London, in 1832, aged eight.[12] While there he was presented to the Duke of Wellington who chatted to him, patted him on

Fig 2.3
Lancaster about 1850. A more industrialised view than that in Figure 1.12. The castle can be seen centre left; a railway viaduct spans the River Lune, and smoking chimneys denote the shift from a trading port to an industrial town. Beyond Morecambe Bay lies the belt of land south of the Lake District that was still part of Lancashire: it would provide Paley and later his partner Hubert Austin with many commissions. (W G Niven collection)

the head, and gave him a guinea as the grandson of Archdeacon Paley, whom the duke evidently admired.[13] Under the school rules a pupil was obliged to leave at age 15, unless he was going on to university or to join the navy. Paley left in July 1838 and became the pupil of Edmund Sharpe, possibly because poor family finances precluded his progression to university. These appear to have been strained around the time that the boy was being entered for Christ's Hospital in 1832, when his father pleaded that his vicarage was 'much reduced in value' and 'that it scarcely amounts to the clear Income of two hundred and fifty Pounds': his private property had also 'lately suffered' being 'reduced to One Hundred Pounds'. However, a good deal of the trouble was self-inflicted; as he admitted, 'I hav [*sic*] Ten Children to maintain'![14] Things should have begun to improve after his appointment in 1835 to the prosperous living of Gretford, near Stamford. His wife Sarah confided to her half-sister, Harriet Butler, 'now better days begin to dawn'.[15] However, Paley did not take up the post immediately, delaying it until 1838 when the rectory had been enlarged sufficiently to house his numerous progeny.[16] He remained at Gretford until his death in 1850, assisted by his son Francis (1826–1909). By that time his fourth son, Edward Graham, was starting to make a name for himself as an architect. But what were the links that brought the 15-year-old Paley to Lancaster (Fig 2.3) and the office of Edmund Sharpe?

The Paleys, the Sharpes and the move to Lancaster

Although F A Paley and Edmund Sharpe were both undergraduates at St John's College, Cambridge, they were *not* contemporaries, and links between the two families must be sought elsewhere. A complex set of family connections takes us back to the late 18th century, when members of the Paley family were still farming around Langcliffe. However, Richard Paley (1746–1808), a second son,[17] left to become a successful soap boiler in Leeds,[18] and he used his new-found prosperity to invest in cotton mills in Leeds and elsewhere, and a cast iron foundry near Wakefield. About 1788 Richard was also a founder of the Bowling Ironworks, near Bradford, where in 1798 he was joined by his nephew, John Green Paley (1774–1860), who subsequently became manager there, achieved great wealth and retired to Harrogate.[19] His social circle included the Buck family of Bradford, which included Sarah, the wife of William Whittaker, whose younger sister Martha would become the mother of Edmund Sharpe. William and Sarah's son and Sharpe's cousin, the redoubtable John William Whittaker, briefly went to the same early school in Halifax (Heath House) later attended by J G Paley's second son Thomas, the third cousin of E G Paley.[20]

After the families of Sarah Whittaker and Martha Sharpe moved to Lancaster in 1823 and 1824, they lived close to the family of Esther Whittaker, Martha's elder sister, and her husband Benjamin Satterthwaite, a prosperous wine merchant. The Satterthwaites' son Thomas (1794–1849) became an invalid after a riding accident in his early teenage years, and was treated on at least one occasion by Robert Paley, a doctor in Halifax and Ripon (brother of John Green Paley).[21] Robert's son, also Thomas (1810–99) – E G Paley's first cousin – went to Sedbergh School and St John's College, and at both he was an exact contemporary of and friend of Edmund Sharpe.[22] Although there were various links between the Paleys and the Sharpes, it seems likely that it was *this* acquaintance with Thomas Paley from Halifax that gave Edmund Sharpe his introduction to the wider Paley family, paving the way to his taking on the young Edward Graham in October 1838.[23]

Edward or Graham Paley?

Edward Graham Paley's first name was that of his uncle Edward. His second name was intended as a link with a prominent Borders family into which his father's eldest sister Jane (1777–1826) had married in 1809 at Halifax, when she became the second wife of the Revd Fergus Graham. He was rector (from 1790) of the two livings of Arthuret and Kirkandrews-on-Esk, adjacent to the Cumberland–Scotland border, which had been held earlier by his father Robert. Fergus Graham owed these appointments to the patronage of his elder brother, Sir James Graham (baronet from 1783), whose seat at Netherby Hall was the centre of a substantial Cumberland estate.[24] Fergus was probably Edward Graham's godfather, and it seems that the Graham connection was a matter of some pride. His second name was the one used in family and social circles but, confusingly and for reasons that are not clear, he employed the first one for his professional affairs. Drawings and business correspondence are variously signed 'Edward G. Paley', 'Ed. G. Paley', and plain 'E. G. Paley', so there is little doubt that his first name would have been the one familiar to clients and colleagues. Occasionally his second name appeared in the public arena, as happened in 1854 when the funeral procession for J W Whittaker was reported in the press: one of the carriages was noted as 'containing Graham Paley, Esq.'.[25] But, of course, Paley was a relative through his marriage to Sharpe's sister (Sharpe being Whittaker's cousin). The personal side of E G Paley's life is represented by far less material than the architectural, but it clearly points to his being known as 'Graham Paley'. Family photographs from the 1860s to the 1890s are nearly all labelled on the reverse 'E. Graham Paley'.[26] Furthermore, around 1878–9 James Pearson Langshaw noted in details of his family history that his son-in-law, Hubert Austin, 'is an Architect and is in partnership ... wth. Graham Paley'.[27]

Private, public and professional life

After their marriage in June 1851, Paley and his wife (Fig 2.4) lived initially at 35 (now 16) Castle Park in the shadow of Lancaster Castle and near to where he would later establish the office which would serve the practice until the end of its days.[28] In 1855 he bought a plot of land on the south side of Lancaster and built a new house, 'The Greaves', to which the family moved on 5 April 1856[29] and where he eventually died in 1895.[30] At the time no other properties had been built across the road, and Paley had a large garden there, known locally as 'Paley's Garden'. Interestingly (and in the light of what has been said about the use of his given names), when streets appeared opposite his house at right angles to the main road, one of them was, and still is, called Graham Street.[31] As their prosperity increased, the Paleys also created a country residence called 'Moorgarth' at Brookhouse,

Fig 2.4
Paley's wife Frances (Fanny) photographed in 1862 by Maull & Polyblank, London. (Austin Family collection)

near Caton, four miles north-east of Lancaster, which had been a workhouse until it closed in 1869 (Fig 2.5).[32] Paley and his wife seem to have had a happy marriage. They had five children: Emily Frances (1852–1918), Margaret (1854–1939), Mary Elizabeth (1856–1939), Edmund Graham (1857–88) and Henry (Harry) Anderson (1859–1946). Paley was a keen churchman, who attended Lancaster parish church regularly. After he purchased 'Moorgarth', he also worshipped at St Paul's, Brookhouse, which had been largely rebuilt to his designs in 1865–7.

Fig 2.5
'Moorgarth', Brookhouse, Caton. Paley's country home outside Lancaster from 1869.

Paley's former master and partner, Edmund Sharpe, was a leading figure in the affairs of Lancaster, helping to shape the town physically, socially and intellectually. Paley never assumed such a high profile yet was, nonetheless, an important man in the town and after his death in 1895 was accorded a civic funeral. His obituary in the *Lancaster Guardian* ran for almost three columns, cataloguing his life and achievements and the major architectural works of his practice – plus a lengthy piece on his ancestors.[33] It described him as 'one of the foremost of our citizens' and spoke, it seems, with genuine feeling 'of his geniality, kind-heartedness and readiness to help in every good work. He was one of nature's gentlemen, always cheerful and kindly; and he was deservedly esteemed and respected by all with whom he came in contact.' Fifteen years after his death the *Lancaster Guardian* accorded him an article in its 'Old Time Worthies' series.[34]

Paley did not involve himself directly in the political life of Lancaster except for a brief period in the 1850s. In 1856 he stood unsuccessfully as the Conservative candidate for Castle Ward,[35] and from 1858 he served three years as a councillor for Queen's Ward, after which he chose not to stand again.[36] He was, however, very much involved in other aspects of life in and around the town, his *Guardian* obituary noting that 'there are few public organisations of which Mr. Paley was not at one time or another an active member'.[37] He was very interested in education, being a member of the committees of St Mary's Schools and the Mechanics' Institute. He was particularly involved with the latter, especially its School of Art, at which he was successively Secretary, Treasurer and President. At the time of his death Paley was on the committee of the Storey Institute (which took over from the Mechanics' Institute), where he promoted art as applied to industry.

He also enjoyed archaeological and antiquarian pursuits. He was a founder member of the Royal Archaeological Institute, for which in 1858 he and Sharpe conducted a tour of sites in and around Lancaster.[38] He was also involved with the Cumberland & Westmorland

Antiquarian & Archaeological Society. Music was a major interest, as it was for both Sharpe and Austin too. He was, with his wife, a member of the Lancaster Choral Society, and played an active part in the musical life of the town.[39] For many years he was a director of the Athenaeum Company (founded by Sharpe in 1848) and a promoter of the Lancaster Philosophical Society. In 1873 he was a founder of the County Club, a gentleman's club in Lancaster, and from 1879 until his death he was a member of the Lancaster Charity Trust.[40]

As a young man Paley was a fine sportsman. As well as being a member of the John O'Gaunt Bowmen, he was associated with Sharpe in the formation of the Lancaster Rowing Club in 1842 and was a prominent oarsman. With Paley (stroke), Sharpe (cox) and Tom Austin among the crews of 1844–7, the club achieved some notable successes over others from Liverpool, Chester, Preston and Fleetwood, both on the Lune and at the Chester Regatta. For the rest of his life Paley retained an interest in the club, becoming an umpire for the Lancaster Regatta from 1853, and at the jubilee banquet in 1893 he jokingly offered to 'find a crew of old 'uns to compete against the young members'.[41]

One public office which occupied him for many years, and which he took over from Sharpe from 1860, was that of Bridgemaster for South Lonsdale Hundred, until control of the county bridges passed to Lancashire County Council after 1889.[42] This required him to submit reports to the Quarter Sessions on the state of bridges and roads within his jurisdiction, which meant that he was well placed to design the new road bridge at the Crook of Lune, Caton, built in 1882–3 after the collapse of the old one in 1881 (Fig 2.6).[43] From 1868 Paley was appointed to inspect the buildings of Lancaster Gaol and the Judges' Lodgings four times a year at a salary of £25 a year.[44]

In 1864 Paley was one of the original committee members involved in setting up what would become the Royal Albert Asylum in Lancaster, one of the great philanthropic endeavours of Victorian England in the North.[45] Working for this organisation, which cared for and educated those with learning disabilities, must have had an added poignancy for Paley since his elder son, Edmund Graham, had been born with severe Down's syndrome. In 1869, aged 11, he was sent for long-term care at the pioneering Normansfield Hospital at Teddington in Middlesex, founded the previous year and run by John Langdon Down, after whom Edmund's condition is now named.[46] The asylum project, the biggest in the entire history of the practice, was heavily supported by Freemasons, which seems to have led Paley to join them (albeit temporarily), unlike Sharpe or Austin, neither of whom became Masons. He was initiated on 3 March 1867 into Rowley Lodge, and appears to have attended meetings spasmodically until October 1870. He held no offices and is not in the list of Lancaster Masons for 1871. In 1870 he also joined the Lodge of Fortitude, the other local lodge operating at the time.[47] Paley rejoined the committee of the Royal Albert Asylum in May 1878 and 'from that time until his death he took a most earnest interest in the management of the Institution', even attending

Fig 2.6
Bridge at the Crook of Lune at Caton, 1882–3, a commission no doubt arising from Paley's role as Bridgemaster of the South Lonsdale Hundred. (Mark Watson)

a meeting less than two weeks before his death though he 'complained of feeling a little out of sorts'.[48] His illness grew worse and turned out to be typhoid fever, from which he died on 23 January 1895, aged 71.[49]

Unlike Edmund Sharpe, who received no formal architectural training and was largely self-taught, Paley served his articles with Sharpe and thus had a proper apprenticeship in the profession. Around 1840 the training in architects' offices could be a hit-and-miss affair, though it seems likely that Sharpe was diligent in his dealings with his pupils. Paley was truly enthused by architecture, evidently passing this on to his elder brother, Frederick, and was a regular member of Sharpe's sketching excursions which led to *Architectural Parallels*, in which his name appears on four of the lithographs.

Like most architects, but unlike his prolix master, Paley wrote nothing, and therefore his buildings must speak for him. Similarly, he played no part for a long time in the affairs of his profession and it was not until 1871, halfway through his career, that he became a fellow of the RIBA. His proposers were T Roger Smith, C F Hayward and Thomas Worthington. Worthington practised from Manchester so he and Paley would surely have known each other as fellow Lancastrian architects, but there is no clue as to the sponsorship from the relatively little-known Smith and Hayward, both of whom practised from London and were closely acquainted.[50] Paley then started to play a modest part in the affairs of the Institute, becoming a member of its council in 1873–4 and again in 1881–4.[51] He was one of the representatives of the RIBA in the funeral procession for G E Street in 1881.[52] At the time of his death, he was one of its examiners.[53]

Fig 2.7
Gateway at Laon drawn by Paley on his continental tour in August 1857.
(Private collection)

Architectural tours

Like many other architects, Paley made tours to the continent which no doubt combined pleasure with the important business of gaining first-hand experience of historic buildings abroad. Although there were very probably more such trips, we know of only two of them, one in 1857 and another in 1862, from a pair of small sketch books that survive in private hands. The earlier tour was an ambitious, month-long affair on which Paley was accompanied, he noted, by a fellow architect, John Bownas Atkinson (1807–74). Atkinson was, with his brother William (1811–86), in a busy York practice which was the successor to that of the great John Carr.[54] Paley and Atkinson were in Brussels on 7 August, and went on to Berlin, down to Prague and thence to Venice. In northern Italy they inspected the sights of Padua, Vicenza, Verona and Milan before making their way through Switzerland and Alsace and then visiting several of the great cathedral cities of northern France (Fig 2.7) before returning probably via Rouen, arriving back in London on 9 September.

In 1862 the trip was a more modest 'French Journey' of a couple of weeks in the company of his fellow architect and friend Robert Johnson, who had just spent a few years in G G Scott's office. Arriving at Rouen on 16 August, they went on to include Paris, Creil, Beauvais, Senlis and Noyon. Paley was back in London on 1 September and took the opportunity to visit the International Exhibition. He noted seeing work by some of the leading designers, manufacturers and artists of the day. Tiles by Godwin's were 'good', as was the carving by James

Fig 2.8
Brunel's still incomplete bridge at Clifton near Bristol, as drawn by Paley on 24 June 1859. He noted the intention to reuse the chains from Hungerford Bridge: over the Thames in London also by Brunel, which was demolished the following year.
(Private collection)

Forsyth: he also looked at work by Thomas Earp and Henry Poole & Sons. The stained glass of the fledgling Morris, Marshall, Faulkner & Co attracted his attention but was noted (rather paradoxically) as 'good tho' mean'.

As he travelled closer to home Paley also sketched buildings and features that caught his eye, and various drawings survive from the late 1830s onwards. June 1859 found him near Bristol drawing the still incomplete suspension bridge across the Avon Gorge at Clifton (Fig 2.8).

The handover of the practice and a new office

As we have seen, Edmund Sharpe made E G Paley his partner in 1845, and thereafter withdrew increasingly from the practice of architecture as he concentrated on other business activities and sanitary reform. From 1847 Paley was shouldering most of the work of the firm, and although the title 'Sharpe & Paley' continued until 1856, when Sharpe left Lancaster for North Wales, Paley's independent work was evident from at least 1849 (Fig 2.9). His marriage in 1851 to Sharpe's youngest sister Frances was probably the signal for Sharpe to withdraw entirely.[55] The two families were now linked by marriage, and the two men would no doubt have kept in touch and continued to meet regularly. Sharpe's local status and Paley's professional role would bring them together as, for example, in 1852 when both found themselves in the procession for the opening of the new Lancaster Grammar School buildings.[56] Paley probably continued to work from Sharpe's old office at St Leonard's Gate for a number of years, but in 1860 he established himself on the second floor at 32 Castle Hill (24 Castle Park from the late 1880s), one of the houses facing Lancaster Castle (Fig 2.10), which would serve the firm until its demise.[57] It had been owned since 1851 and used as a legal office by William Dunn, the Town Clerk. Deeds show that it was owned by Paley from 1871.[58]

The shifting of responsibility from Sharpe to Paley produced no distinctive change in the work of the firm. In the late 1840s both men

Fig 2.9
Paley is named as the architect for a new fish market in Lancaster in this illustration.
(Lancaster Gazette
24 February 1849)

Fig 2.10
Paley moved into part of this building on Castle Hill as his office in 1860. It served the practice until the end of its days, finally being sold to Lancaster Corporation in 1945, the year before Harry Paley's death.
(Mark Watson)

were involved in the remodelling of Capernwray Hall and the rebuilding of Wigan parish church, but who exactly was responsible for what is uncertain. We can be certain, however, that any works between 1851 and 1867 are by Paley alone. As a provincial architect, and the only major practitioner based in the large swathe of country between Preston and Carlisle, Paley was approached to design all types of buildings and take on commissions both great and small. Nonetheless, he is, like Sharpe, best remembered for his churches.

Fig 2.11
Paley built for denominations other than the established church, as here for the Independents at Morecambe in 1862–3.

Paley as church architect

Between 1851 and 1867 the Catalogue in this book reveals that church work outnumbered other commissions in a ratio of about 1.2:1 (*see* Appendix 5). It is even higher if the related projects for parsonages and church schools are added. During this period Paley was responsible for some 36 new or rebuilt churches, predominantly, but not exclusively, for Anglicans. Whereas most Victorian church-building was commissioned on sectarian lines, Paley was unusual in working for other denominations, which no doubt reflects his reputation as the architect of choice in the Lancaster area. For the Independents (Congregationalists) he designed a church in Morecambe in 1862–3 (Fig 2.11), and Sunday Schools in Lancaster in 1856. For Roman Catholics he designed a church at Yealand Conyers, 1852 (Fig 2.12); a complex of church, presbytery and schools at Garstang, 1857–8; and the church (now cathedral) of St Peter in Lancaster and its associated buildings, 1857–9 (this latter project and the Royal Albert Asylum were Paley's two most important commissions).

Although Paley is now best remembered as a partner in the firm of Paley & Austin, he enjoyed a good reputation as a church architect in his own right. After his death, the *Architect & Contract Reporter* carried an article highlighting his church work, illustrating it with engravings of six of his churches, and copying his long obituary from the *Lancaster Guardian*.[59]

In the 13 years between 1838, when Paley joined Sharpe, and 1851, when he became sole principal, a sea change came over church-building, at least for the Anglican and Roman Catholic communions. We have seen some of its effects in the work of Edmund Sharpe, in terms of the abandoning of his beloved Romanesque style in favour of Gothic, and withdrawal from the rudimentary Gothic which dominated church-building around 1840. The Cambridge Camden Society might not have liked Sharpe's terracotta attempt at Decorated architecture in his Rusholme church, but there is no doubt that this was a sincere effort to design in accordance with the stylistic preferences of the mid-1840s and to endow the building with rich detail and dignity rarely met with before 1840.

By 1851 the revolution was complete. In the vanguard of church architecture things were about to move on again as leading architects and their clients built on the achievements of the 1840s by developing Gothic architecture in new directions. In London William Butterfield's great churches of St Matthias, Stoke Newington, and All Saints, Margaret Street, were under construction, both of them in brick (which *The Ecclesiologist* had dismissed as 'a mean material' as recently as 1844),[60] both using decidedly continental elements, and with All Saints providing a high-profile example of the awakening interest in structural polychromy. But not so in central and northern Lancashire. Paley was not an innovator like Butterfield, G E Street or William White, nor one to ignore ecclesiological orthodoxy like E B Lamb or S S Teulon; and he was certainly not a young Turk like the *arrivistes* of the mid/late 1850s, A W Blomfield and J P Seddon.

In general Paley designed, and his clients seem to have required, the kind of church that had become the norm by 1850, inspired by the writings of Pugin and forcefully insisted upon by the Cambridge Camden Society and its less polemical sister society in Oxford. The resulting 'norm' was a church that was quite faithful to medieval English precedents from the later 13th and early 14th centuries, perhaps with a few slightly unusual touches yet ones with a historical pedigree behind them. Internal arrangements required open roofs, bench seating for the congregation, stalls in the chancel, a pulpit to the side of the chancel entrance, a font at the west end, a rise in floor level in the chancel, and no side chapels (what may be a side chapel today would have started life as a chancel aisle fitted up with seating facing north or south). What began with a lead from high churchmen, who were suspected in the early 1840s of having dangerously popish sympathies, had become decoupled from such fears by the 1850s, and thus the great Victorian Anglican church-building movement proceeded along the lines that it did, populating the country with many thousands of medievally inspired buildings, yet ones which were also clearly of their own time.

Edward Graham Paley provided such buildings in large numbers. This was against a background of low churchmanship in the diocese of Chester, which then included the whole of the historic county of Lancashire. Manchester diocese was carved from it in 1848 and followed the same tradition, with its first bishop, James Prince Lee (1804–69), having no time at all for Tractarianism. Nothing is known for certain about Paley's own churchmanship, though he is thought to have been of a Broad persuasion.

Fig 2.12
Yealand Conyers, St Mary (RC), 1852.

Churches of the 1850s

Paley occasionally turned away from almost universally accepted ecclesiological precepts in his use of Perpendicular forms. His rebuilding of St Patrick, Preston Patrick (CuW), in 1852–3 is a case in point (Fig 2.13). Placed prominently and impressively on a hill, the rebuilt church has a north-west tower which reuses genuine later medieval work in its west window, but

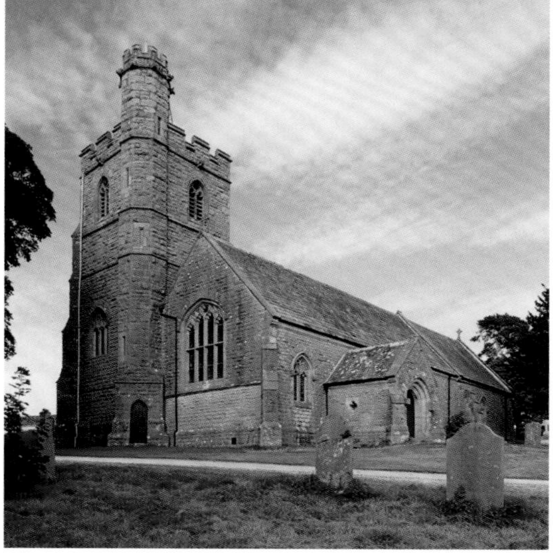

Fig 2.13
Preston Patrick (CuW), St Patrick, rebuilt in 1851–3 incorporating Perpendicular features.
(Mark Watson)

Fig. 2.14
Rylstone (NY), St Peter, before and after rebuilding in 1852–3. Even allowing for any inaccuracies in the sketch (right), the new work is clearly not a copy of what was there before and shows a conscious decision to adopt the Perpendicular style (below).
(Mark Watson)

new, 15th-century-style windows are introduced elsewhere. This might be seen as an act of conservatism to keep the stylistic features of the previous building, along the lines specifically expressed by the parishioners at Wigan who had demanded that their new church, rebuilt in the late 1840s, look just like the old one. Such conservatism certainly seems to have been the reason behind the extensive use of the Perpendicular style in rebuilt churches in Dorset in the 1850s and 1860s, where the style was dominant in country churches, and a sense of continuity seems to have underscored the choice.[61] At exactly the same time, Paley was rebuilding the Yorkshire church of St Peter, Rylstone. Here a sketch of the old church shows no medieval features other than in the tower; yet details of the building are taken almost exclusively from the 15th century (Fig 2.14). Perhaps it is unwise to suggest that Paley had a positive enthusiasm for the style, but he certainly had no aversion to it, unlike those in the forefront of church-building. He would go on to use it for the rebuilding of St Paul's, Brookhouse, near Caton, in 1865–7. The works listed here are relatively minor and perhaps not too much should be made of them, but after Paley was joined by Hubert Austin the firm can be seen as a true pioneer in the rehabilitation of Perpendicular architecture after its ecclesiological exile for a quarter of a century.

Fig 2.15
Thwaites (CuC), St Anne, 1853–4, a large but economical country church.
(Mark Watson)

Shortly after Preston Patrick and Rylstone came St Anne's at Thwaites, 1853–4 (CuC) (Fig 2.15), in the south-west tip of Cumberland, and the most remote commission from Lancaster since Edmund Sharpe's church at Calder Bridge, 1841–2 (CuC). As in other small, hitherto impoverished villages in the southern Lakes and north Lancashire, the old church, dating from 1721, was a rather miserable modern affair. The desire and the means to provide more becoming buildings from the 1850s presented Paley (and Austin) with a string of commissions which would continue into Edwardian times. At Thwaites the new church, although cheap (tender £1,500), is a big building of some muscularity, with plate tracery in the aisle windows and circular clerestory openings. Here Paley added (or, more likely, was told to add) seats with low doors, in clear contravention of ecclesiological propriety, smacking as they did of the by-now-reviled box pews. When in 1858 he came to restore his father's former church at Easingwold (NY), the same thing happened. He was in surprisingly good company, with both Scott and Butterfield having been obliged to put in similar seating on occasion.[62]

Other churches of the 1850s were built at Bacup and Wrightington (Fig 2.16) in 1854, and there were rebuilding and additions at Penwortham in 1855–6. The first two mark the appearance of a favourite Paley feature, the traceried oculus window, which became a regular feature of his repertoire in the 1860s. In the later 1850s the Roman Catholic Church provided Paley with substantial activity. In 1856 Catholics in Garstang were in a position to

Fig 2.16 (far left)
Wrightington, St James the Great, 1854, west end with a wheel window, a favourite device of Paley's.
(Mark Watson)

Fig 2.17 (left)
Garstang, St Mary & St Michael (RC), Bonds, 1857–8. Nave roof.
(Mark Watson)

provide themselves with a new church together with a presbytery and school. Building took place in 1857–8. The church had a continuous roofline over the nave and chancel although they were divided by an arch internally. The architecture is mostly conventional enough, although the roof internally (Fig 2.17) is an impressive four-tier structure with wind-braces and may be seen as a precursor to the many impressive roofs that P&A/A&P would put on their churches.

Paley's last church of the 1850s was St George's, Barrow-in-Furness, of 1859–60 (CuL) (Fig 2.18). Barrow played a hugely important part in the firm's affairs, and further mention of the church is deferred to the account of the town below. By the time it was started, Paley had almost completed his great church of St Peter in Lancaster.

St Peter's, Lancaster

St Peter's was Paley's masterwork as an independent church architect (Figs 2.19, 2.20, 2.21 and 2.22). Catholics had had a chapel in Lancaster since 1799,[63] but by the late 1840s they sought more adequate provision for their needs and in 1847 a three-acre site was secured on sloping ground at Greenfield on the east side of the town. Paley laid out a cemetery here in 1849–50 and designed schools and a convent, built in 1851–3, together with a presbytery (Fig 2.23). A legacy of £2,000 from Thomas Coulston in 1856 became the platform for fund-raising to build an impressive church.[64] Tenders were invited in March 1857 and no time was lost, the foundation stone being laid on 29 April. Two and a half years later, the consecration by the bishop of Liverpool, Dr Alexander Goss, took place on 4 October 1859. The church was raised to cathedral status in

Fig 2.18 (below)
Barrow-in-Furness (CuL), St George, 1859–60. The tower stands at the west end of the south aisle. The Ramsden Chapel beyond the east end of the south aisle was added by Paley & Austin in 1883–4.

Fig 2.19
Lancaster, St Peter (RC), 1857–9, now the cathedral. Watercolour by Robert Rampling, 1877. (Lancaster Cathedral; Mark Watson)

Fig 2.20 (far left)
Lancaster, St Peter, west end.

Fig 2.21 (left)
Lancaster, St Peter, interior looking east.

Fig 2.22 (far left)
Lancaster, St Peter, wooden-vaulted east end, decorated by Thomas Early.

Fig 2.23 (left)
The presbytery at St Peter's.

1924, when the Liverpool diocese was divided.

While not on the sheer scale or with such a magnificent steeple as Joseph Hansom's great Catholic church of St Walburge of 1850–4 in Preston, St Peter's has an equivalent presence in the Lancaster townscape thanks to its soaring, 240ft tower and spire. St Peter's is built on a grand scale, with excellent and extensive detailing, unlike many Catholic churches of the time which suffered from limited funding. The building, in Paley's favoured 'Middle Pointed' style, has tall, six-bay arcades with tall circular sandstone piers and early Gothic foliage capitals, tall transepts and a polygonal, painted, timber-vaulted apse. The two chapels off the south aisle have stone vaulting. The church is a fine, expansive building and was mentioned with some enthusiasm by the German critic Hermann Muthesius in his survey of modern English church-building in 1901.[65] The practice continued a long association with the church, the most notable work being the west gallery on marble piers to accommodate a new organ in 1888, choir stalls of 1899 and a polygonal, stone-vaulted baptistry at the north-east in 1901 by Hubert Austin. This resembles a small chapter house and is richly equipped in its centre with a Connemara marble and serpentine font.

Fig 2.24 (above) Quernmore, St Peter, 1860, interior, Paley's first bare-brick-lined church. (Mark Watson)

Fig 2.25 (above far right) Ince-in-Makerfield (GM), Christ Church, 1863–4, west porch in which, unusually, Paley embraces the lively vigour of mid-Victorian Gothic. (Mark Watson)

Fig 2.26 (right) Walton-le-Dale, All Saints, 1861–2. (Mark Watson)

Fig 2.27 (far right) Bradford (WY), Holy Trinity, 1864–5 (demolished), font. Paley used the same design as that at Walton-le-Dale, All Saints, 1861–2. (BB64/01286 © Crown copyright.NMR)

Some churches of the 1860s

The year 1860 saw the rebuilding of St Peter's, Quernmore (Fig 2.24), four miles east of Lancaster, paid for by William Garnett of Quernmore Park to replace a modest chapel of 1834. A fairly conventional essay in the style of around 1300 with an oculus window at the east end of the aisle, it is the first Paley church with a bare brick interior. His previous ones had plastered walls and thus a very different character. Paley went on to use bare brick again at St Mark's, Preston (1862–3), Egton (CuL, 1864–5) and St James, Barrow (CuL, 1867–9). It occasionally reappears in the work of Paley & Austin although their predilection was to be for bare ashlar.

Paley was rarely given to indulging in the more exotic kinds of High Victorian Gothic, dubbed 'acrobatic Gothic' by the *Building News* and often referred to at the time as having 'GO'.[66] Its repertoire was rich, varied and designed for effect. Strong polychromy, lavish foliage, strange geometry, bold, punched tracery and distorted Gothic forms all made their appearance. Such were the extreme consequences of the development of Gothic initiated in the 1850s. Paley, however, was not immune to this aspect of the taste of his day, and occasionally characteristically High Victorian decorative motifs appear in his work – hence the principal rafters at Quernmore are embellished with notching. However, structural polychromy played no significant part in his architecture, nor, to make a sweeping generalisation, was it used particularly prominently in most of the North West: the ferocious brick polychromy at, say, St Mary, Rufford, of 1869, by Liverpool architects Danson & Davies, seems to have had no appeal whatsoever for Paley (nor indeed for Hubert Austin). Paley's most overt piece of freely treated High Victorian Gothic is the west porch at Christ Church, Ince-in-Makerfield (GM), of 1863–4 (Fig 2.25).

All Saints, Walton-le-Dale (Fig 2.26), south-east of Preston, of 1861–2, is an example of a relatively expensive Paley church, designed in 1860 when it was expected to cost £4,300. As so often, the style was of around 1300, and the church was provided with a broach spire and given a polygonal east end. In the south aisle east wall it has one of Paley's typical wheel windows. Although architecturally fairly conservative, the church is equipped with an inventively Gothic font, the design of which Paley reused at the now-demolished church of Holy Trinity, Bradford (WY) (Fig 2.27), of 1864–5.

Apart from Hansom's famous spire of St Walburge's Catholic church, western Preston has another important landmark in the tower of St Mark's Anglican church. This was built in 1862–3, with the tower coming later in 1866: Paley originally planned a spire but this was not built, and a new tower design was used involving impressive tall openings below the belfry. Externally the body of the church is fairly conventional Middle Pointed, but there is a polygonal apse with gables which allow the sanctuary windows to be heightened (Fig 2.28). The interior (Fig 2.29), now converted to flats, was remarkable for its powerful double hammer-beam roof with the lower beams being carried on slender columns. Galleries were fitted into the transepts, hence the windows on two levels.

The wide, aisleless nave and the galleries at St Mark's, Preston, are strongly suggestive of Low Church worship. An even more dramatic example of such a building is St Andrew's, Livesey, near Blackburn, of 1866–7 (Figs 2.30 and 2.31) where the nave is 38ft wide and, as at Preston, is covered by a vast roof, in this case arch-braced to a low collar. Also as at Preston, there are Paley's usual circular windows in the transepts.

Paley's largest church of the early and middle 1860s was St James', Poolstock, in Wigan, built in 1863–6 (Figs 2.32 and 2.33) and paid for by Nathaniel Eckersley, cotton-mill owner, banker and railway promoter, as a memorial to his

Fig 2.28 (above) Preston, St Mark, built 1862–3 but the steeple design was changed. The apse has gables to enable enlarged windows and the transept shows a typical Paley wheel window. A single roof covers the nave. (Architect & Contract Reporter *53, 1895, 82)*

Fig 2.29 (left) Preston, St Mark. Wide, high roofs are typical of Paley's work in the 1860s, but the double hammer-beam roof carried on iron columns has no parallel in his output. The walls were originally of bare brick. A small gallery can be seen at the west end. (BB82/03512 © Crown copyright.NMR

Fig 2.30 (right)
Livesey, St Andrew, 1866–7. The apse, the steeple beside the chancel, the large nave roof and the transept with a wheel window are reminiscent of the design for St Mark's, Preston (see Fig 2.28). Only the lowest stage of the steeple was built: the intended corner spirelets re-emerge at Manchester, St John, Cheetham (see Fig 3.22).
(St Andrew's Parochial Church Council; Mark Watson)

Fig 2.31 (far right)
Livesey, whose wide nave and central block of seats strongly indicate a Low Church commission. The impressive, tall roof was a Paley speciality in the 1860s (see Fig 2.29).
(Mark Watson)

Fig 2.32
Wigan (GM), St James, Poolstock, 1863–6, a large church in 14th-century dress and paid for by industrial and commercial wealth. Popular Paley devices are the transept wheel window and straight gables over the belfry lights.
(Mark Watson)

Fig 2.33
St James, Poolstock, east end. The chancel decoration and the ornate reredos were added in 1876–7.
(Mark Watson)

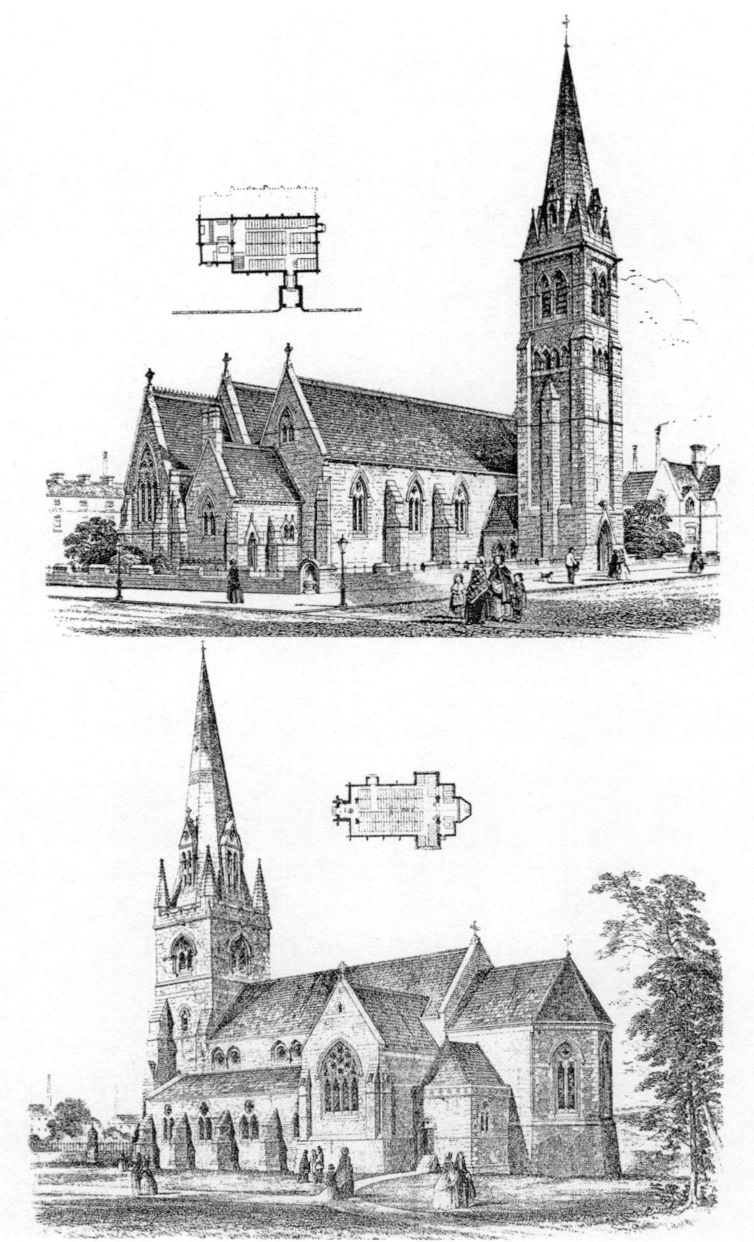

Fig 2.34 (top)
Bury (GM), Holy Trinity, the north-west steeple was never built.
(Architect & Contract Reporter *53, 1895, 84)*

Fig 2.35 (above)
Darwen, St John the Evangelist, Turncroft, 1864, demolished. Paley often used polygonal apses for his chancels at this time.
(Architect & Contract Reporter *53, 1895, 84)*

parents and brother. Built in the Decorated style, it has a prominent west tower with a pierced parapet, and over the belfry windows are straight-headed gables, a feature which Paley made much use of from about 1860. Other substantial town churches included Holy Trinity, Bury (GM), 1863–4 (Fig 2.34), and St John's, Turncroft, in Darwen, 1864 (Fig 2.35), both essays in the customary Middle Pointed. A number of minor, small country churches were also built, although that at Ireleth (CuL) has some interesting detail and occupies a dramatic site (Fig 2.36).

St Peter's, Bolton

Along with St Peter's, Lancaster, Paley's other great independent church project was the rebuilding of Bolton's fairly modest parish church (Fig 2.37) on a scale and with the dignity that befitted this great Victorian textile town. In 1863 a committee had been formed to consider repair or rebuilding, and in early 1864 Paley was called in to report. Peter Ormrod (1795–1875), a cotton-spinner and banker who lived at Halliwell Hall, came forward with an offer to pay for a new building, so it was no doubt to most people's delight that Paley reached the conclusion that repair was not practicable. Paley had already built Ormrod's country house, Wyresdale Hall, at Scorton in 1856–8, and the commissions associated with him are almost certainly due to the extensive social and business connections in Bolton of Edmund Sharpe's wife Elizabeth's family, the Fletchers. The Ormrods also had marriage and business links with the Cross family, funders of St Thomas, Halliwell, a major P&A church in the mid-1870s.

Nonetheless, the prospect of a new building was not universally welcomed. In a letter to the local press in October 1865, one 'Urbanus' argued against rebuilding out of respect for the ancient fabric, and concern about disturbing the dead.[67] However, the following week, the appropriately styled 'Aurora' put forward the persuasive thought that 'a man would be considered insane if he were to choose an old cotton mill in preference to a new one, just because the former was more ancient'.

Ormrod's offer of £30,000 was duly accepted, and the magnitude of his generosity made the press nationally.[68] The old church was demolished in 1866. The new one that rose in its place was finally finished in 1871, by which time the cost had risen to £45,000 (Fig 2.38). The site falls sharply away to the east and north, and the church is a major landmark. The commanding, north-west tower is, at 180ft, the highest in Lancashire and has above the belfry lights the straight-sided gables in which Paley delighted. Pevsner's reviser, Matthew Hyde, sounds a note of caution, rightly suggesting that the 'NW tower is actually too tall for comfort … It is awkwardly jointed into four equal storeys, with too many set-offs to the buttresses.'[69] St Peter's is a grand, assured church with aisles and transepts, although it has never met with great enthusiasm. Pevsner

Fig 2.36 (far left)
Ireleth (CuL), St Mary, 1864–5, overlooking the Duddon estuary from the Furness peninsula. It was paid for by the Duke of Buccleuch, whose already considerable wealth was augmented by the mineral riches of the area. Behind the camera, the hills still bear the scars of mining.

Fig 2.37 (above left)
Bolton (GM), St Peter, the old parish church as sketched by Paley in 1855. Edmund Sharpe was married here on 27 July 1843, as was Fanny Austin's grandfather, John Langshaw, on 2 January 1800.
(Edward & Sara Mason collection)

Fig 2.38
Bolton, St Peter, rebuilt 1867–71 and Paley's largest church commission. The tower, the highest in Lancashire, is the chief landmark in the town, the wealth of which, based on cotton manufacture, would provide further important commissions for Paley & Austin in the years to come.
(Mark Watson)

himself described it in 1969 as 'a confident if conventional piece of work'.[70] It is built of fine ashlar from the Longridge quarries in an early 14th-century style, 156ft long, and, as Paley liked, it is also tall with the nave rising to 82ft. The main view from the town is the west end with a large, seven-light intersecting window. On the south elevation the aisle windows are of three lights and the clerestory has paired windows with ballflower decoration. Paley deploys historical precedents in the window tracery which, Hyde says, 'are from published sources, eg the S transept from Temple Balsall in Warwickshire'. The interior, with a five-bay nave with clustered columns, and a three-bay aisled, stone-vaulted chancel, has a similar character to the exterior – large, grand and yet cool.

Secular commissions

As might be expected of a successful provincial architect, Paley designed a great variety of building types, and secular commissions supplemented his ecclesiastical ones throughout his independent career. Early on there were a number of schools in Lancaster from about 1850, including new premises for the Royal Grammar School (Fig 2.39). There was also a steady stream of village schools starting with one at Bardsea (CuL) in 1851. This was followed by others throughout the 1850s and 1860s – Poulton-le-Sands (today's Morecambe), 1854; Pilling, 1856; Davenham (Ch), 1856–7; Abbeystead, 1857; Ellel, 1858; Glasson, 1860; Singleton, 1862; Allithwaite (CuL), 1863–5, as part of a integrated church, parsonage and school complex; Clapham (NY), 1864; and Arkholme, 1867–8.

Paley (& Austin) also did much work at Rossall School, an Anglican boarding school, founded on the Fylde coast in 1844 (Figs 2.40 and 2.41). After the first commission for a chapel, built in 1861–2, there followed the east side of the quadrangle with a large 17th-century-style gatehouse (Fig 2.42), showing, in Clare Hartwell's words, Paley 'at his most relaxed … with nods to Stonyhurst and Hampton Court, yet [a design] entirely his own'.[71] Rossall commissions would continue into the Edwardian era, ending with a mission church in Manchester in 1909–10, St Wilfrid's Newton Heath, although by this time the firm was obliged to share the work for the school, commissions also going to Henry Littler of Preston (father and son; eg the sanatorium of 1892) and John Bilson of Hull (Modern Schools of 1911). Paley also undertook the first of several commissions for the practice at Giggleswick School in 1849–51 (alterations and modest new building work).

The diversity of Paley's work is represented by such commissions as a music hall in Settle (NY) (Fig 2.43), 1853; cemetery buildings at Lancaster, 1855, and Stalmine, 1856 where,

Fig 2.39
Lancaster, Royal Grammar School, 1851–2. The tower is part of the headmaster's house. The school was attended by both Austins and Langshaws. Down the hill, leading towards the town centre, is the spire of St Peter's church.

Fig 2.40
Rossall School, early sketch by Paley. The design of the gatehouse tower changed on execution.
(David McLaughlin collection)

presumably as a deliberate act of symbolism on the part of those commissioning them, the Anglican chapel is grander and at a higher level than the nonconformist one (Fig 2.44); alterations to accommodate the Mechanics' Institute in Lancaster, 1856; the restoration and reordering of the medieval tower at the former Dalton Castle (CuL) to form a courthouse, also in 1856; a villa at Slaidburn, 1857; an obelisk in Lancaster cemetery as a Crimean War memorial, 1860 (Fig 2.45); (probably) station designs

Fig 2.41
Rossall School, chapel, 1861–2. Photograph of c 1900 taken to showcase the newly installed wall-panelling made by James Hatch & Sons of Lancaster.
(Album of photographs of work by Hatch & Sons, private collection)

Fig 2.42
Rossall School, gatehouse, 1867, and north-east corner of the 'The Square' (quadrangle).

for Edmund Sharpe's Conwy–Llanrwst railway; showrooms and other work at a marble works in Lancaster, 1863; substantial works for the Lancaster Carriage & Wagon Company (Fig 2.46), 1864; a market hall in Barrow (CuL), 1864; and varied work for the Furness Railway Company, which is discussed later.

Paley's also carried out two major country house projects. One was the rebuilding of Wennington Hall in 1855–6 (Fig 2.47), in the Lune Valley, not far from Hornby Castle where he had worked with Sharpe a few years before. The estate had been acquired in 1841 by Richard Saunders, whose son William commissioned

Fig 2.43 (above)
Settle (NY), Music Hall, 1853.
(Mark Watson)

Fig 2.44 (far right top)
Stalmine, cemetery chapels. The Anglican chapel is in the foreground.
(Mark Watson)

Fig 2.45 (right)
Lancaster Cemetery, the Crimea Memorial, 1860.

Fig 2.46 (far right bottom)
The huge works of the Lancaster Carriage & Wagon Company lines the main road leading north-east out of Lancaster. The tower housed a water tank.
(Mark Watson)

Fig 2.47
Wennington Hall, 1855–6. Built in a Tudor Gothic style, it has, like other country houses by Sharpe and Paley & Austin, a large tower towards the rear. The stable block (left) has its own towered entrance.

Paley to replace the previous house which had already been remodelled by Thomas Harrison. Saunders's new home was a two-storeyed, asymmetrical Tudor-style building with several gables, 'entirely relaxed, treated freely as a hall-and-cross-wing composition with a really big castellated tower at the back', as at Sharpe & Paley's Capernwray Hall of nearly 10 years earlier.[72] The composition spreads out on the left, with a stable block connected to the house that has its own tower. Inside there is a staircase hall with a hammer-beam roof and stained glass. Nearby and just across the Yorkshire border, Paley built a much smaller house in 1857–60 for a Mr B H Bent at Low Bentham. 'The Ridding' (Fig 2.48) is a compact, square building, and uniquely in Paley's output is in the Scottish baronial style, presumably something that was requested by the patron. Paley's other major country house, 'Abbot's Wood', near Barrow-in-Furness, is referred to below.

Barrow-in-Furness – a new town of opportunity

Barrow-in-Furness, like Middlesbrough and Crewe, was a Victorian industrial creation. It also provides a microcosm of the work of E G Paley (and subsequently of Paley & Austin), covering diverse and numerous commissions, and even providing sufficient work for the firm to establish a sub-office there in the 1870s. Its importance is such that some background to the town, its promoters and the role of the Furness Railway Company (FR) in its development needs to be given.

At the start of the 19th century, the chief towns of Furness were Dalton and Ulverston, Barrow being just a small village within the parish of Dalton. The catalyst for change was the development of iron ore deposits – very rich at 50–65 per cent iron – in the Furness peninsula. Ore had been extracted in pre-Roman times

Fig 2.48
Low Bentham (NY), 'The Ridding', 1857–60. An essay in Scottish baronial just over the Yorkshire border. (Mark Watson)

and had also helped underpin the great wealth of Furness Abbey in the Middle Ages. Production grew to feed the furnaces of the Industrial Revolution, some of them local but mostly in South Wales, with exports being shipped from various places along the coast, including Barrow itself. The tonnage leaving the area rose from an annual average of under 4,000 in 1800–5 to 100,000 in 1844, but it was an inefficient business so long as transport relied on horses, carts and muddy roads.[73] Industrial expansion really began with the development of iron-making from 1857 and steel from 1864. The population increased more than fourfold between 1851 (4,700) and 1861 (22,500), and had doubled again by 1871 (40,300). This growth led to an explosion of building and architectural opportunities.

What had changed everything was the building of the Furness Railway. Formed in 1844 with the first lines opening in 1846, the FR was not connected to the main railway system until 1857, before which time the quickest and most convenient way from Lancaster to Furness remained, as it always had been, across the sands of Morecambe Bay. The railway was conceived for and initially concerned with the iron ore trade, which it funnelled into the Barrow area. In addition, passenger traffic soon developed and led to Sharpe & Paley's development of the Furness Abbey Hotel. The FR would be the direct source of many commissions for the firm in years to come. The key figure behind the company's creation was William Cavendish, who was the 2nd Earl of Burlington, and (from 1858) the 7th Duke of Devonshire. He adopted Holker Hall as his favourite home and paid great attention to his Furness interests from there. The other chief investor was the absentee landowner, the Duke of Buccleuch; Joseph Paxton was also an original investor. These men provided the principal capital for the enterprise, but the man who transformed the various schemes for the railway and for Barrow into reality was James Ramsden (1822–96).

Ramsden arrived as the FR's locomotive superintendent at the start of 1846, becoming general manager in 1859 and finally managing director from 1865 to 1895. His dynamism and entrepreneurial activities extended far beyond the running of trains, and he played a key part in developing port facilities and steamer services, and also Barrow's key industries of iron and steel and shipbuilding. He also invested substantially in the Barrow Flax & Jute Company (which provided much-needed female employment), and the Barrow Steam Corn Mill.[74] Ramsden also became managing director of the Barrow Haematite Steel Company from 1866, chairman of the jute company from 1869, and managing director of the Barrow Shipbuilding Company from 1888. In 1856 he conceived the idea of a model town with wide main thoroughfares and separate residential and industrial districts,[75] and the spaciousness of the street planning still evident in parts of present-day Barrow can be traced back to Ramsden's ideas. He was a notable benefactor to the town and its institutions, and served on many committees. After Barrow became a borough in 1867 Ramsden served five consecutive terms as mayor until 1872, when he was knighted. That year also saw the unveiling, amid a huge and enthusiastic crowd, of his statue by Matthew Noble which overlooks Ramsden Square (*see* Fig 3.70). One of the larger subscribers to this monument, at 10 guineas, was Edward Paley, who had every reason to be grateful for Ramsden's generous patronage.[76]

The second great figure in the development of Barrow, and who also patronised the firm, was Henry William Schneider (1817–87).[77] Schneider was from a London family of Swiss origin, with extensive mineral exploration and mining interests in England and overseas. He first came to Furness in 1839 and spent 10 years prospecting, not very successfully, for iron ore until the end of 1850 when, just as his funds were drying up and his exploration rights were about to expire, he and his team discovered an immensely rich deposit of ore at Park on the

Earl of Burlington's lands. In 1853 Schneider formed a company with Robert Hannay, a wealthy Scottish landowner, which further developed the Park mine, and built blast furnaces at Hindpool in Barrow on land leased from the Furness Railway. The first two furnaces were blown in during 1859, with others following. The Furness ores, being low in phosphorus, were particularly suited to the newly invented Bessemer steel-making process, which converted iron into steel by forcing air through to remove impurities. Barrow was given a huge boost by the new technology. The Barrow Haematite Steel Company started production in 1865 with Lord Frederick Cavendish (second son of the Duke of Devonshire), Schneider and Ramsden among the original directors. In 1866 Schneider, Hannay & Company was dissolved and its interests assigned to the Barrow Haematite Steel Company which, backed by increased capital, became one of the largest producers of steel in the world. Schneider had previously lived in London, but following the death of his wife in 1862 he moved to Ulverston. After his second marriage in 1864 he moved to Conishead Priory and also built a red-brick Italianate marine residence on Roa Island, which may have been designed by Paley.[78] Later it was Paley & Austin who built him a large (long-demolished) residence, 'Oak Lea', north of Barrow, in 1874.

Paley's work in Barrow – a mansion, the Furness Railway, and two churches

Ramsden's status within the Furness Railway and his place in Barrow society were exemplified by his residence, 'Abbot's Wood', designed by Paley and set on elevated ground above Furness Abbey (Fig 2.49). In 1857 the Furness Railway authorised the expenditure of £2,000 on the building, but it must have cost a great deal more than that.[79] It was ready for occupation in 1859, and was a complex assemblage with many gables and roofs, Gothic and

Fig 2.49
Barrow-in-Furness (CuL), 'Abbot's Wood', 1857–9. Paley deployed Tudor Gothic to create a mansion for a successful Victorian businessman, Sir James Ramsden, the 'father of Barrow'.
(Cumbria Record Office & Local Studies Library, Barrow; Mark Watson)

Tudor details, and a square tower with a much taller stair turret. Another tower stood over the gatehouse entrance, and there were extensive grounds with long walkways with fine views. The grandeur of the building seems out of proportion even to Ramsden's status and likely wealth in the late 1850s. It may also have been used by the railway company as a showcase to display its great success and to serve, perhaps, as a place to entertain clients (just as the shipbuilders, Vickers, commissioned Lutyens to build 'Abbey House' (1913–14) on the other side of the valley). 'Abbot's Wood', apart from some of its estate buildings, was demolished in the 1960s.

Fig 2.50 (right) Grange-over-Sands station, c 1864, one of the firm's many buildings for the Furness Railway Company. (Tim Austin)

Fig 2.51 (below) Barrow-in-Furness (CuL), St James, 1867–9. A brick church with a wide, Low Church nave, aisles, a polygonal apse and mostly 13th-century detailing. All this is typical of Paley, but the innovative transition from tower to spire is a new element in the practice's work and might herald the arrival of Hubert Austin. (Mark Watson)

Building the Furness Abbey Hotel (1847–8) and 'Abbot's Wood' provided the firm with an entrée to a most unusual avenue for a major architectural practice: for almost three decades it designed most, if not all, the buildings needed by the Furness Railway. Most of this work was undertaken during the P&A years and will be considered in the following chapter. However, here we may note three commissions by Paley in the 1860s. The first was Strand station in Barrow, opened in 1863, with James Ramsden driving into it with the inaugural train.[80] The previous year the FR had absorbed the Ulverston & Lancaster Railway, which gave it a through line to the Lancaster–Carlisle main line, so it set about laying a second track with an accompanying station-building programme. Grange-over-Sands, one of the larger stations, appears to be a Paley work from 1864 (Fig 2.50). Anyone alighting there could stay at the imposing, if rather gaunt, Paley-designed Grange Hotel (1866 but extended) on the hillside overlooking the town and Morecambe Bay.[81]

The year that 'Abbot's Wood' was ready for occupation, 1859, saw the start of the first permanent church in Barrow. This too was by Paley. Planning for St George's had begun in 1857. Lord Burlington and the Duke of Buccleuch offered £4,000 for the project, provided that the remaining £2,000 could be raised locally: among those rising to the challenge were Schneider, Hannay & Company. The facing material was sawn slate from the (now) Duke of Devonshire's own quarries at Kirkby-in-Furness, which is contrasted with red sandstone dressings from St Bees. As so often, Paley used details of around 1300. The church opened in 1860, when it included a nave, south aisle and south-west tower with a higher stair turret. However, it was expanded by a north aisle in the late 1860s, followed by the lengthening of the chancel and the addition of the Ramsden Chapel by Paley & Austin in 1883–4.

The rapid growth of Barrow during the 1860s, especially in the Hindpool area, prompted the building of another Anglican church, again designed by Paley. This is one of his finest works. Whereas St George's is a fairly conventional essay in Middle Pointed Gothic, marked out chiefly by its striking grey slate facing, St James's church, which was commenced in 1867 and opened in 1869, is a dramatic red-brick structure that would have done credit to any of the major church architects of the time (Figs 2.51, 2.52 and 2.53). Placed on slightly rising ground above the centre of the town, its spire is a landmark for miles around. The building itself has strong, clean lines, a tall, clerestoried, six-bay nave and a polygonal east end. It draws on the 13th century for its detail, to which is added a little Victorian polychromy over the arch heads, and strong contrasts between the red brick and limestone dressings. Inside, the nave is extremely wide, with fairly narrow aisles. The 'modern' Gothic nature of the building is emphasised by the red brick of the arches and, indeed, originally, the brick would have been even more in evidence as the walls were unpainted (as at Quernmore, 10 years earlier).[82] The Derbyshire alabaster font and pulpit are particularly fine, and were carved by (probably) T R & E Williams of Manchester. Yet the most distinctive feature of St James's is the remarkable transition from the tower to the spire, which rises out of four gables. The arrangement is a variant on Rhenish helm spires, represented in this country by the Saxon steeple at Sompting in West Sussex. The difference is that the Sompting spire is four-sided, while that at Barrow is octagonal. Pevsner, evidently dubious about Paley's capabilities for originality and awed by his new partner, asked, 'Might these top parts of the steeple be an Austin improvement?' Perhaps: it is a fair question, but one to which a firm answer will probably ever be lacking.

The Royal Albert Asylum, Lancaster

Fig 2.52 (above)
Barrow, St James, interior with its wide nave, high-pitched roof, and brick arches on pink sandstone piers. When the walls were of bare brick this interior would have been much more striking.
(Mark Watson)

Fig 2.53 (left)
Barrow, St James, pulpit of alabaster with marble colonettes and standing on a pink sandstone base. The straight-headed gables were a favourite device of Paley's. The font is also a fine piece in alabaster.

The culminating work of Paley's independent career and the largest building ever undertaken by any of our architects was an asylum in Lancaster, half a mile south-west from the centre, and completed in the early years of the Paley & Austin partnership. The town already housed the County Lunatic Asylum, opened on Lancaster Moor in 1816, which later received very substantial additions designed by Edmund Sharpe. But apart from the insane, there were many thousands of mentally retarded individuals who, to use what were then technical terms, were known as 'imbeciles' and 'idiots', the latter more impaired than the former.[83] The provision of specialist education for mentally retarded children had been pioneered on the Continent, and the first provision in England was at a house at Bath in 1846, which took in four children.[84] Other institutions followed, and it was a Lancastrian Quaker businessman, James Brunton, who offered £2,000 in 1864 towards building a substantial asylum for six (later seven) northern counties.[85] It seems he had experienced mental health problems himself and had been a patient of a notable local doctor, Edward Denis de Vitre.

De Vitre, twice mayor of Lancaster and visiting physician at the County Lunatic Asylum, was interested in the care of the mentally ill and promptly set about organising a fund-raising committee. Paley was one of the 10 men who met for this purpose on 14 November 1864. The resulting asylum would become an institution caring for children aged 6 to 15 under an enlightened regime aimed at equipping them for everyday life in the outside world. Much of its funding came from Freemasons, both locally and from further afield, and this extensive Masonic participation in the project seems to have prompted Paley to become a Mason himself.

In May 1866 Paley was appointed as architect. There is no evidence of a competition but – well regarded and well connected – he was a natural choice for the committee. At the time Paley was extremely busy, and in August he confided to Hubert Austin (whom he was expecting to join him): 'I have done nothing at the Asylum & the Committee are beginning to ask for plans!'[86] A vast asylum such as this was really a new building type, and Paley had certainly done nothing like it before. Evidently he considered a possible prototype could be the well-known asylum of 1853 at Earlswood, Redhill, in Surrey, by W B Moffatt, and he had clearly been hoping that Austin could obtain some details about it. His letter to Austin continued: 'Have you been able to get a tracing of the Earlswood plan? Trust you could do this & I will gladly pay any charges of sending a draughtsman. To be any use it should be sent at once. The principal floor plan roughly traced is all I want.'

Plans were finally submitted in October 1866 and work began in 1868, with the foundation stone being laid on 17 June amid lavish Masonic ceremonial by the Grand Master, the Earl of Zetland. In fact this was one of the very rare occasions when Grand Lodge assembled outside of London and the ceremony was witnessed by 4,000 to 5,000 people.[87] Paley, recently initiated as a Freemason himself, carried his plans amid the body of Masons on the procession from the centre of Lancaster. By autumn 1870 the south wing, to be used by boy patients, was ready, and the first intake of 50 arrived in December. The intention was that some 500 patients, both girls and boys, would be accommodated (by 1909 there were 662). The numbers from the various counties were proportionate to the funds subscribed by each. The asylum grounds covered 67 acres on an elevated site commanding magnificent views across Morecambe Bay towards the Lake District.

The asylum was built in a Gothic style on an E-shaped plan: the external walls were faced with local stone and lined with brick, with a small cavity between the two.[88] The symmetrical main façade is 470ft wide with the principal entrance in the centre. From this, the male wing stretched out to the south and the female one to the north. At each end, three-bay blocks were brought forward 60ft and run back east to west for some 184ft. The central part was also extended back eastward for 250ft and included a large dining hall and assembly room. The most striking feature of the complex is the

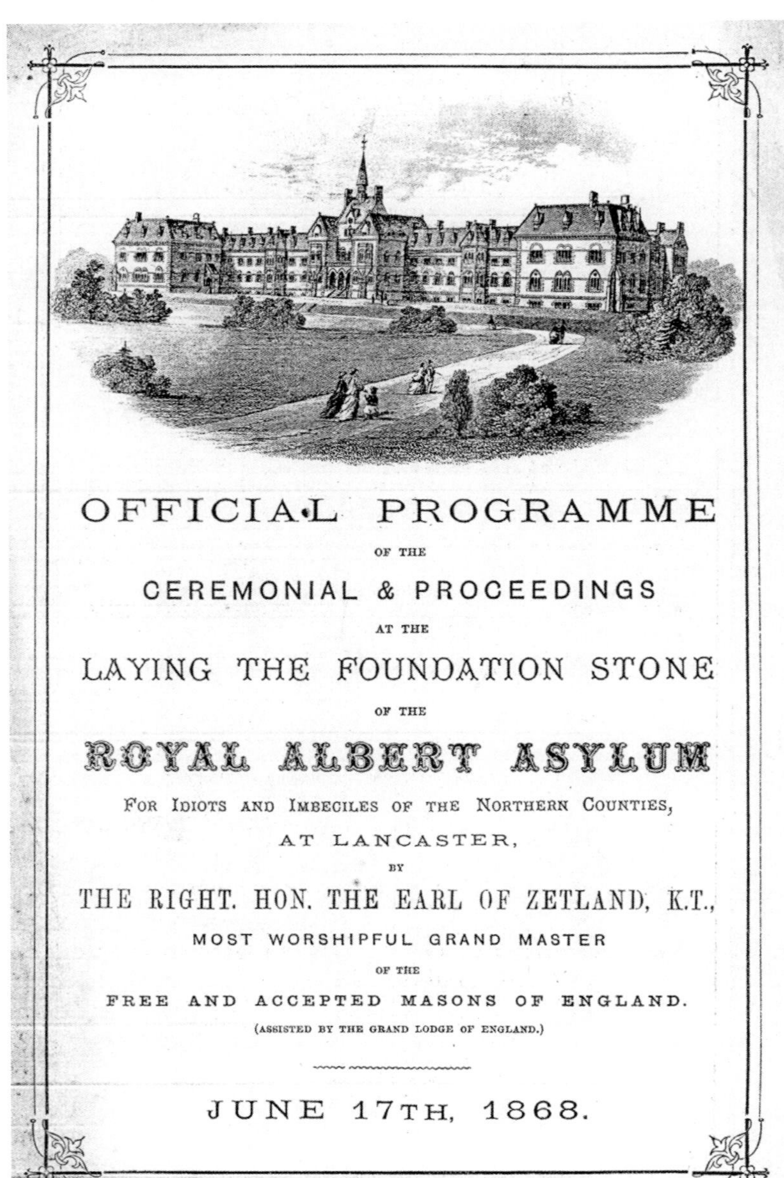
OFFICIAL PROGRAMME

OF THE

CEREMONIAL & PROCEEDINGS

AT THE

LAYING THE FOUNDATION STONE

OF THE

ROYAL ALBERT ASYLUM

FOR IDIOTS AND IMBECILES OF THE NORTHERN COUNTIES,

AT LANCASTER,

BY

THE RIGHT. HON. THE EARL OF ZETLAND, K.T.,

MOST WORSHIPFUL GRAND MASTER

OF THE

FREE AND ACCEPTED MASONS OF ENGLAND.

(ASSISTED BY THE GRAND LODGE OF ENGLAND.)

JUNE 17TH, 1868.

Fig 2.54
Lancaster, Royal Albert Asylum. Front cover of the programme for the laying of the foundation stone in 1868 showing the original design.
(Produced with agreement of the County Heritage Manager, Cultural Services, Lancashire County Council)

Fig 2.55
*Royal Albert Asylum. The revised design, as built, with its dramatic entrance tower. The plan shows female wings left of the central spine, and male to the right. The dining hall, kitchens and workshops/washhouses are arranged successively behind the square administrative area at the central entrance. (*Building News *9 October 1874)*

central tower, which has a tall, steep pavilion roof equipped with lucarnes and corner pinnacles: it bears the date 1873 over the entrance. The local press remarked upon its 'continental character' and regarded it as 'an improvement on the original design' (Figs 2.54 and 2.55). The treatment of the entrance tower forms a majestic centre of gravity to the building (Fig 2.56), and the change in design may well reflect the influence of the newly arrived Hubert Austin. The central area housed an entrance and staircase hall, visitors' reception rooms and administrative offices; to the south lay the superintendent's residence and to the north the matron's apartments. Long corridors connected the principal parts of the building, and modern technology included a good heating and ventilating system, lifts for goods and coals, and an electric bell system for the matron to communicate with distant parts from her apartments. Facilities for the patients included a swimming bath, individual baths, showers, workshops where trades could be learned, a grocer's shop to teach weighing and measuring skills and how to purchase goods, and a farm.

The role of the asylum changed after 1948 when it was incorporated into the National Health Service; long-stay patients became more numerous and the age profile broadened. As with most other asylums, the late 20th century brought about closure, yet unlike many others this grand building was spared demolition or conversion to apartments. In 1996 it was converted into the Jamea Al Kauthar, which provides secondary education for Muslim girls.

An architectural reputation

E G Paley (Fig 2.57) tends to be overshadowed by his partner of nearly 30 years' standing, Hubert Austin, who will enter our story in the next chapter. There is no doubt that, with Austin's arrival, the practice did develop greatly from about 1870 and that many of its buildings are truly inspired. However, it would be wrong to sideline Paley. He was an architect of some talent, who attracted favourable interest during his lifetime and was accorded obituaries in the national architectural press on his death in 1895. One of these was a seven-page piece in the *Architect & Contract Reporter*, which illustrated six of his churches and drew attention to

the fact that 'they all have a distinct character'.[89] His ecclesiastical masterpiece was undoubtedly St Peter, Lancaster, which, for Hermann Muthesius was a 'remarkable' church, and, for Pevsner, 'a fine, aspiring building'.[90] Paley's other churches include a number which stand up well in comparison with the mainstream work of Gilbert Scott. They are mostly harmonious and built in a 'Middle Pointed' style, avoiding the flamboyance of High Victorian Gothic and its interest in polychromy and exotic detail.

Paley produced good secular work too, and it is probably right to see his largest work, the Royal Albert Asylum, as his chief achievement, even if its crowning central tower may well have been influenced by Austin. His country houses, Wennington Hall and 'The Ridding' at Low Bentham (NY), are of some interest, and it is a great pity that his ambitious 'Abbot's Wood', near Barrow, has been lost. Like nearly all other provincial architects, Paley turned his hand to many building types and took on commissions both great and small, and in large numbers. His work is thus extensive throughout northern Lancashire and in that part of Cumbria which, in his day, was still part of Lancashire. After Austin joined Paley, the tempo of the practice increased markedly, yet its scope, rooted in church-building but accommodating many other kinds of commissions of greatly varying size, concentrated in the North West of England. As the *Architect & Contract Reporter* noted in 1895, 'the individuality of the late Edward Graham Paley was, of course, merged in the work of Paley & Austin', and it is usually impossible to determine the relative inputs of the two men. The one certain thing is that the firm produced some great buildings between the late 1860s and Paley's death in 1895.

Fig 2.56 (opposite) Royal Albert Asylum, the entrance tower.

Fig 2.57 (left) Edward Graham Paley, photographed July 1868 by W T & R Gowland, Lendal, York. By this time he had been joined by his partner, Hubert Austin. (Austin Family collection)

3

Paley & Austin, 1868–1886

The practice covered by this book is most famous for work carried out between the late 1860s and the First World War – that is, the years when Hubert James Austin (1841–1915) was a partner. Prior to this, as we have seen, Edward Paley, an experienced, well-connected architect with good churches and houses to his credit, worked as the sole principal following Edmund Sharpe's retirement from architecture in 1851. By the late 1860s Paley's practice was flourishing, particularly owing to securing the enormous Royal Albert Asylum commission in Lancaster, and the rebuilding of Bolton parish church as one of the largest in Lancashire. There were also other new churches, restorations, a large hotel in Grange-over-Sands (CuL), a couple of schools, and houses and shops in Lancaster. He had pupils and assistants to call upon but he evidently felt the need for more help and a suitable partner. The choice was inspired.

This chapter describes Austin's background, and the various links through which he came to join Paley. It then examines the pivotal years around 1870 when the partnership forged ahead, especially with churches of considerable distinction. These often had a new-found muscularity which tended to be uncharacteristic of Paley's work, while there were also innovations such as the rehabilitation of the Perpendicular style and even the occasional use of ornament from the repertoire of the Aesthetic Movement. The partners' ecclesiastical work is discussed first, followed by their secular commissions. The chapter then deals with the partners' work until 1886, when Paley's son Harry joined the firm as a partner and it became known as Paley, Austin & Paley, although this signalled no major gear-shift in the output of the practice. After about this time important secular commissions diminished, and the three decades leading up to the First World War are characterised by the maturing of the firm's late Gothic style for churches, which is undoubtedly attributable to the influence of Austin.

Family background and the Tate connection

Austin's ancestors came from Kent, where they can be traced with certainty to a Jonathan Austen (*c* 1697–1774). Just before his marriage he described himself as a maltster but later became a yeoman farmer at Egerton near Ashford, where the family continued to farm for generations.[1] He and his wife Elizabeth Pope had, among their three children, two sons, George (1743–1820) and Thomas (1749–1809). George remained a farmer but Thomas established himself in a ham and beef business in London near St Martin-in-the-Fields, on the site of what is now Wyndham's Theatre in Charing Cross Road.[2] This business prospered, so that when he died early in 1809 he left his second wife, Jane Smurthwaite, and his son Thomas (1796–1856) (Fig 3.1), who would become Hubert's father, well provided for.

Jane now returned with her son to her Yorkshire roots at Richmond.[3] Here the Revd James Tate (1771–1843) (Fig 3.2), since becoming its headmaster in 1796, had turned the small town grammar school into one of the foremost Classical schools in England. He regularly sent pupils to Cambridge, and in particular to Trinity College, where they were known as 'Tate's Invincibles'. Both Tate and his school play an important part in our story (Fig 3.3). Thomas Austin attended Tate's school, where his education flourished. He then went up to Trinity College, after which he entered the Church, and in 1820 he married Tate's eldest daughter, Jane Eliza (1797–1826), which no doubt aided his career. He was successively curate at Spennithorne (NY) (Fig 3.4), 1820–3, curate at Haughton-le-Skerne (D), 1823–45 (where Hubert was born), and finally, from 1845 until his death in 1856, rector of Redmarshall (D), a living worth a very respectable £400 a year. The induction early in January 1845 was attended not only by his own family, but also by Edmund Sharpe, suggesting a strong personal interest to induce him to make the long and circuitous rail journey (probably via Manchester) in the depths of winter.[4] Thomas and Jane had three children, the eldest of whom, also Thomas (Tom), became an architect, and his brief career together with the part he played in Hubert's development is discussed shortly.

The Tate and Paley families were also well known to one another. James Tate would have known Archdeacon Paley, not least because of his close friendship with Paley's biographer (in 1809), George Meadley.[5] Tate would no doubt have met the archdeacon's son, Edmund, after he became vicar of Easingwold in 1812, together with his wife Sarah. Tate had also long known Samuel Butler, headmaster at Shrewsbury School, who was related to the Paleys through Sarah. Tate and Butler were contemporaries at Cambridge and maintained close contact both as classicists and as headmasters. In 1833 Sarah wrote of 'our friend Mr Tate',[6] and Tate was one of three supporters of Edmund's final appointment as rector of Gretford, Lincolnshire, in 1835.[7] There is no reason to suppose that Tate played any active part in placing Edward Graham Paley with Sharpe, the likely background for which is explored in Chapter 2, but his interest in the Paley family's affairs meant that he would have heard about it soon enough. It is no surprise, however, that Tate's eldest grandson Tom, after being educated at Richmond, went on to join Paley in Lancaster as a pupil of Edmund Sharpe.

After the death of his first wife, the Revd Thomas remarried in 1828. His new bride was Jane Margaret Brougham (1802–66). Known as Margaret, she was descended from the Brougham family of Westmorland, which had strong roots and influential connections in the northern counties.[8] The couple were to have six children, the youngest of whom was Hubert (Fig 3.5). So it was that both the oldest and youngest children of the 'Revd Thomas' became architects. Before moving on to consider Hubert, we should first briefly examine Tom's career since it was intimately linked with those of Sharpe, Paley and, indeed, his own younger half-brother.

Fig 3.1
Thomas Austin (Hubert's father), at Trinity College, Cambridge, c *1820. In 1820 he graduated, was ordained and married Jane Eliza Tate.*
(Austin Paley Archive, Lancaster City Museums, MS LM 86/129; Tim Austin)

Fig 3.2
The Revd James Tate, headmaster of Richmond School, painted c *1832–4 by H W Pickersgill. The* c *£300 cost was contributed to by 'Tates's Invincibles', who would presumably have included the Revd Thomas Austin.*
(By permission of the Master and Fellows of Sidney Sussex College, Cambridge)

Thomas Austin (1822–67), architect

Tom Austin joined Sharpe as an articled pupil probably in the second half of 1841, and was definitely in Lancaster in time for a sketching trip to Furness Abbey in September 1842, together with Paley, R J Withers and Sharpe.[9] Nothing is known for certain of any architectural work by him at this time although he may have been responsible in 1845 for his father's large new rectory at Redmarshall in County

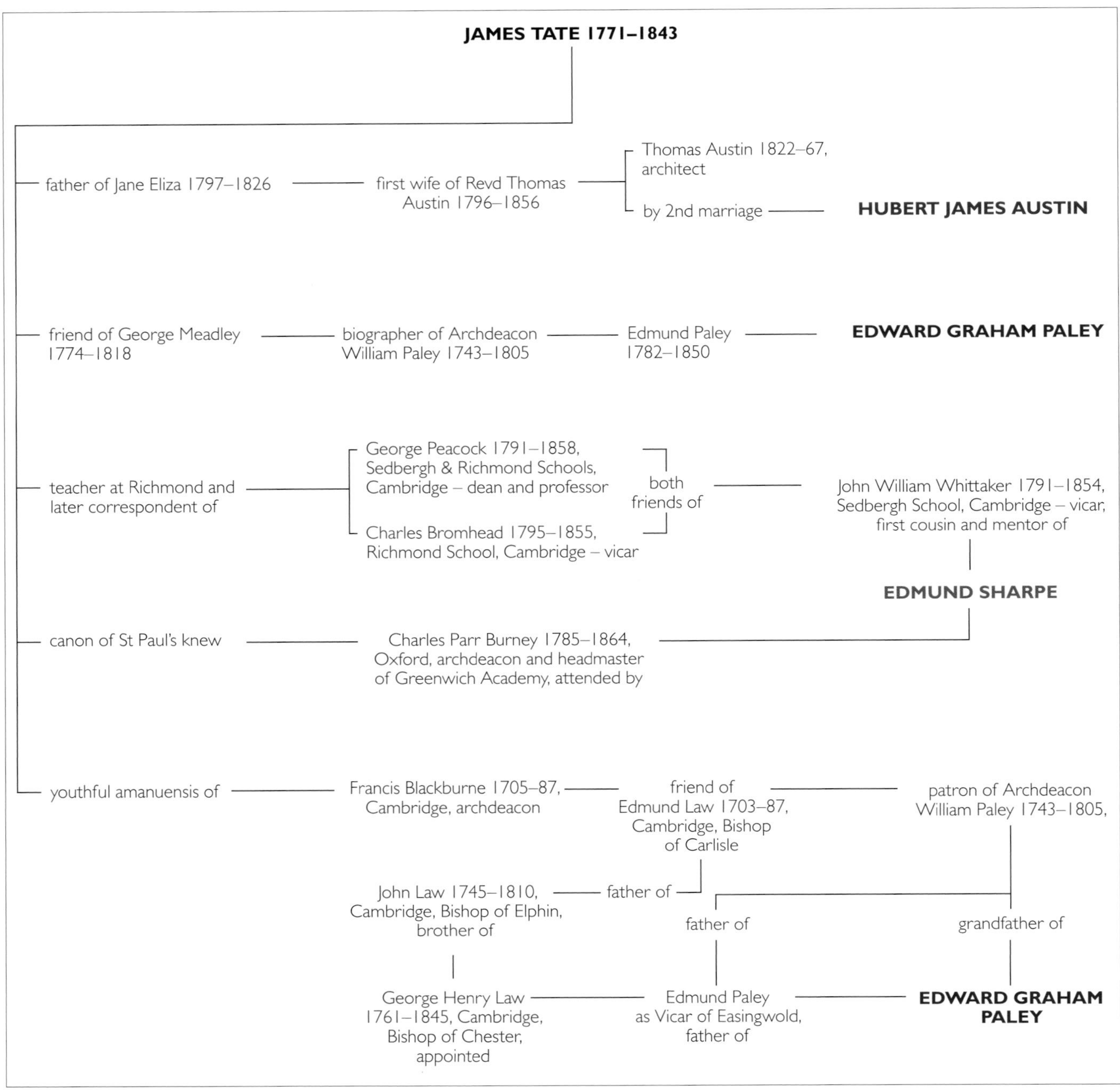

Fig 3.3
James Tate had many personal and professional connections that are bound up with the lives of the principal architects in this book.

Durham (Fig 3.6), along with restoration work at the church there. We might conjecture that he was also the job architect for other commissions in the area – the rebuilding and restoration at St Peter, Bishopton, in 1846–7, and a new church at Thorpe Thewles in 1848–9. Tom was still in Lancaster in the autumn of 1852, when he was secretary of the annual Lancaster Regatta, but by 1853 he was an architect in Newcastle upon Tyne, based at 36 Mosley Street.[10] The architectural opportunities presented by the populous North East may well have been an attraction as there was probably little prospect of a partnership with Paley at this early stage of the latter's career. Moreover, family reasons may have been the immediate spur since Tom's father, most of whose children had now left home, was not well owing to heart problems, and was having difficulty in fulfilling his duties. He died in 1856. Later that year Tom Austin married Anne (known as Annie) Crow at St Mary, Norton, Stockton, where the service

Fig 3.4
Spennithorne, St Michael (NY), 1821, drawn by Revd Thomas Austin when curate there. Tom Austin was born in the rectory (back left of the tower).
(Ann Lendrum collection)

was conducted by the Revd James Tate junior (Fig 3.7).[11] One of his witnesses was his former colleague E G Paley.

Little is known of Tom Austin's early work in Newcastle, but by 1858 he was engaged in the careful restoration of the Augustinian Priory at Brinkburn, Northumberland, for the Cadogan family. In the same year he was one of the founders of the Northern Architectural Association. So too was his friend Robert James Johnson (1832–92). Johnson had been articled to the Darlington architect John Middleton (1820–85) from 1846 to 1853, after which he tried to establish himself in independent practice in Newcastle and then in North Shields.[12] Achieving little success, in 1859 Johnson moved to London to enter G G Scott's office, then the largest and most successful practice in the country. While with Scott he undertook study tours in France between 1860 and 1862, and made drawings which he published in 1864 as *Specimens of Early French Architecture*. In the introduction he acknowledged the help of others, who included Austin and Paley as well as G F Bodley, E R Robson and J J Stevenson, whom he describes as 'several of his fellow travellers'.[13] Paley, Tom Austin and Johnson clearly formed a close-knit circle: Johnson's 1862 tour in northern France, for example, was spent in the company of Paley,[14] while in 1866 Johnson visited Paley during his honeymoon.[15] After the French tour, in 1862 or early 1863, Johnson moved back to Newcastle where he joined Tom Austin to form the partnership of Austin & Johnson, operating from 15 New Bridge Street, where the veteran architect John Dobson (1787–1865) had his office.[16] In 1865, after

Fig 3.5
Memorial window at Redmarshall (D), St Cuthbert, given in 1904 by Hubert Austin in memory of his parents. It was designed by Carl Almquist and made by Shrigley & Hunt of Lancaster, who were favoured by P&A/A&P.
(Tim Austin)

Fig 3.6
Redmarshall rectory, 1845, for the Revd Thomas Austin, father of Hubert, and probably designed by the latter's half-brother, Tom.

Dobson's death, the two of them purchased his practice and finished some of his works.[17] They achieved some success, even establishing branch offices in Middlesbrough and York. Tom's career was, however, short-lived. In 1866, to recuperate from ill health, he travelled with his wife and son Gerald to Australia, where his eldest half-brother, George (1829–72), was living.[18] Here, Tom Austin is thought to have designed a church for the Victorian gold-rush town of Clunes, near Melbourne (built posthumously by 'Austin & Johnson' in 1870–1).[19] But on the return voyage he died, on 24 March 1867, off Ascension Island, and was buried at sea the same day.[20] By that time, his half-brother Hubert's career, which he no doubt helped along

Fig 3.7
Tom Austin and his wife Annie, photographed on a visit to Lancaster in 1864, when they may have settled the matter of Hubert's joining Paley.
(Austin Family collection)

significantly, was about to enter a new and exciting phase. So it is to Hubert's upbringing and entry into architecture that we now turn.

Hubert Austin: early life and training

Hubert Austin was born on 31 March 1841 at Haughton-le-Skerne on the northern outskirts of Darlington, and was the last of the Revd Thomas' nine children (the sixth with his second wife Margaret). Both his parents were fine artists, and no doubt similar skills were instilled in Hubert at an early age (Fig 3.8).[21] His earliest education may have been provided by his father, but by early 1854, when he was 13, he was attending a grammar school in Stockton, a short distance from his home at Redmarshall.[22] Then on 6 August 1856, just after the death of his father, and escorted by his elder brother Henry (Harry), he went to Richmond School, just as all his male siblings had done.[23] Like his elder brothers, Hubert boarded with the Revd James Tate junior (1801–83), who had taken over the running of the school from his father. Hubert did well academically, gaining congratulations from Tate for his success in classics.[24] He was 'head monitor', played football and cricket,[25] and was also in the school choir.[26]

At this time Hubert was becoming exposed to the profession which he would adopt. Apart from Tom establishing his practice in Newcastle, James Tate became curate in 1858 at Holy Trinity chapel in Richmond, where he seems to have initiated a series of restorations, culminating with work by Austin & Johnson in the mid-1860s. Also in 1858 G G Scott was engaged for what turned out to be the very extensive restoration at St Mary's parish church in Richmond. Tate, as a pillar of the established church in the town and a member of the committee which chose Scott,[27] would surely have met the great architect and could well have introduced the young Hubert Austin to him. It seems hardly a coincidence that Johnson entered Scott's office about this time to improve his experience, a move which may have been suggested by Tom Austin and facilitated by both him and Tate.

Hubert left Richmond School at Christmas 1859, and the following February began his architectural training as an articled pupil of his half-brother Tom in Newcastle.[28] The 1861 census shows Tom living in Gateshead, which was now also home to Hubert, his mother, his brother Harry and sister Grace, while his brother Charles was now married and living across the Tyne in Newcastle.[29] In 1862 Hubert won a prize medal in Newcastle for 'Success in Art'.[30]

Hubert Austin was one of seven students to pass the RIBA's Voluntary Examination held on 25–27 January 1864.[31] He then followed in Johnson's footsteps and entered Scott's office on 1 March, spending one year as an improver, and two as an assistant.[32] For the latter he was paid £120 in his first year, rising to £150 in the second.[33] He noted that he worked on the Law Courts competition, 'S Pancras Station' (ie the Midland Grand Hotel), and jobs in Cirencester and Mirfield.[34] In 1864 he was living at 31 Chepstow Place, Bayswater.[35] By 1866 he had moved to number 22 and had been joined nearby by his mother and sister Grace.[36] While with Scott he would have rubbed shoulders with others who would become well-known architects in their own right – Scott's son, John Oldrid Scott, J T Micklethwaite, C J Ferguson (whose Carlisle practice would be active north of the area where Paley & Austin operated), J D Wyatt, and a man who seems to have become a good personal friend, Somers Clarke. Austin played an active part in the early days of Scott's publishing enterprise, the *Spring Gardens Sketch Book* (Scott's office was in Spring Gardens), which reproduced large-scale drawings of British and foreign buildings and their details. Austin might even have suggested the project, which was remarkably similar to

Fig 3.8
The Holy Family, *painted by Hubert Austin's mother, Jane Margaret (née Brougham), c 1834. The faces are believed to be those of herself, her husband, the Revd Thomas Austin, and their first three children. (Tullie House Museum & Art Gallery, Carlisle)*

Fig 3.9
A pair of Austin's drawings of Sussex churches – Iford (right) and Southwick (far right) – reproduced in the Spring Gardens Sketch Book, c *1872. The Iford example may have been an influence for the church at Finsthwaite (CuL) (see Fig 3.32).*
*(*Spring Gardens Sketch Book *4,* c *1872)*

Sharpe's *Architectural Parallels* of the 1840s. In the first volume, issued in 1866–7, Austin was described as the retired honorary secretary (having left Scott's office by the time of publication). He contributed sketches to the first five volumes published down to 1874, and remained a member of the group right up until the eighth and last edition which came out in the 1890s – long after the death of Scott senior.[37] It was probably Austin who also initiated a Lancaster-based version under the aegis of Paley & Austin, the *John O'Gaunt Sketch Book* (*see* p 90), which first appeared in 1874–5 and in which Austin published many sketches from then on.

In 1866 Austin was awarded the RIBA's first Pugin studentship, which he used for travelling in July and September, the month's interval being occasioned by the death of his mother.[38] In July he was in Sussex and Hampshire, and some of the drawings of Sussex churches which appeared in the *Spring Gardens Sketch Book* (Fig 3.9) owe their origin to this time. In September he was in the eastern counties, taking in some of the great late medieval churches there. It may not be too fanciful to suppose that these influenced his adoption, so brilliantly, of the late Gothic style in his own work.

Austin's architectural debut

Hubert Austin's first commission pre-dated his move to Lancaster and was for a church in Ashford, Kent – not far from his ancestral home.[39] The town's population had tripled after the South Eastern Railway sited its locomotive works there in 1847, and although the medieval church had been lengthened by a bay in 1860, more accommodation was considered a necessity. The vicar of Ashford, the Revd J P Alcock, began fund-raising in 1860, but – fortunately for the young Austin – it took until 1864 for this to progress sufficiently to allow for a competition to be held for the design of a new church.[40] Austin was declared the winner from among the 48 entrants in 1865 and built the church with Gilbert Scott's permission.[41]

Money for Christ Church seems to have remained tight, and construction did not take place until 1866–7 (Fig 3.10). Austin put a brave face on the constraints, commenting that the church was 'treated in a plain and substantial manner, so as to avoid ornament at the expense of utility'.[42] The tower, intended to rise above the (otherwise unnecessarily hefty) walls of the south porch, was never built. Taken overall, the church is an unremarkable essay in what Austin

*Fig 3.10 (far left)
Ashford (Kent), Christ Church. Hubert Austin's first church, won in a competition held in 1864 and built 1866–7. The character of the building has altered owing to reordering at the east end and the white paint applied to the stone surfaces.*

*Fig 3.11 (left)
Ashford, Christ Church, vestry and organ chamber.*

described as 'early English to decorated [*sic*]'. The five-bay nave and aisles, and their small lancets, present an austere appearance, though the east and west ends received windows with Geometrical tracery. The interior has standard details from around 1300 and routine fittings. But there is one feature that does mark the building out – a rather dramatic hipped roof over the vestry/organ chamber (Fig 3.11). This has real personality and would be echoed in other works by Paley & Austin in later years.

The move to Lancaster: the man and marriage

On 28 January 1867 Hubert Austin, fresh from his spell in Scott's office, came up to Lancaster to join Paley, whose office he entered the following day.[43] This had been in prospect for some time and was no doubt brokered between Paley and Tom Austin, who maintained a close friendship with each other. Tom and his family are known to have visited Lancaster in 1864,[44] and Hubert's future would no doubt have been an important topic of conversation (indeed, he may well have gone on this visit too). By the summer of 1866, Paley was pressing Hubert to join him as soon as possible, especially to assist with the church at Bolton.[45] At the same time, as we have seen, he was asking Austin to obtain details of Earlswood Asylum to help him with the Royal Albert commission. After some negotiation over terms, the formal partnership came into being on 1 July 1868, initially for 10 years, then renewable for a further 10 years from 1878.

Austin's move from London to Lancaster was rather contrary to the usual direction, which usually saw promising architects migrating from the provinces to the metropolis. In this case the reverse migration is to be understood against a background of the friendship between the Paleys and the Austins, alongside the now plentiful work passing through Paley's well-respected practice. A further explanation may lie in the character of Austin himself, for whom the relative tranquillity of Lancaster would have been more appealing than the hectic life of the capital. His obituary in the *British Architect* emphasised his 'modesty and reserve',[46] and it is perhaps significant that he never joined the RIBA or other professional bodies. His private nature was recalled in 1968 by his son Geoffrey (1884–1971): 'I don't think my father had any friends amongst architects. Perhaps Canon Grenside, vicar of Melling near Hornby, was his greatest friend – in fact he's the only one who ever spent a night with us.'[47]

Alongside historic buildings and archaeology, Austin was interested in music and painting: 'He was an artist to the fingertips, very fond of sketching and watercolour painting,' noted an obituary in the local press.[48] He was also a sportsman, and was remembered as a skilled oarsman and a member of the Lancaster Rifle Club. He was a devout churchman and served as the vicar's warden at Lancaster parish church from 1894 until 1903, when he

Fig 3.12
Wedding photograph: Hubert Austin married Fanny Langshaw on 6 September 1870. The figure left of the bride is the architect Somers Clarke, a friend and colleague of Hubert Austin's from their days together in Gilbert Scott's office. Note 3.50 identifies the other figures. The main house in view is Fenton House, which Sharpe built for himself.
(Nicholas Deane collection)

became a sidesman.[49] Horticulture was a major recreation. Unlike Sharpe, or to a lesser extent Paley, he is not known to have been involved in public affairs other than to have been appointed a Commissioner of Land Tax in 1886.

The links between the Sharpe, Paley and Austin families were firmly sealed in 1870, when Hubert Austin married Fanny Langshaw (1844–1915), a niece of Edmund Sharpe, on 6 September, at St Mary's church in Lancaster (Fig 3.12).[50] Her mother was Sharpe's second sister Emily (1812–93), who, in 1843 (also on 6 September), had married James Pearson Langshaw (1814–96), a well-known surgeon in Lancaster and a former organist at this church, like his grandfather and father before him. At the wedding the best man was Somers Clarke (1841–1926), who was the same age as Hubert and had been with him in Scott's office. A family story has it that Hubert met Fanny (Figs 3.13 and 3.14) when she was doing the flowers at Heversham church. Sadly, such a romantic first encounter seems improbable because, although Paley was commissioned to restore the building in 1867, the two families had no personal connection with the village at the time.[51] In fact there were long-standing connections between the various families, and Fanny and Hubert would easily have met. Her mother's younger sister, Frances, married E G Paley in 1851, and back in the 1830s the Langshaw family was involved in the promotion of Christ Church, Walmsley, built to Sharpe's designs in 1837–9. Fanny's brother George (1848–1901) became an articled pupil of Paley, probably in the mid-1860s, before moving on to a spell in G E Street's office in London and, from 1878, a career as an independent architect. Tom Austin had lived very close to the Langshaws in Lancaster in 1851, and it is quite possible that Fanny met Hubert in 1864 during the visit of Tom and his family to Lancaster.

Fanny and Hubert became engaged in late 1868, when the latter's partnership provided the prospect of a secure financial future: he was congratulated by Sharpe in a letter from Paris.[52] It is not clear where Fanny and Hubert made their home in Lancaster initially but, after success produced rewards, they built a large house, about half a mile from the office, called 'The Knoll' (Fig 3.15).[53] Their attachment to each other is expressed in a terracotta plaque dated 1879 with their initials and a heart placed between them.[54] Fanny shared her husband's love of music, she singing as a soprano at Lancaster Choral Society concerts where Hubert

Fig 3.13 (far left)
Hubert Austin, carte de visite *by Henri Claudet, 107 Regent Street, London, 29 July 1868, the year he became the partner of E G Paley. (Austin Family collection)*

Fig 3.14 (left)
Hubert Austin's wife, Fanny, 1872, photographed at the Ambleside (CuW) studio of Moses Bowness. (Austin Family collection)

played the violin. Geoffrey Austin recalled that his father 'was devoted to his wife & always tried to get home at night however difficult to accomplish from some rural parish he'd had to visit. He was entirely satisfied really with his profession & home life.'[55] In 1899 Austin acquired a country residence, Heversham House at Heversham (CuW), some 13 miles north of Lancaster where he was able to indulge his horticultural interests (Fig 3.16). Then in October 1901 he bought yet another large property, an 18th-century farmhouse, christened by him Kings Worthy Court, in the Hampshire village of that name outside Winchester (Fig 3.17).[56] It is hard to believe that he and his family could have spent much time there, yet in December 1903 and March 1905 he produced plans for significant alterations and additions to it.[57] He also added to the land and, by the time it was sold in 1915, the estate was quite considerable, totalling about 11 acres. Hubert and Fanny were married for very nearly 45 years; she died on 25 February 1915 and Hubert followed her less than a month later on 22 March.

Hubert's two sons, Bernard and Geoffrey, both became architects but played little or no part in their father's practice and, indeed, their relationships with him may have become strained (*see* pp 174–7).

Fig 3.15
'The Knoll', Westbourne Road, Lancaster, 1879, built by Austin for himself and his family.

The partners, their relationship and the office

It is a tragedy that no business records for the practice survive from the 19th century, while the family correspondence tells us nothing about its professional affairs.[58] The family relationships that tied the Sharpes, Paleys and Austins together seem to have been harmonious. E G Paley and Austin remained partners (Fig 3.18) until the former's death in 1895, by which time Paley's son Harry had been with the firm for almost 20 years (articled 1877, partner from 1886), apart from an 18-month spell

Fig 3.16
Heversham House (CuW). View of c *1899 before transformation by Hubert Austin (top). The later, early 20th-century view suggests his interest in gardening (above).*
(Austin Paley Archive, Lancaster City Museums, MS LM 86/129; Tim Austin)

gaining experience in London. The firm was located at 32 Castle Hill (now 24 Castle Park) (*see* Fig 2.10), as it had been since Paley made his office there in 1860. There were, of course, pupils, assistants and clerks (*see* Appendix 2), although we know but few names and nothing is certain about numbers. The most famous picture of a busy Victorian practice is by T G Jackson when remembering his days in Gilbert Scott's office.[59] This he entered in 1858, when Scott's prodigiously successful practice was working at full tilt: 'I think we were twenty-seven in all,' he recalled, and described the office as 'very large'. The Paley & Austin practice was nothing like as busy as Scott's, but we might envisage perhaps half a dozen to 10 men occupied in the office on Castle Hill, depending on the workload.

It is difficult and perilous to try to answer the question, 'What did Paley do and what did Austin do?' As suggested in the discussion of Paley's work in the previous chapter, it *may* be possible to see Austin's hand in the steeple for St James, Barrow (CuL) (*see* Fig 2.51), and the changed design for the great entrance tower at the Royal Albert Asylum in Lancaster (*see* Fig 2.56). It is perhaps no coincidence that its mighty roof is a more elaborate version of the ones Scott had planned for the towers of his Gothic designs for the government offices in Whitehall, a scheme that Hubert Austin would surely have known of. Paley, some 18 years older and more outgoing than his new partner, was well known in local society and no doubt presented the main public face of the practice, at least in its early years. Naturally, it was he who called on the Duke of Devonshire a month after a disastrous fire at Holker Hall (CuL) in March 1871 to discuss rebuilding plans, which would become Paley & Austin's most important country house commission.[60] Yet the modernity of some of the details here almost certainly reveals the hand of the young Austin. Just occasionally Paley is named as the designer, as with the restoration of Farnworth church near Widnes (Me) in 1885, while the following year produced a Paley-designed eagle lectern at a grand estate church at Higher Walton in Cheshire. A tribute to both Paley and Austin in the *Building News* for 1890 helpfully credits Austin with various churches gained in competition.[61] It was he who won the competition for a mountain church suggested by the Bishop of Carlisle in 1872, which led to the design for Finsthwaite (CuL) (*see* Fig 3.32) church of 1873–4. Austin also takes the credit for the firm's greatest executed church, the magisterial St George, Stockport, of 1893–7, where he is actually named as its architect on a relief stone inscription on the interior west wall. Then, at the start of the 20th century, he alone signed the drawings shortlisted in 1903 for the second Liverpool Cathedral competition. But such documented attributions within the practice are unusual.

The *John O'Gaunt Sketch Book*

One project which can be attributed to Austin with some certainty is the *John O'Gaunt Sketch Book*, a publication project very similar to the *Spring Gardens Sketch Book* which he helped to organise while in Scott's office. Both publications were real potpourris of material, ranging from great medieval churches through country houses to details of doorways and ornamental metalwork. The *John O'Gaunt Sketch Book* ran to three volumes, the first dated 1874–5, the second 1876–9 and the third 1879–85, this last wide date range suggesting that the venture was perhaps running out of steam.[62] It seems a curiously old-fashioned project for its time, as there were then so many more journals and architectural books available than when Sharpe brought out his *Architectural Parallels* in the 1840s. The subscribers numbered, successively, just 24, 35 and 34. They can hardly have made it a successful commercial venture and there must have been further, unrecorded sales by the publishers, E & J L Milner of Church Street, who also published one of Lancaster's main newspapers, the *Lancaster Guardian*.

Paley was described, grandiloquently, as 'President'; Hubert Austin was 'Editor'; and Samuel Wright – then a young man serving his articles with the firm and thus beginning a nearly 60-year association with it – as successively 'Secretary' and 'Treasurer',[63] and then again 'Secretary'. Many contributions came from members of the firm and its circle – Austin, Wright,[64] John Harrison, Robert Johnson, and (although not until the third volume) Paley and his son Harry. However, the net was cast much wider, with work published by W A Waddington of Burnley, Alfred Bickerdike of London, C C Hodges of Hexham, Talbot Brown of Wellingborough, and even one offering from Lethaby, together with contributions from others around the country.[65] Subscribers from the architectural profession numbered Gilbert Scott, Somers Clarke, J T Micklethwaite, E W Godwin, Richard Mawson and John Douglas. Others included a few influential and well-known people in Lancashire such as Sir James Ramsden of Barrow, George Marton of Capernwray Hall, Lady Louisa Egerton of Holker Hall and the Revd W B Grenside of Melling, Hubert Austin's close friend. Even though it may have been neither a classic of architectural publishing nor a best-seller, the *Sketch Book* must have done something to keep the profile of Paley & Austin before the architecturally discerning public.

Architecture in transition

The Paley & Austin partnership commenced at a time of considerable flux in British architecture – notably emerging doubts about High Victorian Gothic, the rise of 'Queen Anne', the valuing of refinement, and the resulting more gentle aesthetic which was to characterise the architecture of the later 19th century. Such pervasive shifts only make it more difficult to unpick what may be credited to each of the two partners, yet it is hard to resist the notion that the youthful Austin provided a new creative force. When he arrived in Lancaster at the start of 1867, his head must have been full of discussions in Scott's office (and the profession at large) about the future of architectural style in general, and the way forward for the Gothic Revival in particular.

Fig 3.17
Kings Worthy Court, near Winchester, c 1906–13, bought by and remodelled by Austin. The fledgling planting probably reflects his horticultural interests. The figure is Fanny Austin. (Austin Paley Archive, Lancaster City Museums, MS LM 86/129; Tim Austin)

Three stylistic changes may be discerned in the work of the practice in about 1870 and are mentioned in summary here as a backdrop to the discussion of the firm's buildings in this chapter. First, there is a greater muscularity in some of its church work, at times accompanied by continental overtones, and running somewhat counter to other trends of the day and, indeed, to other facets of the practice's work in the early 1870s. It appears first at Heversham church (CuW) where, as part of a large-scale restoration in 1868–70, the west tower was rebuilt in a strong 13th-century Gothic (Fig 3.19). The plans were drawn up in 1867 under Paley's name, since at that time the partnership was but a future expectation. A severe, early

Fig 3.18
The Paley & Austin logo, as used in the late 1870s.

Fig 3.19
Heversham (CuW), St Peter. The west tower with its muscular 13th-century detailing was rebuilt by the fledgling Paley & Austin practice from 1868. This rather severe, strong treatment may reflect the arrival of Austin as the new partner in the office. (Mark Watson)

13th-century style is also found at St Mary, Walton, to the east of Carlisle, where the details were said to have been modelled on work at Lanercost Priory: the date here is 1869, by which time the Paley & Austin partnership was firmly in place. Robust 13th-century treatment tends to be a feature of P&A work in the 1870s, after which it is but one of the choices in a wider stylistic armoury for churches. Other examples will be examined as case studies shortly.

The second new trend was in an opposite direction which, to us, now seems more in line with the spirit of the time – a move in the direction of a gentler, less ornate architecture which could take on motifs from the Aesthetic Movement or past muster as proto-Arts & Crafts work. Out of this emerges a third strand of crucial importance to church-building which had provided, and would continue to provide, the mainstay of our firm's work. This was the rehabilitation of the Perpendicular style as an acceptable stylistic choice, and one in which, it will be suggested, Paley & Austin, along with Paley's former pupil John Douglas, played a nationally pioneering role.

In their more important and often highly prestigious work, the new partners were concerned with such grander themes as the above. However, before looking at their significant works in more detail, it is worth remembering that they were also, year in, year out, producing a stream of workaday buildings, much like any other architectural practice. The diversity of building types and their range of scale and stylistic variety were extraordinary.

Churches

Two major churches, 1869–71: St Chad, Kirkby, and St John the Evangelist, Cheetham

The first two large churches by the new partnership are both examples of urban churches needed for the industrial areas of (the historic) county of Lancashire. Both are striking instances of the new spirit of design which informed the firm's work at this time.

St Chad's at Kirkby (Me) (Figs 3.20 and 3.21), designed in 1868, replaced a chapel of 1766 and was wholly paid for by the 4th Earl of Sefton. It eventually cost some £12,000 and was built to accommodate 650 people. It is a building of great power, having a mighty saddleback tower placed over the choir. This positioning is decidedly un-English, and creates a composition radically different from a normal medieval crossing. Edmund Sharpe had used it for his first church, St Mark, Witton, but this was a stillborn infant without progeny. This type of planning, which became very popular among Victorian church builders, can better be seen as the offspring of William Butterfield's pioneering church of St Matthias, Stoke Newington, of 1849–53, which, like St Chad's, also has a saddleback tower. The style is suited to the solid massing. The top of the tower has late 13th-century belfry lights, but the other openings are mostly earlier 13th-century lancets. Other parts of the detailing hark back to Norman work, notably in the south doorway. Clearly this is an attempt at a church which suggests 'development' over the period of a medieval century.

The interior of St Chad's is most impressive – long, tall and, as Pevsner commented in 1969, with 'the superb excelsior of the tall high tower arches and the rib-vault inside it high up': his reviser in 2006, Richard Pollard, drew attention to the clustered shafts of the tower arches and was moved to call the interior 'magnificent'.[66] All the capitals, he noted, are different and 'the clerestory is of coupled lancets behind relieving arches which are joined up by narrower intermediary arches to form an arcade'. The walls are finished with fine sandstone ashlar, which would then become the firm's standard wall treatment for practically all of its churches.

As St Chad's was rising to the west of Liverpool, Paley & Austin were building their most important church in Manchester – St John the Evangelist for the northern suburb of Cheetham (Figs 3.22 and 3.23). Like St Chad's, it ranks among the most powerful of all mid-Victorian churches. It was the gift of a wealthy banker, Lewis Loyd (1811–91), whose family came originally from the remote Carmarthenshire valley of Cilycwm (changing their name from Lloyd in the process), and was a memorial to his parents.[67] Lewis's uncle, also Lewis, was a Unitarian minister until 1793, when his marriage to Sarah Jones led him to join her family's Manchester banking business: hence the creation of the Jones, Loyd & Co bank. His three brothers, including in 1808 Edward, the father of our Lewis, also entered the firm. John Jones's four sons had no children and, with their retirement, the Loyd brothers became the senior partners and achieved great wealth. Lewis (senior) was described by a contemporary as 'the richest banker in the City and perhaps the richest man in Europe'.[68] Our Lewis, who at his death left a prodigious estate of £598,798, ran the London branch of the firm. The bank was taken over in 1864 by the London & Westminster, and absorbed into it. The building of St John's took place fairly shortly afterwards, and the two events may be connected if capital was freed up and Loyd was less (or not at all) involved with the business. The choice of Paley & Austin can be put down to long-standing family connections since Edmund Sharpe's uncle by marriage, the Revd Thomas Broadhurst (1767–1851), became a close friend of his fellow Unitarian, Lewis Loyd senior, at the Unitarian College at Manchester, before the latter embarked upon his banking career.[69]

St John's comes from the same stable as J L Pearson's innovative St Peter, Vauxhall, 1863–4, a key building in demonstrating how a noble town church could be built with modest means. Pearson's London church cost only about £8,000,

Fig 3.20 (above)
Kirkby (Me), St Chad, 1869–71, powerfully massed church, built of red sandstone and with a vast saddleback tower over the choir.
(Mark Watson)

Fig 3.21 (left)
Kirkby, the strongly detailed, curved pulpit reminiscent of some of G E Street's work.

Fig 3.22 (right) Manchester, St John the Evangelist, Cheetham, 1869–71, with a continuous roof over the nave and chancel and a distinctive, muscular steeple. (Mark Watson)

Fig 3.23 (below) Cheetham, the interior and its uninterrupted view to the east end. Paley & Austin churches usually have very low or absent chancel screens. The church is stone-faced externally but has bare brick walls internally. (Mark Watson)

and even an early estimate for St John's put the figure at £10,000. Money was not a problem, so more ornament could be provided, while the Manchester church received its fine tower which remained unrealised at Vauxhall. Features which these two great churches have in common are a tall, continuous nave and chancel, an apsidal east end and an early French character. The powerful south-west tower has a remarkable capping, unique in the output of Paley & Austin, of a large, tiled pyramid, split into two tiers and anchored at the corners by turret-like features: however, the latter are reminiscent of the unexecuted spire at Livesey designed by Paley before Austin came on the scene. The church does not seem large from the outside, perhaps because it is dominated by the great bulk of the tower, yet inside it opens up into a vast, high vessel with the nave and chancel run into one. This heroic interior has bare red-brick walls with different designs for the arcades between north and south. Whereas Pearson's church is brick-vaulted throughout, Paley & Austin's has open timber roofs – five-sided over the nave and semi-circular above the chancel area – with large tie beams and king-posts marking out the bays. But in contrast to the beefy architecture, the stalls and pulpit have up-to-the-minute decoration in the form of Nesfield 'pies'. The pulpit (Fig 3.24) also has sunflowers and the tapering, spade-like leaves which are so familiar after the arrival of Art Nouveau some 20 years later.

The Perpendicular revival in the North

Paley & Austin's next major church commission was the rebuilding in 1871–3 of St Mary's in the Lancashire coalfield town of Leigh (Figs 3.25, 3.26 and 3.27). In 1869 Paley was brought in to inspect the medieval church and declared that the tower could be repaired but the rest needed to be rebuilt. This indeed is what happened.[70] Such a story is, of course, commonplace, and was replicated at hundreds, if not thousands, of other churches rebuilt in the first half-century of Victoria's reign. What is remarkable at Leigh is the total commitment to the Perpendicular style at a time when it had been completely out of fashion for a quarter of a century. Ecclesiological diktats had banished it to the shadows as debased and demonstrating a sad decline from the pinnacle of the Gothic achievement of around 1300. Twenty years earlier, Sharpe & Paley had rebuilt Wigan parish church in Perpendicular although in this case they were following the strong wishes of the parishioners to reproduce the style of the previous building. At Leigh the new St Mary's was very different from the previous one, despite being rebuilt on the old foundations.

Leigh parish church is large and grand, and in the mould of late medieval examples in Lancashire and Cheshire, such as Sefton (Me), Deane (GM), Astbury (Ch) and St Helen, Northwich (Ch). The body of the building runs continuously through from nave to chancel, with a prominent range of clerestory windows under an embattled parapet. The distinction between the two areas is expressed externally by more ornate decoration in the eastern area. This transitional area includes a canted porch of the type that first seems to have emerged at Thornton-in-Lonsdale in 1868–70. There is also a large traceried square which is surely an Austin motif and which would become a hallmark of the firm, with innumerable variations in the design, into the 20th century.

Pevsner was not very impressed with St Mary, Leigh, offering a few factual statements about the exterior and noting that the interior lacked 'the spatial thrills of which Paley & Austin were capable later'.[71] In this he is perfectly correct, but it misses the point about the importance of the building which lies in its unashamed adoption of the late medieval style, which is almost certainly due to the influence of the young Austin. This building is the precursor of the large, spacious P&A/A&P town churches of the ensuing decades which draw so much inspiration from the latest medieval Gothic. While in Scott's office Austin would have heard, and perhaps been party to, murmurings against the beloved Middle Pointed of his master from such dissidents as J J Stevenson, J T Micklethwaite and Somers Clarke. However, the rejection of Perpendicular in the years between 1845 and 1870 was by no means as total as is sometimes assumed. In Dorset, for example, the extensive presence of late medieval churches seems to have suggested the use of Perpendicular at this time, even to mainstream figures such as William Slater and R H Carpenter.[72] As we have seen, Paley was certainly not above using it as a perfectly natural style, as at Rylstone (NY) in 1852–3 (*see* Fig 2.14), Preston Patrick (CuW), also of 1852–3, and Brookhouse in 1865–6. Just as there is the vexed question of Gothic revival or Gothic survival in the couple of centuries after the Reformation, we have to ask whether we are dealing with Perpendicular survival or revival in these instances. Mostly such cases can be viewed as responses to local circumstances and/or the survival of the style in the hands of people who were not too troubled by ecclesiological dogma. St Mary, Leigh, however, represents a very conscious and very demonstrative use of the style. There is no comparable example in England from about this time. Its famous, pioneering contemporaries, St Augustine, Pendlebury (GM), of 1870–4 by Bodley, and St Clement, Boscombe, Bournemouth, of 1871–3 by Sedding, use more fluid, less overtly Perpendicular architecture than we see at Leigh church.

Another work which shows Paley & Austin's interest in Perpendicular is their rebuilding of

Fig 3.24
Cheetham, pulpit with its delicate Aesthetic-style floral decoration.
(Mark Watson)

Fig 3.25
Leigh (GM), St Mary, the old church, rebuilt by P&A in 1871–3 apart from the tower.
(Wigan Archive Service, WCLT 87/9)

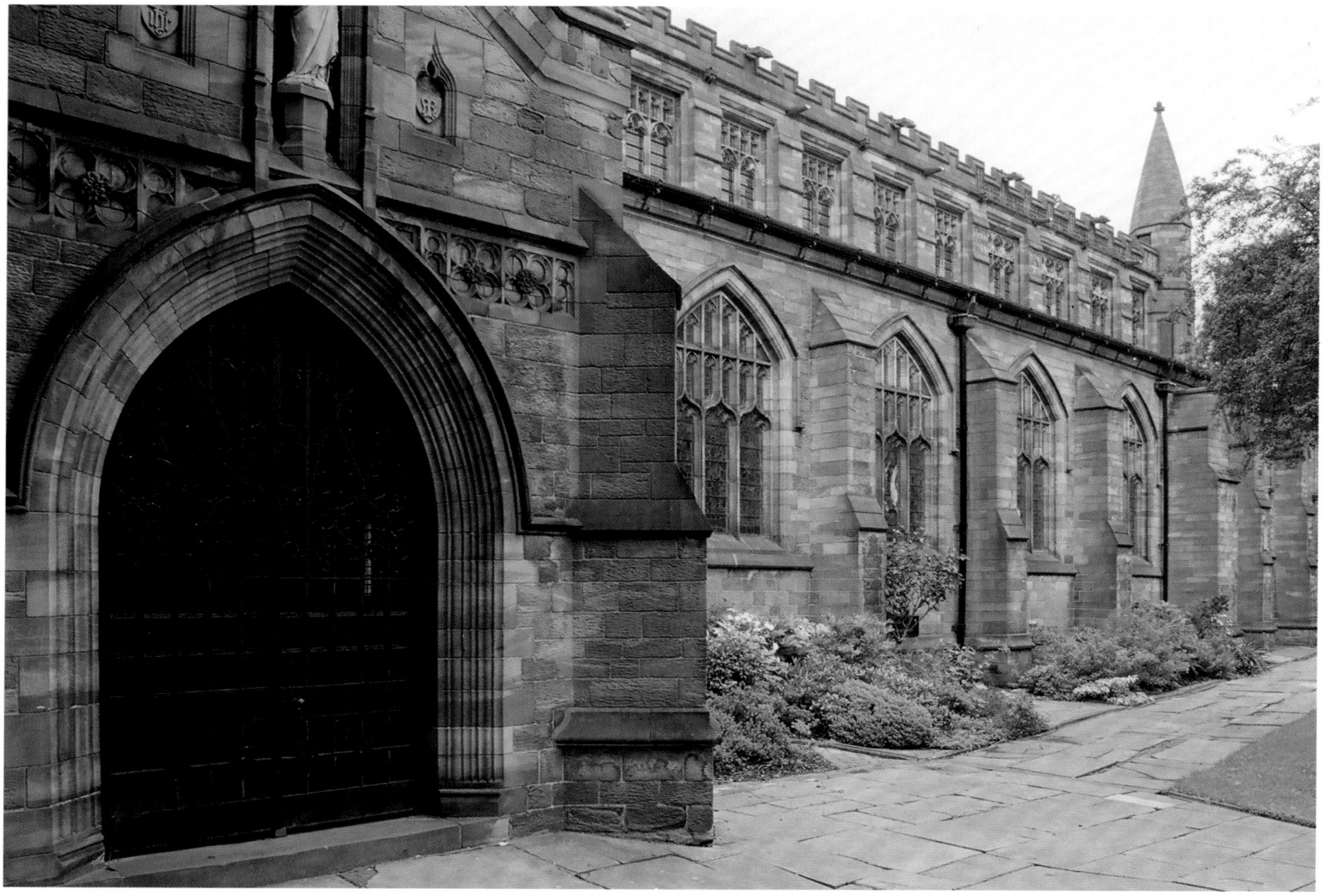

Fig 3.26
Leigh, the rebuilt church with its pioneering use of Perpendicular revival architecture.
(Mark Watson)

All Saints, Daresbury (Ch), apart from the medieval tower, in 1870–2 (Fig 3.28). Old pictures show that the church was not homogeneous – Perpendicular for the most part but with a south chapel having 18th-century-looking details (Fig 3.29).[73] The rebuilt church is a Perpendicular ensemble which is faithful to a church of the late 15th century, apart from the exposed red sandstone ashlar of the internal surfaces, and a Protestant lack of colour (other than in the stained glass windows). P&A/A&P churches, whether new or restored, were also often notable for their woodwork, and Daresbury possesses a fine set of oak benches (Fig 3.30): the various designs in the ends show the firm's facility for producing constantly inventive tracery-work.

Before leaving the issue of the Perpendicular revival, it is worth drawing attention to the work of another north-western architect, John Douglas, especially as he had worked in the firm's office where he was chief assistant to Paley. In 1869 Douglas began the complete reworking of the medieval Cheshire churches of St Alban,

Fig 3.27
Leigh. The area of the nave and chancel junction shows greater elaboration on the latter and the varied Perpendicular forms used by Paley & Austin at the church. A hallmark of the firm is the use of richly traceried squares. The firm also often used diagonally set entrances such as the one seen here.
(Mark Watson)

Tattenhall, and St Mary, Dodleston, and in both cases the churches have full-blown late medieval details. In 1871 Tattenhall became the first church in the newly revived Perpendicular to receive an illustration in the national architectural press, although, sadly, the *Building News* which carried it made no comment about the style.[74] Edward Hubbard, in his study of Douglas, suggests that the choice of Perpendicular may be owing to neither churches being entirely new; yet he rightly regards Douglas' change from his previous High Victorian mode as 'exceptionally *avant-garde* for the date'.[75] With Douglas having worked for the firm (and thus being well known to at least one of its principals), and with both practices located in the north-west and specialising in church work, is it too fanciful to imagine some informal dialogue between Lancaster and Chester on the question of style for church-building for the later 19th century? As far as Paley & Austin were concerned, Perpendicular would become the stock-in-trade style for some of the firm's grandest and most admired buildings as the years rolled on.

In the countryside

The Paley & Austin area of operation embraced both the populous areas of industrial Lancashire and large tracts of countryside which extended into the southern Lakes and the hills of western Yorkshire. The urban areas opened up opportunities for large, imposing churches such as those mentioned above. The rural districts had a variety of needs – old churches that required restoring, relatively modern churches that were felt to need replacing, and places which needed the provision of a church for the first time.

Restoration involved the usual process of renewing worn-out stonework (possibly with some rebuilding), reroofing and reflooring as necessary, removal of box pews and any galleries, the installation of chancel furniture (such as choir stalls and a reading desk) which befitted the changed emphasis in the way services were conducted, and the addition of, say, an aisle or a vestry to provide better accommodation. The firm's activity was considerable and its work similar to that of many other practices up and down the country. Medieval work was carefully preserved where this was considered possible, although towards the end of the century the range of what was considered 'possible' was extended as the conservationist ethos, as epitomised by the Society for the Preservation of Ancient Buildings, came to hold sway. Workaday Georgian pews and galleries were replaced as they were still common enough not to be regarded as of historic interest, a status they only acquired from the very late 19th century. However, high-quality post-Reformation work, such as the chancel screen and pulpit at Daresbury (Ch), was retained in newly restored churches. What was done varied from church to church according to need, budgets and parochial taste, and the Catalogue of works in this book lists churches where restorations took place (*see* Appendix 5). From the early years of the partnership, examples include Heversham (1868–70), Melsonby (NY: 1870–2), Daresbury (Ch: 1870–2), and Llanrwst (Denbighshire: 1874–5).

New and rebuilt country church commissions continued until the First World War, and although they do not number more than 20,

Fig 3.28 (top) Daresbury (Ch), All Saints, sketched by T Raffles Davison after the rebuilding (apart from the tower) in 1870–2. (British Architect *18, 1882, after 392)*

Fig 3.29 (above) Daresbury, prior to Paley & Austin's work. They kept to the Perpendicular style seen in the south aisle, and replaced the 'churchwarden' work in the chapel with 15th-century-style work. (All Saints Parochial Church Council; Mark Watson)

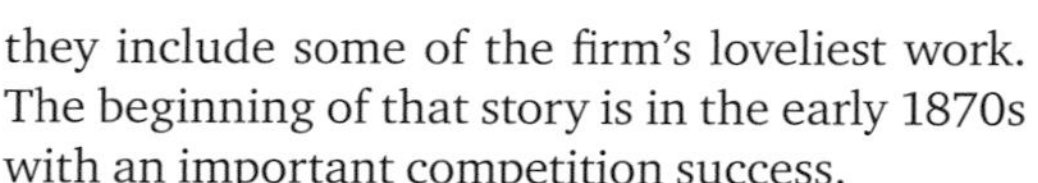

Fig 3.30
The practice excelled in a constant variety of designs for furnishings and fittings. These are four examples of varied designs for the bench ends at Daresbury. (Mark Watson)

they include some of the firm's loveliest work. The beginning of that story is in the early 1870s with an important competition success.

'In Montibus'

The firm's reputation in the Lake District and 'Lancashire over the sands' – all now part of Cumbria – gained a useful fillip from success in a competition in 1872 devised by the Bishop of Carlisle and the Carlisle Church Extension Society (CCES) for the design of 'mountain chapels'.[76] Two members of the committee offered prizes. Henry Schneider, the Barrow iron magnate (who now lived mainly at Bowness on Windermere), offered a first prize of 20 guineas, and E B Wheatly Balme provided the second, worth 15 guineas. The competition attracted 48 competitors who submitted 56 designs.[77] These were then whittled down to 12 and submitted to that prolific assessor of competitions, Ewan Christian. He found the general standard fairly lamentable: 'Some were too costly; some quite out of keeping ... with the rugged character of mountain scenery; some were ill adapted for resisting the penetrating rains of a mountain climate; and others displayed a want of taste' – and so on. His report, endorsed by the CCES, favoured the designs labelled 'In Montibus' which turned out to be the work of Paley & Austin, who thus earned Schneider's 20-guinea prize. The runner up was Charles J Ferguson of Carlisle, one year senior to Austin and his colleague in Gilbert Scott's office nearly 10 years before.

Paley & Austin explained in their submission that 'the designs were based to some extent on the old churches ... in the hilly and remote districts of Sussex and which, with the very simplest manner of construction, exhibit a great variety of treatment, and are admirably suited to the character of the country in which they are placed'. There is little doubt that Austin was the man behind these designs, and there is a close similarity to at least one of the small ancient Sussex churches which he illustrated in one of the numbers of the *Spring Gardens Sketch Book* (*see* Fig 3.9). *The Architect* published three of the designs (Fig 3.31), and of these it was the bell-cote version which was the outright winner, Christian declaring it to be the only one among those exhibited which had 'all the right character'.

When it came to the rebuilding of St Peter, Finsthwaite (CuL) (Fig 3.32), in 1873–4, however, it was not this design but a variant of the central-tower-cum-square-ended-chancel version which captured the imagination of the benefactor, T Newby Wilson of Newby Bridge. This, the first of Paley & Austin's great village churches, replaced a humble predecessor of 1724. It cost Mr Wilson £4,170 and accommodated 200 people. Faced with grey slate, it is very simply detailed but boldly massed, with a powerful tower and pyramid spire crouching between the nave and chancel. Round-arched

Fig 3.31
Three designs entered by Paley & Austin for the mountain chapel competition organised in the Carlisle diocese in 1872, and published in The Architect, *1873. All employ simple round-arched windows and rugged massing, which was evidently deemed fit for the terrain.*
*(*The Architect *20 September 1873)*

windows add to the sense of calculated simplicity, although inside the tower arches are round. Unusually, the internal walls are plastered.

Contemporaneous with St Peter's was the small church of St John the Evangelist, Osmotherley (CuL), a very modest affair costing only about £1,400. It too is built of slate but has a rounded apse to the chancel, lancet windows and a timber bell-cote. St Thomas, Crosscrake (CuW), was built in 1874–5 but is now a sadly altered building. Its striking central saddleback tower was reduced in 1944 owing to structural problems, and was removed completely in 1963–4. It is faced with square slate blocks and has detailing from the late 12th and early 13th centuries.

Other country churches

A brief mention may be made of the eight further country churches by Paley & Austin between the mid-1870s and the mid-1880s. St Luke, Winmarleigh (Fig 3.33), of 1875–6, was built at the cost of John Wilson-Patten, the newly created (from 1874) Baron Winmarleigh, and has a particularly attractive boarded bell-turret and a tall spirelet towards the east end, two transeptal chapels, and stylistically varied detailing incorporating Decorated and Perpendicular work. St Wilfrid, Halton, was rebuilt in 1876–7 except for the west tower, said to date from 1597. The style is Decorated and features of interest include a two-storey porch, arcades with alternating octagonal and clustered piers, and a substantial roof structure. St Peter, Leck, was a rebuild in 1878–9 of a small late 18th-century church, but it was destroyed by fire in 1913 and rebuilt again (it is said) to the original designs by Austin & Paley. St Peter, Scorton, of 1878–9 (Figs 3.34 and 3.35), is a fine landmark on the west side of the M6 motorway, and was built as a memorial to Peter Ormrod, the wealthy cotton spinner from Bolton, who

Fig 3.32
Finsthwaite (CuL), St Peter, 1873–4, where the firm brought to execution the ideas used in the mountain church competition. The building material is tough, angular local slate.

Fig 3.33
Winmarleigh, St Luke, 1875–6. An estate church for the newly created Baron Winmarleigh.
(Mark Watson)

Fig 3.34 (right)
Scorton, St Peter, 1878–9. James Ormrod rebuilt the church as a memorial to his brother Peter. It has a largely timber porch as sometimes favoured by Paley & Austin, a prominent shingled spire, and strong geometry to the tower.

Fig 3.35 (far right)
Scorton, chaste woodwork on the organ case embellished with flourishes of rich tracery.

had paid for the rebuilding of Bolton parish church under Paley some 10 years before and had a residence at Wyresdale Hall nearby. Its distinctive feature is the west steeple with a tall, shingled splay-foot spire and a prominent south-east projection for the stair. St Peter, Mansergh (CuW), 1879–80, replaced a church of 1726 or 1727. It is, thanks to its dark grey stone facing and severe lines, a curiously bleak building, yet its Perpendicular detailing shows how, by this time, the style had become a standard element in the Paley & Austin repertoire. The dominant element is the west tower and its longitudinal saddleback tower. Also of 1879–80 is the incomplete church of St Leonard, Billington, where Decorated and Perpendicular elements mingle and there is an interestingly designed north-east vestry (Fig 3.36). A large west tower with a longitudinal saddleback roof and the two west bays of the nave were never built. In 1880–1 St John, Hutton Roof (CuW), replaced a chapel of 1757. It is also wholly Perpendicular and has a south-west tower-cum-porch and an impressive catslide roof over the nave and north aisle. St Luke, Torver (CuL), of 1884, comes 10 years after Finsthwaite, and is an economical version of the same plan, slightly

Fig 3.36 (far left) Billington, St Leonard, 1879–80, an attractive composition for the vestry. (Mark Watson)

Fig 3.37 (left) Betws-y-Coed (Caernarvonshire), St Mary, 1872–3, a powerful building for the mountainous country of North Wales. (Mark Watson)

smaller but still with a robust central tower. The mighty pyramid roof at Finsthwaite here gives way to a lower, functional capping.

Two small town churches and an estate church

The needs of north-west England in the later 19th century meant that Paley & Austin built more urban churches than rural ones. Before examining the former, there are three fine churches which occupy an intermediate position between the country churches described above and the buildings erected, often on a grand scale, for Lancashire's larger settlements.

The first was not in Lancashire but in North Wales, at Betws-y-Coed (Caernarvonshire), and was built in 1872–3. Here the old church was inadequate for the numbers of summer visitors now frequenting this mountainous area. The resulting church of St Mary is said to have been won in competition with a design by Austin.[78] Knowledge of the job and our firm's interest in securing it may be due to local connections, Edmund Sharpe having lived close by for some years and become a well-known figure. In fact the principal benefactor, the Liverpool businessman Charles Kurtz, bought Edmund Sharpe's North Wales home in 1865. The church is a particularly good example of the powerful, stern architecture of which the firm was capable at this time, the style being 'a mixture of Norman and old English styles', as the local press put it (Fig 3.37).[79] The tower is placed over the choir and has crow-stepped parapets at the angles, while the west wall is punched through with a massive circular window. The interior (Fig 3.38), with bare local stone walling, low, taut piers and unstepped arcade arches, mirrors the strength of the exterior.

In 1882–4 Paley & Austin built the church of St John the Evangelist, Higher Walton (Ch) (Fig 3.39), for the wealthy brewer Sir Gilbert Greenall, who lived at Walton Hall nearby, where they had made various additions in the 1870s, including a clock tower. 'A glorious estate church', says Pevsner's reviser Richard Pollard, 'exquisitely detailed and composed'.[80] The dominant feature is a tall tower with a stone spire. 'Austin', adds Pollard, 'designed

Fig 3.38 (below) Betws-y-Coed. The stern exterior is matched by the interior with its bare stone walls, unchamfered arches in the nave, and architecture of the late twelfth/early thirteenth centuries. (Mark Watson)

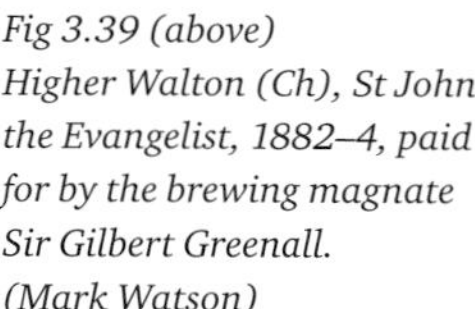

Fig 3.39 (above)
Higher Walton (Ch), St John the Evangelist, 1882–4, paid for by the brewing magnate Sir Gilbert Greenall.
(Mark Watson)

Fig 3.40 (above right)
Higher Walton: the crossing is placed over the east end of the nave rather than the choir. The work of P&A often attracted the attention of T Raffles Davison in his 'Rambling Sketches' for the British Architect. *In the case of this church, he devoted several double-page spreads to it.*
*(*British Architect *12 August 1884)*

some magnificent towers; this is one of the best.' It is unusual in the firm's output in forming a true medieval-style crossing rather than being placed above the choir space. What makes the tower distinctive (and rather different from medieval exemplars) is its emphasis on squared-off forms which are accentuated by the square-topped paired belfry lights. This trait, which can first be glimpsed in some of the details at St Mary, Leigh, would become one of the defining characteristics of later Paley & Austin and Austin & Paley work, and surely shows the hand of Hubert Austin. Another characteristic is the use of chequerwork on the middle stage of the tower, a device which was used on various other occasions. Its first appearance has not been firmly ascertained but the work at Higher Walton was preceded by less demonstrative work on the west and north faces of the tower at Scorton (1878–9). Chequerwork is not a feature of old north-western churches but is, rather, to be found in the late medieval buildings of East Anglia. Hubert Austin would certainly have met with it on his travels as a Pugin Student in 1866, but to attribute such a specific and direct source is to assume too much. It is better seen simply as a matter of late Victorian eclecticism, and one borrowing among many to enhance the design of the firm's churches – which it does splendidly at Higher Walton. The interior befits the exterior and is fitted out at considerable expense (Fig 3.40).

The parish church of St Mary, Dalton-in-Furness, the old 'capital' of Furness, was rebuilt in 1884–5 on a grand scale and at the substantial cost of £11,500 (Fig 3.41). Half of the funds came from the dukes of Devonshire and Buccleuch, the industrialist H W Schneider, and the Barrow Haematite Steel Co, all of whom had prospered from the industrial development of Furness and the growth of its 'new town', Barrow. The site is dramatic, overlooking the valley which runs down to Furness Abbey, and Paley & Austin made the most of it with a tall west tower, where (as at Higher Walton) prominent chequerwork plus traceried flushwork make an appearance. Flushwork (in the form of blind arcading) appears to have entered the Paley & Austin repertoire at St Matthew & St James, Mossley Hill, Liverpool (Me), as far back as 1872–5 (design 1870), Richard Pollard suggesting with some plausibility that it 'is a legacy of Hubert Austin's study tour of East Anglian churches'.[81] Maybe. At Dalton the chancel gable and chapel parapets also have chequerwork. A notable detail is the use of polygonal porches, a device which reappears at other churches by the firm (Hertford, 1893–5, and Widnes, 1908–10). The body of the church is grandly scaled and has tall arcades. The tower is flanked by the aisles and is 'propped' by quadrant arches.

Fig 3.41
Dalton-in-Furness (CuL), St Mary, grandly rebuilt to serve the town that had been the principal centre of the Furness peninsula before the rise of Barrow. Much of the funding came from the old aristocracy and the new businessmen who had prospered through industrial development in the area. Chequerwork and flushwork were popular features in the Paley & Austin repertoire.

Urban churches, 1870–85

In addition to the churches mentioned above, Paley & Austin built some 23 urban churches between 1872 and 1885. These are extremely diverse in origin, scale and architecture. They range from simple, temporary buildings to some of the finest produced in the entire history of the firm. All of them, apart from the firm's only Scottish commission at Greenock (Renfrewshire: 1877–8), a 'railway church' for Crewe (Ch: 1884–5) and a mission chapel in Scarborough (NY: 1885) (Fig 3.42), are (or were) located in the historic county of Lancashire, mostly in the industrial south. Almost all were for Anglicans (or the Scottish Episcopal Church), an exception being a Presbyterian chapel in Barrow (1874–5).

It is possible, in this body of work, to see the evolution of Paley & Austin's church architecture. This follows no simple, linear progression partly because during the 1870s and early 1880s the firm's church architecture developed great freedom of expression which, while still rooted in Gothic, was clearly modern. A significant trend was the move away from the muscularity and severity which was in evidence around 1870, as seen for example at Betws-y-Coed and Kirkby. That aesthetic, which was clearly a deliberate design choice, was given up, as was any interest in Continental forms – there were to be no apses after St John, Cheetham, of 1869–71, until that at the rather exceptional Flookburgh in 1897–1900 (CuL). The shift was away from the 'early' styles of transitional and Early English towards the late Gothic of Perpendicular, often fused with elements of Decorated. A characteristic style emerged which put emphasis on rectilinear geometry and was sometimes (and appropriately) described as 'a squared-off look'. Although found in the 1870s and 1880s, this would become the norm after the mid-1880s for the firm's larger churches.

There was no standardisation of plan. Aisles were usual, although very wide naves – the response to Evangelical preferences – were used to impressive effect. The churches of St George, Millom (CuC: 1874–7), and St James, Salford (GM: 1877–9), have north aisles only. Likewise, the positioning of towers varied. The west end was usual but the by now mainstream tower-over-choir arrangement was also used with fine effect at St Matthew & St James, Mossley Hill, Liverpool (1870–5), and St Peter, Westleigh (GM: 1879–81). The polygonal porches at Dalton-in-Furness (and their later cousins) have been mentioned, while at Mossley Hill there is a

Fig 3.42
Scarborough (NY), St James' mission church. Built in 1885, it has one of Paley & Austin's interesting treatments for a bell-turret (see also *Figs 3.61, 4.50 and 4.57).*
(British Architect *40, 1893, after 24)*

polygonal vestry – a fine feature which later finds a counterpart in the magnificent baptistry of 1901 at St Peter's church in Lancaster.

As was so often the case in the later 19th century, Paley & Austin used brick as a common solution to the problem of building large churches cheaply. This was frequently necessary in the towns of industrial Lancashire but, as will be seen, the firm proved highly adept at achieving grandeur and beauty using what, at the start of Victoria's reign, had been despised as a building material for churches. Stone, however, remained a desideratum wherever funds allowed, with the dull beige stone from Longridge, east of Preston, and red Runcorn sandstone very much in evidence. Internally, Paley & Austin now favoured bare stone or brick, reserving plaster for the smallest and humblest churches.

Roofs were a Paley & Austin speciality and rose far above mere structural necessity. Typically they are robust with heavy tie beams and struts, and add much to the sense of solidity and grandeur of their work. Little has been said so far about fittings and furnishings, yet it is during the Paley & Austin years that they come into their own. It was expected that architects would fit out their churches, and this Paley & Austin did with enormous facility and diversity. Their work is best appreciated through the various illustrations presented here in which can be seen something of their extraordinary inventiveness in the tracery that enlivened their pulpits, screens, seating, panelling and other items.

Space precludes description and illustration of all Paley & Austin's urban churches and a selection of the most important and interesting examples has necessarily to be made: they are dealt with in date order.

Liverpool, St Matthew & St James, Mossley Hill, 1870–5

'[O]ne of the best Victorian churches in Liverpool', thought Pevsner.[82] Designed in 1870 but not consecrated until June 1875, this mighty red sandstone church was built with funds bequeathed by a Liverpool merchant, Mr Glenton, whose first names were used in the dedication (Fig 3.43). His trustees sought their architect through a limited competition in which designs were submitted via Ewan Christian. It is built on a very grand scale in a late 13th-century style with a 'truly monumental crossing tower' (Pevsner again) and pyramidal roof over the choir. It was stated in 1890 that the design was Austin's although the reality is probably not so clear-cut.[83] The flushwork arcading may indeed be a borrowing from Austin's Pugin studentship tour of the eastern counties in 1866, but the windows have straight-headed gables above them (also used in the reredos), a feature which appealed greatly to Paley and was often used by him. The clerestory range is notable for its two-light windows: these are 12 in number and, outside, are read singly, although internally it is clear that there are two to each arcade bay.

The interior is majestic, the centrepiece being the great crossing tower (Fig 3.44). The nave arcades stride towards it, with alternating octagonal and clustered piers supporting conventional double-chamfered arches. On the nave side the crossing arch has four continuously chamfered orders, the middle two of which sit on a slightly awkward demi-octagonal corbel arrangement. Within the crossing the space is bathed in light from north and south windows. The nave seats bear a variety of tracery patterns, as favoured by Paley & Austin when funds permitted. The stone carving was carried out by John Roddis (1838–87) of Birmingham, an artist who secured several commissions through Paley & Austin.

Paley & Austin were evidently proud of their work since they exhibited drawings and models of it in the British Section of the Paris Exhibition in 1878.[84]

Fig 3.43
Liverpool, St Matthew & St James, Mossley Hill, built 1872–5. A very large, grand church for what was a prosperous part of Liverpool, shortly after completion. The polychrome banding, very unusual in Paley & Austin's work, is now far less evident after more than a century of weathering and grime. The vicarage, on the left, is also probably by the firm.
(David McLaughlin collection)

Fig 3.44
Mossley Hill, St Matthew & St James, towards the crossing (over the choir in this case) and east end. The bare stonework and generous proportions give the church sober dignity. Date of photograph uncertain. As so often, there is a simple low stone screen between the nave and chancel.
(OP04390 English Heritage. NMR)

Fig 3.45
Bolton, St Thomas, interior from the south aisle, and just as imposing as the exterior.
(Mark Watson)

Bolton, St Thomas, Halliwell, 1874–5

St Thomas's marks the start of an extremely fruitful period in which Paley & Austin explored a great range of possibilities for building churches in brick. Bolton had already provided Paley with one of his largest commissions, the rebuilding of the parish church which was opened in 1871. Then came the opportunity to build another large church in the town, in the working-class area of Halliwell (Figs 3.45 and 3.46). The chief benefactors were the Crosses, a mill-owning family who lived nearby at Mortfield: the prime mover was Thomas Cross, a bleacher, who gave the site for the church, a school and a vicarage, plus £1,000. This is one of the finest and very early examples of the firm's essays in building an imposing brick church with modest resources. The cost was only £6,400, for which 849 seats were obtained. It is, thought Pevsner, 'in its brick simplicity sensational for its date'.[85] Tucked away in the side streets of north-west Bolton, it is little known yet

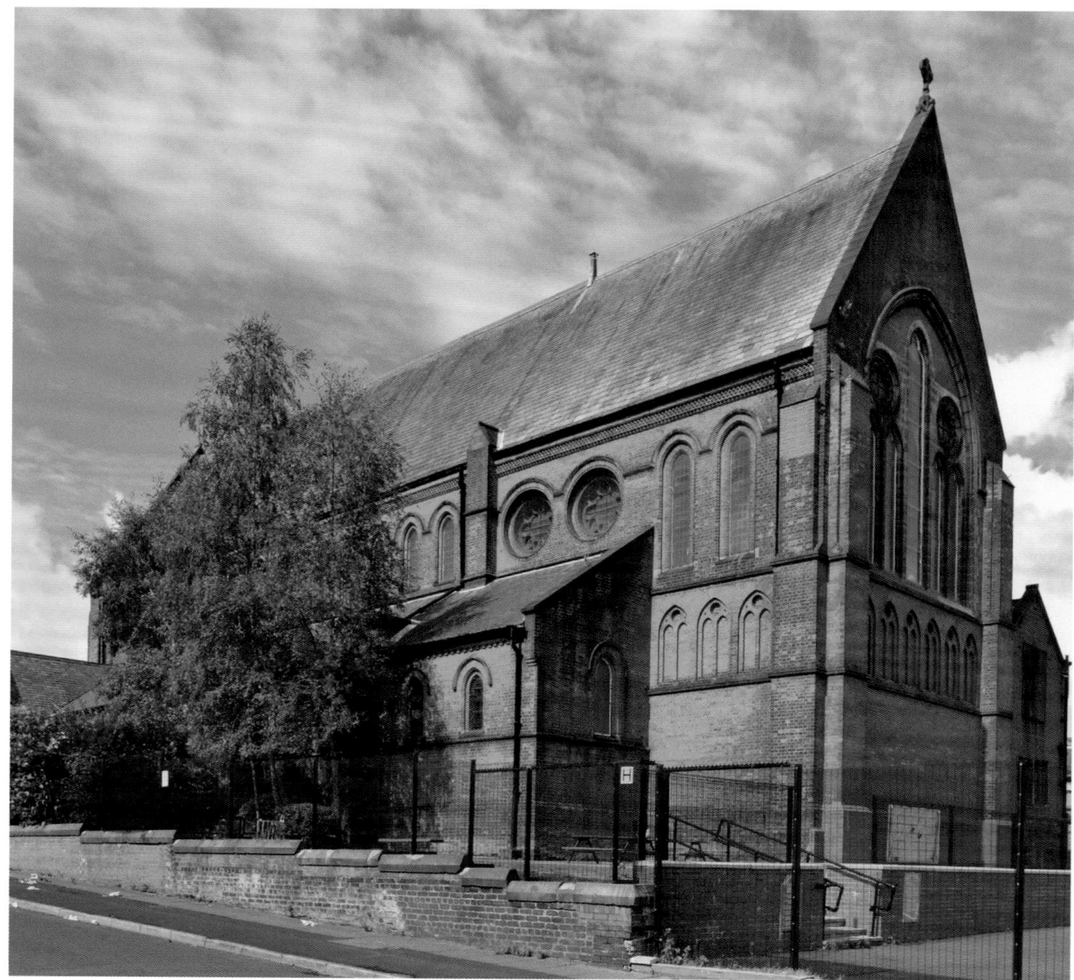

Fig 3.46
Bolton (GM), St Thomas, 1874–5, a monumental brick church for a working-class district. It is in the mould of the famous brick churches by James Brooks that sought to achieve grandeur with modest resources.

may justly be considered a worthy stable companion to James Brooks's great inner-London brick churches. Sadly, the north-east tower never rose above the level of the clerestory.

Economy is achieved by the use of an early 13th-century style. The fenestration is thus very simple, with lancets of various sizes and configurations; the east and west ends also have pairs of oculi. In the clerestory is a striking run of 14 constantly repeated lancets. The interior, like the exterior, is of bare brick, apart from a few buff sandstone dressings and circular piers with transitional capitals. Decoration is minimal, except for the remarkable treatment of the east wall below the windows – brick 'coffering' with tiles set in the recesses depicting, for example, fleurs-de-lys, angels and the Instruments of the Passion.

With its wide nave (28ft 6ins) and lack of elaboration, St Thomas's was surely conceived for Low Church worship. That is certainly to be expected in Bolton which, because of its strong Protestant tradition, earned itself the epithet 'the Geneva of the North'. However, the association between cheap, inferior church-building and Low Church sympathies had long been broken by the time St Thomas's was built. Ornament and the trappings of Anglo-Catholic worship may be lacking, but the architectural setting is grand and a testimony to the effects of the Victorian ecclesiological revolution on Anglican church-building for all persuasions. These will be seen again shortly in two further remarkable Bolton churches.

Atherton, St Michael & All Angels, Howe Bridge, 1875–7

St Michael's was one of a number of churches (such as St Mary, Leigh) built by Paley & Austin in the settlements serving the Lancashire coalfield. In this case the commission came about through family connections – the building being paid for by Ralph Fletcher (1815–86), the younger brother of Elizabeth, whom Edmund Sharpe had married in 1843.

Here Paley & Austin provided a freely treated version of 13th-century Gothic, severe in its details but with complex and visually varied massing on the principal, north side. The aisleless nave and chancel run through at the same level, but with a tall, two-tier flèche towards the east. There is a tall north transept, a single bay chapel west of this (matched on the south), a north-east chapel and a stair-turret at the north-east corner. The porch, like several others by Paley & Austin, is partly timbered. The chancel has a clerestory whereas the nave does not. Inside, despite what the continuous roofline might suggest, there is a strong demarcation between nave and chancel (Figs 3.47 and 3.48). The latter is stone-vaulted and is separated from the nave by a moulded chancel arch on robust corbels while the nave roof is of open tie-beam and crown-post construction. St Michael's is by no means a conventional essay in Gothic and displays much originality in the handling of its plan and massing: it is, as Richard Pollard remarks, one of Paley & Austin's 'most stimulating churches'.[86]

Fig 3.47
Atherton (GM), St Michael & All Angels, Howe Bridge, 1875–7. The fine chancel here is relatively unusual in the firm's output, being stone-vaulted.
(Mark Watson)

Fig 3.48
Howe Bridge, font, an interesting design in polished limestone. It tapers, as do many Paley & Austin fonts. Behind is a plaque to Ralph Fletcher whose grandfather was father-in-law to Edmund Sharpe. (Mark Watson)

Four cheap churches for Barrow, 1877–8

The growth of Barrow-in-Furness (CuL) and Paley's work there has been mentioned in the previous chapter. Subsequently commissions in Barrow multiplied, so much so that the firm set up a sub-office in the town. This, and the firm's numerous secular works in the area, will be dealt with later, but here an unusual church-building project needs highlighting which shows the firm designing humble, completely functional places of worship at a time when it was also building and designing town churches of great splendour. It came about because Anglican church provision in Barrow was being outstripped by the growth in population, which almost doubled from 22,500 in 1861 to 40,300 in 1871 and had grown by almost half again to 58,200 just 10 years later. The problem was tackled in 1877–8 by building four temporary brick and timber churches around the town to a common design, each dedicated, appropriately, to one of the Four Evangelists.

The total cost, including parsonages, was put at £24,000 and was funded by those who had created Barrow and had the greatest stakes in the town. The Duke of Devonshire funded two churches, the Duke of Buccleuch one, Lord Frederick Cavendish gave £3,500, and other major donations came from the town's elder statesmen, Sir James Ramsden (£500) and H W Schneider (£1,000), and the main shareholders of the Furness Railway and Barrow Docks companies. Each church had wooden arcades and was designed to accommodate 520 people. Of the four, one still remains in use for Anglican worship, St Mark's in Rawlinson Street (Fig 3.49), which was soon outgrown by its congregation and enlarged in 1882–3.[87]

Fig 3.49
The firm also built very modest churches when required. This is one of the four identical 'temporary' churches they built to meet the needs of expanding Barrow in the 1870s. It was enlarged in the 1880s and is still in use.

Two brick and terracotta churches in Salford, 1877–9

At the same time that the 'temporary' churches were being built in Barrow, Paley & Austin provided two substantial inner-city churches for Salford. Both were built of common red Knutsford brick with terracotta details. St Clement, Ordsall (1877–8) (Figs 3.50 and 3.51), was paid for by Lord Everton at a cost of £9,000. It is a church of considerable personality, with a bold range of three-light aisle windows (of two different designs), circular clerestory windows, and a rather gaunt, slate-hung flèche at the nave/chancel division. The west end has a remarkable portal which is something of a tour de force in moulded brick (supplied by the Knutsford Brick & Tile Co) and contains a roundel of typically inventive tracery in terracotta (from Costessy, near Norwich). Unusually for a Paley & Austin church (but compare Howe Bridge above), the chancel is vaulted, in this case in brick.

St James, Broughton, of 1877–9, although cheap at £7,000 for 600 seats, is an impressive building (Fig 3.52). There was no money for a proposed north-west steeple tower, but a bell-cote, which was planned in addition, was built over the east end of the nave. The nave and chancel run through at the same level and have little structural division internally. Examples of Paley & Austin's individuality can be found in the projecting stair at the west end, the hipping on the south porch roof, a bold buttress on the south side demarcating the nave/chancel division, and the use of traceried square windows in the chancel and organ chamber. The north aisle was subdivided off from the nave about 1970.

Fig 3.50 (above)
Salford, St Clement, Ordsall, 1877–9. An essay in brick and terracotta for a poor area, and with a striking range of windows in the north aisle.
(Mark Watson)

Fig 3.51 (far left)
Ordsall, west portal: red brick with a terracotta roundel containing ingenious tracery.
(Mark Watson)

North of the Border: St John's Episcopal Church, Greenock, 1877–8

St John's (Fig 3.53) was Paley & Austin's only venture into Scotland and probably came about through a family friendship. It also sheds light on the often slow and tortuous mechanics that

Fig 3.52
Salford, St James, Broughton, also of 1877–9, another economical brick and terracotta church. (Mark Watson)

Fig 3.53
Greenock (Renfrewshire), St John the Evangelist, 1877–9, the firm's only work in Scotland, probably secured through a clerical family friendship. (David O'Hara)

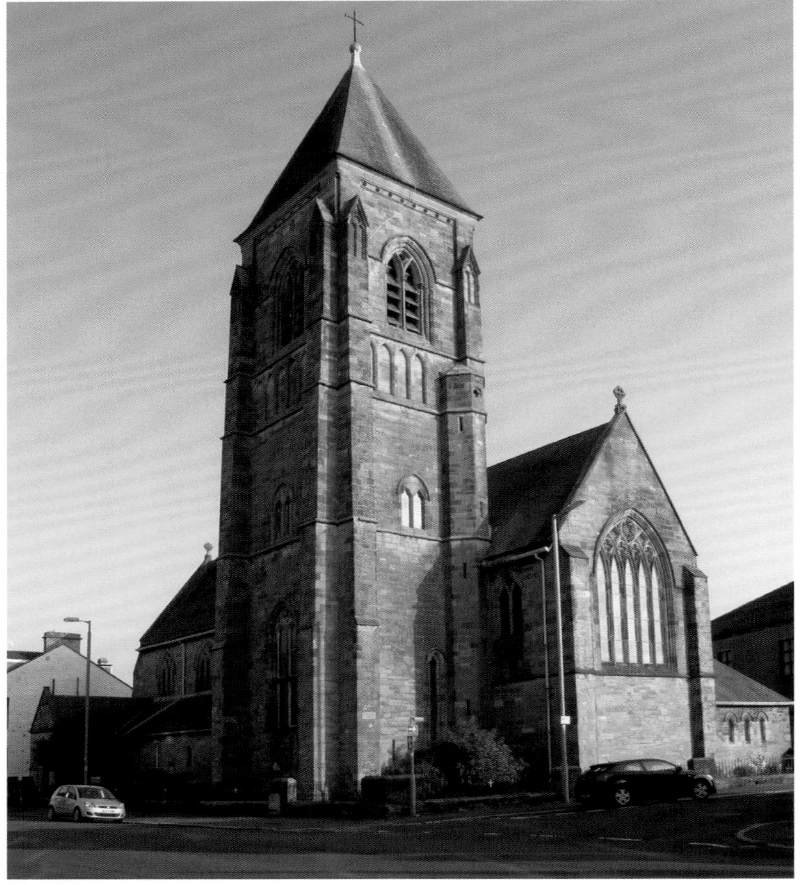

could attend the building of a Victorian church. An Anglican congregation had been established at Greenock (Renfrewshire) in 1823, and by the early 1870s their thoughts had turned to a new place of worship.[88] There was a typically unsatisfactory competition. In 1873 four Scottish and Irish architects submitted drawings of their work.[89] This failed to persuade the building committee to make a choice, so it decided on a competition of these four plus three others, at which point one of the original hopefuls withdrew.[90] The assessor was Ewan Christian (again!), who seems to have been faced with a predisposition on the part of the committee for John Stafford's design. 'I think', said Christian in his report on 10 March 1874, 'the Author would do well to spend time in careful study of the beautiful details in the fine buildings of the North, rather than import from the South.'

Such lack of enthusiasm was shared by Sir Michael Shaw-Stewart, Lord-Lieutenant of Renfrewshire, patron of the church, and the main benefactor, who was unwilling to entrust the work to an architect 'whose designs were condemned by an Ecclesiastical Architect of such recognised professional eminence as Mr Ewan Christian'. It is not clear whether Paley & Austin were among the six entrants but their fortunes looked up when the Revd Julius Lloyd (perpetual curate at St John's from 1871) recommended Mr Paley 'whom he knows to be of honourable character'.[91] He then added an endorsement from the very top of the architectural profession: 'Mr [G E] Street's recommendation is a sufficient warrant for his professional abilities.' It is likely that Lloyd had known the Paley family for some years. His second curacy, from 1858, was at St Peter, Wolverhampton (St), just over a mile from Penn where E G Paley's younger brother, Francis Henry (1826–1909), had been vicar since 1856. One can imagine a friendship between the two men, who were of the same generation, and thus a link to Paley the architect (who would have no doubt visited his brother) and the commissioning of St John's.

Matters moved slowly, and it was only in January 1875 that Shaw-Stewart consented to Paley's being instructed to produce plans. Progress remained dreadfully slow, and it was mid-October before Paley reported that he had seen the site and had 'an idea of the appropriate sort of building for 500–600'. By May 1876 there was even debate about who would deal with the quantity surveying. A Mr Blackmore wrote to Lloyd saying that 'Mr Barr [civil engineer] would be preferable as measurer to one of Paley and Austin's choice, who would tend to favour them in the first measurement which gives [the] first idea of cost'. Haggling over the design went on through 1876, including a contribution in January sent in by Shaw-Stewart from Cannes, where he was no doubt escaping the Scottish winter. Building finally began in 1877, and St John's was consecrated on 28 November 1878.

The church is built in a late 13th-century style and has a strong, south-east tower with a pyramidal roof. The chancel is slightly lower than the four-bay nave which has substantial three- and four-light windows, making for a brightly lit interior. This cannot have been one of P&A's happiest projects, but the firm must have given satisfaction since it was designing stalls for St John's in 1890 and was asked for an additional vestry in about 1897–8.

Atherton, St John the Baptist, 1878–9

On the north side of the Market Place at Atherton (GM) stands one of Paley & Austin's finest churches (Fig 3.54). It replaced a functional box of 1810 and followed on immediately from the firm's nearby church at Howe Bridge. It was

Fig 3.54
Atherton (GM), St John the Baptist, 1878–9. The west end and noble tower were built in 1892 to a modified design. The church dominates the market square and has very distinctive square clerestory windows with varied tracery. (Mark Watson)

Fig 3.55 (above)
Atherton, a pair of the inventive clerestory windows.
(Mark Watson)

Fig 3.56 (above right)
Atherton, west window, dating from 1892. This was probably the first time the firm used detached mullions for large east or west windows, which were later employed at some of its other greater churches.
(Mark Watson)

Fig 3.57 (opposite above)
Bolton (GM), All Souls, 1878–81. This large red-brick church towers above the back streets of the town: it was paid for from the wealth created in Bolton's 19th-century cotton industry.

Fig 3.58 (opposite below)
Bolton, All Souls.
Its founders were strongly Evangelical, hence the immensely wide nave. It is eloquent evidence that Low Churchmanship was not incompatible with building impressively.
(Mark Watson)

built in two stages, with the chancel and three bays of the nave coming first in 1878–9 with the proud tower (to a modified design) and west end in 1892. The five-bay nave and chancel are under a continuous roofline with vertical accents provided by the magisterial tower-cum-porch, the south transept and a stubby south-east turret. At this church we see the maturing of Paley & Austin's handling of late Gothic architecture, medieval in spirit but with an individuality that is clearly their own. The window treatment is particularly varied, with pointed and square-headed forms and what Richard Pollard nicely describes as 'virtuoso tracery'.[92] The treatment of the square windows is particularly original, and the extraordinary handling of the nave clerestory windows will be discussed shortly. On the eastern wall, abutting on to the road and below the large east window, is a lavish display of red and buff chequerwork with carved roses, IHC emblems, leaves and sword designs.

Following a disastrous fire in 1991, the interior was reordered in 1996–7 and the chancel divided off from the rest. This obviously had a major impact on the character of the building, yet nonetheless the nave remains a remarkably impressive space of five tall bays with quatrefoil piers. Across the five bays are spread eight square clerestory windows, in two groups of four each side (Fig 3.55). This syncopation is further complicated by the fact that although the four western windows are mirrored on the north and south, the eastern ones are not. This can only be seen as a playful (or wilful?) attempt to introduce a touch of carefully contrived asymmetry. Another original feature in Paley & Austin's work is the treatment of the great west window, which is almost certainly a design change in the second phase of construction (Fig 3.56). The main mullions are doubled internally with rectangular piercings between the two, a splendid effect which was repeated at St Silas, Blackburn, of 1894–8, St George Stockport (GM) of 1893–7, and the firm's last great town church of St Mary's, Widnes (Me), of 1908–10.

Great Bolton churches: All Souls, Astley Bridge, 1878–81, and St Saviour, 1882–5

The brothers Nathaniel and Thomas Greenhalgh made their fortune in cotton spinning in Bolton. They were ardent evangelicals and sought to use their wealth for the moral and spiritual improvement of the town. In 1877 they built a school, designed by the local architect J J Bradshaw, on land they owned off the Blackburn Road. But that year Nathaniel died, aged 60, leaving his fortune to his brother. The Greenhalgh wealth would provide Bolton with not one, but two of Paley & Austin's finest churches.

The first was All Souls, Astley Bridge, on the north side of the town. Thomas commissioned Paley & Austin to build a church adjacent to the school, and this now forms a major landmark in the area thanks to its mighty west tower (Fig 3.57). It is clear that his Evangelical leanings did not prevent him from commissioning a magnificent church, although they had a very profound influence on the building. The show of a foundation stone-laying was studiously avoided and the desire for a single, undivided congregational space led to a magnificent, aisleless nave 52ft wide and six bays long. The dramatic side walls are pierced by large, high-set three-light windows, filled with tracery fusing Decorated and Perpendicular elements. At the east end of the nave there are three arches: the central one, to the inevitably short chancel, with mouldings dying into the reveals. The chancel terminates in a canted arrangement (rather than a conventional apse), and such a treatment would be used subsequently at a number of Austin & Paley churches. Over the nave is a highly inventive roof structure with tie beams, false fan-vaulting and a raised polygonal central section (Fig 3.58).

Thomas Greenhalgh spent £20,000 on a second Paley & Austin church – St Saviour's: 'one of their noblest churches', declared Pevsner emphatically[93] – but it is no more, having been pulled down in 1975 after a long period of closure (Fig 3.59).[94] Faced in red brick with Longridge stone dressings, like All Souls it had a grand west tower, in this case with large pinnacles (137ft high to the tips) and a stepped, pierced parapet. The east end was square rather than canted, and the plan, being rather more complex than All Souls, gave rise to somewhat more eventful massing. The key feature was large transepts, which led off a widened fifth, eastern bay of the nave, which in turn led into aisles north and south of the chancel. The nave, at an immense 50ft (Fig 3.60), was only fractionally narrower than that at All Souls. The loss of Sharpe, Paley and Austin churches has been fairly modest, but the demolition of St Saviour's is by far the most grievous. Its older sister, All Souls, is redundant but now vested in the Churches Conservation Trust, which began a programme of work in early 2011 to promote community use and secure the future of the building. This will mean removal of the (rather ordinary) nave seating and the installation of various modules, but keeping a clear view to the east end.

Daisy Hill (GM), St James, 1879–81

The Lancashire coalfield area around Atherton and Leigh has some of Paley & Austin's very best churches. St James's, designed in 1878, was for Pevsner 'one of their most masterly performances'.[95] Superficially it is completely simple, with the main body just consisting of a wide unaisled nave and a chancel beyond a chancel arch, but continuing at the same roof level (Fig 3.61). On the north is a transept and a two-bay organ chamber and vestry. Economy was necessary since there was not much money to spend. The £6,500 the church cost was given by two sisters, Mrs Alice Markant and Miss Margaret Haddock, and provided 410 seats. Red brick and terracotta were used with minimal stone dressings.

Fig 3.59
Bolton, St Saviour, (1882–5, demolished 1975), the large and imposing sister church to All Souls.
(Copyright Bolton Council from the Bolton Museum & Archive Service collection, LSO1024)

The greatness of the building lies in its fine proportions and its highly inventive and enormously varied details. The style is essentially Perpendicular yet fused in the windows with flowing Decorated tracery. There is also a good deal of variety, for example in the way the nave south elevation has both three-light windows and a pair of two-light openings; the chancel, on the other hand, has segmental-headed lights. The porch gable has flushwork, while that above the west window has a grid of shaped brick that might have been borrowed from a Baltic church. Dotted around are a few traceried squares, such as had become a hallmark of the firm. But the most remarkable feature of all is the tall bell-turret locked on to the south-west part of the chancel – 'Spanish-Colonial-looking' is how Matthew Hyde, Pevsner's reviser, aptly sums it up. It is of five stages, the

Fig 3.60
Bolton, St Saviour, which shared with All Souls an immensely wide nave and a pair of arches leading east on both sides of the chancel arch.
(Copyright Bolton Council from the Bolton Museum & Archive Service collection, LSO1023)

upper two of them pierced by three bell-openings. The interior has plain brick walling above a timber dado and is an exercise in chaste simplicity, beauty being reserved for the traceried windows (and later reredos and Morris east window). In the chancel extra interest is provided by the detached shafts of the windows.

Leigh, St Peter, Westleigh, 1879–81

As St James's was rising, another major Paley & Austin church was being built scarcely two miles away to the south. Again Pevsner was excited by it, considering it 'one of their most thrilling churches in Lancashire'.[96] At £7,000 it was not

Fig 3.61
Daisy Hill (GM), St James, 1879–81, another red brick and terracotta church for the Lancashire coalfield area. When funding did not permit a tower, Paley & Austin often substituted a bell-turret: the one here is probably their most impressive example. (Mark Watson)

Fig 3.62
Leigh (GM), St Peter, Westleigh, is not far from Daisy Hill and is another confident church, of rather duller red brick and with terracotta replaced by stone. The powerful rectangular-shaped tower sits over the east part of the nave. The square-headed windows are typical of the mature work of the firm.
(Mark Watson)

much more expensive than St James, but it also is a remarkable essay in how to build a splendid church on a tight budget (Fig 3.62). The materials are local, cheap red brick, relieved by red Runcorn stone dressings. The details, as at Daisy Hill, are a mixture of Perpendicular and Decorated. The window openings are mostly square-headed: on the south (main) elevation only the large window lighting the base of the

Fig 3.63
Westleigh, the spacious, red-brick-lined interior.
(Mark Watson)

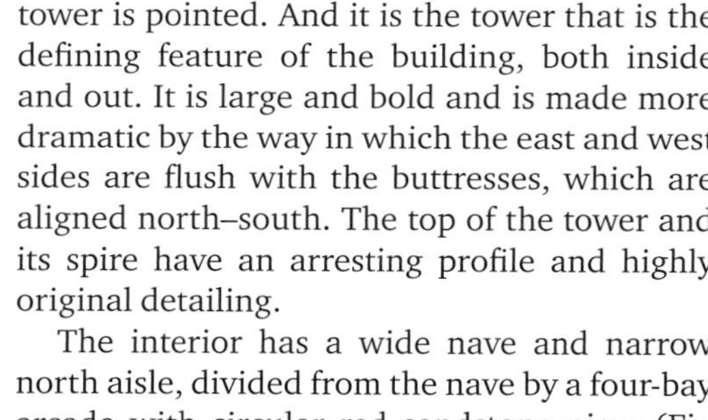

tower is pointed. And it is the tower that is the defining feature of the building, both inside and out. It is large and bold and is made more dramatic by the way in which the east and west sides are flush with the buttresses, which are aligned north–south. The top of the tower and its spire have an arresting profile and highly original detailing.

The interior has a wide nave and narrow north aisle, divided from the nave by a four-bay arcade with circular red sandstone piers (Fig 3.63). The walls, of course, are of bare brick. For all its vast external bulk, the tower is not unduly obtrusive and is placed, unusually, over the eastern part of the nave; it is carried on capital-less, moulded brick arches. The nave roof is a typically robust Paley & Austin tie beam design. The font is an inventive piece with green marble polygonal shafts.

Knutsford, St Cross, 1880–1

The start of the 1880s saw the beginning of a new church for Edmund Sharpe's home town of Knutsford (Ch): the tower was completed in 1887 and the aisles in 1889 (Fig 3.64). Perpendicular in style with a few Decorated flourishes, it is built of intensely red brick with terracotta. Like St Peter, Westleigh, it has a crossing tower over the east part of the nave but here, by contrast, the tower is tall and not so tautly designed, and spreads upwards in a strange assortment of stages ending in a panelled belfry stage and an embattled parapet, the stone of which gives it an odd, stuck-on appearance. Internally there are three nave bays on the north and two on the south, the difference being accounted for by a vestry placed in the south-west angle. The crossing, as at Westleigh, creates a fine effect, beautifully lit by the large north and south windows. Compared with the carefully controlled and harmonious designs of Paley & Austin's churches from this time, St Cross is interesting and unusual for its quirky, almost wayward treatment.

Fig 3.64 (left)
Knutsford (Ch), St Cross, 1880–1, completed 1889 (plus later additions). Bright red brick and terracotta again in evidence. The sandstone top to the tower strikes an incongruous note. (Mark Watson)

Fig 3.65 (below)
Crewe (Ch), St Barnabas, 1884–5, an economical church for railway workers, in cheap red brick with terracotta details. The large gables, and hence enlarged windows, create a light interior and a sense of spaciousness. Shingled bell-turret and spirelet.

Fig 3.66 (bottom)
Crewe, St Barnabas, interior.

Crewe, St Barnabas, 1884–5, and its successor

Hubert Austin's first church, in Ashford, was as a result of the railways. So too was St Barnabas in Crewe (Ch), built for the populace that depended on the London & North Western's workshops nearby. Railway churches and tight budgets went hand in hand, and this one was estimated to cost £4,000 for 500 seats, including the endowment (the final cost is not known). Yet, like the Daisy Hill and Westleigh churches, it is extraordinarily successful, despite (or perhaps because of) the restrictions involved. The material is common red brick with terracotta from Ruabon (Fig 3.65). There is no tower, but a shingled bell-turret adorns the west end. Space and light are created within the church by wide aisles covered by three large transverse gables, allowing for the insertion of a large three-light transomed window in each bay. The arcade arches are correspondingly wide, and the moulded arches die without capitals into slender stone lozenge-shaped piers (Fig 3.66). The chancel and nave are in one, without any structural division, and no unnecessary expense is devoted to the roof, which is a simple five-sided affair with tie beams.

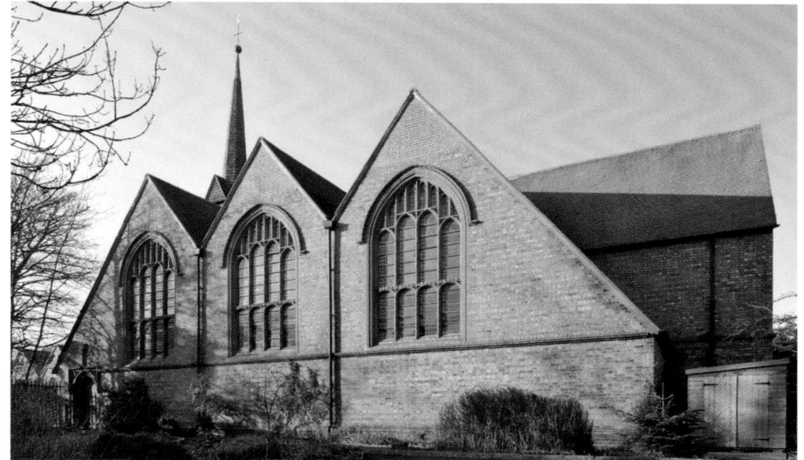

St Barnabas is a remarkable achievement in producing a dignified church at low cost. The experiment was repeated very closely a few years later in the church of St John, Birkdale (Me), of 1889–90 (Figs 3.67 and 3.68). With 318 seats, this was slightly smaller and cost a mere £3,300. The roof at Birkdale is rather more elegant, having a chunky raised tie beam construction, and the piers are graced with capitals (perhaps the curious blocks were intended to be carved).

Fig 3.67
Birkdale (Me), St John, 1889–90, derives from the firm's earlier church in Crewe. Some details have changed such as the use of a little half-timbering, the presence of paired windows in the aisle bays and the design of the bell-turret. (Mark Watson)

Liverpool – the cathedral that never was

One of the most important architectural competitions of the late 19th century was for a cathedral for the new Anglican diocese of Liverpool, carved out of that of Chester in 1880. Plans were afoot by the spring of 1884 to provide it with a worthy cathedral on a site adjacent to St George's Hall, taking the place of St Peter's pro-cathedral in Church Street. An open invitation was issued to architects 'who have been engaged in the erection of churches' to send in examples of their work.[97] In all, 101 portfolios were received; these were quickly reduced to 40, from which the 'principal adviser' to the committee, Ewan Christian (yet again!), recommended 12.[98] This latter list placed Paley & Austin in the company of the greatest architects of the day, including Bodley, Pearson, Waterhouse and Brooks.[99] Unfortunately for our story, Paley & Austin did not make it to the next and final round which whittled the number of competitors down to four architects who were asked to prepare actual designs to be submitted in 1886. These were Pearson (who in fact did not supply a design), Brooks, Bodley and, the winner, William Emerson with his domed Gothic design. Not only were Paley & Austin disappointed but so was everyone else, because the project was abandoned in 1888. There was talk of a scaled-down cathedral which, as *The Builder* commented, seemed a 'rather lame and impotent conclusion to the grand competition scheme'.[100] Even this fizzled out as the project's General Committee seemed unable to raise more than £25,000 towards the £30,000 needed for a reduced scheme, which, as *The Builder* commented, was 'only sufficient for a good sized parish church'.[101] Matters had to wait until the start of the 20th century, when a new

Fig 3.68
Birkdale, St John, interior. The piers have acquired capitals, there is a different east window and red bricks replace buff bricks for the walls, but the planning and general arrangements are very similar to those at Crewe.
(Mark Watson)

competition was organised that would result in Giles Gilbert Scott's mighty building. By this time most of the more successful competitors from the 1880s were dead, but the firm at the centre of the present study, then known as Austin & Paley, entered the lists and distinguished itself as a finalist.

Churches 1867–1885: conclusion

The first 20 years of the Paley and Austin partnership produced a remarkable corpus of church buildings. With the arrival of Hubert Austin in 1867 the practice branched out with designs which were both innovative and varied. The use of stern transitional and Early English characterised some of the partners' early works, yet side by side with these there was an increased interest in the possibilities of late medieval architecture. The potential of brick was exploited to the full from the middle of the 1870s, and by the end of the decade this had produced some extraordinarily assured and creative designs which also made much use of terracotta. The firm's best churches of these years easily stand favourable comparison with the work of the greatest metropolitan church architects of the day.

In parallel with this church-building activity, Paley & Austin were busy with numerous secular commissions, both great and small. They covered almost every conceivable building type, from a great mansion for an important aristocrat, through schools, a few factories, commercial buildings and even buildings that helped the running of mid-Victorian railways. The following pages examine a selection of such work.

Secular works

The building of Barrow

By far the most important concentration of work for Paley & Austin during the 1870s and early 1880s was in Barrow-in-Furness. The background to the town has been described in the previous chapter as it was very significant to Paley's career. He was responsible for the two principal Anglican churches in the town and then, in 1877–8, he and Austin undertook the four temporary churches already discussed.

Barrow was dominated by iron, steel and shipbuilding industries, and there was a serious shortage of work for women. To remedy this, a new enterprise was planned at the end of the 1860s, a flax and jute mill under the chairmanship of Barrow's ubiquitous elder statesman, James Ramsden. The buildings were designed by Paley & Austin, and work on them began in

1870. They were completed in two phases, opening in 1872, and were, a local directory noted a little later, of 'excellent red brick, with bands of terracotta and Yorkshire stone facings' (Fig 3.69).[102] This vast factory on Hindpool Road was closed in the early 20th century, with the main chimney demolished in 1930, and the offices in 1948. Despite its former importance, it is now little remembered.

Fig 3.69
The Barrow Flax & Jute Mills works, 1870–2 (demolished). A foray into factory building by the practice.
*(*North Lonsdale Magazine *3, 1898–9, 155)*

Fig 3.70
Sir James Ramsden presides over the square named in his honour in Barrow-in-Furness. The large building was built under Paley & Austin plans of 1873 for the Lancaster Banking Co. This is said to have been designed by John Harrison, who ran a local office for P&A from the 1870s: he was also said to have designed the base for Ramsden's statue.

The 1870s in Barrow presented great opportunities for the partners, whose stock must have stood very high as they had already built some of the town's most important buildings. They decided to open a sub-office there, run by John Harrison (1837–96), who had worked in the Lancaster office in the 1860s. He moved to Barrow probably in late 1871 or early 1872 and became responsible for some of the design work for the firm locally, including extensive work for the Furness Railway. His first design was said to be the base for Sir James Ramsden's statue in Ramsden Square, unveiled in May 1872, the year Ramsden was knighted (Fig 3.70). Harrison was based at 16 Church Street, which served as both an office and a home. However, the growth of Barrow stalled from the 1870s and the last mention of the firm's having a base in the town is in 1886. Harrison continued to live here, unmarried, but probably maintained an informal association with Paley & Austin and was used as and when a local presence was required. The last case that has been traced is Harrison signing the plans for St Mark's schools in 1888. For further details on him, *see* Appendix 2.

Despite the peaking of Barrow's growth, commissions there continued to come thick and fast until the early 1880s, as the Catalogue abundantly shows (*see* Appendix 5). Apart from work for the Furness Railway and the abortive Town Hall project, jobs included a couple of banks, buildings for Barrow cemetery, vast tenement blocks, a Presbyterian church, schools, villas,

Fig 3.71
Barrow-in-Furness Cemetery, entrance gateway, c 1873. Round-arched openings, and strongly contrasted white limestone and red sandstone.
(Mark Watson)

Fig 3.72
Barrow-in-Furness, tenement blocks, c 1873–4, fronting Michaelson Road, and built for the Barrow Iron Ship Building Company, many of whose workers came from Scotland. The building of other blocks continued into the 1880s.
(Mark Watson)

meeting halls and the School of Art. Three of these are worth singling out. The two banks date from 1873 and were built on Ramsden Square; they are typical mid-Victorian classical commercial buildings and are credited to Harrison in one of his obituaries. Paley & Austin were appointed in 1870 to design the buildings for Barrow's cemetery, which were complete by 1874. The muscular gateway (Fig 3.71) has a family resemblance to the gatehouse for the Royal Albert Asylum. The firm's biggest development in Barrow was the building of a series of 10 tenement blocks on Barrow Island between 1874 and 1884 (Fig 3.72). These are clearly based on Scottish models and the contractor was a Scots firm, Smith & Caird from Dundee. The tenements were to house large numbers of workers at high density, and such a solution seems to have been unique in the north-west of England. It is likely that some Scots would have been brought in to work in the flax and jute mill, but that scarcely explains a housing development on such a huge scale.

Barrow: the town hall that never was

As 1877 opened, Paley & Austin were set fair to undertake a major public building – a new Town Hall for Barrow-in-Furness. But it was a tale of mismanagement, misunderstanding and (no doubt for our architects) misery, which is worth describing as a classic example of how such things can go wrong. In October 1876 a subcommittee was set up 'to select and invite Architects to send in competitive drawings'.[103] There is no sign that it looked beyond Paley & Austin, and on 4 January they were recommended to the General Purposes Committee which four days later gave the go-ahead 'to instruct the Architects accordingly', although no contractual arrangements were actually put in place. Fearing a reaction from other local architects, an agreement had been struck whereby P&A withdrew from competing for a new workhouse the design of which was being sought at the same time.[104] That was indeed a real concession since they had already produced plans which, in the opinion of the mayor, H W Schneider, 'would have been accepted by the Local Government Board'.

On 2 February the full council was called upon to approve the appointment of P&A as architects for the town hall. There was little doubt as to the quality of their submission, with Schneider once again enthusiastic, declaring the plans to be 'the very best ... he had ever seen in his life'. But there was dissent in the air. One councillor, for instance, while seemingly doubtful that the 'architects in the town could produce plans equal to those of Messrs. Paley and Austin', spoke up for the principle of free trade and the right to give local architects a chance. However, the vote went decisively in P&A's favour at 21 to 3. A month later it was all very different after six Barrow architects had sent in a complaint to the council.[105] After much debate the members now voted to rescind the February decision and throw the job open to *local* competition.

However, that is not what happened. The town hall subcommittee was sent away to advertise for competitive plans, and the idea must have dawned that restricting such an important project to local architects was unsatisfactory, so an *open* competition was determined upon. No fewer than 140 architects asked for instructions, and 23 submitted designs.[106] Paley & Austin saw fit not to compete, which is hardly surprising in the circumstances. The entries were submitted in October, and the wide variety of Gothic, Venetian and Renaissance offerings were assessed by Alfred Waterhouse.[107] To add insult to injury as far as P&A were concerned, only one of the six dissident local architects put forward a design.[108] None of the premiated designs went to local men. Third prize went to Leeds architects H Perkin & G B Bulmer and second to T E Collcutt of London. Waterhouse's first choice was a design labelled 'Ima'. Unfortunately the architect had forgotten to enclose his details but he was soon tracked down. And so it was that the proudest building in Barrow came to be designed neither by Paley & Austin (who, of course *did* have an office in Barrow), nor any other local architect, nor, indeed, by an Englishman, but the distinguished Irish practitioner, W H Lynn of Belfast.

Buildings for the Furness Railway Company

The Furness Railway facilitated the development of Barrow, and from an early date the firm, first as Sharpe & Paley and then Paley alone, designed buildings for it. The wide range of the railway company's activities went far beyond running trains, it being a major landowner and developer in the area, which led to a wide range of Paley & Austin-designed structures. Many of these seem to have been designed by John Harrison working out of Barrow. A great deal has been written about the Furness Railway but unfortunately much of what is said about Paley/P&A involvement, while possibly true, seems unsupported by solid evidence. Philip Grosse, writing in 1996, refers to the stylistic impact on the company's buildings 'when [it] commissioned Paley and Austin to carry out future work'.[109] This implies (although probably not intentionally) an overarching contract, which is most unlikely to have been the case.

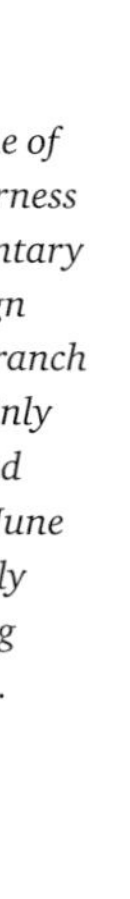

Fig 3.73
Conishead (CuL) is one of the stations for the Furness Railway with documentary evidence for P&A design (designs 1880). The branch line, which served mainly Bardsea and Conishead Priory, opened on 27 June 1883 but closed as early as 1917, the track being lifted for use in France. (Cumbrian Railways Association, Kerr collection, 236a)

Although John Harrison's obituary notices indicate that he/P&A designed most of the stations, it has proved difficult to tie these back to documentary sources.[110] The list of works in the Catalogue (*see* Appendix 5) is almost certainly very incomplete but works have only been included when documentary evidence has been located (Fig 3.73).

Assuming they are indeed by the firm, Paley & Austin station-building continued into the 1870s and 1880s, and one of its characteristics was simple timber buildings with widely projecting eaves set upon stone plinths (Figs 3.74 and 3.75). Associated with the stations are a series of goods sheds, also built to a standard design with a lunette window in each bay, the number of bays depending on the size of shed required. At Seascale, Paley & Austin were certainly responsible for an imposing circular water-tower, designed in 1878 (Fig 3.76). Barrow's main station moved from The Strand to further north in the town and opened in 1882; sadly, no evidence of Paley & Austin involvement has been found in the Barrow building plans or the local press. The Furness

Fig 3.74 (above left) Askham (CuL) station has the widely projecting eaves similar to those shown in Figure 3.75.

Fig 3.75 (above) Even P&A's railway work was captured by Raffles Davison's prolific pen, in this case as part of a sheet of drawings, 'Rambling Sketches No. 19', in the Furness area. (British Architect *21 October 1881)*

Fig 3.76 Seascale (CuC) water tower (far left) and goods shed (left). The former is certainly to a P&A design; the latter is probably by them too and was used at various other stations by the Furness Railway. In between is the church of 1890 by C J Ferguson of Carlisle. (Tim Austin)

Fig 3.77
Barrow-in-Furness, Abbey Approach/Barrow Road, a pair of cottages (design 1872) for the Furness Railway Company. (Mark Watson)

Fig 3.78
Barrow-in-Furness, a former hotel on what was Devonshire Dock Road (plans 1885).

Railway was active in building cottages for some of its employees, and those near Furness Abbey are of considerable distinction (Fig 3.77). Various small hotels were also planned, but these seem not to have been built (such a hotel, not designed for the Furness Railway, survives on Barrow Island as a pub (Fig 3.78)). The last known Furness Railway involvement was a plan for a very basic, minor extension to the Concle Inn at Ramside, in 1886.

Rebuilding at Holker Hall, 1871–5

Minor commissions for the Furness Railway were a world apart from the firm's work at Holker Hall, its most important country house commission, which is, said Pevsner, 'the grandest of its date in Lancashire'.[111] The house was the seat in 'Lancashire over the sands' of William Cavendish, the 7th Duke of Devonshire, who had major investments in the Furness area and did much to promote its development. On 9 March 1871 he and his family were awakened to find much of the house being ravaged by fire.[112] A month later, on 11 April, E G Paley was there to advise. 'He seems to think', recorded the duke, 'that if I settled to rebuild the house as it was the walls might stand but if alterations are made that it will not be worthwhile to keep them.' In the event, the old walls of George Webster's stuccoed Jacobean-style building of 1838–41 came down. In August the duke noted that '[t]he works are due to begin immediately', and they continued into 1875, with some final touches not made until the following year. Raffles Davison reckoned the cost was about £38,000.[113]

Paley & Austin's confident new building, which houses the state rooms, is Elizabethan in style and faced with the variegated red sandstone which the firm so favoured (Fig 3.79). The entrance front, facing east down a slope and not easily seen from a distance (because of trees), has a large, asymmetrically placed porch flanked by turrets with domed and pinnacled cappings. Behind the porch is a tall slim tower

Fig 3.79
Holker Hall (CuL). A couple in the 1870s admire the newly built state wing (right). The work on the left is by George Webster of Kendal, c 1840.
(BB86/07008 English Heritage.NMR)

Fig 3.80
Holker Hall. The Aesthetic-style floral panels on the entrance front inject a note of modernity to a building that otherwise looks back to establish Elizabethan links (cf the decoration at St John, Cheetham, see Fig 3.24). (Mark Watson)

with a copper-covered ogee-topped cupola. To the right is a broad square tower with a lead-covered pyramid. Like the other elevations, the entrance façade has mullioned windows. A real surprise, and presumably due to Austin, is the introduction of square panels carved with Aesthetic-style flowers (Fig 3.80). The corners of the garden fronts are turned through a semi-circular projection and have eventful skylines of large, asymmetrically arranged dormers behind the parapets and the two towers of the eastern front rising behind them.

The porch leads into a long entrance hall (Fig 3.81) with the library and the billiards, dining and drawing rooms leading off it. The latter faces both south and west and has the semi-circular corner projection mentioned. All the ground-floor rooms have elaborately decorated plaster ceilings. At the far end of the hall, beyond polished Furness limestone arches, a cantilevered staircase with richly carved bellies to the balusters leads to the first-floor bedrooms. The soffit of the staircase arch has floral and other circles carved in the sunk panels, which again have a decidedly Aesthetic look to them.

The new work at Holker Hall is full of interest and incident. The three elevations are all asymmetrical and have unexpected touches – for instance, a triangular projection from the library, the semi-circular turning of the corner to the garden, the complex arrangement of the entrance front, and the playful introduction of up-to-the-minute Aesthetic motifs. 'It is', said Pevsner, 'a pleasure to follow the compositional finesse.'[114] Paley & Austin had no further opportunity to do anything like it on so grand a scale. It is a work that must have given them much satisfaction.

Fig 3.81
Holker Hall, the entrance hall with large Elizabethan windows and richly decorated ceiling. An inscription on the fireplace records the destructive fire in 1871 and the rebuilding: the date, 1874, suggests it was one of the last items to be installed. The pair of arches at the far end are of polished Furness limestone. (Mark Watson)

The restoration of Hoghton Tower

Another important country house project was the restoration of Hoghton Tower, some six miles east of Preston and magnificently sited on a hilltop. The de Hoghton family had resided here perhaps since before the Conquest although the present house dates from 1561–2, with extensions and making good in about 1692 to 1702 after Civil War damage. Abandoned as a family residence from 1768, much-needed repair and restoration to the house only took place after Sir Henry, the 9th Baronet, inherited in 1862 and decided to turn it into an 'occasional residence'.

Written accounts imply that work began shortly after Sir Henry inherited, but the available documentation does not begin until the 1870s.[115] Paley & Austin, who were responsible for the most important elements of an admirable restoration, were certainly involved by 1876 and dealing with the key state rooms, notably the banqueting hall (Fig 3.82). Their work is carefully considered, enhancing the qualities of the building and yet subtle and self-effacing in a proto-Arts and Crafts way.[116] In making the plans for the hall in February 1876, for example, the firm suggested a timber ceiling in preference to a plaster one which, they considered, would jar with the bare stonework of the walls (they appear to have removed the plaster from the walls). The work seems to have continued until late 1878, with excellent woodwork by James Hatch of Lancaster, a fine craftsman who was repeatedly employed by the firm. Sir Henry died in 1876 and was succeeded by his brother Charles as 10th Baronet. Sir Charles continued the restoration, but it was not until 1880 that work was sufficiently advanced for him to take up residence, suggesting that perhaps less was done during Sir Henry's time than has been supposed. A lodge on the drive designed in 1876 for Sir Henry by Paley & Austin was built in 1878 (Fig 3.83), with Sir Charles's initials replacing those of his brother. In 1877 the firm was dealing with the dilapidated gateway tower and adjacent walling (Fig 3.84) and in 1879–80 work was carried out on the east wing offices, a new kitchen, the building of an underground service corridor, and various other alterations

Fig 3.82
Hoghton Tower, the Banqueting Hall, restored in the late 1870s. P&A suggested the use of a wooden ceiling, rather than a plaster one.
(Thomas de Hoghton)

Fig 3.83
Hoghton Tower, lodge on the drive up to the house. A plain, yet chaste and elegant house that belies its date. The raised label encloses the initials of Sir Charles de Hoghton and the date 1878.

Fig 3.84
Hoghton Tower, viewed from the inner courtyard entrance. The latter was much restored and rebuilt by the firm.
(Thomas de Hoghton)

estimated to cost £3,503.[117] Visits by Hubert Austin suggest that he was the partner mainly responsible.

Paley & Austin were replaced for later work at Hoghton Tower but for unknown reasons. The estate surveyor, the Blackburn architect James Bertwistle, was busy with alterations, stables and farm buildings in the 1880s, and after Sir Charles's death in 1893 a little-known London architect, Robert Dudley Oliver (d 1923), was brought in from 1896 until completion in 1901. He provided nursery accommodation, a smoking room, a billiards room and the lavish larger drawing room (now known as the ballroom); his work, notes John Martin Robinson, has 'a markedly richer and less disciplined tone than Paley & Austin's'.

Other country house commissions

Paley & Austin secured a regular stream of other large house commissions. At the start of their partnership in 1868–9 they built Sedgwick House (CuL) (Figs 3.85, 3.86 and 3.87), four miles south of Kendal, for William Henry Sedgwick, whose wealth derived from gunpowder works in Westmorland (one of which lay south of the village). The house was the last Paley & Austin country house to have a strongly Gothic imprint, with pointed arches to the porte cochère at the base of a large square tower placed in the centre of the entrance façade, and

Fig 3.85 (left) Sedgwick House (CuL), High Victorian Gothic fireplace in the Great Hall.

Fig 3.86 (below) Sedgwick House (CuL), 1868–9, the firm's last country house with Gothic elements. A large porte-cochère stands in front of the central tower of the main block.

Fig 3.87
Sedgwick House, Great Hall.

Fig 3.88
Leighton Hall, Yealand Conyers, from the east. The 1870 block on the left adds a strong note of asymmetry to the frontage of 1759–61, which itself was Gothicised in 1822–5.

some windows with cusping and tracery. The entrance leads through a lobby to a large, still very baronial three-storey staircase hall. The stable block has a clock tower with a tall, two-stage spire. After 1870 Paley & Austin (and their clients) turned away from any hint of Gothic for their houses.

In 1870 the firm built a simple but elegant extension to Leighton Hall on the left flank of the main façade which, with its tall tower, makes for an effective termination to this side of the house (Fig 3.88). Also in 1870 a more extensive expansion of the 1830s Walton Hall, Higher Walton (Ch), was carried out for the Warrington brewer Sir Gilbert Greenall and included the building of a clock tower. In 1871 the partners undertook a Jacobethan rebuilding in brick of Winmarleigh House, near Garstang, for John Wilson-Patten, later the 1st Lord Winmarleigh. Major changes were made from 1872 to Underley Hall, north of Kirkby Lonsdale (CuW), the seat of the Earl of Bective. With its pierced parapet tower and cupola, and Elizabethan style, it belongs to the same stylistic world as Holker Hall, which was rising once again at the same time. In 1874 a large house, 'Oak Lea' (now demolished), was built for the Barrow industrialist H W Schneider to the north of the town. Also of 1874 is Witherslack Hall, near Levens (CuL) (Fig 3.89), built of harsh local rock-faced limestone with red sandstone dressings. The details are Jacobethan, with extensive mullioned windows. Capernwray Hall, which had been remodelled by Sharpe & Paley in the 1840s, received an extension in 1875–6 of a south-east block attached to the tower and with an attractive clock tower at the east end. Typical of a smaller, but still substantial, country residence is Hampsfield House, near Lindale (CuL), of 1880–2 (Fig 3.90). Also around 1880 the firm carried out a range of modifications at Whittington Hall for Dawson Cornelius Greene. These included a charming octagonal dairy at the Home Farm (Fig 3.91).

The last major country house project for the firm was the remodelling of Thurland Castle at Tunstall in the north-east tip of Lancashire. Paley & Austin were brought in by the owner, Mr North North, after a serious fire in 1876. Work began in 1879, continuing until 1885, with over 100 men on site for some of the time. This spreading, low building is a mixture of Elizabethan with very late Gothic, with numerous mullioned windows and low towers. It 'is surrounded romantically by stone terraces and a moat', comments John Martin Robinson; 'The interior is evocative of the late C19 Arts and Crafts Movement with low comfortable rooms of informal shape and varying size with light oak panelling, De Morgan tiles, heraldic stained glass, simple plasterwork and stone, alabaster and carved wooden chimneypieces.'[118]

Fig 3.89
Witherslack Hall (CuW), 1874, for Frederick Arthur Stanley MP, later 16th Earl of Derby. Sketches by T Raffles Davison.
*(*British Architect *22 August 1881)*

Fig 3.90
Lindale (CuL), Hampsfield House, c 1881, for John Tomlinson Hibbert MP (Parliamentary Secretary to the Local Government Board under Gladstone, 1871–4, 1880–3).
(Mark Watson)

Schools

Schools of various types provided the firm with commissions for the entire span of its century-long existence. Most of the work was architecturally unexceptional, rarely attaining distinction except in the chapels provided to serve the larger schools. In the first two Paley & Austin decades there was the usual crop of small schools, such as an infants' school in Dalton-in-Furness (CuL: 1868), National Schools in Lancaster (1868), schools for a Wesleyan chapel complex again in Lancaster (1873–4), in Barrow (1875, extended 1880), and for St Mary's church, Lancaster (1879). Paley was even chosen in 1883 to be the assessor for a new Board School in Carlisle.

The 1870s saw the start of a 60-year association with Sedbergh School (CuWY), located in a small (then) West Yorkshire country town in lovely hilly surroundings. The school, 22 miles north-east of Lancaster, played an important part in our story: both Edmund Sharpe and J W Whittaker had been educated there, as had members of the Feilden, Fletcher, Langshaw and Paley families. In 1874 a new governing body was set up, one of its members being its old boy, Edmund Sharpe.[119] The following year it appointed a new headmaster, Frederick Heppenstall, under whom the school started to make great strides forward (Fig 3.92). The programme of improvement and enlargement meant a building campaign for which the architects would be Paley & Austin. Nothing is recorded about the reasons for this choice, but we may imagine Sharpe putting in a good word for them, while the partners were without doubt the leading architects in this part of England. At the time they were working at Holker Hall (CuL) for the 7th Duke of Devonshire, father of another governor, Lord Frederick Cavendish, and were extending Underley Hall (CuW), near Kirkby Lonsdale, for yet a third governor, the Earl of Bective.

The existing school buildings and the headmaster's house were extended in 1875–6, a new headmaster's house built in 1877–8, the second master's house in 1877–9, additional classrooms in 1878–9, and a swimming bath and gymnasium in 1884–5. Before his death in 1877 Sharpe seems to have put his experience to good use, for example agreeing in August 1876 to supervise the erection of the master's house and casting his eye over the plans and specifications before the contracts were let. Paley visited the governors to discuss the proposals and so may have been behind the designs; the firm was also sometimes represented by Samuel Wright (1852–1929), who had been articled to the firm and worked in its office for nearly 60 years. In 1881 it was Austin who presented the plans for a swimming bath and gymnasium to the governors. These early works at Sedbergh are modest architecturally, but as the school grew in status (and hence resources) towards the end of the 19th century, the quality of its new buildings also increased, notably the chapel of 1896–7 and the Powell Hall of 1904–6. But these buildings take us into a later period, and one in which E G Paley played no part as he died in 1895. The next chapter picks up the story from 1886, when the practice underwent a further name change to become Paley, Austin & Paley.

Fig 3.91 (above) Whittington Hall, dairy, c 1880. It contains marble shelving and tiled panels of the Four Seasons.

Fig 3.92 Sedbergh (CuWY), Sedbergh School. Entrance for the second master's house, School House.

4

Paley, Austin & Paley / Austin & Paley, 1886–1915

By the middle of the 1880s the Paley & Austin partnership was firmly established as a leading architectural practice in the North West and one whose churches could stand comparison with those of any other architects in the country (Fig 4.1). The next 30 years until the First World War and the death of Hubert Austin in 1915 were prolific ones. Churches still formed the greater proportion of the more important commissions, but as was to be expected from any accomplished provincial architectural practice, there were numerous other works in a wide range of building types and styles. Some of them were very minor indeed. Just as Paley & Austin were not above planning a small extension to a public house for the Furness Railway so, at the start of the 20th century, Austin & Paley could be designing lock-up shops for the local Co-operative Society while, at another drawing board, Hubert Austin might be preparing his design that would be short-listed for Liverpool's new Anglican cathedral.

After Hubert Austin joined the practice in 1867 there was a perceptible shift in the quality

Fig 4.1
Lancaster in the Paley, Austin & Paley years. Winter view by Hubert Austin, 1892, watercolour. It was probably painted from the east side of the River Lune on the area known as the Green Ayre, and shows Skerton Bridge. (Francis Sandison collection)

and variety of the firm's architecture. No such change took place again, despite the entry of Paley's son into the practice in 1886 and E G Paley's death in 1895. Rather, the firm built upon its achievements thus far, with the reputation of the practice resting chiefly on its churches. In the country these were to be some of the firm's loveliest creations, and in the towns, although the pace of building slackened somewhat, especially from the start of the 20th century, many fine churches were also built, including the greatest of them all, St George's, Stockport.

Paley, Austin & Paley

Henry Anderson Paley (1859–1946), known as Harry, was the fifth and last child of Edward Graham Paley and his wife Frances, Edmund Sharpe's youngest sister.[1] Harry had three sisters, Emily, Margaret, and Mary, and also a brother, Edmund, who suffered from Down's syndrome and died young in 1888. Harry's earliest education was no doubt in Lancaster, where he later attended Castle Howell School in Queen's Square before moving in 1873 to Uppingham School in Rutland. He did not go on to university, and on leaving school in 1877 joined the family firm where he was articled until 1881. He then went to the office of T E Collcutt (1840–1924) in London for an 18-month spell to broaden his experience. He passed the RIBA qualifying examination in 1884 and became an ARIBA the following year, having been proposed by his father, Collcutt and the little-known London architect Cole Alfred Adams.[2] Then, in 1886, Harry was made a partner with his father and Hubert Austin.

The practice now became known as Paley, Austin & Paley, although the shorter 'Paley & Austin' was still frequently used. There is no pattern to this: in 1890 a series of illustrations of the firm's work in the *British Architect* are simply signed Paley & Austin. Likewise the original drawings for, say, an important 1890s church at Waterloo outside Liverpool are signed 'Paley & Austin', yet drawings for St George's, Stockport, where Austin is known to have been the man behind the design, are signed 'Paley, Austin & Paley'.[3] Other drawings, too, are signed with the longer title. Just as the name of the practice had some fluidity about it, so too there is usually no way of knowing who was responsible for which jobs. In fact the question probably has little meaning given the likelihood of close and collaborative working arrangements within the office. Certainly Harry Paley's obituary in the *JRIBA* is not to be trusted since, taken by itself, it would have us believe that he was the architect of St George's, Stockport.[4]

Harry Paley, like his father, seems to have been a sociable and gregarious individual with varied interests. His obituary in the *Lancaster Guardian* explained that he was 'keenly interested in field sports, an enthusiastic angler and at one time a very good shot'.[5] It went on to describe his particular pride in a crayon drawing presented to him of a 50lb salmon he landed on a Norwegian fishing trip. A 20lb pike which he caught in the Lune was similarly memorialised. He was a member of the Lune Board of Fishery Conservators, the Lancaster Museum Sub-Committee and the Lancaster Charity Trustees. He became treasurer of Lancaster Cricket Club in 1879–81 and a committee member in 1886–92, and a long-term member of the County Club. As a young man he was a member (along with others in the firm) of the John O'Gaunt Bowmen. He is also said to have been a good photographer and a member of the Lancaster Photographic Society from its inception in 1890. After his death he was remembered as a large, kindly and jovial man who was held in high regard in his native town.

In 1888 Harry Paley married Katherine Margaret Gosselin, the eldest daughter of Major Nicholas Gosselin who held a Home Office appointment in Lancaster from 1884 to 1888 and then returned to London. After residing briefly at Dallas Court in Lancaster, the couple moved to the Manor House at Halton, then to Escowbeck Cottage at Caton, finally settling in 1902 at his father's residence near Brookhouse, 'Moorgarth' in Littledale. They had one daughter Katharine (Kitty) Helena, who never married following the death of her fiancé in the First World War (Fig 4.2). The years after the war when Harry Paley was the sole principal in the firm are dealt with in the next chapter.

The death of E G Paley

It is uncertain just how much work Paley senior was responsible for in the latter years of his life but it would seem clear that the chief creative force in the practice was Hubert Austin (Fig 4.3).

Paley's end came on 23 January 1895 when he died at his Lancaster home, 'The Greaves'. He had been suffering from typhoid fever for 20

Fig 4.2 (right)
Edward Graham Paley and his granddaughter Kitty, October 1891. He died a little over three years later on 23 January 1895. (Austin Family collection)

Fig 4.3 (far right)
Hubert Austin, 1890, photographed by Davis & Sons, Lancaster. (Austin Family collection)

days although the cause for its appearance was, according to his *Lancaster Standard* obituary, not discovered. His place as a well-respected and prominent citizen in the town was recognised by flags being flown at half mast on the Town Hall and other public buildings. He was laid to rest in Lancaster Cemetery. At his death he was a very prosperous man indeed, leaving an estate of £71,939 – far more than any of the other partners. When probate was granted in March, this event and the sum involved were reported in the press as far afield as Huddersfield, Leeds, Liverpool and Manchester.[6] Although being a successful architect would have underpinned his security, such a large sum, which would have made him a multi-millionaire in present-day terms, is surely testimony to a lifetime of wise and profitable investments.

Fig 4.4
Sedbergh (CuWY), St Andrew. New nave seating. The cue for the 17th-century style is work of the period at the church. Similarly, the firm almost always used balusters for the many altar rails they installed in new or restored churches, such detail being usual when altar rails came into common use in post-Reformation churches. (Mark Watson)

The firm's achievements at the end of the 19th century and in the early 20th now need to be described. As in the previous chapter, churches, which formed by far the most significant part of its output, will be discussed first.

Churches

Between 1886 and 1915 the practice built or rebuilt 52 churches and restored or repaired many others.[7] Fifteen of the new and rebuilt ones (including a couple of mission churches) were in villages. Four school chapels were also built, at Sedbergh (CuWY) (twice), the Ripley Hospital, Lancaster, and St Bees (CuC). The urban churches were an extremely varied collection. At the simplest level there were humble mission churches and, at the other end of the spectrum, a series of mighty town churches, mostly in populous parts of industrial Lancashire.

Restoration work and additions also continued although the great age of restoration was largely over (fortunately, some might have said), partly because by the mid-1880s most churches had undergone extensive schemes, and also a less interventionist ethos of the kind promoted by the Society for the Preservation of Ancient Buildings was beginning to hold sway. There were some thoroughgoing schemes such as that at Sedbergh church (CuWY), in 1885–6, where the south aisle and arcade were rebuilt, the galleries removed, and new floors, roofs and fittings installed (Fig 4.4). Similarly extensive work took place at St James, Tatham, in 1886–7, where a £2,800 legacy from William Foster of Hornby Castle (and a desire on the part of his sons to memorialise him) led to much rebuilding, new fenestration, ceiling removal, refitting and reflooring, as well as an east window by Burlison & Grylls and a reredos by Aldam Heaton. At St Margaret's in Hornby itself the nave dated from 1815–17 and hence was ripe for the complete remodelling it received in 1888–9. Other substantial schemes included those at St Andrew, Dent (CuWY), in 1889–90, St Bartholomew, Colne, 1889–91, St Michael, Bootle (CuC), 1890–1, and St Alkelda, Giggleswick (NY), 1890–2. Thereafter there were markedly fewer such schemes, with the only 'thorough restorations' (to use a mid-Victorian phrase) apparently being at St Luke, Farnworth, near Widnes (Me), in 1894–5, St Mary, Mellor, 1897, St Mary, Acton (Ch), 1897–8, and St Margaret, High Bentham (NY), 1901–2. There was still a crop of rebuildings of much-despised churches dating from the 18th and very early 19th centuries, but the medieval work that had survived until the 1890s was unlikely to be at risk. The Catalogue of works at the end of this book is replete with church work from the mid-1880s, but much of it consists of piecemeal schemes or the provision of individual items of furnishings or fittings (*see* Appendix 5).

Village churches of the 1880s

The firm produced only two village churches in the later 1880s. One was St John the Baptist, Pilling, of 1886–7, on flat ground to the south of the Lune estuary with a west steeple forming a landmark from the other side of the river. For a modest village it is a strikingly ambitious aisled structure, costing £7,000. It replaced a building of 1721, and the new church would be entirely at home in a town. Various Paley & Austin motifs are brought into play – arcaded flushwork at various points, chequering on the porch and very inventive tracery in the east window (Fig 4.5). Inside, the chancel arch dies into the responds, the piers are concave-sided, and the woodwork is of a typically high standard. At the east end there is a clerestory on the chancel and a subtle and ingenious architectural treatment with the north and south sides being differently arranged (one arched bay to the north, two to the south), together with imaginative traceried treatment in the sedilia. Pevsner was impressed. 'The fertility of Paley & Austin', he exclaimed, 'remains astonishing.'[8]

Fig 4.5
Pilling, St John the Baptist, 1886–7. Decorated and Perpendicular motifs sit side by side.

The church of the Good Shepherd at Tatham Fells, in deeply rural, hilly country north-east of Lancaster, replaced an earlier building of uncertain date in 1888–9 (Fig 4.6). It is in the tradition established at Finsthwaite (CuL) in 1873–4 of an aisleless church with a strong central tower over the east end of the nave and big buttresses between the nave and chancel. At £1,200, it is a much cheaper building than its predecessor and the simple detailing produces a church suggestive of the 16th century.

Village churches of the 1890s

The 1890s were something of a golden decade for the firm's country churches. The first was St Bartholomew, Barbon (CuW), of 1892–3 (designs 1891), which replaced a church of 1813. There was more money to spend than at Tatham Fells (£3,000, primed by a £1,000 legacy), so here there is a crossing tower of considerable height, and two-bay aisles flanking the eastern parts of the four-bay nave; the tower has quasi-transepts for seating (south) and an organ chamber (north) (Fig 4.7). Internally, the building is a delight (Fig 4.8). The body of the church opens out into the small aisles, and beyond is the crossing, brightly lit from the side. The style is generally Perpendicular detail (by now so often the style of choice for the firm) but mixed with round and pointed arches internally to create a sense of historical evolution.

Fig 4.6
Tatham Fells, The Good Shepherd, 1888–9, a small church for a remote village, with a characteristic, robust central tower.
(Mark Watson)

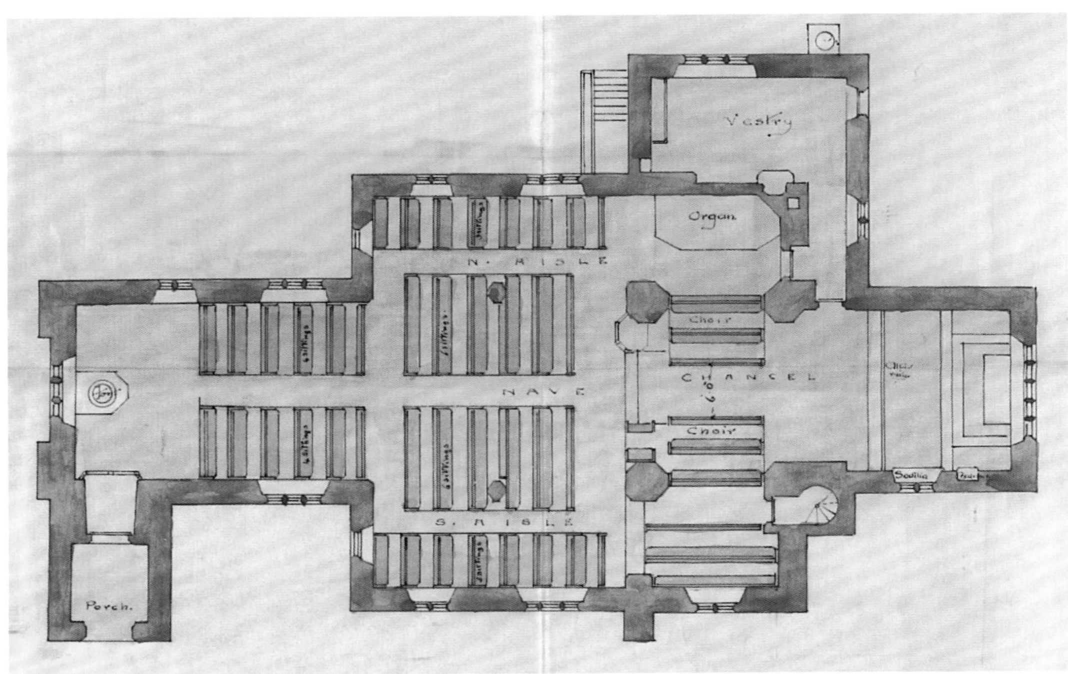

Fig 4.7
Barbon (CuW), St Bartholomew. The firm's church planning was generally fairly conventional, although the short aisles it used (as here) are an interesting variant on the usual and create a modest amount of extra seating and a fine internal effect. Entrances were usually placed in the west bay to make the most efficient use of space. (Lambeth Palace Library, ICBS 09604)

Fig 4.8
Barbon, 1892–3, a delightful village church interior with mixed round and pointed arches and simple but elegant fittings.

There was still more money available for St Peter, Field Broughton (CuL), which in 1892–4 replaced a church of 1745 a mile away (Fig 4.9). The donors were a local family, the Hibberts, and the church was partly intended as a memorial to Harriet Hibbert's late husband. This is one of the firm's very best village churches, and is, as usual, Perpendicular in its details. It has a similar plan to that at Barbon, with a crossing tower (but with a shingled spire), and a nave which is expanded into a small aisle (in this case just one bay) at its east end, in front of the transepts (Fig 4.10). The crossing forms a glorious centre to the church, brightly lit from side windows and yielding complex vistas of arches and half-arches (Fig 4.11). All the arches die into their respective responds, and ornament is employed with the usual restraint, being reserved for points of beauty such as the stall and bench ends (Fig 4.12). The roof is a robust raised tie beam affair and is typical of the strong, reassuring roofs which Paley & Austin deployed in their country churches.

In complete contrast to St Peter's, the year 1894 saw the building of a 150-seater mission church at Sunderland Point (Fig 4.13), a strange and evocative place cut off at high tide from the rest of the peninsula on the north side of the River Lune. Rather less mundane is St Mary, Borwick, a small Perpendicular memorial church of 1894–6 built to a single-cell plan. St Mark, Dolphinholme (Fig 4.14), of 1897–8,

Fig 4.9
Field Broughton (CuL), St Peter, 1892–4, a large country church with a crossing tower and shingled spire.
(Mark Watson)

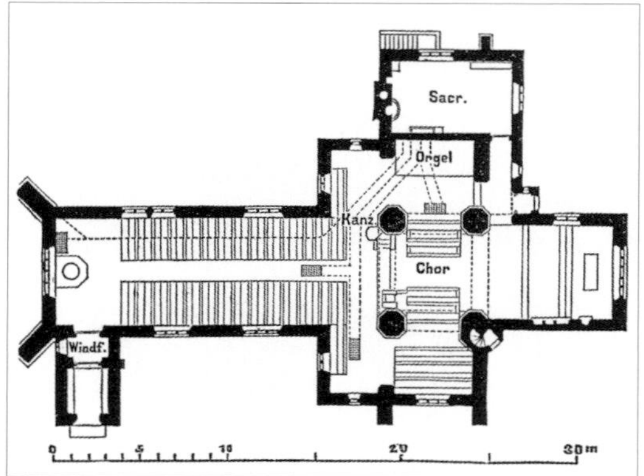

Fig 4.10
Field Broughton, plan whose key feature is the central tower over the choir. The seating south of the crossing and chancel is for children. (Muthesius 1901, 44)

replaced a 'very unsightly' church of 1839–40 at the fairly modest cost of about £3,300. It marks the return to the highly successful formula of a powerful central tower, in this case straddling the choir, with a north aisle to the nave. As usual, the crossing is illuminated by side lighting. Here Austin & Paley play stylistic games, with imaginatively treated tracery in the south windows versus simple square-headed lights in the north aisle, and pointed arches to the crossing versus round arches to the aisle. The nave roof has, once again, massive raised tie beam trusses (Fig 4.15). At Slyne, a rather suburban

Fig 4.11
Field Broughton, the crossing, brightly lit from the side windows and where arches and half-arches create a complex sense of space. The nave has a heavily timbered roof, typical of the firm. (Mark Watson)

Fig 4.12
Field Broughton, bench end, displaying the free, flowing tracery that was a speciality of the firm. (Mark Watson)

village to the north of Lancaster, St Luke's church was built in 1898–1900 with another of the firm's unmistakable central towers, and is also characterised by a large catslide roof over the north aisle which is continued, embracing the tower, over the vestry to the east end.

As the churches at Dolphinholme and Slyne were rising, Austin & Paley were also building St John the Baptist in Flookburgh (CuL), a village close to Holker Hall. In 1872, Lady Lucy Cavendish had described the old church of 1777 as 'a mean conventicle [which] is almost unbearable. It insults the majesty of God.'[9] However, its inadequacies were borne and the insult remained for another 20 years. Then, led by Victor Cavendish, a grandson of the 7th duke (for whom Paley & Austin had rebuilt the state wing at Holker Hall), and his wife Evelyn, a new church was built between 1897 and 1900. The cost was about £12,000, which provided a very substantial building. It is articulated in three main parts – nave, slightly lower choir and an apsidal sanctuary. With its use of 'early' detail in the round-headed windows and massive west tower with saddleback roof, it has a severity which is more akin to Paley & Austin work of around 1870 (Fig 4.16).

Fig 4.13
Sunderland Point, mission church, 1894. This gaunt brick church, on a bleak part of the Lancashire coast, was built at the same time that the firm's greatest building, St George, Stockport, was rising. The Point was very important as an outport for Lancaster about two centuries earlier. (Mark Watson)

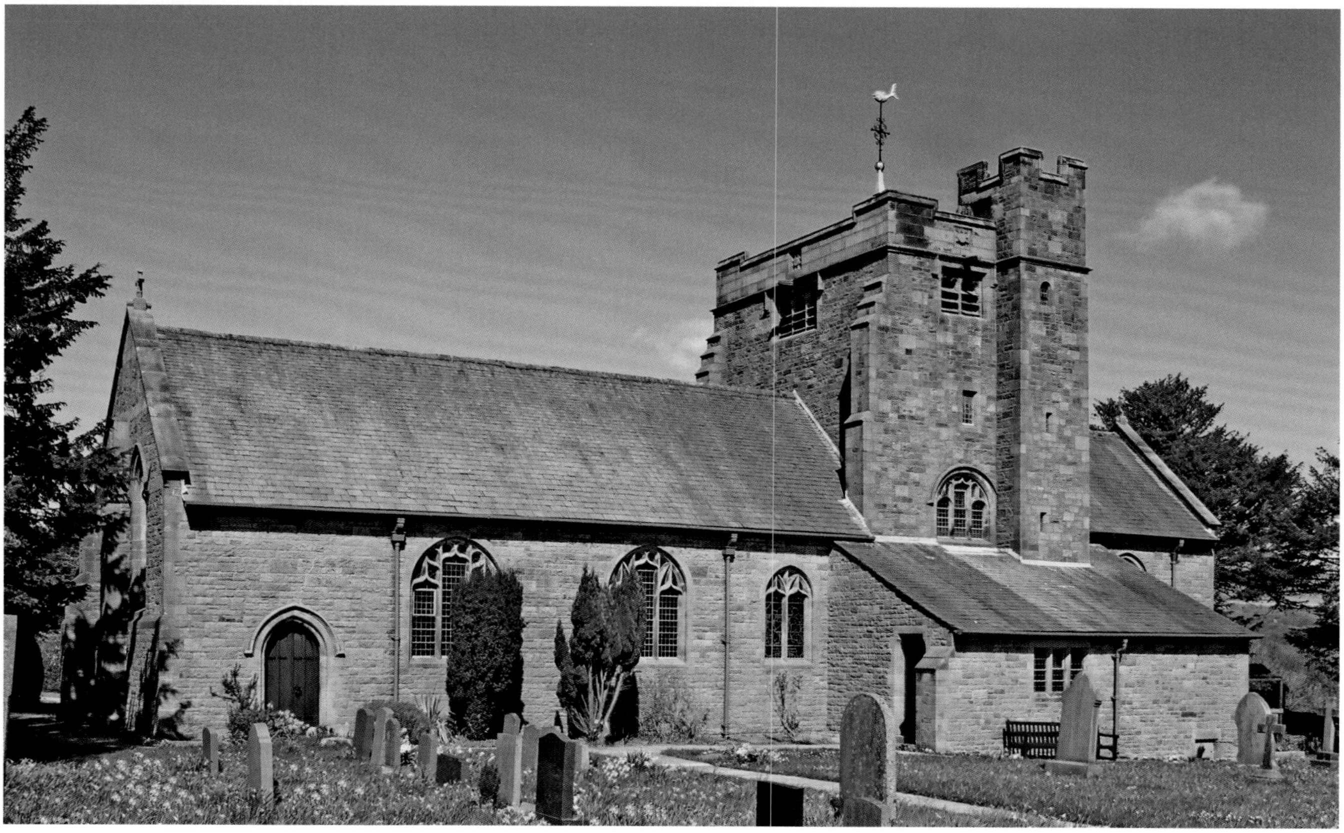

This makes the church rather unusual in the firm's output at this period, as does the use of a semi-circular apse for the first time since St John, Cheetham. The interior at Flookburgh is also rather different from the firm's other late Victorian country churches (Figs 4.17 and 4.18). The aisles cover only the eastern parts of the nave as at Barbon and Dolphinholme, and the strongly defined choir space, while not having a tower over it, reads as if it did, with arches to the east and west.

Fig 4.14
Dolpinholme, St Mark, 1897–8, uses the firm's successful central tower formula and has typically inventive tracery in the windows. (Mark Watson)

Fig 4.15
Dolpinholme: as at Barbon (see Figs 4.7 and 4.8) there is a short north aisle (but no south aisle) and a juxtaposition of round and pointed arches. The nave is crowned by a heavily braced raised tie beam roof which is almost barn-like in character, suggestive of the world of Arts & Crafts architecture.
(Mark Watson)

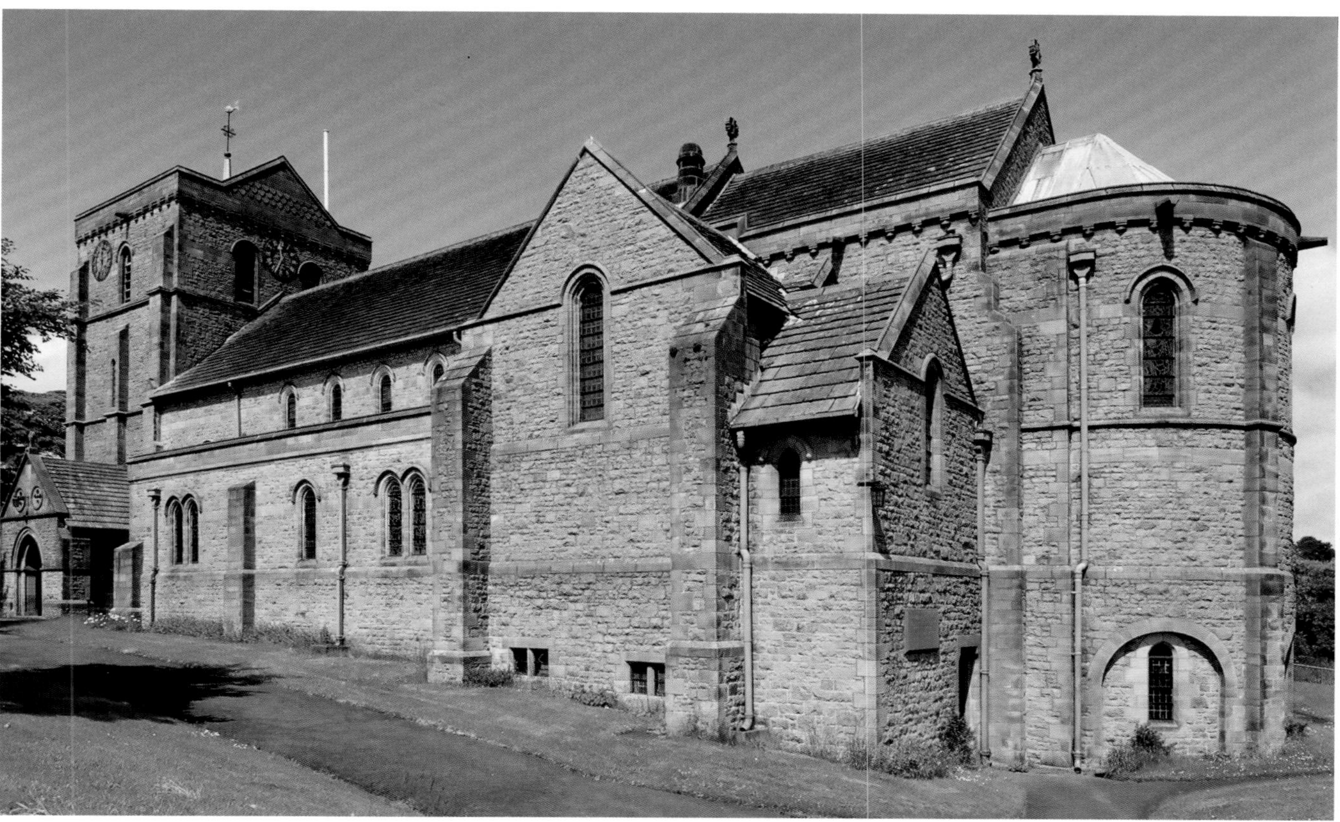

Fig 4.16
Flookburgh (CuL), St John the Baptist, 1897–1900. The muscular detailing with its use of round arches (apse) and early 13th-century lancets is more characteristic of the firm's work at the start of the Paley & Austin partnership. (Mark Watson)

St Oswald, Preesall, across the River Wyre from Fleetwood, was designed in 1896 by Austin, according to a drawing signed by him in the church. Finished in 1899, it is a modest yet very charming building (Fig 4.19). Unlike all the other village churches so far mentioned in this chapter, it is built of brick to which are added sandstone bands. Near the west end a shingled bell-turret straddles the nave ridge. There is a south aisle with concave piers as at nearby Pilling. Unusually, the nave and aisle walls are of brick whereas the chancel is faced with red Runcorn sandstone.

Village churches, 1900–15

No Austin & Paley country churches were built at the start of the 20th century until All Saints, Barnacre, of 1905–6 – a memorial to Thomas Henry Rushton from his wife and children. The building is plain, with late medieval square-headed windows and varying numbers of lights (the south chapel is an addition by Harry Paley in 1937). The one demonstrative feature is the massive, rectangular west tower with its prominent buttresses (Fig 4.20). Over the nave and chancel runs a continuous roof ridge, although an internal division is achieved by means of an arch. The interior is plain to the point of austerity, the one striking feature being a detached mullion to a pair of north windows.

St John, Ellel, replaced a church of 1800 on a different site in 1906–7. It was the last village church with a large central tower to be built before Austin's death (although Harry Paley reused this plan). This one stands over the choir on massive round piers into which the arches die away. A notable feature is the strong asymmetry between the two sides of the chancel and the existence of a clerestory on the north side of the nave but not the south: such asymmetry is a favourite device in the work of the firm. Other features include the oft-used side lighting into the tower space, and the very varied designs for the fenestration.

St Mark, Natland (CuW), like so many other of the firm's country churches, replaced a humble modern predecessor, in this case one of 1825 by George Webster (Fig 4.21). It was another memorial church, this time to William Dillworth Crewdson of Kendal (1838–1908), who had given a substantial amount towards the rebuilding. It was also to be the last major village church before Austin's death and was erected in

Fig 4.17
Flookburgh, looking west. Bare stone walls, simple, chaste furnishings, aisles that do not run the full length of the nave, and a sturdy tie beam roof. The straightforward, baluster altar rails are typical of the firm.

1909–11. So it is fitting to quote Pevsner's admiring judgement: it is, he said 'as good as any of the churches by the best church architects of those years, say Temple Moore'.[10] Similarly, J O Scott and C Hodgson Fowler, who assessed the plans for the Incorporated Church Building Society in 1908, wrote simply: 'Highly approved.'[11] It is, of course, foolish to regard this as a sort of valedictory summing up, since Austin would hardly have intended it to be his last such church! Nonetheless, the building has much that brings together elements of the practice's late church architecture. There is a stout west tower with a higher stair turret, although it is less individual than most Austin & Paley towers. As at Barnacre, the roof runs continuously over the nave and chancel, but inside the two are demarcated by an arch with dying chamfers. The other adjacent arches – which are of varying heights and widths – are similarly treated. Such large round piers were used at Ellel, but in St Mark's they are deployed on a truly monumental scale at the west end as supports for the tower. Austin & Paley devices also include imaginative fusions of Decorated and Perpendicular window tracery, a plain sturdy tie beam roof (to a segmental-shaped ceiling) and beautiful, chaste oak fittings with delicate ornament. But as with all fine architecture, this building is more than the sum of its parts: it exemplifies what the best of the late Gothic Revivalists were striving to do – to build modern churches beautifully in the *spirit* of medieval architecture.

Fig 4.18
Flookburgh, font, which reflects the 12th-century/early 13th-century character of the building: of polished fossiliferous limestone. (Mark Watson)

Fig 4.19
Preesall, St Oswald, completed 1899. A simple, but well-proportioned and well-detailed church of brick plus stone bands, a shingled bell-turret and a break in angle between the nave and aisle roofs.
(Mark Watson)

Fig 4.20 (far left)
Barnacre, All Saints, 1905–6. The massive west tower.

Fig 4.21 (left)
Natland (CuW), St Mark, 1909–11, a simple but refined interior with a combination of arches dying into piers and slim, conventional capitals. The roof is typical of the Austin & Paley years.
(Mark Watson)

School chapels

The Ripley Hospital chapel is, along with the Royal Albert Asylum and Paley's St Peter, one of the firm's three most important works in Lancaster itself (Fig 4.22) and is part of a complex of buildings across the Ashton Road to the north of the asylum. Thomas Ripley, a merchant who traded out of Liverpool and Lancaster, left on his death in 1852 a large sum of money to establish a charitable orphanage and school along the lines of the Bluecoat School in Liverpool, aimed especially at providing for children whose fathers had been lost at sea. His wishes were put into action by his widow, Julia, and building started in 1856 although the school did not open until 1864. The architect was *not* Paley, as might be expected, but a Liverpool man, John Cunningham (1799–1873), who may have been recommended to Mrs Ripley through connections there. She died in 1881, having set up a trust for the school with her quarter-of-a-million-pound fortune. Her trustees used this to develop the school, employing Paley & Austin (& Paley) to make various additions in the mid-1880s, including the entrance lodge. The major work, however, was the chapel, designed in 1884–5 and built in 1886–8, and linked to the school by an arcaded walkway.

Cunningham had used unusual and rather unappealing polygonal stonework to face his building; this was continued by Paley & Austin for the sake of uniformity. The chapel is tall, with high-set windows beautifully fusing Decorated and Perpendicular forms. Below them the walls are enlivened by broad, blind segmental arches. Over the chancel/nave junction is a tall and elegant flèche. What really counts is the interior: beyond the ante-chapel is a long nave with a three-bay south aisle, although, as in some of the firm's parish churches of this time, this does not cover the western third of the nave. The nave is strongly asymmetrical, having an arcade on the south, and blind walling on the north (expressed outside by the segmental arches) below high-set windows. A wall passage runs through the deep reveals of the windows. The chancel stalls are some of the richest woodwork that the practice ever produced (Fig 4.23).

Sedbergh School (CuWY), as explained in the previous chapter, became a regular source of work for the firm from the mid-1870s, and would continue to be so until its very last years. A chapel of sorts already seems to have existed, and in 1890 plans were made to extend it. At first these took the form of a temporary wooden building put up by James Hatch, the Lancaster builder and carpenter who found

Fig 4.22
Lancaster, Ripley Hospital chapel, 1886–8. A grand setting for services in a philanthropic institution. (Mark Watson)

much employment on Paley & Austin projects. However, this hardly befitted a rising public school, and perhaps it was a blessing in disguise when a mighty wind caused much damage to the building in 1893 so that a new one was deemed desirable. The grand, long new chapel rose in 1895–7, at a cost of £7,827 (Fig 4.24). It is lower than that at the Ripley Hospital but shares with it a flèche marking out the division between the nave and chancel. There is something here of the rectilinear forms so much in vogue in the Austin & Paley years – the stepping of the parapet at the east and west ends and the crenellation-like hood over the tall clerestory. This clerestory and the very low aisles form the ruling design features of the interior. The aisles are mere passages, of the kind that were popularised by late Gothic Revival architects and became very common for church-building between the wars.[12] Here Austin & Paley use the device effectively to combine practicality and beauty: the aisles form a fine architectural feature, and also allow rapid access to the seats for the large number of boys who were obliged to occupy them on Sunday mornings and other occasions.

St Bees' School (CuC) had been employing Paley & Austin since 1882 when the practice produced plans for the headmaster's house. The chapel was started in mid-1906 and shares characteristics with both the Ripley Hospital and the Sedbergh School chapels. There are aisles with segmental headed arcading (cf Sedbergh) which covers just the eastern part of the aisles (cf Ripley Hospital). There is also by now an inventive and eclectic mix of detailing with, among other things, round-arched openings in the south aisle, broad mullioned clerestory lights with cushion capitals, and decidedly Art Nouveau hopper-heads. In addition, there is a weighty south-east tower with a transverse saddleback roof which looks as though it could have been at home defending a minor Scottish castle.

Fig 4.23
Ripley Hospital chapel, stalls.
(Mark Watson)

Fig 4.24
Sedbergh (CuWY), Sedbergh School, chapel.
(Mark Watson)

Urban churches of the late 1880s

As for rural churches, Paley, Austin & Paley also found the late 1880s a fairly quiet time for town church commissions, in contrast to the productive years around 1880 and the highly successful 1890s. The most important work was St Mary, Ince-in-Makerfield (GM), of 1887 (Figs 4.25 and 4.26). In its location on the Lancashire coalfield lay the seeds of the church's destruction, since it was demolished in 1978 because of mining subsidence. It belonged to that group of churches represented by Paley & Austin's two Salford churches of 1877–9, and St James, Daisy Hill (GM: 1879–81), being cheaply built of red stock brick yet having real character and individuality.[13] It was strikingly crowned towards the east end by a bell-cote, itself crowned by a tall, slender spirelet. The plan was also very unusual for the firm in having passage aisles divided from the nave by segmental arches, thus forming a precursor (although in a very different church) for the chapel at Sedbergh School.

Fig 4.25
Ince-in-Makerfield (GM), St Mary, 1887 (demolished), a remarkable church in terms of its outlines, passage aisles and landmark bell-cote/ steeple.
(BB77/02421 © Crown copyright.NMR)

St John, Birkdale (Me), was planned in 1888 and built in 1889–90. It is a close derivative of St Barnabas, Crewe (Ch), and is mentioned along with that church in the previous chapter (*see* pp 117–18). Following on from the church at Ince, it helps to demonstrate the diversity and inventiveness of the firm in providing dignified places of worship for a modest outlay.

St John, Cloughfold, in Rawtenstall, dates from 1889–90, the result of the practice winning a competition assessed by Ewan Christian (cf the 'mountain church' competition of 1872). Although it has not been demolished like the Ince church, it has undergone the indignity of

Fig 4.26
Ince-in-Makerfield, interior looking east. A modest budget led to a bare brick interior but the clean lines would not have been out of place in the 20th century.
(BB77/02423 © Crown copyright.NMR)

being turned into a shoe warehouse. Nor was the building ever completed: the north-west tower-cum-porch never rose more than 10 feet from the ground. It is, however, a very typical example of the firm's town churches of the time – large, long and with big late Perpendicular clerestory windows providing a well-lit nave – and belongs to the substantial group of town churches that helped to enhance the firm's reputation in the 1890s. There is not space to describe all of these, so the following are selected and illustrated to highlight the firm's most important works, and to provide a representative view of its output during this important decade.

Rawtenstall, St John, Crawshawbooth, 1890–2

This imposing church was built with substantial funding from a calico printer and quarry-owner, Thomas Brooks (1825–1908; from 1892, Baron Crawshaw), and his wife, and eventually cost nearly £12,000 (Figs 4.27 and 4.28). It is a fine example of the firm's large, late medieval type of building pioneered at St Mary, Leigh (GM), in 1871–3, and at St John, Atherton (GM), in 1878–9. The detailing is Perpendicular, with two clerestory windows per nave bay that together with the large east and west windows create a light interior, faced as so often with red sandstone, in this case from Rainhill (Me). In the angle of the south aisle and transept is an obliquely set porch of the kind favoured by the firm. On the north-east there stands a large, proud tower with massive pinnacles. The interior at the east end is an example of the complexity of planning that we have met previously at, for example, St Peter, Field Broughton (CuL), with arches of varying heights and opening in different directions. The dropping of the sills to the chancel clerestory is a simple but unexpectedly interesting device. St John's also has an early example (probably the first significant case) of what would become a favourite feature for Austin & Paley – carved, black-letter inscriptions. These were usually in Latin, sometimes in English. Here they appear on the outside of the tower and also in the vicinity of the tower inside the church, and are taken from Psalm 148 – the *Laudate Dominum*. Such inscriptions recur on most of the firm's major churches from now on.

Waterloo, Christ Church, 1891–9

In many ways similar to St John, Crawshawbooth, is Christ Church, Waterloo, just to the north of Liverpool, a commission which Paley, Austin & Paley secured after a limited competition had failed to produce an acceptable design. It, too, is a big, grand church and, said Pevsner, 'an outstanding design' (Fig 4.29).[14] The language is very similar to St John's, with a massive north-east tower (rather more elegant than St John's), Perpendicular detailing (as in the inventive tracery), and typical devices such as chequerwork and inscriptions on the tower (*Laudate Dominum* again) (Fig 4.30). The west end has a small canted projection for the font, something unusual in the practice since they did not normally favour western baptistry projections (a feature which had entered the repertoire of Anglican church-building from the

Fig 4.27 (below left) Rawtenstall, St John, Crawshawbooth, from the NE, dominated by the massive tower. (Muthesius 1901, after 44)

Fig 4.28 (below) Rawtenstall, St John, plan. The space south of the tower and chancel is occupied by children's seating. (Muthesius 1901, 44)

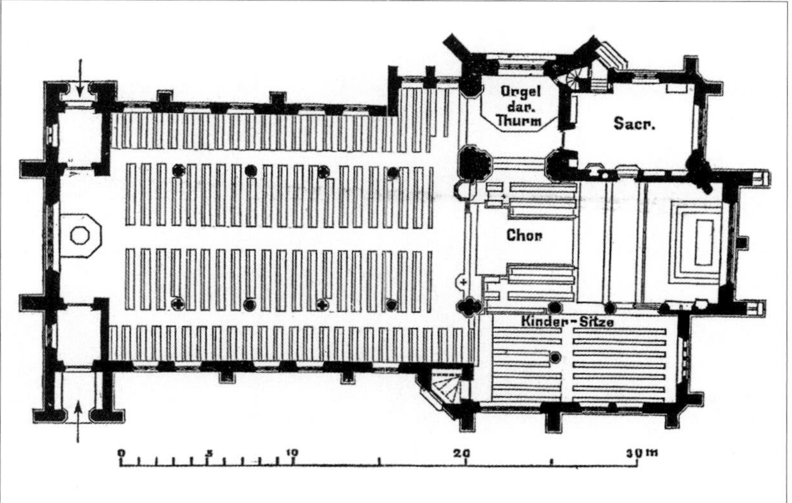

Fig 4.29 (above) Waterloo (Me), Christ Church, from the NW. Although the architectural details are different, the church is planned similarly to that at Rawtenstall. The tower is said to have served as a navigational marker for ships entering the Mersey. (Muthesius 1901, after 44)

Fig 4.30 (above right) Waterloo, Christ Church, the lavishly and ingeniously detailed top to the tower. Gothic letter inscriptions, as here over the belfry windows, were commonly used on the firm's churches from the 1890s. (Mark Watson)

1860s). The interior, now stripped of its fittings following redundancy, has great dignity, and – unusually for the firm – a timber sexpartite vault. On the boundary wall of the churchyard are gate-piers with Gothic tracery designs verging on Art Nouveau, which are mirrored elsewhere in Austin & Paley work (Fig 4.31), as at St George, Stockport (*see* Fig 4.38); similarly, 'almost Art Nouveau' is how the south transept window at All Saints, Sutton, St Helens (Me) of 1891–3, struck Richard Pollard.[15]

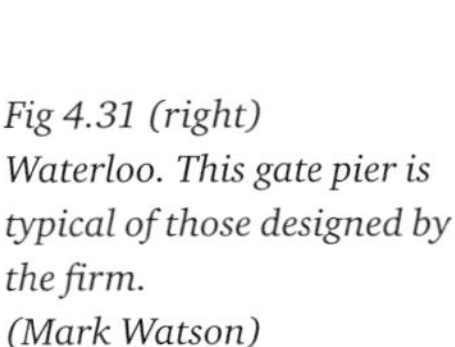

Fig 4.31 (right) Waterloo. This gate pier is typical of those designed by the firm. (Mark Watson)

Hertford, All Saints, a church for the Home Counties, 1893–5 (or, how to choose an architect)

Early on 21 December 1891 the old parish church of Hertford was gutted by fire, leaving only the walls of the nave and the tower standing – and these in a dangerous condition. The replacement which rose on its site was the firm's only new church work in the south of England in its entire hundred-year history. A possible reason will be advanced later, but first it is worth looking at how the selection came about since unusually detailed information is available from the local press.[16]

A vestry meeting quickly voted in favour of an open competition for a new church, and a building committee was set up. However, just before the competition was put in motion, 'one or two gentlemen on the Committee, who had consulted with some architects, [suggested] that it would be better to appoint an architect as assessor'. So an approach was made to the president of the RIBA to suggest three suitable names. One of these was the great James Brooks, who inspected the site in February 1892 and strongly advised against an open competition as 'the best architects would not compete'. They should either get leading church architects to submit portfolios *or* they should simply select one architect. The committee, obviously keen on playing the field, chose the former option.

With great rapidity seven architects were approached and six submitted portfolios which were displayed at the Shire Hall on 8–9 March.[17] Paley, Austin & Paley's work was favoured, beating off a strong field of Blomfield, Bodley & Garner, Jackson, J O Scott, and, strangely it seems, James Brooks & Son.[18] An inspection of the site took place and, although it is not known which of the partners attended, the initial enthusiasm was clearly confirmed: 'the Committee', it was reported, 'formed such a favourable opinion of them that it was thought they should be entrusted with the work of preparing plans'. The firm's appointment was settled at a vestry meeting on 31 March, fund-raising continued apace, and the foundation stone was laid on 25 March 1893. The dedication took place on 20 February 1895 – but without the fifth, western bay of the nave, tower and the aisles flanking it, which had to wait until 1904–5.

Hertford thus received a big-boned, grand Perpendicular building entirely characteristic of the firm, in the mould of others it had built or was about to build in the north-west (Figs 4.32 and 4.33). Typical details included chequer-work, inscriptions below the chancel parapet, exposed ashlar internally, and much intricate and inventive blind tracery in various parts of the building. This incongruous import does not seem to have attracted any criticism at the time, although, seven decades on Pevsner was completely taken aback. It was, he said, 'the penalty of going to a Northerner ... [and] completely alien in Herts'.[19] Not only did the stone (flecked Runcorn sandstone from Weston Point [Ch]) come from the north, but so also did some of the contractors. The main building contract went to Smith Bros of Burnley, who had built St John, Crawshawbooth, while the woodcarving was undertaken by James Hatch & Sons (Fig 4.34). The stone carving went to the large and important Midland firm of Robert Bridgeman & Sons of Lichfield, who had been supplying work to various churches by the practice since the late 1880s.

It is curious that the firm went for this job, since they entered no other church competitions so far from home.[20] It is one of several distant commissions, grouped together in Appendix 4, which often owe their origins to personal

Fig 4.32 (above)
Hertford, All Saints, 1893–5, a large town church typical of the firm's work in the North West but transposed to the Home Counties. The fine tie beam roof can be seen to good effect here.

Fig 4.33 (left)
Hertford, the clerestory and its series of projections and recessions.

Fig 4.34
Hertford, bench end for a corporation seat carved by Hatch & Sons of Lancaster, the carvers most patronised by the firm.

connections. In this case there may even be a touch of old-boy sentiment at work between E G Paley, Christ's Hospital and Hertford. Paley entered Christ's in London back in 1832. It had a 'feeder' school in Hertford, but the school records make it clear that he did *not* go there, although his older brother Edmund did (in 1829).[21] Interestingly, just as the church was being started, Christ's decided to move out of London to the clean, open country near Horsham in Sussex. Paley & Austin entered the competition for the new buildings (*see* Appendix 4).

The abortive bell-tower for Coventry, 1891

St Michael, Coventry, subsequently Coventry Cathedral, was a magnificent late medieval church until bombed in 1940. It enters our story in the mid-1880s amid an intense debate on what to do about the bells and the church's glorious steeple.[22] Essentially there were grave doubts about rehanging the bells in the steeple, which rested on whether this would be sufficiently strong for them to be rung in full peal without considerable (and archaeologically undesirable) reinforcement. An offer from a wealthy solicitor and industrialist, George Woodcock, to pay half the cost of a new bell-tower had encouraged this course of action – an idea which was in fact far from new, having been mooted as far back as 1793.

Fig 4.35
Coventry, St Michael, the proposed bell-tower, drawn by Hubert Austin. It is linked to the church by a passage, cut through by an archway.
*(*The Builder *20 June 1891)*

The matter taxed some of the great names of the day – J O Scott (who was in charge of the steeple restoration), J L Pearson, the fiercesome Lord Grimthorpe and, in 1889, a group of five architects assembled from the Incorporated Church Building Society's panel of Consulting Architects – R H Carpenter, Ewan Christian, James Brooks, J P Seddon and William White. In due course the great Alfred Waterhouse and Norman Shaw were also brought in to advise. A delegation came to Coventry in November 1890 to assess the matter at first hand and soon issued a report which came down in favour of a detached campanile.

The advisers' report also clearly reflected the widespread mistrust within the architectural profession about competitions, suggesting that it would be better to commission an architect of 'undoubted ability and experience'. Exactly what lay behind the choice of Paley, Austin & Paley to supply the design is not known. However, it clearly shows the respect for their work on the part of senior figures in the profession, and must have been based on knowledge of their churches. Their design (Fig 4.35) met with great praise. Reviewing it in March 1891, Ewan Christian thought it 'very beautiful' and Norman Shaw 'admire[d] it exceedingly'.[23] After the plans and specifications arrived in Coventry on 12 May 1891, the *Coventry Standard* printed a euphoric notice and gave the credit specifically to Austin:

> Of the loveliness of the conception there can be no question. It is an inspiration, bridging over all the difficulties of site and surroundings, pure in style, and harmonising most completely with the existing group of buildings ... and yet characterised by freedom and originality of treatment ... Mr. Austin, for it is no secret that to him the credit belongs ... has produced a design which cannot fail to remove the anxiety of those who were fearful lest an inharmonious structure should be erected.

But on 18 May, the very day the plans went on show to the public, tragedy struck. George Woodcock died after a brief illness. His £200,000 estate went to his widow, and, although she offered £5,000 to the parish to use as it saw fit as a memorial to her husband, enthusiasm for the bell-tower evaporated. Finally, in 1895, the bells were rehung in the old steeple, where they were chimed rather than rung. They were recast in 1927 and, having survived the war, were finally rehung for ringing in 1987 in a new chamber some 50ft from the ground.

The failure to build the tower is significant in two ways. First, it meant Coventry was denied what would have been a very fine landmark building. Second, had it been built the Paley & Austin name would have become much better known. In 1918 St Michael's became Coventry Cathedral, which was destroyed, apart from the steeple, in 1940, and a new building on an adjacent site was built between 1955 and 1962 amid enormous public interest. Had it survived the Blitz, as it probably would have done, the bell-tower could have become part of the potent story of the destruction and rebirth of Coventry and the reconciliation that was associated with it. However, the design remained on paper, although something of its character pervades the next commission from much the same time.

Stockport, St George, Heaviley, 1892–7

St George's is the largest, grandest and most expensive church the practice ever built and is the masterwork of Hubert Austin (Figs 4.36, 4.37, 4.38 and 4.39). Built between 1892 and 1897 in a sharp angle between the Buxton Road and Bramhall Lane, it is one of the largest and greatest of all Victorian churches. There is no doubt that Hubert Austin was its creator. It was he who dealt with the trustees from the outset in 1890, and it is he who is given credit for the building in a relief inscription at the west end. It is also his name that appears as the designer on the Raffles Davison drawings exhibited at the Royal Academy in 1897, even though they were shown officially under the Austin & Paley name. It must have been a very special and moving experience for this deeply religious man to erect such a magnificent building to the glory of his God: his gift of the holy table in 1897 surely symbolises a very personal involvement.[24]

The project originated in a dispute over churchmanship.[25] The Revd Arthur Symonds became rector of St Thomas, Stockport, in 1887 but his High Church practices offended the more Evangelical members of his congregation. In 1890 four men, with the requisite money or enthusiasm, resolved to do something about it and in March the following year they secured approval from the Bishop of Chester, Francis Jayne, for a new parish. These four founding trustees were Wakefield Christie-Miller, a landowner and property developer (by then living in London); Arthur Sykes, a close relative of Christie-Miller's, a former mayor, and partner in the family bleachworks; Robert Green, manager of the huge Christy hat factory in the town (who also looked after Christie-Miller's affairs in Stockport); and finally a former churchwarden at St Thomas', Major George Fearn (1845–1911) (Figs 4.40 and 4.41), 'Major' being an honorary title conferred in 1887 after 27 years of volunteer service with the 4th Stockport Rifles. Christie-Miller gave the site, but the building work, which also included schools and a vicarage, was funded by Fearn, whose fortune came from Bell & Co's Hempshaw Brook Brewery, where he was both a partner and manager.[26] He was a man of obsessive modesty, so much so that he did not even attend the consecration in 1897, and certainly was uncomfortable (though maybe secretly pleased!) with the dedication insisted upon by his fellow trustees. His name is said not to have been revealed until after the consecration service. Fearn's decision to build the church (and associated buildings) may have been prompted by the death of his father in 1886 and his mother in 1888. The tenders accepted in November 1891 amounted to £41,372 for the church alone, and the whole project, with the schools and vicarage, is said to have come to nearly £80,000.

The trustees' minute book records how in December 1890 they looked over 'plans &c of Churches built by Messrs Paley & Austin', having been recommended to do so by solicitors Parry, Gammon & Farmer who advised the bishop.[27] Fearn wanted a building on a grand scale, insisting on seating for 1,200 when the bishop thought that 1,000 would suffice. The trustees also insisted on the very best Runcorn stone. Contracts were awarded to separate trades, the largest being that for the mason's work, taken by W Thornton of Liverpool for £31,300. A Clerk of Works, John Hindmarch, was appointed in January 1892 when the ground works began.[28] It was over a year before the foundation stone was laid in March 1893 by Lord Egerton with full Masonic ritual (cf the Royal Albert Asylum). Much of the work was finished in 1895, with the spire being completed in September that year – at 230ft it is the tallest in the Manchester area. Consecration by Bishop Jayne eventually took place on 25 February 1897.

St George's is built on an epic scale with the full panoply of aisles, crossing tower (over the choir), and transepts, the northern one of which takes in half of the north chapel. The latter must not be envisaged in a High Church context, but rather as a morning chapel, something that became acceptable to Anglicans generally towards the end of the 19th century for small services. Side chapels such as this had became detached from the notion of Popery, as had the building of a such a magnificent church, something that would have aroused Protestant suspicions 50 years before. Now, at St George's, despite its staunchly Protestant origins, it was possible to depict the Virgin and Child on a stall end, while other saints and angels feature there too (Fig 4.42), as they do on the reredos (although the strong message of the latter is of redemption through Christ).[29]

Architecturally, St George's synthesises everything in the firm's mature style for urban churches such as late, freely treated Gothic, yet rooted firmly in the Perpendicular; 'squared-off', rectilinear forms; very rich tracery; relief inscriptions; chequerwork; and the spacious character of the interior, which was a hallmark of its large town churches. The use of detached internal mullions for the east window is a fine device previously used for the first time by the firm in the completion of St John, Atherton, 1892 (although, of course, Austin may already have had St George's in mind). Over the chancel there is stone vaulting, which they had sometimes used when money was available (eg St Michael, Howe Bridge, Atherton, 1876). The crossing space is side-lit and the clerestory is extended to the east end. In the nave there are two clerestory lights to each bay below

Fig 4.36 (opposite) Stockport (GM), St George, 1892–7. Hubert Austin's perspective, reproduced from Academy Architecture. *(*Academy Architecture *1897(i), 39)*

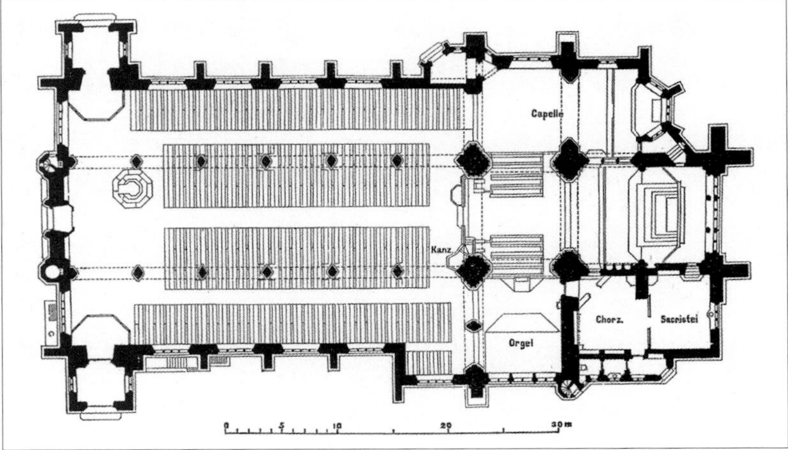

Fig 4.37 (above) Stockport, plan. North of the crossing and chancel is a chapel: the organ is placed in the south transept, and south of the chancel is a pair of vestries. Like other major PA&P churches, the plan is quite conventional and the church depends for its majesty upon its noble scale, fine proportions and careful detailing. (Muthesius 1901, 45)

Fig 4.38 Stockport, interior shortly after the opening. (BL14814a English Heritage. NMR)

and, internally, the reveals of the clerestory are opened up by wall passages. As Figure 4.38 shows, these, along with the panelling in the arcade spandrels, the complex section of the piers, the multiple mouldings of the arches (the outer orders of which die before reaching the capitals) and the panelling on the crossing piers (later used at St Mary, Widnes, 1908–10), create a display of great richness yet a calm majesty.

St George's has always had its admirers. Just four years after its consecration, as we shall see,

Fig 4.39
Stockport, the richly decorated south porch. The gate-piers are similar to those at Waterloo (see Fig 4.31).
(Mark Watson)

it was greatly praised in Hermann Muthesius's survey of recent English church-building. In 1956, when Victorian architecture was generally still deeply unfashionable, Cecil Stewart, in his *The Stones of Manchester*, could praise it thus: 'The whole is a beautifully worked out composition: refined and perfect ... It provides a suitable finale to the Gothic Revival in Manchester.'[30] In one of his later Buildings of England volumes (*Cheshire*, 1971), it was for Pevsner 'even nationally speaking, a masterpiece', although he tempered this with a slightly sour 'of the latest historicism, designed just before the most original younger architects began to turn away from the strict Gothic Revival'.[31] A further 40 years on it is still an astonishing work. St George's recaptures the spirit and grandeur of major late medieval town churches, reinterpreted with originality and complete naturalness for a leading industrial town at the end of the 19th century. It is as magnificent as anything the Gothic Revival ever achieved.

Fig 4.40
The grave of George Fearn (died 1911) is marked by a version of the spire at the church he paid for. It is thought to have been designed by Hubert Austin. (Mark Watson)

The last Victorian town churches

There are too many other churches by the practice in the prolific 1890s to treat all of them in detail, so some general comments with examples must suffice. By this time all the elements of the firm's church architecture were in place, and were being deployed with enormous facility. If there were such a thing as a typical late church, it would be on the lines of All Saints', Hertford, although perhaps not quite so large – in other words Perpendicular in style, with a prominent clerestory, aisles, ample provision for vestries and an organ chamber, perhaps a morning chapel, and a tower, probably at the west end, but perhaps to one side or over the choir. The different arrangements either side of chancels sometimes led to markedly asymmetrical elevations. Naves and chancels sometimes had continuous rooflines, although the division internally would be clearly demarcated; sometimes the chancel apex was stepped down from the nave. Externally, squarish, 'blocky' geometry and large, square-headed windows were often in evidence. Square panels with pierced or blind tracery (as pioneered at St Mary, Leigh (GM), at the start of the 1870s, *see* Fig 3.27) were a stylistic hallmark, as were other details such as chequerwork, and doorways set obliquely across angles in the building. Although red brick might be used for cheapness, the material of choice was, ideally, red sandstone which would be left bare internally. Roofs were usually robust tie beam structures but were not highly decorated. Furnishings often displayed inventive treatment of tracery and other decoration: fonts might be 'blocky' in form and thus stylistically related to the external architecture.

Such generalisations are immediately subject to exceptions, and one such is the church of St Matthew, Highfield in Wigan, built in 1892–4 as a memorial to Beatrice Blundell (d 1884) by her husband, Henry (1831–1906), owner of the Pemberton Collieries, and Conservative MP for Ince to 1892 and again from 1895. Very unusually for a work by the partners at this time, it is in an Early English style and thus of a very different character from churches like those at Waterloo or Hertford, and more akin to the strong Paley & Austin designs of the 1870s. The north side is treated like some of the firm's village churches, with an aisle which flanks just the eastern parts of the nave.[32] There is a variety of good furnishings and fittings, for example the sedilia have trefoiled heads to accord with the 13th-century character of the architecture. Although this was a memorial church, funds may well have been tight since it was not designed until seven years after Beatrice's death and completion did not take place until 1909–10, by which time Henry too had died.

Fig 4.41
Major George Fearn. (St George's Parochial Church Council; Mark Watson)

Fig 4.42
Stall ends designed for St George's, Stockport, in the James Hatch & Sons workshop in Lancaster, awaiting delivery. (Album of photographs of work by Hatch & Sons, private collection; Mark Watson)

Two fine churches from the mid-1890s are St Mary Magdalene, Alsager (Ch), of 1894–6 (but design by Austin, 1884), and St Silas, Blackburn, of 1894–8. The former, where the chancel is lower than the nave, remains incomplete, since its western steeple, embraced by the aisles, never rose above the nave. It has a fine east window, combining Perpendicular mullions and reticulated tracery, and the south chapel, by means of its tall, square-headed windows (Fig 4.43), contrasts with the rest (with its pointed lights). The assured interior is typically light and spacious, and has arches which die into their piers (Fig 4.44). The font is an angular piece which, while Gothic, owes almost nothing to the Middle Ages and is typical of the kind of design the firm applied to such fittings at this time (Fig 4.45). The Blackburn church was more fortunate, in that its massive west tower (minus the originally intended spire) and south-west porch were eventually completed, albeit in a second building campaign in 1913–14. Here too the aisles flank the tower. This combined with the lack of a clerestory mirrors Paley & Austin's work in the rebuilding of St Mary, Dalton-in-Furness (CuL), 10 years earlier (*see* Fig 3.41). The south chapel has striking tall, square-headed windows which closely resemble those at Alsager. At the east end of the chapel is a stair turret with a stone spirelet (Fig 4.46), a feature occasionally found at other of the firm's churches. St Silas's is an interesting case of how reactions to buildings can vary. Pevsner was downbeat about it, remarking that it displayed Paley & Austin's 'seriousness and dignity but nothing of their spatial ingenuity'.

Fig 4.43 (left)
Alsager (St), St Mary Magdalene, 1894–6, tall, elegant square-headed windows in the south chapel. (Mark Watson)

Fig 4.44 (below)
Alsager, a spacious urban interior. As so often with the firm's later churches, the arches have no capitals. (Mark Watson)

Fig 4.45 (below left)
Alsager, the blocky sandstone font. (Mark Watson)

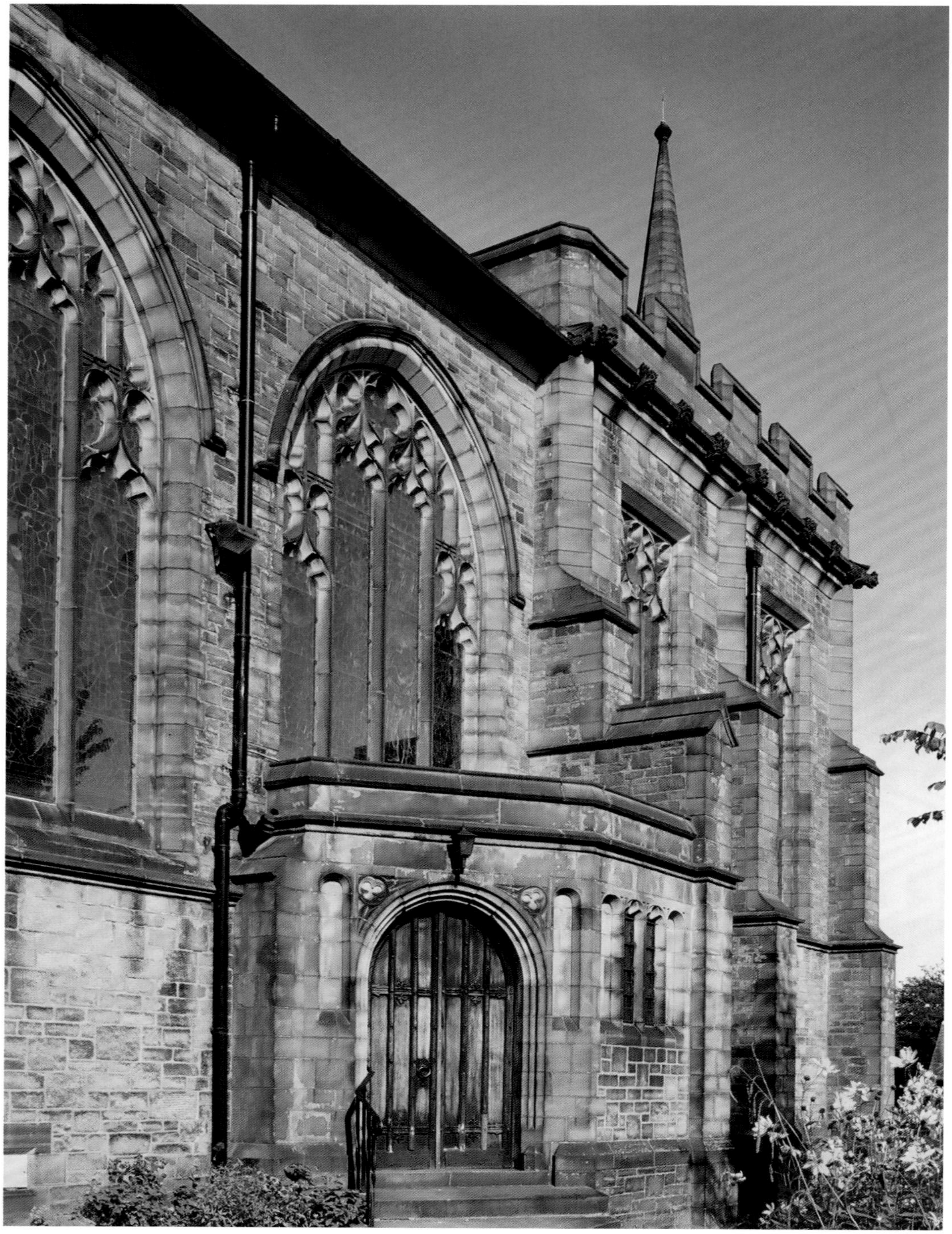

Fig 4.46
Blackburn, St Silas, 1894–8, south aisle and chapel. (Mark Watson)

Fig 4.47
Blackburn, St Silas, foundation stone, 1894, typical of the design used by the firm at this time. (Mark Watson)

However, more charitably (and rightly so), Pevsner's reviser, Clare Hartwell, says of the interior that 'the effect is one of spaciousness, nobility and grandeur imparted by the handling of the proportions'.[33] The east end bears a foundation stone of typical design (Fig 4.47).

There were to be several other town churches in the concluding years of Victoria's reign. St Barnabas, Morecambe, of 1898–1900, remained incomplete, lacking two bays of the nave and the west tower (which was meant to be embraced by the aisles), the south aisle not being built until 1913 (Fig 4.48). As at St Silas, Blackburn, there is no clerestory, and again the chapel is distinguished from the rest by square-headed windows. Another Morecambe church built at the same time was St John the Divine, Sandilands, 1898–1901, which like St Barnabas is Perpendicular but with a crossing tower which, with the intended spire, has remained unfinished. St Anne, Hindsford, Atherton (GM), of 1898–1901, is an aisled church without a clerestory. It presents its north elevation to the road, and has rather wilful massing with a low, chunky tower (with a chapel below) squeezed in the angle between the transept and chancel. Much use is made of tall, square-headed windows. The church was converted into flats in 2003–4. Very unusual among Austin & Paley's churches from this time for the use of materials is St Thomas, Lytham St Anne's, of 1899–1900 (Fig 4.49). It is built of fiery red brick (no doubt suggested by its widespread use in local housing), with extensive displays of contrasting buff stone. It was won in competition in 1892 but progress was slow. The first campaign omitted the two west bays of the nave and the north-west tower (with an odd and ungainly recessed top stage), which is linked by a passage to the second bay of the north aisle. Another, cheaper brick church is St Alban, Altrincham (Ch), of 1900, where the east end and two bays of the nave were the only parts built. Its distinguishing feature is the large bell-cote facing east on the north side (Fig 4.50).

Hermann Muthesius and *Die neuere kirchliche Baukunst in England*

The German architect Hermann Muthesius (1861–1927) came to England as a cultural attaché in 1896 to report on the architectural scene. The most famous result was his survey of domestic architecture, *Das englische Haus*, published in 1904, the year he returned to Germany. He also made a study of church-building, and in 1899 and 1900 placed before his German readership an in-depth series of essays on modern churches in the *Zeitschrift für Bauwesen*. These were republished with extra text and illustrations in Berlin in 1901 as a book, *Die neuere kirchliche Baukunst in England*. The research must have been conducted at a busy pace and was no doubt much dependent on what material was readily available. Hence there are omissions, such as a work by Temple Moore and J T Micklethwaite, and he also came to a conclusion which saw J L Pearson towering above all others in his pantheon.[34] Magnificent architect that he was, it is questionable whether modern architectural history would place him so easily above what was evidently a second tier. This consisted of Bodley (& Garner), James Brooks, J D Sedding, Norman Shaw, G G Scott junior – and Austin & Paley.[35]

Fig 4.48
Morecambe, St Barnabas, as intended and illustrated in the British Architect, *1893. Partially built 1898–1900. There are vestries at the east end and a chapel north of the chancel. The tower is flanked by entrance spaces as, for example, at St Mary, Dalton-in-Furness, some years before.*
*(*British Architect *40, 1893, after 112)*

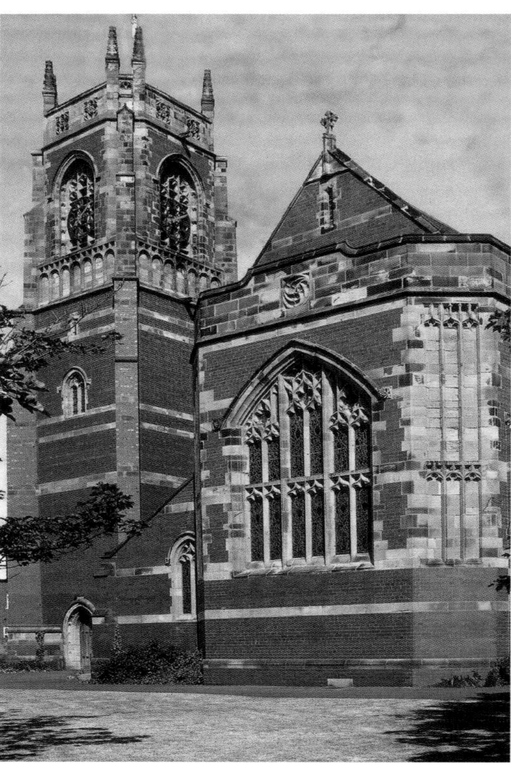

Fig 4.49 (right)
Lytham St Anne's, St Thomas, 1899–1900, west end, with a tower/porch linked to the north aisle and a canted projection at the west end of the nave.

Fig 4.50 (far right)
St Alban, Altrincham (Ch), 1900. Only the eastern parts were built, including a large, slender bell-cote of the kind favoured by the firm.
(Mark Watson)

Whatever its idiosyncrasies may be, Muthesius's book is a perceptive one and there is no doubt that he rated Austin & Paley's work very highly indeed. His admiration for Paley's St Peter's in Lancaster has already been noted and, in all, he illustrated no fewer than eight of the firm's churches, the same number as for Brooks and twice as many as for Pearson himself.[36] Having just discussed the church work of James Brooks, he puts Austin & Paley's work on a par with it but notes that it is entirely different (*grundverschieden*) from it. This is perhaps an odd point to make, since the early Paley & Austin churches (which are illustrated by Betws-y-Coed and one of their mountain church designs) have a toughness which is very apparent in Brooks's output. Muthesius draws attention to the excellence of their village churches and notes the characteristic placing of a tower over the choir. He refers his readers to the illustrations to appreciate the quality of the firm's work, and does not single out buildings, other than the recently completed and splendid (*prachtvolle*) St George, Stockport. Having made such an impression on such an important commentator as Muthesius, it is not surprising that Austin & Paley were also able to make a mark on the most important church competition of the 20th century.

Liverpool Cathedral – a second attempt

The start of the 20th century saw the resurrection of plans to build a new Anglican cathedral in Liverpool. These had foundered in the 1880s, owing, as the *Building News* put it bluntly, to a 'lack of funds and enthusiasm'.[37] The scheme was revived in 1901 for a different site, St James's Mount, where the cathedral stands today. In the autumn of that year architects were invited to submit anonymous portfolios of their work, not necessarily including designs specific to the new cathedral. The *Building News* had its reservations about such a process, arguing that 'designs for parish churches, colonial and other cathedrals, do not furnish sufficient evidence of the author's skill to design an edifice worthy of our age'.[38] The deadline, set initially for December, was soon extended to 30 June 1902, and two highly eminent assessors, Richard Norman Shaw and G F Bodley, were appointed. Between July and September they sifted through 103 entries, 33 of which were specific to the project. They drew up a shortlist of five to produce designs – Austin & Paley, Charles Nicholson, Walter Tapper, Malcolm Stark (a relatively little-known Scot)[39] and the 22-year-old Giles Gilbert Scott, who was already being tipped 'in well-informed quarters' as the likely winner even as the designs hung on display in the Walker Art Gallery in May 1903.[40]

The award to Scott (who, on account of his youth and lack of experience, was obliged to work with the veteran Bodley) was generally applauded; but it deprived Austin & Paley of the commission for the cathedral for a second time, the firm having previously lost out in the 1880s competition (*see* pp 118–9. Its design (Figs 4.51, 4.52, 4.53 and 4.54) – in reality, by Austin[41] – received a mixed reception in the architectural press. A 'design of remarkably fine proportion in plan and skilful draughtsmanship', opined the *Building News*.[42] It admired the width of the nave, which, at 62ft, was 12ft

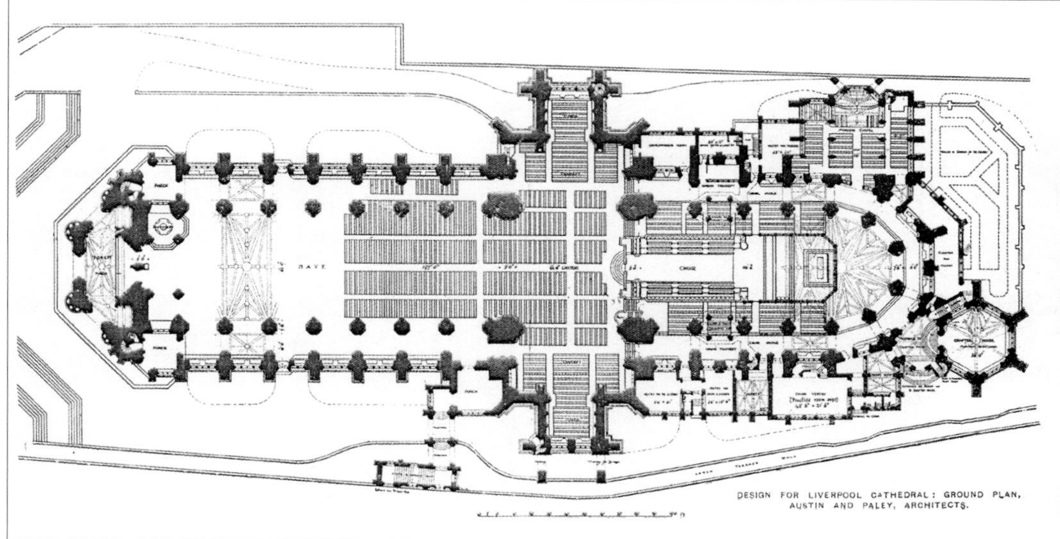

Fig 4.51 (below left) Liverpool Cathedral competition. The plan for Austin & Paley's entry reproduced in the Builder's Journal, *1903.* (Builder's Journal & Architectural Record *17, 1 July 1903)*

Fig 4.52 (below) Liverpool Cathedral, the north elevation displaying a marked increase in richness towards the east end. This drawing shows how the central dome would have been rather obscured by the transept towers but it displays Austin's ease at working with late medieval architecture on a very grand scale. (Builder's Journal & Architectural Record *17, 1 July 1903)*

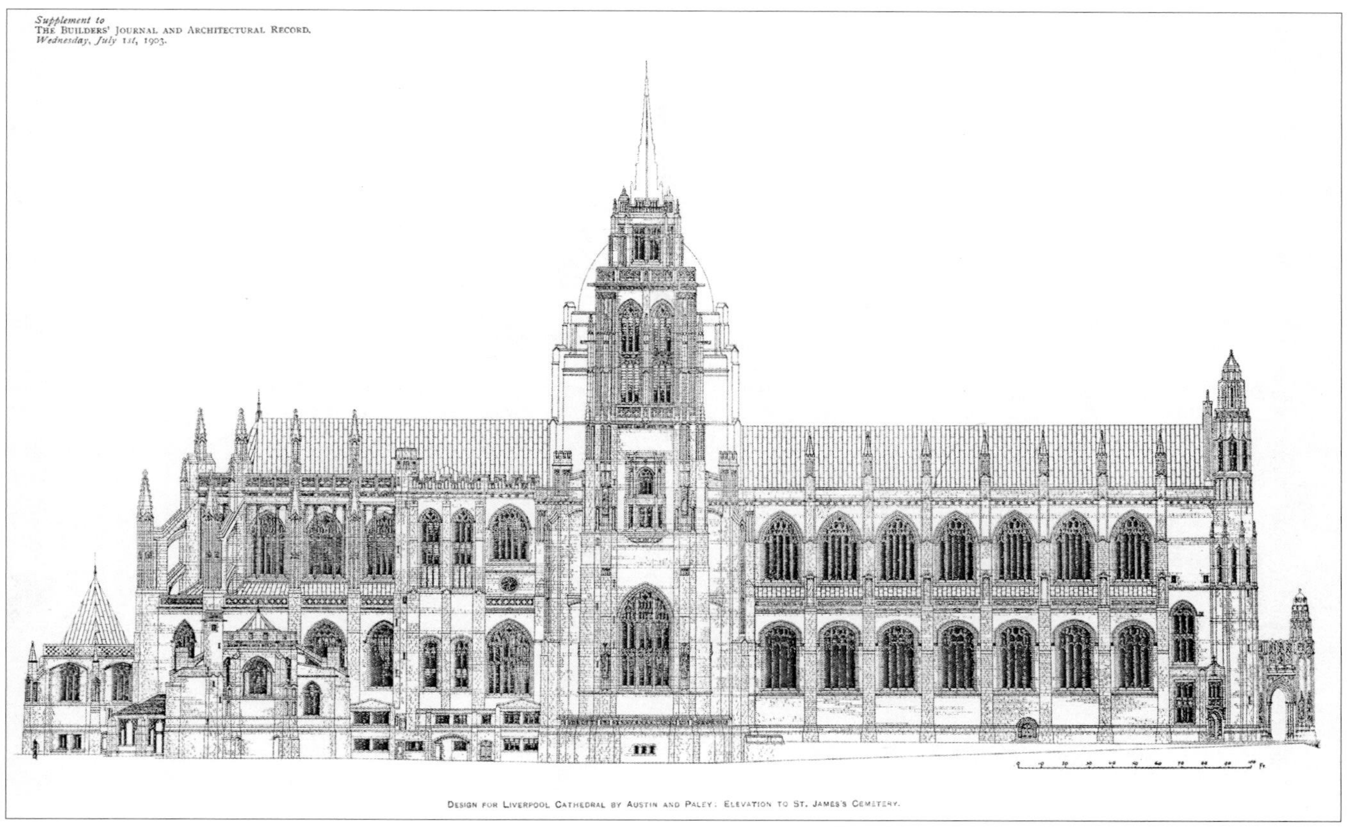

wider than Scott's. But there the favourable comparisons ceased, with the lower height of Austin's nave (105ft against Scott's 114ft) giving 'a wider and less dignified proportion to the church'. The real problem with the Austin & Paley design, which was rightly picked up not only by the *Building News* but also by *The Builder* and the *Builders' Journal & Architectural Record,* was the relationship of the tall transept towers which competed with the domed crossing. The *Builders' Journal* was much more critical than the *Building News*, also stating that in 'the detail there is great monotony and want of effective proportion'. Nor, taking what seems a rather old-fashioned argument in the early 20th century, did it like 'the hidden-iron-girder construction ... [which] seems ... singularly out of place as not conforming to the construction which prevailed in Gothic times, which would seem to be desirable in the case of a design based upon medieval detail'.[43] The writer felt, rather harshly, that this was a magnifying up of parish church work, and recalled the firm's Stockport church 'with greater pleasure'.

*Fig 4.53 (above) Liverpool Cathedral, Austin's sketch of the projected building from the north-west showing the relationship of the transept towers and central dome when viewed obliquely. (*British Architect *59, 1903, after 556)*

Fig 4.54 (right) Liverpool Cathedral, Austin's sketch of the vista across his great crossing towards the south-west. His signature appears in the bottom left-hand corner. (British Architect 59, 1903, after 556)

Town churches, 1901–15

Austin & Paley's urban church commissions continued unabated down to the First World War. New and rebuilt churches varied in scope, including a basic mission building in Lancaster in 1906–7 and several replacements for earlier, smaller and humbler buildings, as with St Michael, Middleton (GM), in 1901–2, and St Mary, Walney Island, Barrow (CuL) (Figs 4.55 and 4.56), of 1907–8 which took the place of a Sharpe & Paley church of 1852–3. There were also new churches beyond the inner suburbs as with St Andrew, Starbeck, Harrogate (NY) (Figs 4.57 and 4.58), in 1909–10 and St Margaret, Halliwell, Bolton (GM) (Fig 4.59), of 1911–13.

The churches mentioned, and others of the period, do tend to display the distinction to be expected from the drawings boards of Austin & Paley. They do not, however, require the particular attention which is needed for the firm's last two major urban churches. St Michael & All Angels in Ashton-on-Ribble, a middle-class suburb of Preston, was started in 1906–8 when the eastern end and part of the nave were built. The west end followed in 1915, but the south tower remained unbuilt. The building is very much in the Austin & Paley tradition, but the east end introduces the device of canted corners to the sanctuary, which has a flat, parapeted roof projecting beyond the gable over the main body of the chancel (Fig 4.60). Inside, below this gable, is an arch to the sanctuary. This therefore looks like a normal chancel arch but placed further east. Where

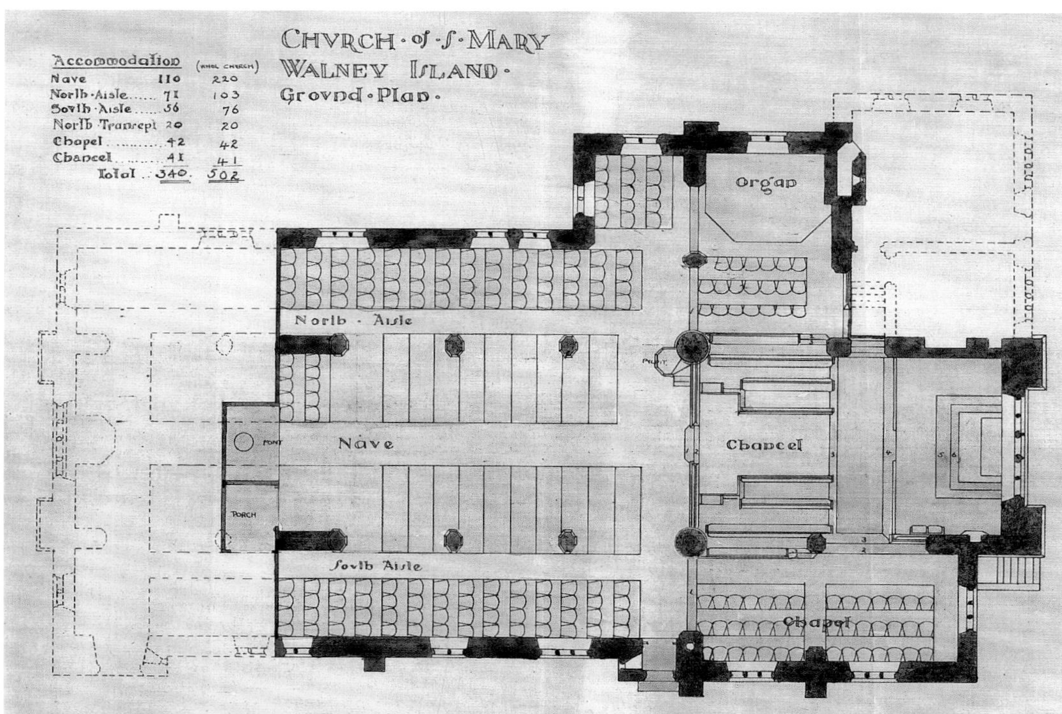

Fig 4.55
Barrow-in-Furness (CuL), St Mary, Walney Island, 1907–8 (plan by A&P, 1911). The dotted areas were not completed until 1930–1. (Lambeth Palace Library, ICBS 10737)

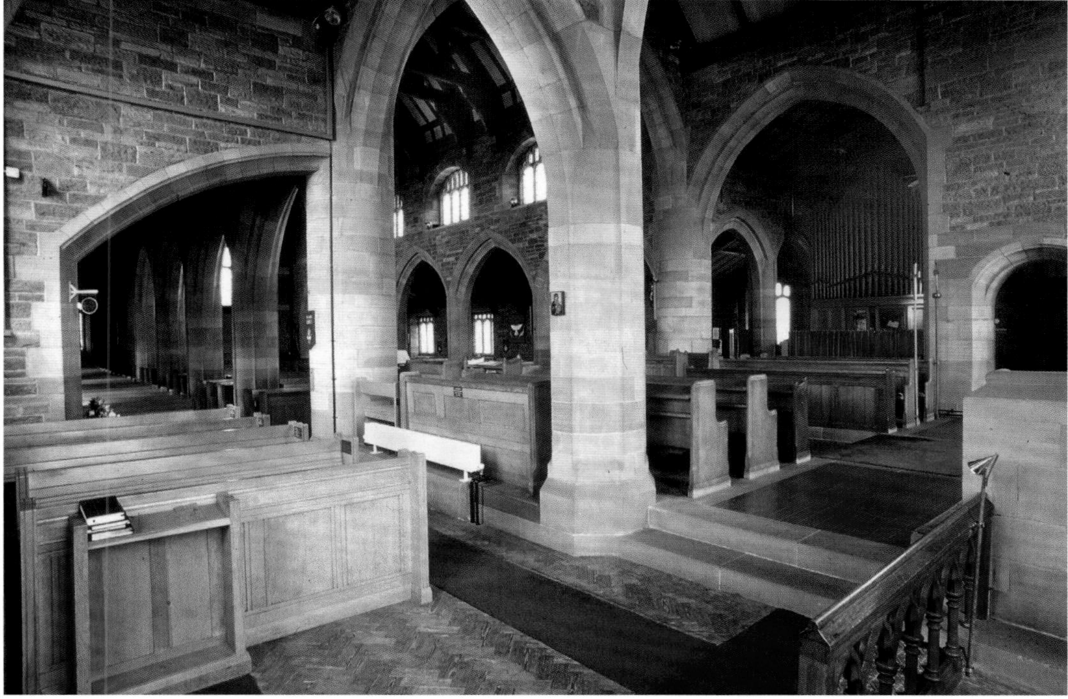

Fig 4.56
Walney Island. The numerous arches and their different forms in the area of the crossing create a sense of spatial complexity. View looking north-west from the south chapel.

the chancel arch should be are panelled responds (cf the crossing arches at Stockport), crowned on each side by a canopied (unoccupied) niche. The canted east end/projecting sanctuary arrangement was also used at St Wilfrid, Newton Heath, Manchester, an urban mission church founded by Rossall School and built in 1909–10.

The last great church masterpiece by Austin & Paley was St Mary, West Bank, Widnes (Me) (Figs 4.61 and 4.62), built in 1908–10 to replace one of 1858 on a different site. The main benefactor was Thomas Sutton Timmis, a soap manufacturer, who, with his six children, gave £8,000 towards the total cost of £16,669. Sutton Timmis's business associate F H Gossage, of the firm of William Gossage & Sons, gave a further £4,000. The commanding west tower, embraced by the aisles, is a major landmark beside the Mersey. Built (inevitably in this area) of pink sandstone, the church has many of the Austin & Paley hallmarks, combined

Fig 4.57 (right)
Harrogate (NY), St Andrew, Starbeck, 1909–10, with bell-cote and canted west end.
(Mark Watson)

Fig 4.58 (far right)
Starbeck. Detached mullions adds to the visual complexity and the light and shade.
(Mark Watson)

Fig 4.59 (below)
Bolton (GM), St Margaret, Halliwell, 1911–13 one of the last churches built before the First World War. It continues the traditions of the Perpendicular style, large clerestory windows and blocky massing. No tower was ever intended.
(Mark Watson)

Fig 4.60
Preston, St Michael & All Angels, Ashton-on-Ribble, 1906–8, with its canted east end of the chancel and incomplete tower.
(Mark Watson)

here in a typically individual and imaginative fashion. The style is Perpendicular (as always at this time) but with infusions of lovely Decorated tracery. A *Te Deum* frieze runs along the clerestory, and there are also inscriptions over the west doorway, on the doors themselves, and on that most optimistic of church fittings, an outside pulpit set in the churchyard wall overlooking the road! Other Austin & Paley themes appear in the north porch, such as chequerwork and a canted entrance. The nave has five bays (with concave-sided octagonal piers) plus one-bay transepts entered through very lofty arches. It is from this viewpoint that the true glory of St Mary's appears, with its great spatial complexity and diverse elements. At the entrance to the chancel is a pair of great round panelled piers, from which spring the arches to the transepts and the chancel arch itself. Beyond this is an arch to the sanctuary, as at St Michael, Ashton-on-Ribble, and beyond this the east window has detached pierced mullions of the kind first appearing in the firm's work at St John, Atherton (GM), in 1892, and St George, Stockport (Ch), 1892–7. The arches on the north side of the chancel are extremely tall, while those on the south are very low, allowing for massive clerestory windows. The church thus becomes a magnificent essay in space and light, equal to, if very different from, the best churches of the time by such masters as Giles Gilbert Scott and Temple Moore.

Secular works

The activity of the firm was very much dominated by church work in the last 15 years of the 19th century and the first 15 of the 20th. There were also secular commissions in considerable numbers, although examination of the Catalogue (*see* Appendix 5) shows that, for the most part, these are generally minor, and in many cases around Lancaster, quite simply mundane.

Country houses played no part at all in the work of the practice during this period, the last new one of any substance having been the rather plain, four-square Hampsfield House near Lindale (CuL) in 1880–2 for J T Hibbert (1824–1908), MP for Oldham and staunch supporter of Gladstone (*see* Fig 3.90). This was also the time of Paley & Austin's last major country house restoration, Thurland Castle, which was being restored and remodelled after a fire in 1876. This shift in the pattern of commissions seems to reflect two factors: first, that there was

Fig 4.61 (right) Widnes (Me), St Mary, West Bank, 1908–10. West end with canted north porch.

Fig 4.62 (far right) West Bank, the chancel entrance, north transept and organ chamber. The east window has detached mullions like those at Atherton (see Fig 3.56).

less work going on in country houses from the latter part of the 19th century, and second, that the primary focus and reputation (and interest?) of the practice was ecclesiastical.

Public buildings

With two exceptions, the Storey Institute (1887–91, 1906–8) and the Infirmary (1893–6) in Lancaster, there were no major public commissions either. Paley & Austin had made extensive additions to Lancaster's old town hall in 1871–4 but the new one of 1906–9 went to E W Mountford, who had an impressive track record with such buildings at Sheffield (1890–7), Battersea (also 1890–7) and Hitchin (1900–1). It was paid for by James Williamson (1842–1930), from 1895 the first Baron Ashton, whose family fortune was based on the production of oilcloth for floor coverings, earning him the nickname 'Lord Linoleum'. At the time of his elevation to the peerage he was employing 2,500 people in Lancaster, making him the town's biggest employer by far. His father, also James, who had founded the business in the 1840s, gave a park to the town which his son completed. Within it he built the most grandiloquent piece of family self-commemoration in this country, the Ashton Memorial, whose baroque rotunda and copper dome form such a prominent landmark from the M6. This commission went to John Belcher in 1904 and was built, with J J Joass, in 1907–9. Belcher was honoured with the RIBA Royal Gold Medal in 1907. The Ashton Memorial and Lancaster Town Hall are two baroque extravaganzas which belong to a very different architectural world from Hubert Austin's and it is easy to imagine that he might have felt the former to be a rather vulgar display with which he was out of tune.

In fact the firm was never commissioned to carry out any work for the Williamsons, possibly because it did so for their smaller rivals, Storey Brothers, with whom there were personal links. In 1835 the Storey family had migrated to Lancaster from Bardsea on the Furness peninsula, and as far back as 1841–2 Edmund Sharpe had used Storey (probably John) & Lawrence to build a chapel at the County Lunatic Asylum. In 1847–8 John Storey had been one of the contractors on Sharpe & Paley's remodelling of Hornby Castle. John's brother William (1823–79) had worked with James Williamson senior in the 1840s, but set up his own business in 1848 and

Fig 4.63
Lancaster, Storey Institute, 1887–91, 1906–8. Jacobean in style and one of the firm's major public buildings in Lancaster. Their offices lie behind the Institute and face Lancaster Castle.

was joined by his brother Thomas (1825–98) in 1851 making table baize and other products similar to those produced by James Williamson & Son. Thomas also worked for a while for Sharpe as a railway surveyor and the commercial manager for both the 'Little' North Western Railway and the Phoenix Foundry. Family ties were sealed when in 1873 Edmund Sharpe's second son, also Edmund, married Alice, one of William Storey's daughters. Edmund junior had joined Storey Brothers when the Sharpe family returned to Lancaster from the continent in 1866, and continued to work for the firm all his life, becoming manager of the Moor Lane cotton mills, and eventually (by purchase) lord of the manor of Halton, living at Halton Hall (to which he added the surviving Victorian wing).

Storey Brothers acquired the important White Cross Mills in Lancaster in 1856 and employed Paley & Austin for the top of the 250ft-high brick chimney (built 1876–8). In 1887 Thomas Storey turned to Paley, Austin & Paley for his great gift to his adopted town: this was prompted by the Queen's Golden Jubilee for which, as mayor, he had organised the celebrations. It consisted of an enlarged and better equipped replacement for the Lancaster Mechanics' Institute, and was built in 1887–91 on the corner of Meeting House Lane and Castle Hill, right behind the PA&P offices (Fig 4.63). The purpose, as with all such institutions, was 'the promotion of art, science, literature and

Fig 4.64 (above) Lancaster Infirmary, 1893–6. As at the Storey Institute, 17th-century detailing enriches this building, which lies on the south side of the city centre.

Fig 4.65 Hornby village institute, 1914.

technical instruction', and the building was provided with lecture rooms, a reading room, library, picture gallery, a school of art and a music room. It was renamed the Storey Institute in 1891 and expanded further in 1906–8 by Austin & Paley, when Thomas's son Herbert provided a further £10,000 to extend the premises up Castle Hill to provide more rooms for the teaching of science, domestic economy, art and commerce. The institute forms a prominent block on the way out of the town centre towards the station. It is neo-Jacobean in style, with ranges of paired and single windows spread over two floors and an attic which has shaped-gabled dormers. At the corner it is anchored by a polygonal tower-like feature with a dome capped by a tall spike.

The new Lancaster Infirmary was built in 1893–6 to designs by Paley, Austin & Paley (Fig 4.64), its chief focus being a fine octagonal tower over the main entrance. It has been added to constantly over the years, and provided work for Harry Paley until the end of his career. The building is still very much in use today. The firm also built the North Lonsdale Hospital in

Barrow (CuL), in several phases from the early 1880s, but this is almost entirely demolished, having been replaced by a new hospital to the north of the town.

The last public building before Austin's death was an attractive Jacobethan village institute at Hornby in 1914 (Fig 4.65).

Schools and related buildings

Schools of all kinds kept the firm busy, and their school chapels have already been mentioned. The practice seems to have monopolised any work in Lancaster. There were extensions to Christ Church schools and the Royal Grammar School, both in 1887; a major addition the following year to the Royal Albert in the form of a recreational hall (plus a new wing in 1898–1901); a Roman Catholic school for St Peter's church in 1895–7; alterations at St Thomas's Schools in 1896; additions to a girls' school in Middle Street, 1897; Nazareth House, a Catholic home for 'waifs and strays', in 1898–1902 (Fig 4.66); unexecuted plans for a school in South Road, 1901; and additions to a school in the suburb of Skerton also in 1901 and to the Grammar School in 1906. Schools also formed part of the complex of buildings at St George, Stockport (Fig 4.67), with building work going on into the Edwardian years. In terms of style, these and other school work looked back to the 16th and 17th centuries, taking their cue from the foundation of grammar schools and the development of Oxbridge colleges at that time.

Fig 4.66
Lancaster, Nazareth House, 1898–1902, a Roman Catholic venture to care for 'waifs and strays': a large building with repetitive 16th-century detailing of gables and mullioned windows.

Fig 4.67
Stockport, St George's Schools, across the road from the church, c 1900. As at Nazareth House, there is a multiplicity of gables and mullioned windows.
(Mark Watson)

Fig 4.68
Christ's Hospital School, the hall and dining room, from the competition drawings made for the firm by T Raffles Davison.
*(*British Architect *3 August 1894)*

One of the major competitions of the 1890s was for Christ's Hospital School. The decision had been made to move to a 1,200-acre site near Horsham, Sussex, and in 1892 an invitation to design the new buildings was issued to the architectural profession. It elicited 131 responses, which were assessed by Ewan Christian.[44] These were to be whittled down to four to produce actual designs, but the number was later increased to six after protests from the profession that four was too small a field. In 1894 five entries were received from Austin & Paley, T G Jackson, T E Collcutt, Carpenter & Ingelow and the eventual winners, Aston Webb & Ingress Bell, whose designs met with approval not only from the governing body of the school but also from the architectural press.[45] The *Building News* commented that all the designs were 'creditable to their authors' and felt able to add that the competition was 'conducted so fairly and decided so justly'.[46] The Austin & Paley proposals were placed second and were specifically attributed to Hubert Austin (Fig 4.68).[47] They envisaged brick buildings and a Perpendicular style for the main hall, chapel and dining room and a late 16th-century style for the others. The *Building News* merely commented that they were 'an able design', but *The Builder* was extraordinarily hostile, criticising the planning and declaring that the firm 'would have been more successful if they had devoted to practical considerations some of the trouble which they have bestowed on the production of a considerable number of charming perspective drawings'.[48]

Any work at Sedbergh School (CuWY) was monopolised by the partners and continued in a steady stream down to the Great War and beyond. The years 1904–6 brought the biggest work there, the Powell Hall and six classrooms associated with it (Fig 4.69). Contemporary with this was a large extension to Leeds Grammar School, 1904–5, won in competition and having a severe grid-iron appearance to it

(Fig 4.70). It is hard to resist the analogy with repetitive computer-aided designs of the late 20th century. St Bees School brought happier buildings: in addition to the chapel, there were the headmaster's house, library and laboratories in 1907–8. Minor work was undertaken also at the Clergy Daughters' School at Casterton (CuW) in 1896, and at Rossall School in the 1890s and 1900s.

An interesting project of this period was a new building for the Keswick School of Industrial Arts in 1893–4 (closed 1984), set up in 1884 by Canon Hardwicke Rawnsley (1851–1920) and his wife, Edith (née Fletcher), Edmund Sharpe's niece by marriage, and a bridesmaid at the wedding of Fanny Langshaw and Hubert Austin in 1870.[49] Rawnsley was a passionate defender of the Lake District, a friend of Beatrix Potter and John Ruskin, and co-founder of the National Trust. The school promoted Arts & Crafts principles of manufacture and was noted for its metalwork, the teaching of which was supervised by Edith. The architecture draws on Lakeland domestic work and the frontage bears appropriate words by Robert Browning: 'The Loving Eye and Patient Hand ...'.

Paley, Austin & Paley also built a surprisingly far-away commission at Llandovery College, Carmarthenshire, with an extensive east range, dining hall and rooms above, 'in a well-detailed northern English C17 style ... [in] Red sandstone'.[50] How this job was secured is uncertain but a possible source could be the architect/surveyor Neander Gesenius Lewis (1864–1937), who worked in Lancaster for about 20 years from the mid-1880s; he had been born and brought up close by. Another, rather less distant scheme, at Shrewsbury School, seems to have been due to a family connection. In 1913–14 there were extensions to the swimming baths and the house of a housemaster, Arthur F Chance, one of whose pupils had been Geoffrey Austin, son of Hubert, who is discussed below.[51]

Fig 4.69 (above) Sedbergh School (CuWY), Powell Hall, 1904–6, scholastic Tudorbethan once again in evidence. (Mark Watson)

Fig 4.70 (below) Leeds Grammar School extension, 1904–5. The hard rectilinear style contrasts with E M Barry's original Gothic building on the left.

Fig 4.72 (opposite)
The Lancaster & Skerton Co-operative main store in central Lancaster. Its beehive symbol features at the top of the canted corner. The shop fronts have been removed from the ground floor.

Commercial buildings

There were at this time various commercial commissions in both Lancaster and Barrow (CuL), but mostly minor. One of the more significant was for new workshops and showrooms in North Road, Lancaster, in 1902 for a cycle maker turned car manufacturer, William Atkinson (Fig 4.71). This was one of the earliest motor garages and showrooms in the provinces. However, the most regular source of work from 1900 was the building programme of the Lancaster & Skerton Co-operative Society (the title seems to have varied over time). This produced numerous small shops dotted over Lancaster and as far as Morecambe and Heysham, even down to a temporary wooden affair in Skerton (1901). The major project was a large store and hall in the centre of Lancaster on the corner of Church and New Streets (Fig 4.72). Like the Storey Institute, it is in a free neo-Jacobean style, and has tall dormer windows, in this case under segmental heads. The ground floor is now an arcaded loggia, having been created when the shop fronts were removed (as at 2011 the ground floor is a Chinese restaurant). The smaller shops have mostly long ceased to be Co-ops but, as at the big Lancaster store, their carved beehives of industry still proclaim their origins (Fig 4.73). The last Austin & Paley Co-op was built at Bare in Morecambe, in 1914.

Succession

At the outbreak of what was to turn into the Great War, Hubert Austin was a man of 73 (Fig 4.74). Harry Paley was already a partner in the firm and it might be expected that Austin's own sons would have joined him. His eldest, Bernard Tate (1873–1955), was educated at Magdalene College, Cambridge, and after graduating in 1895 he did indeed study architecture in his father's firm, and is said to have served his articles there.[52] In 1901 he married Emma Dowd (1867–1937), whom he met in Lancaster but who was born, like her father, in Tipperary; in doing so Bernard had a serious falling out with his father, which probably explains why he never became his partner.[53] His brother Geoffrey later remarked very simply that he was 'in the office for a year or two and left'.[54] He went to Liverpool to practice in about 1902, probably with Grayson & Ould, and later worked as chief assistant to James Lomax-Simpson (1882–1977), who began practice in 1905. In 1910 Lomax-Simpson became chief architect to William Hesketh Lever, later Lord Leverhulme, and Bernard was Simpson's deputy at Lever Brothers.[55] He worked on many buildings at Port Sunlight. In 1911 he was living at Egerton Park, Rock Ferry, close to Port Sunlight. He also worked with Simpson on the Unilever Building at Blackfriars

Fig 4.71
Lancaster, former shop, workshop and showroom premises for William Atkinson, North Road, 1902. Originally a cycle maker, he became a very early British car manufacturer with his John O'Gaunt model.

Parksafe
County Court
Castle & Priory
Tourist Information

Fig 4.73
A former Co-operative store, Sibsey Street/Westbourne Road, Lancaster, a building Hubert Austin would have passed on his way to the office.

Bridge, London, from 1929. He had moved to Shortlands, Kent, by 1930, still working for Unilever until he retired in 1939 to Otford (Kent), where he lived until 1954. He died at Sydenham in 1955.

The war led to a rift in the relationship of

Fig 4.74
Hubert Austin, 1914, painting (from a photograph) made by James Bacon & Sons, photographers and miniature painters, probably at their Edinburgh premises between 1921 and 1934, when Geoffrey Austin and his wife, Mary, were living at St Andrews.
(Ann Lendrum collection)

Geoffrey Langshaw, Hubert's youngest son, with his father, as he set about joining up. This finally prevented continuity of the partnership through the Austin line, not just during the war, but, importantly, after it.

Geoffrey was born in 1884 and after education at Lancaster Grammar School went on to Shrewsbury, a school with a long connection to the Paley family. In 1903 he began his articles with Walter Brierley in York and then returned to Lancaster in 1907 to work with his father's firm. He married on 8 July 1908 Mary Hutton Bowes-Wilson.[56]

In 1913 Geoffrey was the architect for the extension to the swimming baths of Shrewsbury School and in 1914 for the extension to the house of Arthur Chance, his school housemaster and godfather to his youngest son, Tony.[57] He was made a junior partner in January 1914. In 1968, recollecting his work after an interval of over 50 years, he dismissed it rather pithily: 'I think you can ignore the brief connection I had with the firm – it was of no account whatsoever.'[58] This recollection was no doubt coloured by what follows.

On 5 September 1914, on the dais at a large recruitment meeting in the Ashton Hall, Lancaster, was Edmund Sharpe junior (1847–1925), Geoffrey's mother's first cousin, and three of his wife's relatives. A few days later Geoffrey was pictured walking down Castle Park, having vol-

From
Austin & Paley ~~& Austin,~~
H. A. PALEY.
Architects,
TELEPHONE 614.
Lancaster.

Fig 4.75 (far left) Captain Geoffrey Austin, 1916, painting, again from a photograph, by James Bacon & Sons, and probably made at the same time as the painting of his father. (Ann Lendrum collection)

Fig 4.76 (above) A transitory practice. The firm had stationery printed to include Geoffrey Austin as a partner. When he did not join the firm after the war, an amendment was necessary. From a letter about plans for alterations to his father-in-law's house in Lancaster. (Lancashire Record Office, MBLA/acc 5167/10/3064)

unteered.[59] Rather surprisingly in the light of the general, modern perception of Great War patriotism, his action incurred the very considerable displeasure of his father.[60] The row undoubtedly rumbled on over the winter because Geoffrey did not formally sign up until February 1915, as a private in the King's Own Royal Lancaster Regiment,[61] at which point he resigned from the firm.[62] This was just before the death of his mother on 25 February and that of his father on 22 March. In the meantime, on 12 March, he was appointed to a commission in the 4th Loyal North Lancashire Regiment (Fig 4.75).[63]

In 1915 his battalion became part of the 170th Brigade, 57th Lancashire Division, and in late 1916, by which time Geoffrey was a captain, it went for final training at Aldershot. There it was inspected by King George V, watched by Geoffrey's family. They all spent Christmas together at Aldershot. On 8 February 1917 the battalion reached France for active service.[64] Without doubt Geoffrey was with them on the early morning of Friday, 26 October, at the start of the horror that was 2nd Passchendaele (3rd Battle of Ypres) with appalling casualties in a morass of mud for virtually no ground gained.[65]

Geoffrey continued his war service until the early summer of 1919. In May his father-in-law Thomas had alterations carried out at the new family home, 'Fairlight', on the Haverbreaks estate in Lancaster.[66] The family had moved in by August. His fifth child, Ann Brougham, was born there in April 1920. He never returned to architecture (Fig 4.76) and the firm, explaining in a letter 48 years later, again succinctly, 'that there was no "money" for ecclesiastical work [to fund salaries]'.[67] Whatever arrangements had been made with Harry Paley after Hubert's death had almost certainly been settled in the two years that he had served in England before going to France.[68] In April 1921 Geoffrey obtained the post of Secretary to the Council of St Leonards School for Girls in St Andrews, Scotland, a post he held for 35 years until 1956.[69] He died in October 1971, aged 87, leaving 12 grandchildren.

So it was that when peace returned after 1918 no members of the Austin family were part of the firm that Hubert had joined 50 years before. He died on 22 March 1915, after a three-day illness, at 'The Knoll', the Lancaster home he had built for himself and his much-loved wife, Fanny.[70] He lies in Lancaster Cemetery, not far from Edmund Sharpe and E G Paley. His estate, at £38,997, was substantial, although far less than Paley's, with whom he had developed such a successful and respected partnership. Hubert's sons, for different reasons, pursued other paths and the firm's torch was carried on by Harry, E G Paley's son, until it was finally extinguished at the end of the Second World War.

5

The last years of the practice: Harry Paley

The First World War, though not as economically cataclysmic as the Second, led to serious hardship and deprivation in its later years. Initially, the firm's building projects planned or started before the war continued to be built, hence the completion of churches during 1915 at Basford (St), Leck and Ashton-on-Ribble. The same year also saw the installation of an Italian marble reredos at St Silas, Blackburn, and a couple of private commissions, one of which was for alterations at Hubert Austin's former home in Lancaster for its new occupier. But commissions stalled in 1916, and during the following year came the first example of what was to remain the staple fare for many architects over the next few years – memorialisation of the fallen and sometimes also those who had served. After the war the practice never regained its late 19th-century level of activity, yet it seems to have enjoyed reasonable success in its north-western heartland. Ecclesiastical jobs were numerically dominant and they formed the mainstay of the practice, just as they had done since its foundation almost a century before.

Harry Paley and the practice

The firm now had but one principal, Harry Paley, the fifth and last child of E G Paley, and he ran the business with the aid of Thomas Baines (1863–1946), James Tarney (1867–1959) and J B Slinger (1896–1986), details of whom are given in Appendix 2. There were perhaps others in the office as clerks or assistants, but no details are known. Paley came from a comfortable professional background which his father had in large measure created, and his family was well-integrated into Lancaster society. Some details of his close involvement in the life of the town are given in the previous chapter, and these would have helped him in gaining commissions. Like his father, Harry was a very sociable individual and an enthusiastic field sportsman who enjoyed the life of a quasi-country squire (Fig 5.1). He lived at his home, 'Moorgarth', in Brookhouse, to the north-west of Lancaster, with his wife Katherine and their one daughter, Katherine Helena (1889–1966), known as Kitty, who never married following the death of her fiancé in the war.[1] Nothing is known of any contact between Hubert Austin's sons and Harry Paley after the war, but communication was continued for nearly 50 more years between their daughters.[2]

Harry Paley perpetuated the name of his firm as Austin & Paley (Fig 5.2) even though the Austin involvement died with Hubert in 1915. The same, of course, had happened with the retention of the Sharpe & Paley name from 1851, when Edmund Sharpe withdrew from the practice. There was nothing particularly unusual about this: instances of nationally celebrated practices doing the same are 'Sedding & Wilson' after J D Sedding's death in 1891, and 'Temple Moore & Moore' after the former died in 1920.[3]

After the great achievements and enormous reputation of the practice in the late 19th century and the Edwardian years, it is easy to see the interwar period as an anti-climax. In a sense it was, yet the firm was not totally undistinguished. In the Buildings of England volume for North Lancashire (2009) there are some nine interwar Austin & Paley entries, which are an indication of some measure of worthiness. Admittedly this is exceeded in the ratio of over four to one by the pre-war Austin & Paley, but such a tally is much more than most firms styling themselves 'architects' in the interwar north-west managed to achieve.

Nor was the level of activity insignificant, and from the mid-1920s the workload began to pick up. The better survival rate of records for

Fig 5.1
Harry Paley in a shooting party at Hawkshead Farm, Halton Park, c 1930. He is believed to be the man on the far left. (Bill Hosfield collection)

this time means we have more detailed, systematic information about what the firm was doing than for any previous period, and this includes information about various minor jobs which swells the Catalogue and gives a rounded picture of its activity (*see* Appendix 5). Harry Paley and his associates seem to have been running a reasonable successful practice. The surviving records consist of three volumes which found their way into the offices of the Lancaster stained glass manufacturers Shrigley & Hunt and are now in the Lancashire Record Office.[4] They consist of a specification book, 1925–39; accounts for jobs, 1927–42; and reports, estimates, tenders and correspondence, 1928–40. Analysis of these records reveals over 160 jobs, with the peak of activity coming in the early 1930s; three-quarters of the jobs were in the historic county of Lancashire.[5]

War memorials, schools and other secular work

As mentioned, the immediate post-war years provided most architects with few opportunities other than commemorating those who fell or served in the war. With well over a million dead and wounded, most British families were touched directly or indirectly by tragedy, lead-

From
Austin & Paley,
(H. A. Paley)
Architects,
Lancaster.
Telephone 614.

Fig 5.2
The firm's post-war letterhead.

ing to permanent commemoration on an unprecedented scale. Monuments to the fallen were already being commissioned before the end of the war. Private Joseph Cockroft, killed while on sentry duty in France on 17 July 1916, was remembered through an A&P-designed brass tablet at Christ Church, Lancaster, in 1917; in the same year, but rather more grandly, Colonel Henry Blundell was commemorated at St Matthew, Highfield, in Wigan, by a stone reredos. There then followed commemorative crosses, tablets, screens, a baptistry and other items paid for by the living to remember the dead (Fig 5.3). Most memorials were in place by about 1921, but sometimes provision could take a surprisingly long time if fund-raising was slow or a committee argued about what form a memorial might take (and at what cost). A&P's last war memorial commission was a shrine in 1924 for the roll of honour in Lancaster parish church, housed in the chapel of the King's Own Royal Lancaster Regiment – which itself had

Fig 5.3
Pilling churchyard, war memorial, 1919–20, executed by A O Thoms, whose firm built a great many Harry Paley commissions.
(Mark Watson)

been built in 1903–4 under Hubert Austin as a Boer War memorial.

Public schools were places where the Great War touched raw nerves, since so many former scholars and young staff with bright futures had gone off to slaughter. The firm's closest association was with Sedbergh School, where it had been responsible for works both large and small for 40 years. This association nearly came to an end just after the Great War – even perhaps because of it. The new contenders for work were Thomas Worthington & Sons of Manchester. Three of Thomas's sons had been at Sedbergh, one of them being wounded in the war, and another, after distinguished service at Gallipoli and in France, dying of his injuries.[6] The third brother, John Hubert (1886–1963), began practice as an architect in 1913, became professor of architecture at the Royal College of Art in 1923, and was knighted in 1949. He had been at Sedbergh in 1900–5.

Whatever the background may have been, the governors' minutes for 20 May 1920 note that 'it appeared desirable that Mr. [Hubert] Worthington should be School Architect as soon as possible and … That on the completion of the new Science Building Messrs. Austin & Paley should be informed, sufficient notice being given, that their services would no longer be required.' So Worthington it was who designed the war memorial cloisters, which were dedicated in 1924. A&P found themselves in competition with Worthington's for a new boarding house in 1923–4, but in the end this job went to them (A&P) and the threat that seemed very real in 1920 lifted. The firm continued to work for the school until global warfare loomed for a second time. Works identified in the Catalogue encompass a boarding house in 1924–6, lodges in 1927–9, a sanatorium in 1929–30, and various classrooms and dormitory accommodation in the 1930s (*see* Appendix 5).

Other schools provided work too. Leeds Grammar School, where Austin & Paley had originally made a large extension in 1904–5, built laboratories in 1924–6 and swimming baths in 1926–9. Giggleswick (NY), where the firm first worked about 1850, commissioned plans for a porter's lodge in 1929 and a sanatorium in 1929–30.

Much of this school work was fairly utilitarian. So too was a long list of works at the Royal Lancaster Infirmary between 1928 and 1941, with new accommodation for nurses, wards, operating theatres, dining rooms and various other extensions. Other secular work chiefly involved additions and alterations to private houses.

Churches

Harry Paley's main achievement as sole principal, and the one he would have no doubt claimed for himself, was his new churches. In many cases they still remain incomplete. They drew unashamedly on the firm's work from the end of the 19th century and Edwardian years. They are often described as conservative, and indeed they are. On the one hand, one senses an architect who was at ease with the firm's tried and trusted formulae; on the other, his clients seem to have had little or no appetite for innovation – as was usually the case in English church-building at the time. Economy was also the order of the day, but such economy was not necessarily synonymous with meanness. The clean lines and paring down of ornament, which had been the trend in church-building since about 1870, were ideal for the task in hand, lending themselves to the achievement of buildings of subdued elegance. So it was that Paley built roomy churches, sometimes in stone, sometimes in brick, with bare internal wall treatment and using late Gothic detailing. Externally he sometimes resorted to blocky geometry and large clerestories, while internally his arches usually tended to die, without capitals, into piers and responds. He continued to use the sturdy roof structures favoured by the pre-war A&P practice, and was keen on canted east ends which secured visually satisfying terminations to east ends at no real cost.

The first substantial church after the war was not built until 1925–6 (plans 1923), when the mid-18th-century church at Becconsall was replaced on a new site given by Major T Fermor-Hesketh. Harry Paley's design, which would have cost some £6,500, was scaled back, and the projected spire was replaced by a saddle-back roof of the kind the firm had used at Flookburgh and Broughton-in-Furness (both CuL) about 1900. The church is fairly small, aisleless and conservative, using Decorated and Perpendicular tracery, and a timber porch, all of which might have been deployed at an Austin & Paley church of the 1890s.

Harry Paley's next church is probably his masterpiece, even though it remains incomplete at the west end and with its tower never realised. St Stephen-on-the-Cliffs in Blackpool (Figs 5.4, 5.5 and 5.6) was designed in 1924 and built

Fig 5.4
Blackpool, St Stephen-on-the-Cliffs, 1925–7, a fine interior in the mature A&P tradition with a canted east end and a complex array of arches of varied sizes and shapes.
(Mark Watson)

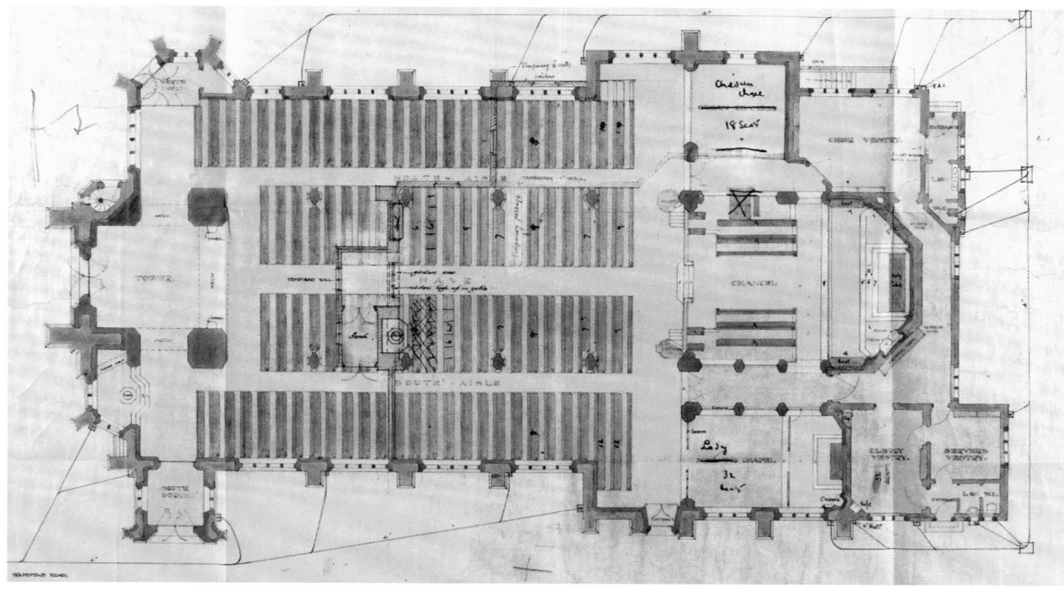

Fig 5.5
Blackpool, St Stephen, plan March 1925. The walls across the nave and aisles show the extent of the intended first phase. Building never went into a second, leaving the church incomplete.
(Lambeth Palace Library, ICBS 11782)

S. Stephen on the Cliffs, Blackpool.

Rev. F. B. FRESHWATER - - - Vicar,
Mr. D. L. HARBOTTLE, Mr. J. CHADWICK, Churchwardens, Treasurers.
Mr. P. HOGLEY - - - Hon. Secretary Church Council.

PROPOSED NEW CHURCH

Messrs. Austin & Paley, Architects, Lancaster.

An Appeal to raise £14,000

Fig 5.6
Blackpool, St Stephen, as intended on a 1920s appeal for funds.
(Lambeth Palace Library, ICBS 11782)

in 1925–7, and was the first church to be consecrated in the new diocese of Blackburn (created in 1926 out of Manchester). It is faced with brick and appears very utilitarian, yet inside it has the spatial qualities of Austin & Paley's best late Victorian and Edwardian churches, with complex planning and vistas in the eastern parts. There are four tall arches south of the chancel (which has a canted east wall), then a passage for circulation, and a three-bay arcade in two tiers to the south chapel. Typical features include the use of Perpendicular detailing, dying arches, large clerestory windows, and, of course, bare pink sandstone.

St Stephen's was quickly followed by St Hilda's for the large village of Bilsborrow, a fine building from a single campaign in 1926–8 (Fig 5.7). It follows the well-established A&P tradition of a substantial tower over the choir, in this case with a prominent stair turret at the south-east corner. It rather lacks some of the tautness of the firm's village churches of the 1890s and 1900s, but typical motifs include the squared-off

Fig 5.7
Bilsborrow, St Hilda, 1926–8, where Harry Paley used the successful A&P formula of a large central tower and aisles which flank only part of the length of the nave.

detailing on the tower, inscriptions (*Laudate Dominum*) over the bell-openings, and the free mixing of Decorated and Perpendicular tracery. The interior has massive, rounded crossing piers, side lighting to illuminate the tower space, and dying mouldings – all in the A&P tradition.

A number of suburban churches were built around 1930 but none was finished at the first attempt. St Luke, Orrell (Me), was started in 1927–8 with three bays of the nave. The east and west ends were finished in 1938, but still without a projected south-west tower. As at Blackpool there is a three-sided east end, and the usual Perpendicular detailing with dying arches and bare sandstone internally. The restrained but elegant fittings (Figs 5.8 and 5.9) are typical of Harry Paley's output. St Stephen, Whelley, in Wigan (GM) (Figs 5.10 and 5.11), was also built in two phases, the eastern part in 1928–30, and the west end in 1937–8. The Perpendicular style, arches dying into lozenge piers, bare internal sandstone and large clerestory are all again stock items. It also has a prominent bell-cote to the south-east.

There was also the new church of St Barbara in the Coventry suburb of Earlsdon (Figs 5.12, 5.13 and 5.14). Paley was involved from 1927 over the selection of the site and in June 1928 was instructed to prepare plans. The church was eventually built in 1930–1. What brought Harry Paley to a job so far from Lancaster is unclear, and the fact that his father had been involved, with Sharpe, in the design of the mother church of St Thomas over 80 years earlier seems unlikely to have had anything to do with it. Perhaps there was a social connection with the machine-tool manufacturer Sir Alfred Herbert, who was the chief benefactor and who paid for the Lady Chapel as a memorial to his wife. Despite such patronage the church has remained incomplete, although it is still quite an impressive, restrained, albeit conventional piece of work. The building is a moderately large Perpendicular essay, the intention being to provide dignified accommodation at modest cost but without the expense of a tower. In this respect the church is similar in conception to one of A&P's last churches before the outbreak of war, St Margaret, Bolton, 1911–13. In conjunction with the brick walling – and, no doubt to reduce cost – artificial stone (Croft Adamant) was employed for the dressings. This was meant to

Fig 5.8 (below left)
Orrell (Me), St Luke, stalls, late 1930s.
(Mark Watson)

Fig 5.9 (below)
Orrell, font and the firm's trade-mark foundation stone.
(Mark Watson)

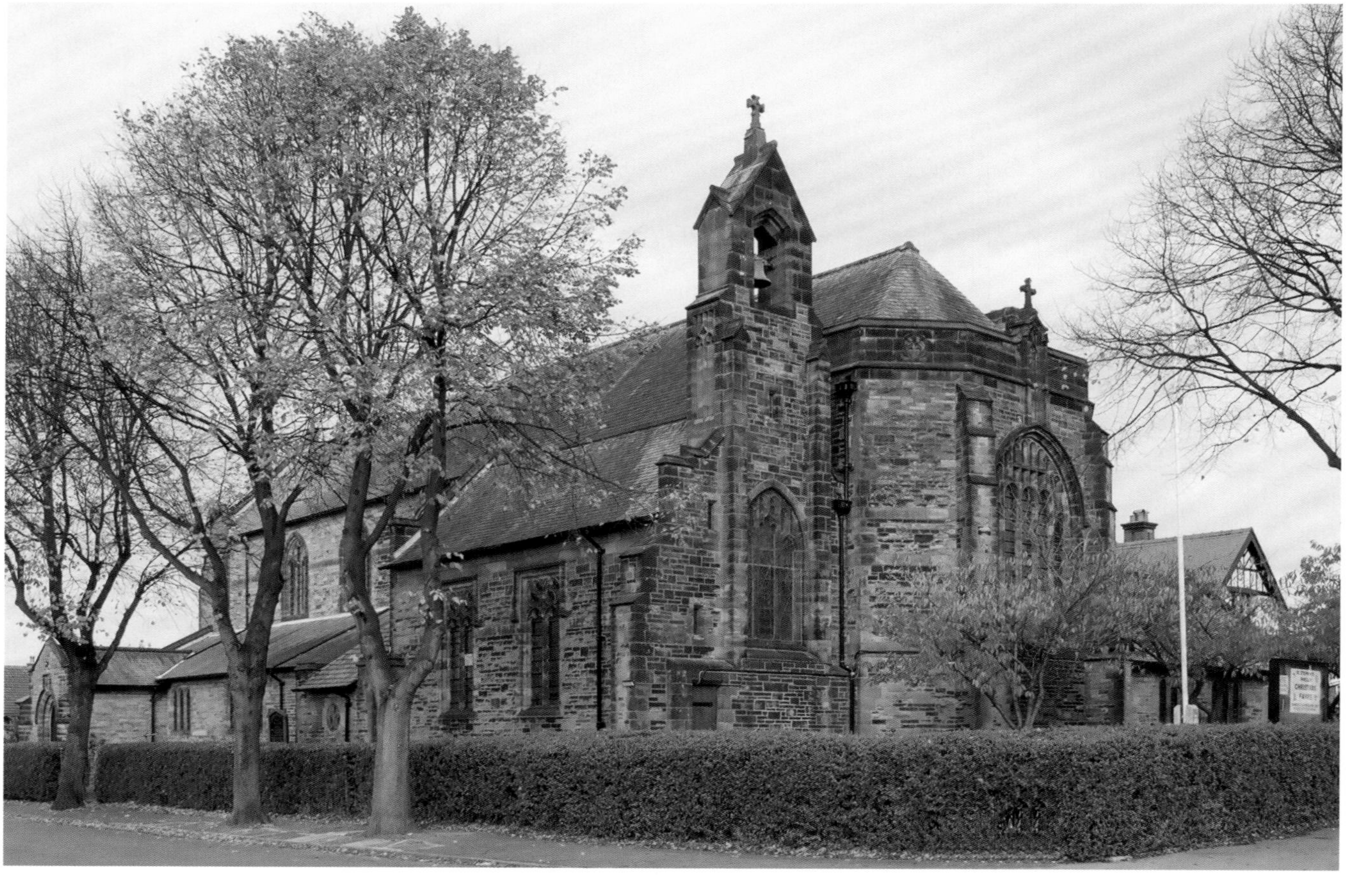

Fig 5.10
Wigan (GM), St Stephen, Whelley, 1928–30. Like its Blackpool namesake, it has a canted east end and was never completed.
(Mark Watson)

resemble Hall Dale stone, and the interior work was tooled to enhance the deception, so it is hard to distinguish it from the real thing.[7] To handle this distant project Paley took on a local 'advisory architect', Harold T Jackson, who doubled as Clerk of Works and made site inspections every few days.

Fig 5.11
Wigan, Whelley. The use of inventive details and tracery was continued by Harry Paley.
(Mark Watson)

St Barbara's led on to a second commission in the Coventry suburbs, St Barnabas, on the opposite, north side of town, and built in 1932–3.[8] The formula of brick walling and artificial stone (in this case from the Leicester-based Constone Company) was repeated, with Jackson again supervising the work. Jackson's papers show that Paley was responsible simply for running up the design of the main structure. It was a *very* modest, plain Perpendicular affair, much cheaper than St Barbara's, and also never completed at the west end. When asked by the *Architects' Journal* for pictures, Jackson was obliged to report that the vicar 'wishes me to state that the building is devoid of architectural interest and that I was called in by the Church Council to make such improvements to the interior as was possible and to design interesting furniture and fittings to redeem the poverty of design in the structure'.[9]

St Thomas, Blackpool, of 1930–2, also remained incomplete after the east end and three and a half bays of the nave and aisles had been built. It has a routine Perpendicular brick exterior but a bare sandstone interior of surprising

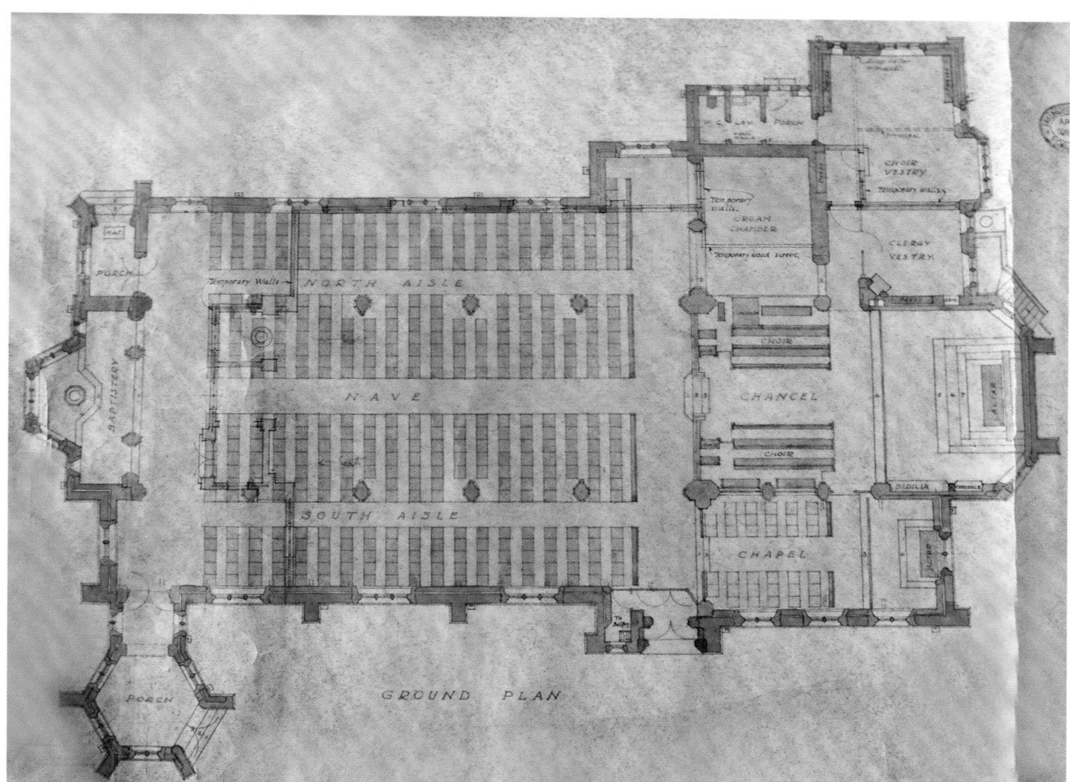

Fig 5.12
Coventry, St Barbara, Earlsdon, plan August 1929. The west end was never built.
(St Barbara's Parochial Church Council)

Fig 5.13
Earlsdon, south-east parts: the square-headed windows in the chapel have a family resemblance to those at Alsager (see Fig 4.43) and Blackburn, St Silas (see Fig 4.46) while the Gothic-letter inscription over the entrance, the traceried square to the left of the doorway and the blocky parapets are all A&P trademarks.

Fig 5.14
Earlsdon, interior.

Fig 5.15
Blackpool, St Thomas, 1930–2. Like other churches by Harry Paley, this one remains incomplete. (Mark Watson)

Fig 5.16
Blackpool, St Thomas. An unconventional detail in a generally conventional church: the springing of the nave arches. (Mark Watson)

dignity and with several inventive touches (Figs 5.15 and 5.16). St John the Evangelist, Abram (Me), built in 1935–7, replaced an adjacent church of 1838. Like Becconsall, it has a saddleback tower. Richard Pollard, in the revised Buildings of England volume, follows Pevsner's first edition comment in calling the building 'very conservative'. However, he has to admit that 'the practice was still capable of producing a dignified interior'.[10] The fittings are entirely in the elegant, well-established tradition of the firm (Figs 5.17 and 5.18).

The Abram church proved to be the last new church to be designed by the firm. There were some other later church commissions, such as the finishing off of the north aisle at Alsager

Fig 5.17 (far left) Abram (Me), St John the Evangelist, stall end, 1937. (Mark Watson)

Fig 5.18 (left) Abram, pulpit, 1937. (Mark Watson)

(St: 1936–7), the nave and aisles at Whelley (GM: 1937–8), and the completion of a church by R Knill Freeman – St Mary Magdalene, Ribbleton, in Preston. This last work was first proposed in 1936 and limped along into the war, the final certificate not being issued to the Incorporated Church Building Society, which provided a small amount of the funding, until May 1942.

Last days

The last time the Austin & Paley name is known to have appeared professionally is, appropriately, in relation to church work. In 1944 James Tarney sketched a couple of suggestions for enlarging the small church of St Anne at Haverthwaite (CuL).[11] It was hardly a time for such things to be done, and Tarney suggested that 'proper estimates are tried out after the War is over'. The end of the war came, but nothing was done at Haverthwaite. Nor did the practice carry out any further work. Harry Paley had retired, although when he did so is uncertain. One of his contractors remembers his retiring in 1936 after rebuilding work at Burton-in-Lonsdale church (NY).[12] Yet, given the quite numerous commissions down to the outbreak of war, this date is perhaps premature. Although in his late seventies, he may well have kept up part-time practice with his colleagues Tarney and Baines. Finally, however, the offices on Castle Park were sold by Paley on 1 September 1945 to Lancaster Corporation. The records of the firm were destroyed although, it seems, churches with which the firm had been connected were offered relevant drawings for a small fee; some, it is said, did take up the offer.[13] Then on 19 April 1946, Harry Paley died suddenly at his home in Brookhouse, aged 86. He was buried in the churchyard at nearby St Paul's, Brookhouse, where he was joined three years later by his wife Katherine, and later still by his daughter Kitty. The architectural dynasty of Sharpe, Paley and Austin was no more.

APPENDIX 1
EDMUND SHARPE: ENGINEER, BUSINESSMAN AND REFORMER

Edmund Sharpe is best known today for his work as an architect and architectural writer; however, these activities formed but a part of an intensely varied and interesting life. The following account examines his wider place in the life of Lancaster and then takes a roughly chronological look at his non-architectural ventures.

Sharpe and early Victorian Lancaster

Lists published in the *Lancaster Gazette* over a 20-year period from 1836 of attendees at the gatherings of Lancaster's various societies show Sharpe playing an active part, and rubbing shoulders with those of power and influence. He had a great love of music so it is appropriate that his name first appears in September 1836 as one of 12 people charged with arranging the first concert of the Lancaster Choral Society.[1]

Sharpe also joined the Lancaster Literary, Scientific & Natural History Society, and in January 1837 delivered 'a very interesting paper on bridges' and subsequently lectured on other topics.[2] He was a committee member from 1839 to 1842, when his future brother-in-law, James Pearson Langshaw, was one of the two curators. He also attended meetings of the Heart of Oak Club, the social hub of the Lancaster Conservative Association.[3] Other appearances are as secretary and treasurer of the short-lived Lancaster Institution for the Encouragement of the Fine Arts; steward at a fancy dress ball in the Assembly Rooms in honour of Queen Victoria's coronation; and, in April 1840, as a committee member for the newly formed local branch of the Protestant Association – clear evidence of his Low Church leanings.[4]

On 1 November 1841 Sharpe was elected a councillor for Castle Ward along with Dr Edward Denis de Vitre (1806–78), a leading physician who also played a central role in the affairs of Lancaster: he and Sharpe would be closely associated in several capacities.[5] Sharpe stood unopposed until 1850, when he was returned for a further three-year term. In May 1842 he was elected a Port Commissioner, although this was by then a largely honorary recognition of social standing.[6] However, he does seem to have had some maritime interests as a press report in 1842 mentions a vessel of his carrying stone being lost on its way to Fleetwood.[7] In 1843 he was appointed a Council representative on the Police Commission, and a visitor of the National Schools. On 9 November 1848 he was elected as Lancaster's Mayor.

Sharpe joined in Lancaster's sporting activities, beginning with the oldest group, the John O'Gaunt Bowmen. At their gala day in September 1840 he won the large silver arrow for the best score at 90 yards.[8] The ball and dinner the next evening seems to have eclipsed even that of the Heart of Oak Club in Lancaster's social calendar. The Sharpe family seems to have attended this annual event right through until leaving Lancaster in 1856, as did the Langshaws and the Fletchers, and later the Paley family. In 1849 Tom Austin made an appearance; and in 1855 the list of guests included Mrs Gaskell and two of her daughters.

In June 1841 Sharpe helped to found the Lancaster Lunesdale Cricket Club, but barely a year later, in September 1842 'on the motion of Mr. Edmund Sharpe … was dissolved, and out of it, there and then was formed the first Lancaster Rowing Club'.[9] But Sharpe's cricketing days were not over, and he seems to have played regularly for a Lancaster 1st XI in the early 1850s. Meanwhile, the Rowing Club flourished with Sharpe, Paley and Tom Austin all playing an active part and R J Withers acting as secretary for the Lancaster Regatta until 1852 (succeeded by Austin).

In the spring of 1843, Edmund Sharpe purchased for £500 the Theatre Royal, known today as The Grand (Fig A1), the third-oldest provincial theatre in Britain, dating from 1782.[10] Sharpe spent £680 converting it into a music hall and a museum which housed the collection of the Literary, Scientific & Natural History Society. The conversion seems to have been a philanthropic gesture by Sharpe with the building hosting various concerts, religious meetings, readings and lectures. Here in November 1843 Sharpe the musician and churchman gave a lecture on 'Congregational Singing ... With Illustrations, in four parts, by 70 Voices'.[11]

In December 1848 Sharpe founded a new literary, music and scientific society known as the Lancaster Athenaeum. He offered his music hall for its varied programme and he himself gave a number of lectures on subjects as diverse as bells, music, medieval architecture and the Crimean War. Excursions were made to such places as Lowther Castle, Ullswater, Knowsley Hall and one of Sharpe's most beloved buildings, the ruins of Furness Abbey. The success of the Athenaeum was such that the accommodation in the music hall became inadequate. So in 1856 Sharpe began an apsidal-ended extension with a gallery, thus doubling the capacity of the hall which reopened to the cheering strains of Haydn's *Creation* in December 1857.[12]

In the summer of 1851, accompanied by the mayor (Henry Gregson) and the town clerk, Sharpe went to Balmoral to arrange a visit to Lancaster by the royal family on its return journey to London.[13] This duly took place amid great excitement on 8 October and involved the party driving through four temporary triumphal arches designed by none other than Sharpe & Paley. In its fulsome preview, the *Lancaster Gazette* had noted these were to be 'in the best possible taste ... One will bear the royal arms, another the county arms, and the third the borough arms, and each will be decorated with a great number of flags, all national, and the whole of them surmounted by the royal standard.'[14] During the tour of Lancaster Castle the royal family were conducted up the tower by Edmund Sharpe, who answered various questions put to him.

Fig A1
The Theatre Royal, St Leonard's Gate, Lancaster (now The Grand), purchased by Sharpe in 1843 and the scene of many entertainment and cultural events, including lectures, concerts and meetings, some arranged by Sharpe himself. (Mark Watson)

Railway-builder: south from Lancaster

Despite his flourishing architectural practice, Sharpe was soon widening his business interests. In April 1836 the Lancaster & Preston Junction Railway Company was formed to build a 20-mile stretch of line which would eventually become part of the west coast route to Scotland. The route was engineered by Joseph Locke (1805–60), a leading railway civil engineer, who had started out as an assistant to George Stephenson. Tenders were sought in January 1838 for each of the four sections of the new line. Sharpe put in a successful bid for the masonry work (Fig A2) on the six-mile stretch south of Lancaster, while a Peter Perry of Chester-le-Street, Co Durham, secured the earthworks. Locke then made a decision which was to have serious consequences for the young Sharpe. He refused to accept two separate tenders, and insisted that the contract for *both* masonry *and* earthwork be made with either Sharpe or Perry – he didn't mind which. In the event, the contract was made with Perry, who subcontracted the masonry work to Sharpe.

By the AGM in June 1839, all was not well.[15] Perry was in financial difficulties and the railway company had taken over his work. Sharpe had set out zealously to fulfil his part of the contract, but the crisis meant that he had not been properly paid and was understandably annoyed.

In advance of the AGM, to explain his position, he published the correspondence between himself and the company secretary, Edward Bolden.[16] He explained: 'I opened two entirely new Quarries [at Greaves and Ellel], at very considerable expense [Fig A3]. I purchased six new quarry cranes and six complete sets of quarry tools. I bought five horses and carts and had upwards of one hundred men regularly at work, for a period of fifteen weeks before I received a farthing from the company.' Sharpe's action was something of an affront to the directors but, nonetheless, the day before the AGM, the company sought to draw a line under the sorry business with an offer to pay Sharpe for the work thus far completed. Sharpe accepted, but still caused heated exchanges at the AGM which rumbled on far into the evening. After the meeting and, over the next month, a vitriolic exchange of correspondence appeared in the *Lancaster Gazette,* largely initiated by Edmund Sharpe, who clearly felt let down, betrayed, hurt and even insulted by those he had formerly considered his friends. Yet, not one to bear a grudge, only three years later, in the closely-knit world of Lancaster, Sharpe was serving alongside George Burrow, the railway company chairman (of a family close to the Langshaws), on the committee of the Lancaster Literary, Scientific & Natural History Society, and in 1843 joined other directors as a member of the Police Commission.

The 'Little' North Western Railway

In 1845, as the railway boom gathered pace, Edmund Sharpe joined with others to promote what became known as the 'Little' North Western Railway (to distinguish it from the much larger London & North Western formed the same year). The aim was to link industrial Yorkshire with the north Lancashire coast and provide a route to meet the projected Lancaster to Carlisle line near Milnthorpe with a branch running south to Lancaster down the Lune Valley. It would stimulate trade in industrial Yorkshire through imports and exports via the west coast which, in the process, would help revive the port of Lancaster. The bill for the railway received Royal Assent in June 1846, and the first sod was cut six months later on 31 December. Twelve directors were appointed, with Sharpe as company secretary at £600 a year. Then, at the first AGM a month later, he received a special vote of thanks and was appointed general manager as well as secretary, with company offices at his house in Fenton Street, Lancaster.

The contentious issue was how to improve

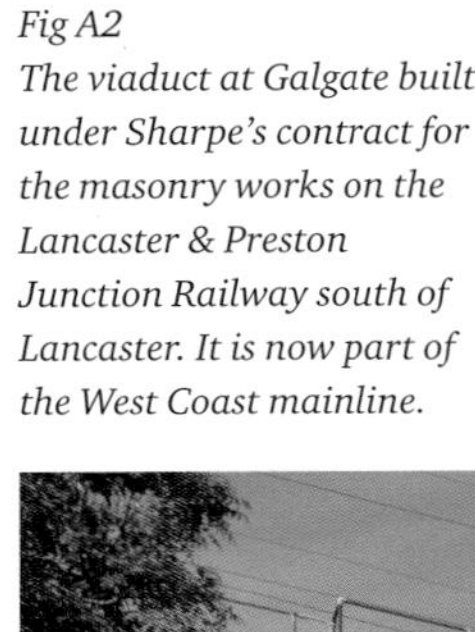

Fig A2
The viaduct at Galgate built under Sharpe's contract for the masonry works on the Lancaster & Preston Junction Railway south of Lancaster. It is now part of the West Coast mainline.

Fig A3
'Lancaster Stone Quarry. Augt 29. 1837', *drawn by Emily Sharpe. Her brother Edmund opened two such quarries for his work on the railway south of Lancaster. The view looks out towards Morecambe Bay. (Austin Paley Archive, Lancaster City Museums, MS LM 86/129; Tim Austin)*

the link to the sea. Three possibilities were considered: improvements to the River Lune; alterations at Glasson Dock, six miles downstream; and a ship canal from Morecambe to Lancaster. Despite Sharpe's zeal for the last venture, nothing came of any of them, largely owing to cost. The final solution, thrashed out during 1845–6, was building port facilities at Morecambe with a railway link to Lancaster. To this end the Morecambe Harbour & Railway Company had been established but it was promptly taken over by the 'Little' North Western after October 1846. Sharpe was a key player in both enterprises, and engaged in puzzling, if not conflicting, financial manoeuvrings. He had been the initiator of the ship canal idea but then became a director of the Harbour Company, whose interests should have been at odds with his role as a Lancaster Quay Commissioner and town councillor. Indeed, in the takeover of the harbour company by the 'L'NWR, for which the directors were largely the same people, Sharpe seems to have been in negotiation with himself!

In April 1847 Sharpe resigned as secretary to tender for constructing part of the line – four miles from Morecambe to Lancaster and a further 10 up the Lune Valley to Wennington. This produced a somewhat awkward situation since Sharpe, as company secretary, no doubt had had access to existing tenders. However, the issue was resolved after the directors asked the resident engineer, John Watson, to scrutinise matters. His recommendation to accept Sharpe's tender of £100,000 (excluding the bridge over the Lune at Lancaster) was quickly seized upon since it was well below the Parliamentary estimate and other tenders. The Lancaster–Morecambe line was opened in June 1848 with a wooden jetty at Morecombe handling iron ore from Furness, cattle from Ireland, and passenger traffic from as far afield as Scotland. The Morecambe Harbour scheme was scaled down on execution but the port thrived for over 30 years. A large hotel to designs by Sharpe & Paley was built in 1847–8 (Sharpe laid the foundation stone) and a stone quay was developed from 1853, although Morecambe would never rival the other major Lancashire ports. On 31 October 1849, Sharpe's 40th birthday and in his last week as mayor, the first train left Morecambe for Wennington, and the line was officially opened on 17 November.[17]

In 1849 Edmund Sharpe even joined the 'L'NWR board and was promptly appointed to the key Executive and Finance Committees. His involvement took an unusual turn when he offered to take over running the line, resigning as a director and becoming its traffic manager from September: 'The company's minutes indicate that he was to provide all the locomotives, rolling stock, and operating staff, to work a service between Skipton and Lancaster, at 11d. per mile run, the passenger trains to run at an average speed of 22 m.p.h.'[18] As the completion of the main line drew near, the company realised that it still lacked the necessary rolling stock to satisfy the Board of Trade. Sharpe again provided the answer: the company let its carriage works to him for seven years and 'immediately gave him an order for a hundred goods wagons, at £75 each, five carriage trucks at £85 each, twenty cattle wagons at £100 each, and two horse boxes at £120 each'.[19] At the same time the company turned down an offer from Sharpe to lease the line at £500 per week for a term of seven years.[20]

Sharpe's employment with the 'Little' North Western was abruptly terminated at the end of January 1852 after technical problems with some of the locomotives and rolling stock.[21] Also a two-year dip in company fortunes from 1850 led to joint arrangements with the Midland Railway, which began working the 'L'NWR's lines from June 1852 (it finally absorbed them in 1871). Sharpe had been trading on a substantial scale. At the termination of his contract he was paid £21,000 for locomotives and rolling stock in his possession, together with severance compensation of £5,600.[22]

The Liverpool, Crosby & Southport Railway

Sharpe was briefly connected with the Liverpool, Crosby & Southport Railway which was approved in 1847, partly opened in 1848 and fully opened in 1851.[23] He was for a short time company secretary to the railway, which at first leased its rolling stock and right of entry to its Liverpool terminus from the Lancashire & Yorkshire Railway Company. At some point the L&Y, seeking to put pressure on the smaller company, announced that it would stop leasing it rolling stock. Sharpe had seen this coming and had made surreptitious arrangements to confound the L&Y's plans by supplying locomotives and carriages. The railway was eventually amalgamated with the L&Y in 1855, but not before Sharpe had submitted proposals in May 1854 to construct a North Docks branch to run from Marsh Lane station through the village of Bootle to the south-east corner of the Prince's Dock in Liverpool.[24] Sharpe would initially have to bear all the £90,000 costs (excluding the enabling bill) and, once again, he offered to work the whole line himself for a fee of £10,500 per annum, on a 14-year contract. A truncated version of the new line opened in 1855 but bore little resemblance to Sharpe's initial proposals.

The Phoenix Foundry

In mid-1852 Edmund Sharpe became proprietor of the Phoenix Foundry in Lancaster, some 300 yards east of the music hall, and begun in 1827 as the Lune Foundry on Cable Street. For a brief period, between October 1852 and December 1853, it was administered by a partnership between James Atherton and Thomas Storey (later Sir Thomas of Storey Brothers), both of whom had worked for Sharpe on the 'Little' North Western Railway. In 1853 the foundry gained the contract for iron piping for the new Lancaster water supply and in August 1855 it received its first order for shells for use in the Crimean War, the quality of which was much praised.[25] After Sharpe's death in 1877 the foundry remained in the family, being run by his eldest son, Francis, who in 1880 married E G Paley's second daughter, Margaret. It lasted into the early 20th century as Sharpe & Co.[26]

The struggle for sanitary reform

From the mid-1840s Sharpe embarked upon two large projects which would occupy him for almost nine years. One was a railway-building venture to be considered later. The other was the improvement of Lancaster's woeful sanitation, which had led to a cholera outbreak in 1843 (the same year that Sharpe was appointed to the Police Commission, whose responsibilities included sanitation).

After the setting up of the Health of Large Towns Commission in 1844, a group of Lancastrians asked it to investigate conditions there and Professor Richard Owen, the distinguished anatomist and himself a Lancastrian, was appointed to the task. His damning report in July 1845 told of appalling conditions. Two years later nothing had happened, so Sharpe instigated a petition (collecting more than 1,600 signatures personally) to the Commission in November 1847.[27] Robert Rawlinson, another Lancastrian and a well-qualified civil engineer, was then appointed to look into matters again. His report took a year to appear, by which time Lancaster had set up, in October 1848, its own Sanitary Committee, comprising members of the Police Commissioners, Town Council and Poor Law Guardians.[28] Then, on 9 November, Edmund Sharpe was elected mayor, and with the threat of Asiatic cholera looming again he galvanised the Committee into achieving numerous small-scale but cumulatively significant sanitary improvements throughout the town. Rawlinson's eventual report set out two overarching needs: a new sewerage system, and a reliable supply of wholesome water. Sharpe welcomed the report, yet (as he explained in a 50-page book chronicling sanitary reform in Lancaster, published in the last year of his life; Fig A4) Rawlinson's plans seemed to him overly expensive and he doubted whether the proposed water supply would be adequate in either quality or quantity.[29]

In the same month, November 1848, Sharpe and his co-belligerents met the newly formed General Board of Health in London, and were told that if mortality in Lancaster exceeded 23 in 1,000 inhabitants a year, the board would send in an inspector and, if necessary, impose a new Local Board of Health, thus taking matters away from the ineffective Police Commissioners. Sharpe and his colleagues established that mortality was indeed above the threshold and informed the General Board accordingly. A Scot, James Smith, was immediately appointed as inspector and discovered (predictably) that 'all the localities that were unhealthy and filthy [when Owen] ... made his inspection ... are unhealthy and filthy still'.[30] Smith's report recommended implementing Rawlinson's plans, but this was far from welcome to various 'interested parties' in the town who foresaw the effect on their pockets, albeit spread over a long period of time.[31] 'This alarm', Sharpe later recalled angrily, 'predominated over every other consideration; the fear of cholera was, in fact, overcome by the fear of increased taxation; and the opponents of sanitary reform won an easy victory.'[32]

However, the General Board of Health would have none of this, and included Lancaster in an Act transferring the powers of the Police Commissioners to the Town Council. The resultant Local Board of Health first met on 22 August 1849, presided over by Sharpe as mayor, whose understandable satisfaction was tempered by the fierce local opposition. In September 1849 he convened a meeting at his house which selected six pro-reform candidates for the forthcoming municipal elections, and 'four of the strongest opponents of Sanitary Reform' were successfully ousted.[33] Then in December he published *A Proposal for Supplying the Town of Lancaster with WATER, and for improving its SEWERAGE*, in which he offered to undertake the resewering work himself for the sum of £5,500. Ever the resourceful businessman, he also offered to deliver 200,000 gallons of clean water a day from the River Lune for £6,450.

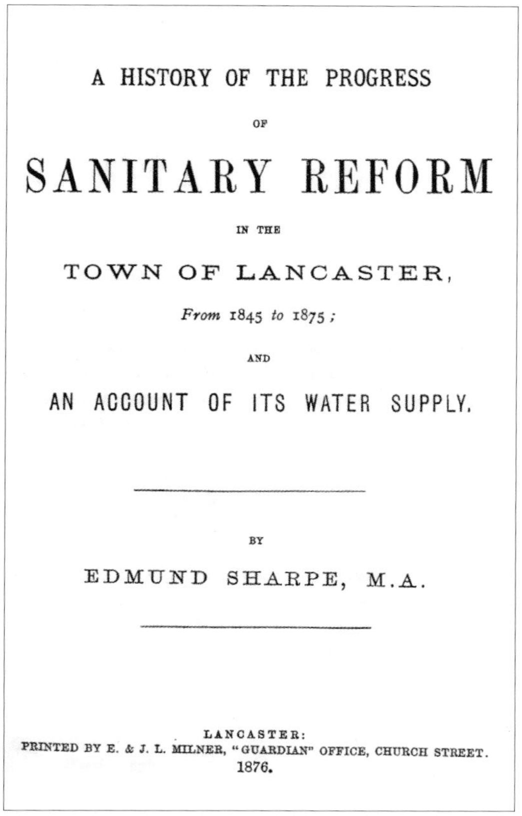

Sharpe's proposals were well received, but matters drifted on until April 1850, when Rawlinson was again appointed to prepare plans. Delay ensued once more; public interest waned and by the spring of 1851 had turned into opposition once more. Sharpe too was highly critical of Rawlinson's proposals, concluding that they would yield much less than the desired 200,000 gallons of water a day. The final solution appeared from an unexpected quarter.[34] The labour master at the Lancaster workhouse, a

A HISTORY OF THE PROGRESS

OF

SANITARY REFORM

IN THE

TOWN OF LANCASTER,

From 1845 to 1875;

AND

AN ACCOUNT OF ITS WATER SUPPLY.

BY

EDMUND SHARPE, M.A.

LANCASTER:
PRINTED BY E. & J. L. MILNER, "GUARDIAN" OFFICE, CHURCH STREET.
1876.

Fig A4
The title page of Sharpe's account of sanitary reform in Lancaster, published in the last year of his life. (John Hughes collection)

young man called Bartholomew Dodding, a former gamekeeper on the Wyreside Fells some six miles south-east of Lancaster, had noticed abundant springs of pure water issuing from Littledale Fell to the north of the River Wyre. After meeting with initial scepticism, he discussed his observations with Richard Hinde, a local sanitary reformer, and the two men, along with Edmund Sharpe, visited the area to gauge the flow of the streams, which amounted to a magnificent 800,000 gallons a day. Matters now moved forward, and in June 1852 a parliamentary Act empowered the Lancaster Corporation to draw 300,000 gallons daily from the Wyresdale Fells.

Progress with the water supply led to demands for improving Lancaster's sewerage. The immediate catalyst was a damning report in May 1852 from the Board of Guardians showing a shocking death rate of over 50 per 1,000, which Sharpe ascribed to 'the want of a complete and perfect system of sewerage'.[35] The obvious answer was a system of drains flushed by water, now about to be available in abundance. In October 1852 the battle for reform was finally won when agreement was reached on both the water supply and new sewerage projects (to avoid digging up the streets twice). The first water arrived from the Grizedale springs in June 1854 amid scenes of jubilation, and the waterworks were finally complete in 1855. Meanwhile, with victory in sight, Edmund Sharpe attended fewer meetings of the Local Board of Health and the Town Council, finally resigning his seat in November 1853.

A move to North Wales

In 1856 Edmund Sharpe moved with his family to the Conwy Valley in North Wales, leasing a house for two years before buying a large, Italianate property called 'Coed-y-Celyn', just under a mile south of Betws-y-Coed. Although he still had major business interests in Lancaster, his personal ties with the town had been loosened by the death of his mother the year before. Presumably now a wealthy man, he seems to have been attracted by the idea of a being a person of substance in an attractive area of countryside which conveniently offered a new business opportunity and where, possibly, there were family connections. Sharpe's aunt Mary had married Dr Peter Holland of Knutsford, whose brother Samuel (1768–1851) had been well established in Liverpool commerce and also had extensive slate-producing interests in the Blaenau Ffestiniog area, later taken over by his son, also Samuel (1803–92). At a time when Welsh slate was roofing the world, a railway down the Conwy Valley to export slate and minerals by joining the Chester & Holyhead line seemed highly desirable, while the rapidly developing North Wales tourist trade was seen as a further source of lucrative summer income.

Such a line had been mooted in 1853–4, but not until Sharpe became involved and carried out detailed survey work was much progress made. In a 32-page printed letter to the President of the Board of Trade in 1857, he made a bold attempt to promote the idea of narrow-gauge railways in mountainous districts, using the Conwy Valley by way of illustration.[36] Nothing came of this, but a draft prospectus for such a line was produced with Charles Holland (brother of Samuel junior) as one of the provisional directors and Edmund Sharpe as engineer. In the event, the parliamentary bill in 1860 was for a standard gauge line for which Sharpe now became, at once, consulting engineer,[37] financier and contractor. The first sods were cut on 27 August and the 10½-mile line from Llandudno Junction to Llanrwst was opened on 17 June 1863, by which time it had become part of the mighty London & North Western.[38] Sharpe and his new railway must have created quite an impression, and his praise was hymned by a quarryman-poet from Blaenau Ffestiniog, Rowland Walter (bardic name Iono-ron Glan Dwyryd). Among his 98 lines, Ionoron sings of the shout of the crowd on opening day – 'Virtuous Sharp[e]'![39] Yet Sharpe did not hear the enthusiasm. He had already, in April, moved with his family to the Continent, where they would stay for the next three years.[40] The first of two projects there, which would run concurrently, was a pair of tramways in Geneva.

The Geneva tramways

In 1861 the London firm of Charles Burn & Co secured a contract to build a four-mile horse-drawn tramway from the centre of Geneva to the district of Carouge to the south (Fig A5).[41] Its success encouraged Burn to propose, in 1862, a line east to Chêne-Bougeries, about six miles from the centre, to be extended eventually a further four miles to Moillesulaz on the French border. While matters progressed, Burn announced in April 1863 that his sole associate in this enterprise was now Edmund Sharpe, who was planning to spend some months in Geneva and had already rented a large property on the road to Chêne.[42] The contract for the second line was awarded nominally in the name of 'Charles Burn & Co.' but effectively to Edmund Sharpe, who accepted its terms on 18 July from Paris. Here he had rejoined Burn after spending some time at Chamonix for his health. Thereafter, the two dissolved the partnership on 1 December 1863, leaving Sharpe as sole concessionaire, having paid Burn compensation of a princely £7,600.

Curiously, Sharpe seems to have operated mainly from Paris, where he was also supervising (apparently not very well) the building of a railway in the south of France. Nevertheless, in March 1864 a public circular in Geneva stated that Edmund Sharpe was now the sole operator for the existing Geneva–Carouge line, and the sole contractor for the Geneva–Chêne line. In October he asked to transfer the contract to the Commercial Bank of Geneva, which was agreed on 4 June 1865. Thereafter, the city authorities naturally dealt with the bank's administrators, and Sharpe's name disappears from the official record.

A technical report for the Geneva authorities shows how Sharpe introduced an innovation for the second line of flat rails with a third, grooved rail between them to receive a guide wheel which the operator could retract at will. This enabled him to leave the tracks and steer the carriage around unexpected obstacles or bring it to one side of the road to deposit passengers. The author of the report mentioned that this system was already operating in Manchester and that this was its first known application on the Continent.[43]

The last railway venture – Perpignan to Prades, France

Sharpe's last railway venture was in southern France, and was as disastrous, if not more so, than his first, south of Lancaster. Ideas had been mooted in 1858 to link Perpignan, near the Roussillon coast, with Prades, 26 miles away in the Pyrenees. As in the Conwy Valley, this was to be primarily an industrial line, bringing exports from and raw materials to inland metal industries. Sharpe tendered for its construction to the French government, which made a grant of 1,999,000 francs towards it.[44] On 29 August

Fig A5
Trams still run in Geneva on the routes originally laid out by Edmund Sharpe. This is the stop at Carouge in 2010.

1863, exactly two months after securing the second Geneva tramway, Sharpe was awarded the concession (Fig A6).

Physically the line presented no particular difficulties, with few major works. The conditions required Sharpe to form a company to capitalise the railway, complete the work within two years and, as soon as possible, operate the line.[45] As it turned out, all this was hopelessly optimistic and by the end of 1865 hardly anything had been achieved. Sharpe's subcontractors were in difficulties and Sharpe himself spent most of his time in Paris rather than Perpignan, maybe in order to deal with the finances of the project. Perhaps because of the stress involved, his health failed, causing him to take a long convalescent break in Italy.

On 4 December 1865 – when the enterprise should have been complete – the chief engineer, Monsieur Giret, gave the glum report to the Préfet at Perpignan that 'Little progress has been made ... only the [first] section between Perpignan and Millas has been undertaken'. The local landowners, he said, had been uncooperative and Sharpe had been 'unable to deal amicably with [them] ... so that it has not been possible to establish construction sites except at a few points'.[46] No limited company had been

PREFECTURE DES PYRÉNÉES-ORIENTALES.

CHEMIN DE FER
DE
PERPIGNAN A PRADES.

ARRETÉ.

Nous, PRÉFET du département des Pyrénées-Orientales, Officier de la Légion-d'Honneur, etc.,

Vu la demande du sieur Edmond Sharpe, concessionnaire du chemin de fer de Perpignan à Prades, tendant à obtenir l'autorisation d'entreprendre les études du tracé définitif dudit chemin de fer;

Vu le décret de concession du 29 août dernier et la loi du 16 septembre 1807;

ARRÊTONS:

ART. 1er. — Les Ingénieurs et tous autres agents employés par le sieur Edmond Sharpe aux études du tracé définitif du chemin de fer de Perpignan à Prades, sont autorisés à pénétrer dans les propriétés clôses et non clôses, à poser au besoin des jalons, signaux, bornes et repères, à couper les haies, branches d'arbres, arbres, etc., etc., qui porteraient obstacle aux opérations dont il s'agit et qui doivent s'exécuter sur le territoire des deux arrondissements de Perpignan et Prades.

ART. 2. — Les propriétaires des terrains sont tenus en conséquence, sous les peines de droit, d'en laisser le libre accès auxdits ingénieurs et agents et de n'apporter aucun obstacle à la pose comme à la conservation des jalons, signaux, bornes, repères, etc., à la charge par le sieur Edmond Sharpe de pourvoir au paiement des indemnités qui pourraient être dues pour les dommages causés. Ces indemnités seront réglées, à défaut d'accord entre les parties, conformément aux prescriptions de la loi du 16 septembre 1807.

ART. 3. — MM. les Maires sont invités à user au besoin de toute leur autorité pour faciliter aux ingénieurs et autres agents du sieur Sharpe les opérations auxquelles ils sont appelés à procéder.

Perpignan, le 20 octobre 1863.

LE PRÉFET,

Cte E. DE COETLOGON.

Perpignan, Imprimerie de Mlle. A. TASTU.

Fig A6
Public notice announcing Sharpe's concession to build the Perpignan-Prades railway and the rights of access for his surveyors. (R Jolley collection; John Hughes collection)

formed, and the first instalment of government money (333,000 francs) could not be paid to Sharpe until he was in a position to show he had expended three times that amount – which he had not. He planned, said Giret, 'to use his own capital and personal credit to build about two thirds of the line, that is as far as Bouleternère'. Eventually, after public anger had erupted in 1867 in the still-railwayless communities around Prades, Sharpe renounced his concession, probably at considerable financial loss. Eventually the first 16 miles of track was inaugurated in December 1868, and one of those in attendance, whether hero or villain, was 'M. Sharpe, entrepreneur de l'exploitation'. As if symbolic of the whole dismal story, even this opening was premature and services had to be suspended until January 1870. The complete line to Prades did not open finally until 3 January 1877.

Sharpe established at least one other business interest in France. He applied for a concession in 1869 to work iron ore mines at Escaro-Sud in the Pyrénées-Orientales, close to the Spanish border, which was granted in 1873.[47] It passed after Sharpe's death to his children, and was sold in 1885 for 520,000 francs by his eldest son, Francis, representing his siblings.

Electoral reformer

On returning to Lancaster in 1866 Sharpe involved himself in a local political issue which took on a national dimension. At the general election the previous year Lancaster sent two Liberals to Parliament: E M Fenwick (later to be a co-governor with Sharpe at Sedbergh School), and H W Schneider, industrial magnate of Barrow. They were found guilty by a Royal Commission of bribery and corruption in apparently 'buying' votes. In consequence, Lancaster (along with Reigate) was disenfranchised under the 1867 Reform Act, and remained so for nearly 20 years.

Sharpe objected that this penalised the 'innocent' electors, who had not succumbed to financial inducement, along with the 'guilty'. So in March that year, whilst staying with his distant relatives the Feildens at Bonchurch on the Isle of Wight (possibly for health reasons), he penned a long letter to Disraeli, Chancellor of the Exchequer in Lord Derby's third Ministry, putting forward his proposals for electoral reform. Characteristically, he had this printed and distributed in pamphlet form by the office of the *Lancaster Guardian*.

Sharpe's proposals were not altogether dissimilar from those Disraeli himself put forward the same year. They were based on a long lecture Sharpe had given in May 1859 at the Lancaster Music Hall, where, at his oratorical best, he had championed the rights of the middle classes, and showed a surprising dislike and distrust of the secret ballot. A mixed reaction had ensued, with a lengthy leader in the *Guardian* energetically rebutting some of his ideas.

In his letter to Disraeli, having established population and property in equal measure as the twin foundations of representation, Sharpe addressed the difficulty of obtaining the necessary balance between them: the number of votes exercised by any elector should be in proportion to the rates he paid, up to a maximum of six. Had this been the case in 1865, he argued, Lancaster would never have been disenfranchised. In the event, Sharpe's pleas attracted no governmental attention – if indeed they ever reached Disraeli, who never replied. Such a reverse would no doubt have disappointed Sharpe but such things were relatively rare in his rich and varied life. Entering the last decade of his life, he would have been able to look back on a lifetime filled with many achievements as politician, engineer, businessman, writer and architect.

APPENDIX 2
PUPILS AND OTHERS ASSOCIATED WITH THE OFFICE

The office was a busy one and took on assistants and pupils from its very early years, the first being E G Paley, who joined Edmund Sharpe in October 1838. As is the case with all other Victorian architectural practices, no comprehensive list of pupils and assistants exists, and the following has been assembled from a multiplicity of sources.[1] It is impossible to say how complete it is, but it probably includes all the significant names who passed through the office and into the annals of architectural history: Tom Austin, John Douglas and R J Withers. Some of the lesser figures moved on to independent careers and added to the country's building stock but, in common with the vast majority of architects, did not produce work that attracts particular attention. Apart from those listed here, there would have been many assistants, improvers, surveyors and clerks who remained unnoticed, but whose work was essential to the functioning of the office and making its achievements possible.

Much use has been made of the RIBA's *Dictionary of British Architects, 1834–1914* (*see* Brodie *et al*, 2002), although individual facts therefrom are not usually referenced here.

Edmund Sharpe / Sharpe & Paley

Austin, Thomas, 1822–67. *See* p 81–4.

Brown, Walter Talbot (1852–1931). Accompanied ES on his last Continental tour as an assistant, 1877. Articled to E F Law of Northampton, 1869–74. Contributed to the first volume of the *John O'Gaunt Sketchbook,* 1874–5 (and the next two, 1876–85). Pugin student, 1877. Established practice in Wellingborough (Northamptonshire), probably in 1877, and with his partner from 1880, J W Fisher, was a very successful local architect, practising as W Talbot Brown & Fisher.

Douglas, John, 1830–1911.[2] Articled mid/late 1840s and afterwards chief assistant to EGP. Son of a builder and joiner (also John, *c* 1799–1862) of Sandiway (Ch), who was employing 48 men at the 1851 census. Set up practice in Chester either 1855 or 1860, according to Hubbard's book on Douglas (*see* Hubbard 1991, 22). Later in partnership with D P Fordham 1884–97, and C H Minshull 1897–1909. Hubbard does not explain his 1855 and 1860 dates: Douglas's first work was a garden ornament at Oakmere (Ch) in 1856, but CS (pers comm) points out that this very minor work was for a friend of his father's and is no indicator of Douglas's having set up in Chester[3] until 1859 when 'John Douglas, architect of Chester' purchased land at Hartford (Ch) on which he built a house, 'Mersey Vale', 282 Chester Road (ex info Peter Howell). He married (on 25 January 1860) and, on balance, it seems likely that he stayed with Paley until a year or two before his marriage. First appears as occupying 6 Abbey Square in 1860, which was initially both home and office (and later just an office).

Henman, William, 1846–1917. Began practice in Stockton-on-Tees 1871. His obituary in the *JRIBA* (1917 ser 3 24, 223) says that after being articled to his father (1866) he later 'assisted Edmund Sharpe with his work on Architecture' (cf Brown, Johnson and Wood), presumably drawings and research for his writings, lectures and/or Architectural Association excursions.[4] Henman was not one of the three research assistants he took to Italy in the 1870s.

Taylor, William, 1829–71. Born at Lancaster. 'Architect's clerk' at 1851 census. Sometime assistant of ES: said to have joined Walsh (*below*) in Blackburn,[5] where he was an architect at the 1861 census.

Walsh, Thomas Harrison, 1815–59. Born at Blackburn. Eldest son of Thomas Walsh, builder and joiner,[6] who undertook carpentry at St Mark, Witton, 1836–8. A Mr Walsh was one of those whose life was saved by Tom Austin when the boat crewed by members of the practice overturned in the mid-1840s.[7] He was with S&P when the latter worked on St Mary, Lancaster, 1848–9. In 1844 he married Elizabeth (d 1854), sister of Joseph Shrigley, and they built 'Mawdale' (now 'Rivendell') on the corner of Westbourne Road and Milking Stile Lane in 1849. 'Architect' in 1851 census. Master of the Lodge of Fortitude Dec 1853. Moved to Blackburn after the death of his wife where he was later joined by Taylor (*above*).[8] There in 1855, he designed the Bank Top Schools, 1855-6, and buildings at Blackburn Cemetery (opened 1857), where his father was Clerk of Works.[9] At his death, lived at Whalley.

Withers, Robert Jewell, 1824–94. Born at Shepton Mallet, Somerset, but educated from age 10 at Newport, Isle of Wight. Articled to Thomas Hellyer of Ryde, Isle of Wight, from 1839 (there at 1841 census). Went on a trip to Furness Abbey with Tom Austin, ES and EGP in Sept 1842. His name appears on five of the lithographs for Sharpe's *Architectural Parallels*, 1842–6. Hon Secretary Lancaster Regatta, 1846–7. Commenced practice Sherborne, Dorset (where his parents had moved), 1848; moved to London 1851. ARIBA 30.4.1849; retired from RIBA 1860, yet was a FRIBA 19.12.1864. His churches received enthusiastic notices in *The Ecclesiologist*.

Wood, Walter James, b c 1855. Articled to W M Teulon & Cronk.[10] Assistant to ES on his drawings in Britain and abroad (cf Brown, Henman and Johnson). In offices of Harman & Harrison, John Tavenor Perry and Frederick Henry Reed. Commenced independent practice 1878 Prittlewell, Southend, Essex. ARIBA 20.3.1882.

E G Paley

Harrison, John, 1837–96. P&A's representative in Barrow-in-Furness (CuL). Born in Lancaster, the son of a stonemason (also John), was an errand boy in 1851, but styled 'Architect' in the 1861 census. Seems likely his training was with EGP and, since he went on to design for the firm, he probably undertook articles with him. At 1871 census still living in Lancaster, and Masonic records indicate he moved to Barrow the following year.[11] His first professional involvement there is said to be the design for the base of Sir James Ramsden's statue, unveiled 21.5.1872, although there is some doubt about this.[12] His combined home and office was at 16 Church Street, where the 1881 and 1891 censuses record him as unmarried, but by his death in 1896 he had moved to 10 Strand. Oversaw the construction of P&A buildings in the area and, indeed, designed many of them. His obituary in the *Barrow Herald* 8.4.1896, says: 'Most of the railway stations on the Furness Railway are built to the design of this firm, Mr Harrison having had sole charge of the work of erection.' But three days later the paper had an editorial notice saying that 'Mr. Harrison has had to do with the designing of very many of the buildings in and about Barrow'. The same edition carried a longer obituary, which stated specifically: 'Most of the railway stations on the Furness Railway were built to Mr. Harrison's designs and under his care.' Not only that: 'He also designed the two banks in Ramsden Square, and among other professional work of Mr. Harrison's we might mention the Dalton Parish Church, St James' Church Barrow, the new chancel to St George's Church, Barrow, the restored Eskdale Church, the pretty lodge across the [railway] line from Abbotswood, and many other of the chief buildings in the district.' Some of these attributions, notably Dalton church, may be an embellishment of the facts, but nonetheless Harrison seems to have been a much-trusted member of the firm. Obituary notice in the *Barrow News,* 3.4.1896, said he had been the 'local representative for Paley and Austin in Barrow for over 25 years', [13] although the last formal mention so far discovered of the firm's having a base in the town is in 1886.[14] But, as so often with architectural practices, a loose association with Harrison was probably kept up.

Johnson, Richard Wright, 1844–1909. Articled *c* 1859 ('Apprentice to an Architect' at 1861 census).[15] In a series of almost weekly advertisements on the front page of the *Lancaster Gazette* Nov 1877–Feb 1878, he announced himself as a former pupil of EGP, 'and for the last ten years Principal Draughtsman to the late Edmund Sharpe, M.A., F.R.I.B.A.' and gave his (presumably new) address as 'Temple Chambers, 28 Church Street, Liverpool'.[16] This suggests that he was commissioned to undertake drawing work for ES's various publications and lectures (cf Brown, Henman and Wood), leaving Lancaster for Liverpool after his employer's death in May 1877. Late 1879 moved to 36 Prescot Road, Old Swan, describing himself as an 'Architect, Illuminator, Draughtsman, &c'.[17] Last noted as an 'Architect and Surveyor' 1894.[18]

Langshaw, George, 1848–1901. Younger brother of Fanny Langshaw (who married Hubert Austin). Articled to EGP (nd, *c* 1865), then three years in G E Street's office. Commenced practice 1878. ARIBA 9.1.1882, when one of his proposers was EGP, the others being T E Collcutt and T W Cutler.[19] In 1881 based at 16 Red Lion Square, London, lodging with the architect John Henry Eastwood (1843–1913) who began practice that year. After moved to Ockham (Surrey), where he lived with his brother Pearson Charles (1851–92), a land agent: both buried at Brookwood Cemetery. No works by him are mentioned in the *Buildings of England CD-ROM*, 1995.

Ralph, William Chasen, 1848–1913.[20] Articled to EGP 1864: remained as an assistant until 1875. With John Douglas 1875–90. Commenced independent practice in Wigan 1890. FRIBA 1903.

Paley & Austin

Ainslie, Wilfred, 1859–1936.[21] Articled 1877. Improver to Ewan Christian 1881. Clerk of Works Grayshott Hall (Hampshire), 1886–7. In independent practice with John Henry Townsend Woodd (1855–1939) 1887 until *c* 1914. FRIBA 1903.

Baines, Thomas, 1863–1946. 'Architect's clerk' at the 1881 census. Did drawings of the Priory church, Lancaster, in 1882; contributed to the *John O'Gaunt Sketch Book*, vol 3, 1879–85; and produced photographs of Nazareth House, Lancaster, 1902. Periodic survey work at Sedbergh School for A&P, *c* 1898–1900.[22] 'Building Surveyor' at 16 Hubert Place at 1901 census (same address 1911, when Bulmer's *Directory*, 1911, calls him 'Assistant Architect'). Clerk of Works for perhaps 30 years, including for a shop by A&P, 1902.[23] Worked with HAP as an assistant and surveyor. Last recorded involvement was signing a report on Preston parish church in Nov 1939.[24]

Barlow, Luke, 1853–1933. His father, Thomas Varley Barlow, was employed at Edmund Sharpe's Phoenix Iron Foundry, Lancaster, where he was a 'clerk' in 1861, and 'manager' by 1871.[25] His obituary in 1911 noted that 'Mr. Sharpe largely left the management to Mr. Barlow' and this rising career may have helped pave the way for his son's pupilage with P&A from 1869.[26] Was a Freemason from 1877, when he was initiated into the Duke of Lancaster Lodge (no 1353).[27] Remained as an assistant until 1881. EGP, his chief sponsor for RIBA associateship, described him as 'a painstaking pupil and afterwards a valuable assistant in the office'.[28] Then assistant to Edmund Kirby, Liverpool, 1882, and John Lowe, Manchester, 1883–94. Passed RIBA qualifying exam 1894. EGP signed the ARIBA nomination papers on 22.12.1894, but had died by the time Barlow was elected on 11.3.1895.

Practised independently in Manchester from 1894, in which year he won the Lancaster market hall extension and hotel competition assessed by HJA.[29]

Beckett, Richard Thomas, 1867–1937. Articled 1886–90. Passed RIBA qualifying exam 1890. ARIBA 16.6.1890, when one of his proposers was EGP; re-elected 1911, resigned 1920. In the office of John Douglas (*see* p 198) 1890–4. In 1894 set up in practice either with Edmund Rathbone of Liverpool[30] or independently in Hartford (Ch). Partnership with Rathbone dissolved 1911 and set up in practice in Chester until 1914. Did not return to architecture after service with the Royal Engineers 1915–22.

Hall, John Compton, 1863–1937.[31] Educated at King William's College, Isle of Man. Articled to J Medland & Henry Taylor, Manchester, from 1880. Then went to London to gain experience with William White, 1884–5. With P&A 1885–8, when he set up a partnership in London with William Oswald Milne (1847–1927). FRIBA 1901.

Milne, Charles, 1856–1927. Aged 14 at the 1871 census, and was described as 'Architect', living with his parents at 28 Castle Hill, near P&A's offices. Ten years later still at the same address and described as 'Architect's Assistant'. Contributed a drawing to vol 3 of the *John O'Gaunt Sketch Book* (1879–85); this, along with the proximity of P&A's office, suggests he worked there. His older brother Edward (b 1851) contributed to vol 1 of the *Sketch Book* (1874–5).[32] Died at Preston, where he had been at the 1901 census.

Perkin, Joseph Craddock, *c* 1862–1942.[33] Articled 1877; remained an assistant until 1883. Assistant to Horace Cheston of London 1883–5. Commenced practice 1885 while remaining as assistant to Cheston; then in partnership with him 1892–1913. FRIBA 1905.

Tarney, James, 1867–1959. Educated at Lancaster Grammar School. Did not serve articles with P&A but worked in the firm for over 60 years – and was the last man to run the practice from 1936 to 1945, retiring aged 80. His obituary[34] says he designed the Morecambe war memorial, and St Christopher, Bare, also in Morecambe,[35] as well as the bishop's throne and canons' stalls at Lancaster Cathedral, and the King's Own Chapel at St Mary's, Lancaster (the latter attribution is wrong since it was the work of HJA). It adds that he was involved with the restoration at St John, Sandilands; St Lawrence; St Barnabas; and Emmanuel Free Church of England, all in Morecambe. Lived at Morecambe for 66 years.

Tonge, James Humphreys, 1866–1943. Born in Stafford. Son of John, a builder from Stockport. By 1881 living in Barrow-in-Furness where P&A had an office and where the census notes that his father was a Clerk of Works. Soon associated with P&A, perhaps initially in Barrow with John Harrison (q v). Contributor to the *John O'Gaunt Sketchbook* 3, 1879–85. By 1892 studying in York at the School of Science and Art. Won Silver and Gold Medals in National Art competitions in 1892 and 1893. Believed to have been associated then with Demaine & Brierley, a firm with which EGP had contact from at least 1857. In the late 1890s moved to Chester where in 1901 he was an 'Architect's Assistant', working, it is believed, for John Douglas (q v). By 1911 working in Cardiff as 'Architect, Chief Assistant'. Died in Middlesex.

Wright, Samuel, 1852–1929. Educated at Lancaster Grammar School. Articled *c* 1866–73 ('Architect's Pupil' at 1871 census); worked as an assistant until *c* 1891, when he joined his father William in Wright & Son, surveyors. Continued close links with the PA&P/A&P firm, his obituary noting that he was 'associated with it for nearly 60 years'.[36] Sometimes gave his address as the A&P offices. Unlike the other chief members of the firm who were Anglicans, he was a staunch Methodist. Was P&A's representative for Sedbergh School by 1875,[37] and worked for them as an architect but more often as a surveyor and Clerk of Works. In his own right designed Wesleyan churches at Skerton; the Greaves, Lancaster;[38] and West End, Morecambe, as well as the Queen Victoria Hospital, Morecambe. Lived at Morecambe and had a long history of public service, being a member of the Local Board until it was replaced by an urban district council of which he was chair for three years, during which time he designed improvements to the promenade. Mayor 1906–7, trustee of Morecambe Queen Victoria Hospital, trustee of Green Street Wesleyan church (which he attended) and three other churches on the Morecambe Wesleyan circuit. JP for Lancashire from 1916 and, after its establishment in 1919, sat on the Morecambe Bench. For many years a member of Morecambe cricket and golf clubs. His funeral was attended by HAP and James Tarney.

Wright, William, 1826–1905. Born at Toft, Knutsford (Ch). Worked for P&A from *c* 1855 until *c* 1891, when he set up a company with his son Samuel. 'Architect's Clerk' in 1861, and 'Architect's Assistant' 1871, his role seems to have been as a surveyor ('Building Surveyor' in the 1881–1901 censuses). Acted as Clerk of Works at, for example, St Thomas, Blackburn, 1864–5. Many of the building plans for schools submitted to the Lancaster Council are signed by him.[39]

Wright, William Oswald, 1881–1951. Born Morecambe, son of Samuel Wright (q v). 'Articled clerk' in 1901; 'Architect and Surveyor's Assistant', 1911. In the First World War he became a major in the Territorial Army. Did not rejoin the staff after the war.

Paley, Austin & Paley

Armstrong, Walter Thomas, 1876–1954.[40] Born and died at Lancaster. Son of John, Skerton schoolmaster. Student 1891 at the new Storey Institute's School of Science & Art. Articled 1891: remained as an assistant until 1898. Assistant to Grayson & Ould 1898–9, to Robert Marmion 1899–1902, and Daniel Powell 1902–3 (all of Liverpool), and J C Mount of Lancaster from 1903.

Passed RIBA qualifying exam 1906. ARIBA 4.3.1907; two of his sponsors were Edward Ould and James Lomax-Simpson (with Grayson & Ould before 1905). Ould was a past pupil of John Douglas (*see* p 198). Many links to Bernard Austin's joining Grayson & Ould in 1902 and then Lomax-Simpson in 1905 (*see* p 174).

Lewis, Neander Gesenius, 1864–1937. Born in Carmarthen, son of a Baptist minister. Not confirmed as a pupil or assistant in the firm, but by 1891 living in Lancaster and described as 'Architect & Surveyor', and in 1901 in Morecambe as 'Architect'. May have been involved with A&P's work at Llandovery College, 1901–3. Died at Lewisham (then Kent).

Austin & Paley

Austin, Bernard, 1873–1955. *See* pp 174–6

Austin, Geoffrey Langshaw, 1884–1971. *See* pp 176–7

Barrow, John William, 1885–1952.[41] Articled 1900–7; remained as an assistant 1907–10. Assistant to J H Martindale, Carlisle 1911; Cumberland County Architects Department 1911–12; and to E T Dunn of Ilford from 1912. Passed RIBA qualifying exam 1912. ARIBA 1913. In 1914 in Bradford City Architect's Department.

Hinton, Charles Allen, 1893–1918.[42] Youngest brother of J G Hinton (*below*). Mentioned as staff in HJA's obituary, Mar 1915. The only member of the firm identified as losing his life in the First World War, after distinguished service and bravery in the field. Articled *c* 1907–14 ('Architect's apprentice' in 1911). Commission 2nd Lt 1/5th King's Own Royal Lancaster Regiment, Oct 1914. Arrived France 15.2.1915, very possibly the week that Geoffrey Austin joined the regiment. Transferred to Royal Engineers (North Midland Division) Jan 1916. Awarded MC (Jan 1918) & Bar (Mar 1918) 'for conspicuous gallantry and devotion to duty'. Died 22.5.1918 France; buried Fouquières-lès-Béthune (Captain, Adjt 46th (North Midland) Division).

Hinton, John Garfield, 1882–1946.[43] Brother of C A Hinton (*above*). Articled 1896–1903 and remained as assistant 1903–4. Assistant to P Morris of Exeter 1904–5, and to Hampshire Education Architect 1903–13. By 1914 working for Birmingham Education Department. Passed RIBA qualifying exam 1912. ARIBA 1913 when HAP was one of the proposers.

Slinger, John Bowness, 1896–1986. An assistant in 1915[44] and a principal mourner at HJA's funeral.[45]

Thompson, John, 1859–1931. Building surveyor 1881–1901 and a long-serving clerk in the office. For many years the Thompson family were neighbours of William Wright (*above*).

APPENDIX 3
CONTRACTORS AND CRAFTSMEN

It was common and, indeed, is to be expected that 19th-century architects would have their favourite builders and craftsmen. A close working relationship meant that each party had a reasonable idea of what to expect from the other, which must have enabled many a Clerk of Works to sleep more peacefully at night knowing that the contractor he was supervising had been tried and was trusted by his employers. The P&A/A&P practice was no exception and we find the names of their contractors and craftsmen constantly recurring. Not only Lancaster firms were involved, but also those others local to further-flung commissions.

The Catalogue in this book identifies contractors and craftsmen when known (*see* Appendix 5). Perusal will show that often, instead of there being a single main contractor (contracting 'by the great', in 18th-century parlance) two, three or even more separate trades are listed. In the pre-P&A period – that is, before 1868 – in cases where it is known who was responsible for the work, separate trades contracting outnumbered 'by the great' by about five to four. After that, until 1914, although separate trades were still responsible for the construction of many of the firm's buildings, this method was outnumbered by single-contract work by more than two to one. After the First World War almost all the contracts for Harry Paley's buildings were taken by single contractors.[1] Whether this reliance on multiple-trade contracting in the early to mid-Victorian period was in any way peculiar to the firm or to the north-west must, at present, be a matter of conjecture.[2] An obvious reason for letting a job to separate trades rather than a single contractor is that the latter bears all the risk and is likely to reflect this in a price greater than the sum of individual tenders. But it was E G Paley himself who supplied another reason when dealing with work at Sedbergh School (CuWY) in 1876–7. He reported to the governors that all-in bids for the Second Master's house would work out at some £10,000, whereas by dividing up the trades up the job could be built for £8,748.[3] Some months earlier he had advanced the interesting argument that a main contractor would probably sublet work, which would lead to less easy control than in the case of a series of individual, direct contracts 'as a contractor for the whole work might, and probably would, sublet and make his own terms with the sub-contractors, who would not be so amenable to the Clerk of Works as when contracting directly with the Governing Body'.[4] How typical local building processes were must await further investigation of the Victorian building trades.

Strong links between the firm and particular contractors is not much in evidence until the start of the P&A era but this is no doubt partly because the names are not known. We find Messrs Storey & Lawrence working on a couple of significant Edmund Sharpe jobs (the Lancaster Lunatic Asylum *c* 1840, and Capernwray Hall *c* 1845), while Thomas Cross's debut appearance as a plasterer and slater at Sharpe & Paley's rebuilding of the chancel at Bolton-le-Sands in 1847 is the first of a long series which his successors reprised down to 1911. The regularity with which the same names keep appearing is not surprising since they were the leading practitioners within their trades, well known to the architects and their clerks of works, and were no doubt experienced in how to judge their pricing. A striking instance occurs with a major contract to build the Rodgett Infirmary at the Royal Albert Asylum in Lancaster. Tenders were invited in the press in January 1881 from as far afield as Liverpool, Manchester and Leeds, but the four (separate trade) contracts all ended up going to the Lancaster regulars – Baynes (building), Hatch (woodwork), Cross (slating and plastering) and Calvert & Heald (plumbing and heating).

The following pages give summary details of the main contractors, craftsmen and artists who worked on jobs for the firm where details are known.

Lancaster

Christopher Baynes, stonemason, builder, and quarrymaster
Christopher Baynes (1811–85) was a leading figure in the Lancaster building industry. The Catalogue in this book (*see* Appendix 5) notes 10 instances of his involvement on jobs between 1849 and 1882, the largest of which by far was the building of the Royal Albert Asylum in Lancaster from 1867: it is likely that he would also have been engaged on other projects where his name is not recorded. Censuses show a peak of activity in 1871, when he was employing 134 men and 21 apprentices as well as farming 41 acres. He was operating from premises in Penny Street at the time of his death. About 100 men in his employ attended his funeral.[5]

Baynes seems to have had close associations with ES, being a vice chairman at the latter's leaving dinner in March 1856 with others, including Charles Blades (*below*) and James Hatch (*below*).[6] He was on the General Committee for ES's Scotforth church in 1873.[7] He was closely associated with St Thomas's church from its opening in 1841, being a churchwarden for 21 years and a teacher at the Sunday School for 43, and 'lived a life of simplicity and Christian integrity that would be long remembered in this parish and town'.[8] He was predeceased by his two wives, both named Eleanor, and his only daughter Annie, and bequeathed the business to his nephew William Warbrick (*see* p 204), whose mother was his first wife's sister.

Charles Blades, timber merchant, joinery, carpentry work, building

Charles Blades (1818–93) was a self-made man who became one of the elite that ran the town. He was born at Aysgarth (NY), and as a child moved with his family to Lancaster where, aged 13, he was apprenticed to James Monks (1795–1872), joiner and wheelwright.[9] Moving to Liverpool, he spent two years as assistant to the great dock engineer, Jesse Hartley. Back in Lancaster he became a partner with his friend James Hatch (*below*) in late 1841 and remained with him for about three years. Blades then took over their premises in Dalton Square, which he occupied until his death. His firm became the largest timber importer in the area, with timber stores at Glasson Dock, and in Nelson Street and Bulk Road, Lancaster. It had sawmills and a planing shed for floorboards. As well as selling timber wholesale, Blades supplied carpentry and joinery services to the building trades. The first job for the firm was carpentry and joinery for S&P's North Western Hotel at Morecambe, 1847–8. His obituary says he built all the stations on the 'Little' North Western Railway from Morecambe to Skipton, and also on the Furness Railway. The biggest commission was the woodwork for the Royal Albert Asylum in Lancaster, from 1867. Although in competition with Hatch's from the early 1870s, Blades continued to carry out work on many P&A jobs until his death, the last being the supply of chancel fittings at Preston Patrick (CuW) in 1892. He had no children to succeed him.

Charles Blades was a key man in Lancaster's affairs, a councillor from 1861, alderman from 1881, and mayor four times.[10] He was a major shareholder in the Lancaster Carriage & Wagon Co, founded in 1863, its vice chairman from 1866 to 1880, then its chairman. He was also a director of the Lancaster Banking Co. He attended St Mary, Lancaster, and then, in his later years, St Anne's.

Calvert & Heald, plumbers and glaziers

Charles Calvert (1844–96) and James Heald (1850–1919) set up in business in 1878 on the retirement of Willan & Cleminson (worked on four EGP/P&A jobs from 1856) in their premises (13 Market Street) and with their recommendation: Calvert had been in their employ for 21 years.[11] Recorded as working on seven P&A/A&P jobs, 1881–98. Heald was very successful, moving to Castle Park by 1901 ('Ironmonger' in the census), serving as mayor 1904–5, and leaving £45,000.

T (and E) Cross (& Sons), slaters and plasterers, builders' merchants

Thomas Cross (1794–1853) set up in business in 1827.[12] After his death, his widow Elizabeth (1795–1880) and three sons ran the firm as E Cross & Sons; the sons were John (1825–1901), William (1827–1908) and Thomas (1831–1902). The firm first enters our story with slating and plastering at S&P's rebuilt chancel at Bolton-le-Sands, 1847, and plasterwork at their Midland Hotel, Morecambe, 1847–8. At the 1871 census the firm was employing 21 men and 9 apprentices. From the mid-1880s the firm traded again as T Cross & Sons and would be carried on by Thomas senior's grandchildren. It continued to work on P&A/A&P commissions into the 20th century, the last known work being slating and plastering work at St Mary, Lancaster, in 1911. There was also a branch of the firm in Liverpool run, in 1889, by Thomas Cross, the eldest son of John.

Gillow & Co, furniture makers

This famous firm of cabinetmakers had been founded in 1728 by Robert Gillow (1704–72), who made furniture from mahogany brought in through the port of Lancaster.[13] A London office opened in 1769 as the firm developed a national reputation, supplying some of the country's richest families. The Gillow family sold out in 1813 and by 1881 the firm had moved to new premises between North Road and St Leonard's Gate. A loose financial arrangement was developed with Waring of Liverpool, but in 1903 the firm was formally constituted as Waring & Gillow. As makers of fine furniture, Gillow's were responsible for the furnishing at the P&A's rebuilding of Holker Hall (CuL) in 1871–5.

James Hatch & Sons, joiners and builders

This large and regionally very important firm provided building and woodwork services for many buildings by Paley & Austin. Educated at the Lancaster National Schools, James Hatch (1818–95) was apprenticed to his father John, a millwright.[14] In 1841 he went into partnership with Charles Blades (*above*), first in Meeting House Lane and then in Dalton Square.[15] After three years the partnership was dissolved, with Blades remaining at Dalton Square and Hatch moving to premises in Cable Street, then to larger premises on the Green Ayre. Hatch moved his business again in 1848 to Queen's Square, off King Street, where the firm remained till after his death. He retired in 1885 and died in February 1895, less than three weeks after E G Paley. He was a popular, much respected and important figure in Lancaster where he was a leading employer. He was a churchwarden at St Thomas's for 30 years, and for over 20 years was a Freemason, being treasurer of Fortitude Lodge and its master in 1858. His standing in Lancaster was further enhanced by a long record of public service. From 1867 until his death he was a town councillor: he was elected an alderman in 1884 and the following year mayor, and at his death he was 'father' of the council. From 1885 the firm was run by two of his sons, John (1847–1922) and William Henry (1855–1942).[16] In 1903 they expanded the business by taking over W Warbrick's masonry business. John died in 1922, and the firm carried on until 1925 when Henry, a bachelor, closed it down. His final act was to pass the business over to two of his foremen, Charles Thompson and Richard Jackson.

The business had two sides to it. The building side seems to have specialised in churches and chapels, for which they were praised in 1894 as 'giving satisfaction to all concerned'.[17] Second, there was its work in wood, which was deployed in a great many P&A commissions. At its height Hatch's workshop covered over an acre, where joinery and woodworking were carried out (*see* Fig 4.42). Employment was provided to over 100 people making the enterprise comparable with the better-known Harry Hems workshop in Exeter. The firm made wooden products for domestic and industrial purposes but is of greatest importance here for its output of ecclesiastical furnishings of all kinds, although there were secular commissions too, including woodwork for Sedbergh School and the restored Hoghton Tower. Compiled probably just before or just after the Great War, 'A List of Churches at which J H & Sons have been employed' is a handwritten record of just over 200 places where the firm had supplied work.[18] The geographic spread is very similar to that of P&A/A&P's activities, running up from Cheshire to southern Cumbria. Most outliers of work are directly linked to the architects' commissions, for instance, as at St John, Greenock; All Saints, Hertford; St James, Scarborough; St Andrew, Starbeck, Harrogate; and Worksop (presumably St Anne). However, there are one or two far-flung jobs which, so far as is known, have nothing to do with them – at All Saints, Ipswich; Chigwell; and Woodford (the latter two being in Essex and near to each other).[19] James Hatch's first known commission for EGP was not until 1852, when he supplied woodwork for the restored church of Burton-in-Lonsdale (NY). Then comes the joinery for a Wesleyan chapel in Lancaster (1873–4), and the pulpit and stalls at P&A's great church of All Souls, Bolton (1878–81), where the carving work was undertaken by the Lancaster firm of Miles & Morgan; then in 1881 Hatch acted as the main contractor for extensive works at Bolton-le-Sands church. Thereafter the firm must have enjoyed almost continual employment on P&A/A&P jobs.[20]

A O Thoms, builders

Arthur Ogelvie Thoms (1876–1963) was the son of James, a master builder, and founded his business in 1902. By the time of its closure in 1986 it was the oldest building firm in Lancaster.[21] It was based in Wheatfield Street, but expanded in 1955 by taking over the joinery business of R S Wright & Sons (*below*) in Queen Street and moved its operations there.

Thoms did the masonry work for A&P with additions to Claughton church, 1904, at Ellel church, 1906–7, alterations to St Mary, Lancaster, 1911, and some rebuilding at Blawith (CuL) church, 1914. But real success came in the post-war period, and Thoms built the majority of Harry Paley's more substantial projects.

W Warbrick, stonemason and builder

The son of a stonemason, William Warbrick (1832–97) was employed on many P&A contracts from 1886, having been bequeathed the business of his uncle Christopher Baynes (*see* p 202), for whom he worked for 38 years and became his manager.[22] His father, James, was in business, *c* 1851, near Brock Street, with the father of John Harrison, the firm's Barrow manager (*see* p 199). His premises were in Penny Street – no doubt the same as those occupied by Baynes. Warbrick was prominent in the Masonic world, a Liberal in politics, and a member of Lancaster Council.[23] In 1903, some years after Warbrick's death, the business was taken over by James Hatch & Sons (*see* p 203).

R S Wright & Sons, builders and joiners

This firm, run by Roger Squires Wright (1817–92), was in existence by 1861 when Wright employed 12 men and 4 apprentices. By 1871 it had expanded to employ 16 men and 8 apprentices. In the early 1870s it undertook joinery work for P&A's extensions to the town hall (1871–4) and carried out masonry work in alterations to the Presbyterian chapel in St Nicholas Street in 1874. It was operating for building and joinery work from Queen's Square in 1886, but it does not occur again in the P&A record until 1891, when it carried out the joinery for extensions to Scotforth church. At the 1881 census Roger Wright employed 10 men and 7 boys. Rather surprisingly for what appears to have been a successful business, Wright, who had retired by 1891, left an estate of just £464 on his death in 1892. By 1914 the firm acted as timber merchants and builders and would find regular employment on contracts for HAP's buildings, for example, Bilsborrow church, 1926–8, alterations at Lancaster Infirmary, 1931, and adding a new chancel to Glasson church, 1931–2. The last work for A&P was removing woodwork from the chancel of St Mary, Lancaster, for safekeeping in the Castle in 1940. The firm was taken over by A O Thoms (*above*) in 1955.

Stained glass in Lancaster

Lancaster was home to two stained glass firms of more than local significance – Shrigley & Hunt and Abbott & Co – and their glass found its way into large numbers of P&A/A&P buildings. That it did so is more than a matter of chance, as is suggested, for example, by the appearance of S&H glass at a far-flung P&A commission like St John the Evangelist in Greenock. The firms seem to have worked to the benefit of each other, but the association seems rarely to have been direct, either artistically or commercially. The link was by no means absolute: in 1877 P&A initially recommended Morris glass and work by Burlison & Grylls to those considering memorial windows at Greenock.[24] A month later, after saying 'Ballantine's glass has never been quite satisfactory', they suggested 'a newer firm Powell Bros, Leeds'.[25] But in the end it was Shrigley & Hunt who took up the work.

Abbott & Co

The Abbott firm was founded in 1860 and was run by William Abbott (1837–1904). Initially it was a plumbing and glazing business in Penny Street, but by the 1890s the firm was making stained glass, and after changing location several times had set up in Chapel Street by 1910. It remained here, although taken over by Cosalt of Fleetwood in 1976, and the workshop was removed to Fleetwood in 1996. The firm carried out various plumbing and glazing works on P&A/A&P buildings (1873–4 is the earliest in the Catalogue – *see* Appendix 5), but its stained glass can also be found in many of the firm's churches.

Shrigley & Hunt

The Shrigley business of 'painters, carvers and gilders' had been founded in Lancaster in 1750.[26] In the 19th century it went through various partnerships and name changes. Arthur William

Hunt (1849–1917), who had been apprenticed to Heaton, Butler & Bayne from about 1867, took over the business in 1873–4 from Eliza (née Hudson), the widow of Joseph Shrigley (1825/6–69), and stained glass production began in 1875. The premises were a few yards down Castle Hill from P&A's office and close links were developed between the two firms. These must have been personal as well as business-like. Arthur Hunt, for example, was sometime churchwarden at St Mary's, where Hubert Austin also was a warden for seven years until 1903, and then a sidesman. However, Geoffrey Austin wrote of his father that he 'knew Mr. Hunt well but you'd not describe him as a friend – they didn't come into contact except in relation to business'.[27] And Paley & Austin it was who designed Hunt's house, 'Longlands', on the west side of Lancaster in 1884. But to say 'Paley & Austin … was their most important client', as has been claimed, implies direct contractual links which the almost non-existent evidence does not support.[28] The architects, who had quite enough work in hand already, do not seem to have gone in for the specialist, artistic business of stained glass designing and most probably suggested to any clients seeking windows that they would do well to contact S&H (or Abbott's). Assuming that the rather conventional glass was to their tastes, what was the point of their looking further? S&H had highly competent designers on its books, notably Carl Almquist and Edward Holmes Jewitt. The firm outlived A&P, continuing beyond the Second World War, albeit on a much smaller scale than in its late 19th-century heyday. A fire destroyed cartoons and records in 1973 after which its head, Joseph ('Jo') Fisher, continued a one-man business from his home in Lancaster until his death in 1982, when the business went into voluntary liquidation.

It is said that Joseph Shrigley had an account with Paley in 1858.[29] The S&H records give few clues to the relations between the firm and P&A. Financial transactions between them are very limited, with the surviving invoice and cash book for 1874–1881 detailing very minor items including what appear to be various items of, probably, personal expenditure by Paley.[30] The only significant sum is £484 for decoration at Singleton church *c* 1880.[31] Of course, any windows or schemes of decoration finding their way into P&A churches would have been charged directly to P&A's clients, but no records of such work have come down to us. However, three valuable books of specifications, accounts, reports and correspondence have been preserved for the years 1927–41, when Harry Paley was in charge, and are often the only record we have of the work involved. They were presumably passed over to S&H after the A&P business was wound up, which would be suggestive of close links between the two firms – perhaps it was thought that the background information about the buildings might be of some use to the glassmakers.

Beyond Lancaster

Most commissions in and near to Lancaster were contracted to local firms. Those further away usually went, unsurprisingly, to others. A few names reappear for major projects in the Catalogue – firms such as James Duckett of Burnley, James Garden of Dalton-in-Furness, William Winnard of Wigan (*see* Appendix 5). We know little about these firms but there are four for which some information is available:

Brassington Brothers, builders, Settle

Brassington Bros was a medium-sized building firm established in Settle before 1886 and which closed in 1959.[32] Henry's brother Joe ran a branch in Sedbergh but the workshop (Bridge End Mill) and sawmill was in Settle. As well as building work, they undertook joinery and woodwork. Their first engagement on an A&P job was, as Brassington Bros & Corney, the building of the new chapel at Sedbergh School in 1895–7. They continued to obtain contracts for Harry Paley jobs after the First World War until Paley retired in 1936. After this they did several woodworking jobs for James Tarney, who ran the office at the end of its life.

Robert Bridgeman & Sons, carvers, Lichfield

It seems to have been the death of John Roddis (*see* p 206) that prompted the switch to Bridgemans for a number of commissions. The first was in 1888 for the statues of Victoria and Albert placed on the front of the new Winmarleigh Hall at the Royal Albert Asylum in Lancaster. At least 10 further commissions followed down to the Great War. It is not clear under what circumstances the patronage went to Bridgemans but it involved work in both stone and wood. At All Saints, Hertford (1893–5), the split was stone carving to Bridgemans and wood to Hatch. Curiously at St Lawrence, Morecambe (1899), Hatch's made the stalls but the carving on them was undertaken by Bridgemans. After Hubert Austin's death, they worked on at least four Harry Paley jobs down to the effigy of Sir John Robinson at St Anne, Worksop (Notts), 1931. A large archive still exists for the firm but, sadly, access to it was denied to me: hopefully future researchers will be more fortunate.

William Gradwell, builder and contractor, timber merchant, brick and tile manufacturer, Barrow-in-Furness

The rise of William Gradwell (1820–82) as a self-made man to status and fortune is bound up with the phenomenal growth of Barrow during the first 40 years of Victoria's reign.[33] With little education, he came to Roose, near Barrow, in 1844, and set up as a joiner. His first important contract was a wooden pier at Piel (Roa Island), completed in 1847, which did much to stimulate goods and passenger traffic in the area. He established an imported timber trade with a sawmill, developed housing in Barrow, and built the Duddon estuary railway viaduct. In 1855 he moved his business to Hindpool, Barrow, and set up a brickworks in Dalton Road capable of turning out 75,000 bricks a week. Large swathes of the town were built by him, including many buildings designed by P&A, beginning in 1867–9 with St James's church. The last major Gradwell/P&A buildings were the North Lonsdale Hospital, 1882–7, and the additions at St George's church in 1883–4, although William junior made the alterations to HJA's house at Heversham, 1899. Like Lancaster builder James Hatch (*see* p 203), Gradwell took an active interest in the affairs of the town and its surroundings. He was a councillor, an alderman, and in 1881–2 mayor. He died near the end of his mayoralty and the business continued to be run by his son, son-in-law and nephew.

John Roddis, wood and stone sculptor, Birmingham
John Roddis (1838–87) was born at Sutton Coldfield and followed in the footsteps of his father, Thomas, listed as a carver at the 1841 census. John developed a successful career, latterly based at 45–47 Aston Road North, Birmingham.[34] At the 1861 census he was employing 8 men and 2 boys, and by 1881 13 men. He was first employed by P&A for carving and sculpture at Kirkby (Me: 1869–71),[35] and at Liverpool, Mossley Hill (1870–5), for statues on the south porches at Daresbury (Ch: *c* 1872) and Leigh (GM: *c* 1873) churches, and subsequently on important work at three of the firm's major churches (All Souls and St Saviour, Bolton (GM); and Higher Walton (Ch)). He was a very prominent supporter of the Liberal cause. After his death, aged only 49, P&A's patronage seems to have shifted to Bridgemanws of Lichfield (*see* p 205).

APPENDIX 4
DISTANT COMMISSIONS AND THEIR ORIGINS

For the whole of its 100-year history, the activity of the practice was very much concentrated in the North West – Lancashire, Cheshire, and spilling over into southern Cumberland and Westmorland, the western parts of Yorkshire, and northern Staffordshire – as Figure 0.2 demonstrates. The vast majority of commissions would have come from word-of-mouth recommendation by satisfied clients, from people looking at other work by the firm, or from being chosen as a well-known name in a commercial directory. Personal connections also played an important part and were certainly responsible for launching Edmund Sharpe's architectural career so speedily and successfully.

As regards those jobs far removed from the firm's north-western heartland, it seems worthwhile to isolate them, and to explain the often interesting backgrounds to them. Further details of the commissions and references for them are given in the Catalogue under the appropriate dates (*see* Appendix 5).

Buckinghamshire
Fawley, St Mary, restored 1882–3; *Fawley Court,* extended 1883. William Dalziel Mackenzie (1840–1928), a barrister, was lord of the manor and owner of Fawley Court. His father Edward (1811–80), born at Witton, Blackburn, had on retirement purchased the estate in 1853 from the 'Freeman' family, owners since 1680. He had been a partner in the extremely successful railway contractors Brassey & Mackenzie. They would have been well-known to ES from his railway-building activities with the 'L'NWR. Mackenzie's older brother William (1794–1851) and Thomas Brassey (1805–70) had been brought together by the engineer Joseph Locke, who was very well known by ES in respect of the latter's work on the Lancaster to Preston line (*see* Appendix 1). However, it surely cannot be a coincidence that the eldest son of the last 'Freeman' family owner became in 1863 the husband of Isabella Merivale (1844–1911), the niece of the Revd Charles Merivale (*see below*, Essex), who had initiated the first Oxford and Cambridge Boat Race at Henley in 1829. The Fawley estate adjoins the Thames midway down the Henley Regatta course. As skilled rowers ES and EGP may well have visited the Regatta which had begun in 1839.

Cambridgeshire
Stanground, St John the Baptist. Design for reredos and altar rails, *c* 1860 (perhaps there was other work too). There were many Paley family links to the area: EGP's great-grandfather lived at Peterborough 1735–45, while a canon, and was vicar at Helpston 1735–99; his grandfather was born and baptised there in 1743 and his father was rector at Gretford 1838–50. His brother, Frederick Apthorp Paley (FAP), lived there 1856–60. The vicar of St John's, Stanground, 1842–85, Robert Cory (1801–85), was a half first cousin through their mothers. He, like FAP, was at Shrewsbury School under headmaster Samuel Butler. Thomas Paley (1810–99), EGP's first cousin, the school and college friend of ES, was rector at Ufford-cum-Bainton 1847–81.

Cumbria
Calder Bridge (CuC), St Bridget. Replaced a medieval church (still standing at Beckermet), 1841–2. A very long way from the core area of ES's activity, this commission probably came via his pupil EGP, whose family had enjoyed a long friendship with the Senhouse family of Cumberland. Mary Senhouse was the wife of the chief benefactor, Captain Thomas Irwin of Calder Abbey. A letter of EGP's mother, Sarah, in 1834 shows that they knew the family. This link goes back to *c* 1769 and the Carlisle days of EGP's grandfather, Archdeacon William, and his patron Bishop Edmund Law, whose wife's mother was Bridget Senhouse. EGP's uncle, and putative godfather, Fergus Graham's first wife Johanna's mother was Mary Senhouse, niece of Bridget. There had also been recent links *c* 1830 at Shrewsbury School (*see below*), attended by Humphrey Senhouse, son of Johanna's first cousin, at the same time as EGP's brother Frederick.

Walton (CuC), St Mary. 1869. No background known.

Derbyshire
Mickleover. Work at residence (Mickleover Manor) for C E Newton, *c* 1860. No background known. Now converted to flats.

Durham, County
Redmarshall, St Cuthbert. Restored 1845; *Redmarshall, rectory*, rebuilt 1845; *Bishopton, St Peter*, restored 1846–7; *Thorpe Thewles, Holy Trinity* 1848–9 (design 1847). The Revd Thomas Austin was rector of Redmarshall, 1845–56. His son Tom had joined ES probably in the second half of 1841 and remained with the firm until 1852. Both Bishopton and Thorpe Thewles are less than two miles from Redmarshall.

Essex
Lawford, St Mary. Restored 1853. Connection between ES and the Revd Charles Merivale (1808–93), rector 1848–69, who may well have been introduced by George Langshaw (*see* p 26) who was at

St John's, 1825–9. Merivale was also an undergraduate at St John's College, Cambridge, 1826–30, which ES attended from October 1829. Both men rowed for the Johnian Boat Club (Merivale initiated the first Oxford and Cambridge Boat Race in 1829), ES becoming a member in February 1830. In 1869 Merivale became Dean of Ely. *See also* Warwickshire, Coventry, St Thomas, for another ES/university link.

Hertfordshire
Hertford, All Saints. Church rebuilt (after a fire), 1893–5. Commission won in competition in 1892. PA&P never competed for another church job so far from home. They may have been suggested as entrants by James Brooks, who had been brought in to supervise the competition. He had been one of the advisers for the proposed bell-tower at St Michael, Coventry, which PA&P were selected to design. Why they took a keen interest, at a very busy time in the practice, is perhaps slightly curious. Improbable as it may seem, this might link back to EGP's youth, and a deep affection for his old school, Christ's Hospital, which he entered in London back in 1832. This had a 'feeder' school in Hertford and, although he did *not* go there, his older brother Edmund did (in 1829). Interestingly, the firm also competed for the new Christ's Hospital buildings in Sussex (*below*).

Leicestershire
Bottesford, St Mary the Virgin. Restored 1847–8 (plans from 1846). Apparently linked to ES's cousin, the Revd J W Whittaker, who in 1821–2 was chaplain to the Archbishop of Canterbury, Charles Manners-Sutton, whom he impressed considerably. The archbishop was a cousin of the patron, the 5th Duke of Rutland, and a cousin of the three rectors at Bottesford from 1782. Whittaker may well have met the second of these, Charles Roos Thoroton, rector 1821–46. He died on 14 February 1846 and his successor, the Revd Frederick John Norman (until 1888), lost little time in calling in S&P, whose plan for proposed seating is dated June 1846. The rebuilding of the steeple in 1865, however, was carried out under G G Scott.

Nottinghamshire
Worksop, St Anne. New church 1911–12. No background known.

Shropshire
Shrewsbury, St Mary, vestry 1884. *Shrewsbury School: possible baths* 1887, *extended* 1913; *extension for house of A F Chance* 1914. The Paley family connections to the school went back to Samuel Butler, headmaster 1798–1836 and to EGP's brother Frederick, a pupil 1827–33. The school had moved to a new site in 1882, and buildings designed by A W Blomfield. However, EGP may have hoped for work here and this is perhaps supported by the minor work carried out in 1884 at St Mary's, historically used for the old school Sunday services. Geoffrey Austin went to Shrewsbury School 1897–1903, and this link surely accounts for the swimming baths extension, and undoubtedly the alterations to the house of his former housemaster (and godfather to his youngest son).

Sussex
Christ's Hospital, Horsham. Competition entry 1894. PA&P were runners up for this very large and prestigious commission. There is no information on why they entered, but a possible explanation, unlikely as it may seem, is suggested in the discussion of All Saints, Hertford (*above*).

Westham, St Mary 1876–7; *Willingdon, St Mary* 1878; *Wilmington, St Mary & St Peter*, 1882–3. Three restorations at villages all very near Eastbourne where the 7th Duke of Devonshire was a major landowner (and developed the town). He was patron of the livings at Westham and Wilmington. P&A were well known to him since they had recently rebuilt the state wing at his seat, Holker Hall (CuL), and no doubt a kindly word secured them the first job. In turn, favourable reports from Westham presumably lay behind the Willingdon commission.

Warwickshire
Coventry, St Thomas. New church 1848–9 (plans 1846). The connection appears to be William Drake, who went up to St John's College, Cambridge, in 1831, where ES was an undergraduate. He was second master at Coventry Grammar School and lecturer at St John the Baptist, Coventry, 1841–57. He was also examiner in Hebrew at London University 1840–65, so a further link may be through his fellow Hebraist, the Revd J W Whittaker, who was ES's cousin and did much to promote his career. It was Drake who wrote to the ICBS in 1843 enquiring about applying for funds for St Thomas's (file 3310), and in 1846 despatched the application (file 3772); no other involvement with St Thomas' is known, and by 1846 the district has its own minister (the Revd Stephen Cragg, an Oxford man). *See* Essex, for another ES/university link.

Coventry, St Michael. Bell-tower design 1891. PA&P seem to have been selected by the eminent advisers to the project – James Brooks (*see* Hertford *above*), Alfred Waterhouse, Norman Shaw, Ewan Christian, J P Seddon, William White and R H Carpenter. This says much for the standing of the firm within the profession at the time.

Coventry, St Barbara, Earlsdon. New church 1930–1. No background known.

Coventry, St Barnabas. New church 1932–3. A follow-on job from St Barbara's.

Yorkshire
Bridlington Priory (St Mary). Restoration from 1846. No background known.

Scarborough. All Saints Schools, 1880; *St James' mission chapel,* 1885; *St James's church institute,* 1893; *St James's church,* 1894. No background known.

Ireland

Desborough Hall (Co Tipperary). Metalwork verandah, *c* 1855–70. No background known. House demolished and rebuilt in the 20th century.

Isle of Man

Douglas, Christ Church. Lectern, *c* 1855–70. *See* Catalogue (Appendix 5) for what little is known.

Scotland

Renfrewshire

Greenock (Renfrewshire), Episcopal Church of St John the Evangelist. New church 1877–8. The firm was recommended by the Revd Julius Lloyd (1830–92), the perpetual curate (1871–80). His second curacy had been at St Peter's, the main church in Wolverhampton (St), 1858–62, then at nearby Trysull 1862–6, and he would surely have come into contact with EGP's younger brother, Francis Henry, who was curate 1851–6, then vicar 1856–74 at Penn, just over a mile away.

Wales

Caernarvonshire

Betws-y-Coed, St Mary. New church 1872–3. Won in competition with a HJA design. ES had lived just to the south of the village between 1856 and 1863, and also had relatives involved in local mining activities. Such links with the area no doubt provided the stimulus to enter the competition. One of the chief benefactors of the new church was Charles Kurtz, a Liverpool businessman to whom ES sold his house in 1865.

Carmarthenshire

Llandovery College. Extension 1901–3. The only known link to the area is through Neander Gesenius Lewis (*see* Appendix 2), born in the area, and probably working for PA&P by 1891.

Denbighshire

Capel Garmon, St Garmon. Restored, 1862–3 (plans 1861). This village is just two miles from Betws-y-Coed and three from ES's residence. This small commission must have come EGP's way through his former partner's influence.

APPENDIX 5
CATALOGUE OF WORKS AND PROJECTS

This catalogue is arranged chronologically. Wherever possible, the dates quoted are those of construction. If the only dates established are those of plans and/or invitations to tender, this is made clear. It is worth noting that some dates may not be as precise as they appear. For example, commencement dates for churches are often derived from the laying of foundation stones, but groundworks and the lower stages of construction may have begun many months before. Similarly consecrations, which suggest obvious terminal dates, sometimes took place a long while after construction and fitting out had been completed.

Counties. Places are in the modern ceremonial county of Lancashire (or are very well-known towns and cities), unless otherwise stated in brackets. A list of county abbreviations is given on page viii.
Names of houses are given in inverted commas to avoid any confusion with local place names.
Demolition, alterations and change of use, if known, are noted. Lack of such information, however, does not guarantee that a building still exists or remains largely unchanged.
A note on completeness. The lack of any comprehensive archive for the practice means that this Catalogue of its activities has been compiled from a wide variety of sources. These are given in square brackets, with primary sources (including contemporary newspapers) being listed first. Secondary sources have been used when they are thought to be reasonably trustworthy. It is unlikely that any major commissions have been omitted, but it is a near certainty that there are (perhaps many) minor works which have not yet come to light. On the other hand, the sheer ubiquity of the firm's work in its core geographic area and the high reputation it enjoys has occasionally led owners, custodians and others to claim that the firm was responsible for buildings when in fact it was not. Some published misattributions are listed at the very end of this Catalogue, following a list of unconfirmed but reasonably plausible attributions.
Scope of the entries. The vast number of the practice's works means that, for reasons of space, it is impossible to give details of the style, materials and plans of individual buildings. The exception to this regrettable necessity is in the case of lost buildings, where some details are occasionally provided for the record.

1836–7
Bamber Bridge, St Saviour, Cuerden. Plan signed by ES 9.5.1836 when the cost was estimated at £1,360. Land given by Robert Townley Parker MP of Cuerden Hall, who also gave £200. 650 seats. Consecrated 3.10.1837 [ICBS 1933: *LGaz* 7.10.1837: *Preston Chronicle* 7.10.1837: *K* 1913, 100: Abram 1877, 741: BE].

The National School E of the church is in the same Lombardic Romanesque style and is probably by ES (quoted as such by JP, citing Jolley), but no original documentary evidence has been found. Hunt [1997, 160] gives the date as 1839, JP as 1839–40. However, an undated printed leaflet (with 1836 correspondence in the ICBS file) appealing for funds for the unbuilt church mentions a 'commodious School House, which is *now* [original emphasis] in progress'.

1836–8
Blackburn, St Mark Witton. ES's first church commission but completed after Bamber Bridge. Initial plans by Nov 1835. Consecrated 10.6.1838. £1,700 of which £400 came from the Chester Diocesan Society for Building Churches; £300 from the ICBS; £200 from Joseph Feilden of Witton House who laid the FS. 669 seats. CC – John Ibbotson (masonry), Thomas Walsh (carpentry). CW – Edward Harrison [ICBS 1933: *BS* 12.10.1836: *LGaz* 9.6.1838]. E window by Thomas Willement dated 1838 [*BS* 12.10.1836: *Blackburn Times* 20.5.1938: Walmsley 1986, 5].

1837–8
Chatburn, Christ Church. Land given by William and Dixon Robinson. Estimated cost of building £950. Seating for 364. £250 grant from the ICBS. 'It is highly probable', observed the *BS*, 'that the village Church of Chatburn is the first that has been commenced in the reign of ... Queen Victoria'. It also noted that ES 'was engaged in thirteen similar undertakings' [ICBS 2144: *BS* 28.6.1837: *LGaz* 1.7.1837, 22.9.1838]. Victoria succeeded to the throne at 2am on 20 Jun, the FS being laid with Masonic ceremonial at 3pm on 22 Jun.

Cowgill (CuWY), St John the Evangelist. New church. Seats for 250. FS laid by the geologist Adam Sedgwick [*LGaz* 8.7.1837, 3.11.1838].

Howgill (CuWY), Holy Trinity. Replaced a chapel of *c* 1685 on a different site. Cost put at £470 in 1837. 130 seats. The prime mover was the Revd Isaac Green, second master at Sedbergh School from 1831 and incumbent at Howgill until his death in 1875. Site given by Stephen Sedgwick [inscription: ICBS 2299: *LGaz* 8.7.1837, 3.11.1838].

1837–9
Walmsley (GM), Christ Church, Egerton, Bolton. Replaced a chapel 'rebuilt or generally repaired A. D. 1771' seating 126. Plans 1836. Estimated cost £2,150: actual £3,557. £300 granted by the ICBS. 512 seats [ICBS 2101: *LGaz* 28.12.1839, 4.1.1840]. Transepts and chancel 1867 (architect unknown). The National School at the foot of the hill has the same, unusual channelled

stonework and may be ES's work [BE].

1837–45
Blackburn, Holy Trinity, church and schools. FS 5.10.1837 [*LGaz* 7.10.1837] but plans were still not finalised. Furthermore 'the depressed condition of trade and manufacture' seems to have led to little progress but by Nov 1842 the scheme was ready to proceed again. Sunday School opened 1843 and licensed for worship. Complete by 2.6.1845: consecrated 12.7.1846. £5,019 of which the CBC gave £1,519. Seats for 1,626 (of which 834 were free). Tower 1853; spire never built. School beyond E end of the church opened 1843 (closed 1962, later demolished). Church redundant in 1981 and vested in the CCT 1984 [*BS* 11.10.1837: ICBS 2200: Whittle, P A 1852 *Blackburn as it is*. Blackburn, 82–3: Port 2006, 334: Slater 1895: Varah, E C 1946 *A Memorial of the Centenary of the Church of Holy Trinity, Blackburn*: McClintock, M E 1992 *Holy Trinity Church, Blackburn, Lancashire*. Redundant Churches Fund guidebook].

1838
Holcombe (GM), Emmanuel. An application for rebuilding in 1840 to the ICBS says ES examined the existing church. Correspondence starts Oct 1838 when it was proposed to build a church seating 900 people (with galleries) or 700 (without): these worked-up numbers may imply an architect's involvement, but no mention is made of ES in all of this [ICBS 2401]. The scheme evidently lapsed until a new church by Thomas Holmes of Bury was built in 1852–3 [BE].

Lancaster, County Lunatic Asylum. ES was architect to the asylum by Sept 1838, when he was involved in new arrangements for the water supply [*LGaz* 22.9.1838].

1838–9
Bickerton (Ch), Holy Trinity. Plans by Feb 1838: estimated cost £500 (final cost £700). Land given by Sir Philip de Malpas Grey Egerton. 268 seats. £120 grant from ICBS. Consecrated 7.1.1840. Baptistry 1911, replacing the W porch which was moved to the N side (architect unknown) [ICBS 2280: LBS 56842: Gater, E 1990 *Holy Trinity Church, Bickerton*, quoted in Hughes 2010, 1, 134].

Lancaster & Preston Junction Railway, 15 bridges on line S of Lancaster. Included the Galgate viaduct and skew bridge; also an iron bridge. ES contracted for the masonry works on the line and a Peter Perry of Chester-le-Street (D) for the earthworks. In a dispute over workmanship the directors cancelled ES's contract, leaving six bridges uncompleted by him [ES 1839 *Correspondence between Edmund Sharpe Esq. and the Directors of the Lancaster and Preston Junction Railway Company*. Lancaster: *LGaz* 27.6.1840].

1838–40
Stalybridge (GM), St George. FS 1.9.1838 (as also next entry), consecrated 24.6.1840. £4,012 (estimated at £3,960 in Sept 1838); of this £2,712 was granted by the CBC. Seating for 1,022 [*LGaz* 8.9.1838: Port 2006, 331: BE].

1838–41
Dukinfield (GM), St John the Evangelist. FS 1.9.1838 (as also previous entry). Cost estimated at £3,200 in Sept 1838: actual cost £3,299 (including £2,599 from the CBC). 1,234 seats [ICBS 2603, 2312: *LGaz* 8.9.1838: Port 2006, 331].

1839
Lancaster, bridge across River Lune. Repaired and repointed [*LGaz* 15.6.1839].

Lancaster, County Lunatic Asylum. IT for 1,800 yards of cast iron pipe [*LGaz* 13, 20.7.1839].

***c* 1839**
Marthall (Ch), All Saints. *LGaz* [4.1.1840], is the only source for an ES attribution and comes in a list of 11 churches by him quoted by the newspaper from a report in the *Conservative Journal*. Built by Wilbraham Egerton, later Lord Egerton of Tatton, on his land for his tenants [*The History of the Church*, Marthall, leaflet (nd)].

1839–40
Bretherton, St John the Baptist. New church. £1,058 (including £250 from the CBC). Application to ICBS in 1838; funds were being raised by Mar 1838. Note that the ICBS file number is sequential with that for Mawdesley (*below*) and the designs for the two churches are very similar. Site given by George Arthur Legh Keck. 400 seats [ICBS 2360: *LGaz* 31.3.1838, 20.4.1839: Port 2006, 334].

Farington, St Paul. New church. ES appointed by Dec 1837. IT Jun 1839. £1,700 including £500 from the CBC. 479 seats [*BS* 19.6.1839: *LGaz* 15.6.1839: Port 2006, 334]. ES was probably responsible for the parsonage (demolished and replaced) [ex info CS].

Glasson, Christ Church. New church [*LGaz* 2, 9, 16.2.1839, 13.4.1839, 18.2.1840, 27.6.1840].

Mawdesley, St Peter. Design 1838. In 1839 estimated cost £950 for 400 seats. Site given by Sir Thomas D Hesketh [ICBS 2359: *LGaz* 20.4.1839, 4.1.1840].

Wray (nr Hornby), Holy Trinity. Complete 3.6.1840 but not consecrated until 1.7.1841. £2,021 [*LGaz* 6.4.1839, 13.4.1839, 1.6.1839, 4.7.1840: Anon *Jubilee of Holy Trinity, Wray. July 1st, 1891* (leaflet)].

1839–41
Wigan (GM), St Catherine, Scholes. £3,180 of which £962 was provided by the CBC. Land given by John Woodcock of Springfield Hall. Seating for 1,113. CC – Messrs Harrison, Horwich (masons), Turner, Pemberton (joiner), J Halliwell, Wigan (painter). Consecrated Jun 1841. [*LGaz* 4.1.1840: Port 2006, 335: Bithell, B 1991 *The First 150 Years of St Catharine's Church, Wigan, 1841–1991*, 6–9]. Retains the original plan, box-pews and galleries and is the most intact of Sharpe's churches.

1839–42
Stainforth (NY), St Peter. Design and IT 1838. Consecration not until 29.9.1842: unclear whether this means building took a long time or that the consecration was delayed. Built on the initiative of the Dawson family of Settle and Hornby Castle [*LGaz* 29.12.1838, 5.1.1839, 4.1.1840, 8.10.1842: BE].

1839–45
Lancaster, County Lunatic Asylum. A series of extensions. 1840: for slating and plastering at additional buildings; also for cast iron

window frames [*LGaz* 22.8.1840, 3.10.1840]. 1841: two new wings, IT Dec 1840 [*LGaz* 5.12.1840, 10.9.1845]. 1841–2: chapel 'after the Italian [in style]'; a screen prevented male and female patients from seeing one another but both had sight of the clergyman. C – Storey & Lawrence [*LGaz* 23, 30.10.1841, 30.4.1842]. 1842–5: additional buildings, 'called Workshops, at the South end' to accommodate 50 extra patients at a cost of £1,500. New workshops, dormitories and wall round the asylum [*LGaz* 20.4.1840, 18.5.1840, 10.8.1844, 12.4.1845, 10.9.1845]. Ex info JMH: in total, as many as nine extensions may have been built 1835–55, of which all but two have been demolished: he notes five wings were built 1839–45, of which three have been demolished: the chapel and remaining wings have been converted to flats.

1840
Capernwray, chapel. For Mr & Mrs George Marton of Capernwray Hall. Accommodation for 100. The W gallery formed the family pew [*LGaz* 3.10.1840, 10.10.1840, 17.10.1840].

Fleetwood. ES invites applications from people wishing to lease or purchase land to obtain the particulars from him (he adds that the plans for the new town and harbours can be inspected at his premises) [*LGaz* 18, 25.4.1840].

Wray (nr Hornby), bridge at Fournessford. Now called Furnessford Bridge: grid ref SD 635669. IT [*LGaz* 22.8.1840].

1840–1
Briercliffe, St James. New church. Designs 1838. Estimated cost £1,280 for 515 seats. Land given by the Duke of Buccleuch. Retains N, S and W galleries. CC – Benjamin Chaffer; joinery by Waddington. [ICBS 2312: *LGaz* 4.1.1840: Frost, R 1984 *Briercliffe Parish Church: A History and Guide to the Church of St James the Great*, 8–9, 13]. Refitted 1881 (architect unknown).

Lancaster, St Thomas. New church. Design 1839. Land given by George Marton of Capernwray Hall; the endowment of £1,100 by Elizabeth Salisbury. Intended to seat 1,100 [*LGaz* 24.8.1839, 21.9.1839, 28.12.1839, 4.1.1840, 1.2.1840, 7.3.1840, 29.6.1840, 13.2.1841].

Lancaster, Union Workhouse. ITs for porter's lodge, vagrants' lodging and walling [*LGaz* 10, 31.10.1840]. IT for various works [*LGaz* 28.11.1840, 5.12.1840, 12.12.1840, 19.12.1840, 6.2.1841]. *PG* [9.9.1843], indicates additions were made in 1840–1.

Morecambe (then known as Poulton-le-Sands), Holy Trinity. Replaced a 'wholly inadequate' chapel of 1745. In Sept 1840 estimate over £1,200 for 498 seats (including 320 free). CC – Rawes & Wilson (masonry), William Fox (slating & plastering), William Till (joinery), Isaac Jackson (painting). [ICBS 2407: *LGaz* 14.3.1840, 30.5.1840, 6, 20.6.1840, 19.9.1840, 12.6.1841, 7.3.1891, 25.7.1891: Bingham, R K 1990 *Lost resort? The Flow and Ebb of Morecambe*. Milnthorpe, 99].

1841
Runcorn (Ch), Christ Church, Weston Point. For the Weaver Navigation Trustees. *c* 400 seats. C – John Gannon, Knutsford. Redundant from 1997 [LBS 486911: ex info JMH].

Lancaster, Castle. Heating and ventilating work for warming and airing the Castle courts [*LGaz* 13.2.1841: *PG* 9.9.43].

1841–2
Calder Bridge (CuC), St Bridget. Replaced a medieval church (still standing at Beckermet). Plans submitted to the ICBS 1840. Built at the sole expense of Captain Thomas Irwin of Calder Abbey. Under £1,900. Not consecrated until 24.6.1844 [ICBS 1928: *Eccl* 2, 1843, 23: Bulmer 1901, 614].

Lancaster. Plans presented to the Town Council for 'a parapet' (ie a pavement) by the riverside [*LGaz* 7.5.1842].

Northwich (Ch), Holy Trinity, Castle. For the Weaver Navigation Trustees for the watermen under the Weaver Churches bill. *c* 430 seats. C – Joseph Clarke, Altrincham [*LGaz* 17.10.1840, 10.7.1841: ex info JMH: BE].

1842
Lancaster, County Lunatic Asylum. Chapel 'of the Grecian order' in course of erection. C – Storey & Lawrence [*Preston Chronicle* 30.4.1842].

1842–4
Davenham (Ch), St Wilfrid. Rebuilt except for the tower and spire which were repaired. Estimated cost at outset £2,150. Nave lengthened by a bay, heightened and widened and N, S and W galleries inserted. Accommodation increased from 601 to 910. C – Thomas Dean who was paid £1,835 for his work [CALS, P6/7/12b: ICBS 3050: *Eccl* 7, 1847, 118].

Lever Bridge (nr Bolton, GM), St Stephen & All Martyrs. Design 1841. Terracotta church for John Fletcher, owner of the Ladyshore coal mines at Little Lever from which the clay came. Land given by the 2nd Earl of Bradford. Terracotta also used for the altar, bench ends, organ case, font, parts of the pulpit, etc. Chief benefactor – John Fletcher. Cost £2,600. 471 seats (though ES said in 1876 that the number was 350). Consecrated 26.6.1845 [*Bolton Free Press* 28.6.1845: *B* 34, 1876, 553–4: *Eccl* 3, 1844, 86–7: *Illustrated London News* 1.2.1845: typescript guide (nd)]. Openwork spire demolished 1937; octagon and top of tower demolished 1966. Vicarage (demolished) by ES a little later than the church [typescript guide].

1843
Cockerham, vicarage and wall. For the Revd John Dodson [datestone: *LGaz* 1, 8, 15.4.1843].

Lancaster, Music Hall, St Leonard's Gate. Created out of the Theatre Royal of 1782 and made into a 'beautiful little Music Hall ... through the liberality and public spirit of our townsman E. Sharpe, Esq.'. It also housed the museum for the collection of the Lancaster Literary, Scientific & Natural History Society [*LGaz* 22.4.1843: Betjemann, A G 1982 *The Grand Theatre, Lancaster: Two Centuries of Entertainment*. Lancaster University, Centre for North-West Regional Studies, Occasional Paper 11, 20ff].

Lancaster, Barn Close, sale notice of land on Penny Street/Dalton Square. Suggests surveying and/or estate agent activity on the part of ES [*LGaz* 10.6.1843].

Lancaster, 'Greaves House', Greaves Road. [CS: *LGaz* 3.8.1844, 9.7.1881]. For Samuel Simpson who had social and business connections with ES. His family had old trading links with ES's uncle Satterthwaite's family, and trading and marriage links with the Salisbury and Dodson families associated with ES's commissions at St Thomas, Lancaster and Cockerham. In 1847 Simpson's sister-in-law married ES's brother-in-law, Pearson Fletcher. Although no documentary evidence identifies ES as architect of this Tudor-style property, the personal links suggest this as a near certainty [ex info TBA].

New Bailey Bridge (now Albert Bridge): over the River Irwell, Manchester/Salford (grid ref SJ832984). Plans for rebuilding by ES adopted [*LGaz* 14.1.1843]. ES plans unexecuted: bridge built 1844 to a design of George W Buck civil engineer, Manchester [*LGaz* 17.6.1843]. Curiously Buck issued invitations to tender in the *LGaz* between 6.4.1843 and 20.5.1843, no doubt to the irritation of ES. A report in *LGaz* [7.9.1844] quotes the opinion that ES 'was ill-treated by the committee'.

1843–4
Kirkham, St Michael. Tower and spire, 150ft high, built of Longridge stone [*Preston Pilot* 18.11.1843: *Eccl* 3, 1844, 23–4: BE].

Knowsley (Me), St Mary. For the 13th Earl of Derby [RIBA Y5/218–9: *Eccl* 2, 1843, 75–6: BE]. As *Eccl* reviewed it in Jan 1843, designs must have been in existence in 1842.

Winsford (Ch), Christ Church, Over. For the Weaver Navigation Trustees for the use of the watermen. *c* 420 seats. Demolished 1882 owing to subsidence from salt-mining; replaced by a new church by Richard Beckett [RIBA Y5/202–3: ex info JMH: BE].

1844
Knutsford (Ch), gaol chapel. On 14 Oct 'Mr. Sharpe attended with plans for the making of a New chapel [unexecuted] and Governor's House [as at 2006 tourist and newspaper offices]' [CALS, Visiting Magistrates' Minute Books, ex info JMH].

Lancaster, stone arch over the Mill Dam in continuation of the existing arch. IT [*LGaz* 23.3.1844].

***c* 1844**
Lancaster, house, Fenton Street. House built by ES for himself (he acquired the site of nos 14–16 in 1843) [ex info JMH].

1844–8
Capernwray, Capernwray Hall. Remodelling of a house of 1805 for George Marton. Designs by Jan 1844. Main body of the old house kept and refenestrated. Large W wing added with dining room and drawing room; centre of the old house turned into a three-storey, top-lit staircase-hall: tower built. E stable and service block 1848. C – Storey & Lawrence [drawings at the house: *LGuar* 13.1.1844: 1848 datestone on courtyard clock turret]. Since 1946 a Christian holiday and conference centre.

1845
Lancaster, County Lunatic Asylum. Two new wings, one at each end of the N front, had been contracted for to accommodate 150 extra patients at a cost of £3,500 but a new proposal was made to enlarge them and take over the superintendent's existing house, thus accommodating 388 additional patients at a cost of £9,440: new house to be built for the superintendent. The scheme was initially abandoned but the wings were built soon after [*LGaz* 12.4.1845: ex info JMH].

Preston, St George. New chancel. Minton's tiles laid [LL MS21, 10r].

Redmarshall (D), St Cuthbert. Restored. Work attributed to Thomas Austin, for his father, the rector, also Thomas [*Archaeologia Aeliana* ser 3 10 1909, 240].

Redmarshall (D), rectory. Rebuilt for the Revd Thomas Austin partly reusing materials from the previous building. Also attributed by *Archaeologia Aeliana* to Thomas Austin for his father. £1,326. £600 of which came from Queen Anne's Bounty. CC – Bulmer (stonemason), Fletcher (bricklayer), Atkinson (joiner), Bowness (slater), Johnson (plumbing etc). CW – Richardson [*Archaeologia Aeliana* ser 3 10 1909, 240: Bell, D & S 1994 'The Two Former Rectories of Redmarshall'. *Durham Archaeological Journal*, 10, 63–8].

1845–6
Manchester, Holy Trinity, Rusholme. Design 1844. Terracotta, aisled church for Thomas Carill-Worsley of Platt Hall. Design 1844. 650–700 seats. £4,000 (excluding the stained glass). Tower and spire 170ft high, completed 1850, C – Henry Sellers. CW – Edward Harrison [*Manchester Guardian* 27.6.1846: *B* 34, 1876, 553–4: *Eccl* 9, 1849, 137–8].

1845–50
Wigan (GM), All Saints. Rebuilt except for tower, Walmsley chapel and two turrets between the chancel and nave. The first phase (1845–7) was the chancel, Lord Crawford's chapel and the Legh chapel. Total cost £15,065: the Revd H J Gunning paid for the chancel and Lord Crawford for the rebuilding of his chapel. Sculpture and ornamental stone-carving by John Gibbs Oxford, painting by J Shrigley, Lancaster and Brice Grant Dean, Wigan: corporation benches at W end carved by Rattee, Cambridge, tiles by Minton. Reredos (1847) carved by John Thomas. C – Edward Harrison, Blackburn. CW – Hughes [LL MS21, 1r-2v, 3v-4r; LL 2, 94, 102, 110: *Wigan Times* 9.8.1850: *Eccl* 6, 1846, 117: Colling, J O 1957 *The Parish Church of All Saints, Wigan: A Short History and Guide*. Wigan, 2–15].

1846
Blackburn, new Market Place. Second place for S&P's competition entry (£10 premium). Plans estimated at £7,800 with buildings proposed so that they could be built in three phases. However, the Improvement Commissions preferred the design of a Mr Flanagan (who won a £15 premium) [*BS* 18.3.1846].

Conistone (NY), St Mary. Chancel added and nave and aisle much rebuilt in a Norman style [BE, *West Riding: Leeds etc*]. Three drawings of sections, elevations and fittings signed by S&P, Dec 1846 [in possession of the Revd John Potter, vicar, at Jun 1963, ex info JMH/R Jolley: whereabouts not now known].

Prestolee (GM), Holy Trinity. Plans for a new church estimated at £2,235 for 423 seats but excluding a projected tower and spire

[ICBS 3824]. Scheme presumably abandoned as the present church was built in 1859–62 to designs by George Shaw of Saddleworth [BE].

1846 onwards

Bridlington (EY), Priory (St Mary). Restoration. S&P prepared plans in 1845 and charged £78 3s 0d. Work does not seem to have started until at least May 1846 when alternative schedules of work were drawn up – one for the building to be 'thoroughly repaired', the other 'in case the building be entirely restored'. *Eccl* in Oct 1847 reported that 'very much has not yet been done' but notes restoration of part of the W front masonry and rebuilding of its gable, restoration of three bays of the nave (with new roof of raised pitch), clerestory reopened on the N and reglazed. W window probably opened at this time. CC – John Holderness (mason), Benjamin Popplewell (smith), John Cameron (plumber). Holderness was paid £672 for work in 1846–7 plus a further £172 in 1848–9. Six terracotta angels for the hammerbeam ends made by 'Willocks & Co, Terra Cotta Works, nr Manchester': cost £11 4s 0d in 1846). A total of £1,125 was spent 1846–53 but it is unclear how closely S&P were involved with the work since they do not appear in the accounts after their bill in 1845 [ERYAO, PE 153/50–5: *Hull Packet* 30.10.1846: *Eccl* 8, 1847–8, 125–6]. Thereafter restoration under G G Scott who was appointed in 1855 and work began in mid-1856: by mid-1858 over £3,500 had been spent [ERYAO, PE 153/56].

1846–7

Bishopton (D), St Peter. N aisle added; S wall rebuilt above window level and refenestrated. Norman chancel arch replaced by a pointed one. E wall rebuilt [guide, nd: LBS 350376].

1847

Bolton-le-Sands, St Michael (now Holy Trinity). Chancel rebuilt. Over £600 at the expense of John Holden in memory of his wife. E window by Wailes. CC – John Storey (masonry), Wilson Law (joinery), Cross (slating & plastering) [*LGaz* 27.11.1847, 21.9.1889]. BE gives 1846: but, as the chancel was finished in Nov 1847, it seems likely that the work was completed within that year.

Lancaster, County Lunatic Asylum additional offices. IT [*LGaz* 6, 13.6.1847].

Lee Bridge, Over Wyresdale (1 mile NE of Abbeystead: grid ref SD 568552). IT for rebuilding bridge over the River Wyre [*LGaz* 9.1.1847: ex info JMH].

1847–8

Barrow-in-Furness (CuL), Furness Abbey Hotel and station. Disused manor house on the site of the main gatehouse of Furness Abbey converted for the FR. Work likely to have been complete in 1848 as a directors' minute for 21 Nov says it was to be let for £100 a year to Mr Parker of the Sun, Ulverston [FR directors' minutes, National Archives, microfilm RAIL214/4: *LGuar* 26.1.1895: Norman 2001]. Demolished 1953 and/or 1954 apart from part of the N wing.

Bottesford (Leics), St Mary the Virgin. Plans from 1846. Nave, aisles and transepts restored: reseated, new aisle roofs, gallery removed, tower screen inserted, new pinnacles, refloored, refenestrated and W window opened. £2,235: the Duke of Rutland gave £600, the Revd F J Norman £500, and the ICBS £110 [Record Office for Leicestershire, Leicester & Rutland, 1D41/42, 2, 3a-b; DE 829/64 (seating plan); DE829/65/4–5, 11: ICBS 3823: *Leicester Chronicle* 15.5.1847: *Leicester Journal* 22.10.1847: *Eccl* 9, 1847, 268]. *Eccl* notes 'curious frescoes' discovered over the chancel arch but they were not deciphered.

Morecambe, North Western Hotel (the 'Midland' from 1871). For the 'Little' North Western Railway. Its minutes for 14.6.1847 say 'Mr. Paley submitted his plans for the erection of an hotel'. *c* £4,800. CC – C Baines (masonry), C Blades (carpentry & joinery), T Cross (plastering); Shrigley & Jackson (painting). Demolished 1933 to make way for Oliver Hill's Art Deco Midland Hotel [LL MS 21, 12v-17r: *LGaz* 16.9.1848: Guise, B & Brook, P 2007 *The Midland Hotel*, 3].

1847–9

Ince (Me), Ince Hall. Italianate style. Extended for Eliza Jane Park a widow and the younger daughter of Edmund Yates, Sharpe's godfather. At least £7,448 plus (in 1848) £1,452 spent on the stables. CC – J Dean (mason), R Wilson (joiner), Cross (plastering) [LL MS21, 8v-9v, 10v, 11v-12r, 19r-21r: *BS* 4.7.1891: *LStd* 25.1.1895: Robinson 1991, 46]. Demolished in the mid-20th century.

Morecambe to Wennington railway. ES supervised building of line for the North Western Railway Company. ES acted as contractor for the Morecambe to Lancaster and Lancaster to Wennington sections. In 1849 IT for stations which, presumably, ES (or S&P) designed [*LGaz* 2, 9.6.1849: Fawthrop, R A 1992 'The North Western Railway Company: Railway Company Politics in Cumbria and Lancashire' (unpublished typescript): ex info JMH].

St Helens (Me), St Nicholas, Sutton. Over £3,900 of which £1,270 was contributed by King's College, Cambridge, to commemorate the 400th anniversary of its foundation. Consecrated 4.6.1849 [*PG* 5.6.1847: LL MS21, 11r: ex info JMH].

1847–51

Hornby, Hornby Castle. 'Extensive alterations and improvements after a design replete with taste and beauty, by Mr Edmund Sharpe' for Pudsey Dawson. In fact EGP was probably largely responsible for much of the work. Design 1846. At least £1,300. Front rebuilt and projecting wings added, portico built with oriel window over, round tower replaced by a square one. CC – John Storey, Bolton-le-Sands: also Mr Wilson, Mr Cross, and Mr Howson [LL MS21, 3v: *LGaz* 5.12.1846, 16.10.1847]. Illustrated in *B* [8, 1850, 402]. The *JRIBA* 3 ser 2, 1895, 334, says 'the entire superintendence of the improvement to the frontage of Hornby Castle' was entrusted to EGP.

1848

Heversham (CuW), St Peter. Drawings of pulpit, reading desk and ornamental work [CRO(K), WPR 8/9/21].

***c* 1848**

Kirkham, vicarage. Work for the Revd G L Parsons (probably alterations) [LL MS21, 22r].

1848–9

Coventry (Warwicks), St Thomas, Albany Road. Plans 1846. Five-bay nave, bell-turret at NW corner, aisles, chancel and vestry. £3,450 of which £630 was provided by the Coventry Archidiaconal Society, £230 by the Church Building Commissioners and £320 by the ICBS. Seating for 576 or 710. CC – George Taylor: carving by Gibbs Oxford. £3,721 (£600 from the Coventry Archidiaconal Society, £320 from the ICBS £230 from the CBC). Stone given by Lord Leigh from his estate [ICBS 3310, 3772: Port 2006, 342, 162–3: Palmer, M S 1949 *'A Hundred Years Old': The Story of the Parish of St Thomas from 1848 to 1949*. Gloucester]. Redundant 1974, demolished 1976.

Lancaster, St Mary. Internal work: work on the roof by Mr Batty [LRO PR 3262/4/2].

Lancaster, Savings Bank Church Street/New Street. Modifications. £828 [LL MS21, 17v-18r; LL 2, 5; LL PL/2/64: *LGaz* 27.5.1848].

Ribby-cum-Wrea, St Nicholas' church and schools, Wrea Green. Church cost *c* £1,600. In 1857 pulpit, organ chamber, vestry and stalls added but no architect named [LL MS21, 27r: Barrett 1886, 750: BE].

Thorpe Thewles (D), Holy Trinity. Design 1847. Replaced an isolated church 1½–2 miles away which was to have the chancel and N vestry retained for funerals. Described by the Revd William Cassidi as 'extremely pretty & very much approved, the design I believe taken from Binstead in the Isle of Wight'. Estimated cost £600. Seating for 175. The church measured 68ft E–W and 23.5ft N–S [ICBS 3842: Durham University Library, DDR/EA/CHC/3/G/6]. Demolished because of decay and damp under a faculty of 1885 [Durham University Library, DDR/EJ/FAC/3/274] and replaced by another church by R J Johnson, 1886–7.

Warton, St Oswald. S arcade piers rebuilt. Chancel S arcade also rebuilt and arches raised slightly to match those in the nave S arcade, CC – John Storey, Bolton-le-Sands (masonry); T Cross, Lancaster (plastering) [LRO PR 572].

1849

Bolton (GM), St Peter. Window on S side of the chancel in memory of William Bolling, MP for Bolton (ES's son Alfred married his granddaughter Rosamond). Stained glass by Wailes but no evidence that S&P were involved in the design of the latter [*LGaz* 15.12.1849: ex info JMH].

Cottages for Mr Bateman. Tender from C Baynes, £306. Not known if work carried out. Location unknown [LL MS21, 25r].

Crook of Lune, 'The Hermitage'. House for John Sharp, a prominent Lancaster solicitor. Estimate £1,800. Tender in at £1,200 [LL MS21, 26r: ex info JMH].

Heysham, St Peter. Proposals for £520-worth of work involving seating. Tender from C Baynes, £480 [LL MS21, 24r].

Lancaster, proposed fish market. Design by EGP [illustrated in *LGaz* 24.2.1849].

Preston, St George. Pulpit, given by T M Lowndes [*LGaz* 10.3.1849].

Lancaster, 'Mawdale' (now 'Rivendell'), Westbourne Road/Milking Stile Lane. House probably by ES's assistant Thomas Walsh for himself [date in stained glass: 'Lancaster Fifty Years Ago: January 1852–December 1853'. *LGuard* Jan 1904].

1849–50

Lancaster, Charity School for Girls, Middle Street. Rebuilt on an enlarged site. Mr & Mrs Richard Newsham of Preston gave £300 towards the cost [*LGuar* 9.6.1849, 13.4.1850]. Later enlarged by P&A, nd [ex info JP]. Converted to flats 2007.

1849–51

Giggleswick (NY), Giggleswick School. Alterations costing £721 including a new porch, 22 windows; also £400 for new buildings [LL MS21, 28r]. Work including a library and room for modern languages, completed early 1851 [*LGuar* 15.3.1851]. Demolished 1960.

1850

Lancaster, RC cemetery. Laid out by S&P. Consecrated 28.8.1850 [ex info JP].

Tonge, schools and master's house. IT [*BS* 16.1.1850].

1850–1

Lancaster, National Schools, St Leonard's Gate. IT 1850, opened Jan 1851 [*LGuar* 18.5.1850, 18.1.1851]. Demolished.

1850–4

Ringley (GM), St Saviour. Church of 1826 or 1827, rebuilt 1850 apart from tower which was heightened 2ft in 1854. £2,530 (estimate); land given by 13th Earl of Derby who also gave £500; font and pulpit given by R S Sowler of Stand. 662 seats (initially estimated at 621). Consecration delayed until 1854 [ICBS 4271: LL 2, 78: Port 2006, 335: BE: ex info JMH].

1851

Bardsea (CuL), school and school house. [LL 2, 34]. The LL 2 drawing is undated but *K* [1913, 103] mentions a new school and school house built in 1851 by the Revd and Mrs T E Petty which surely must refer to the same building.

Bolton-le-Sands, St Michael (now Holy Trinity). Pulpit and reading desk [*LGaz* 28.9.1889].

Lancaster, RC Infants' School, Moor Road. Plans [LRO, MBLA acc 5167/18a: *LGuar* 13.9.1851].

Lancaster, four temporary triumphal arches, for a visit by the royal family to Lancaster on 8.10.1851 [*LGaz* 4.10.1851].

Lever Bridge (nr Bolton, GM), school for St Stephen's church 'about to be erected'. To accommodate 400 scholars. Cost estimated at £1,000 towards which J & W Gray of Wheatfield contributed £500: site given by the 2nd Earl of Bradford. To 'correspond in design and materials with the church and parsonage, which are built of Ladyshore terra-cotta' [*B* 9, 1851, 578].

1851–2

Lancaster, Free (from 1852, Royal) Grammar School, East Road. £8,000; statue of Queen Victoria over the entrance sculpted by Duckett of Preston. CC – Dugdale, Lancaster in association with

Taylor (masonry), Cross (slating & plastering), Hewson (plumbing & glazing) and Barrow & Stewardson (painting) [*LGaz* 29.3.1851, 3.5.1851, 10.5.1851, 2.10.1852: *LGuar* 17.5.1851, 2.10.1852].

1851–3
Preston Patrick (CuW), St Patrick. Report on church. Estimated cost in 1851 £850. IT Mar 1851. 1,386 seats [CRO(K), WPR 42/1/4/5, 7: LL 2, 35: ICBS 4336: *LGuar* 22.3.1851, 22.10.1853].

1852
Yealand Conyers, St Mary (RC). Paid for by Richard Thomas Gillow of Leighton Hall. £1,100 to £1,200 [*PG* 14.8.1852: Bulmer 1913].

Lancaster, St Thomas. NE steeple added, chancel lengthened and W gallery converted to an organ loft. Over £4,000. E window by Warrington; chancel floor and reredos tiles by Minton; *corona lucis* with 48 jets in chancel by Skidmore; pulpit, stalls etc by Rattee of Cambridge; organ case made by James Hatch [*LGuar* 1.5.1852: *LGaz* 1.5.1852, 27.11.1852, 18.12.1852, 1.5.1875].

Lancaster, new house for the master of St Thomas's School. Application to the Board of Health [LRO, MBLA acc 5167/26a: *LGaz* 7.8.1852].

Lancaster, presbytery for proposed new RC church. Plans 1851 [LRO, MBLA acc 5167/10a: ex info CS].

Lancaster, counting house and show rooms. Parliament Street, for the Phoenix Foundry. Application to the Board of Health [*LGaz* 20.11.1852].

c 1852
Lancaster, St Peter's RC Convent. For the Sisters of Mercy from St Ethelburga, Liverpool. Application to build reported in 1852. Also schools [*LGaz* 13.3.1852: *LGuar* 6.10.1859: Lambert 1991].

1852–3
Barrow-in-Furness (CuL), St Mary, Walney Island. Designs probably 1851: estimated cost £520 for 184 seats. Aisleless chapel with octagonal bell-turret replacing one of *c* 1690 which itself replaced an earlier one [ICBS 4396: *LGaz* 5.3.1853: *LGuar* 5.3.1853: old postcards in church]. Design for font, nd [LL 2, 9]. Replaced by an A&P church 1907–8 and then demolished.

Rylstone (NY), St Peter. Rebuilt. £1,000 or £1,100 towards the total of £1,700 was bequeathed by Richard Waddilove of Rylstone (d 1850) [inscription: LL 2, 80–1, 118: ex info Peter Leach]. Sketch in the church notes it was 'restored' in 1852; notice says bells installed 1853. The visual evidence suggests that it is largely, if not wholly, rebuilt.

Settle (NY), Music Hall. Announced in 1850 that it was to be built to S&P's plans and that the benefactor was the Revd John Robinson. C – James Winskill, Hutton Roof [*LGaz* 20.7.1850, 5.2.1853: *LGuar* 22.10.1853: Mitchell, W R *et al* nd *Settle's Victoria Music Hall*, 43].

1852–65
Lancaster, St Mary. Protracted work including estimates for a new vestry, removal of galleries, and reseating, reflooring, new communion rails, heating etc. £1,850 was spent 1855–65 [LRO, PR 3262/4/19].

1853
Blackburn schools. S&P appointed as architects 'for a Central National and Sunday School' [*BS* 7.9.1853].

Easingwold (NY), St John the Baptist & All Saints. Restored: porch in memory of EGP's father who was vicar here 1812–39 [inscription: *BN* 58, 1890, 721: JP]. Design for reredos and repewing, nd [LL 2, 22, 77].

Lancaster, foundry, stables and other works at the Phoenix Foundry. Application to the Board of Health [LRO, MBLA acc 5167/30a: *LGaz* 5.2.1853].

Lancaster, reservoir: IT for excavation of 3,500 cubic yards to create a reservoir 'on the Knot, near Stanley Farm'. Plans and specifications available at the S&P offices: perhaps on land belonging to Lancaster Asylum since 'the Clerk of Works at the Lancaster Lunatic Asylum will attend … to point out the Site, Xc' [*LGaz* 12.2.1853].

Lawford (Essex), St Mary. Chancel restored: new E window design, roof and stalls [*Ipswich Journal* 19.11.1853]. This far-away commission must have arisen through ES: he and the rector, the Revd Charles Merivale, were at St John's, Cambridge, in 1830 and both rowed for the college.

Lever Bridge (GM), St Stephen & All Martyrs. Gravestone for Annie Sophie Fletcher (d 19.7.1853), [LL 2, 1 at back of volume]. She was the niece of ES's wife so the design may be his.

Urswick (CuL). Design for gable cross [LL 2, 31].

1853–4
Thwaites (CuC), St Anne. Replaced a chapel of ease, commenced 1721, consecrated 1725, on opposite side of the road. Report 1851, design 1852. Land given by W Postlethwaite of 'The Oaks'. Tender £1,500; cost £1,678, all subscribed by the parishioners. CC – Thomas & Henry Harrison (builders), George H R Young, Ulverston (mason), Charles Blades (carpentry) [CRO(B), BPR 15/C/4/1–10: *Cumberland Paquet* 13.6.1854: BE: Johnson, D nd (2000) *The Story of St Anne's, Thwaites*]. Design for lychgate, Jun 1854 [LL 2, 19]. Design for pulpit, nd [LL 2, 11].

1854
Bacup, Christ Church. Paid for by Revd James Heyworth of Henbury Hill near Bristol from a legacy of his uncle James Heyworth. Over £3,000. Seating for 500 [*Manchester Times* 16.8.1854].

Kildwick (WY), St Andrew. Design for pulpit and reading desk [LL 2, 18].

Lancaster, depot for the 1st Regiment of the Royal Lancaster Militia, South Road. IT [*LGaz* 13.5.1854: JP].

Morecambe (Poulton-le-Sands), schools and master's house. IT [*LGuar* 21.10.1854].

Wrightington, St James the Great. Probably designed in 1853. Not consecrated until Jul 1857. Seating for 400 [ICBS 4727: *LGuar* 1.8.1857].

1855

Lancaster, cemetery buildings. IT for two chapels, lodge and gardener's cottage Dec 1854. IT for third chapel Mar 1855. Cemetery opened Oct 1855 [*LGaz* 3.11.1855: *LGuar* 16.12.1854, 24.3.1855].

Lancaster, Girls' National School. IT for new floor, desks and 'other smaller alterations' [*LGuar* 9.6.1855].

1855–6

Lancaster, 'The Greaves', Belle Vue Terrace, Greaves Road, Scotforth. House built by EGP for himself [Fanny Langshaw diary 1856, ALA].

Penwortham, St Mary. Plans 1853. Nave rebuilt and aisles added, chancel roof restored, chancel arch inserted, tower arch opened and W gallery added. C – Thomas Duckett, Preston (font) [records at church (ex info CS): *PG* 28.5.1853: *K* 1913, 796: *VCH* 6, 1911, 53].

Wennington, Wennington Hall. Tudor Gothic house for William A F Saunders [LL 2, 31: *LGuar* 5.5.1855]. Now a school.

1855–8

Lancaster, St Mary. Restoration work including a new W gallery. Box-pews removed and new seats put in [*LGaz* 1.12.1855; McClintock, M 2003 *Lancaster Priory*, 18].

c 1855–70

The following are designs from among undated drawings in the second and third volumes of the firm's drawings formerly in Lancaster Reference Library (now in LRO). The style and context of other drawings in the album suggest that they probably date from the 1850s through to the early 1870s. Designs for individual items may indicate more widespread work, evidence for which has not been traced.

Burnley, St Peter. Seats for chancel, S aisle and Townley chapel [LL 2, 177–8].

Dalton (CuL), cemetery. Reading desk [LL 2, 73].

Desborough Hall (Co Tipperary, Ireland). Metalwork verandah [LL 2, 87]. House demolished and rebuilt in 20th century [ex info CS].

Douglas (Isle of Man), Christ Church. Lectern [LL 2, 192]. No Christ Church existed in Douglas but did so in both Laxey and Maughold, but both these churches were designed by Ewan Christian. The connection may be through the Revd Samuel Simpson, vicar of St Thomas, Douglas, until 1867, who knew EGP [ex info CS and Peter Kelly].

Hornby. Market cross [LL 2, 17].

Kirkby Lonsdale (CuW). Memorial fountain [LL 3, 27].

Lancaster, cemetery. Monument [LL 2, 172].

Lancaster, 'Ryelands'. Tile design for T R Dunn [LL 2, 98].

Lancaster, Town Hall. Inner entrance [LL 3, 33]. Possibly for the 1871–4 works.

?Llansanffraid Glan Conwy Station (Clwyd). Drawing states '… saintfford', probably a variant of Llansanffraid Glan Conwy (2 miles from Conwy) for the Conwy-Llanrwst line for which ES was engineer [LL 2, 62].

Lytham, St Cuthbert. Enlargement of belfry windows [LL 2, 56].

'Malham Tarn House' (NY). Verandah or gallery [LL 3, 22]. For William Morrison [ex info CS].

Manchester, Cathedral. Restoration of rood screen [LL 2, 51].

Mickleover (Derbys), residence for C E Newton. Plan and woodwork in entrance hall, design for fireplace etc in dining room [LL 2, 125–6]. The work was at Mickleover Manor, now converted to residential accommodatuion [ex info CS].

Mirfield (WY). Altar rails, pulpit, reading desk and altar [LL 2, 93, 105, 111, 120].

Preston, All Saints. Top of tower (with cupola) [LL 2, 36]. A cupola exists.

Stanground (Cambs), St John the Baptist. Reredos and altar rails [LL 2, 23].

1856

Airton (NY), 'Newfield Hall', Malhamdale. Opened [construction must have started at least in 1855]. House built for William Nicholson Alcock. Cost £36,000. Attribution to EGP from his obituary in *LGuar* 26.1.1895. Other details from www.kirkbymalham.info/KMI/calton/newfield.html (accessed 30.11.2011). Now a holiday fellowship centre.

Dalton-in-Furness (CuL), Dalton Tower (or 'Castle'). First plans 1854. Extensive internal reordering of the court facilities in this 14th-century building. The three storeys were reduced to two. Jury room created on the ground floor with a court room and ante-room above with a wooden staircase between the two [CRO(B), BD/BUC/62/6: LL 2, 42–3].

Lancaster, Athenaeum. Alterations [Betjemann, A G 1982 *The Grand Theatre, Lancaster: Two Centuries of Entertainment*. Lancaster].

Lancaster, Independent (Congregational) Sunday Schools, High Street/Middle Street. IT Oct 1855 [*LGaz* 13.10.1855]. £1,261. CC – T & H Hanson (masonry), Shaw & Parkinson (joiners), T Walker (slater & plasterer), Willan & Cleminson (plumbers & glaziers), R Charnley (ironfoundery & heating apparatus) [Trinity United Reformed Church minute book 1856: *LGuar* 23.8.1856].

Lancaster, Mechanics' Institute. Moved to the top of Market Street and alterations to the building there by EGP to accommodate it. A room created for the School of Art on the higher floor at the front and another large room at the back for a school room for elementary classes. £250 or more [*LGuar* 16.2.1856]. The Institute had been founded 1824.

Preston, St John the Divine. Caen stone font, given by three daughters of Edward Gorst of Preston. Carved by A E Jackson, York. [*LGuar* 20.12.1856]. Possibly groining for tower [LL 2, 3]. Design for altar, nd [LL 2, 174].

Stalmine, two cemetery chapels and entrance gates. IT [*LGuar* 29.2.1856, 26.4.1856].

Unknown location. Conservatory [LL 2, 15].

Unknown location. Red granite grave cover for W L G Bagshawe (d 1854) [LL 2, 19].

1856–7
Capernwray, chapel. SW tower and chancel added to ES's chapel of 1840: new W window inserted [drawings at Capernwray Hall: 1857 datestone on tower].

Davenham (Ch), school. On triangle of land between the Hartford and Northwich roads: land given by John H Harper of Davenham Hall. *c* £2,125. C – Thomas Dean [CALS, P6/14/41–64b].

Pilling, National Schools. [*LGuar* 12.1.1856, 19.1.1856, 19.4.1856]. The first notice was on 12 Jan which implies designs in 1855. A drawing dated Sept 1857 suggests work was still progressing then [LL 2].

1856–8
Scorton, 'Wyresdale Hall' (now 'Wyresdale Park') [Robinson 1991, 255: CS]. Enlarged 1863 [datestone]. Client – Peter Ormrod who later commissioned EGP to rebuild St Peter's, Bolton.

1857
Abbeystead. IT for school [*LGuar* 18.4.1857]. Lancaster. Sends 'the Magistrates assembled at Lancaster sessions … [a] report upon the state of the Buildings etc'. Signed 'Edward G. Paley for Edmund Sharpe … January 3 1857' [LRO 3523/10 QSP].

Lancaster, Music Hall. IT for alterations [*LGuar* 16.5.1857]. Involved an apsidal extension with a gallery.

Slaidburn. Design for villa [LL 2, 103], identified as 'Whiteholme' for Miss King-Wilkinson [ex info CS]. Design for gate piers (nd) for a cottage at Slaidburn [LL 2, 31].

1857–8
Garstang, St Mary & St Michael (RC), Bonds. Also presbytery, schools and master's house. Church with seats for 600. C – Harrison, Wilson & Walker, Lancaster, and Waterhouse, Garstang [*LGuar* 2.5.1857, 9.5.1857, 20.6.1857: *PG* 21.8.1858: Slater 1895, 348]. Slater gives cost as £7,000 for church and schools; *PG* and *LGuar* say *c* £3,000 [probably for church only].

Preston, St John the Evangelist. Reredos [*PG* 30.1.1858].

1857–9
Barrow-in-Furness (CuL), 'Abbot's Wood'. House for James Ramsden. Outlay of up to £2,000 authorised by the FR: occupied by 1859. Demolished *c* 1964 [FR directors' minutes, National Archives microfilm RAIL214/4, 27.2.1857: *LGuar* 26.1.1895: ex info Aidan Jones of CRO(B)].

Lancaster, St Peter and associated buildings (RC). Cost £15,000 (£2,000 bequeathed by Thomas Coulston). Seating for 600. Chancel ceiling decorated by [Thomas] Early, high altar and Lady Chapel altar by Stirling (or Sterling) of Liverpool, Caen stone altarpiece in Whiteside chapel by Lane of Birmingham, altarpiece in Coulston chapel by E E Geflewski, Liverpool. CC – Duckett, Preston (masonry), R Wilson, Lancaster (carpentry), John Cross, Lancaster (slating & plastering), Thomas Dickinson, Lancaster (plumbing & glazing), J Shrigley, Lancaster (painting) [LRO, RCLn 3/1–15: LL 2, 1, 6–7, 18, 21: *LGuar* 14.2.1857, 6.10.1859: *PG* 8.10.1859: Lambert 1991].

1857–60
Low Bentham (NY), 'The Ridding'. House remodelled for B H Bent in the Scottish baronial style [*LGuar* 18.4.1857: LBS 324056: ex info W H Gardner]. The IT refers to the house being in Wennington whereas, in fact, it is just across the Yorkshire border in Low Bentham. Designs for W and S elevations in possession of the owner are signed and dated by EGP.

1858
Claughton, rectory. IT [*LGaz* 26.6.1858].

Clitheroe, Standen Hall. Possible alterations suggested by a drawing dated Nov 1858 of bay windows in the drawing room [LL 2, 36].

Easingwold (NY), All Saints & St John. Restored [guide: JP].

Ellel, National and infant schools. IT [*LGaz* 21.8.1858].

Grange-over-Sands (CuL), parsonage. IT [*LGaz* 29.5.1858].

Lancaster, cemetery, registrar's residence. Designs [LL 2, 33, 209].

1859
Burton-in-Kendal (CuW), Dalton Hall. Enlarged and interior remodelled in a classical style. Destroyed by fire and rebuilt to a new design by Clough Williams-Ellis, 1973 [Robinson 1991, 269]. For Edward George Hornby who married Sarah Yates, niece of ES's godfather, Edmund Yates [ex info JMH].

Cartmel (CuL), National Schools with separate residences for the master and mistress. IT [*LGaz* 19.11.1859].

Cockerham, schools. New classroom and other alterations. IT [*LGaz* 26.11.1859].

Lancaster, house on land adjoining the Royal Grammar School, East Road. For the Revd T F Lee (headmaster). Application to the Local Board of Health and IT [LRO, MBLA acc 5167/76a: *LGuar* 10.6.1859]. Probably the house immediately N of the school bearing a shield dated 1860.

Ormskirk St Peter & St Paul. New E window given by John Pemberton Heywood, banker of Liverpool. C – T Livesey, Scarisbrick [*PG* 12.11.1859].

Preston, St John the Divine. Organ case by Kirtland & Jardine of Manchester [*LGuar* 5.11.1859].

Unknown location. Design for an ash sieve for 'XXXham House' dated Oct 1859 [LL 2, 61].

Unknown location. Design for a Gothic memorial fountain for Mr Philips [LL 2, 205]. Also a design of 1860 for a Renaissance-style, wall-mounted drinking fountain [LL 2, 201].

1859–60
Barrow-in-Furness (CuL), St George. IT in Nov 1857 for an unspecified church but undoubtedly what was to become St

George's. Chief benefactors – the Dukes of Devonshire and Buccleuch, who in 1857 had guaranteed £4,000 towards the cost if £2,000 was subscribed by others for the parsonage and endowment. Other benefactors – Schneider, Hannay & Co, and Harrison, Ainslie & Co. Built of Kirkby slate from the Duke of Devonshire's quarries with St Bees sandstone dressings. CC – Thomas Duckett, Preston (mason), William Blades (carpenter), E Cross & Sons (plasterers), Willan & Cleminson (plumbers) and Shrigley & Seward, Lancaster (painters) [*LGaz* 10.5.1884: *LGuar* 21, 28.11.1857, 4.6.1859: Anon (Church Congress), 73: Leach 1872, 100: Richardson 1881, 102–3].

Singleton, St Anne. Rebuilt. IT and plans 1858. Old church demolished 1859. Paid for by Thomas Miller of Preston. CC – James Duckett (masonry), C Blades (joinery), E Cross & Sons (flagging & slating), and James Walmsley (plumbing, glazing & plastering): pulpit and font carved by Blinston of Chester [inscription: LRO, PR 3224/4/36–9: *LGaz* 27.11.1858: *PG* 10.12.1859, 14.7.1860: Anon 1960 *The Church of St Anne, Singleton*]. Miller was a Preston mill-owner who had purchased the Singleton estate.

c 1850s

Appleby (CuW), church uncertain. Design for organ case and porches [LL 2, 34, 47].

Bury, All Saints, Elton. Drawing of a font cover (£5 to Jackson of London); this might suggest other work took place [LL 2, 37].

1859–61

Holker Hall (CuL). Alterations [BE].

1860

Blackburn, Holy Trinity. Galleries reconstructed. 200 extra seats obtained. New stalls. Organ moved to behind pulpit. Over £1,000 [*BS* 2.5.1860]. *c* 1860: screen [LL 2, 71].

Glasson, schools. IT for additions and alterations [*LGaz* 28.4.1860, 5.5.1860].

Knowsley (Me), St Mary. Transepts [BE]. Pulpit design Nov 1860 [LL 2, 10].

Lancaster, St Peter (RC). Font, carved by Huling of Liverpool [*PG* 16.6.1860].

Lancaster, Crimea War memorial. Design 1856. A letter from 'A Working Man' in *LGuar* 14.5.1859, complained that the monument had still not been erected. For an obelisk 34ft high, EGP made no charge. Estimated cost £120–£140. C – C Baynes, Lancaster [*LGuar* 27.12.1856: *LGaz* 14.7.1860, 10.11.1860].

Quernmore, St Peter. Replacement of a chapel of 1834 designed by W Coulthard. Additional land to double the site area given by W G Bradley. Cost of building *c* £3,000 paid entirely by William Garnett of Quernmore Park. 320 seats. CC – C Baynes, Lancaster (masonry), Sandham, Quernmore (woodwork), Cross & Sons (slating & plastering), J Shrigley (painting & varnishing), J Parkinson (plumbing & glazing), pulpit carved by Bell & Coupland [LL 2, 116: *LGaz* 22.12.1860: *BN* 7, 1861, 19: Anon nd [*c* 2004] *The Parish Church of St Peter Quernmore: A Brief History*]. A reference in Nov 1859 [*LGuar* 5.11.1859] and the laying of FS in Feb 1860 suggest a design in 1859.

***c* 1860**

Casterton (CuW), Holy Trinity. Chancel added [BE].

1860–1

Lowton (Me), St Mary. Design 1855–7, estimated to cost £1,215 for 345 seats [ICBS 5020: LL 2, 72–3: BE].

Rossall, Rossall School, new studies, master's house and servants' quarters (now Mitre House). Preparatory school planned but not built [*LGaz* 19.5.1860: Bennett 1990].

1861

Hindley (GM), schools, probably for All Saints' parish. Designs Feb 1861 [LL 2, 197,199: ex info the Revd Dr I Carter, May 1997].

Wigan (GM), All Saints. Tower heightened [BE]. The plan at the end of the main restoration in 1845–50 had been to case the existing tower and add a storey [*Wigan Times* 9.8.1850].

Yealand Conyers, St John. Unexecuted plan to add a N aisle, costing £400, to increase the seating by 85 to 309 (plans probably of 1860) [ICBS 5680].

1861–2

Aldford (Ch), St John the Baptist. To be rebuilt to EGP's designs at the expense of the Marquess of Westminster [*Cheshire Observer* 2.2.1861]. Nothing came of this, and the present church of 1866 is by John Douglas.

Hoddlesden, St Paul. EGP engaged by Aug 1860 when he was looking at possible sites [LRO, PR 3081/4/21]. Geometrical style church with four-bay nave (72ft × 25ft) and N aisle (20ft wide). Built of local stone: roofed with slates from Over Darwen. Tower and spire intended to be 130ft high. To seat 650 at a cost of *c* £4,000. C – James Duckett, Burnley. [LRO, PR 3081/4/27: *BS* 31.7.1861, 3.6.1876: *Preston Herald* 3.8.1861]. Demolished 1975.

Rossall, Rossall School, chapel. Estimate £4,400 [Rossall School drawings collection, ex info DM: Bennett 1990].

Walton-le-Dale, All Saints, Higher Walton. IT and plans 1860 at estimated cost of £4,300 to seat 604. Body of the church cost £4,000. Miles Rodgett of Darwen Bank gave the site, and the cotton firm of Rodgett Bros £1,000 towards the building. EGP gave a stained glass window (Healing of the Sick Man). C – Cooper & Tullis, Preston [ICBS 5596: *Lancaster Observer* 20.7.1861: *PG* 17.7.1861, 29.11.1862, 9.7.1864: *BN* 6, 1860, 542; 7, 1861, 19: Abram 1877, 741]. The consecration was delayed until Jul 1864: designs were made for altar rails in Nov 1863 [*BN* 11, 1864, 548]. The demolished vicarage was probably by EGP.

1862

Gressingham, St John the Evangelist. Restored; porch removed, S wall rebuilt with buttresses and new windows, new E window (Perpendicular style), new lights on N clerestory, chancel arch restored, reseated, refitted, ceiling removed, chancel tiled. *c* £300. Chief benefactor – F F Pearson. CC – J Foxcroft of Wray (stonework), W B Smith, Hornby (woodwork), Walker, Lancaster (plastering), A Hargreaves, Lancaster (plumbing & glazing) [*LGuar* 29.3.1862]. The scale of the work suggests it must have begun in 1861.

1862
Singleton, school. Design Aug 1862 [LL 2, 85].

Lancaster, unspecified building near the Royal Grammar School. IT [*LGaz* 20.9.1862].

1862–3
Barrow-in-Furness, Strand station. [CRO(B), BTBR 1/16: Andrews 1996, 8].

Blawith (CuL), St John the Baptist. Design 1860 £1,600; 169 or 171 seats. Chancel built by subscription as a memorial to the Revd Richard Harrison [LL 2, 69, 74: *LGaz* 24.3.1860: *North Lonsdale Magazine* 2, 1896–8, 185–6: *VCH* 8, 1914, 362: file at CCT]. The contents and fabric of the old church were sold off in 1869 and it was left to become 'a picturesque ruin' [*Soulby's Ulverston Advertiser* 29.4.1869: *North Lonsdale Magazine* 2, 1896–8, 185]. Closed 1986: vested in the CCT.

Capel Garmon (Denbighshire), St Garmon. IT 1861. Restored and reseated: S wall rebuilt, windows renewed and new porch and N vestry. £880. Seating increased by five to 150. BW implies, incorrectly, that it is entirely rebuilt. [ICBS 5735: *North Wales Chronicle* 25.5.1861: *ChBldr* 1864, 8: BW, 115]. In 2006 a builder's store.

Morecambe, Independent (Congregational) chapel, Clark Street. Seating for 350 [*LGaz* 23,5 1863, 30.5.1863 (with illustration)]. Converted to offices.

Preston, St Mark. Design probably 1861. Longridge stone for the exterior and also the interior dressings, CC – Cooper & Tullis (masonry), Mr Bamber (joinery). £6,594 (including site but spire not built [*PG* 26.4.1862, 26.9.1863: *BN* 8, 1862, 154; 11, 1864, 859, 861–2: *Eccl* 25, 1864, 50–1: Slater 1895, 585]. Tower by William Johnson of Howden 1870 [Fleetwood-Hesketh 1955, 167] although BE does not question EGP's authorship. Converted to flats in the late 20th century.

1862–4
Ince-in-Makerfield (GM), Christ Church. Design from early 1860 when seating for 750 was envisaged. C – James Fairclough, Wigan [LRO, PR 3081/4/16: *PG* 23.4.1862]. By early 1861, 677 seats were planned and costs of £5,000 expected (the site had been given). IT also issued early 1861 [ICBS 5750: LL 2, 101, 119: *BN* 7, 1861, 149: BE].

1863
Glasson, master's residence at school. IT [*LGaz* 11.7.1863].

Heysham, St Peter. N aisle 'etc' [*LGaz* 4.7.1863: Bulmer 1913, 248].

Lancaster, showrooms and new buildings at Fawcett's Marble Works, Green Ayre. IT [*LGaz* 16.5.1863].

Lancaster, Castle. Proposed alterations (unspecified). IT [*LGaz* 1.8.1863].

Melling, St Wilfrid. Organ case [*LGaz* 24.10.1863].

1863–4
Over Kellett, St Cuthbert. Restored: ceiling removed, chancel arch reinstated, E end rebuilt, to increase seating by 35 to 295 but pews of 1816 retained. £330 [ICBS 6235: *BN* 11, 1864, 330: Bulmer 1913, 364: BE].

1863–5
Allithwaite (CuL), St Mary's church, parsonage and schools. IT for parsonage and schools Jun 1863. Miss Mary Winfield Lambert of Boarbank Hall (d 1857) bequeathed £2,500 for the church, £1,000 for the schools and £1,500 for the parsonage. C – C Baynes (masonry), R Storey, Cark and R Wright, Lancaster (joinery), T Dickinson, Lancaster (plumbing), G Taylor (slating & plastering), Downward, Ulverston (painter). CW – H Gorton. *Eccl* called it 'A good church'. [*LGaz* 20, 27.6.1863, 15.10.1864: *UM* 1.7.1865: *Eccl* 26, 1865, 232: Ellis, D C 2006 *A Brief Guide to St Mary's Church, Allithwaite*, 1–2].

Bury (GM), Holy Trinity. S aisle and NW tower and spire of EGP's original design not carried out. The 14th Earl of Derby gave the site and £1,000 to the endowment fund. Cost *c* £5,500. 627 seats. C – Ellis & Hinchcliffe. Chancel furniture and lectern by Blades, Lancaster. [LL 2, 63: *Bury Guardian* 22.4.1865: *PG* 22.4.1865: *ChBldr* 1865, 128: LBS 493405: Lee, F *The Church of the Most Holy and Undivided Trinity, Bury: A Celebration for the Feast of Dedication, April 19th 2001*]. Rectory perhaps by EGP too.

1863–6
Hindley (GM), St Peter. IT 1860. £9,507 (including £1,100 towards the endowment and £200 to the repair fund: £3,781 paid by Alfred Pennington: £1,650 by other members of his family); seating for 689. FS 19.10.1863. Partly floored with Maw's 'mosaic tiles'. CW – Stephen Hodgson. Chancel fittings by Gilbert French, Bolton. Sculpture by Mr Gregg. C – James Neill, Bradford [LRO, PR 3081/4/16: ICBS 5608: *LGaz* 24.10.1863: *Wigan Observer* 19.10.1866: *BN* 6, 1860, 542: *ChBldr* 1867, 46].

Wigan (GM), St James, Poolstock. FS 3.9.1863. Built at the sole cost of Nathaniel Eckersley of Standish Hall, cotton mill owner, banker and railway promoter, in memory of his father, mother and brother. CW – Stephen Hodgson. Chancel wall paintings by Hardman. CC – William Winnard & Son, Wigan, J Gregg, Manchester (carving), Preston (joinery), Edmond & Son, Manchester [brass inscription in church: *Wigan Courier* 22.9.1866: *BN* 10, 1863, 690: Slater 1895, 1081: Anon (Eckersley) 1892 *Memoir of the late Nathaniel Eckersley, Esq., D. L. of Standish Hall, Wigan*: Fishburn, A 2005 *St James with St Thomas, Poolstock: A Short Guide*].

1864
Aughton, St Saviour. £590. Seating for 100 [*BN* 11, 1864, 569: *ChBldr* 1864, 185].

Clapham (NY), school. Memorial to J W Farrer [inscription: North Yorkshire County Record Office, ZTW III 11/169, letter 30.5.1864].

Crayke (NY), St Cuthbert. Restored and N aisle built. £1,000 [*ChBldr* 1864, 187: *Eccl* 26, 1865, 232: BE].

Darwen, St John the Evangelist, Turncroft. EGP had been engaged by Aug 1861 [LRO, PR 3081/4/25]. Paid for by Mrs Graham. Spire 146ft 6ins high. CC – James Duckett, Burnley or Preston (masonry), Whittle, Darwen (carpentry), R Entwistle, Darwen (painting & plastering), Bradshaw, Darwen (plumbing & glazing), Lavers & Co, London (decorative painting). CW for spire – Stephen Hodgson, Blackburn. Drawing for pulpit dated Oct 1863 [LL 2, 100, 110: *BS* 24.6.1863: *BN* 11, 1864, 568–9: *ChBldr* 1864, 186–7: Slater 1895, 278]. Closed. A school was opened in 1865 but no architect's name mentioned [*BN* 13, 1866, 538].

Lancaster, Asylum chapel. IT [*LGaz* 23.1.1864].

Lancaster, Phoenix Foundry. Plan for large extension for E Sharpe & Co [LRO, MBLA acc 5167/150a].

Walton-le-Dale, St Leonard. Chancel restored at the expense of Sir Henry de Hoghton and Richard Assheton. Reroofed, refloored and refitted. Bath stone reredos. C – Hatch (stalls) [*PG* 16.4.1864]. The extensive nature of the work suggests it probably was begun in 1863.

1864–5

Barrow-in-Furness (CuL), market hall with town hall above accommodating 1,000 people. £7,000. A Mr Phillips probably acted as the CW [*BH* 18.11.1865: Mannex 1882, 333: *K* 1913, 105]. Demolished *c* 1970.

Blackburn, St Thomas. First design for brick church Sept 1859 but, against EGP's wishes, stone was insisted upon. FS Sept 1860 but the plans and not even the orientation settled. 'Discouraged by this deficiency of funds in the beginning of 1862, and apprehensive of increasing difficulty, arising from the threatening "cotton famine", the works were suspended.' Work began in spring 1864. Originally designed for 766 seats but increased to 1,054. £4,469. C – James Duckett, Burnley (building work), William Baron, Blackburn (carpentry & joinery). CW – W Wright [ICBS 5591: LRO, PR 3081/4: *LGaz* 4.11.1865]. Demolished.

Bradford (WY), Holy Trinity, Leeds Road. Plans 1863 when cost estimated at £3,565 for 638 seats. Stone, five-bay aisled church with SE tower and later (1871) broach spire. [ICBS 6043: NMR photos BB64/1277–87: BE]. Demolished 1966.

Egton-cum-Newland (CuL), St Mary, Penny Bridge. Nave and S aisle. Cost of £1,000 paid by Countess Blücher von Wahlstadt. CC – W Troughton, Mr Butcher, and T Wearington [*SUA* 23.2.1865: CGT[ownley] 1898 *An Account of the Church and School of Egton-cum-Newland*. Ulverston, 5–8].

Ireleth (CuL), St Mary. Land given by John Todd of Kirkby Ireleth, otherwise built and furnished by the Duke of Buccleuch. £2,044. 200 or 300 seats. CC – J Garden, Dalton, and Cook Ulverston. The work had apparently been planned for some time since tenders for rebuilding were submitted in Apr 1863 [CRO(B), BD/BUC/52/7: *BH* 1.7.1865: *UM* 1.7.1865].

Lancaster, works for Lancaster Waggon Co Ltd, Caton Road. Adjacent to the Midland Railway at Bulk. C – J Hatch (for part of the work) [*LGaz* 5.3.1864, 14.5.1864: *BN* 11, 1864, 215].

Woodland (CuL), St John the Evangelist. Replaced a church of *c* 1689; design probably 1862. Nearly £1,000. 150 seats. CC – Usher & Dixon, Hawkshead (walling), George Butcher, Ulverston (mason), E Coward, Coniston (joiner), E Redhead, Coniston (plumbing & glazing), Green, Dalton (plasterer) [ICBS 6006: LL 2, 106, 108, 112, 117: *BH* 23.9.1865: *UM* 15.9.1865: *ChBldr* 1866, 82].

1864–6

Ulverston (CuL), St Mary. Medieval tower retained but the church of 1804 was rebuilt. *c* 1,400 seats. CW – Henry Reay. CC – W Troughton (builder), George Butcher (stonemason), William Braithwaite (plumbing, glazing & painting), J W Grundy (carpentry & joinery) [CRO(B), BPR 2/W/4/5: LL 2, 132: *UM* 3.11.1866: Bardsley, C W 1885 *Chronicles of the Town and Church of Ulverston*, 140–1: Slater 1895, 1031].

Lancaster, house for J L Bradshaw. IT [*LGaz* 25.11.1865].

c 1864

Grange-over-Sands (CuL), station. For the FR [plaque at station]. LBS 460552 suggests *c* 1877.

1865

Broughton-in-Furness (CuL), 'Eccle Riggs'. Tudor-style house for Richard Assheton Cross MP [datestone: Robinson 1991, 180]. Now offices.

Little Lever (GM), St Matthew. Replaced a church of 1791 [BE].

Staining (near Poulton-le-Fylde), school-chapel. FS Jun [*PG* 3.6.1865].

1865–6

Walton-le-Dale, All Saints, Higher Walton. Capitals of the arches (left incomplete when the church was built) carved by H S Miles who had executed the carving at Preston Town Hall [*PG* 2.12.1865].

1865–7

Caton, St Paul, Brookhouse. IT for rebuilding 1863. Estimated cost £4,000. CC – Robert Foxcroft, Caton (masonry), Charles Blades, Lancaster (carpentry), Willan & Cleminson, Lancaster, (plumbing & glazing): tower not rebuilt [*LGaz* 14.11.1863: BE: ex info, ebook, Caton chapel, http://tioli.co.uk/pdfs/Chapter1v0.2.pdf (accessed 28.1.2012)].

1866

Barrow-in-Furness (CuL), St James's schools. [*BH* 29.12.1866].

Capernwray Hall. Design for SW lodge [drawing at Capernwray Hall].

Kirkby Lonsdale (CuW), St Mary the Virgin. Restored at the cost of the Earl of Bective (Lord Kenlis). Reseated, reroofed, S porch. A pillar removed in 1806 to give a better view of the pulpit replaced. Wrought-iron screen and font inserted and (probably) the alabaster and mosaic reredos. Chancel floored with Godwin's tiles. Designs 1865 [LL 3, 13, 26: *LGaz* 30.12.1865, 6.1.1866, 14.4.1866: Mellor, M 2001 *The Church of St Mary the Virgin, Kirkby Lonsdale, Cumbria*].

Grange-over-Sands (CuL), Grange Hotel, Station Square. IT Dec 1863. Built for the FR [*LGaz* 26.12.1863: LBS 460550].

Lancaster, shop front, Church Street. For Mr Helme [LRO, MBLA acc 5167/193a: *LGaz* 20.10.1866, supplement].

Lancaster, Poor Law Union offices, Penny Street. Plans for new board room and alterations [LRO, MBLA acc 5167/187a and A319].

Lancaster, new house Quernmore Road, Bowerham. Plan for Miss Hinde [LRO, MBLA acc 5167/188a].

Morecambe, Holy Trinity. S aisle [drawing in the church signed by EGP, ex info JP].

Whalley, Whalley Abbey. Proposals for development of the NW wing, probably commissioned by John Taylor (d 1867) [LRO, DDWT box 24: ex info Clare Hartwell].

c 1866
Lancaster, 'Quarry Hill' (now 'Brunton House'), Higher Greaves. Alterations to house (built 1852 to J A Hansom's designs for Miss Elizabeth Dalton) purchased by ES for his own occupation [Hewitson 1990, 149: ex info CS, JMH and JP].

Lancaster, Moor Hospital chapel. [*LGaz* 26.6.1875].

1866–7
Ashford (Kent), Christ Church. Fund-raising started 1860. Designs by HJA (while in Gilbert Scott's office) for a competition in early 1864 which attracted 48 entrants: won 1865. Built for the workers in the South East Railway Co's workshops, it became known as 'the railwayman's church'. £4,219. Land given by G Jemmett, lord of the manor. *c* 600 seats (all free). C – Steddy, Joy & Steddy. CW – W King [ICBS 6268: *Kentish Express* 11.5.1867: *B* 22, 1864, 274: *Eccl* 26, 1865, 54].

1866–9
Churchtown, St Helen. Restored. £1,372. C – Richard Robinson & Proctor, Preston (carpentry). The work may have been drawn out: the restoration committee was formed as far back as 1864. In Oct 1866 work had not yet begun and it was reported that reseating and W gallery removal were to be included [LRO, PR 2446: *PG* 13.10.1866].

1867
Barrow-in-Furness (CuL), St George. N aisle added, increasing the seats to nearly 1,000. C – James Garden, Dalton [Anon (Church Congress), 74].

Cartmel (CuL), Priory. Plan for reseating 1863 (but seats not assigned till 1867). '[V]ery carefully restored by Mr. Paley' (*Eccl*). Restored; walls stripped of plaster, galleries removed, new seats, organ (by F W Jardine of Manchester), font, pulpit, reading desk reglazed with Hartley's cathedral glass [CRO(K), WPR 89/1/3/10–12: *LGaz* 7.9.1867, 2.10.1867: *Eccl* 29, 1868, 313].

Lancaster, corner of Damside Street/New Road. Plans for Lancaster Banking Co to change office into a house [LRO, MBLA acc 5167/201a].

Lancaster, shop and warehouse, Church Street. Plan for the Lancaster & Skerton Co-operative Society [LRO, MBLA acc 5167/214a].

Rossall, Rossall School. E range which continues the design of the N one; three-storey gatehouse [LBS 184736].

1867–8
Arkholme, schools. Erected by Mary and Eliza Alice Cort in memory of their father, the Revd Robert Cort, who was born in the village [*BN* 27.6.1868].

Stockton Heath (Ch), St Thomas. Replacement for a church which had been converted from a school room *c* 1839. In 1865 estimated cost £5,395 to seat 650. Main benefactor – Gilbert Greenall MP. N aisle never built. Chancel, N transept, and aisle E windows by Clayton & Bell, two W windows by Heaton & Butler, baptistry window by Gibbs & Co [ICBS 6412: LL 3, 23: *BN* 26, 1868, 646–7: BE]. The tower was added later.

1867 or 1868
Lupton (CuW), All Saints. [LL 2, 158: *LGuar* 19.9.1868: Bulmer 1913, 469: BE].

1867–9
Barrow-in-Furness (CuL), St James. W tower and spire, six-bay nave and aisles. *c* £7,650. 950 seats. CC – W Gradwell (main), Gregg, Blackburn (carving), Williams, Manchester (font and pulpit in Derbyshire alabaster), A Seward (heating apparatus). The IT was in Sept 1866 [LL 3, 5r, 11, 24: *Barrow Advertiser* 20.5.1869: *BH* 1, 8.9.1866; 22.5.1869: Richardson 1880, 295: *K* 1913, 105]. Design for organ case Feb 1870 [LL 2, 150]. 'Williams' refers presumably to Thomas Richard & Ewan Williams, a leading firm of Manchester sculptors and carvers.

Giggleswick (NY), Giggleswick School, Boarding House ('The Hostel') and master's house. IT Nov 1866. Estimate £6,400. Now much rebuilt internally [LL 2, 139: *LGaz* 17.11.1866: ex info W Brooks].

1867–71
Bolton (GM), St Peter. Rebuilt. The cost of £45,000 was paid by Peter Ormrod JP, cotton spinner and banker, of Halliwell Hall. EGP was asked in Jan 1864 to report and concluded that it could not be permanently repaired, and rebuilding was being planned 1864–5; in Nov 1865 Ormrod's offer of £30,000 for rebuilding was accepted. Faculty Feb 1866, and old church demolished same year. At 180ft the tower is said to be the highest in Lancashire. In 1867 the church was still expected to cost £30,000. Built of Bradshaw stone, but Longridge stone for the tower. Chancel roof decorated by Clayton & Bell. E window by Hardman & Co erected by public subscription to record Ormrod's gift; E window N chancel aisle by Wailes [EGP is not thought to have been involved with the glass designs]. C – Cooper & Tullis, Preston; woodwork by Blades, Lancaster; seats carved by George Dunley, Lancaster. CW – Mr Waites [LL 2, 88, 219: *Bolton Guardian* 1.7.1871: *LGaz* 2.12.1865, 8.7.1870; *BN* 14, 1867, 313; 21, 1871, 15: guide (early 1990s)]. Reredos 1878 [BE].

1867–73
Lancaster, Royal Albert Asylum (renamed the Royal Albert Institution in 1909). 'For the care and training of idiots and imbeciles belonging to the seven northern counties.' Contracts let May 1867 and excavations begun: FS laid May 1868. It was not intended for the most acute mentally ill cases, including 'epileptic, paralytic, or insane persons, nor those who are incurably hydrocephalic; idiocy combined with blindness and deafness is also a disqualification'. EGP appointed in Apr 1866 and presented plans in Oct. CW – Combe. CC – Baynes of Lancaster (masonry), Blades, Lancaster (woodwork), James Walmsley, Preston (plumbing), Johnston Bros of Carlisle (plastering). *c* £80,000. First phase (the N

or boys' wing) opened 1870, having cost £30,000. Main benefactors: Revd & Mrs Richard Brooke of Selby; John Bairstow of Preston, bequest of £5,000; Dr Waddington, Dean of Durham, bequest of £5,000; James Brunton of Lancaster, £2,000; and Henry Kelsall of Rochdale, £1,000 [*LGaz* 28.4.1866, 6, 13.10.1866, 17.9.1870: *LGuar* 13.6.1868: *BA* 5, 1876, 260 + illustration: Slater 1895, 412]. Bulmer, [1913, 34], noted the cost had been £204,300, and the estate covered 205 acres.

1868
Dalton-in-Furness (CuL), infants' school. CW – W Wright. C – James Garden, Dalton [*BH* 28.3.1868].

Burton-in-Lonsdale (NY), parsonage. IT [*LGuar* 13, 20.6.1868]. Built by 1870 [*B* 28, 1870, 391].

Grimsargh, St Michael. IT Aug 1867. The chancel and N aisle added in 1840 to a chapel of 1716 were retained but the nave was rebuilt and W tower added at the expense (£3,000) of the Revd John Cross. 220 seats [*PG* 17.8.1867: Barrett 1886, 690: Carbis, guide, 5, 8–9].

Lancaster, St John's National Schools, Cable Street/Nile Street. £2,080. Additions and alterations. C – John Shaw [LRO, MBLA, acc 5167/231a: NS/7/1/7457: *LGaz* 30.1.1869: ex info CS]. Demolished.

St John's Chapel (D), Town Hall. [BE].

Tatham Fells, parsonage. IT [*LGuar* 16, 23.5.1868].

Ulverston (CuL), vicarage. IT [*BH* 29.8.1868, 5.9.1868].

1868–9
Burnley, St James. Steeple and other changes [DM].

Goosnargh, St Mary. Restored and nave rebuilt, reseated, reroofed, and galleries removed. Plans to strip the wall plaster were unexecuted. £1,938 of which £435 came from the dean and chapter of Christ Church, Oxford. C – Joseph Shaw, Lancaster. Moves to restore were made in 1867 [LL 3, 17: *LGaz* 26.6.1869: *BN* 17, 1869, 17: Slater 1895, 363: Cookson, R 1878 *Goosnargh: Past and Present*. Preston 121–9]. Designs for alabaster reredos Dec 1869 [LL 3, 23] (although present reredos is of wood), and lectern Jan 1870 [LL 2, 161] suggests finishing-off work continued into 1870.

Lancaster, new bank for the Lancaster Banking Co, Church Street. IT May, FS Oct so work would have continued into 1869 [LRO, MBLA acc 5167/242a: *LGuar* 23.5.1868, 30.5.1868, 24.10.1868].

Sedgwick (CuW), Sedgwick House. For William Henry Wakefield [CRO(K), WPR 7/9/2/5 (designs for chimney pieces, 11.11.1868): LL 2, 140–1, 143, 148; LL 3, 6–9, 12: BE].

Windermere (CuW), 'Browhead'. Designs for house for E Cohen including a clock tower Dec 1869 [datestone: LL 2, 138; LL 3, 2, 15, 16, 25: ex info CS]. A school since 1924.

Woodland (near Broughton-in-Furness, CuL), parsonage. [*BH* 10.10.1868: *LGuar* 27.6.1868]. As the FS was laid in Oct 1868, it is almost certain work would have continued into 1869.

1868–70
Burton-in-Lonsdale (NY). All Saints. Rebuilt at the expense of Thomas Thornton of Brixton Hill, London 'for the benefit of his native place'. Estimate £7,000–£8,000. C – James Garden, Dalton-in-Furness [LL 2, 152–3, 188–9, 195; LL 3, 19–21, 28, 41: *LGuar* 15.2.1868, 23.5.1868: *B* 28, 1870, 391: *BN* 15, 1868, 367].

Heversham (CuW), St Peter. Restored. Tower rebuilt at expense of Mr & Mrs Argles of Eversley; N arcade rebuilt, chancel arch largely rebuilt, roofs of chancel, N and S aisles renewed, reseated. Plans formulated 1867 [CRO(K), WPR 8/1/3/3; WPR 8/9/3–20: *LGaz* 26.11.1870]. Faculty late Jan 1868 [*LGuar* 25.1.1868] and restoration seems to have started on the nave (rainwater heads dated 1868) but the IT for rebuilding the tower was not until Jan 1869 [*LGuar* 2, 9.1.1869]. Tower designs 1869 [CRO(K), WPR 8/9/11].

Thornton-in-Lonsdale (NY), St Oswald. Rebuilt apart from the tower and three Norman arches. £5,000 willed by Felix Slade (1790–1868) after whom the Slade School of Fine Art was named and who often resided at 'Halsteads', a house nearby. [LL 2, 155, 160, 162; LL 3, 18: *BN* 18, 1870, 330: church guide leaflet, 2005: BE]. IT Jul 1868 signed by EGP [*LGuar* 25.7.1868] but *BN* [18, 1870, 330] refers to P&A, as the practice had then become. Designs for pulpit May 1869 [LL 3, 18], and altar and lectern Jan 1870 [LL 2, 155, 160].

1868–71
Lancaster, St Mary. Chancel restored; new vestry and organ chamber (1870); altar rails made by James Hatch [LRO, PR 3262/4/19/16: *LGuar* 11.1.1868, 18.1.1868].

1869
Bamber Bridge, St Saviour. Proposal to reseat and enlarge from 450 to 650 seats at an estimated cost of over £3,400. Application to the ICBS Jan 1869 (so plans may be 1868) but no evidence for any work done [ICBS 7106: *BS* 21.7.1869]. The existing chancel and transepts 1886–7, by T Harrison Myers of Veevers & Myers, Preston [ICBS 9135: *B* 52, 1887, 52: Hunt 1997, 161].

Claughton, St Chad. New E window [tracery] designed by HJA and paid for by a £270 legacy, including a Holiday design for the glass which was made by Heaton, Butler & Bayne. At the same time new altar, tiles and gable cross but no indication if HJA was involved [*LGuar* 6.2.1909].

Lancaster, St Mary. Chancel restored; reseated, refloored, stone steps and base provided for pulpit. C – Charles Blades [*LGaz* 4.12.1869].

Over Kellett. IT for building a farmhouse called 'Addington' for S Booker [*LGaz* 2.10.1869].

Thelwall (near Warrington, Ch), All Saints. Designs for pulpit and reading desk [LL 2, 135, 137].

Thornton-in-Lonsdale (NY). IT for enlargement of schools [*LGaz* 17.7.1869].

Walton (CuC), St Mary. *c* £2,000. Details modelled on Lanercost Priory to which the living once belonged. CC – James Ferguson & Sons, Great Orton (masons), Rutherford, Brampton (carpentry);

E window by Wailes [*B* 27, 1869, 792].

Winwick (Ch), St Oswald. Restored and spire rebuilt under EGP. £122 [LL 2, 68: LRO, DDSr 10/3, f3: *BN* 58, 1890, 721].

1869–70
Lancaster, County Hotel, Station Road. 19-bedroom hotel for T Cross & Son. Plan 1868 [LRO, MBLA acc 5167/240a: *LGaz* 12.2.1870: ex info CS].

1869–71
Kirkby (Me), St Chad. Replaced a chapel of 1766. FS laid Mar 1869 by which time much of the outside walls had been built. Paid for wholly by the 4th Earl of Sefton (in 1869 estimated at £10,000, but rose to £12,000). 650 seats. Stone from the earl's own quarries. CC – E Garbutt, Liverpool, sole contractor: carvings and sculpture by John Roddis: some woodwork by Haigh & Sons, Liverpool. Godwin's tiles in nave and aisles [LL 2, 173, 191; LL 3, 44: *Birmingham Daily Post* 18.10.1871: *LGaz* 3.4.1869: *Liverpool Mercury* 1.4.1869, 5.10.1871: *BN* 16, 1869, 323; 21, 1871, 276]. Design 1868 (or earlier) since *BN* [15, 1868, 545] notes the contract for building as being open (referred to as 'Kirby near Prescot' but there can be no doubt this is the same place as Kirkby).

Manchester, St John the Evangelist, Cheetham. Estimate £10,000. Built and endowed at cost of Lewis Loyd of Monk's Orchard, Beckenham, near Croydon, who had been a member of the banking house of Jones Loyd & Co, London. To seat 600. C – J Robinson, Hyde [*B* 27, 1869, 292: www.cilycwm.com/ci_history.php (accessed 30.11.2011)]. The narthex was added in 1894, presumably by A&P [BE], but this is not certain.

1870
Barrow-in-Furness (CuL), North Lonsdale Hospital, School Street. The hospital had been founded in a single building in 1866. P&A drew up plans for enlargement in 1870 and these were much revised in 1873. They do not seem to have been acted upon [CRO(B), BT/HOSP/NL7: Leach 1872, 117–18].

Cartmel (CuL), St Mary. Design for altar [LL 2, 215].

Desborough (Ireland), church, Design for pulpit [LL 3, 30r].

Higher Walton (Ch), Walton Hall. Extension and offices for the Warrington brewer (later Sir) Gilbert Greenall including a wing terminating in a square tower containing a billiard room and guest rooms. Most of the P&A work was demolished *c* 1990 but the clock tower survives [*LGuar* 26.2.1895: displays at the Walton Hall Heritage Centre: BE]. Designs for doors [LL 3, 11] and oriel window [LL 3, 14].

Lancaster, Mechanics' Institute, Castle Hill/Meeting House Lane. Plans 1868: approved and built 1870 [LRO, acc 5167/A0281: ex info CS]. Demolished for PA&P's Storey Institute of 1887–91.

Lancaster, 'Croftlands', Westbourne Road. Three attached properties, probably built for William (1820–79), eldest son of William Satterthwaite who sold the land to EGP to build his house, 'The Greaves' (*see* p 217 and Chapter 2, note 29), who probably occupied the west one, with the central one occupied by HJA, and the east one by John Chippindall senior (friend of HJA's wife's family). The plan is unsigned but it seems inconceivable that HJA did not make the design [LRO, MBLA acc 5167/307a: 1871 census: ex info TBA]

Leighton Hall. New three-storey wing with a billiard room below and bedrooms above. The large S-facing window is a 20th-century insertion [ex info Mrs S Reynolds].

Stalmine, vicarage. IT [*LGaz* 30.4.1870]. Detail of design [LL 3, 30r]. The IT for the schools, however, was signed by Thomas Risby, Manchester [*LGaz* 16.7.1870].

***c* 1870**
Brookhouse, 'Moorgarth', Caton. Former workhouse purchased 1869 by EGP and turned into a residence for himself. Now divided into two properties [ex info JMH].

1870–2
Barrow-in-Furness (CuL), mill and warehouses for the Barrow Flax & Jute Mills Co, Hindpool Road. Planning commenced 1869, construction in 1870; opened 1872. Superintendant of the works in 1870 – Mr Worrall [*Barrow Advertiser* 19.5.1870: *LGaz* 2.4.1870: *North Lonsdale Magazine* 3, 1898–9, 155: Mannex 1882, 35]. Intentions in Oct 1871 to complete it, thus more than doubling capacity [*Barrow Pilot* 21.10.1871]. Demolished.

Bowness (CuW), St Martin. Restored; new chancel and vestry, saddleback tower top and stair turret, reseated; alabaster reredos by Bell & Almond of London; chancel woodwork and organ screen by Brownrigg & T T Holmes who also did part of the roof; woodwork in the body of the church by J Holmes, executed by Blades of Lancaster [*BN* 21, 1871, 202: BE]. Design for pulpit, nd [LL 2, 179].

Daresbury (Ch), All Saints. A specification had been prepared by EGP in 1866 (new one Oct 1870). Much rebuilt except for W tower. Slightly lengthened and clerestory continued to the E end; new timber N porch and vestry. The Good Shepherd in the S porch gable carved by John Roddis. £6,000. C – Peter Swindells & Thomas Little, Manchester [CALS, P66/6/9–14: LL 2, 176: LL 3, 29: *BA* 18.8.1882: *BN* 22, 1872, 362–3]. Possibly a new vicarage too.

Melsonby (NY), St James. Chancel rebuilt, new nave roof, porch and vestry added, new font [LL 1, 90: N Yorks County RO, MIC 1997/2184, 2202, 3001–57; MIC 2007/350–5: ex info J R W Frost].

1870–5
Liverpool, St Matthew & St James, Mossley Hill. Design 1870. Built with funds bequeathed by M J Glenton; his trustees invited a limited number of architects to submit designs through Ewan Christian. *c* 800 seats. FS 10.8.1872. £12,000 (or £25,00 in another account) for church and parsonage. CC – Winnard, Wigan, stone-carving (including font and reredos) by John Roddis, Birmingham [FS: LL 2, 17; LL 3, 44: *LGaz* 24.6.1875: *BN* 19, 1870, 464; 29, 1875, 23]. Vicarage probably by P&A [BE].

1871
Arnside (CuW), vicarage. IT and specification May 1871 [*LGaz* 27.5.1871, 22.7.1871: CRO(K), 39/1/5/2].

Barrow-in-Furness (CuL), Royalty Theatre (Star Music Hall). The

Barrow building plans register and the envelope containing plans CRO(B), BBP 39, say 'music hall, Cavendish Street, for Mrs Atkinson', but the plans now in the envelope are for a shop (*see* under 1872). The Theatre Royal, Albert Street, was reopened after rebuilding in 1868 [*BH* 19.9.1868]. Closed pre-1939 and the Roxy cinema built on the site [ex info Margaret Bainbridge to JP, 1998].

Bradford (WY), Holy Trinity. Spire built. Chancel arch rebuilt and tower underpinned because of subsidence due to old coal workings. C – Messrs Beanland, Bradford [*LMerc* 19.1.1872].

Burton-in-Kendal (CuW), St James. Removal of W gallery chancel N wall, demolished and organ chamber/vestry built, seated, pulpit remodelled, new font (Lancaster stone bowl, Purbeck marble shafts), chancel laid with 'Goodman's' (presumably Godwin's) tiles. At the consistory court re the faculty, HJA said the designs were his. CC – C Baynes (stonework), Hatch (woodwork), Harrison (font). [*LGaz* 21.10.1871].

Collyhurst (GM), church, parsonage and schools. Competition entry among six invited architects. The winner Lowe of Manchester: P&A unplaced [*B* 29, 1871, 164].

Lancaster, St Mary. Choir vestry [DM].

Lancaster, shop front, Market Street/Frances Passage. For T D Smith. Plan [LRO, MBLA acc 5167/42].

Stalmine, St James. Design for a finial [LL 3, 30]. Presumably other work was involved.

Walton-le-Dale, All Saints, Higher Walton. Spire added. £600 or £650 [Abram 1877, 741: Barrett 1886, 590].

Windermere (CuW), St Mary. Restored, and chancel and vestry added: reseated, alabaster and mosaic reredos (given by H W Schneider), E window glass restored by Ward & Hughes under the supervision of C Watson, Secretary of the Society of Antiquaries, CC – Bell & Almond (reredos), Brownrigg & T T Holmes (chancel and organ screens), John Holmes (working under Blades of Lancaster for other woodwork). Faculty 1870 which include increase of seats to 656 from 536. Plans drawn by EGP no doubt in 1869 [*Barrow Advertiser* 6.1.1870: *LGaz* 9.9.1871].

Winmarleigh, Winmarleigh Hall. For John Wilson-Patten, MP for N Lancs (from 1874 1st Baron Winmarleigh), who moved there from Bank Hall, Warrington. Design stated to be by EGP: the firm had been appointed by Jan 1870 [LL 2, 182–3; LL 3, 31: *LGaz* 29.1.1870, 16.7.1892: *LGuar* 16.7.1892]. P&A probably responsible also for the school, *c* 1870.

1871–2

Knowsley (Me), St Mary. Memorial chapel to the 14th Earl of Derby. £3,000 (of which £800 or £1,000 was accounted for by the monument: figure carved by Matthew Noble, base by John Roddis, Birmingham). C – Burroughs & Son of Knowsley [LL 2, 168–9: *LGaz* 13.1.1872: *BN* 22, 1872, 44].

Wolverhampton (St), St Bartholomew, Penn. Nave and S aisle extended E, chancel and S chapel built [memorial plaque to F H Paley in chancel: Hampton, R 1997 *St Bartholomew's Church*. Penn: BE]. Appears to have been much other restoration work at the time. For the incumbent, the Revd Francis Henry Paley, younger brother of EGP, who was curate-in-charge 1851–6 and vicar 1856–74.

1871–3

Leigh (GM), St Mary. Rebuilt except for tower. EGP reported in 1869 that the tower could be repaired but the rest needed rebuilding; estimated at £8,000. Final cost variously put at £9,750 (*Wigan Observer*) or over £10,000. Seating for 710. Total cost £8,738. Chancel laid with Godwin's tiles; gas fittings and altar rails by Hart, Son, Peard & Co. C – Hugh Yates, Liverpool. CW – Whaite or S Waites of Bolton [LL 1, 38; LL 2, 184–6: *LGaz* 20.5.1871: *Leigh Chronicle* 20, 27.5.1871: *BA* 2, 1874, 233 + illustration: *Wigan Observer* 22.2.1873: *B* 28, 1870, 331: *BN* 17, 1869, 467; 20, 1871, 395: Slater 1895, 426]. Statue of Virgin and Child over porch carved by John Roddis, 1873 [www.vads.ahds.ac.uk/large.php?uid=75443 (accessed 30.11.2011)].

1871–4

Lancaster, Town Hall. Extensions. Police offices and cells opened 1872, followed by a new court room. *c* £7,000 excluding the site. CC – Thomas Harrison (masonry), Roger Wright (joinery), Thomas Dickinson (glazing & plumbing), H Hartley (plastering), Shrigley & Hunt (painting & decorating). CW – Heap. By the end of 1874, £10,232 had been spent which covered a superintendent's house, a police station with four cells, a surveyor's office, a sanitary office, magistrate's room, beadle's room, etc [*LGaz* 26.8.1871, 1.10.1874, 2.1.1875].

1871–5

Holker Hall (CuL). Rebuilding for the 7th Duke of Devonshire to a new design of a wing of 1840 destroyed by fire on 10.3.1871. Negotiations were conducted by EGP. Work began in autumn 1871 but prices were not settled until 1872. The fabric was effectively complete in 1874. C – James Garden of Dalton who was paid £15,084. Fitting and furnishing (eg furnishings by Gillow & Co; fireplaces by the Ashford Marble Works near Bakewell) went on even into 1876. *c* £38,000 [diary of the 7th Duke of Devonshire (at Chatsworth House), vols 21–3: LL 3, 33–4: LRO, DDCa 13/331–8: *BA* 16, 1881, 407, 514 + illustrations: *Country Life* 3.7.1980, 20–1]. Entrance lodge probably by P&A, *c* 1875; possibly the school near the gate.

1872

Barrow-in-Furness (CuL), plans for a shop on Ramsden Square for Smyth & Co dated Jul 1872 [CRO(B), BBP 39: these plans are misplaced in an envelope under this reference, although the plans register and envelope for the plans relate to a music hall and 1871].

Barrow-in-Furness (CuL), base for statue of Sir James Ramsden, Ramsden Square. Designed by John Harrison [*BH* 11.4.1896].

Blundellsands (Me), St Nicholas. The building committtee consulted EGP in connection with the entries from a limited competition among local architects; the award was made to 'Messrs Hay' [presumably W H & J Hay of Liverpool] [*BN* 22, 1872, 402]. However, the church consecrated in 1875 was designed by T D Barry & Sons [*BN* 27, 1875, 415].

Chorley, Town Hall. EGP assessor in the competition: won by J J Bradshaw of Bolton [*PG* 18.5.1872]. However, BE notes the Town

Hall is by Ladds & Powell, 1875–9.

Hindley (GM). IT for schools [*BN* 13.9.1872, ix]. The FS for parochial schools laid in 1873 (but no architect(s) named) [*BN* 24, 1873, 521]. Designs for fireplaces, nd [LL 2, 197, 199].

Lancaster, Castle. IT for a building with 63 cells [*LGaz* 16.3.1872, 23.3.1872].

Lancaster, shop, Penny Street [LL3, 32]. The plan for this is associated with LRO, MBLA acc 5167/10 and is for a new bakehouse for Whewell & Holmes' baker's shop: it is undated but plan 11 is of 1872 [ex info CS].

Lytham, St Cuthbert. Chancel built [BE: JP].

Ulverston (CuL), St Mary. Estimate by EGP for rebuilding N aisle and general repairs [*LGaz* 7.9.1872].

From 1872

Underley Hall (nr Kirkby Lonsdale, CuW). Major alterations for Thomas Taylour, Earl of Bective, including a 100ft tower and the whole of the mansion from the two windows south of the tower. [LL 3, 38: *BN* 58, 1890, 721: Morris, F O (ed) nd [*c* 1880] *A Series of Picturesque Views of Seats of Noblemen and Gentlemen of Great Britain and Ireland,* vol 4. London, Edinburgh & Dublin, 73]. Became a school in 1948: from 1976 one for for boys with social, emotional, etc difficulties.

1872–3

Betws-y-Coed (Caernarvonshire), St Mary. Competition winning design by HJA. Seating for 1,500. £5,000. C – Gethin Jones, Penmachno. Chief benefactors – Charles Kurtz of Liverpool (a businessman to whom ES had sold his N Wales property in 1865), the Gwydir Estate, the Revd J W Griffith of Betws-y-Coed (£1,000). Consecrated Apr 1873 so work was no doubt in progress in 1872 [LL 1, 37: *North Wales Chronicle* 26.4.1873: *BN* 24, 1873, 521; 108, 1915, 348]. Tower completed 1907.

Lytham St Anne's, St Anne, Heyhouses. New church. Paid for by Lady Eleanor Clifton on land given by her husband. £4,229. CC – G Smith, Great Marton, sole contractor [*LGaz* 8.6.1872: ICBS 9030: Slater 1895, 462: Anon 1937 *The Parish Church of S. Anne's, St Anne's-on-the-Sea*, 4–5: Holliday, E 1973 *The Parish of St Anne, St Annes-on-the-Sea*]. R Knill Freeman of Bolton, not P&A, seems to have been responsible for the N aisle, transept and vestry of 1885–6, and tower of 1890. S vestry 1903–4.

Whitehaven (CuC), Bransty station. Designs [CRO(W), TBR 1/1/7, 1/8/16].

1872–4

Giggleswick (NY), Giggleswick School, science area including a 'chemical room' and chemistry lecture theatre [datestone: ex info W Brooks].

1872–7

Livesey, St Andrew. EGP design. Estimated cost £4,500 but this rose to £6,000 (excluding site which was given by Benjamin Swain of Feniscliffe who completed the fittings at his own expense). The FS was laid Dec 1866 [*BS* 26.12.1866: *PG* 29.12.1866] but the scheme must have stalled since an IT was issued in 1872. 652 seats. C – Ashworth & Broughton. Tower incomplete and broach spire never built. Not consecrated until 1877 [*LGaz* 20.3.1872, 17.2.1877: *BN* 14, 1867, 19: Anon (Livesey) 1926 *S Andrew's Parish Church: Handbook of the Grand Bazaar*]. Declared redundant 2010.

1872–8

Bradshaw (GM), St Maxentius. IT 1863, but the FS was not laid until 1872 and work proceeded slowly and with difficulty; design by EGP [*BN* 10, 1863, 560, 580: ex info the Revd David M Dunn]. Tower of old church retained on the old site.

1873

Barrow-in-Furness (CuL), pair of cottages, in angle of Abbey Approach/Barrow Road for the FR Plans Nov 1872 passed by Barrow Council 8.1.1873 [CRO(B), BBP 317].

Barrow-in-Furness (CuL), pair of cottages at Furness Abbey western gate. For the FR. Plans 1872: passed by Barrow Council 8.1.1873 [datestone: CRO(B), BBP 329].

Barrow-in-Furness (CuL), bank for the Cumberland Union Banking Co, Ramsden Square (NE quadrant). Plans submitted to council and IT [CRO(B), BBP 557 (but plans missing): *BN* 28.2.1873, ix; 14.3.1873, ix]. Designed by John Harrison according to an obituary notice [*BH* 11.4.1896].

Barrow-in-Furness (CuL), bank for the Lancaster Banking Co, Ramsden Square (SE quadrant). Plans submitted to council and IT [CRO(B), BBP 391 (but plans missing): *BH* 18.10.1873]. Designed by John Harrison according to an obituary notice [*BH* 11.4.1896]. Now offices.

Barrow-in-Furness (CuL), porter's cottage. Furness Abbey station for the FR: design Mar 1873 [CRO(B), BBP 366].

Clifton, St John the Evangelist, Lund. IT for building the church and tower 1872 [*PG* 4.5.1872]. The church had been built in 1824–5 with a chancel (by J A Hansom) added in 1852: tower 1873 [BE]. It seems the P&A work ended up being restricted to the building of a W tower.

Halsall. St Cuthbert. Chancel restored and repaved at cost (£2,000) of the Revd T H B Blundell, the late rector [*K* 1913, 528: DM].

Kearsley (Farnworth, GM), St John the Evangelist. Chancel and porches built, church restored. Cost £4,000. Reopened Sept 1873 [ex info Revd D T N Parry; Slater 1895]. However, BE says 'there is some confusion because the church asked for plans from both Freeman & Cunliffe and Paley & Austin'. CS explains that Freeman completed the church 1878 [pers comm].

Kildwick (WY), St Andrew. Restored [*B* 108, 1915, 312: guidebook by B A Wood].

Lancaster, Christ Church, schools. [LRO, MBLA acc 5167/112].

Lancaster, Centenary Congregational Church, St Leonard's Gate. Converted from an 18th-century house, school created in the basement [minute book 1873, at church: LRO, MBLA acc 5167/97: *LGuar* 1.11.1873]. Design for pulpit Jul 1873 [LL 3, 39].

Lancaster, St Mary. Organ case for the enlarged organ. C – Hatch [*LGaz* 24.5.1873].

Liverpool, vicarage for St Matthew & St James, Mossley Hill [datestone: *LGuar* 26.1.1895: *BN* 19, 1870, 464].

Morecambe, station, Northumberland Street. Elements of this station designed in 1873 were incorporated in the Promenade Station of 1907 by Thomas Wheatley [JP: BE].

Windermere (CuW), 'Chapel Ridding'. New villa with stables and lodge for Edward Gibson. Commission probably gained via John Fletcher (founder of Lever Bridge church, 1842–4) who now lived close by [datestone: LL 1, 95: ex info TBA and CS]. Now apartments.

1873–4

Barrow-in-Furness (CuL), cemetery. P&A appointed 1870. Chapels consecrated Jun 1873 so work may well have begun in 1872. £5,300. C – James Garden. A cottage and gateway were tendered for in Jul 1873, and entrance lodges and a gateway in Oct 1873. The gates and railings were the subject of an accepted tender (£135) from T Ashworth of Burnley in Jul 1874. The registrar's house, mason's yard and cottage were placed at the E corner [CRO(B), BBP 520: *B* 14.6.1873, 12, 19.7.1873, 11.10.1873, 11.7.1874: Leach 1872, 35, 122]. Gateway, lodge and RC chapel survive. Landscaping by Edward Kemp, Birkenhead.

Barrow-in-Furness (CuL), tenement block of 'workers' dwellings' for the Barrow Iron Ship Building Co in the SE angle of Michaelson Road/Island Road. Known as Devonshire Buildings. Earliest plans Jan 1872. The building was nearly complete by Sept 1874 when a plan was submitted to the council for a further block in the NE angle. C – Smith & Caird, Dundee. Trescathric notes ten blocks were built, mostly of four-storey flats. JP gives 1881–4 for the blocks on Steamer/Barque/Brig/Schooner Streets [CRO(B), BBP 595 and 750: JP: Trescathric 1985, 26–7].

Broughton-in-Furness (CuL), St Mary Magdalene. Plans by EGP Aug 1872. Designed for 499 seats. Restored, including much rebuilding and adding a new nave and chancel to the N of the existing smaller ones. Plaster stripped from walls; reseated and W gallery removed. *c* £3,029 or £3,071 (R Assheton Cross MP subscribed £1,000). Local stone plus St Bees stone for the outside dressings: interior faced with Runcorn stone. Seats for over 480. CC – Thomas Garner, Broughton (mason), Coward & Sons, Coniston (woodwork) [CRO(B), BPR 6/C9: ICBS 7576: *BH* 1, 8.2.1873, 24.10.1874: *LGaz* 24.10.1874].

Finsthwaite (CuL), St Peter. Replaced church of 1724. One of four designs (published in *The Architect* 20.9.1873) submitted for the Carlisle Diocesan Church Building Society competition for a mountain chapel (C J Ferguson was second): P&A won this competition, judged by Ewan Christian. Nave and chancel with tower between. 200 seats. £4,170, paid for by T Newby Wilson of Newby Bridge; chancel windows by Holiday, executed by Heaton & Co. CC – Berry, Barrow (masonry), T Wearing, Ullswater (woodwork), Mills, Barrow (stone-carving), Holmes, Lancaster (wood-carving). CW – Goldstraw [CRO(K), 101/1/3/8–9: LL 1, 37: *BH* 15.2.1873, 12.12.1874: *LGaz* 12.12.1874: *The Architect* 10, 1873, 147: *B* 31, 1873, 472: *K* 1913, 500].

Lancaster, Presbyterian chapel, St Nicholas Street. Interior renewed, reroofed, new windows, new semi-circular chancel at W end, original entrances walled up and new ones created N and S at junction of chancel and nave, new vestry on S. *c* £1,500. CC – Lancaster & Trafford (masonry), Roger S Wright (masonry), Shrigley & Hunt (tablets and cathedral glass in chancel), W Abbott (plumbing & glazing), Hartley (slating & plastering) [LRO, MBLA acc 5167/154: *LGaz* 28.11.1874]. Demolished *c* 1965.

Lancaster, Wesleyan chapel and schools, Sulyard and Bryer Streets. IT Jun 1873. Over £6,000; accommodation for 520 on the ground floor and 506 in the galleries (excluding children and choir); schools in basement. CC – I & J Mawson (masonry), James Hatch (joinery), Abbott (plumbing), Blezard (painting), Hartley (slating & plastering). CW – [W or S] Wright [*LGaz* 21.6.1873, 29.11.1873, 2.1.1875]. Slater [1895, 411] says 1877–8 (£8,074) but the later *LGaz* account suggests it was basically complete in Dec 1874.

Osmotherley (CuL), St John the Evangelist. Design 1872. *c* 150 seats. Site given by Mark Whineray; A Brogden MP gave 200 guineas. *c* £1,400. C – T F Tyson, Ulverston [ICBS 7382: *Soulby's Ulverston Advertiser* 16.7.1874: Bulmer 1911, 368].

1874

Barrow-in-Furness (CuL), 'Abbot's Wood'. Plan for addition to Old North Lodge for Sir James Ramsden [CRO(B), BBP 547].

Bolton-by-Bowland, school. [LSMR, PRN10102-MLA10102].

Grappenhall (Ch), St Wilfrid. Restored including new floors and roofs. *c* £4,000 [*Liverpool Mercury* 22.9.1874: *Cheshire Observer* 26.9.1874].

Lancaster, County Hotel. Plans for alterations and/or additions. Listed in the Lancaster building plans [LRO, MBLA acc 5167/261] but original drawings too fragile to be produced.

Witherslack (CuW), Witherslack Hall. For Frederick Arthur Stanley MP, later 16th Earl of Derby. £17,000 [datestone: *BA* 22.7.1881 (illustration), 16 (1881), 407: BE: ex info B Till]. Since 1972 a special needs school.

c 1874

Euxton, dedication unknown. Plans for new chancel and N aisle: unexecuted [Walsh, H 1983 *Euxton Parish Church: A Brief Description of The Village and Church of Euxton*, 30].

1874–5

Barrow-in-Furness (CuL), Trinity Presbyterian church, School Street. For a mainly Scots congregation formed in 1865. IT Jun–Jul 1873 but FS not laid till Mar 1874. Land given by Sir James Ramsden. Over £5,000 plus hall, £1,400. Seating for 730. C – W Gradwell. CW – Paterson [CRO(B), BDFCP/T: *LGaz* 8.1.1876: *BH* 28.6.1873, 5, 12.7.1873, 28.3.1874, 10.7.1875: Richardson 1880, 307: Richardson 1881, 114–15]. Closed 1971.

Barrow-in-Furness (CuL), 'Oak Lea', Sowerby Wood, Hawcoat. Queen Anne-style house with 14 or 17 bedrooms for H W Schneider. Built of Stainton limestone with sandstone dressings. C – Garden of Dalton. [*LGaz* 27.11.1875: *LGuar* 26.2.1895: Banks 1984, 84, 88 n7]. Destroyed by fire 1913 leaving the gate lodge and coach house [ex info A Jones].

Bolton (GM), St Thomas, Halliwell. Mostly funded by the Cross family: the prime mover was Thomas Cross, a bleacher, cotton spinner and banker, who gave the site and £1,000. Reredos given by his son James Percival Cross of Catthorpe Towers near Rugby (Warwicks). £6,400. 849 seats. CC – Cottam of Croston (main), Miles of Barrow (carving). CW – Waites. NE tower not completed [*Bolton Guardian* 24.7.1875: *BN* 29, 1875, 128: Kirkman, H 1949 *The Parish Church of Halliwell, St Thomas 1875–1950*, 12].

Crosscrake (CuW), St Thomas. Replaced a church of 1773. Site and some funds given by W H Wakefield (a banker). *c* £3,000 [CRO(K), WPR 65/1/4/3 (tower design): Bulmer 1913, 530–1]. Design for font, nd [LL 1, 92].

Hornby, court room and police station (opposite the drinking fountain). P&A appointed as architects Dec 1873: estimate £2,000. IT May 1874. £2,300. CC – Thomas Harrison, Lancaster (mason), Harper Bros, Settle (woodwork), W Abbot, Lancaster (plumbing & glazing) [*LGaz* 6.12.1873, 16.5.1874].

Lancaster, St Mary. Alterations to the stalls [*LGaz* 30.1.1875].

Little Ouseburn (NY), Holy Trinity. N aisle and E wall rebuilt (E window reset higher), organ chamber, chancel heightened, new fittings, roof reslated [*Yorkshire Gazette* 24.7.1875: *LGuar* 26.1.1895: BE].

Llanrwst (Denbighshire), St Mary. Chancel of church of 1841–2 tripled in size eastward. Reseated: £925 including two chancel windows by Ward & Hughes: largest benefactor – the Revd J Boulger of Pennant. C – Samuel Parry [ICBS 7683]. Demolished and the stone altar moved to the N aisle of St Grwst's, Llanrwst.

Manchester, St Margaret, Burnage. Three-bay nave, chancel and S aisle. Seating for *c* 200. Site given by Lord Egerton of Tatton. Other major benefactors – Canon and Mrs Tonge and the Birley family. Cost £4,000 [Pollard 2000, 6].

Scotforth, St Paul. Design by ES: appointed 1873. £3,491: chief benefactor – Richard Newsham of Preston, 300 seats. ES was another important contributor and the church was erected under his personal supervision. Terracotta made by Cliff & Sons, Wortley, Leeds. CC – C Baynes, Lancaster (masonry), William Huntington (woodwork), E Cross & Sons (slating & plastering), Willan & Cleminson (plumbing & glazing). CW – Mitchel [*sic*] Holmes. Consecrated 18.2.1876 [*LGaz* 15.8.1874, 5, 19.2.1876: guide: Slater 1895, 416]. The first moves to build a church here made in 1870 (ES had made the second largest subscription by May that year) [*LGaz* 7.5.1870]. P&A had submitted a plan and elevation in 1871 for a church [*LGaz* 8.4.1871] and an IT was issued on 20.12.1872 [*LGaz* 21.12.1872, 28.12.1872].

Whittington. IT for schools and teacher's residence: Datestone 1875 [*LGaz* 23.5.1874, 30.5.1874].

1874–6

Giggleswick (NY), Giggleswick School. Extensions on the N and S of the boarding house. IT Dec 1873: classrooms built in 1876 ('The Hostel') [*LMerc* 16.12.1873: ex info W Brooks].

Millom (CuC), station. Designs [CRO(B), B/TBR/1/141].

1874–7

Millom (CuC), St George. P&A appointed 1873 when they produced a design. *c* £12,000 of which £7,186 was given by the Millom Ironworks. Five-acre site given by the Earl of Lonsdale [*BH* 27.7.1874, 29.5.1877, 2.6.1877: Bulmer 1901, 586: [E H Isaac], 1977 *The Parish of St George Millom*]. The vicarage, begun in 1874, is probably by P&A (the detail on the datestone is suggestive of HJA's hand). Design for font, nd [LL 1, 92]. Vicarage now an old people's home.

1874–8

Ulverston (CuL), station. 1874 passenger station rebuilt [CRO(B), BD/MA E181; ex info Leslie Gilpin] 1875: design for stables. C – James Garden [CRO(B), BTBR/1/81; BD/MA box 5/278]. Mr Gilpin notes ancillary buildings were built over a period down to 1878.

1875

Barrow-in-Furness (CuL), Cambridge Street Schools, Salthouse. Accommodation for 250 children. C – Saddler, Wood & Andrews. [*BH* 28.8.1875: Richardson 1881, 120].

Blackpool, St John. EGP assessor for competition. Won by Ladds & Powell, London [*B* 33, 1875, 813].

Cark-in-Cartmel (CuL), station buildings on up platform. [CRO(B), TBR/1/65: Grosse 1996, 41]

Lancaster, Edward Street, plans for conversion from a Wesleyan school into Catholic Apostolic church [LRO, MBLA acc 5167/97 & 188: ex info CS].

Morecambe, Holy Trinity. New pulpit, reading desk and lectern. C – Veevers of Morecambe [*LGaz* 28.11.1875].

Sandside (CuL), verandah at end of waiting room for the FR. Design [CRO(W), TBR 1/1/40].

Whittington, St Michael. Largely rebuilt at the expense of Colonel D C Greene of Whittington Hall [Bulmer 1913, 440: BE].

Unknown location, 'Rockfield'. Design for vane on tower (no doubt an indication of more substantial work) [LL 3, 45].

c 1875

Millom (CuC), Dunningwell Hall. For Captain Charles John Myers [*LGuar* 26.2.1895: www.dunningwellstatues.co.uk (accessed 9.10.2010)].

Skipton (NY), Ermysted's Grammar School. EGP was approached in Jan 1873 for a school to replace one on a different site. Designs available in Apr. Cost estimated at £8,285 in May 1874; most of the building carried out in the second half of 1875. In Jun 1877 a payment of £313 was made to P&A [ex info Douglas Grant].

1875–6

Capernwray, Capernwray Hall. SE block (including a billiard room and a single-storey corridor attached to the tower) [drawings at Capernwray Hall].

Sedbergh (CuWY), Sedbergh School. School buildings and master's house enlarged: in Mar 1875 budget for the former up to £500 and the latter £1,750: final total £3,935. Other minor works probably carried out [SSGM, 1875–6: LM, 99.60].

Winmarleigh, St Luke. Built at sole cost of Lord Winmarleigh, *c* £2,000 or £2,800. CC – J Collinson, Nateby (brickwork plastering, tiling), Wilkinson & Kirkby, Longridge (masonry) [*LGaz* 13.2.1875, 26.2.1876: *BN* 30, 1876, 283: Bulmer 1913, 302]. The FS laying in Feb 1875 suggests the designs would have been made in 1874. N chapel later.

1875–7
Atherton (GM), St Michael, Howe Bridge. £7,000 paid by Ralph Fletcher (1815–86) [Lunn 1971, 189]. Consecrated 8.2.1877 which suggests possible completion 1876.

Lancaster, Royal Grammar School, new buildings. IT Dec 1874. New three-storey wing with basement (new classrooms, laboratory, dormitories for 22 boys). £4,834 excluding the chemistry laboratory and heating apparatus; laboratory given by Councillor Bradshaw [LM, 99.60: *LGaz* 5.9.1874, 12.9.1874 19.9.1874, 29.9.1877, 24.9.1881].

1876
Barrow-in-Furness (CuL), Millwood House, Millwood Lane. Addition for Edward Wadham, agent for the Furness estate of the Duke of Buccleuch, to a house of *c* 1860 by Edward Browning of Stamford: kitchen, servants' area; three bedrooms on first floor [CRO(B), BBP 1089; BUC BD 39/38].

Burnley, St Matthew, Habergham Eaves. Unsuccessful competition design; competition won by W A Waddington of Burnley [Ashworth 1979, 8].

Hoddlesden, St Paul's vicarage. £2,100. CC – Lloyd & Millward (builders), Whittle (joiner). Fundraising to complete the church tower was also taking place [*BS* 3.6.1876].

Lancaster, dwelling for J L Bradshaw. IT [*LGaz* 17.6.1876].

Leyland, St Andrew. Organ case [*PG* 22.7.1876].

Scotforth, parsonage. IT: replies to be sent to E Sharpe junior (not P&A) [*LGaz* 29.1.1876].

1876–7
Halton, St Wilfrid. Rebuilt except for tower: replaced work of 1792. *c* £3,500. CC –Robert Clarkson, Carnforth (masonry), Tennant, Lancaster (joinery), Cross & Son (slating), Willan & Cleminson (plumbing & glazing) [*LGaz* 5.8.1876, 13.10.1877: LSMR, PRN393-MLA393: BE].

Westham (E Sussex), St Mary. Restoration and reseating. Plans 1875 when cost was put at £3,000. Seating increased from 297 to 403 [ICBS 7941: *BA* 2.11.1883]. This far-flung commission no doubt arose because the patron of the living was the Duke of Devonshire, an important and recent client of the practice.

1876–8
Darwen, St Cuthbert. Design 1874. Estimated cost £4,500 for 419 seats; final cost £5,925 though *K* 1913 gives cost as £8,382 (including site). 462 seats. W bay of nave, and NW steeple (square turning to octagonal) not built. CC – Kay & Buckledge, Darwen (main), James Lloyd & Millward, Darwen (joinery and internal fittings). E window by Wailes [ICBS 7934: LL 3, 46: *BS* 12.2.1876: *BN* 34, 1878, 148: Kershaw 2004]. W bay of nave and (to new design) W tower with saddleback roof 1907–8 by R W Smith-Saville, borough engineer. This is no doubt the £7,000 extension referred to in K [FS: *LGaz* 21.8.1875: *K* 1913, 467: Kershaw 2004].

Hoghton, Hoghton Tower. Restoration for Sir Henry de Hoghton including that of the banqueting hall in which a timber ceiling was added with carpentry by James Hatch. Design of ceiling in tenants' hall, 1876 [papers at Hoghton Tower: *Country Life* 30.7.1992, 51–2].

Lancaster, White Cross Mills, ornamental top to 250ft-high brick chimney. C – C Baynes [loose printed sheets from a book listing chimney constructions in LL, control ref M0341666LC]. Demolished.

Morecambe, St Lawrence. Estimated cost £8,680 plus £780 for parsonage. 610 seats planned. NW tower and spire planned but not built. Chief benefactors – F Grafton of Heysham Hall, Mrs Ripley of Springfield Hall and Mrs Royds of Heysham. CC – J & T Mawson, Lancaster (masonry), J Hatch (carpentry & joinery), C Nelson, Bradford (plumbing & glazing), Pycocks, Leeds (tiling) [ICBS 8047: *LGaz* 12.8.1876, 4.9.1878: *B* 34, 1876, 912: Fidler 1973–4, 56].

1877
Askam-in-Furness (CuL), station. Design [CRO(B), BTBR/1/137].

Barrow-in-Furness (CuL), hydraulic engine house at Ramsden Dock. C – W Gradwell [CRO(B), BTDH/2/7].

Barrow-in-Furness (CuL), town hall. P&A withdrew from a competition for a new workhouse on the understanding that they would have work for the new town hall, but no such understanding existed [*BH* 17.3.1877].

Bolton (GM), St Peter. Oak reredos paid for by the widow of Peter Ormrod. C – James Hatch with carving by John Roddis, Birmingham [*Birmingham Daily Post* 22.10.1877: *LGaz* 26.9.1877].

Liverpool, Eye & Ear Infirmary, Myrtle Street. P&A assisted the committee on evaluating the plans of the eight architects who submitted designs [*Liverpool Mercury* 7.8.1877].

1877–8
Alderley (Ch), St Mary. Restored including floor lowered, S arcade underpinned, reseated, plaster removed from walls. Estimate £520 [CALS, P142/6/4, 6].

Barrow-in-Furness (CuL), four temporary brick and wood churches (St Matthew, Harrogate Street; St Mark Rawlinson Street; St Luke, Salthouse Street; St John, Island Road). Cheap brick churches with wooden arcades, each built to the same design and seating 520. Total cost £24,000. The Duke of Devonshire gave money for two and the Duke of Buccleuch money for one, Lord Frederick Cavendish £3,500, H W Schneider £1,000, Sir James Ramsden £500, and major shareholders of the FR and Barrow Docks also gave large amounts. The first church, St John's, was opened in Nov 1877: C – David Caird who also built St Matthew. C – W Gradwell (St Mark and St Luke). All four churches were dedicated on 26.9.1878 [CRO(B), BBP 1160, 1172: *BH* 1.12.1877, 28.9.1878: Anon (Church Congress), 80–4]. St Mark's survives.

Barrow-in Furness (CuL), vicarages for St Matthew, St Mark and St Luke. Notice given for commencement in Dec 1877, so construction would have taken place mainly or wholly in 1878 [CRO(B), BBP 1225–7].

Greenock (Renfrewshire), St John the Evangelist (Scottish Episcopal Church). Replaced a church of 1824. First designs 1875. Just over £7,000: Sir Michael Shaw Stewart Bt gave £1,500 plus land to enlarge the existing site. CC – Hugh Steel (mason); Crawford & Fulton (joiners), J Robertson & Co (slating); Maclean & Barclay (plumbing) [*Greenock Telegraph* 24.10.1877: list of parish documents held at parish].

Manchester, St Mary, Hillkirk Street, Beswick. Built partly as a memorial to Bishop Prince Lee. Had a seven-light W window and was aisled. Estimate £8,700. Seats for 600. C – Cordingley & Stockford, Manchester [*Manchester Times* 21.7.1877: *LGaz* 22.6.1878: *BA* 28.9.1883: Fidler 1973–4, 58]. Demolished *c* 1963.

Ormskirk St Peter & St Paul. Plans 1876. Refloored, some reseating, new heating system. The reseating seems to have been spread over several years [Ockenden 2002, 43–5].

Orton (CuW), All Saints. Restored: chancel and N aisle rebuilt. £651. C – Bland [copy of letter from HJA, 13.2.1879, DM collection: LBS 74091].

Salford (GM), St Clement, Ordsall. Given (with the site and parsonage) by Lord Egerton. £9,000. Terracotta from the Costessy Works, Norwich; bricks from the Knutsford Brick & Tile Co. C – Wilson, Hulme Bridge: brickwork subcontracted to Mr Williams and masonry to Graham & Son, Ancoats. CW – Potts [*Cheshire Observer* 21.9.1878: *Salford Weekly Chronicle* 21.9.1878: *BA* 11.2.1881: *BN* 35, 1878, 332].

Sedbergh (CuWY), Sedbergh School, headmaster's house. With accommodation for 40 boarders. Design and tenders 1876. Total tender price £9,937 (includes Clarkson & Son, Carnforth, £5,136 for building; Huck & Son, Endmoor, Kendal, £2,470 for joinery & carpentry). CW – Allen of Skipton [datestone 1877 over entrance: SSGM, 1876–8]. Remained the headmaster's house until 1967. Now known as School House.

1877–9
Salford (GM), St James, Higher Broughton. Estimated cost £7,000. Site and £2,800 given by Samuel Clowes. Seating for 600 adults. Common red brick from the Knutsford Brick & Tile Co plus terracotta dressings. C – Foreman & Todd, Broughton [*Manchester Times* 4.8.1877: *LGaz* 5.4.1879: *BN* 33, 1877, 115: ex info Tim Ashworth, Salford Local History Library]. BE considers the vicarage must also be by P&A.

Sedbergh (CuWY), Sedbergh School, Second Master's house. Now known as Sedgwick House. With accommodation for 40 boarders. Total tender price £8,748 (includes Thomas Pattinson, Bowness, £4,652 for building; Richard Carter, Little Horton, Bradford, £2,167 for joinery & carpentry). CW – Allen of Skipton [SSGM, 1877–9: *LGaz* 30.6.1877].

1878
Barrow-in-Furness (CuL), plans for a cottage and weigh house at bottom of Ramsden Street [CRO(B), BBP 1310].

Barrow-in-Furness (CuL), baths, minor alterations to frontage, Abbey Road (corner of Bath Street) [CRO(B), BBP 1253].

Hensingham (CuL), vicarage and offices. IT [*BH* 13, 20, 27.7.1878].

Hoghton, entrance lodge at Hoghton Tower. Designed for Sir Henry de Hoghton (d 1876), 1876, built for his brother, Sir Charles [papers at Hoghton Tower, private collection].

Holmrook (CuC), cottages, reading room and smithy. For C R Fletcher Lutwidge [RIBA, R6a: 29502. E/21: *BN* 30.1.1880]. Date uncertain but presumably of about this time: Holmrook Hall, design for turret on stables [LL 1, 6]. Turret now removed and the hall largely demolished in the 1940s.

Lancaster, Royal Grammar School. Plans for new school room and reading room. Plans approved Mar 1879 [LRO, MBLA acc 5167/324].

Lancaster, hotel. For the King's Arms & Royal Hotel Co. HJA assisted with the competition adjudication. 19 entries. Won by Holtom & Connon, Dewsbury & Leeds [*LGaz* 11.12.1878: *B* 36, 1878, 1287].

Morecambe, proposed rectory. Plans passed [*LGaz* 13.7.1878].

Seascale (CuC), station building, water tower and weigh house. For the FR. Designs [CRO(W), TBR 1/1/32]. The goods shed is no doubt by P&A too and is to a design used at other stations.

Willingdon (E Sussex), St Mary. Restored [www.sussexparishchurches.org/content/view/182/34/ (accessed 30.11.2011) quoting *Chichester Diocesan Kalendar* 1878: 2, 75].

1878–9
Atherton (GM), St John the Baptist. Design 1877. Replaced a church of 1814, itself a rebuilding of one of 1723. Chancel and three bays of nave £10,000 (£3,200 given by Fletcher, Burrows & Co [formerly John Fletcher & Sons], colliery owners). C – William Winnard, Wigan [MRO, L177: *Manchester Times* 3.1.1880: Fletcher 1923, 14, 20–2].

Leck, St Peter. Church of *c* 1770 rebuilt. £3,000 (estimate was £2,480). 224 seats. C – J Hatch (organ case, reredos, altar, lectern which were carved by Miles & Morgan, Lancaster [ICBS 8265: *LGaz* 23.8.1879: Bulmer 1913, 432].

Sedbergh (CuWY), Sedbergh School, three new classrooms. Tender £5,261 (includes Thomas Pattinson, Bowness, £3,074 for building; Robert Grime, Settle, £1,057, for joinery & carpentry) [SSGM, 1878–9].

1878–80
Billington, St Leonard. Replacement for the old church on a different site. Design 1877. Tender £3,089, eventual cost £4,350. 346 seats. C – Thomas Hacking, Clayton-le-Moors (but not mentioned in the reopening report where Messrs Stones of Blackburn are named as the contractors): J Hatch (woodwork). One bay of the nave and the tower and spire were omitted (with these the total cost would have been £6,000) [ICBS 8220: *BS* 21.9.1878: *PG* 18.9.1880: *BN* 35, 1878, 290: Slater 1895, 1069]. P&A are said to have restored the old church in 1879.

1878–81
Bolton (GM), All Souls. £23,000. Funded by Thomas Greenhalgh

of Thornydikes, Sharples, from funds bequeathed by his brother, Nathaniel (d 1877), a cotton spinner in Halliwell. 800 seats. Nave 52ft wide. Windows at E end by Clayton & Bell; those in tower by Shrigley & Hunt. Reredos carved by John Roddis, Birmingham. Pulpit and stalls by James Hatch with carving by Miles & Morgan, Lancaster. Gas pendants by Hart, Peard & Co. CC – Cordingley & Stopford, Manchester (contract £16,500 excluding stained glass, chancel fittings, font, organ and boundary walls). CW – Potts [LL 1, 48: MRO, L117/2/1–31: *Bolton Chronicle* 2.7.1881: *BN* 48, 1885, 631, 711: *K* 1913, 253: 'ALH' [1981] *A Short History of All Souls' Church, Bolton 1881–1981*]. Vested in CCT 1987. The schools, begun in 1877, designed by J J Bradshaw, Bolton, not P&A.

1878–9

Grasmere (CuW), St Oswald. Restoration scheme by EGP not approved as it only provided 350 seats [*BH* 1.2.1879]. Proposals also included a new vestry [CRO(K), 91/1/3/17].

Scorton, St Peter and vicarage. A memorial to Peter Ormrod of Wyresdale Park (who had paid for the rebuilding of Bolton parish church) by his brother James. £13,000 to £15,000. 250 seats. Chancel floor by Craven, Dunnill & Co. E window by Burlison & Grylls. CC – Wilkinson & Kirby, Longridge; carpentry by Blades, Lancaster; six bells by Warner's foundry. CW – J Mills [MRO, L117/2/1–3: *LGaz* 5.7.1879: *BN* 36, 1879, 399: Slater 1895, 350: BE]. Vicarage (now 'Ghyllwood'), dated 1879 over entrance.

Thorpe Bassett (EY), All Saints. Restored. N aisle (which had been demolished) rebuilt on its old foundations: blocked medieval arcade opened out, chancel rebuilt and vestry and porch added; tower rebuilt because of higher elevation of nave roof. Over £2,000 (£1,255 from Lady Cholmley). C – John Brown, York [*LMerc* 24.4.1879: *York Herald* 30.8.1879: *BN* 36, 1879, 491: *K North & East Ridings [of] Yorkshire* 1893, 498].

1879

Foxfield (CuL), station. Plans 1877 [CRO(B), BTBR/1/118/10: CRO(K), WDSo 108/A 2513/Wagner 6; WDSo 108/A 2652/ Shillcock roll 10].

Kildwick (WY), St Andrew. IT for new boundary walls and reglazing on S side [*LMerc* 10.5.1879].

Lancaster, 'The Knoll', Westbourne Road. House by HJA for himself [datestone with initials of HJA and his wife: LRO, MBLA acc 5137/339 (21.5.1879)].

Lancaster, premises for T D Smith, Penny Street. IT for rebuilding [*LGaz* 15, 22.2.1879].

Lancaster, additions to 1 Lindow Street. IT [*LGaz* 26.4.1879, 3.5.1879].

Ormskirk St Peter & St Paul. N and S galleries removed, chancel refurbished, organ built over vestry [Ockenden 2002, 46].

Scotforth, school. IT [*LGaz* 8.2.1879].

Walton-le-Dale, new vicarage. IT [*PG* 22.3.1879].

1879–80

Hoghton, Hoghton Tower. Work on offices, a new kitchen, building and underground service corridor, and various other alterations estimated to cost £3,503 (seems to have risen to £4,640 on execution. CC – T Duckworth (masonry), J Hatch (carpentry), Walmsley (plumbing & glazing). Client – Sir Charles de Hoghton [papers at Hoghton Tower, private collection].

Kirkby Malham (NY), St Michael. Restored [*LGuar* 26.2.1895: BE].

Lancaster, St Mary's School, St George's Quay. Converted from an old mill offered by Storey Bros at 'considerably less than its real value'. Overall cost estimated at £1,500 in Sept 1879. Plans approved Jan 1880 [*LGaz* 20.9.1879: LRO, MBLA acc 5167/350A].

Mansergh (CuW), St Peter. Church of 1726 or 1727 rebuilt. Design 1879. 148 seats. *c* £2,000 (original estimate £1,848) mainly contributed by the late William Wilson of Rigmaden Park: other contributions from Trinity College, Cambridge, the Earl of Bective and the vicar of Kirkby Lonsdale. CC – Atkinson, Kirkby Lonsdale (masonry), W Huck & Sons, Endmoor (woodwork), Moorhouse (plumbing), Pycock Leeds (slating) [FS: ICBS 8406: *Kendal Mercury* 27.8.1880: *LGaz* 15, 22.3.1879, 4.9.1880]. Porch 1903 [BE] but no architect named.

Wray (nr Hornby, La), Holy Trinity. Plans 1876 and IT issued for reseating and chancel rebuilding. Chancel, organ chamber and porch cost £1,000 of which £500 was given by Mrs Hardacre; total cost £1,307 [LRO, PR 3338/4/2, 3, 12–19: *LGaz* 8.2.1876, 8.2.1879: Bulmer 1913, 419–20].

1879–81

Daisy Hill (GM), St James. Designs 1878. £6,500. Sole benefactors – Mrs Alice Markant and Miss Margaret Haddock (sisters). C – Parnell, Wigan. CW – W Parnell [MRO, L128: *BA* 11.2.1881: Fidler 1973–4, 64].

Leigh (GM), St Peter, Westleigh. £7,000. 460 seats [dated rainwater heads 1879: LL 1, 16: *BA* 11.2.1881: Fidler 1973–4, 64–5].

1879–88

Tunstall, Thurland Castle. Extensive restoration for Mr North North after a fire in 1876. The firm 'worked in a sensitive mixture of Gothic and Elizabethan ... the interior is evocative of the late C19 Arts and Crafts movement with low comfortable rooms of informal shape and varying size with light oak panelling. De Morgan tiles, heraldic glass, simple plasterwork and stone, alabaster and carved wooden chimney-pieces. The library, ballroom and billiard room are particularly good' [Bulmer 1913, 427: BE: quote from Robinson 1991, 245]. CC – C Blades (woodwork); Bayliff, Kirkby Lonsdale (masonry) who had over 100 workmen on the site. HJA's obituary refers to two restorations: the second maybe the additional work referred to by JP in 1888 [*B* 108, 1915, 312: JP]. Interiors illustrated by three Bedford Lemere photographs in *The Architect* 1.2.1895. Now converted to gated apartments.

1880

Barrow-in-Furness (CuL), Cambridge Street Schools, Salthouse. Addition begun [Richardson 1881, 120].

Barrow-in-Furness (CuL), addition (drawing room, hall and entrance) to Mr Humphreys' house, Cavendish Park. Plans [CRO(B), BBP 1400].

Barrow-in-Furness (CuL), stables for St George's vicarage. Plans [CRO(B), BBP 1409].

Carnforth, station. Waiting room and parcel office added at N end of present station buildings. IT 1878 [*BH* 25.5.1878: *LGaz* 1.6.1878: ex info Philip Grosse].

Dacre (CuC), 'Ennim Bank'. IT for alterations and additions [*Carlisle Journal* 5.3.1880, ex info Denis Perriam].

Lancaster, shop for Mr Knipes, Penny Street. [LRO, MBLA, acc 5167/354].

Newton, Newton Hall. Largely rebuilt for Mr North North of Thurland Castle who would make Newton Hall his principal seat in 1885. Lodge also by P&A [Robinson 1991, 223: BE].

Scarborough (EY), All Saints' Schools. Red Brick Tudor style. £3,600. C – Pabury & Son, Scarborough [*York Herald* 18.12.1880].

Ulverston (CuL), Holy Trinity. Chancel [BE].

Ulverston (CuL), hydraulic engine house at canal bridge. C – W Gradwell. Plans [CRO(B), BD/MA E168]. Demolished.

1880–1

Barrow-in-Furness (CuL), plans for two semi-detached villas, Michaelson Road. Plans for the Barrow Iron Ship Building Co [CRO(B), BBP 1451].

Barrow-in-Furness (CuL), Victoria Hall, Rawlinson Street. First phase. *c* £1,300. For St Mark's school to accommodate 600 children. C – W Gradwell. CW – Matthew Stables [CRO(B), BBP 1415: *BH* 20.1.1881]. Expanded 1888 [datestone], presumably by P&A.

Great Harwood, St Bartholomew. Nave lengthened by a bay, new chancel, vestry and organ chamber: new pulpit. Accommodation increased from 377 to 470 built. £2,000 [*BS* 12.11.1881].

Hutton Roof (CuW), St John. Replaced a chapel of 1757 'of most unecclesiastical character'. Design early 1878, perhaps late 1877. IT 1878. £2,500. It was intended to start building in Mar 1879 but this was delayed until Mar 1880. CC – John Berry, Hutton Roof (stonework), W Huck & Sons, Endmoor (joinery), Moorhouse & Co, Kirkby Lonsdale (plumbing & glazing), Hartley, Lancaster (slater) [CRO(K), WPR 21/1/2/3: ICBS 8278: *Kendal Mercury* 2.7.1880: *LGaz* 12, 19, 26.10.1878, 3.7.1880: Bulmer 1913, 467].

Knutsford (Ch), St Cross. Designs 1879: slightly modified to reduce cost. £7,580 after completion of the tower (1887) and aisles (1889). C – James Hamilton, Altincham [CALS, P189/5/2: Fidler 1973–4, 66].

By 1881

Barrow-in-Furness, Furness Abbey station and 'A Cabin' at Furness Abbey. [Drawn by T Raffles Davison in *BA* 21.10.1881].

1881

Arkholme, vicarage. [Ex info Angus Taylor to JP].

Barrow-in-Furness (CuL), Gateway Cottage, Cricket Field, Barrow Island. Plans [CRO(B), BBP 1506].

Barrow-in-Furness (CuL), new ferry station. Walney Island. Plans [CRO(B), BBP 1562]. Demolished.

Bolton-le-Sands, St Michael (now Holy Trinity). New, wider N aisle, vestry, doorway, oak porch, pulpit, and font, floor lowered, gallery removed, tower arch opened, old windows in nave replaced by four-light traceried ones, reseated, chancel retiled and refitted. 450 seats. CC – James Hatch (main contractor), C Baynes (mason), Parkinson (plumbing & glazing), Hall & Son (slating & plastering), all of Lancaster [*LGaz* 6.8.1881: *BN* 41, 1881, 215].

Boot (Eskdale, CuC), St Catherine. Restored, reseated (seats increased by four to 126) and vestry added. £750 [ICBS 8649: Bulmer 1901, 560].

Carlisle (CuC), Grammar School. P&A among eight practices invited to compete but they, like Cory & Ferguson, declined the invitation [*LGaz* 7.5.1881].

Eskmeals (CuC), station. Plans [CRO(B), BDY 198: CRO (Carlisle), TBR/1/1/6].

Hornby, Hornby Castle. Additions and alterations [LBS 182390].

Kirkby-in-Furness (CuL), vicarage. Now 'Beckside Grange'. IT [*BH* 30.4.1881].

Lancaster, plans to convert the old Corn Market into council committee rooms and offices [*LGaz* 19.3.1881].

Lancaster, Christ Church Schools. Plans to increase accommodation by 260 places. Estimate £1,000 [*LGaz* 9.4.1881, 18.6.1881].

Lancaster, cottage for Miss Michaelson, High Street. Plans for alteration [LRO, MBLA acc 5167/404].

Lancaster, 'The Greaves', Belle Vue Terrace, Greaves Road, Scotforth. Alterations to EGP's house for himself [ex info CS].

Lindale (CuL), 'Hampsfield House'. For John Tomlinson Hibbert MP (Parliamentary Secretary to the Local Government Board under Gladstone, 1871–4, 1880–3). T Raffles Davison noted it 'is now completing', *c* £7,000 [*BA* 16, 1881, 407 + illustration]. So may well have been started prior to 1881.

Lytham, St Cuthbert. Plans to enlarge N aisle. Seating would be increased by 115: estimated at £1,000 (or £1,500 for oak seats). Also plans to add an organ chamber and vestry [*PG* 23.4.1881, 10.9.1881].

Scorton, schools. IT [*LGaz* 18.6.1881].

1881–2

Lancaster, Royal Albert Asylum Rodgett Infirmary. £4,000 donated by Edward Rodgett of Darwen Bank Preston. CC – C Baynes (masonry), J Hatch (joinery), E Cross & Sons (slating & plastering), Calvert & Heald (plumbing & glazing). [*LGaz* 26.2.1881, 30.9.1882: *PG* 15.1.1881, 30.9.1882].

Manchester, St Margaret, Burnage. Bell-cote added [Pollard 2000, 6].

Ormskirk St Peter & St Paul. Work on W tower completed and bells rehung [Ockenden 2002, 46].

Whitehaven (CuC), Bransty station. Proposed additions [CRO(W), TBR 1/1/7].

Windermere (CuW), St Mary. Chancel, tower and W end. £4,600 (£1,000 subscribed by Mr Pollard of London) [CRO(K), 104/66–7:

BH 26.2.1881, 5.3.1881: *LGaz* 15.11.1882]. Plans for new S transept [CRO(K), 104/68].

1881–4
Ormskirk St Peter & St Paul. Restoration of the Derby Chapel [Ockenden 2002, 47].

1881–7
Blackburn, St Mark Witton. ES's church expanded [no doubt by the transept] on N side [*VCH* 6, 1911, 34: Fleetwood-Hesketh 1955, 133, who also mentions that the Feilden mortuary chapel (S side) was added *c* 1879 but no architect named, although a sketch is included in LL 3]. *Blackburn Times* [20.5.1938], says reseated 1889 (no architect named).

1882
Barrow-in-Furness (CuL), 'Abbot's Wood'. Proposed new morning room for Sir James Ramsden [CRO(B), BBP 1676]. Built on the SE corner.

Barrow-in-Furness (CuL), plans for coffee tavern, Michaelson Road/Bridge Road (NE corner) [CRO(B), BBP 1683].

Corney (CuC), St John the Baptist. Reseated, refloored, externally repaired. P&A 'locally represented' by Mr Harrison of Barrow. Estimated cost £398. CC – Watson (masonry), Huddart (joinery), Eilbech (plastering) [ICBS 8729: *BN* 43, 1882, 649].

Darwen, mission church, Culvert. Plans. To seat 400. Estimate £1,000 [*BS* 8.7.1882].

Lancaster, new workshops, Castle Hill for W Hunt of Shrigley & Hunt. IT [*LGaz* 11.2.1882: ex info CS].

Lancaster, Royal Grammar School, new swimming baths. IT [LRO, MBLA acc 5167/494: *LGaz* 25.3.1882, 1.4.1882].

Lytham, St Cuthbert. N aisle, vestry and organ chamber added. £1,200. C – Saul, Preston [LRO, PR 3220/4/114: *BN* 43, 1882, 185].

Morecambe, St Lawrence. Alabaster pulpit. C – James Heap, Lancaster [*LGaz* 15.4.1882].

Seascale (CuC). Plan for additions to houses [CRO(W), SRDED 3/1/41].

Seascale (CuC). Plans for stationmaster's cottage [CRO(B), BD/MA box 5/27: CRO(W) TBR 1/1/34].

Skipton (NY), Ermysted's Grammar School. Design for gymnasium and pool [ex info Douglas Grant].

Ulverston (CuL), Holy Trinity. Design for reredos [LL 1, 39].

Yealand Conyers, St John. IT for new chancel and reseating. Design 1881 [*LGaz* 7, 14.1.1882].

1882–3
Barrow-in-Furness (CuL), St Mark. Proposals to enlarge in Oct 1881 temporarily abandoned in favour of a permanent church [*BH* 1.10.1881, 3.12.1881]. But then proposals for an extended S aisle were approved by Barrow Council in Aug 1882 adding 300 extra seats (total became 1,062): faculty granted 26 Oct. C – executors of W Gradwell, £1,500 including organ [CRO(B), BBP 1677: BPR 4/I2/5: *BH* 16.9.1882, 31.3.1883: Anon (Church Congress), 83]. A permanent church was never built.

Caton, bridge over River Lune. Replaced a bridge of *c* 1805 which collapsed in 1881. Contract £8,500. C – Benton & Abraham Woodiwiss, Manchester & Derby. P&A had submitted designs in 1881, as had A W Kershaw [inscription: *LGaz* 17.12.1881, 11.8.1883]. EGP's obituary [*LGuar* 26.1.1895] credits him with the design, and he is named as architect in a report of the Lancaster Quarter Sessions [*LGaz* 17.10.1883].

Fawley (Bucks), St Mary. Restoration; nave walls raised, tower arch rebuilt, new nave roof, new windows, N transept and vestry built, S transept refaced and opened up to the nave by a new arch. Font, 1884 [RIBA PB175: Tyack, G 1986 *Fawley, Buckinghamshire; a Short History of the Church and Parish*, 13]. A drawing for a lychgate costing £125 [LL 1, 50] is undated but no doubt is from the same scheme.

Wilmington (E Sussex). S aisle added, S transept removed, W gallery demolished, new floors, altar, altar rails, seats, stalls, desk and lectern [E Sussex RO, PAR 510/4/1–5: *BA* 21.12.1885]. This far-flung commission no doubt arose because the patron of the living was P&A's existing important client the Duke of Devonshire.

1882–4
Higher Walton (Ch), St John the Evangelist. For the brewer, Sir Gilbert Greenall of Walton Hall. £17,500. Sculpture carving on reredos by John Roddis, Birmingham; other parts by Miles & Morgan, Lancaster. E, W and transept windows by Shrigley & Hunt. C – J Fairhurst, Whitley. CW – Perkins [LL 1, 3: *BA* 12.12.1884: *BN* 46, 1884, 227: displays at Walton Hall Heritage Centre]. BE and JP date as 1882–5 but Raffles Davison's sketches in *BA* suggest it was complete by the end of 1884.

1882–5
Bolton (GM), St Saviour, Astley Bridge. Design 1882. *c* £20,000; the gift of Thomas Greenhalgh using funds bequeathed by his brother, Nathaniel. 804 seats. Aisleless nave 50ft wide, 86ft long: transepts, double aisles to chancel, W tower 137ft high. Carving and sculpture by John Roddis. Seven-light E window by Burlison & Grylls, W window by Shrigley & Hunt. C – Collins & Son, Warrington. CW – E Potts [LL 1, 33: RIBA PB129/3: *LGaz* 23.2.1884: *BA* 24, 1885, 266 + illustrations: *BN* 48, 1885, 631, 711; 49, 1885, 550: *K* 1913, 253: 'ALH' [1981] *A Short History of All Souls' Church, Bolton 1881–1981*]. With the schools and vicarage the cost is said to have been £30,000 [*Bolton Chronicle* 26.9.1885, which does not mention the architect(s) responsible]. Demolished 1975.

1882–7
Barrow-in-Furness (CuL), North Lonsdale Hospital. Plans from Mar 1882. IT 1883. C – W Gradwell [CRO(B), BT/HOS/NL 7–8: *BN* 45, 1883, 149: *LGaz* 7.7.1883]. A note in the CRO(B) register listing, BT/HOS/NL 7–8 notes that construction began in 1885 and that the building was in use by 1887. But given the detailed plans in 1882–4 work almost certainly began before 1885 and the fact that there is correspondence about the detailed matter of ventilators in Oct 1885 suggests that occupation may have

followed fairly soon afterwards. Closed 1989, demolished 1990.

1883
Barrow-in-Furness (CuL), plans for 36 cottages, Adelaide Street. For W H Jackson [CRO(B), BBP 1753].

Barrow-in-Furness (CuL), plans for pair of semi-detached cottages, Thwaites Flat. For the FR [CRO(B), BBP 1798].

Barrow-in-Furness (Cu)L, proposed hotel, Barrow Island. For F H Weyergang on Devonshire Dock Road: not built [CRO(B), BBP 1845].

Barrow-in-Furness (CuL), proposed hotel, Holker Street. For James Thompson. Unexecuted plans [CRO(B), BBP 1846].

Barrow-in-Furness (CuL), plans for new porch at St James's school [CRO(B), BBP 1872].

Barrow-in-Furness (CuL), plans for vicarage; first designs 1881 [CRO(B), BBP 1876].

Barrow-in-Furness (Cu), plans for houses, reading room, officers' room, armoury etc on the Strand for the FR [CRO(B), BBP 1765].

Barrow-in-Furness (CuL), plans for Exchange Hall, Hindpool Road [CRO(B), BBP 1777].

Carlisle (CuC), Board Schools competition. EGP was assessor. Winner – George Dale Oliver, Carlisle [*B* 43, 1883, 497].

Conishead Priory (CuL), station. Plans 1880 [CRO(B), BD/MA E178; BDX 53/10/3; BTBR 1/2/7].

Fawley (Buckinghamshire), 'Fawley Court'. New wing (with study, billiard room, smoking rooms and bedrooms) and terraces (intended in 1883 to be 'constructed round the whole mansion on two levels') [*LGuar* 26.2.1895: *K* 1883]. Commissioned by William Dalziel Mackenzie, a barrister and lord of the manor. E J Climinson, 'Fawley Court' in Ditchfield, P H (ed) 1901 *Memorials of Old Buckinghamshire*, 87, adds that 'the bricks being scraped and refaced; its whole appearance is most handsome and infinitely more so than when whitened'.

Fleetwood, St Peter. E end built, £3,000 [Slater 1895, 338: BE].

Lancaster, Royal Grammar School. Plans (Jul) for gymnasium and carpenter's shop [LM, 99.60]. Additions [LRO, MBLA acc 5167/553].

Lancaster, 'Ryelands', Owen Road, Skerton. Extension [LSMR, PRN4632-MLA4632]. Home of James Williamson: *LGaz* [15.7.1885] notes that P&A had been responsible for 'a fine conservatory'.

Lancaster, St Leonard's Gate. Plans for workshops for Gillow & Co [LRO, MBLA acc 5167/548].

Lancaster, two shops, Upper Church Street. Gothic style, four storeys: for Preston & Co, grocers [*LGaz* 10.3.1883]. Building application and IT had appeared in 1881 for rebuilding shops for T Preston in Church Street (presumably this work was delayed) [LRO, MBLA acc 5167/403: *LGaz* 2.7.1881].

Lancaster, Woodville Street, plans for eight terraced cottages for R Cross & Son [LRO, MBLA, acc 5167/602, /605, /610, /654 (ex info CS)].

Great Ouseburn (NY), St Mary the Virgin. Restored. S chapel [*LGuar* 26.1.1895: JP].

Seascale (CuC). Plans for villa for the Revd Charles E Johnston dated Nov [CRO(B), BD/MA/5/28].

Stalmine, St James. IT for restoration and building a new chancel [*LGaz* 16.5.1883].

1883–4
Barrow-in-Furness (CuL), St George. Chancel lengthened 12ft and Ramsden Chapel added on S side: seating provided in the latter for members of the Corporation for civic occasions. C – W Gradwell [CRO(B), BBP 1843: *BH* 10.5.1884: Anon (Church Congress), 74].

Barrow-in-Furness (CuL), proposed hotel on Barrow Island for John B Robinson on corner Anchor Road/Ramsden Dock Road with stables nearby [CRO(B), BBP 1844]. Revised plans, 1884 [CRO(B), BBP 2003]. Unexecuted.

1883–6
Northwich (Ch), St Helen, Witton. Restored: N aisle and vestries added, baptistry created. In 1883 cost estimated at £7,520 when it was intended to increase seating by 47 to 742 [LL 1, 19: ICBS 8801].

1884
Barrow-in-Furness (CuL), Masonic Hall, Abbey Road. £1,200–£1,400. Design Sept 1883 by John Harrison of the P&A office [CRO(B), BBP 1946: *BH* 28.6.1884].

Barrow-in-Furness (CuL), St Mark. 'Vestry' for classes, prayer meetings etc added. *c* £300. C – exors of W Gradwell [*BH* 1.3.1883].

Barrow-in-Furness (CuL), School of Art, Abbey Road (corner (N) of Bath Street). Designs Sept 1884 so no doubt building went on into 1885 [CRO(B), BBP 2015]. Seems to have been incorporated into Woodhouse & Willoughby's Technical School of 1900.

Barrow-in-Furness (CuL), hotel for Mrs Clarkson, Roose Road. Unexecuted plans [CRO(B), BBP 2004].

Barrow-in-Furness (CuL), hotel for James Thorp, Ferry Road. Unexecuted plans [CRO(B), BBP 2011].

Darwen, St Barnabas. New church. £1,462. 360 seats. CC (all of Darwen) – J Orrell & Sons (masonry), Holden Baron (slater), R Jackson (plasterer), H C Jephson (plumbing & glazing) [*BN* 47, 1884, 236]. A cheap church which may have been intended as a temporary building.

Grange-over-Sands (CuL), St Paul. Design for pulpit, Dec 1884 [LL 1, 4–5].

Lancaster, 'Longlands'. House for Arthur W Hunt, proprietor of Shrigley & Hunt [LRO, MBLA acc 5167/572: *LGaz* 5.1.1884: *BA* 34, 1890, 60 + illustration: Waters 2003, 11].

Liverpool, Cathedral. P&A succeeded in reaching the second stage of the competition in which some hundred architects who had sent in portfolios of three designs of other churches were whittled down to 10. They failed to make it to the short list of four (G F Bodley, James Brooks, J L Pearson and, the eventual winner in

1886, William Emerson) [*B* 46, 1884, 740; 47, 1884, 251, 316].

Llanrwst (Denbighshire), St Grwst. Restored: reseated and W gallery removed, N aisle added, new rood-loft stairs, and stalls. P&A were involved by May 1882 when they produced a seating plan of the existing building but mention in 1881 (ICBS) of plans for a N aisle may suggest they were consulted that early. The work estimated at £2,000, was to be done from Aug 1884. Seating increased to 362. £2,300. C – S Parry of Llanrwst [plan in church, and picture there captioned as showing the church before 1884 restoration: ICBS 8778: *Rhyl Guardian* 27.11.1889: *BN* 15.8.1884, xvii: BW, 234].

Ribby-cum-Wrea, St Nicholas, Wrea Green. IT 1883. Steeple. £1,300. C – Fielding & Sons, Blackpool. Design probably 1883 [LL 1, 24: *LGaz* 16.5.1883: *BN* 43, 1883, 772; 46, 1884, 656; 47, 1884, 484: Barrett 1886, 750].

Shrewsbury, St Mary. N vestry [BE].

Thornton-in-Craven (WY), house, Fence End. IT [*LMerc* 5.7.1884].

Torver (CuL), St Luke. Rebuilt, replacing a church of 1849 (design probably 1847) by Miles Thompson of Kendal. Designs 1883. 150 seats, £1,350 [ICBS 3796: CRO(K), 52/1/2/8; 52/6/8, 14: *BH* 25.10.1884: *BN* 44, 1883, 609: Slater 1895, 379].

Windermere (CuW), 'The Grange', off Lake Road. Plans for additions to detached house [CRO(K), WSUD/W/W1/919]. Now three dwellings.

1884–5

Crewe (Ch), St Barnabas. New church for the London & North Western Railway Co near to its workshops. Designs existed before the end of 1883. 500 seats. Estimate £4,000 (including endowment). Terracotta dressings made by J C Edwards, Ruabon. C – A P Cotterill, Crewe [*BN* 45, 1883, 387; 46, 1884, 386; 49, 1885, 687]. School and vicarage probably by P&A too.

Dalton-in-Furness (CuL), St Mary. Rebuilt, replacing a church of 1825–6 and 1830 by George Webster. P&A appointed and plans presented 1882. E window from the previous church reused in N aisle. *c* 700 seats. £11,550 (the dukes of Devonshire and Buccleuch gave £2,500 and £1,000 respectively, H W Schneider £1,000, Barrow Haematite Steel Co £1,000). C – James Garden (contract signed Mar 1883); woodwork carving by Miles & Morgan, Lancaster: E and W windows by Burlison & Grylls [CRO(B), BPR 1/C5/12, PP.48, 50–1: *BH* 6.6.1885, 12.12.1885: ex info the Revd S Skinner].

Sedbergh (CuWY), Sedbergh School, swimming bath and gymnasium. Designs from 1881 when HJA presented plans to the governors [SSGM, 1884–5].

1884–6

Giggleswick (NY), Giggleswick School. Classrooms extended, including a hall above and classrooms below, and building of a covered playground [ex info W Brooks]. C – Brassington & Corney(?). Quantity surveyor – William Wright [JB/JP].

Lancaster, Ripley Hospital. Additional schoolrooms, dormitories, laundry, swimming bath and entrance lodge. Built under a bequest by Mrs Julia Ripley. £17,000. Designs start Apr 1883. Design for entrance lodge 1884. [LRO, MBLA acc 5167/597, 597: LM, 99.60: *LGaz* 24, 31.5.1884, 10.11.1888: Slater 1895, 412]. BE says the W arm (for boys) was extended in 1883–9.

Sedbergh (CuWY), Sedbergh School, sanatorium. Tender price £1,590 (including Richard Greenwood, Sedbergh, £880 for building, William Huntington, Lancaster, £372 for carpentry). CW – James Cushing [SSGM, 1884–6]

1884–7

Pilling, St John the Baptist. Replaced a church of 1721 on a different site. £7,000. Plans in 1883 to rebuild at a cost of £4,000. 410 seats [LRO, PR 3243/4/62–73: LL 1, 25: *LGaz* 10.11.1883: *Liverpool Mercury* 21.6.1884: Bulmer 1913, 300; *K* 1913, 798].

1884–9

Rossall, Rossall School. NW corner and W side of The Square completed with school house buildings [ex info Clare Hartwell].

1885

Alsager (Ch), school for St Mary Magdalene's church. P&A appointed Jul 1884 (HJA visited the site for a school and church, and produced a perspective drawing of both in 1884) [drawing in church: CALS, P102/4/1, 1: ex info A M Shaw].

Barrow-in-Furness (CuL), plans for hotel on Devonshire Dock Road. For J Thompson (now corner Ferry/Stanley Roads) [CRO(B), BBP 2097]. Now the Crow's Nest pub.

Cartmel Priory (CuL), tomb chest to support the figure of Lord Frederick Cavendish, carved by Thomas Woolner. C – James Heap [*BH* 29.8.1885].

Farnworth (nr Widnes, Me), St Luke. Proposed to complete the restoration; architect – EGP. To include reseating, gallery removal, whitewash removal, and some new roofing. EGP had already restored the tower [*BN* 49, 1885, 108].

Lancaster, St Mary. Supervised installation of two Ward & Hughes windows (nearest N and S windows in chancel clerestory to the chancel arch [*LGaz* 4.4.1885].

Manchester, St Margaret, Burnage. Clergy vestry, reredos and organ screen [Pollard 2000, 6]. *BN* [50, 1886, 764], says P&A commissioned to design a reredos so a date of 1886 is perhaps to be preferred.

St Bees (CuC), St Bees School, school house [BE, 1967, 184].

Scarborough (NY), St James' mission chapel. C – George Scales, Scarborough [*Scarborough Gazette* 23.7.1885: ex info Dr K S Walker].

Whittington, Whittington Hall, Home Farm. Restored and a tea room and octagonal dairy added (the latter with with marble shelves and tiled panels of the Four Seasons) [LSMR, PRN15954-MLA15927: Robinson 1991, 251].

1885–6

Bolton-by-Bowland, St Peter & St Paul. Restored with new roof and parapets [LSMR, PRN295-MLA295; BE, *W Yorks*].

Sedbergh (CuWY), St Andrew. Restored: S aisle and arcade rebuilt; parts of other upper walling rebuilt. Floor lowered, gallery removed, new roofs. New pulpit, desk altar rails, altar, all made by Gillow. £4,200 [*LGuar* 24.7.1886: Gladstone, R nd *Saint Andrew's Church, Sedbergh*].

1885–8
Chadderton (GM), St Luke. Chancel. The nave and aisles of 1882–5 are by Stott & Sons, Oldham. In 1883 the chief benefactor, James E Platt, offered to build the chancel in memory of his wife provided he could use his own architect and design. No progress had been made by Jun 1885 but church was consecrated Nov 1888 [ICBS 8734].

1885–91
Ormskirk St Peter & St Paul. NE part of church rebuilt to match the chancel and Derby Chapel, chancel heightened 5ft, larger vestry with organ chamber over, chancel reroofed as were the Scarisbrick and Bickerstaffe Chapels, E wall rebuilt and W window enlarged, nave rebuilt and reroofed, W gallery removed (1890), S porch (1891), S aisle refenestrated. There seems to have been a hiatus in the work in 1888–90 [inscription in porch: Ockenden 2002, 47–51].

1886
Barrow-in-Furness (CuL), Concle Inn, Ramside. Plans for wing at rear for the FR, comprising a kitchen, bar parlour and shed: a club room over [CRO(B), BBP 2207].

Barrow-in-Furness (CuL), entrance and lodge for the Barrow Shipbuilding Co to its engineering works on Devonshire Dock Road [CRO(B), BBP 2226].

Barrow-in-Furness (CuL), St Mark. Plans for alterations to porch [CRO(B), BBP 2247].

Halsall, St Cuthbert. Restored. Citation for faculty 1884. Reroofed, nave and aisles largely rebuilt, reseated, S porch rebuilt. £7,000 [LRO, PR 277: *K* 1913, 528].

Higher Walton (Ch), St John the Evangelist. Eagle lectern (EGP named as the designer), executed by Hart, Peard & Co. Pulpit to P&A design executed by James Heap [*LGuar* 11.12.1886].

St Bees (CuC), St Bees School. [BE]. *BN* [43, 1882, 722] noted that the headmaster's house was to be added.

Scorton, St Peter. Design for altar, 12.11.1886 [LL 1, 15].

Whittington, Whittington Hall. Plans for rearrangement of stables [Copeland 1981, 31].

1886–7
Tatham, St James the Less. Restoration paid for by William Foster's sons, William, Robert, Frederic and Herbert. New organ chamber and vestry; walls and buttresses on S and E rebuilt, new windows, fittings, floor, ceilings removed, E window by Burlison & Grylls, altar cloth and reredos designed by Aldam Heaton. £2,800 bequeathed by William Foster of Hornby Castle. CC – Heap, Lancaster (alabaster reredos), J & J Dawson, Kirkby Lonsdale (masonry), John Greene, Lancaster (joinery), H Slinger, Bentham (slating & plastering), J Moorhouse, Kirkby Lonsdale (plumbing & glazing), Miles & Morgan, Lancaster (carving alabaster reredos [inscription: LRO, PR 2920/4/8–9: *LGaz* 18.6.1887: Slater 1895, 393]. Design for oak alms box, nd [LL 1, 8]. The top of the tower must surely be P&A's work.

1886–8
Lancaster, Ripley Hospital, chapel. Built under a bequest by Mrs Julia Ripley. CC – W Warbrick (masonry), C Blades (carpentry & joinery), T Cross & Sons (slating), T Miles & Son (wood- and stone-carving), all of Lancaster [LM, 99.60: LRO, MBLA acc 5167/814: *LGaz* 10.11.1888: *BA* 34 (1890), 76 + illustration by T Raffles Davison]. Designs Jan 1884 and another set Jul 1885 [drawings in Lancaster Museum *c* 1970, catalogued by DM].

1887
Bolton (GM), St Peter. Corporation pew to be proceeded with [*BS* 8.1.1887]. Fraser-Powell memorial stalls at W end of church [*BS* 25.6.1887].

Davyhulme (GM), St Mary. Competition design. P&A placed second after George Truefitt by the assessor Alfred Darbyshire of Darbyshire & Smith. Third place awarded to W H M Ward of Manchester [*BN* 54, 1888, 61].

Ince-in-Makerfield (GM), St Mary. IT 1885. New, large stock brick church with red brick dressings. John Pearson and Thomas Knowles, who owned collieries and ironworks locally, contributed £5,000 each. Replaced 1978 as P&A's church was suffering from subsidence and rot [*Liverpool Mercury* 14.3.1885: *BA* 27.5.1887: Anon 2000 *St Mary's Church, Ince-in-Makerfield: A Millennium Album*, 2–3: BE, 1969, 129; BE, 220].

Knutsford (Ch), St Cross. Tower completed. Tender £2,104. C – James Hamilton [CALS, P189/5/2, 999].

Lancaster, Christ Church. Font cover. C – Gillow & Co [*LGaz* 16.4.1887].

Lancaster, Christ Church schools. Addition of a classroom approved [LRO, MBLA acc 5167/815]. Another addition [LRO, MBLA acc 5167/441].

Lancaster, Royal Grammar School, sanatorium. IT 1885. Estimated at £2,154. C – W Warbrick [LRO, MBLA acc 5167/775: LM, 99.60: *LGaz* 5.3.1887]. Additions to headmaster's house: new dining room and nurseries above. IT estimates work at *c* £800 [LM, 99.60: *LGaz* 3.6.1885, 30.4.1887, 21.5.1887].

Lytham, St Cuthbert. Seating and new gallery front [LRO, PR 3220/4/116–17: *BN* 54, 1888, 65].

Whittington, Whittington Hall. Alterations for Dawson Cornelius Greene including the billiard room, secondary staircase, and garden loggia intended to lead to an unexecuted private chapel [LSMR, PRN15967-MLA15930: Robinson 1991, 251].

Winmarleigh, St Luke. Enlarged by a N aisle and vestry. Sole benefactor – Lord Winmarleigh. C – J Collinson & Sons, Garstang [*LGaz* 23.4.1887: Barrett 1886, 776].

1887–91
Lancaster, Storey Institute. A new school for 'the promotion of art, science, literature and technical instruction'. Paid for by Sir Thomas Storey as a Jubilee memorial, including a reading room, library, a science lecture room, laboratory, music room, a picture

gallery, school of art and caretaker's house. CC – W Warbrick (masonry), C Blades (joinery), Hartley & Sons (slating & plastering), Calvert & Heald (plumbing & glazing), Eaton & Bulfield (painting), Percy Wood (carved busts on the frontage) [*LGaz* 13, 20, 27.8.1887, 8.10.1887, 24.10.1891, 7.11.1891: *BA* 34, 1890, 76 + illustration].

1888

Barrow-in-Furness (CuL), Lancaster Banking Co, 23 Church Street. Plans for minor additions of a scullery and bathroom. Application signed by J Harrison, presumably on behalf of P&A [CRO(B), BBP 2391].

Barrow-in-Furness (CuL), villa for Thomas Butler. Application (approved Feb 1889) signed by John Harrison [CRO(B), BBP 2412].

Barrow-in-Furness (CuL), St Mark. Plans for schools, signed by John Harrison [CRO(B), BBP 2433].

Blawith (CuC), St John the Baptist. EGP reported on settlement at W end and proposes rebuilding from the bottom of the W window. Some parishioners favoured a tower but this was rejected because of expense [*BarrN* 25.5.1888].

Halton, St Wilfrid. Alabaster reredos. C – James Heap, Lancaster [*LGaz* 30.3.1889].

Heversham (CuW), St Peter. Drawings of organ case [CRO(K), WPR 8/9/26].

Lancaster, St Peter (RC). Cleaned, painted and generally renovated: organ gallery built by Blades, on eight granite pillars erected by James Heap, Lancaster [*LGaz* 12.1.1889].

Lancaster, Royal Albert Asylum Winmarleigh recreation hall. IT Aug/Sept 1886 but work did not start until 1888. 52ft wide × 79ft long to the foot of the orchestra. *c* £6,000. CC – W Warbrick (masonry), W Huntington (joinery), R Hall & Son (slating & plastering), Hithersall (plumbing). Statues of Queen Victoria and Prince Albert on the front carved by R Bridgeman, Lichfield, in Longridge stone [*LGuar* 28.8.1886, 4.9.1886, 4.8.1888, 22.9.1888: *BN* 54, 1888, 517: *The Times* 18.9.1888].

Lancaster, Henry Gregson Memorial club house and lecture room, Moor Lane. Plans and IT [LRO, MBLA acc 5167/896: *LGaz* 7.7.1888].

Morecambe, mission church, West End. Plans for a church costing £650 [*LGaz* 19.5.1888].

Overton, vicarage. IT [*LGaz* 7.7.1888].

From 1888

Leigh (GM), St Mary. Glazing scheme planned with Shrigley & Hunt but remained incomplete for lack of funds. E window designed by E H Jewitt of Shrigley & Hunt [Waters 2003, 76].

1888–9

Hornby, St Margaret. Nave of 1815–17 largely rebuilt, the outer walls lowered, clerestory and arcades (without capitals) inserted, arches on either side of chancel rebuilt, reroofed, refloored, vestry turned into an organ chamber, and a new vestry built; work by estate workmen supervised by Mr Jowett; work paid for by Colonel Foster of Hornby Castle and his brothers. CC – Gillow, Lancaster (reredos, organ case, altar, altar rail, seats in chapel), Heap (marble and tile pavement), Shrigley & Hunt (painting of reredos, design and painting of E window), Anthony Bell & Sons, Lancaster (font); cost estimated at £3,000 in Feb 1888 [LL 1, 22, 45: *BarrN* 18.2.1888: *LGaz* 25.5.1889: White, A J nd [*c* 1990] *A Short History and Guide of St Margaret's Church, Hornby*, 2, 4].

Prestwich (GM), St Mary. Specification 1887. Chancel, organ chamber, vestries. Wilton [N] Chapel extensively restored. Designs for pulpit and screen (to be estimated for by R Bridgeman). C – William Southern & Sons [LL 1, 40, 51: MRO, L160/2/36/1–5: *BA* 41, 1894, 150 + illustration: *BN* 14.6.1889, xvii: local information: BE].

Tatham Fells, The Good Shepherd. Church of *c* 1840 rebuilt. Cost under £1,000. Seats for 140. Chief benefactors – children of William Foster of Hornby Castle. CC – J Cumberland, Low Bentham (masonry), J Holmes, Mewith (joinery), W Greene, Bentham (plumbing & glazing), H Slinger, Bentham (slating & plastering) [LL 1, 31: *LGaz* 23.6.1888, 11.8.1888, 15.6.1889: *BN* 56, 1888, 888: Slater 1895, 394: Bulmer 1913, 436]. *K* [1913, 1151] gives the date of old church as 1745 and cost of new one as £1,200.

1888–90

Sedbergh (CuWY), Sedbergh School, a further master's house and additions to classrooms. CW – R Young [SSGM, 1888–90].

1889

Abberley (Worcs), probably St Mary. Designs for chapel seats [LL 1, 20]. The owners of Abberley Hall from 1867 were the Jones family, colliery owners and cotton manufacturers from Oldham (who also used John Douglas for estate buildings) [ex info Alan Brooks, 25.7.2007, and CS].

Salesbury, Wilpshire. Proposed orphanage for Blackburn. EGP acted as the competition assessor, selecting the design of Briggs & Wolstenholme of Blackburn [*BS* 20.7.1889, 31.8.1889].

Knutsford (Ch), St Cross. Church completed by building the aisles. Estimate £1,010. C – James Hamilton. Final cost of the church £7,580 [CALS, P189/5/2, 9].

Lancaster, Christ Church. S aisle built to P&A's plans of some years before, *c* £1,000 for 152 seats. CC – W Warbrick (masonry), Blades (joinery), Calvert & Heald (plumbing), T Cross & Sons (plastering) [LRO, MBLA acc 5167/968: *LGaz* 9.3.1889, 23.11.1889].

Lancaster, High Street. Plan for three-sided extension of sitting room and bedroom at house for Miss Michaelson and addition of WC etc in yard [LRO, MBLA acc 5167/941].

Sedbergh (CuWY), St Andrew. Design for pulpit, Dec 1889 [LL 1, 49].

Witherslack (CuW), St Paul. Reredos [*LGaz* 16.2.1889].

1889–90

Birkdale (Me), St John. New church. £3,300. 318 seats. N aisle and vestries not built [*K* 1913, 983; ex info Stuart Baker].

Dent (CuWY), St Andrew. Plans 1888 for thorough restoration and refitting [CRO(K), WPR 70/1/4/5]. Cost £2,700 [*BN* 58, 1890, 270]. C – Brassington & Corney (joinery & slating [JB/JP].

Rawtenstall, St John, Cloughfold. Proposal to build a church in 1886 [*BN* 50, 1886, 242]. Competition in 1888 assessed by Ewan Christian. 500 seats. £5,000. CC – Warburton & Andrews, Accrington (woodwork), George Hanson, Rawtenstall (excavation & mason's work) [LL 1, 29, 44: MRO, L76: ICBS 9319: *BN* 55, 1888, 602: Slater 1895, 647]. Of the tower only the base was constructed. As at Feb 2010 a shoe warehouse.

1889–91
Colne, St Bartholomew. Restored. Plans 1888. Nearly £7,000. N aisle rebuilt as a double aisle, organ chamber and vestries added, screens, reseated, choir stalls, pulpit and altar added. CC – T Baines (main), J & M Hawley, Colne (masonry), J Hatch & Sons (joinery) [LL 1, 64: *LGaz* 25.4.1888: *BN* 60, 1891, 696: LRO, PR 3172/14/57: Slater 1895, 264].

Cound (Shropshire), St Peter. N vestry which reused a 13th-century priest's doorway [BE].

Hornby, Hornby Castle. Restored: additions and alterations works [*LGaz* 7.12.1889: LBS 182390] for Colonel William Henry Foster.

Ormskirk St Peter & St Paul. Reroofing and rebuilding of the nave completed.

1880s
Giggleswick (NY), Giggleswick School. Science area extended [ex info W Brooks].

1890
Barrow-in-Furness (CuL), North Lonsdale Hospital. Plans for alterations and additions [CRO(B), BBP 2623].

Barrow-in-Furness (CuL). Five dwellings in St George's Square for H Wilkinson and others [CRO(B), BBP 2624].

Greenock (Renfrewshire), St John. Design for stalls, £155 [LL 1, 54].

Lancaster. Sheds for W Hunt [LRO, MBLA acc 5167/1044].

Lancaster, Ripley Hospital. Organ case. C – C Blades; carving by H T & S Miles. [*LGaz* 12.4.1890].

Lancaster, new lodge, Springfield Park. IT [*LGaz* 6.8.1890].

Leigh (GM), St Mary. Refitting in the chancel including an altar and reredos. CC – J Hargreaves (stonework), J Hatch & Sons (oak), Shrigley & Hunt (colour decoration) [Rogan, J 1972 *Leigh Parish Church*, 2: BE]. Also undated drawings survive for a pulpit and screens round the chancel [LL 1, 23, 32, 60].

Sedbergh (CuWY), Sedbergh School, chapel. Plans in 1889 for an extension to the existing chapel seem to have turned into ones for a new temporary wooden building. C – J Hatch & Sons, Lancaster who tendered at £826 [SSGM, 1889–90: *BN* 58, 1890, 684]. *See also* 1895–7.

Whalley, St Mary. Report on proposed restoration, estimated at £2,000 [*LGaz* 14.6.1890: *BN* 58, 1890, 854].

By 1890
Whittington, Whittington Hall. Plans for 'proposed layout of the gardens' including a sick room [Copeland 1981, 31].

c 1890
The following are mostly derived from undated drawings in the first volume of A&P drawings formerly in Lancaster Reference Library (now in LRO). The style and context of other drawings in the album suggest they probably date from the 1880s or 1890s.

Bakewell (Derbys), drinking fountain. Design [LL 1, 11].

Cartmel Priory (CuL). Design for memorial tablet [LL 1, 20].

Casterton (CuW), Holy Trinity. Design for pulpit and lectern [LL 1, 66].

Heversham, St Peter. Design for monument in Levens chapel [LL 1, 30].

Lancaster, St Peter (RC). Design for organ in S transept [LL 1, 27].

Millom (CuC), St George. Design for alabaster reredos [LL 1, 36].

Salford (GM), St Clement, Ordsall. Designs for chancel seats and font [LL 1, 1, 7].

Stalmine, St James. Design for font [LL 1, 7].

Probably 1890s
Whittington Hall, West Hall Lodge. Copies S lodge by G Webster [LSMR, PRN15982-MLA15944].

1890–1
Bootle (CuC), St Michael. Restored. Plans 1888 when a faculty allowed heightening of the chancel and vestry walls by 2ft, and erecting a vestry and organ chamber on the N. External render removed, much renewal of dressed stone, new seats, roofs and floors, windows glazed with cathedral glass, tower of 1850 completed [LL 1, 10: *BarrN* 3.3.1888: *Cumberland Pacquet* 12.11.1891].

1890–2
Giggleswick (NY), St Alkelda. Restored including new roof. The faculty provided for reseating, gallery removal, vestry rebuilding, replastering, reflooring, rebuilding or repair of N arcade, making uniform the clerestory windows, and general repairs [*LGaz* 25.1.1890: *BN* 57, 1890, 547: LBS 323793]. A £3,000 restoration was proposed in 1888 but no architect mentioned [*LGuar* 10.3.1888]. C – Brassington & Corney (masonry, slating & plastering) [JB/JP].

Rawtenstall, St John, Crawshawbooth. Local stone with Yorkshire stone dressings outside; red Rainhill stone inside. The land (donated in 1888) and £3,000 for the building (plus £1,000 for the endowment) came from Thomas Brooks (from 1892, Baron Crawshaw), calico printer, and his wife. In 1890 cost estimated at £6,800 but rose to £7,500 by the time the FS was laid owing to problems with the foundations: the final cost for the fitted-out church rose to nearer £12,000. Seating for 616. CC – Smith Bros, Burnley (masonry), Pickup & Birtwistle, Crawshawbooth (joinery and carpentry), T Cross & Son, Lancaster (slating), H Braithwaite & Co, Leeds (plumbing & glazing). CW – J H Atkinson, Rawtenstall

[LL 1, 57: *Rawtenstall Free Press* 29.10.1892: *BA* 33, 1890, 439–40 + drawing: Slater 1895, 648]. Later fittings such as reredos (*c* 1909) and font cover (*c* 1918) probably by A&P too.

1890–6
Atherton (GM), St John the Baptist. Completed (including 120ft-high tower). Contract £6,012. Seats increased to 850 [MRO, L177: *BN* 58, 1890, 570: Fletcher 1923, 23: Lunn 1971, 190].

1891
Barrow-in-Furness (CuL), 'Abbot's Wood'. Plans for addition of inglenook fireplace for Sir James Ramsden [CRO(B), BBP 2816].

Coventry (Warwicks), St Michael. Designs for detached tower to house bells from the medieval tower about which there were fears regarding stability. Slightly revised after comments from E Christian, R N Shaw and A Waterhouse suggested the link to the church was somewhat weak in design. Scheme abandoned following the death of the chief benefactor, George Woodcock in May 1891 [RIBA PB254/4: *BA* 44, 1895, 200–1: *B* 20.6.1891: Pickford 1987, 49–55].

Dalton-in-Furness (CuL), St Mary. PA&P to design frame for brass plate commememorating names of the committee members for the rebuilding in 1884–5 [CRO(B), BPR 1/C5/12, 53].

Lancaster, Primrose District mission church, Dale Street. Mission church for Christ Church. Plans and tenders accepted. To accommodate 300, approved 1.5.1891. Estimate £1,165. C – W Warbrick (masonry), Hatch & Sons (joinery), Hartley & Son (slating & plastering), W Huthersall (plumbing & glazing [LRO, MBLA 5167/1/1132, 1142: *LGaz* 6.5.1891].

Lancaster, Skerton Hotel, Skerton. For Mrs Perkin: also addition of manure shed and pig sties at rear [LRO, MBLA acc 5167/1046, 1113].

Scotforth, St Paul. W end extended by three bays and transepts formed for extra 150 seats. Design 1890. £930. CC – W Warbrick (masonry), R S Wright & Sons (joinery), R Hall & Son (slating & plastering), Calvert & Heald (plumbing), George Blezard (painting) [*LGaz* 12.4.1890, 6.8.1890, 2.12.1891: *BN* 61, 1891, 887]. Design for font and sanctuary lamp, nd [LL 1, 35].

Melling, St Wilfrid. Restored for Canon W B Grenside, including reseating. £1,100 [Gibson, M 1989 *Melling Church: A History and Guide*]. Grenside was a close friend of HJA.

1891–3
St Helens (Me), All Saints, Sutton. New church: crossing tower not completed. Largely (?wholly) paid for by Pilkingtons, glass manufacturers. 600 seats. Estimated at £6,800. C – Samuel Webster, Bootle [inscription: *BN* 61, 1891, 31, 40, 217: local information].

1891–8
Stockport (GM), St George, Heaviley. Church, church schools and vicarage, Heaviley. Designed by HJA who was approached in Dec 1890. First designs for the church Dec 1891. Site and land adjoining given by Wakefield Christie-Miller; buildings paid for by George Fearn. Tenders accepted Nov 1891 totalling £41,372 (masonry £31,300, joinery £7,897, slating £153, plumbing, £1,399, glazing £623). FS 17.6.1893. Accommodation planned for 1,200 but seating only provided for 1,040. Consecrated 25.2.1897. CC – W Thornton & Sons, Liverpool (masonry), James Hatch & Sons, Lancaster (joinery), Pickles Bros, Leeds (slating), H Braithwaite, Leeds (plumbing & glazing). E and W windows by Shrigley & Hunt paid for by Christie-Miller and Fearn respectively; reredos of Derbyshire alabaster and font carved by Robert Bridgeman & Sons, Lichfield (contract £600 [reredos], £65 [font]). CW – John Hindmarsh. Infant school contract (£4,176) let Oct 1891, opened Dec 1893: C – Joseph Broadhurst, Stockport. Vicarage contract (£2,142) let Dec 1896, dedicated May 1898. C – William Pownall. Dates of mixed school (estimate £7,000) not ascertained. Total cost of the church and other buildings said to be nearly £80,000 [CALS, P303/4505/205: LL 1, 53, 93: RIBA PA5; PB310/2, 8: *Builders' Journal* 5, 1897, 45–6: *BN* 60, 1891, 827; 64, 1893, 855; 72, 1897, 364; Jones 1997]. Vicarage ruinous as at 2009.

1891–9
Waterloo (Me), Christ Church. Replaced a church of 1840 by Arthur & George Williams which was said to be structurally unsound by the late 1880s. A limited competition in 1891 was held but none of the designs was considered satisfactory and PA&P were appointed. £21,956: major benefactor – James Barrow of Beach Lawn, Waterloo (£8,375). C – George Woods & Son, Bootle: woodwork by W Goulborn. Nave and baptistry 1891–3; chancel 1894; tower 1899. [RIBA PB254/3: *BN* 61, 1891, 593: *Liverpool Mercury* 19.10.1891, 3.12.1891, 4.12.1899: Brandwood, G 2000 *Christ Church, Waterloo, Merseyside*. Churches Conservation Trust guide, 1–2]. It was wrongly reported that Birkett & Langham had won [*BN* 60, 1891, 466] but PA&P made it clear in *B* [60, 1891, 378], that this was not the case. Redundant 1988, now vested in the CCT.

1892
Spalding (Lincs), probably St Mary & St Nicholas. Screen on N of chancel [DM].

Preston Patrick (CuW), St Patrick. Plans 1891. 'Chancel built and church beautified in memory of Mary Keightley of Old Hall, d. 1891.' C – C Blades (stalls, pulpit and lectern) [inscription: CRO(K), WPR 42/1/4/11: NADFAS, 2001: BE].

Warton, St Oswald. Restored [JP: BE].

1892–3
Barbon (CuW), St Bartholomew. Replaced a church of 1813. Design 1891. Four-bay nave, two-bay aisles, crossing tower, S transept; £3,000 (£1,000 of which came from a legacy from Mrs Eastham for a church for her native village) with contributions from Sir U Kay-Shuttleworth (£650), Lord Bective and others. Site give by Mrs Hollins, Mrs Thorpe and the Misses Wilson of Whelprigg. E window given by Lady Kay-Shuttleworth. Stalls carved by J M Kirkbridge [*LGuar* 16.9.1893: *LStd* 7.4.1893: ICBS 9604: Bulmer 1905, 344; 1913, 463].

Knowsley (Me), St Mary. Enlarged vestry on S side. New E window [BE].

1892–4

Field Broughton (also known as Broughton East: CuL), St Peter. Replaced a church of 1745 a mile away. Design 1891. £7,500 or £8,000 paid for by Harriet Margaret Hibbert and her trustees as a memorial to her husband, Thomas Hibbert, and by Henry Hibbert of Broughton Grove. Shingled spire 110ft high. CC – J Hatch & Sons, Lancaster, Thoms of Grange (mason). [CRO(K), WPR 86/1/3/7–9, 24; 86/1/8/7: *LStd* 6.7.1984: Bulmer 1905, 203: *K* 1913, 500].

Wigan (GM), St Matthew, Highfield. New church. Design 1891. Memorial church paid for by Colonel Henry Blundell-Hollinshead-Blundell MP, owner of the Pemberton Collieries in memory of his wife, Beatrice (d 1884). Cost over £10,000. C – J Hatch & Sons, Lancaster [inscription in chancel: LL 1, 74, 78: *BN* 61, 1891, 278: Cooke 1993, 42–7].

1893

Cartmel (CuL), St Mary. Design for churchyard gates, Sept [LL 1, 80].

Heversham (CuW), St Peter. Design for oak lychgate [LL 1, 76].

Horsham (W Sussex), Christ's Hospital. Competition design by HJA. *c* 150 applications received which it was intended to whittle down to four entrants. The committee and assessor, Ewan Christian, decided to go for six in view of the importance of the scheme: one of the six objected to this change in the rules and withdrew leaving PA&P in the field with Carpenter & Ingelow, T E Collcutt, T G Jackson and the eventual winners Aston Webb & Ingress Bell, to whom PA&P were runners-up [*B* 63, 1892, 523; 64, 1893, 345; 67, 1894, 100–1 + illustrations: *BA* 42, 1894, 23, 78 + illustrations: *BN* 66, 1894, 805, 884; 67, 1894, 7, illustrations 20 Jul].

Lancaster, Drill Hall, St Leonard's Gate/Phoenix Street. For the 1st Volunteeer Battalion of the Royal Lancaster Regiment. Estimate £2,500. Plans 1892, submitted to Lancaster Council 1893 [LRO, MBLA acc 5167/1296: *LGaz* 30.3.1892]. Now used as a church.

Lancaster, three shops and houses, Penny Street. For William Bland. Plans [LRO, MBLA acc 5167/1337].

Lancaster, Ripley Hospital. Plans (Apr and Jun) for a two-storey addition and alterations [LM, 99.60].

St John in the Vale (CuC), St John. Reordered [ex info G Darell, son of an earlier rector via JP].

Scarborough (EY), St James, church institute [*Scarborough Evening News* 21.7.1894]. Demolished 1950s [ex info Dr K S Walker].

1893–4

Morecambe, Sunday school and church premises for St Lawrence's church, Edward Street. York dressed stone and rubble. Gothic, two storeys. Work supervised by S Wright. C – John Edmondson, Morecambe [*LGaz* 9.9.1893, 5.5.1894: *LStd* 8.9.1893].

Keswick (CuC), Keswick School of Industrial Arts, Crosthwaite. For Canon Hardwicke Rawnsley and his wife Edith (née Fletcher, niece by marriage of ES). Plans by Mar 1893. Estimated cost £1,300. C – T & I Hodgson and F & W Greeen, both firms of Keswick. Closed 1984, now a restaurant [LL 1, 56: Haslam, S E 2004 *John Ruskin and the Lakeland Arts Revival, 1880–1920*. Cardiff, 95–7: BE].

Wesham, Christ Church. New church. £3,350. P&A involved as early as 1889. Design 1892. E end not built. 229 seats [LL 1, 25: RIBA PB129/2: ICBS 9623: *BN* 58, 1890, 305: Anon nd [1994] *Wesham Church, established 1894: Centenary 1894–1994*: Bulmer 1913, 333].

1893–5

Hertford, All Saints. Replaced a church destroyed by fire on 21.12.1891. In 1892 portfolios of designs were submitted by Sir A W Blomfield, James Brooks & Son, T G Jackson, and Bodley & Garner, but the committee appointed PA&P who presented their plans 12 May. Cost was estimated at £6,000 but by Dec 1894 had risen to over £15,000. FS 25.3.1893; dedicated 20.2.1895. 1,007 seats. £16,898 plus architects' and Clerk of Works' costs. C – Smith Bros of Burnley, woodwork by J A Hunt, Hoddesden; stone-carving by R Bridgeman, and wood-carving by Hatch & Sons. CW – A Fincham [LL 1, 28: *Hertfordshire Mercury* 5.3.1893, 2.4.1893, 14.5.1893, 8.10.1893: *B* 2.3.1895: *BN* 61, 1891, 923; 62, 1892, 418, 763; 67, 1894, 486: Lovejoy, J A nd [1950s] *The Story of All Saints' Hertford*. Gloucester, 10–11].

1893–6

Lancaster, Infirmary, South Road. £25,000 [Slater 1895, 412]. Sketch plans first prepared 1889. Original estimate £17,000 (excluding childrens' ward (£1,200) paid for by W Smith MP) but lowest tender in Jan 1893 amounted to £19,305 plus the cost of site making £21,800. £5,000 given by J Williamson MP. IT 1890; FS not laid till Jul 1893. CC – W Warbrick (masonry), W Huntington (joinery), Cross & Son (slating & plastering), Calvert & Heald (plumbing & glazing), G Blezard (painting) [LRO, MBLA acc 5167/1292, 1320, 1393: *LGaz* 9.8.1890, 8, 15.7.1893, 21, 28.3.1896: *LStd* 7, 14.7.1893]. *LGaz* [8.7.1893] and *LStd* [7.7.1893] name EGP as the architect in a report of the arrangements for the FS laying but this may simply be because he was there representing the practice.

1894

Bury (GM), St Mary. Design for stalls: memorial to the Revd Frank Edward Hopwood [LL 1, 41: *Manchester Times* 26.10.1894].

Fence, 'Hoarstones', Old Laund Booth. Alterations for Mr Hartley, including right-hand bay, and extension backwards of left-hand section [LSMR, PRN667-MLA667].

Finsthwaite (CuL), St Peter. Stained glass window commissioned from Shrigley & Hunt, designed by Carl Almquist, E H Jewitt, G P Gamon and E J Prest [Waters 2003, 3].

Lancaster, Common Garden Street. HJA assessor of competition for market hall extension and hotel. Paid £10 10s. First prize awarded to Luke Barlow of Manchester [*LGaz* 2.6.1894: *BN* 67, 1894, 6].

Lancaster, Ripley Hospital. Design for reredos Mar 1894 [LL 1, 68].

Leigh (GM), St Mary. Design for tower screen Mar 1894 [LL 1, 87, 94].

Scarborough (NY), St James. Aisles, W porch, and N vestry added. Designs 1893. Seats increased from 200 to 350. £2,000. C – James Bland, Scarborough [LL 1, 62: *Scarborough Mercury* 4.8.1893: *Scarborough Evening News* 21.7.1994: *BA* 40, 1893, 22 + illustration: ex info Dr K S Walker].

Sunderland Point, mission church. Red brick 41ft × 17ft; capacity *c* 150 and also suitable for use for parish meetings. Cost *c* £250. C – Willis Bros, Morecambe [*LGuar* 9.11.1894: *LStd* 9.11.1894].

1894–5
Farnworth (nr Widnes, Me), St Luke. Restoration; W and S galleries removed, plaster stripped, chancel and Cuerdley chapel roofs repaired, vestry demolished and new ones added, new floors and seating; £4,011. C – Woods & Son [*LGaz* 20.6.1894: *BN* 67, 1894, 819].

Lancaster, Christ Church. W baptistry as a memorial to the Revd Philip Bartlett. CC – T Mawson (masonry), Wright & Sons (joinery), R Bridgeman, Lichfield (carving of angels in the screen), Calvert & Heald (plumbing etc). IT Sept 1894 [*LGuar* 6.10.1894, 14.12.1895: *LStd* 13.12.1895].

Lancaster, St Mary. Clergy vestry [DM].

1894–6
Alsager (Ch), St Mary Magdalene. New church. First phase built following an HJA design of 1884. Estimate £5,450: between 1889 and 1896 £6,344 was collected for the building. To have 450 seats out of an eventual 700. C – John Fielding, Altrincham. Church opened 8.1.1897. Only the E bay of the N aisle built [drawing and framed donations record in church: LL 1, 55: *Crewe Guardian* 13.1.1897: *BN* 67, 1894, 450: Shaw, A M *in St Mary's Church News* (Mar 1984): ex info A M Shaw]. Tower and spire never built.

Borwick St Mary. Paid for by William Sharp of London in memory of his wife Clara (d 1889). LStd (wrongly) says designed by 'a London architect'. Edward Sharp of Linden Hall gave the pulpit. C – J Hatch & Sons. The stained glass W window was in place Oct 1895 so the church may have been complete that year and consecration delayed to 24.6.1896 [inscriptions: *Carnforth News* 2.7.1896: *LGuar* 24.5.1894: *LStd* 26.6.1896: LSMR, PRN26267-MLA26210].

1894–8
Blackburn, St Silas. New church, built except for W tower and spire. £10,000 (£1,750 given by W Tattersall of Quarry Bank). Seats for 609. CC – B Graham & Sons, Huddersfield, Dent & Marshall, Blackburn (joinery), some interior stonework including the pulpit by R Bridgeman, Lichfield, wood-carving by Mills, Manchester. CW – M Whewell, a member of the building committee. W tower and S porch built 1913–14 but spire abandoned. A design by P&A had been accepted as early as Oct 1878 [LL 1, 59, 75: *K* 1913, 134: Whalley 1990, 7–14]. *BN* [50, 1886, 242], notes a proposal to build a church of St Silas, Blackburn.

1895
Ambleside (CuL), St Mary. Reredos by Shrigley & Hunt (mosaics), R Bridgeman, Lichfield (woodwork) [LL 1, 79: BE].

Lancaster, St Peter's boys' school (RC), Balmoral Road. Plans (Nov) for 1,000 scholars [LRO, MBLA acc 5167/1486: (Blackburn) *Weekly Standard* 9.11.1895].

Lancaster, St Peter (RC). Plans for addition to presbytery (now Bishop's House) [LRO, MBLA acc 5167/1429].

Lancaster, St Luke, Skerton. HJA produced plans for a chancel estimated at £550/600 [*LGuar* 18.5.1895].

Over Peover (Ch), St Laurence. Refurbishment [*K* 1914, 517].

***c* 1895**
Hertford, house. By HJA for T J Sworder. £3,800 including the stables [LL file of prints etc]. Sworder was a Hertford solicitor who was hon secretary to the building committee for Hertford, All Saints, and owned land on the Queen's Hill Estate nearby where plots were being sold in the early/mid-1890s. The house was probably 'Balsalms', where he moved in 1898 [Hertfordshire Archives & Local Studies, D/EL3389–99: White, S 2010 'All Saints' Church: the Disastrous Fire of 1891'. *Hertford & Ware Local History Journal*, 8].

1895–7
Lancaster, St Peter's School, Balmoral Road. For 350 boys. *c* £5,500. CC – Robert Thompson (masonry), Hatch & Sons (joinery), Cross & Sons (plasterers), J Kay (plumber), Eaton Bulfield (painting); IT Oct 1895, FS Dec 1895 [*LGuar* 19.10.1895, 12.12.1895, 27.2.1897].

Sedbergh (CuWY), Sedbergh School, chapel. Replacement of the 1890 chapel damaged by wind in 1893. First plans 1894. IT Mar 1895. C – Brassington Bros & Corney, Settle: tendered price of £4,098. Final cost (noted in 1900 as £7,827 [SSGM, 1894–7, 1900: *LGuar* 23.3.1895: *LStd* 13, 22.3.1895: *KCN* 16.10.1897].

1896
Buxton (Derbys), St James. Spire and W end taken down after being condemned by A&P as unsafe [*Sheffield & Rotherham Independent* 27.2.1896].

Casterton (Cu), Clergy Daughters' School. IT for new classrooms and gymnasium [*LGuar* 18.7.1896: *LStd* 17.7.1896]. A new founder's wing had been tendered for in 1863 but architect(s) not named [*BN* 10, 1863, 403].

Eccles (GM), St Mary the Virgin. Alabaster credence [LL 1, 18].

Grindleton, St Ambrose. Sedilia and credence [NADFAS, 2005].

Lancaster, St Thomas's Schools. Following a report from a school inspector in Aug 1894, plans produced for alterations, including a room and classroom for infants, a cloakroom for infants, a cloakroom for girls, and improved lighting and ventilation for the boys' school. Approved by the Education Department. [*LGuar* 24.10.1896].

Lancaster, additional sheds for Mr Hunt [LRO, MBLA acc 5167/1549].

Silverdale, St John. Organ case (made by Hatch & Sons) for organ made by Abbott & Smith, Leeds [*LGuar* 10.4.1896].

1896–7
Altrincham (Ch), St George. Nave and aisles, replacing work of

1799. Design 1895 [Breton, B 1999 *The Story of St George's Altrincham*, 46–50].

Staveley (CuL), St Mary. Plans 1896. Pews removed, reseated, reroofed, five-bay oak arcade inserted to replace rubble piers. Estimate £1,000 [*Carnforth News* 13.8.1896: notes in church]. Pulpit dated 1899 looks like A&P work.

1897
Barrow-in-Furness (CuL), North Lonsdale Hospital, laundry. Design and specification 1896 [CRO(B), BT/HOSP/NL 8].

Bootle (CuC), village cross. [BE].

Casterton (CuW), Holy Trinity. Reredos. C – R Bridgeman, Lichfield [*Lunesdale Magazine* 1897, ex info Margaret Mellor].

Lancaster, Bowerham School. Classroom [LRO, MBLA acc 5167/1629].

Lancaster, Girls' Blue Coat School, Middle Street. IT for additions [*LGuar* 30.10.1897, 6.11.1897: *BN* 73, 1897, 712]. As tendering was late in the year, work would have continued into the following one.

Lancaster, Royal Albert Asylum Storey Home for nurses [LSMR, PRN31022-MLA27813].

Lymm (Ch), market cross. Repairs. Design Aug 1897 [LL 1, 65].

Mellor, St Mary. Renovated; the Dodgson monument placed inside the church and a substitute erected over the family vault, the Hargreaves, Dodgson and Troy windows protected with sheet glass, organ added by Edwin Smith of Blackburn, new font. CC – J Hatch & Sons; font carved by Varley, Blackburn, the cover by Harry Hems [*BN* 74, 1898, 57]. BE suggests the E lancets are apparently from the P&A restoration, 1899 [*sic*].

Morecambe, Holy Trinity. New chancel, organ chamber and vestries; additional 69 seats. Drawings 1896. Estimate £1,160 [drawings in church, ex info JP: *LGuar* 6.2.1897, 21.8.1898].

Rossall, Rossall School. Alterations to N range of quadrangle [LBS 184734]. Drawing for proposed alteration to school room, Feb 1897 [Rossall School drawings collection, ex info DM].

c 1897
Halton, Manor House. Home of HAP. New wing added to rear and internal alterations [ex info JP].

1897–8
Acton (Ch), St Mary. General restoration; N wall of N aisle rebuilt, new heating chamber and apparatus, clerestory of 1757 rebuilt, plaster ceilings removed, refloored, reseated, new pulpit, new porches and doors. Chief benefactors – Lord Tollemache (rector) and Sutton Timmis [*BN* 75, 1898, 317: *B* 108, 1915, 312: BE].

Dolphinholme, St Mark. Replaced a 'very unsightly' church of 1839–40. Design 1896. *c* £3,300 (estimate £2,601 in 1896). 497 seats. C – J Hatch & Sons, who subcontracted the rubble masonry to Thoms of Grange-over-Sands. Consecrated 25.1.1899, so no doubt the work was completed in 1898 [ICBS 9954: *LGuar* 2.10.1897, 28.1.1899].

Greenock (Renfrewshire), St John. A&P invited to draw up plans for an additional vestry [list of documents held in the parish].

Grindleton, St Ambrose. Rebuilt except for tower and S side [BE].

Lancaster, Ripley Hospital. Single-storey wood- and metal-working classrooms, and also a gymnasium. Designs and IT Aug 1897 [LM, 99.60: *LGuar* 21, 28.8.1897].

Winsford (Ch), St Chad, Over. Vestries and organ chamber [ICBS 9983].

1897–1900
Flookburgh (CuL), St John the Baptist. Replacement for a church of 1777 on a different site and a memorial. New site given by the Misses Harrison of Flookburgh House. Main benefactors – members of the Cavendish family, especially Victor Cavendish MP and his wife Evelyn. *c* £12,000 (original estimate £8,000). CC – Anthony Blair, Allithwaite (masonry), Bradwell & Co, Barrow (carpentry), Chippendale, Grange-over-Sands (slating), A Moorhouse, Kirkby Lonsdale (plumbing and glazing) [CRO(K), WPR 79/1/2/4: *KCN* 11.12.1897: *BN* 73, 1897, 670, 866; 79, 1900, 571].

1898
Barrow-in-Furness (CuL), North Lonsdale Hospital. Plans (Sept) for new medical wing for women and children [CRO(B), BT/HOSP/NL 8]. Demolished.

Bolton-le-Sands, St Michael (now Holy Trinity). White alabaster reredos in memory of the Revd J D Grimke carved by R Bridgeman & Sons, Lichfield. *c* £600 [*LGuar* 21.5.1898].

Bretherton, St John the Baptist. Restored [dated rainwater head: *B* 75, 1898, 321].

Burnley, St Andrew. Additions to chancel and new vestries. Plans 1897 [LRO, PR 3100/4/4–10].

Bury (GM), St Paul. Side galleries removed, nave roof repaired, new choir stalls and font [*BN* 75, 1898, 90].

Galgate, new farmhouse called 'Hampson', Hampson Green. For W G Welch. IT published 1 Jan so the design is of 1897 [*LGuar* 1.1.1898: ex info CS]. Confusingly the *LGuar* [5.2.1898 and 12.2.1898] published an IT for alterations and additions to an unspecified building at Hampson Green: uncertain if these two schemes are related.

Lancaster, St George (Marsh Mission Church), Willow Lane. Brick school/chapel and three classrooms, £2,100. 300 seats. Main contractor – J Hatch & Sons, W Harrison (brickwork), T Cross & Sons (plastering), T Riding (painting), Calvert & Heald (plumbing) [*LGuar* 9.7.1898]. Demolished *c* 2000.

Lancaster, Ripley Hospital. Design (Mar) for single-storey sanatorium [LM, 99.60].

Melling, St Wilfrid. Design for sedilia, May 1898 [LL 1, 67].

Prestwich (GM), church. Design (Mar) for a church with six-bay nave and passage aisles. Apparently unexecuted [LM, 99.60].

1898–9
Billington, St Leonard. Reredos. C – J Hatch & Sons, carving by R Bridgeman, Lichfield [(Blackburn) *Weekly Standard* 4.2.1899].

1898–1900
Morecambe, St Barnabas. New church. Plans had been prepared as far back as 1893 when the cost was estimated at £4,895. IT Aug 1896 but the FS was not laid till Jul 1898. Total cost estimated at £6,500, but initial scheme was to provide 400 seats at a cost of £3,500, involving the chancel and three bays of the nave and structures on the N. These new parts would be joined to the existing temporary church; in the event, five bays of the nave and aisles were built at a cost of £4,214. C – John Edmondson, Morecambe [ICBS 9782: *LGuar* 11.3.1893, 29.8.1896, 23.7.1898, 8, 7.7.1900].

Slyne, St Luke. New church. 180 seats. £2,358. CC – John Dawson, Kirkby Lonsdale (masonry), Holmes & Son, Arkholme (joinery), Abbott & Co, Lancaster (plumbing & glazing), Cross & Sons, Lancaster (tiling) [FS: *LGuar* 2, 9.7.1898, 4, 7.7.1900: *B* 79, 1900, 112].

1898–1901
Atherton (GM), St Anne, Hindsford. New church. Design 1898. £9,000; land given by Lord Lilford. Seats for 450. Converted to flats 2003–4 [*BN* 74, 1898, 159: Lunn 1971, 191: *K* 1913, 86: BE].

Lancaster, Royal Albert Asylum Ashton Wing. CC – J Thoms, Grange-over-Sands (masonry), J Season, Leeds (slating), O Lister, Ilkley (plastering & glazing), Seward & Co, Lancaster (plumbing & heating), E Payne, Lancaster (painting). Architects' estimate £15,000 but lowest tender was £19,440 [*LGuar* 23.4.1898, 30.4.1898, 25.6.1898, 1.10.1898, 28.9.1901].

Morecambe, St John the Divine, Sandylands. New church. *c* £7,000; site given by Revd C T Royds; reredos and altar given by Mrs John Royds. Seating for 600. C – John Edmondson, Morecambe [inscription: *LGuar* 21.5.1898, 19.10.1901]. In late 1898 the intention was to build only the nave and N aisle [*LGuar* 10.12.1898]. Crossing tower and spire never built.

Waddington (WY), St Helen. Largely rebuilt except for tower [BE].

1898–1902
Lancaster, Nazareth House. For the Sisters of Nazareth of Hammersmith; RC home for waifs and strays. CC – B Graham & Sons, Huddersfield (masonry), T Hird, Keighley (most of the carpentry; he had been the orginal main contractor), J Hatch & Sons (joinery), Hill & Nelson, Morecambe (slating), O Lister, Ilkley (plastering) [LRO, MBLA acc 5167/1738: *LGuar* 26.11.1898, 3.12.1898, 25.1.1902, 15.2.1902].

1899
Accrington, St Peter's vicarage. Plans being made for proceeding Oct 1898 [(Blackburn) *Weekly Standard* 15.10.1898].

Arkholme, St John the Baptist. Plans 1895 for over £2,000 of work which included a W tower (not built). Restored; wall-plaster removed and walls pointed inside and out, roof reslated, ceilings removed, N wall rebuilt and new windows inserted, and part of S side similarly dealt with, new S porch, and on the N organ chamber and vestry, chancel extended 18ft, window inserted in W wall, new floors, seats, screen and pulpit; CC – J Dawson, Kirkby Lonsdale (masonry), W Holmes & Sons, Arkholme (joinery), Slinger, Ingleton (slater & plasterer), Moorhouse, Kirkby Lonsdale (plumbing, glazing & heating apparatus) [ICBS 9978: *LGuar* 8.8.1896, 24.6.1899].

Halton, Halton Hall. E wing [ex info Bill Hosfield/JP]. Robinson [1991, 193], mentions 'A C19 wing designed by Paley & Austin' but gives no date.

Heversham, Heversham House. Alterations by HJA for himself. C – W Gradwell jnr, Barrow-in-Furness [ALA].

Keswick (CuW), Keswick School of Industrial Arts. Proposed additions [CRO (Carlisle), DB 111/23].

Lancaster, Church Street. Rebuilding front of E & J L Milner's business premises [*LGuar* 25.2.1899].

Lancaster, St Peter (RC). Chancel stalls, carved by R Bridgeman, Lichfield [LL 3, 77: BE].

Lancaster, Infirmary, consulting room. Plans [LRO, MBLA acc 5167/1774].

Morecambe, St Lawrence. Stalls. C – J Hatch & Sons, carving by R Bridgeman, Lichfield [*LGuar* 14.10.1899].

Preesall, St Oswald. New church. *c* £3,450; land given by Mrs Elletson of Parrox Hall. Plan and perspective signed by HJA, dated Jan 1896 [drawing in church: Bulmer 1913, 212: BE].

Rossall, Rossall School. IT for museum. Quantity surveyor – Wright & Son [*B* 10.6.1899, 582: *Manchester Guardian* 3, 10.6.1899].

1899–1900
Lytham St Anne's, St Thomas. New church. Designs 1892 for a competition: P&A selected from a field of three. Plans had 'already been adopted' by 1895. Cost put at £8,760 for 804 seats in 1898. Tower, porch and two bays of nave not built; this reduced scheme provided 600 seats (whole scheme for 800). CC – Smith Bros, Burnley, and J Hatch & Sons, Lancaster [ICBS 10134: *B* 64, 1893, 69: *BN* 79, 1900, 9: Slater 1895, 462]. *Academy Architecture* [1896, 62], shows a turret and spirelet at SW corner of the chancel and no tower.

Woodplumpton, St Anne. Restoration: new windows, N aisle reroofed, arcades repaired, and vestry extended [LRO PR 3250 /4/6, 4/8]. 1908 – vicarage extended [ex info JP].

1900
Altrincham (Ch), St Alban, Broadheath. Chancel and two bays of nave and aisles built [BE].

Barrow-in-Furness (CuL), North Lonsdale Hospital. Design for screen to servants' hall [CRO(B), BT/HOSP/NL 8].

Blackburn, St James. A&P recommended the design of A R Gradwell of Blackburn (from among those by various architects') for a tower to be built under a £1,000 bequest from John Bolton. To be 85ft high plus a slated spire, taking the overall height to 120ft [(Blackburn) *Weekly Standard* 15.12.1900].

Lancaster, warehouse and stables, Bulk Street, for the Lancaster & Skerton Co-operative Society. IT [*LGuar* 24.2.1900, 3.3.1900].

Sedbergh (CuWY), Sedbergh School. Alterations to Mr Mackie's house including extension to the boy's dining room and alterations to the bathroom. Estimated at £1,077. C – Richard Greenwood [SSGM, 1900].

1901
Cartmel (CuL), Aynsome Agricultural Experimental Station, chemical laboratory and model dairy. For J S & T M Remington [datestone: undated prospectus in CRO(B), BDTB 67/75, 2, 3: *Furness Year Book 1902*, 256].

Whittington. Design for iron gable cross [LL 1, 91].

1900–1
Balterley (St), All Saints' mission church. Built as a memorial to Thomas Fletcher Twemlow [*B* 108, 1915, 312: DM].

Broughton-in-Furness (CuL), St Mary Magdalene. SW tower built at the expense of Lord Cross, replacing one of 1781 [*BN* 80, 1901, 750: Greenhalgh, W 1990 *The History of the Church in Broughton-in-Furness*, 17, 19]. Design similar to that at Flookburgh.

1901
Lancaster, St Peter (RC). New baptistry. CC – J Hatch & Sons, and Boulton & Sons, Cheltenham (sculpture), Singer & Sons, Frome and London (ironwork), Shrigley & Hunt (windows). Plans and IT 1899 [LRO, MBLA acc 5167/1742: *LGuar* 18.3.1899, 21.9.1901].

Lancaster, shops and business premises, Church/New Streets. For the Lancaster & Skerton Equitable Industrial Co-operative Society, IT Dec 1900 [datestone: *LGuar* 24.11.1900, 1.12.1900].

Lancaster, Skerton, temporary shop of wood. For the Lancaster & Skerton Co-operative Society. [*LGuar* 18.5.1901]. *BN* [80, 1901, 886], notes IT for rebuilding shops at Skerton for the Society. *LGuar* [22, 29.6.1901], has a tender notice for rebuilding shops and business premises for the Society.

Lancaster, stables, Bryer Street. Plans for the Lancaster & Skerton Co-operative Society [LRO, MBLA acc 5167/8/1964].

Lancaster, two lock-up shops, Lune Street, Skerton. Plans for the Lancaster & Skerton Co-operative Society [LRO, MBLA acc 5167/8/1985].

Lancaster, infants' school, off Main Street, Skerton. Additions for the Lancaster School Board. Plan and IT [LRO, MBLA acc 5167/8/2032: *LGuar* 16, 23.11.1901].

Manchester, St Margaret, Burnage. N aisle. £1,300 [FS: *BN* 80, 1901, 216: Pollard 2000, 7]. Design for pulpit, Nov 1901 [LL 1, 81]. Design for font, nd [LL 1, 90].

1901–2
High Bentham (NY), St Margaret. New chancel, transepts, organ chamber and vestries; plaster ceiling in nave removed, nave reseated, tower screen, pulpit. £2,014. CC – W Bayliff, Kirkby Lonsdale (masonry, Cumberland & Holmes (or Cumberland Bros), Bentham (joinery), John Jackman, Bentham (slating and plastering), W H Greenep, Bentham (painting and plumbing), pulpit made by T Marshall, Bentham. It was intended to rebuild the rest of the 1837 church when funds allowed [*LGuar* 20.4.1901, 8.6.1901, 27.7.1901, 14.6.1902].

Middleton (GM), St Michael. New church. E end and first bay of nave. Replaced a church of 1839. Paid for by the local brewer, J W Lees [BE].

Whicham (CuC), St Mary. Vestries, three new nave windows, reseating and general repairs [ICBS 10264].

1901–3
Kildwick (WY), St Andrew. Chancel extended and nave restored [guidebook by B A Wood: BE].

Llandovery (Carmarthenshire), College. E range, school house and dining hall: alterations to old buildings [*B* 108, 1915, 312: BW]. A&P had been instructed 1899: intended to complete the work by Sept 1900 to include new dining hall and kitchen, four new classrooms, and additional dormitories: estimated £5,500-£6,000. IT Oct 1899 [*Western Mail* 2.8.1899: *North Wales Chronicle* 12.8.1899, 21.10.1899].

Rawtenstall, St Paul, Constable Lee. IT 1900. Original design (with large tower over choir) Nov 1899. IT 1901. 332 seats. Initial estimate £5,000, final cost £7,000 [ICBS 10279: (Blackburn) *Weekly Standard* 23.6.1900: *BN* 80, 1901, 178: *K* 1913, 891: ex info Mrs M Hamer].

1902
Caton, shop and two houses. For the Lancaster & Skerton Co-operative Society. IT [*LGuar* 31.5.1902].

Heversham (CuW), St Peter. Plan of gas pipe installations [CRO(K), WPR 8/9/28].

Lancaster, St Mary. Gothic arch revealed by HJA at W end. Also doorway opened at W end as a memorial to John Hatch (no architect named but presumably HJA). CC – William Harrison (masonry), Hatch & Sons (woodwork) [*LGuar* 8.3.1902].

Lancaster, Church Street. Plans for large additions and alterations for the Lancaster Banking Co. Plan 1901 [LRO, MBLA acc 5167/8/2041: ex info CS].

Lancaster, Co-operative store, Skerton. £1,200. CC – T Mawson (building), R Wilson (joinery), J Liver (slating & plastering), W Abbott (plumbing), W Townley (painting). CW – T Baines [*LGuar* 21.6.1902].

Lancaster, North Road. Shop, workshops and showrooms for Mr Atkinson [LRO, MBLA acc 5167/8/2151]. William Atkinson, a cycle maker, became a very early, small-scale car manufacturer, building the John O'Gaunt model in Lancaster [ex info CS/J Minnis]. Now the Green Ayre pub and a shop.

Lancaster, St Mary. HJA and his wife rebuilt the S porch as a memorial to the latter's parents; design by HJA, estimated at £1,500; faculty applied for 1902 [*LGuar* 5.4.1902].

Liverpool Cathedral. Competition entry by HJA shortlisted by the assessors, R Norman Shaw and G F Bodley [RIBA PA142/1–5; PB290; PB310: *B* 84, 1903, 556 + illustrations].

Overton, St Helen. Restored; plaster removed from walls, new floors, steps and seats, roof repaired, 'plain stone mullions' inserted in three windows. £650. HJA named as architect. Plans no doubt 1901 as faculty to be applied for Apr 1901. C – Brassington Bros & Corney, Settle; plan signed by A&P (Dec 1902) dates the various phases of the church [drawing in church: *LGuar* 22.3.1902, 25.10.1902: *BN* 80, 1901, 26 Apr, xix].

Rossall, Rossall School. Narthex to chapel and NW porch [Rossall School collection/ex info DM].

1903
Barrow-in-Furness (CuL), North Lonsdale Hospital. Plans for new operating room [CRO(B), BT/HOSP/NL 8]. Demolished.

Caton, St Paul, Brookhouse. Reredos presented by Miss Mary Greg, executed by Hatch & Sons, decorated by Shrigley & Hunt [*LGuar* 2.1.1904].

Field Broughton (or Broughton East) (CuL), vicarage. IT [*LGuar* 7, 14.9.1901]. Accounts for work dated Oct 1903. CC – Thoms & Sons, Grange-over-Sands, Parke Bros, Kendal (joiners), T Cross & Sons, Lancaster, and J W Braithwaite, Grange-over-Sands [CRO(K), WPR 86/1/4/14].

Lancaster, Bowerham Road. Plans for shop and warehouse for Lancaster & Skerton Co-operative Society [LRO, MBLA acc 5167/8/2261].

Lancaster, Covell Cross. Unveiled Jun 1903 [LL 1, 42: *LGuar* 26.6.1903: RIBA PB310/2, 8]. The sources cited make it very clear that the date is 1903; yet strangely, the inscription refers to 1902.

Lancaster, Gregson Memorial Hall. Plans for new club room, billard room, reading room and lavatory [LRO, MBLA, acc 5167/2231].

Lancaster, High Street. Plans for alterations to drains and new WC for Miss Michaelson [LRO, MBLA acc 5167/8/2183].

Lancaster, St Peter's Schools (RC). Plans for new club room [LRO, MBLA acc 5167/8/2231].

Pilling, vicarage. Plan of stable block [LRO, PR 3243/2/5].

1903–4
Lancaster, St Mary. Outer N aisle built as a memorial to soldiers of the Royal Lancaster Regiment who fell in the Boer War. The old windows were resited in the new aisle: five were intended to have memorial glass. *c* £3,500. Stained glass by Shrigley & Hunt (E window), Powell & Son (W). CC – J Thoms (masonry), J Hatch & Sons (joinery), R Wilson (plumbing & glazing), T Cross & Sons (slating) [LRO, DDSr 10/3, ff13–15: *LGuar* 2.8.1902, 15.11.1902, 14.5.1904, 23.7.1904].

Ulverston (CuL), St Mary. Chancel extended by one bay: chancel fittings and storm porch to S aisle [inscription: BE].

Worsthorne, St John. Faculty 1902 for new tower and font. Tower given by Sir John O S Thursby in memory of his father Sir J H Thursby. Old vestries at W end removed and seating continued up to the W wall. C – Adam Parker, Burnley [LRO, PR 3114/4/11–12: *Burnley Express* 9.7.1904: *B* 108, 1915, 312].

1903–5
Kings Worthy (Hampshire), 'Kings Worthy Court'. Plans for alterations and additions by HJA for himself, Dec 1903 and Mar 1905 [Hampshire RO, 39M73/BP/320, for both]. HJA purchased this property in Oct 1901. It was sold in May 1915 after his death [ex info Peter Finn, Worthy History Group: APA].

1903–6
Skelmersdale (Me), St Paul. Replaced the old church, closed in 1897 'owing to [its] ruinous condition'. Designs 1902. First phase excluding porches, parish room and upper part of three-stage, embattled tower NE tower. 575 seats. Largest benefactor – Earl of Lathom. CC – J Thoms & Sons, Lancaster (masonry), J Rothwell & Sons, St Helens (other trades) [ICBS 10418: Anon nd [*c* 1903] *Skelmersdale and its New Church*].

1904
Claughton, St Chad. N aisle and porch added, new buttresses on W and S sides, refloored, plaster ceiling removed, new seats, tracery in S windows, floors, pulpit and lectern, *c* £900. CC – A O Thoms (masonry), R S Wright & Sons, Lancaster (joinery), W J Cross, Morecambe (slating), A Moorhouse, Kirkby Lonsdale (plumbing & glazing) [*LGuar* 12.11.1904]. Now disused.

Knowsley (Me), St Mary. Tower screen [BE].

Lancaster, Dallas Place, surgery and residence for Dr P F Mannix. IT [*LGuar* 28.5.1904, 4.6.1904].

Lancaster, Greaves Road, new shop for Lancaster & Skerton Co-operative Society. Plans and IT [LRO, MBLA acc 5167/2316: *LGuar* 11.6.1904, 18.6.1904].

Morecambe, St Barnabas. Font [*LGuar* 16.7.1904].

1904–5
Hertford, All Saints. Church completed by building the W end and tower. Contract £10,366 making the total cost of the church £28,148 [*Hertfordshire Mercury* 4.11.1905].

Leeds, Grammar School, Moorland Road. Large extension. Won in competition [*B* 108, 1915, 312: BE].

Lytham St Anne's, St Thomas. Church completed with tower, porch and two bays of nave; seats increased to 670 [guide: ex info D Buckler].

1904–6
Sedbergh (CuWY), Sedbergh School, Powell Hall and six classrooms. First design 1903. Total cost £11,920 (£3,000 given by Sir Francis Powell) [LM, 99.60: SSGM, 1903–7: *LGuar* 16, 23.4.1906].

1905
Brathay (CuC), Holy Trinity. Additions [ex info DM via JP].

Lancaster, Infirmary. Plans for pavilion room [LRO, MBLA acc 5167/2425].

Pilling, vicarage. Proposed alterations and additions [LRO, PR 3243/2/4].

Wray. Proposal for a memorial to R G W Howson (stone in the churchyard and tablet in the church) [*LGuar* 16.12.1906].

1905–6

Barnacre, All Saints. Built as a memorial to Thomas Henry Rushton by his wife and children. IT 1904 [carved inscription inside tower: *LGuar* 30.4.1904, 7.5.1904: Bulmer 1913, 289].

Broughton (nr Preston), St John the Baptist. Chancel, vestries, organ chamber and restoration [*BN* 91, 1906, 725: Fleetwood-Hesketh 1955, 135]. W gallery demolished.

1905–8

Preston, St Michael & All Angels, Ashton-on-Ribble. Main benefactors – Mr & Mrs William Birley (£2,000) and Frank Calvert [JP]. First phase (chancel, organ chamber and part of nave) cost estimated at £6,047 (including stalls, benches and heating apparatus. C – R Rathbone & Sons, Atherton [FS: *PG* 6.10.1906: *BN* 91, 1906, 242; Crosby, A nd [1995] *The Church of St Michael and All Angels, Ashton on Ribble*].

1906

Bolton-by-Bowland, school. Classrooms added on N [*BN* 27.4.1906, xiv: BE, *W Yorks*].

Kirkby Lonsdale (CuW), 'Green Close', Town End [BE]. For Dr Matthews [JP].

Knutsford (Ch), St Cross. Enlargement of vestries. Contract £265. C – J & J Beaumont, Knutsford [CALS, P189/5/11].

Lancaster, Royal Grammar School. Plans and IT for physical laboratory and other alterations [LRO, MBLA acc 5167/9/2453: *LGuar* 18.11.1905].

Lancaster, Royal Lancaster Infirmary. New 'light' room adjoining the outpatients' Department. *c* £250. A memorial to Lady Ashton paid for by Lord Ashton's workers [*LGuar* 14.7.1906].

Lancaster, St Mary's mission church, Willow Lane. Plans for vestry additions [LRO, MBLA acc 5167/9/2468, 2483]. Demolished.

St Bees (CuC), St Bees School, chapel. FS dated 18.6.1906 so work probably went on into 1907 [BE].

***c* 1906**

Winsford (Ch), St Chad, Over. Restoration. Plans probably 1897 (grant application to the ICBS) involving increasing the seating by 56 to 368 and installing a heating apparatus. Estimated cost £899. Work certified as complete in Mar 1907 [ICBS 9983].

1906–7

Balderstone, St Leonard. NW tower and spire [LRO 3072/4/8, /33: *BN* 90, 1906, 372].

Broughton, St John the Baptist. Sedilia and piscina designed by HJA (1906). Oak reredos and gradine (1907): C – Hatch & Sons, Lancaster [NADFAS, 2003].

Ellel, St John. Replaced a church of 1800 on a different site. PA&P were consulted in 1894 when alternative plans were made for a new church and restoration of the old one. Site given by C H Maxsted of Windermere (HJA seems personally to have approved the site); chancel built by William Gibbins of Hampson as a memorial to his wife, Catherine. Designs Sept 1903; next drawings dated Feb 1906; FS Jul 1906; 380 seats (on chairs). Cost *c* £5,000. Proposed spire never built. CC – A O Thoms, Lancaster (masonry), J Hatch & Sons (woodwork), R Hall & Sons (tiling), Rushton & Pitch (plumbing & glazing), C J Allen ([?stone] carving) [inscription: drawings in parish: *LStd* 27.5.1904: *LGuar* 28.7.1906, 21, 28.9.1907, 5.10.1907: *BN* 91, 1906, 132].

Lancaster, mission chapel, Ridge Lane, Bulk. HJA was architect. 200 seats. £600. C – Edmondson, Morecambe [LRO, MBLA acc 5167/9/2498: *LGuar* 9.2.1907]. Demolished.

1906–8

Lancaster, Storey Institute. Extensions almost doubling the size. Major benefactor, H L Storey who in 1904 had offered £10,000 for the work to commemorate the accession of Edward VII but plans were delayed owing to uncertainty about the effect of the 1902 Education Act. IT Nov 1905. £10,500; land given by the council. CC – R Thompson (masonry & joinery), T & J Till (slating & plastering), Hatch & Sons (wood fittings) [LRO, MBLA acc 5167/9/2464: *LGuar* 7.10.1905, 18, 25.7.1908, 19.9.1908].

1907

Betws-y-Coed (Caernarvonshire), St Mary. IT for tower completion [*BN* 92, 1907, 675]. An IT had been issued in 1902 [*BN* 82, 1902, 78] but nothing, apparently, was done.

Blackburn, St Mark. Designs for renovation and redecoration of roof, and for alterations to chancel [*Blackburn Weekly Telegraph* 19.7.1907].

Broughton (nr Preston). Oak reredos given by Miss Lucy Wilson. Carving by Hatch & Sons with figure carving by Caleb Allen (both of Lancaster).

Fleetwood, bank for the Lancaster Banking Co [Anon (Stancliffe Estates), 32].

Lancaster, Christ Church. Storey chapel created in memory of Mrs Edward Storey, taking the place of the old organ chamber (organ moved to the S transept); paid for by Edward Storey and his children. C – Hatch & Sons [*LGuar* 12.10.1907].

Lancaster, Moor Lane/Woodville Street. Plans to convert dwelling and shop into lock-up premises for the Lancaster & Skerton Co-operative Society [LRO, MBLA acc 167/9/2583].

Morecambe, Lancaster & Skerton Co-operative Society, stables. IT [*LGuar* 16.2.1907].

Silverdale, village institute. £500–£600 [*LGuar* 30.11.1907, 14.12.1907].

Skelmersdale (Me), St Paul. Alabaster pulpit, carved by C J Allen, Lancaster [*LGuar* 13.7.1907].

Stockport (GM), Heaviley, St George's schools [Jones 1997, 25].

Tunstall. Restored, *c* £1,000; new vestry, reroofed (the original idea to repair the roof was abandoned because of its poor condition), walls cleaned, masonry pointed, organ chamber enlarged. CC – J Hatch & Sons, T Cross & Sons, J Dean & A Moorhouse of Kirkby Lonsdale [*LGuar* 28.12.1907].

1907–8

Barrow-in-Furness (CuL), St Mary, Walney Island. Replaced a S&P chapel (*see* 1852–3) to serve the greatly expanding population of

Vickerstown created by Vickers Ltd for their workers: land given by the company [CRO(B), BPR 20/C/16: *BN* 93, 6.7.1907, xv; 93, 1907, 529].

1907–10
St Bees (CuC), St Bees School, headmaster's house, library and laboratories [BE].

1907–11
Kendal (CuW), St George. Chancel. HJA published a design in 1904 when an appeal for a complete rebuild was made [Anon (Stancliffe Estates), 40: BE].

1908
Haverthwaite (CuL), St Anne. Plans for internal rearrangement and lengthening of chancel [CRO(K), WPR 90/41].

Newland, Newland Hall, near Galgate. Rear kitchen wing [ex info Colonel Carey Outram to JP].

Unsworth (GM), St George. IT for vestries and porch [*BN* 94, 1908, 372].

c 1908
Bolton (GM), St George. Assessors for the 'restoration scheme' [*B* 108, 1915, 312]. The church was given a new chancel and S chapel in 1908–10 by James Lomax-Simpson to whom Bernard Austin was an assistant. A&P were presumably assessing that scheme but nothing is known for sure.

1908–9
Bretherton, St John the Baptist. Chancel and vestries added [*BN* 2.7.1909, xiv: *B* 108, 1915, 312].

1908–10
Widnes (Me), St Mary, West Bank. Replaced a church of 1858 on a different site. IT Sept 1907. Site cost £5,400: total £16,669 of which T Sutton Timmis and his six children gave £8,000, William Gossage & Sons £3,000, and F H Gossage £1,000. 770 seats [*BN* 20.9.1907, xvi: Anon nd [1960] *Widnes Parish Church of St Mary; a Short History and Description Published on the 50th Anniversary of the Consecration*: Diggle, G E 1961 *A History of Widnes*, 121].

1909
Alderley (Ch), St Mary. Design for tower screen: also churchwardens' seats and lighting estimated for by Isaac Massey & Sons, and probably other minor work [CALS, P143/6/8].

Over Kellett, St Cuthbert. Restored: walls covered with roughcast and dormers inserted [Bulmer 1913, 364].

Skipton (WY), Holy Trinity. N, S and W galleries removed, N transept and vestries added. Design 1908 [*B* 94, 1908, 343; 97 1909, 649]. C – Brassington & Corney. CW – T Baines [JB/JP].

Tatham Fells, The Good Shepherd. Lychgate [*LGuar* 19.6.1909].

1909–10
Birkdale (Me), St John. N aisle and arcade, and vestries. £2,000 bequeathed for the endowment and enlargement by George Cheetham Hussey (d 1903). 186 extra seats planned. A&P had drawn up a plan in Jan 1905 for this work which was somewhat revised in Jun 1908. CC – Halliwell Bros (masonry), Buck & Hodson (bricklayer), J Marshall (tiling & plastering), Thomas Stucliffe (plumbing & glazing) [inscription at W end: *Southport Guardian* 19.6.1909: ex info Stuart Baker].

Leigh (GM), St Mary. Choir vestry on N [BE].

Manchester, St Wilfrid, Newton Heath. Mission church for Rossall School. Initial plans probably 1907: detailed designs from Mar 1908. Four-bay nave and aisles, projecting W baptistry, and canted E end. 504 seats [drawings formerly at church catalogued by DM: ICBS 10861: BE]. Font design Jan 1911 [LL 1, 100].

Harrogate (NY), St Andrew, Starbeck. Replaced a small school-cum-mission building of 1889 seating 200. Seating for 608. £6,800. Chief benefactors – W Freeman JP (£500), William Sykes (£400), G Richardson (£200). CC – Isaac Dickinson, Harrogate (masonry), John Tomlinson, Leeds (joinery), J Woodfield, Wakefield (plumbing & glazing), F Fortune, Harrogate (plasterer) [ICBS 10858: *B* 97, 1909, 343: *BN* 99, 1910, 349: Jones 1985, 12–25].

Wigan (GM), St Matthew, Highfield. Nave and S aisle extended W at cost of Cuthbert B H Blundell. Over £2,000. C – R Rathbone & Son, Atherton. The work was consecrated in Jul so it may well have been begun in 1909 [BE].

1909–11
Natland (CuW), St Mark. Replaced a church of 1825. In memory of William Dillworth Crewdson of Kendal (d 1908) who had given a large sum towards the rebuilding cause. A&P had been consulted by Jul 1908 and considered that adding N and S aisles and making repairs was a possibility, but strongly recommended rebuilding, proposing 259 seats at a cost of £4,910 or £5,010. IT Nov 1908 [CRO (K), WPR 25/1/2/4: ICBS 10850: *LGuar* 3.10.1908, 14, 21.11.1908]. 1910–11 designs for altar, altar rails, reredos, lectern and font [LL 1, 83–6, 99, 100].

1910
Lancaster, St Mary. Pulpit repaired [LRO, PR 3262/4/19].

Lancaster, 'Netherleigh', Westbourne Road. Plans for a music room and study Apr 1910 [LRO, MBLA acc 5167/2794: *LGuar* 23.4.1910]. Plans and IT for a garage and converting a stable into a cottage Oct 1910 [LRO, MBLA acc 5167/9/2819]. Both for Mr Robert Helme, brother of Norval Helme, MP and mayor. Now subdivided. Gardens by T H Mawson & Sons for 'Netherleigh' and HJA's house, 'The Knoll', carried out about the time of these works [LRL, DDPC 4/2/32]

Leigh (GM), St Mary. Tower refaced [BE].

c 1910
Grasmere (Cu), St Oswald. Letter [11.1.1911] from T Cross & Sons re certificate from A&P for second instalment for contract for roughcasting etc [CRO(K), WPR 91/1/3/18].

1910–14
Cockerham, St Michael. Church of 1814 rebuilt: medieval tower retained and tower arch opened. Scheme to rebuild the chancel mooted in 1908. Cost £5,000 of which £3,050 was contributed by

Frederick James Harrison from Hare Appletree and the Harrison Shipping Line of Liverpool in memory of his ancestors who had been yeomen in Cockerham. C – J Hatch & Sons [inscription: *LGuar* 31.10.1908, 12, 19.2.1910, 8.10.1910: *The Times* 21.12.1914: Bulmer 1913, 265].

Kendal (CuW), St George. Additions. PA&P had reported on the need for a new E end in 1894 and A&P did so again in 1904. Chancel, organ chamber and vestries; design 1904 (if not earlier); IT Mar 1910 [ICBS 10628: *LGuar* 12, 19.3.1910: BE].

1911

Barnacre, parsonage. IT [Datestone: *LGuar* 10.6.1911: *BN* 16.6.1911, xii].

Bolton (GM), church, Heaton. Reference to a tender being open for a church by A&P [*The Times* 23.8.1911].

Lancaster, St Mary. Nave reroofed (plaster ceiling removed), plaster removed from nave W wall and W side of chancel arch, chancel floor raised and sanctuary extended W, new heating apparatus; A&P had reported their proposals in Sept 1910. £2,500. CC – A O Thoms (masonry), Hatch & Sons (joinery), T Cross & Sons (slating & plastering). R Wilson (plumbing & glazing), J Hargreaves (marble work) [*LGuar* 24.9.1910, 26.8.1911, 25.11.1911].

Lancaster, 49 Market Street. Plans to convert shop into a bank for the Preston Savings Bank [LRO, MBLA acc 5167/10/2856].

Manchester, St Margaret, Burnage. Unexecuted plans to complete the church at the W end (including a tower and extra W bay) and add a morning chapel [Pollard 2000, 10].

Middleton (GM), St Michael. Nave completed [FS dated 20.7.1911 at W end (hence work may well have gone on into 1912)].

Sedbergh (CuWY), Sedbergh School. New carpenter's shop. A&P's fee £26 5s [SSGM, 1911–12].

Skelmersdale (Me), St Paul. Plans to complete by adding a porch, baptistry and vestry as a memorial to the Earl of Lathom: apparently not carried out (*see* 1925) [*BN* 100, 1911, 436].

Stockport (GM), Buxton Road Cemetery, monument. Over the grave of George Fearn, founder of St George's church, a replica of the church's tower and spire by HJA. [Anon nd [*c* 1980] *St George's Church, Stockport, consecrated 25th February 1897*, 2].

1911–12

Bradford (WY), St Margaret, Thornbury. £8,264 of which £5,000 was given anonymously for the fabric. CC – Isaac Dickinson, Harrogate (masonry), R S Wright, Lancaster (carpentery and joinery), and T & J Till, Lancaster (slating & plastering) [papers in parish: *BN* 100, 1911, 577]. Demolished 1991.

Great Harwood, St John [Anon (Stancliffe Estates), 48: BE]. Tender 1910 [*BN* 16.12.1910, xi]. Demolished 2010.

Worksop (Notts), St Anne. [*BN* 24.2.1911, xiv: ex info the Revd F T Beech].

1911–13

Bolton (GM), St Margaret, Halliwell. Work begun Nov 1911, FS 1912 [FS: *K* 1913, 253]. N vestry not built. The date of 1903 in BE and JP is incorrect.

1912

Barnoldswick, Holy Trinity. Design for competition assessed by J O Scott [LRO, PR 3440/4/89/1–2].

Lancaster, shop and dwelling, Sibsey Street/Westbourne Road. For Lancaster & Skerton Co-operative Society. Plans and IT [LRO, MBLA acc 5167/10/2863: *LGuar* 27.1.1912].

Lancaster, Church Street. Plans for alterations for the Manchester & Liverpool District Banking Co [LRO, MBLA acc 5167/10/2864].

Lancaster, Gregson Memorial Lecture Hall, Williamson Street. Plans and IT [LRO, MBLA acc 5167/10/2888: *LGuar* 8.6.1912].

Lancaster, Territorial Army hall, Phoenix Street. Plans for alterations [LRO, MBLA acc 5167/10/2915].

Lydiate (Me), St Thomas. Chancel, S chapel, N vestry etc [BE].

Milnthorpe (CuW), St Thomas. Alterations to W end. Design for dossal [CRO(K), WPR 88/1/2/17–18].

Sedbergh (CuWY), Sedbergh School, Malim Lodge (now the Bursary) [SSGM, 30.1.1913].

1912–14

Arnside (CuW), St James. Plans for alterations and addition of S aisle [CRO(K), WPR 39/1/4/2; BE].

1913

Bolton (GM), church, Deane. Report by A&P saying extensive repairs needed, including rebuilding of the clerestory [MRO, L85/2/16/1–4].

Field Broughton (CuL), St Peter. Plan of drains round church [CRO(K), WPR 86/1/3/10].

Heysham, shops and nine houses for Lancaster & District Co-operative Society, Main Street/Barrow Lane. IT [*LGuar* 6.12.1913].

Lancaster, Lancaster Cricket & Bowling Club, Lune Road. Plans for alterations to pavilion [LRO, MBLA acc 5167/10/2932].

Milnthorpe (CuW), St Thomas. Proposed new vestry [CRO(K), WPR 88/1/2/19].

Morecambe, St Barnabas. S aisle and organ chamber added. Design 1912 when the cost estimated at £1,502 to increase seating by 116 to 515 [ICBS 11176].

Newland, Newland Hall near Galgate. Billiard room, entrance hall [ex info Colonel Carey Outram to JP].

1913–14

Aughton (Me), St Saviour. Parclose screen [BE].

Blackburn, St Silas. Porch and W tower (104ft high) built but the originally intended spire was abandoned. C – E Lewis & Sons, Blackburn. Cost over £6,000 [Whalley 1990, 8, 14–15].

Manchester, rectory for St Wilfrid, Newton Heath. [22 drawings formerly at the church, catalogued by DM].

Shrewsbury, Shrewsbury School. Extension to swimming baths

and to the school house of his former housemaster, A F Chance. Job architect Geoffrey L Austin [ex info Shrewsbury School archives].

Standish (GM), St Wilfrid. E vestries [LRO, PR 3134/4/17–20: BE].

Thornton, Christ Church. Chancel added to a church of 1836 [*LGaz* 1.10.1836: BE].

1913–15
Leck St Peter. Rebuilt after a fire in Oct 1913. IT Nov 1913. *c* £5,000 [LL 1, 17: *LGuar* 25.10.1913, 29.11.1913: *Lancaster Observer* 1.4.1915]. C – Brassington & Corney (joinery, slating and plastering). CW – T Baines [JB/JP].

1914
Blawith (CuC), St John the Baptist. Chancel arch and top part of E wall rebuilt. £196. C – A O Thoms [CRO(B), 18/W3/4–7].

Goosnargh, St Mary. Pulpit, replacing one of 1707 [information in church].

Grange-over-Sands (CuL), St Paul. Plans to rebuild [CRO(K), WPR 100/W 4]. Unexecuted.

Grange-over-Sands (CuL), Wesleyan chapel. IT for vestry [*LGuar* 18.4.1914].

Hornby, institute. IT [*LGuar* 21.2.1914].

Lancaster, Prospect Street. Plans for new warehouse at premises of the Lancaster & District Co-operative Society [LRO, MBLA acc 5167/10/2957].

Morecambe, shop, Beach Street, Bare. For the Lancaster & District Co-operative Society. IT Dec 1913 [datestone: *LGuar* 6.12.1913: *BN* 105, 1913, 890].

Sedbergh (CuWY), Sedbergh School. Plans for new boarding house. Not executed because of war [SSGM, 1914].

1914–15
Basford (St), St Mark. E end and three bays of nave and aisles [Bragg 1995, 29–43]. A design existed in May 1903 for an aisled church with SE tower and spire (and A&P-style square-headed windows in the aisle) shown on publicity for a 'Grand Bazaar' but no architect is noted [Bragg 1995, 27]. A report in 1907 indicates a new church costing £6,000 was planned but again no architect(s) named [*B* 93, 1907, 653]. The temporary W wall was rebuilt and the church finished off in 1971 by Charles R Lewis [Bragg 1995, 96–102].

1915
Blackburn, St Silas. Alabaster reredos, made in Italy [church guide *c* 2000, 15].

Caton 'Moor Cottage', Brookhouse (now 'Neville House'). Alterations for Mark Rathbone [Garnett, E 2007 *The Dated Buildings of South Lonsdale*, 2 edn, 61].

Lancaster, East Road. Plans for alterations and additions for the Revd M K Cooper [LRO, MBLA acc 5167/10/3006].

Lancaster, 'The Knoll' [HJA's former home], Westbourne Road. Plans for new cloakroom, lavatory and bay window for Annie E Helme [LRO, MBLA acc 5167/10/2995].

Preston, St Michael & All Angels, Ashton-on-Ribble. W end 1915. Upper part of tower never built [Crosby, A nd (1995) *The Church of St Michael and All Angels, Ashton on Ribble*].

Singleton, St Anne. Stalls, reading desk vestry cupboard and screen. Proposed new lights in nave dormer and W windows [LRO, PR 3224/4/32–5, 40].

1916
Darwen, St Barnabas. Proposed N aisle [LRO, PR 3141/4/11, 13–15].

Lancaster, Royal Lancaster Infirmary. Plans for temporary ward [LRO, MBLA acc 5167/10/3010].

1917
Lancaster, Christ Church. Memorial brass to Private J W Cockroft (died on service in France) [*Lancaster Grammar School Magazine* Mar 1917, ex info CS].

Wigan (GM), St Matthew, Highfield. Hollington stone reredos in memory of Colonel Henry B H Blundell. C – R Bridgeman & Sons, Lichfield [Cooke 1993, 77–8].

1918–19
Atherton (GM), St John the Baptist. Correspondence from A&P regarding a proposed memorial chapel [MRO, L177/2/6/1–6].

1919
Atherton (GM), St Michael, Howe Bridge. Stalls [BE].

Beetham (CuW). War memorial Celtic cross in village. C – A O Thoms. Unveiled 18.1.1920 so no doubt largely complete in 1919 [ex info Ian Lewis: BE].

Burton- in-Kendal (CuW), St James. Faculty for war memorial cross in churchyard [ex info Ian Lewis].

Kirkby Lonsdale (CuW). A&P to be commissioned to design a war memorial, probably in the churchyard [*LGuar* 10.5.1919].

Lancaster, Christ Church. 25ft-high Derbyshire stone war memorial cross in churchyard. £400. CC – A O Thoms; sculpture by Frank Birch and G H Leader of Lancaster [*LGuar* 20.12.1919, 17.1.1920].

Lancaster, 'Fairlight', Brettargh Road, Haverbreaks (now 'Emmanuel House'). Plans for alterations for Thomas Bowes-Wilson [LRO, MBLA acc 5167/10/3064]. Occupied until Apr 1921 by Geoffrey Austin, Hubert's son and Thomas's son-in-law, and his family.

Lytham St Anne's, St Anne. Baptistry [DM card index].

***c* 1919**
Great Salkeld (CuC), St Cuthbert. War memorial cross [*K* 1929, 240].

1919–20
Pilling, St John the Baptist. 26ft-high Stancliffe stone war memorial cross in churchyard. C – A O Thoms [*LGuar* 6.3.1920].

Preston, St John. Designs for war memorial cross and tablet [LRO, PR 2845/27/3].

Sedbergh (CuWY), Sedbergh School. Science Building [SSGM, 1919–20].

1920
Bolton (GM), All Souls. Oak and alabaster war memorial on N side of nave [conservation plan for the Churches Conservation Trust, 2007, 26].

Cross-a-Moor, Swarthmoor, Ulverston (CuL). War memorial cross, sculpted by Fairbairn & Hull of Barrow. Identical to that at Barbon (CuW) [ex info Ian Lewis].

Halton, memorial cross (of Stancliffe stone) and village institute. Together they constitute a war memorial. *c* £2,000. CC – A O Thoms; sculpture by H F Birch and G H Leader (cross): building work (presumably the institute) Wright & Sons [*LGuar* 3.4.1920: Dennis, J (ed) 2006 *The Last Post: War Memorials of Lancaster and Morecambe*, 82–4].

Lancaster, George Street. Plans to convert two shops into a bank for the District Bank [LRO, MBLA acc 5167/10/3129].

Lancaster, Penny Street/Brock Street. Plans to convert two shops into a bank for the District Bank [LRO, MBLA acc 5167/10/3131].

Over Wyresdale, Tarnbrook. War memorial cross. *c* £100. Site given by the Earl of Sefton. C – A O Thoms [*LGuar* 30.10.1920].

Pendleton (GM), St James. Wall memorial tablet and low chancel screen [MRO, L115/3/32/1–23].

Lytham St Anne's, St Anne. War memorial baptistry. £1,600. C – A O Thoms [guidebook 1973, 6].

Sedbergh (CuW), Sedbergh School. Designs (also in 1920) in connection with Powell Hall [LM, 99.60]. HAP was involved with new panelling at Powell Hall in 1925 [SSGM, 1925].

c 1920
Kirkby Lonsdale (CuW), St Mary's churchyard. War memorial with Norman detailing [BE].

1921
Ambleside (CuW), St Mary. War memorial cross in churchyard sculpted by Birch & Leader, *c* £450 [ex info Ian Lewis citing parish magazine, Apr 1921].

Barbon (CuW). War memorial cross in village. Identical to that at Cross-a-Moor, Swarthmoor, Ulverston [ex info Ian Lewis].

Basford (St), St Mark. Sicilian marble tablet for memorial window in N transept. C – Robert Bridgeman & Sons, Lichfield [Bragg 1995, 46, 51].

Caton. War memorial cross by HAP. £650. CC – A O Thoms and J Parkinson [*LGuar* 9.7.1921].

Harrogate (NY), Christ Church. War memorial cross outside the church [Jones 1985, 17].

Hornby. War memorial cross by HAP. £180. Used stones from the old market cross for a base [*LGuar* 6.8.1921]. Inscription says 're-erected 1920'.

Morecambe, war memorial, Promenade. Designed by James Tarney, 1920. C – Kirkpatrick Manchester [*LGuar* 19.6.1959: ex info CS].

Staveley (CuL). War memorial cross in village [ex info Ian Lewis].

Stockport (GM), St George, Heaviley. Screens to N and S of the organ chamber [Jones 1997, 26].

1922
Preston, St John. Proposed S aisle and vestries [LRO, PR 2845/27/5].

Staveley (CuW), St James. Plans for new aisle and organ chamber [CRO(K), WPR 68/1/4/2].

1923
Ulverston (CuL), St Mary. War memorial chapel. Plans 1921 [CRO(B), BPR 2/I/2/30: BE].

1924
Lancaster, St Mary. Shrine to contain roll of honour of the King's Own Royal Lancaster Regiment Chapel [*The Times* 20.6.1924].

Little Lever, St Matthew. Tower completed 1924 [inscription].

1924–5
Dalton-in-Furness (Cu), St Mary. Estimate and preliminary plan for proposed side chapel [CRO(B), BPR 1/C/24/1].

1924–6
Leeds, Grammar School. Elementary science and biology laboratories. £7,802 + £488 architect's commission [LRO, DDSr 10/1 fols 56–60; 10/3, fol 8].

1924–c 1926
Sedbergh (CuWY), Sedbergh School. New boarding house. C – A O Thoms (tender £20,634) [SSGM, 1924–5]. The completion date has not been firmly ascertained. The annual accounts show a total cost rising to £24,554 in 1927–8 but it seems unlikely that building work would have spread over four years.

1925
Acton (Ch), St Mary. Specification for tower repairs in Sept so work may have gone on into 1926 [LRO, DDSr 10/1, fols 63–4].

Cartmel (CuL), Priory. Specification for repairs and pointing internal walls in Nov so work probably continued into 1926 [LRO, DDSr 10/1, fol 65]

Penrith (CuC), Burbank House. Specification for alterations and additions [LRO, DDSr 10/1, fols 61–2].

Skelmersdale (Me), St Paul. Probably the porches, vestries and baptistry (*see* 1911) [ICBS 10418]. Upper part of tower never completed.

Rishworth (WY), St John the Divine. Plans for a new church. A&P estimated at £5,500. After the lowest tender came in at £7,500, their scaled-back plans were thought 'so unsatisfactory' and out of keeping for this moorland district that the building committee turned to Walsh & Maddock of Halifax who were held to have 'greater local knowledge' [ICBS 11680].

Skipton (NY), Holy Trinity. Repair after fire in 1925: new N transept roof and organ case. C – Brassington, Sons & Co. CW – T Baines [JB/JP].

1925–6
Barthomley (Ch), St Bertoline. Chancel rebuilt or remodelled for Robert Offley Ashburton, Marquess of Crewe, in memory of his two sons, and uncle, Hungerford Crewe. New roof and chancel arch widened [inscription: Richards, R 1947 *Old Cheshire Churches*. London, 45n].

Becconsall (aka Hesketh), All Saints. Design 1923. Replacement for a small church of 1765. Site given by Major T Fermor-Hesketh. 263 seats. Initially it was planned to spend £4,500: completion of A&P's design would have cost £6,500. Saddleback roof substituted for the planned spire. ICBS grant of £400 in 1924 [ICBS 11610: FS: inscription: *PG* 8.12.1923].

Manchester, St Margaret, Burnage. W end, baptistry and S and SE porches. Reordered 1998 [Pollard 2000, 10, 12].

Newton-le-Willows (Me), St John the Baptist, Earlestown. Nave of C T Whitley & Fry's church of 1875–8 extended by half a bay and base of tower built. *c* £6,000. 90 extra seats [ICBS 11668: BE].

Pennington (Cu), St Michael. A&P produced a scheme, apparently for a complete rebuild of a church of 1826, in 1917 but this was too expensive (£2,100 above A&P's estimate of £4,000). Further plans in 1920 which it was hoped to complete for the centenary in 1926. Specification 1924. Polygonal chancel added, ceiling removed, tower arch opened, new windows inserted, reseated and widespread restoration. Final cost £5,708. C – A O Thoms [CRO(B), BPR 24/1/37–39: LRO, DDSr 10/1, fols 1–19: ICBS 11485]. *See also* 1934.

1925–7
Blackpool, St Stephen-on-the-Cliffs. Design 1924. Chancel, Lady Chapel, vestries, transepts and three bays of nave and aisles built; 400 seats; £20,000. The full scheme, with five-bay nave and aisles, would have seated 800 and cost £35,000. C – A O Thoms, Lancaster [inscriptions: LRO, DDSr 10/2, fol 12: ICBS 11782: appeal leaflet (1925): *A Short History of S Stephen-on-the-Cliffs*: *Church Times* 27.5.1927].

1926
Beetham (CuW), St Michael & All Angels. Memorial (date of death 1926), altar rails [NADFAS, 2004].

Blawith (CuL), St John the Baptist. Repairs to N and W walls; two buttresses added on S of nave [CRO(C)B), BPR 18/W/3/18–20: LRO, DDSr 10/1, fols 66–7: file at CCT].

Lancaster, Drill Hall, St Leonard's Gate/Phoenix Street. For 6th Battalion King's Own Royal Regiment. Specification for decoration and cleaning [LRO, DDSr 10/1, fols 68–9].

Lancaster, Stanmore Drive, Haverbreaks. Plans for detached house, for the Misses Delahunt and Stanley by James Tarney [LRO, MBLA acc 5167/3539, ex info CS].

Southport (Me), Holy Trinity. General repairs [DDSr 10/3, fols 151–4].

Standish (GM), St Wilfrid. Gatehouse [LRO, PR 3134/23–6: BE].

1926–7
Bilsborrow, St Hilda. Specification Mar 1925. £11,640. C – R S Wright & Sons, Lancaster [FS: LRO, DDSr 10/1, fols 36–55; 10/2, fol 10].

Orrell (Me), St Luke. Design 1924. Partly built. C – C O Hallett of Stockport [LRO, DDSr 10/2, fol 8: drawing dated Jun 1924 (FS: DM collection): BE].

1926–9
Leeds, Grammar School. Memorial swimming baths. £14,750. C – J T Wright & Sons. Also workshops [LRO, DDSr 10/2 fol 24; 10/3, fol 9].

1926–31
Middleton (GM), St Michael. Tower. £6,656. C – Grundy, Sons & Co, Middleton [LRO, DDSr 10/2, fol 71].

1927
Slyne, 'Beaumont Cote'. Additions and alterations plus a pair of cottages for T C Butler. C – A O Thoms [LRO, DDSr 10/2, fols 1–5].

1927–8
Preston, St John the Divine. Renovation in churchyard [LRO, DDSr 10/2, fol 6].

Sedbergh (CuWY), Sedbergh School. Quatrecentenary memorial lodge and gateway. First designs 1926. [SSGM, 1926–8].

Wesham, Christ Church. E end and S porch: nave reseated; seats increased by 89 to 317. £5,650. C – Charles Hallett, Stockport [ICBS 11756: LRO, DDSr 10/2, fol 17: RIBA PB129/2: Anon nd [1994] *Wesham Church, established 1894: Centenary 1894–1994*].

1928
Atherton (GM), St Michael, Howe Bridge. Reseated. £1,056. C – R S Wright & Sons [LRO, DDSr 10/2, fol 15]. The W screen, dated 1928, looks like A&P work.

Caton, Institute. Additions. £905. C – A O Thoms [LRO, DDSr 10/2, fol 13].

Lancaster, St Peter (RC), Rearrangement of sanctuary floor, screen and steps. £862. C – A O Thoms [LRO, DDSr 10/2, fol 11].

Morecambe, Holy Trinity. Minor repairs. £253. C – Edmondson Bros, Morecambe [LRO, DDSr 10/2, fol 7].

Sedbergh (CuWY), Sedbergh School. Entrance lodge and gates. £2,608. C – A O Thoms [LRO, DDSr 10/2, fol 14].

1928–9
Basford (St), St Mary. New vestries. £1,450. C – S Heath & Sons [LRO, DDSr 10/1, fols 70–3; 10/2, fol 18].

Sedbergh (CuWY), Sedbergh School. Porter's lodge. C – Greenwood Bros (tender £799) [SSGM, 1928–9].

1928–30
Wigan (GM), St Stephen, Whelley. First designs 1919; others 1925 or 1926. Land given by Lord Crawford. First phase (E parts and two bays of nave and aisles, estimated at £12,000 in Feb 1926). FS Nov 1928, consecrated 9.4.1930. By Sept 1930, £9,863 had been spent; 293 seats. C – Webster & Winstanley. A SW tower was considered as a possibility (eg on a drawing of 1927) but was never built [drawings at church: LRO, DDSr 10/2, fols 39–40: ICBS 11726: Walmsley, G A 1994 *The History of St Stephen's Parish and Church*, 7].

1928–41
Lancaster, Royal Lancaster Infirmary. Protracted series of commissions. 1928–30: nurses' home. 1930: estimates to build a new maternity and children's ward (£11,185) and extend kitchen. 1931: expenditure of £11,256 on alterations and additions; C – A O Thoms: alterations and additions to nurses' home; £8,109; C – R S Wright & Sons. 1931–2: 10 bedrooms, bathrooms and offices on second floor; £1,366; C – R S Wright & Sons. 1931–3: new operating theatres, private and isolation wards; £11,048; C (and for subsequent works) – A O Thoms. 1933–4: staff dining rooms, stores and other works; £3,295: and nurses' home extension; £5,016. 1933–5: new wards and X-ray block; £14,049. 1935: workers' committee rooms, South Road; £546. 1935–6: alterations and additions to the accident entrance and massage block; £2,927. 1940–1: air raid protection £680. 1941: decontamination unit; £146 [LRO, DDSR 10/2, fols 51–3, 72, 108, 119, 126–8, 151, 194; 10/3, fols 7, 54, 59–60, 66].

1929
Arnside (CuW), St James. Specification for alterations to choir and nave seating [LRO, DDSr 10/3, fol 23].

Carnforth, new HQ for the 5th King's Own Royal Regiment. *c* £4,000. C – T W Huntingdon Ltd, Lancaster [LRO, DDSr 10/2, fols 26–8].

Casterton (CuW), Casterton School. Additional storey to classrooms. £257. A – A O Thoms [LRO, DDSr 10/2, fol 30].

Giggleswick (NY), Giggleswick School. Specification for new porter's lodge [LRO, DDSr 10/1, fols 76–87; 10/3, fol 19].

Lancaster, Christ Church schools. Additions and alterations: tenders in 1928. £4,368. C – W Knowles [LRO, DDSr 10/2, fol 22; 10/3, fol 6].

Lancaster, Penny's Hospital. Chapel restored. £430. C – Thompson & Jackson [LRO, DDSr 10/2, fol 16].

Sedbergh (CuWY), Sedbergh School. New gymnasium floor; £436; C – R S Wright & Sons. New lodge to Winder House; £817; C – Greenwood Bros, Sedbergh [LRO, DDSr 10/1, fols 88–9; 10/2, fols 23, 29].

Skerton, St Luke's Junior Schools. New school. £7,273. C – A O Thoms [LRO, DDSr 10/2, fol 21].

Winwick (Ch), St Oswald. Specification for restoring the Gerard Chapel, including new windows and rebuilding the buttresses [LRO, DDSr 10/1, fols 90–1].

1929–30
Ashton-in-Makerfield (GM), St Thomas. New vestry. £506. C – Kearsley & Gee, Ashton-in-Makerfield. [LRO, DDSr 10/2, fol 41; 10/3, fol 34].

Giggleswick (NY), Giggleswick School. Sanatorium: sketch plans 1928: £6,259: C – H V Robinson. Extension to chemical laboratory: £992: C – Brassington, Sons & Co [LRO, DDSr 10/2, fols 32, 34, 44–5; 10/3, fols 1, 18, 20, 37].

Worksop (Notts), St Anne's vicarage. Tenders Sept 1928 [LRO, DDSr 10/2, fols 33, 47; 10/3, fol 5].

1929–31
Burnley, St Matthew, Habergham Eaves. W A Waddington's church of 1879 largely rebuilt after a fire on Christmas Day 1927. Plans 1928 following the previous plan and reusing a little of the old walling. £14,093. Seating for 620. C – A O Thoms of Lancaster; woodwork by Clegg Bros, Burnley [ICBS 11902: LRO, DDSr 10/2, fol 49; 10/3, fols 16–17, 55; 10/3, fol 35: *Burnley News* 4.4.1931: Ashworth 1979, 46–54].

Lytham St Anne's, St Anne. General repairs. £372. C – John Tinker & Sons, Huddersfield (1929). Tenders for further work (1930). Memorial vestry [LRO, DDSr 10/2, fol 19; 10/3, fols 49–50: JP].

Sedbergh (CuWY), Sedbergh School. Sanatorium. R S Wright & Sons (tender £5,725). Cost £6,537 [LRO, DDSr 10/2, fols 82–3; 10/3, fols 20,33].

1930
Bilsborrow, vicarage. £2,188. C – J Turner, Preston [LRO, DDSr 10/2, fol 31].

Cartmel (CuL), Priory. Report and specification for minor restoration [LRO, DDSr 10/1, fols 107–8; 10/3, fols 42–6: SSGM, 1929–30].

Melling, 'Church Gates'. Additions and alterations for Miss Rose. £1,008. C – A O Thoms [LRO, DDSr 10/2, fols 42–3].

Preston, St John the Divine. General repairs and decoration including new ceilings in nave, chancel and chapel; £802; C – T Croft & Sons, Preston. Decoration (£366) by T H Kellett, Preston. A&P had reported on the roofs in 1929 [LRO, DDSr 10/2, fols 35–7; 10/3, fols 21–2].

Sandbach (Ch), St Mary. New vestry and N porch. £1,331. C – Webster & Winstanley. Specification 1929 [LRO, DDSr 10/1, fols 92–3; 10/2, fol 46; 10/3, fols 38–41].

Staveley (CuW), St James. Proposal for a dormer window: unexecuted [CRO(K), WPR 68/1/4/28].

1930–1
Barrow-in-Furness (CuL), St Mary, Walney Island. Completed by a fourth, W bay to the nave, S porch, and vestry. Plans 1929. £4,597. C – A O Thoms [CRO(B) BPR 1/M/9/12: LRO, DDSr 10/2, fol 58; 10/3, fol 62]. S&P's 1852–3 church (still standing to the S after the first phase was built in 1907–8) was then demolished.

Coventry, St Barbara, Earlsdon. Correspondence from 1928: designs 1929. 'Advisory architect'/CW – Harold T Jackson of Coventry. Lady Chapel paid for by the industrialist Sir Alfred Herbert in memory of his wife, Florence. £17,644. C – E Harris & Son, Coventry. W 2½ bays never built. The Lady Chapel cost £975 plus £1,190 of work by R Bridgeman & Sons [papers at church: LRO, DDSr 10/1, fols 94–106; 10/2, fols 57, 61–2; 10/3, fols 11, 31, 36, 113: RIBA PB427/10].

Lancaster, St Peter's Schools, Senior Division. £5,450 of repairs etc. C – A O Thoms [LRO, DDSr 10/2, fols 65–6; 10/3, fol 51].

Lytham St Anne's, St Anne. Memorial clergy vestry on NE. £377. C – John Sutchcliffe & Sons Ltd, St Anne's [LRO, DDSr 10/2, fol 50].

Sedbergh (CuWY), Sedbergh School, Sedgwick House. Tutor's rooms. C – William Potter, Sedbergh [LRO, DDSr 10/2, fol 48; 10/3, fol 47].

1930–2
Blackpool, St Thomas. Specification Jan 1929. £10,326. C – T Croft & Sons, Preston [inscription: LRO, DDSr 10/1, fols 20–35; 10/2, fol 74; 10/3, fol 25].

1931
Lancaster, St Peter (RC). General repairs, *c* £440. Various contractors [LRO, DDSr 10/2, fols 67–70].

Long Whatton (Leics), All Saints. Baptistry as a memorial to Lord Crawshaw. Carving by R Bridgeman & Sons, Lichfield [LRO, DDSr 10/1, fols 109–10; 10/3, fol 91].

Lytham St Anne's, St Cuthbert. Memorial morning chapel for Mrs Mellor; C – A O Thoms [LRO, DDSr 10/2, fol 56].

Melling, St Wilfrid. Estimate for chancel step handrail [LRO, PR 2898/3/13].

Warton, Pringle Head (house). Enlarging scullery, new bedroom, pantry, etc for Miss Welch. £233 [LRO, DDSr 10/2, fol 55].

Worksop (Notts), St Anne. Reredos (estimate £710) and monument (estimate £2,055 including the effigy) to Sir John Robinson of Worksop Manor, the founder of the church. Executed by R Bridgeman & Sons, Lichfield; figure of Sir John carved in Carrara marble by Albert Toft of London. Given by Dame Eveline Maude Robinson who also presented the memorial windows [LRO, DDSr 10/3, fols 30, 78–80].

1931–2
Bolton (GM), St Thomas, Halliwell. New vestries. £882 [LRO, DDSr 10/2, fol 73].

Feniscowles, Immanuel. Reseated and other fittings added. Work estimated at £1,216 in 1931 [LRO, DDSr 10/2, fols 80–1; 10/3, fols 63–4, 76; PR 3147/6/12–15].

Glasson, Christ Church. New chancel and vestry in memory of Matthew and Mary Simpson and their daughter, Caroline. £2,007. C – R S Wright & Sons [inscription: LRO, DDSr 10/2, fol 76].

Orrell (Me), vicarage. £2,655. C – James Gaskell. First tenders in Aug 1930 [LRO, DDSr 10/1, fol 113; 10/2, fol 79; 10/3, fols 57, 72].

Ribby-cum-Wrea, St Nicholas, Wrea Green. Marble chancel floor, steps, and choir seats [LRO, DDSr 10/2, fol 77; 10/3, fol 82].

Winwick (Ch), St Oswald. Tower restored. £463. C – A O Thoms. Tenders for new vestry, porch and offices [LRO, DDSr 10/2, fol 75; 10/3, fols 73–4, 90].

1932
Bretherton, St John the Baptist. New nave floor. £256. C – A O Thoms. Electric lighting [LRO, DDSr 10/1, fol 118; 10/2, fol 84; 10/3, fol 106].

Newton-le-Willows (Me), St John the Baptist, Earlestown. Tenders for vestry, porch and offices [LRO, DDSr 10/3, fol 104].

Kendal (CuW), 'Heaves'. General repairs etc. for Lady Ashton. £2,011. Mansard roof added. C – J Howie & Sons, Kendal [LRO, DDSr 10/2, fols 86–91; 10/3, fols 84–6: BE]. Now Heaves Hotel.

Preston, St John the Divine. Repairs to tower and spire. £320. C – G Read & Sons, Preston [LRO, DDSr 10/2, fol 85].

Standish, St Wilfrid. Woodwork repairs. £100. R S Wright & Sons. New chimney stack to clerestory. £162. C – Peter Moss, Standish [LRO, DDSr 10/2, fols 78, 92; 10/3, fol 99].

Waddington, St Helen. Screen [NADFAS, 2002, which also attributes the rood screen to A&P and dates as 1st quarter C20].

Wennington, 'Cravens'. Work estimated at £1,282 for W M Saunders [LRO, DDSr 10/3, fol 94].

1932–3
Coventry, St Barnabas. Design 1931. W end not completed. Supervising architect Harold T Jackson of Coventry who designed various furnishings. £5,388. C – E Harris & Son, Coventry [V&A + RIBA Architecture Partnership, JaHT/1–5: LRO, DDSr 10/2, fols 117–18; 10/3, fol 83].

Grange-over-Sands (CuL), St Paul. Chancel, chapel, vestry and S porch. £6,160. C – A O Thoms. Glazing by Shrigley & Hunt [LRO, DDSr 10/1, fols 114–15; 10/2, fols 111–12; 10/3, fol 121].

Preston, St Matthew. Chancel completed. £2,637. C – A O Thoms. Decorations; £151; C – T H Kellett [LRO, DDSr 10/2, fols 96, 106–7; 10/3, fols 92–3, 105, 111–12].

Rawtenstall, Crawshawbooth, St John. Lady Chapel created with screen to S transept. Tenders for woodwork 1931 [LRO, DDSr 10/2, fol 64: Anon 1992 *A Short History of Crawshawbooth Parish Church*, 7].

Scotforth, St Paul. New chancel floor, alterations to choir seats and other minor work [LRO, DDSr 10/2, fols 102–3; 10/3, fol 107].

1933
Blackburn, new chapel at the Bishop of Blackburn's house. £1,179. C – E Lewis & Sons [LRO, DDSr 10/2, fol 109].

Broughton, St John the Baptist. Two tables with 'carved apron foliate design' [NADFAS, 2003].

Cockerham, St Michael. Repairs. Report on tower 1932 [LRO, DDSr 10/2, fol 104; 10/3, fol 109–10].

Heysham, rectory. Alterations. *c* £884 [LRO, DDSr 10/2, fols 97–101].

Lancaster, Grammar School. Plans Nov 1932. New two-storey dormitory block. £1,476. C – R L Dilworth [LM, 99.60: LRO, DDSr 10/1, fol 117; 10/2, fols 113–15].

Natland (CuW), St Mark. Plans and sections for electric lighting scheme [CRO(K), WPR 35/1/2/5].

Singleton, St Anne. Oak panelling and altar. Roof repairs, £55 [LRO, PR 3224/4/41–2: LRO, DDSr 10/2, fol 93; 10/3, fol 114].

Warton, 'Pringle Head'. Extension to dining room and verandah for Miss Welch [LRO, DDSr 10/2, fol 110].

Morecambe, St Christopher, Bare. Plans 1932. £5,957. Chancel, nave, N aisle, NE tower, N porch: S aisle never built. C – A O Thoms [LRO, DDSr 10/2, fols 122–4; 10/3, fol 120; MBMO/HE, plan register, vol 2, refs 125–7, 130: ICBS 12156].

1934

Oldham (GM), St Stephen. Specification and tenders for cleaning and decoration [LRO, DDSr 10/1, fols 119–21; 10/3, fol 127].

Pennington (Cu), St Michael. New organ chamber and aisle. £666. C – A O Thoms [LRO DDSr 10/2, fol 121].

Preston, St Michael & All Angels, Ashton-on-Ribble. Organ case, screen and floor for organ [LRO, DDSr 10/1, fol 117; 10/3, fol 132].

Winwick (Ch), St Oswald. New vestry, porch and entrance. £232. C – Harry Fairclough of Howley, Warrington. Tenders Jan 1932. [LRO, DDSr 10/2, fol 120; 10/3, fol 90].

1934–5

Lancaster, nurses' home, Regent Street. New bedroom and bathroom wing for the Lancaster & District Nursing Society. £1,064. C – A O Thoms [LRO, DDSr 10/2, fol 129; 10/3, fol 140].

Sandbach (Ch), St Mary. Clerestory windows reglazed by Shrigley & Hunt. £167 [LRO, DDSr 10/2, fol 125].

Thornton-in-Lonsdale (NY), St Oswald. Major repairs and refitting after a fire in Feb 1933. *c* £9,000. Tenders from Nov 1933. CC – Brassington, Sons & Co, Settle (joinery) and A O Thoms [LRO, DDSr 10/2, fols 131–2, 141–4; 10/3, fols 22, 124–5].

1935

Becconsall (aka Hesketh), All Saints. Tower completed. £721. C – A O Thoms [plaque in church: LRO, DDSr 10/2, fol 130; 10/3, fol 143]. Reredos and panels in morning chapel. C – R S Wright & Sons, Lancaster [LRO, DDX 1657/3].

Burnley, St Matthew, Habergham Eaves. Pulpit [guide, 83].

Carleton Hall, near Penrith (CuC). Alterations and new entrance hall, staircase, 'etc'. estimated at £1,600 [LRO, DDSr 10/3, fol 147]. Now Cumbria Police HQ.

Preston, Christ Church, Fulwood. Repairs, marble chancel pavement, choir stalls (by Thompson & Jackson), decorations etc [LRO, DDSr 10/2, fols 135–40; 10/3, fols 144–5].

Poulton-le-Fylde, St Chad. Decorations. £141. C – Arnold Berry, Cleveleys [LRO, DDSr 10/1, fols 122–4; 10/2, fol 133; 10/3, fol 150].

Southport (Me), Holy Trinity. Decorations and general repairs. £197. C – Heyes Bros, Southport [LRO, DDSr 10/2, fol 134; 10/3, fols 151–4, 161].

1935–7

Abram (Me), St John the Evangelist. Replaced a church of 1838 on the adjoining site. Seating for 478. £11,113. C – A O Thoms [LRO, DDSr 10/2, fols 162–3; 10/3, fol 146, 174–5, 187–8].

1936

Bolton (GM), St Margaret. Report on general repairs [LRO, DDSr 10/3, fols 183–4].

Eaton (near Tarporley, Ch), St Thomas. Refitted with new marble sanctuary floor (by J & H Patteson), reredos, pulpit, stalls, low chancel screen, formation of organ chamber. Woodwork by Thompson & Jackson, Lancaster [LRO, DDSR 10/3, fols 170–1].

Ellel, 'Foxholes', house at Hampson. 'New garden room etc'. *c* £1,047. C – A O Thoms and others [LRO, DDSr 10/2, fols 153–6: ex info CS].

Lancaster, Middle Street School. Report on fabric [LRO, DDSR 10/3, fol 166].

Levens (CuW), St John the Evangelist. Report on condition [LRO, DDSr 10/3, fols 156–8].

Preston, Christ Church. Proposals for new floors and fittings [LRO, DDSr 10/3, fol 173].

Rishton, St Peter & St Paul. Proposals for reredos, altar and rails for the Soldiers' and Children's Chapel [LRO, DDSR 10/3, fol 181].

Standish (GM), Grammar School and girls' and infants' schools. Reports on suggested repairs [LRO, DDSr 10/3, fols 164–5].

Thornton-le-Fylde, Christ Church. Report and specification for nave and tower [LRO, DDSr 10/1, 10/3, fols 128–9, 144–54, 159–160].

Tunstall, 'Tunstall House' (dower house of Thurland Castle). *c* £1,860 of work. C – A O Thoms and others [LRO, DDSr 10/2, fols 145–50; 10/3, fol 163]. Involved new dining room with bedrooms over as an east wing for Thomas Butler-Cole of Beaumont Cote [ex info CS].

1936–7

Alsager (Ch), St Mary Magdalene. N aisle completed. £1,939. C – Stephen Heath & Son, Newcastle [LRO, DDSr 10/2, fol 165: ex info A M Shaw].

Lancaster, shop premises for S B Wilding & Sons, Damside Street. £862 [LRO, DDSr 10/2, fol 164; 10/3, fols 148, 182].

Sedbergh (CuWY), Sedbergh School. New dormitory over tutor's room. *c* £460. CC – various [LRO, DDSr 10/2, fols 157–61]. Proposals for alterations at Powell Hall; these were shelved but reconsidered in 1938–9 then abandoned because of war [SSGM, 1936, 1939].

1936–9
Lancaster, Priory Hall for St Mary's church, China Street. Design 1933. In 1934 it was envisaged that there would be a large and a small hall. Designs no doubt settled in 1935. £5,828. C – A O Thoms [datestone: LRO, DDSr 10/2, fols 181–3; 10/3, fols 123, 155, 162, 167, 179–80, 214: *LGuar* 12.1.1934].

Orrell (Me), St Luke. Completed at E and W ends. £8,578. Webster & Winstanley, Wigan. Chancel fittings (£496: J Parkinson & Sons, Lancaster) [LRO, DDSr 10/1, fols 130–43; 10/2, fols 172, 180; 10/3, fol 189].

After 1936
Stainforth (NY), St Peter. Altar rail by J Tarney [JB/JP].

Tosside (NY), St Bartholomew. Altar rail by J Tarney [JB/JP].

1937
Barnacre, All Saints. S chapel added as a memorial to James Lever Rushton. £1,252. C – A O Thoms [LRO, DDSr 10/2, fol 166; 10/3, fol 193: ex info in church].

Bolton (GM), St Saviour. Report on general condition [LRO, DDSr 10/3, fols 210–2].

Dalton-in-Furness (CuL), St Mary. Report on the fabric [CRO(B), BPR 1/C/5/23/2: LRO, DDSr 10/3, fols 207–8].

Preston, Christ Church, Fulwood. Chapel of Remembrance [LRO, DDSr 10/3, fol 197].

Scotforth, St Paul's School. New staff room and cloakroom extension etc. £661. C – A O Thoms [LRO, DDSr 10/2, fol 167].

Wesham, Christ Church. Design for English altar: estimates (lowest £114) based on patterns and prices provided by Watts & Co [LRO, DDSr 10/3, fol 198].

1937–8
Sedbergh (CuWY), Sedbergh School. New common room and classroom. £850. C – Greenwood Bros, Sedbergh. New day and music rooms and other minor works. *c* £1,840. CC – various [LRO, DDSr 10/2, fols 173–6, 187].

Wigan (GM), Whelley, St Stephen. Nave and aisles completed to W and choir vestry added. £5,243. C – Webster & Winstanley [LRO, DDSR 10/2, fol 170; 10/3, fol 190: Walmsley 1986, 7].

1937–9
Slaidburn. Proposal for a 'central school', estimated at £4,650 to £4,800 (1937) and £5,764 (1939) [LRO, DDSr 10/3, fols 204–6, 218].

1938
Atherton (GM), St Michael, Howe Bridge. Vestry at E end. £1,338. C – A O Thoms [LRO, DDSr 10/2, 177].

Lancaster, St Peter's Cemetery (RC). Re-erect churchyard cross. £165 [LRO, DDSr 10/2, fol 178].

Lancaster, 'Westbourne'. New bathroom and other work for Douglas Phipps Sturton, solicitor at 16 Castle Park. [LRO, DDSr 10/2, fols 168–9].

Preston, St John the Divine. Proposed verger's house. Lowest tender £865 [LRO, PR 2845/27/12; DDSr 10/3, fol 211]. Unexecuted [ex info CS].

Sedbergh (CuWY), Sedbergh School. Tenders (lowest £528) [LRO, DDSr 10/3, fol 213].

1938–9
Garstang, St Helen. New chancel floor and minor alterations; reredos removed. £216. C – T Croft & Sons, Preston [LRO, DDSr 10/2, fol 184].

Rochdale (GM), Christ Church, Healey. Drawing for new altar and retable for Mrs Mary Taylor [LRO, DDSr 10/2, fol 185].

Singleton, St Anne. Vestry £775. [LRO, PR 3224/4/43, 43; DDSr 10/2, fol 171].

1938–41
Preston, St Mary Magdalene, Ribbleton. First proposals Aug 1936. New E end (chancel, organ chamber, chapel, N and S aisles, vestries); intended to add 220 seats to the original 150. £7,322 or £7,918. C – T Croft & Sons, Preston. Certificate of completion to the ICBS 5.5.1942 [ICBS 12431: LRO, DDSR 10/3, fol 172; PR 3310/4/23, 27, 28, 43].

1939
Bolton (GM), St Margaret. Tenders (lowest £1,240) for choir vestry [LRO, DDStr 10/3, fol 219].

Crewe Green (Ch), St Michael. Specification for reredos, panelling organ case, choir frontals, prayer desk heating and alterations to floor. Estimate £709 [LRO, DDSr 10/1, fols 166–8; 10/3, fols 220, 222–4].

Ellel, St John. Churchyard gates and boundary wall. £92. C – A O Thoms [LRO, DDSr 10/2, fol 189].

Lathom, St James. Vestries. £542. C – F Riding & Sons, Ormskirk. Tenders 1938 [LRO, DDSr 10/2, fol 191; 10/3, fol 215].

Standish (GM), St Wilfrid. Tower floor. £226 [LRO, DDSr 10/2, fol 186].

1939–40
Glasson, Christ Church. Vault built for the executors of J H Dalton of Thurnham Hall. £297. C – A O Thoms [LRO, DDSr 10/2, fol 192].

1940
Bolton-le-Sands, Holy Trinity. Proposed organ chamber at E end of N aisle. Estimated at £450 in June [LRO, DDSr 10/3, fol 227].

Lancaster, St Mary. Take down reredos and stalls and move to the Castle for safe-keeping [LRO, DDSr 10/2, fol 194].

Lancaster, garage at presbytery for Canon Brimley. £221. C – A O Thoms [LRO, DDSr 10/2, fol 193].

1944
Haverthwaite (CuL), St Anne. Proposal in Oct for a three-sided apse and N vestry with linking porch signed by J Tarney writing on behalf of A&P. Another sketch plan suggests a square-ended E extension and a N aisle 'divided from the nave by a simple wooden arcade'. No formal estimate made and suggests 'proper estimates

are tried out after the War is over'. [CRO(K), WPR P90/40; 46]. Not executed.

Undated work

Lancaster, Masonic Hall. Listed by JP among ES's works: original source unknown.

Barrow-in-Furness (CuL), 'Dale Ghyll', Hawcoat. Listed among P&A works in EGP's obituary in *LGuar* [26.1.1895].

Barrow-in-Furness (CuL), 'ship works'. Listed in EGP's works in his obituaries in *LStd* [25.1.1895] and *LGuar* [26.1.1895]. These credit it to EGP alone: this should be treated with caution since the obits also credit him with the Barrow jute mill but this was built in the P&A years. It is unclear what this 'ship works' job was.

Over Peover (Ch), St Laurence. Screen to S chapel [*K* 1913, 517].

Undated works listed among 'chief works of "Mr. Austin and the firm"'

Mentioned in HJA's obituary in *The Builder* [108, 1915, 312] but for which no other sources are presently known. The list of works is rather eccentric: they are described as 'chief works' but many in the list are distinctly minor and the following need to be treated with caution. No dates are given.

Barton-on-Irwell (GM), schools.

Keswick (CuC), Keswick High School.

Lichfield (St), St Michael, prayer desks.

Medlar, Christ Church. In fact relates to the church at Wesham, which was referred to as Medlar when the first phase was built [ex info CS].

Tonge, 'new chancel, vestries, side chapel etc.'. No work traced in churches at Tonge Fold or Tonge Moor, Bolton.

Whitefield (presumably GM). The obituary seems to suggest a new church but none is known.

Uncertain attributions

c 1838
Lancaster, 'West Bank', later 'Parkfield', Greaves Road. Classical villa [attributed by CS]. Most probably for William Satterthwaite [ex info TBA].

1841–2
Barnton (Ch), Christ Church. For the Revd Richard Greenall. Seating for 200. £1,400. Attributed to ES by the Revd G Buchan, although no supporting evidence has been found. However, Greenall was a Weaver Navigation Trustee for whom ES built three other churches [Buchan, G 1992 *Christ Church*, *Barnton*: ex info JMH]. ES built three churches for the trustees but in a letter to William Whewell, 7.4.1842 [Trinity College, Whewell Archive, Cambridge, Add.MS.a/212/64], he wrote: 'I have … just completed three out of the four Weaver Churches.' It seems strange for him to miscount: could he have been thinking of Barnton as the fourth one?

1845–6
Aldingham (CuL), St Cuthbert. 'Nave rewindowed 1845–6, and the N aisles added by *Edmund Sharpe*' [BE]. This attribution was added at a late proof stage and the publishers have been unable to explain its origin. Despite considerable subsequent archival and newspaper research by TBA no reference to ES has been discovered. Nonetheless, ES is a prime candidate since his cousin, the Revd J W Whittaker, must have known the rector, Dr John Stonard: were both accomplished Hebrew scholars and JWW included the name Stonard in that of his tenth child, Elizabeth Stonard Whittaker (b 1838). 'Nave rewindowed' is misleading since there are two aisles and no clerestory.

1846–7
Lancaster, 'Dallas House', Dallas Road (then Dallas Place). For and occupied (by Jul 1847 until his death) by Dr James Stockdale Harrison (1797–1879), surgeon, medical teacher and later senior partner of Pearson Langshaw, who succeeded him as surgeon to Lancaster gaol in 1854. Family links and stylistic similarities would suggest S&P as designers. JP gives a date of 1853 for a house in Dallas Road but this seems unlikely [ex info CS and TBA].

1849
Caton, Littledale Hall, Brookhouse. Jacobethan house for the Revd John Dodson, 'almost certainly designed by E G Paley' [Robinson 1991, 216]. Dodson's 1843 vicarage at Cockerham was designed by ES. Now a rehabilitation centre. The Free Church on the estate is probably by EGP too.

1850s
Davenham (Ch), St Wilfrid. W steeple rebuilding. EGP referred as architect to a parish meeting in 1857 but unclear if he did rebuild the steeple [various authors 1986 *Davenham: 900 Years of Work and Worship*, 22–5].

1854
Barrow-in-Furness (CuL), Furness Abbey Hotel. Extension [CRO(B), BDX 248/1 but S&P not named].

Burnley, St Peter. EGP's *LGuar* obituary [26.1.1895] gives this church as one he worked on (but no date given). JP gives 1854. A restoration did take place in 1863–4 involving reseating, chancel extension, new pulpit, font, clerestory, floor, arcades and roof but the architect was Miles Thompson of Thompson & Webster of Kendal [ICBS 4704].

1860
Poulton-le-Fylde, St Chad. Chancel and apse [JP]. BE gives 1868 for apse but does not name an architect.

1862
Coniston (CuL) station, Swiss chalet style [JP: Andrews, M & Holmes, G 2005: *The Coniston Railway*. Pinner, 16, state date as 1879; p 3 cites P&A as architects. No primary evidence located].

1862–3
Barrow, railway offices, St George's Square [JP]. Drawings said to exist in CRO(B) have not been located.

1863–4
Bolton-le-Sands, St Michael (now Holy Trinity). Restoration [JP].

1864
Heysham, St Peter. Restored and N aisle added (according to local tradition) [ex info JP, 2010].

Rhodes (GM), All Saints. BE notes this is attributed to EGP by Terry Wyke but finds this 'hard to believe'.

1865–70
Rossall, Rossall School, (former) indoor baths. 'Presumably by Paley' [BE].

1860
Davenham (Ch), St Wilfrid. Lychgate [JP: DM].

'1869+'
Greenodd (CuL) and Haverthwaite (CuL), stations [JP].

1860s
Barrow-in-Furness (CuL), Roa Island. Italianate marine villa for H W Schneider. The late Angus Taylor told JP the architect was EGP and gave the date as 1861 with the billiard room as 1865. Taylor's source has not been traced. 1861 date seems too early and Banks [1984, 68] suggests the building followed Schneider's second marriage in 1864 to Elizabeth Turner, daughter of the vicar of Lancaster.

1870
Davenham (Ch), St Wilfrid. Chancel, transepts [JP].

c 1870
Knowsley Hall (Me). Staircase possibly by P&A (replaced by Romaine-Walker, 1908–12) [BE].

1871–2
Barrow-in-Furness (CuL), 'shipworks for Ashburner' [JP]. EGP's obituary lists a 'large ship works' but it is in a list of works that are by him working alone after 1851 [*LGuar* 26.1.1895].

1872
Barrow-in-Furness (CuL), Cavendish Park villas [JP].

1872–4
Beetham (CuW), St Michael. Restored incl (added?) porch [JP, 79–80]. However, *LGuar* [10.4.1875] says the restoration was in 1873–5 by Joseph Bintley of Kendal. But to complicate matters, HJA's obituary in *B* [108, 1915, 312] lists an undated restoration at the church by 'Mr. Austin and the firm'. Perhaps this relates to a later scheme: the fenestration is characteristic of the practice.

1873
Bootle (CuC), station. 'Likely to have been undertaken' [JP].

1874
Barrow-in-Furness (CuL), plans for eight pilots' cottages on Piel Island for the Duke of Buccleuch [CRO(B), BBP 776]: cited by JP but drawings not signed.

Leyland, St Andrew. Restored [JP]. CS (pers comm) mentions that an old guide book refers to work by P&A.

1876
Whitehaven (CuC), colliery schools [JP].

1876–8
Barrow-in-Furness (CuL), Piel Castle. Restoration: turret and staircase for the Duke of Buccleuch [JP].

1879
Hindley (GM), St Peter. Organ case 'looks distinctly Paley & Austin' [BE].

1881
Barrow-in-Furness (CuL), Ramsden Dock station and warehouse. Plans [CRO(B), BTDH/2/8–9] unsigned but the station is credited to P&A by JP who dates as 1882: P&A involvement seems likely in view of their extensive commissions for the FR (but *see* 1882).

Clitheroe, St Mary Magdalene. Restored [JP].

Whittington, 'Pearson House'. '1881, with C17th remains, probably by Paley and Austin'. Inscription 'DG [Dawson Greene] 1881' [LSMR, PRN15965-MLA15928].

1882
Barrow-in-Furness (CuL), Central Station. [JP, and Grosse 1996 44]. £15,000 [*BH* 3.6.1882]. P&A did so much work for the FR but sadly no contemporary evidence has come to light showing that they designed what would have been by far their most important station for the FR.

Lancaster, Waring & Gillow's showrooms, North Road. 'Probably by Paley and Austin' [LSMR, PRN15944-MLA15907]. Now a nightclub.

1884
Walton-le-Dale, All Saints' school. [JP].

1884–9
Rossall, Rossall School, NW corner and W side of The Square completed with Tudor-style buildings [ex info Clare Hartwell].

1887
Shrewsbury, Shrewsbury School. Swimming baths [despite mention in BE no confirmation can be ascertained from the school archives].

1891
Bowness-on-Solway (CuC), St Michael. N transept [JP]. BE says probably added at 1891–2 restoration but gives no architect.

1897
Casterton (CuW), Clergy Daughters' School. New hall [*LGuar* 23.10.1897]. Architect(s) not named but A&P are likely contenders as they did other work here.

St Helens (Me), St Nicholas, Sutton. Tower added, reseated, new chancel furnishings and mosaic floor. Possibly S transept. The tower and nave seats are dated by plaques while the style of the stalls is characteristically A&P. They would have been a natural choice having built All Saints', Sutton, in 1891–3. Congregational seating (at least) paid for by Charlotte Auguste Anne Hughes of Sherdley Hall (she laid the FS of the tower) [inscriptions for date and patronage].

c 1900
Bury (GM), Holy Trinity. N vestry. Stylistically could be the work of A&P (added to an EGP church of 1863–4).

Kirkham, St Michael. Gate piers at entrance to churchyard are typical of others by A&P with their Art Nouveau-style detail.

Lancaster, Priory Hotel, Chapel Street. 'Additions ... probably by Paley & Austin' consisting of a 'rectangular plan on the corner of Cable Street' [LSMR, PRN15722-MLA15722].

c 1904
Redmarshall (D), St Cuthbert. Two headstones in churchyard commemorating HJA's siblings and his father with lettering characteristic of HJA. The suggested date of *c* 1904 arises from the fact that HJA gave windows at this time commemorating his parents.

1905
Kirkby Lonsdale (CuW), market cross. Possibly by A&P [visual evidence: inscription for date]. JP notes 'alterations'.

c 1910
Lancaster, Church House, 96 Church Street. 'In 1910 it was bought by trustees, among whom were Henry A Paley and Geoffrey L Austin (who presumably designed the alterations), and converted into a Church House' [LSMR, PRN15768-MLA15731].

1911
Grasmere (CuC), 'Michael's Fold'. Extension for the Misses Paley [unsigned drawing dated 1911 shown to JP]. EGP's daughters, Emily and Mary, are recorded at their house in Caton at the 1911 census and must have moved to Grasmere soon afterwards [TBA].

Read, St John the Evangelist. W steeple 'probably Austin & Paley, whose tower and spire at nearby St Leonard, Balderstone ... has similarities' [BE].

1914
Pudsey (WY), St James, Waterloo. New church [JP].

1915
Singleton, St Anne. Stalls: stylistically like A&P woodwork [inscription for date].

1920s
Singleton, St Anne. Vestry (N) [ex info John Highton, churchwarden].

Work wrongly or probably wrongly attributed to Sharpe, Paley and Austin

1835–6
Blackburn, Feniscowles, Immanuel. Sometimes attributed to ES, notably by Makinson, H nd *History of Feniscowles Church*, 6–8, and a display board in the church: the former says the original design was by the Revd J W Whittaker but 'before work began [this was] rejected, and another one, designed and superintended by Mr. Sharp [*sic*] of Lancaster used instead'. The board, JMH advises, once had Whittaker's name on it but this was later changed to Sharpe's. A report in the *Preston Chronicle* [23.8.1834], says the foundation stone was to be laid within a month but this did not take place until 5.2.1835. There was further delay, it seems, as the consecration did not take place until 10.10.1836. An account in *BS* [12.10.1836], *does* name Sharpe as architect but this was apparently corrected by a printing of a supplement dated the same day naming Whittaker (which seems plausible since ES did not return to England until the autumn of 1835). The *BS* corrected report and the fact that ES (who was not exactly shy of publicity) never referred to the church in correspondence suggests he probably did no more than offer advice to his cousin Whittaker. The relative involvement of the two men will probably for ever remain uncertain, but, in the opinion of the present author and his colleagues, extensive ES design involvement is most unlikely.

1836
Heysham, 'Heysham Tower'. Extended and altered [JP] but in 1836, just back from his continental tour and with only churches in his sights, ES is unlikely to be the architect. No architect given in Robinson 1991, 198. Ex info CS: George Webster wrote that he was not the architect: CS suggests John James Myers of Preston was responsible.

1836–8
Warrington (Ch), Walton Hall. Credited to ES on http:en.wikipedia.org./wiki/Walton_Hall, _Cheshire (accessed 30.11.2011) which cites *Walton Hall & Gardens* (Warrington Borough Council). No evidence has come forward to support this and, as with Heysham Tower, ES seems an unlikely candidate. CS suggests the Cheshire architect George Latham as a more likely designer on stylistic grounds: he also had country house experience by this time, which ES did not.

1840s
Osgodby (EY), Osgodby Hall. Burton, T 1888 *The History & Antiquities of the Parish of Hemingborough*. York, 329, says G P Dawson, the owner from 1844, 'made additions to the house under the guidance of Mr Edmund Sharpe, then of York and in 1854, he added a large embattled square tower'. This is repeated in *VCH* [1976, *East Riding*, 3, 65], where ES is now credited with the tower evidently through a careless reading of Burton. The BE account is more circumspect saying 'enlarged ... in the 1840s, reputedly to the designs of Edmund Sharpe'. There is no evidence ES was involved and David Neave, author of the BE entry, now suggests [pers comm, 3.10.2006] Richard Hey Sharp of York is possibly the architect.

1843–4
Dolphinholme, Wyreside Hall. JP says 'New front' in classical style but no evidence has been traced. Robinson [1991, 256], notes 'substantial reconstruction' in 1843 but does not name an architect, nor does BE. CS suggests the architect is Arthur W Mills of Manchester.

1853
Rossall, Rossall School. N range of quadrangle [LBS 184734]. The architect is E H Shellard and the date 1852–3 [ex info Clare Hartwell].

1859–61
Chorley, St Laurence. Restoration work: JP gives 1859–61. The enlargement, completed Sept 1860, was in fact designed by Charles Verelst of Liverpool and built 1859–60 [ICBS 5435: BE].

1864
Blackburn, St Thomas, school [JP]. The school was built to designs by James Bertwistle of Blackburn at a cost of £3,014: FS Apr 1867 [LRO, PR 3081/11/9, 14, 15].

1869–70
Brindle, St James. Chancel plus renovation [JP]. However, a plan dated Mar 1869 showing new walling for the vestry, S chapel and porch is signed by Brade & Smales of Kendal [PR 3118/4/4]. CS (pers comm) says the chancel is of 1878 and by P&A.

1874
Morecambe, Wesleyan chapel, Green Street [JP]. In fact it is by Milnes & France of Bradford, 1875–6, £6,500 [*LGaz* 5.8.1876].

Seathwaite (CuC), Holy Trinity. JP, but *BH* [22.5.1875], reporting the consecration, says the architect was [Thomas] Bennett of Barrow.

1878
Yarm (NY), St Mary Magdalene. JP refers to 'Restoration and enlargement' but a report in *B* [36, 1879, 491], names the architects as Alexander & Henman of Stockton-on-Tees. HJA's obituary *B* [108 1915, 312] says 'enlargement' but no evidence found.

1881
Altham, St James. Chancel [BE, 1969] or chapel [JP] rebuilt. No evidence the chancel was rebuilt [ex info Clare Hartwell].

1883
Poulton-le-Fylde, St Chad. Restoration [JP]. The restoration, reseating and organ case of 1881–3 appear to have been carried out by J S Crowther of Manchester; he was paid £64 15s 1d for his services [LRO, PR 3222/4/41/63].

1890
Colton (CuL), Holy Trinity. Restored [JP]. The architects were Little & Farmer of Ulverston: date should probably be 1889–90 [ICBS 9383: *LGaz* 7.6.1890].

1894
Worsthorne, St John the Evangelist. New chancel, £564, the gift of Sir John Thursby [JP: LRO, PR 3114/1/31], but BE credits it to W B Colbram.

1902
Lancaster, Alexandra Hotel. Stylistic grounds [JP] but CS advises (pers comm) it is by C J Ashworth.

1904
Redmarshall (D), St Cuthbert. New church [JP]. This church is medieval.

1908
Lancaster, Greaves Wesleyan chapel. Sometimes claimed as A&P's but S Wright was almost certainly the architect, and not working for A&P [obituary of S Wright, *LGuar* 9.3.1929].

1914–15
Cockermouth (CuC), St Michael. HJA's obituary in *B* [108, 1915, 312], says the practice's 'most recent work is the rebuilding, completed two months ago, of [this] ancient church'. This is a confusion with St Michael, Cockerham, which was dedicated on 20.12.1914 [*The Times*].

1931
Aldingham (Cu), St Cuthbert. Repairs to windows and walls [JP]. A&P produced a report on the church in 1931 but the substantial reinforcement works carried out that year were under Hicks of Hicks & Charlewood of Newcastle upon Tyne (the descendant firm of Austin & Johnson) [LRO, DDSr 10/3, fols 68–70: ICBS 12056].

NOTES

Introduction

1 BE: *South Lancashire*, 1969, 45.
2 Ibid, 44.
3 Examples of other highly regarded provincial practices in the North include those of John Douglas of Chester, and, on the other side of the Pennines, the Sheffield firms of Weightman & Hadfield, and T J Flockton. Also, in Newcastle, R J Johnson, who at one time was in partnership with Tom Austin, is well regarded. These practices could handle a wide variety of work and, certainly in the case of Weightman & Hadfield, their reputation extended far beyond their locality.
4 Lancashire:1.052m 1821, 1.667m 1831; Middlesex: 1.144m 1821, 1.567m 1831.
5 I explore such issues in 'Many and varied: provincial architects in Victorian England and Wales' in Ferry, K (ed) 2009 *Powerhouses of Provincial Architecture*. London: Victorian Society, 3–14.
6 Yet, as the catalogue of the great Norman Shaw's works reveals, he was not above minor house extensions or even a warehouse or church hall (Saint, A 2010 *Richard Norman Shaw*. New Haven & London, 425–56): I am grateful to John Minnis for drawing my attention to this (GB).
7 Vol 19, i–viii. The list was based on and slightly corrected from *Kelly's Building Trades' Directory*.
8 It is sometimes suggested that Sharpe built Heysham Tower, Heysham, 1836, but no evidence has come to light. No architect is given by Robinson 1991, 198.
9 See the various editions between 1849 and 1860 of *Masters's Guide to the Churches where the Daily Prayers are Said in England, Wales, Scotland, and Ireland*, in relation to population data from censuses.
10 *Bolton Evening Guardian* 19.1.1875.
11 They are in the LRO under reference DDsr 10/1–3.
12 7th Duke of Devonshire's diaries at Chatsworth House, vol 21, entry for 11 Apr.
13 Letter 21.8.1968 to DM.

Chapter 1

1 He was also organist at Knutsford parish church. Francis's father and grandfather (both also Francis) were musicians in Stamford, Lincolnshire, his father also being a town wait and earlier a pupil of J C Bach.
2 Daniel was a very successful Manchester cloth merchant. After his death in 1792, his eldest son William (father of JWW) went bankrupt in 1794, causing significant changes in the lives of his wider family, leading to his mother and sisters moving to Knutsford in 1795.
3 Frances and her sisters Catherine, Mary and Martha took over the school in August 1803.
4 Mary married on 21.1.1809 and Martha on 2.2.1809. Their sister Frances had married the Revd Thomas Broadhurst there on 26.7.1804.
5 This correspondence dating from 1803 to 1830 was acquired in the 1950s by Edward Hall, a manuscript and book collector and dealer, and divided up between various repositories. Hall transcribed many letters relating to Knutsford as '*Cranford* Again: The Knutsford Letters, 1809–1824' and deposited the result in Manchester Central Library, Languages & Literature Dept, in May 1957. These were retyped in 1980 with new pagination, quoted here as 'Hall, …'. The letters are deposited with the WAS at Leigh (GM), EHC204/M1005 ('The Knutsford Letters, 1808–1829': originals numbered in pencil by Hall). Other Whittaker letters there are under M1006A, B C, D. The ability to use this correspondence here has been much aided by transcripts made initially by Hall, then by Robert Jolley, and finally, and significantly, by Ray Jackson (TBA).
6 Manners-Sutton (as archbishop) held the advowson.
7 Catherine Whittaker to JWW, 19.3.1815, WAS, and Hall, 64 (*see* n5).
8 When her mother Elizabeth (née Holland) died in 1811 she was sent to live with the latter's sister, Mrs Hannah Lumb in Knutsford.
9 Chapple, J A V & Pollard, A 1966 *The Letters of Mrs Gaskell*. Manchester, letter 9, 17.7.1838, Elizabeth Gaskell to her sister-in-law Elizabeth. ES may have composed some 'pretty manuscript duet quadrilles' which Elizabeth Stevenson copied for a friend (Chapple, J A V 1997 *Elizabeth Gaskell: the Early Years*. Manchester, 196.
10 Catherine Whittaker to JWW, 17.8.1815, WAS, and Hall, 68.
11 Martha Sharpe to JWW, first letter on subject, 29.11.1820, WAS.
12 Martha Sharpe to JWW, 17.12.1821, WAS, and Hall, 128 (*see* n5).
13 Martha Sharpe to JWW, 11.5.1823, and Hall, 156.
14 ES to JWW, 7.9.1826. CHLLD, MS 6753.
15 Martha Sharpe to JWW, 10.12.1826, CHLLD, MS 6870.
16 Martha Sharpe to JWW, 22.10.1829, about her son refers to 'his friend Paley', WAS, letter 64.
17 Although he did not leave Sedbergh until June 1829.
18 On Benjamin Satterthwaite's death, Whewell wrote: 'to me his loss has its especial sorrow, for he was one of the very oldest of my friends; a friend who sought me out at the very beginning of my course' (letter, 13.12.1850, to Dr Thomas Mackreth of Halton, husband of Elizabeth Langshaw, Pearson Langshaw's eldest sister), quoted in Douglas, J M 1881 *The Life and Selections from the Correspondence of William Whewell*. London, 376).
19 Martha Sharpe to JWW, 12.8.1824, CHLLD, MS 6861, and Hall, 178 (*see* n5).
20 Martha Sharpe to JWW, 17.8.1824, WAS.
21 Letter ES to JWW, 29.8.1824, WAS.
22 Bullen 2004, 143.
23 Pevsner, N 1972 *Some Architectural Writers of the Nineteenth Century*. Oxford, 45.
24 Ibid, 45–6.
25 Bullen 2004, 144, from which the following information is also taken.
26 Rickman Diaries, RIBA British Architectural Library.
27 Letter Rickman to Whewell, 7.10.1832, Trinity College, Cambridge, R.6.11/32. Rickman was a Quaker and uses the Quaker style of dating '10 mo 7 1832' (ie 7.10.1832). Thus ES was *not* in

Birmingham twice with Rickman as Bullen 2004, 145, suggests as a result of a misreading of the date as 10 May.

28 *Transactions of Royal Institute of British Architects* 1874–5, 25, 219.

29 Cambridge University Library, Oo. VI.95–97.36.

30 For the German/French debate, *see* Lewis, M J 1993 *The Politics of the German Gothic Revival: August Reichensperger.* New York: Architectural History Foundation and MIT Press, 76–85.

31 Many places visited by Sharpe were listed by Whewell in his 1830 study of German architecture as ones he had visited.

32 *B* 28, 1870, 821–2.

33 Trinity College, Whewell archive, Cambridge, R.6.11/6.

34 Lewis, M J 1993 *The Politics of the German Gothic Revival.* New York: Architectural History Foundation and MIT Press, 12

35 Trinity College, Whewell archive, R.6.11/7.

36 Ibid.

37 Translated by Priestley & Weale as *An Essay on the Origin and Progress of Gothic Architecture*. A further translation by W H Leeds appeared in 1836 as *Moller's Memorials of German Gothic Architecture*.

38 His name would seem to be Bayer, judging by a later reference in his letter to 'my friend Mr. Bayer', and their plan was to meet at Frankfurt in May and travel to Worms and Speyer, on into Alsace, through France to Basel and Constance and reach Italy before winter.

39 He probably brought the dog out from England. In a letter to ES, 13.5.1834 (Manchester Archives & Library Service, transcribed by R I Jackson, 1996), Whittaker concludes 'With kind remembrances to Tartar', wording that suggests his familiarity with the animal.

40 Trinity College, Whewell archive, R.6.11/8. It would have been passed on to Whewell.

41 His first name and date of appointment are taken from Bullen 2004, 147.

42 Hence it is known as the *Schottenkirche, Schottenkloster* or *Schottenstift*. ES refers to it as 'The Scotch Ch.', adding, 'No German ever entered this brotherhood since the time of its foundation 1070.'

43 Trinity College, Whewell archive, R.6.11/9.

44 Ibid, R.6.11/10, from which the following details are taken.

45 The identity of this society is uncertain. ES also met 'old Dr. Stieglitz, Dom Probst, and author of one of the earliest treatises in Germany on Gothic architecture, at Leipsig: he received me very kindly, & complimented me so far as to make me a present of the last edition of his work.'

46 Letter to Rickman on 26.12.1834 written in another hand by some unknown amanuensis (Trinity College, Whewell archive, R.6.11/3).

47 Once again written in another hand.

48 Trinity College, Whewell archive, R.6.11/11.

49 Lewis 1993, n 19, 81.

50 Letter to Rickman, 26.12.1834, Trinity College, Whewell archive, R.6.11/3.

51 Benjamin Dockray who spoke about it at the dinner in Sharpe's honour when he left Lancaster in 1856 (*LGuar* 8.3.1856).

52 When he wrote two letters in Latin to the vice chancellor at Cambridge.

53 12,613 at the 1831 census; 13,531 in 1841. For the wide area now covered by Lancaster City Council the figures were 30,897 in 1831 and 32,998 in 1841. The townships of Scotforth and Skerton only became part of Lancaster in 1900.

54 Ex info (to TBA) Melinda Elder, author of 1992 *The Slave Trade and the Economic Development of 18th-century Lancaster*. Halifax.

55 Winstanley M 'The town transformed' *in* White, A (ed) 1993 *A History of Lancaster.* Keele, 148.

56 Letter Martha Sharpe to JWW, from Penny Street, 2.12.1837, CHLLD, MS 7007.

57 Borough of Lancaster, burgess lists, registers of electors, 1838–9, 1839–40, CHLLD; also *LGaz* notice, 4.5.1839.

58 Borough of Lancaster, burgess lists, register of electors, 1843–4, CHLLD; also *LGaz* notice, 12.6.1843. His police rate bill of 1849–50 shows he still *owned* the offices in St Leonard's Gate, which had two tenants, perhaps two of E G Paley, Tom Austin and John Douglas. By April 1851 all three were living separately in lodgings.

59 Fenton House deeds (ex info Andrew White).

60 Obituaries scrapbook, 1923/32, fol 28, CHLLD.

61 Directories and newspapers, *c* 1848–52, suggest there was another office in Cable Street/Parliament Street, at a time when ES had withdrawn from architecture and was still engaged in other enterprises.

62 Letter, 21.12.1835, Trinity College Library, Cambridge; Whewell archive, R.6.11/12. Rickman had written, he said, to dissuade him 'from entering the Profession; but his chief arguments rested on the annoyances & mortifications incident to it, and my want of practical information. I am fully prepared to submit to the former, and determined to acquire the latter as others have done before me.'

63 MALS, L97/1:9/1.

64 Sarah Yates (1804–86) had married in 1827 Edmund George Hornby. His father was the earl's first cousin, his mother was the earl's sister, and his father's sister was the earl's wife. They would later live for over a decade at Castle Park, Lancaster, where they were well known to the Sharpe and Langshaw families. A daughter would later marry a Feilden, thus closing the family circle.

65 A full account was given in *BS* 12.10.1836: various different groups, including, it seems, four bodies of masons numbering over 300, set off from various points and united into a single procession: 'the splendour of the whole affair was never surpassed in Blackburn'.

66 *BS* 13.6.1838. It added: 'The steeple we understand, is to be elevated a great deal higher than originally intended, Joseph Feilden esq., most liberally undertaking to defray the expense.'

67 Dated 21.11.1835, in the ICBS file 1933.

68 An undated (but located with 1836 correspondence in the ICBS file 1933) printed leaflet appealing for funds for the unbuilt church mentions a 'commodious School House, which is *now* [original emphasis] in progress'.

69 Adam Sedgwick's brother, John, was incumbent at Dent, a chapelry of Sedbergh, and had been at St John's, Cambridge, at exactly the same time as JWW. Sedgwick and Whewell's many tours together included the study of ancient buildings.

70 His father, John, had been curate at Howgill and had been schooled at Sedbergh.

71 MALS, L99/2:5/1: the incumbent, Lowther Grisedale, was then lodging in Bolton with first cousins of the mothers (who were sisters) of Edmund Langshaw and John Fletcher.

72 George was admitted to Cambridge from Lancaster Grammar School at barely 16. Before taking up his place he spent time at Sedbergh School. At St John's, Cambridge, his career was excellent – 21st Wrangler and two university prizes, before becoming a Fellow in 1830.

73 Sharpe also designed baseless piers at St John the Evangelist, Dukinfield (GM), 1838–41.

74 So suggested Bumpus, T F 1903 *Holiday Rambles among the Cathedrals and Churches of North Germany.* London, 226.

75 Whewell Archive, Trinity College, Cambridge, Add.MS.a 214/86.

76 MALS, L99/2:5/3. The CBC paid £2,712 out of the £4,012 cost (Port 2006, 331). In 1848 Sumner was elevated to the archbishopric of Canterbury, in succession to William Howley.

77 Greenall was the twin brother of (later Sir) Gilbert (1806–94). The latter built

Walton Hall in 1836–8 but ES was not the architect: later, however, P&A were brought in for the extensions of 1870.

78 The 12th Earl was Hornby's grandfather. His sister married in 1798 the future 13th Earl, and his brother Edmund in 1796 married the earl's sister. A son of this latter union was Edmund, who married in 1827 Edmund Yates's niece Sarah.

79 She was Eliza Jane Yates (1799–1856) and he the Revd William Waldegrave Park (1806–42). Their granddaughter Frances Eliza Griffith (1874–1953) married in 1900 Sir Gilbert Greenall (1867–1938), Richard Greenall's nephew, and the second Sir Gilbert Greenall, the 1st Baron Daresbury.

80 CALS, LNW/2/10.

81 The CBC paid £2,599 of the £3,299 cost (ibid).

82 BE, 336.

83 *LGuar* 26.1.1895.

84 The girls never married, lived their whole life together, and are buried together at Lancaster, close to their father. They lived for some years at 'Broadlands', Ambleside. Francis (1845–99) became proprietor of his father's Phoenix Foundry and in 1880 married his cousin Margaret, EGP's second daughter, living first in Lancaster in February 1866 and then in Caton. Edmund junior (1847–1925) joined Storey Bros in Lancaster and in 1873 married Alice Storey (1851–1926), before becoming a senior manager and board member. Both elder boys were educated at Rossall School, which their uncle 'Old' Ralph Fletcher had helped to found. Alfred (1853–1935) was educated at Haileybury College, trained as a lawyer, and in 1881 married Rosamond Bolling (1856–1943), daughter of the Revd E J Bolling, second incumbent at Lever Bridge church. After an abortive attempt at sugar-planting in Fiji with his cousin Walter Fletcher, he became a big-game hunter in Central Africa. Then a colonial civil servant, was knighted in 1903, and was Governor of Nyasaland (now Malawi), 1907–10.

85 Information on wedding attendees courtesy of Nicholas Deane, great-great-great grandson of Catherine Langshaw and Charles Merriman (TBA).

86 Trinity College Library, Cambridge; Whewell Archive, Add. MS. a. 212/64.

87 The Catalogue in this volume (*see* Appendix 5) cannot be squared with such an exact number. There is no reason to believe ES was exaggerating and it is likely that, given the frequent long delay between initial discussions and work beginning, the apparently later works in 1843–4 can legitimately be added in. To get to 31 one could add in Capernwray chapel (1840); Lancaster County Asylum chapel (1841–2, *see* 1839–45); and Barnton (Ch, 1841–2: unconfirmed attribution).

88 Cole, D 1980 *The Work of Sir Gilbert Scott*. London, 21.

89 Scott, G G 1879 *Personal and Professional Recollections* (facsimile edn Paul Watkins 1995), 85–8 (86).

90 The number is dated April 1842 so it had just come out (*Eccl* 1, 1842, 91–105 (91)).

91 The multi-talented Willis (1800–75), Jacksonian Professor of Natural Philosophy at Cambridge from 1837, had already published on medieval architecture.

92 Letter dated 4.9.1853 (*see* list on p IX of *A Visit to the Domed Churches of the Charente*, AA Memoir, 1882). ES wrote that he 'visited all the churches in Sussex of ancient date which are worthy of notice except two', as his contribution to the project.

93 *Eccl* 1, 1842, 21 (published Nov 1841).

94 *Eccl* 2, 1843, 23 (published Oct 1842). 'In other respects', the acerbic journal commented, 'it is truly a *modern* [its emphasis] Early-English building. The lowest stage of the Tower is absolutely ludicrous: each face presents a very tiny triplet, blank, and almost close to the ground.'

95 Ibid, 75–6.

96 BE, 1969, 150.

97 *Eccl* 3, 1844, 23–4 (24).

98 Ibid, 86–7. Opened formally on 18 February, but not consecrated until 26 June.

99 *B* 34, 1876, 553–4: *BN* 30, 1876, 565–7. It was entitled 'On the adaptability of terra cotta to modern church work: its use and its abuse'. In the article ES himself uses the term 'Pot Church'. The lecture was given later, on 16.6.1876, at the Architectural Association (*BN* 30, 1876, 618–19).

100 ES described the material thus: 'These deposits, in the form of small hard nodules, are generally found in the coal measures of that district. On exposure to the air they disintegrate and fall to pieces, and are then ground to powder, under heavy rollers, formed into a paste-like clay.'

101 Whether Penson stole a march on ES depends on exactly at what stage in the building history of Christ Church, Welshpool, terracotta was introduced. Penson also used terracotta at St Agatha, Llanymynech, Shropshire, 1843–4.

102 Cole, D 1980 *The Work of Sir Gilbert Scott*. London, 23.

103 Church history by Leonard, M *c* 1971 *The Family at Platt: The Story of the Church Family at Holy Trinity (Platt) Rusholme, 1846–1971*.

104 MALS, M35/6:6/2.

105 *B* 34, 1876, 554: *BN* 30, 1876, 566.

106 *B* 34, 1876, 554: *BN* 30, 1876, 566.

107 *B* 3, 1845, 571–2.

108 *B* 9, 1849, 137–8.

109 ERYAO, PE 153/50. Account paid on 4.11.1846.

110 *Great Exhibition of 1851: Official Descriptive & Illustrated Catalogue*: vol 1 (of 3), 331; Class 7: Civil Engineering, Architecture & Building Contrivances. It was exhibit 223.

111 *Preston Chronicle* 9.9.1843. Made up of the £52 10s salary plus £400 for the building of two wings at the asylum, £34 4s for plans and specifications at the Castle, £105 10s for plans for a new bridge, £10 10s salary as Bridgemaster, £68 10s for travelling expenses and measuring and surveying, £3 10s for postage etc.

112 Escolme, R D 2001 *The Big House: Capernwray Hall, Hall Garth and Swarthdale House: The Country Houses of Over Kellet*. Privately Printed, 12.

113 Eg Hornby Castle (C16), Gresgarth Hall (1805–10) and Whittington Hall (1831–2).

114 *JRIBA* 3 ser 2, 1895, 334.

115 BE, 2009, 347. Access was denied during research for the present study (GB).

116 Quoted by Jolley 1966, 116.

117 *Eccl* 4, 1845, 135–6; 7, 1847, 106.

118 Vol 1, chap 28, para xviii.

119 *B* 9, 1850, 480.

120 As noted in the list of ES's published works in the Architectural Association's Memoir to celebrate Sharpe, 1882 *A Visit to the Domed Churches of the Charente, 1875*, viii–ix.

121 Thomas Storey, first chairman of the company, had worked for ES on the 'Little' North Western and at the Phoenix Foundry.

122 *B* 28, 1870, 678–9.

123 No report seems to have been made of the 1871 tour. That of 1872 was reported in *B* (30, 1872, 660–1). The 1873 tour seems to have gone unreported too.

124 RIBA Archive, letters to Council 1835–77.

125 Reported in *Transactions of the Royal Institute of British Architects* 1874–5, 25, 217–19.

126 Part 1, Jan 1874; part 2, Feb 1875.

127 RIBA Archive, letters to Council 1835–77.

128 AA Memoir, 1882, 3, in *A Visit to the Domed Churches of the Charente, 1875*.

129 His estate was valued at under £14,000, a quarter of that left by EGP in 1895. This is less than one might expect after a lifetime of business ventures, but not all of these succeeded.

Chapter 2

1 In April 1851, Elizabeth Gaskell wrote to her daughter Marianne: 'Monday … expect Mrs Langshaw (Emily Sharpe) from Knutsford. … [she brings children]

to buy a present for their Aunt Fanny who is to be married' (Chapple, J A V and Pollard, A (eds) 1997 *The Letters of Elizabeth Gaskell*, Manchester, letter 95, 152).

2 Ellis, C and N (and Langcliffe Millenium Group) 2000 'Paley of Langcliffe' *in Langcliffe: Glimpses of a Dales Village*. Settle, 13–19. A John Paley was buried at Langcliffe in 1597, having died, perhaps, of the plague which ravaged the area in 1597–8. Even further back some Paleys are recorded in the Craven muster to fight at Flodden in 1513. Other family history information has been kindly provided by John Massey Paley, who is descended from the Revd James Paley (1783–1863), the third son of the Archdeacon (TBA).

3 This was becoming the normal 'Paley of Langcliffe' university and the stepping stone to a comfortable career in the Church. William's uncle John had been the first to follow this route, although other local Paleys are recorded as going there as early as 1616.

4 Paley, E 1825 *An Account of The Life and Writings of William Paley*, vol 1. London, 22–3.

5 It opens with the idea that anyone coming across a watch lying on a heath would conclude that it had been made by human agency. Likewise, a study of nature shows a divine intelligence at work.

6 At his death in 1805 Archdeacon Paley left four sons and four daughters by his wife Jane, possibly the daughter of James Hewitt, Carlisle wine merchant, and his wife Jane. Paley had no children by his second marriage to Catherine Dobinson (d 1819, aged 76) of Carlisle, probably the daughter of Thomas Dobinson and Catherine Hutchinson.

7 Born at Cawthorne, near Barnsley, and baptised 11 November at Carlisle. It is not known why he was born at Cawthorne, but in 1809 he went there as curate on his first clerical appointment. Probably he was named after his father's 'first and best patron', Bishop Edmund Law of Carlisle (1769–87), father of his close Cambridge friend and colleague John Law.

8 This was probably for two reasons: (a) the connection of the Senhouse family, who were related to the College founder; and (b) to the preferences given there to natives of Cumberland and Westmorland.

9 Edmund was appointed sometime between the death of his predecessor on 16 July and his marriage on 4 October. Though strictly the patronage of Easingwold lay with the new Bishop of Chester, George Henry Law, son of Bishop Law, enthroned on 28 July, the clergy list of parishes in the York diocese given in Torr's MSS (York Minster Library) shows that Edmund was chosen by Archbishop Edward Venables-Vernon of York, previously Bishop of Carlisle.

10 Frederick Apthorp Paley married, as his second wife, Selina Broadhurst, a first cousin of ES. She was the daughter of the Revd Thomas Broadhurst, Unitarian minister, and Frances Whittaker, the youngest sister of Martha Whittaker, ES's mother. Her brother Edward went to Shrewsbury School and Cambridge just before her husband, and was at Cambridge with ES.

11 EGP's letter quoted by W M Fawcett says this was 'about 1839 to 42', but it must have been early in this period in view of F A Paley's membership of the Cambridge Camden Society by mid-1840.

12 Guildhall Library, London, MS 12818/15, MS 12818A/100, 150. Edmund went there in 1830 after first attending the feeder school at Hertford in 1829 (ibid, MS 12818/15, MS 12818A/9, 130).

13 Recounted in his obituaries in the *LStd* 25.1.1895, and *LGuar* 26.1.1895.

14 Guildhall Library, London, MS 12818A/100, 150.

15 BL, Add MS 34590, fol 417, 20.11.1835. In 1848 the Gretford rectory was worth £525 a year, when a typical living was worth anything between £100 and £300 (figures from the *Clergy List*).

16 He had enlarged the vicarage at Easingwold earlier (Gill, T 1852 *Vallis Eboracensis: The History and Antiquities of Easingwold and the Forest of Galtres*. London; reprint parts, 1974, Easingwold, 93).

17 Of George (1708–65), elder brother of William Paley the headmaster, who married Mary Lawson, ie the same family as Isobel mentioned above who was George's grandmother.

18 Then not a mean occupation, but associated with entrepreneurs. He has been described as the man 'who led the industrial revolution in Leeds', and a man of 'endless enterprise but apparently limited vision'. Eventually, unfortunately, he went bankrupt! (Fraser, D 1980 *A History of Modern Leeds*. Manchester: Manchester University Press, 144: Langcliffe Millenium Group).

19 He was in Bradford for about 40 years and at one time he had two partners, John Sturges and Thomas Mason. At his death he owned most of the land around Langcliffe, although he had retired to Harrogate and had no direct contact with the village.

20 JWW's younger sister Sarah danced with Thomas at George IV's coronation celebrations in 1821, and it is probable that the families had met at parties at Sarah Buck's family home, 'Townhill'. The earliest dated connection is in 1808 in a letter of Sarah's to her son JWW, in which she writes: 'I took a walk to Bowling Hall the other day … Mrs Sturges made an affectionate enquiry after you' (letter 24.11.1808, WAS, EHC/M1006D).

21 Younger brother of John Green Paley. Letter Martha Sharpe to JWW, 3.8.1827, CHLLD, MS 6873.

22 Tom Paley arrived in Lancaster to meet Benjamin Satterthwaite and Edmund Sharpe in January 1828, very possibly in consequence of the above meeting (letter of Edmund and Martha Sharpe to JWW, 6.1.1828, CHLLD, MS 6755).

23 Edmund Paley and his family were well known to the Yorkshire Paleys. His younger sister Mary was the wife of Robert Paley (they were second cousins – married Carlisle 1807) and his younger brother Edward's wife, Mary Anne Paley (his second cousin – married Leeds 1815), was the first cousin of Robert Paley. His eldest sister Jane married Fergus Graham at Halifax in 1809, then the residence of Robert and Mary Paley. His elder sister Elizabeth's husband 'William Priestley' was born in Halifax. Later Robert and his family lived at Ripon some 14 miles west of Easingwold, and were there at the visit of Thomas Satterthwaite in 1827. Edward Paley and his family lived 6 miles west of Easingwold at the small village of Brafferton from at least 1817 to 1828, all their children being born there, and later at Ripley some 16 miles south-west. Thus round about 1830 three Paley families lived in close proximity.

24 The family connection is probably because Archdeacon Paley was a close friend of the family of Fergus's elder brother Sir James Graham and an influence on the upbringing of his statesman son of the same name (*see below*). In 1823 and 1825 Fergus assisted Edmund with baptisms at Easingwold, the first time about three weeks before the baptism of Edward Graham. He was appointed a prebendary canon of Ripon Cathedral in 1824 (his brother was MP for Ripon, 1798–1807). Fergus's nephew Sir James (also Ripon MP 1847–52) was Home Secretary in Sir Robert Peel's last government, 1841–6. Graham Land in Antarctica is named after him. He had been the First Lord of the Admiralty when it was first explored and claimed for Britain in 1832. In the later 19th century his estate covered an immense area – over 25,000 acres.

25 *BS* 16.8.1854. When the report was recycled in the LGuar three days later 'E.' was added before the name.

26 In albums in family possession (AF); part of an archive now in parts in the ALA and APA archives. The latter also has death notices of two of Paley's three daughters from the local press, where the styling 'E. Graham Paley' is usually adopted.
27 Langshaw (1814–96), a Lancaster surgeon, married Emily Sharpe (1812–93), the second sister of ES (ALA, nd but *c* 1878/9 on internal evidence). For Langshaw family history, *see* Goold, M 2008 *Mr Langshaw's Square Piano*. London.
28 It was two doors down from 37 (now 12), the home of Frances's mother Martha Sharpe from about the mid-1840s (possibly from 1843, when both Edmund and Emily Sharpe married) until her death on 26.7.1855. At the 1851 census Paley was living at 21 Castle Hill (near 23, which became the offices of Shrigley & Hunt).
29 Fanny Langshaw's diary 1856 (ALA). It was sold by William Satterthwaite (1790–1866), of a family distinct from but connected to that of ES's uncle Benjamin, and thought to be from the same hamlet, Colthouse, near Hawkshead (CuL) (CHLLD, Reserve Stock, Satterthwaite family, genealogical file).
30 The house was sold in 1903: Lancaster Council Records, 67/1.
31 Ex info CS.
32 Ex info Mrs C Workman.
33 26.1.1895.
34 15.1.1910.
35 *PG* 18.10.1856: it was a close contest, EGP securing 161 votes and his rival 168. EGP's father and grandfather were both Whigs.
36 He represented it along with R Hinde (*LGaz* 6.11.1858, 2.11.1861).
37 *LGuar* 26.1.1895.
38 *LStd* 24.1.1895.
39 The Choral Society was established in 1836 and was revived in 1857 when Paley was on the committee (*LGaz* 4.4.1857).
40 Ex info George Niven.
41 Quoted in his obituary, *LGuar* 26.1.1895.
42 Sharpe's letter of resignation is dated 31.12.1859 (LRO, QSP/3584/25). Presumably from 1856 he returned to Lancaster regularly to look after his business interests and could no doubt have combined this with periodic inspections of the hundred's roads and bridges. EGP's appointment was noted in the *PG* (2.7.1859), which pre-dates Sharpe's letter. The salary was a modest £2 10s a year.
43 EGP reported in 1880 that its design and construction had been poor and that it was in bad condition (*LGaz* 3.7.1880).
44 *PG* 19.12.1868.
45 On being appointed architect for the project, he retired. After it was built he returned to the committee in 1878 and continued to serve the asylum until his death.
46 London Metropolitan Archives, Normansfield Hospital Records, H29/NF/B/1/2; Conor Ward, O 1998 *John Langdon Down 1828–1896, a Caring Pioneer.* London; ex info Ward to TBA 7 and 8.10.2009, and ex info Heather Cadbury to TBA October–November 2009. Edmund Graham died at Normansfield in 1888 of tuberculosis and is buried in Teddington cemetery. EGP's first cousin, Dr Edward Paley (1825–86), son of his uncle Edward, was a lunatic asylum administrator from 1851 to 1883 (in 1863–83 at the wretched Yarra Bend Asylum in Melbourne where by strange coincidence HJA's eldest brother, George Brougham, died in 1872).
47 Ex info the late George W Watkins (to JP), who stated that Paley's sponsors were Henry Ball and Dr Moore (probably John Daniel Moore), and from Peter Mason (ex info to GB, 21.12.2009).
48 *LGuar* 26.1.1895. He was chairman of a branch establishment for private patients known as Brunton House, previously occupied by ES and his family from 1866.
49 The local press obituaries a few days later say the cause had not been established. His death certificate says 'Typhoid Fever 20 days'.
50 Hayward's obituary in the *JRIBA* 1905, 12, 582–3, says he worked 'in association' with Smith and that they had both been in the Hardwicks' offices.
51 *JRIBA* 3 ser 2, 1895, 334.
52 *Morning Post* 30.12.1881, 5: among EGP's distinguished fellow RIBA mourners were Charles Barry, James Brooks, Ewan Christian, Alfred Waterhouse and Thomas Worthington.
53 *LStd* (25.1.1895), says that he was a RIBA 'gold medallist', but this is a confusion with ES.
54 Possibly there were family links; there were many Carr families in the Giggleswick area, some with marriage connections to the Paleys of Langcliffe, the closest in time (to EGP) being headmaster William Paley's younger brother John, who married a Grace Carr, and contact might have been carried on with an Atkinson connection (could EGP have had his interest in architecture stimulated by the Atkinsons?). HJA's son, Geoffrey, would train with Walter Brierley (1862–1926), who carried on the practice from the Atkinson era.
55 Commercial companies commonly retained the names of their founder, and architectural practitioners sometimes did so when the identity of a distinguished former principal might confer prestige: Sedding & Wilson, Sir Arthur Blomfield & Son, and Temple Moore & Moore are examples after the deaths of their founders.
56 *LGaz* 2.10.1852.
57 Borough of Lancaster, Burgess Lists 1842–65, register of electors for MPs, freeman and property (CHLLD). EGP's occupancy of the second floor is mentioned in dispute over the borough voting list reported in *LGaz* 27.9.1862, 5.
58 When Paley moved in the only occupant was Edward Winder, a legal clerk, and his wife. Dunn left the area in 1862 but his legal office remained, probably until 1871. After 1871 Edward Winder and his second wife, Elizabeth, remained as occupants. Winder died in 1878, and three years later Paley took out a mortgage on the property (White, A 2000 *The Buildings of Georgian Lancaster*. Lancaster, 45, 72 n 99), but Elizabeth remained an occupant as caretaker until her death in 1893 (thanks to Andrew White for a summary transcript of the deeds to TBA Aug 2010).
59 *LGuar* 53, 1895, 82–6.
60 *Eccl* 3, 1844, 87.
61 Eg Melbury Bubb 1854 (by R J Withers); Evershot, 1866 (R H Shout of Sherborne); Thornford, 1866 (N aisle added, S wall nave refaced by Slater & Carpenter). A Wiltshire example is Kilmington, 1868–9 (by J P St Aubyn: the chancel had been rebuilt in 1863–4). Perpendicular work was strongly represented in Middlesex and the rebuilding of St John, Isleworth, in 1855–6 by James Deason is probably a nod to local traditions.
62 Scott at Sewerby (EY) in 1846–8, no doubt at the instigation of the squire with whom (Scott noted) he had 'difficulties', and also at West Meon, Hampshire 1845–6; William Butterfield at Trumpington, Cambridgeshire, mid-1850s ('unfortunately' said *Eccl* 18, 1857, 197), and Scottow, Norfolk 1858.
63 Various details of the church are taken from Billington, R N and Brownhill, J 1910 *St Peter's, Lancaster: A History.* London & Edinburgh, and also BE. The 1799 chapel survives as the Palatine Hall in Dalton Square.
64 His uncle, Gabriel, was a prosperous tanner, currier and shoemaker in Lancaster, who had been a director of the Lancaster & Preston Junction Railway.
65 Muthesius 1901, 43.
66 *BN* 11, 1864, 780.
67 *Bolton Chronicle* 7.10.1865.
68 An item in the *Manchester Courier* was culled for reports in newspapers as far afield as Hampshire, Suffolk, Nottinghamshire, Hull, Leeds and the London-based *Morning Post* (29.11.1865),

Standard (28.11.1865) and *Lloyd's Weekly Newspaper* (3.12.1865).

69 BE, 137.

70 BE, 1969, 79.

71 BE, 583.

72 BE, 684.

73 Banks 1984, 12.

74 Andrews, M J 1954–5 'The History of the Railway at Barrow-in-Furness'. Unpublished thesis for diploma course in railway history, City Literary Institute, University of London, 43.

75 Andrews, M J 1996 'The Development of the Furness Railway' *in* Battye & Peascod (eds), 12.

76 Subscription list in the *Barrow Pilot* 13.5.1871.

77 For a biography, *see* Banks 1984.

78 *See* Catalogue (Appendix 5), attributed works.

79 FR directors' minutes, National Archives microfilm RAIL214/4, 27.1.1857.

80 Andrews 1997, 12.

81 Most of the investors in the Grange Hotel Co were directors of the FR: the company aimed to raise £20,000 but only managed £17,000, probably resulting in the failure to complete the N end (ex info from Peter Robinson citing the company records in the National Archives). EGP is listed among the directors and shareholders in 1864 (*LGaz* 13.8.1864, 5).

82 Pevsner, BE, 56, found the brick arches an 'astonishing feature – astonishing for its date'. This is an odd judgement: Street had used brick arches at his St James the Less, Pimlico, of 1859–61 and the feature had already been taken up by provincial architects as in the case of Joseph Goddard's remarkable church at Tur Langton in Leicestershire, 1866–7.

83 After the establishment of IQ testing by the German psychologist Wilhelm Stern (1871–1938) in 1912, imbeciles came to be categorised as those with an IQ of 20 to 49 and idiots with an IQ below 20. 'Morons' were another recognised category with an IQ of 50 to 69.

84 *LGaz* (20.6.1868), in which the account of the foundation stone-laying of the Royal Albert Asylum gives a brief history of previous efforts to educate the mentally subnormal. The first efforts seem to have been in France, followed by Germany and Switzerland.

85 Park House, Highgate, London; Earlswood Asylum, Redhill, Surrey, 1853; Baldoven Asylum, Dundee, 1855; the Eastern Counties Asylum, Colchester, 1859; a Scottish national asylum at Larbert, near Stirling, 1863; and another, small one at Starcross, near Exeter, 1863.

86 Letter, EGP to HJA, 26.8.1866 (ALA).

87 Thanks to Peter Mason for stressing the Masonic significance of the occasion. It even stimulated a group of men to become Masons so they could 'take part in the proceedings at the laying of the foundation stone': one such initiation on 13.5.1868 was of John Harrison who would go on to run P&A's office in Barrow (information from Lodge of Fortitude 281, minutes 1865–76, 80, ex info Jack Baxter).

88 This and other information is from a detailed description in the *LGaz* 17.9.1870. Remarking on the cavity-wall construction, it said this was to render 'the interior perfectly dry and warm by cutting off all communication with the ever-changing external temperature'.

89 *Architect & Contract Reporter* 53, 1895, 82–6 (82).

90 Muthesius 1901, 43: BE 1969, 155.

Chapter 3

1 Canterbury Cathedral Archives, marriage licences 1726–50, bond and allegation, Jonathan Austen, 23.5.1743: Centre for Kentish Studies, Maidstone, Egerton parish church records, Poor Law assessments and churchwarden's accounts, 1736–74.

2 The business, known as Finch's, operated *c* 1776–1836 and appears in *The Epicure's Almanack* of 1815, effectively London's first *Good Food Guide*. It was started by Thomas' uncle by marriage, John Finch. Thomas worked with him and later with John's son Thomas, the business being continued until its closure by Thomas' nephew, also Thomas, elder son of his brother George.

3 Jane had been born in 1765 in Yorkshire, baptised at St James', Melsonby, near Richmond (restored by P&A, 1870–2). At Richmond the Smurthwaite family were involved in trade and local politics.

4 ES arrived late on 8.1.1845 and the next day dined with the family. The party also included Francis James Crow, who that year became the administrator of the Queen Anne's Bounty, whose money built or helped to build the new rectory at Redmarshall (his daughter married Tom Austin in 1856). On his way back to Richmond on 11.1.1845, James Tate jnr took ES to Darlington station (JTD).

5 Tate knew Meadley through contact with abolitionists whose cause was also of great interest to Paley. Details on Tate from Wenham, L P 1991 *Life of James Tate, 1771–1843, Master of Richmond School, Yorkshire, and Canon of St. Paul's Cathedral, London*. North Yorkshire Record Office, publication 46.

6 British Library, Add MS 34588, fol 254. Also in 1834 Tate wrote to his son, now the headmaster at Richmond, saying 'two sons of Edmund Paley are at Christ's Hospital' (North Yorkshire Record Office, letters and papers of James Tate, ZJT).

7 BL, Add MS 34590, fol 417, 20.11.1835

8 Her father, James Brougham, was a London surgeon, and from the Askrigg (NY) branch of the family. Her mother, Grace (née Idle) was the daughter of a Penrith innkeeper.

9 RIBA, ES, for *Architectural Parallels*, 1848, studies of Furness Abbey, PB182/30–45.

10 He shared the premises with John Hutton, a hatter and tailor, whose business ran there for about a century. Hutton was the great-uncle of Mary Hutton Bowes-Wilson, who married Geoffrey Austin, HJA's youngest son. Mary's father Thomas Bowes-Wilson, who married John Hutton's daughter Maria, also attended Richmond Grammar School at the same time as Hubert.

11 Annie (1834–1901) and her elder sister Jane played key roles in the meeting in 1854 at Gateshead of the suffragists Dr Elizabeth Garrett Anderson and Emily Davies, a meeting later said to have been a 'turning point in history' that 'effected the entrance of women to higher education, medicine and politics'. Later, after Tom's death, Annie was the third mistress, from 1870–2, of Girton College (at its original home at Hitchin). Emily Davies attended Annie's wedding in 1856 (JTD).

12 For Johnson's career, *see* Faulkner 1995.

13 Ibid, 4, 9 n4. Whether 'fellow travellers' is to be interpreted in a literal sense seems unlikely and in most causes means those who had also made the journey.

14 They arrived in Rouen on 16 August and took in Paris, Creil, Beauvais, Senlis and Noyon, with Paley returning to London on 1 September (Paley sketchbook in private collection).

15 Letter, EGP to HJA, 24.8.1866 (ALA).

16 Tom had carried out work for Dobson since at least 1860. Dobson had effectively retired from practice in 1862 after a severe stroke (Faulkner, T & Greg, A 2001 *John Dobson: Architect of the North East*. Newcastle upon Tyne, 178, 180).

17 In 1866 W S Hicks (1849–1902) joined them as an articled pupil: he became a partner of Johnson 1875 (Brodie *et al* 2002, 1, 902).

18 George Brougham Austin married and emigrated to Australia in 1851. His son, George Brougham Hubert Austin, became an architect with the Melbourne City Works Department, his main recognised work being the Romanesque Old Magistrates' Court, 1911. He was also a bicycle manufacturer and an inventor, designing what was probably the world's first automatic aeroplane in 1913 (ex info

Shirley Flockart, Constance Blake, Beverley Parton, and Brighton Historical Society, all of Melbourne).

19 Lewis, M (ed) 1991 *Victorian Churches: Their Origins, their Story and their Architecture.* East Melbourne, 150.

20 Letter from Anne Austin to her aunt Mary Webster, 13.4.1867 (ALA).

21 Similarly talented were his half-brother Tom, his half-sister Margaret and his sister Jane Eliza, for all of whom some work survives. On his death Hubert left behind a large number of watercolour paintings.

22 Letters to HJA from his father, 23.2.1854, 27.2.1855, 19.2.1856 (ALA). The school, built in 1848 in Skinner Street, was run by John Spiers Sladden, born 1811 in Kent, a mature graduate of Trinity College, Dublin.

23 On 1.8.1844 Harry went to Richmond School, the same day as Charles Dodgson (Lewis Carroll). Present that day were six Austins: Harry, his elder brothers George and Charles, his parents Thomas and Margaret, and his younger sister Jane Eliza (JTD).

24 Letter, 6.7.1859, from James Tate junior to HJA (ALA).

25 Richmond Grammar School record (now lost), copied, nd (*c* 1920s/30s) by HJA's daughter Hilda (ALA).

26 JTD.

27 Ibid.

28 Manuscript on the flyleaf of what is said to be HJA's copy of Johnson's *Specimens of Early French Architecture*, now in the RIBA British Architectural Library (SR 72.033.4/5 [44]). The sheet has been lost but a photocopy remains in the Austin biography file at the library. Also JTD.

29 Margaret Austin moved to Gateshead, via Norton, after the death of her husband (JTD).

30 'Local Prize for Success in Art awarded by the Department of Science and Art, Stage 3B'. The medal survives in the possession of TBA. The Department of Science & Art was a government body which functioned from 1853 to 1899, promoting education in art, science, technology and design in Britain and Ireland.

31 *Architects', Engineers' & Building Trades Directory 1868*, 37.

32 *See* n3.28.

33 On two scraps of paper in ALA Austin recorded two years' worth of payments from Scott from March 1865. These suggest (understandably) that he was not paid during his time as a Pugin student.

34 *See* n3.28. St John the Baptist, Cirencester, restored by Scott 1865–7, and he built St Mary, Mirfield, 1869–7. The latter date is not necessarily surprising in view of the often long delays between initiation and the execution of a scheme. Two other jobs are indecipherable.

35 ICBS 6268.

36 HJA's address is in the probate details at the death of his mother in August 1866. His mother (with Grace) lived then at 22 Chepstow Place (previously at 14 Pembridge Villas), near two of her Idle cousins at 53 Chepstow Place (will of Jane Margaret Austin, 28.2.1866, proved London, 11.9.1866).

37 It is not dated but lists individuals who were members between 1882 and 1890.

38 Diary in RIBA/V&A collection X(079)P 726.54(42). There is a tradition that he also visited the Low Countries, but there is no evidence that he did so on the occasion of the Pugin studentship: that he did so later is clear from drawings he made.

39 He probably visited the area on a family visit to Egerton in 1847 (Thomas Austin, sketches of the Lake District, North Westmorland, North Yorkshire and Kent, Abbot Hall Art Gallery, Kendal, Acc. no. 02539/84).

40 The funds were 'almost entirely provided by subscriptions from the shareholders of the South Eastern Railway Company' (unprovenanced newspaper cutting among papers at the church dealing with the 1917 jubilee services).

41 *B* 48, 1864, 247.

42 Quoted in the *Kentish Express* 4.5.1867, three days after the consecration.

43 *see* n3.28.

44 Photograph album in family possession (AF: *see* Bibliography).

45 Letter, EGP to HJA, 24.8.1866 (ALA). At the banquet following the consecration of the rebuilt church on 6.7.1871, EGP 'warmly eulogised the part Mr. Austin had taken in the work' (*LGaz* 8.7.1871).

46 *BA* 83, 1915, 159–60 (160).

47 Letter, Geoffrey Austin (GLA) to DM, 21.8.1968. GLA continued (with evident feeling), 'Rarely some relation would come for a day or two, which gave him no pleasure!'

48 *LGuar* 27.3.1915.

49 (Blackburn) *Weekly Standard* 31.3.1894, which notes that the people's warden was James Hatch.

50 She was to have been christened Frances (after Frances Whittaker and Frances Sharpe) but received the name Fanny after, it is believed, an error in the name was conveyed to the clergyman at the font: what had been done could not be undone! In the photograph (with relationship to the bride, if applicable): back row: John Chippindall (Langshaw family friend), Sarah Mary Merriman (bridesmaid, 1st cousin, daughter of Catherine Langshaw, Pearson's sister), Pearson Charles Langshaw (brother), Somers Clarke (best man), Fanny Langshaw (bride), James Pearson Langshaw (father), Hubert Austin (groom), Emily Langshaw (mother), Edith Fletcher (bridesmaid, 2nd cousin, daughter of John Fletcher), Francis Sharpe (1st cousin, son of Edmund Sharpe): front row: Henry Fletcher Pooley (2nd cousin), Emily Sharpe (bridesmaid, 1st cousin, daughter of Edmund Sharpe), Emily Paley (bridesmaid, 1st cousin, daughter of EGP), Margaret Deane (bridesmaid, 1st cousin, daughter of Marianne Sharpe), Emily Deane (bridesmaid, 1st cousin, daughter of Marianne Sharpe), George Langshaw (brother), and, at the front, Jack the dog (unrelated!).

51 However, the first presentation of the plans to the church committee in February 1867 did occur after Hubert had joined the practice.

52 Letter, 8.1.1869, from Hotel Buckingham, Paris, in which Edmund described Tom Austin as 'my dear old friend' (ALA, reproduced in Hughes 2010, 601).

53 At the 1871 census they were staying with the Revd Frederick Binyon and his family, friends of the Langshaws, at Burton-in-Lonsdale (NY) parsonage, recently built to P&A's designs. In June 1871, at the birth of their first child, Mabel, they were living at one of the three properties that made up 'Croftlands' (then new, probably number 2) on the north of Westbourne Road. Their next four children were all born there.

54 Although the initials and date of 1879 are very clear on a terracotta plaque on 'The Knoll', in 1881 the family was living at 'Mayfield' (never identified) and this was where the youngest child, Geoffrey, was born in 1884. 'The Knoll' appears in an 1886 directory so it may have undergone a name change about 1885. A device similar to 'The Knoll' plaque appears in a stained glass window at the top of the stairs at Heversham House (*see below*).

55 *See* n3.28.

56 Ex info Peter Finn of the Worthys Local History Group to TBA July 2010.

57 Hampshire RO, 39M73/BP/320. *VCH Hampshire* 4, 1911, 430, lists him as occupying it. The property was sold on his death by his executors (APA).

58 The latter is now in the ALA but is uncatalogued.

59 Jackson, B H (ed) 1950 *Recollections of Thomas Graham Jackson 1835–1924*. London, New York, Toronto, 58.

60 Vol 21 (entry for 11.4.1871) of the 7th Duke of Devonshire's diaries at Chatsworth House.

61 23.5.1890, 721. At Mossley Hill, 1872–5, Betws-y-Coed, 1872–3, Crewe, 1884–5,

Rawtenstall, Cloughfold, 1889–90, and Crawshawbooth, 1890–2.

62 The British Library holds copies (reference 1736.d7).

63 The term 'treasurer' suggests that the practice may have underwritten the project and that it was probably one of hobby publishing for Paley and his partner.

64 Wright was particularly prolific. In volume two he contributed or shared contributions to 14 of the 72 illustrations; in volume three it was 8 out of the 72.

65 A lithograph, dated May 1880, of lead rainwater heads.

66 BE, 1969, 131: BE, 2006, 213.

67 I am grateful to Alwyne Loyd, great-great nephew of Lewis Loyd, for family details which are amplified by research by TBA and JMH (GB).

68 Quoted by Alwyne Loyd.

69 Broadhurst was minister at the chapel at Blackley, north Manchester, 1791–3, where Lewis Loyd and his wife met. In 1803 Frances Whittaker, ES's aunt, became superintendent of Belvedere House, a residential academy for young ladies in Bath, and was joined there by three of her elder sisters, including ES's mother. In 1804 Frances married Broadhurst at St Swithin's, Walcot, he having been minister at Trim Street Chapel since 1797. They had nine children: the youngest, Selina Frances (1818–1907), became the second wife of Frederick Apthorp Paley, elder brother of EGP. In 1836 Edward Loyd laid the foundation stone of St Luke, Cheetham Hill, Manchester, half a mile from where his son would build St John's.

70 Apart from the tower, BE points to the 'sloping W wall' as 'real Perp' and remarks how 'the roof-line and arcade imposts of the previous nave appear in the [nave W] wall, illustrating how very much lower it [the old church] was. The N aisle roof is real Perp too, reused from the old N aisle.'

71 BE, 1969, 136.

72 Slater at Chetnole 1865; Slater & Carpenter at Thornbury 1866; also R J Withers used it at Melbury Bubb 1854.

73 The picture reproduced is held at the church where there is another, curious one embroidered out of human hair and thought to be of the 18th century. It shows a date of 1773 on the chapel, and also 'churchwarden' Y-tracery window in its east wall. When I (GB) wrote about this church in Ferry (ed) 2009, 92, I said the rebuilt work 'seems to owe little to what there was before'. I was then unaware of the picture reproduced here, which is from a vantage point different from that of the hair picture and shows little original Perpendicular work.

74 3.2.1871: text on pp 115–6.

75 Hubbard 1991, 129.

76 The competition and designs were reported on in *The Architect* 10, 1873, 147. The competition had been suggested by the bishop of Carlisle the previous year.

77 Ibid. In a notice about HJA's work the *BN* (58, 1890, 721), seems to have mistranslated this as '56 competitors'.

78 Ibid.

79 *North Wales Chronicle* 26.4.1873.

80 BE, 629.

81 BE, 439.

82 BE, 1969, 230.

83 *BN* 58, 1890, 721.

84 *LGaz* 11.5.1878, quoting from the Official Catalogue. Later A&P were one of the eight silver medallists in the Architecture Section at the 1900 Paris Exhibition: gold was won by Belcher, Collcutt, Emerson, Lutyens and Webb (*The Standard* 17.8.1900).

85 BE, 1969, 88.

86 BE, 141. BE, 1969, 72, was curiously and unfairly dismissive, referring to it in comparison to the firm's two other churches in Atherton as 'of course a minor church'.

87 The matter of accommodation is a little confused. Although said to have been designed for 520 people originally, when St Mark's was enlarged it was announced that the seats would be increased by 300 to 1,062.

88 Tom Dyer, a member of the congregation at St John's, kindly supplied me with copies of the sheets listing the parish documents.

89 Rowand Anderson of Edinburgh, Alexander Ross of Inverness, John Starforth (writing from Dumfries but said in the RIBA *Dictionary of British Architects, 1834–1900*, to have practised from Edinburgh) and John Langon of Belfast.

90 This was Anderson. The identity of the additional three is not known.

91 That they were not is suggested by a letter from the aggrieved Rowand Anderson to the Revd Lloyd, 24 July 1877, enclosing a note of charges for preparing his designs as the building committee had now appointed an architect. 'This action', he wrote, '... is a distinct breach of faith with the competitors.' If P&A had been competition entrants, it is hard to see how he could have been so upset. Whether he ever got his £52 10s for plans and 10 guineas for travel is not recorded.

92 BE, 136.

93 BE, 1969, 84.

94 Fidler (1973–4, 71), says that during the closure period the fittings were stripped out, with the light fittings sold to Manchester University and the stalls finding a home at St Chad, Farndon (Ch).

95 BE, 1969, 104.

96 BE, 1969, 136.

97 *BN* 46, 1884, 810.

98 *BN* 47, 1884, 251, 300.

99 Others in the list were Somers Clarke & Micklethwaite, J O Scott, A W Blomfield, Slater & Carpenter, and the eventual winner, William Emerson.

100 *B* 54, 1888, 173.

101 Ibid, 278.

102 Mannex 1882, 35.

103 Barrow Borough Council, General Purposes Committee Minutes 1871–82, meeting 20.11.1876.

104 This part of the story is told from the pages of the *BH* of 10 February and 7 March, which printed verbatim the proceedings of the full council's minutes and the General Purposes Committee minutes.

105 The six architects were John Y McIntosh, James Murchie, Sam Wood, Howard Evans, Thomas Bennett and John Turner (listed in that order). None of them designed any buildings of much distinction, the only ones finding their way into the Cumbrian BE volume being Bennett (Imperial Hotel, Barrow, 1874–5); McIntosh (Dalton-in-Furness Town Hall, 1884, Barrow Conservative Club (French chateau style), 1897–9 and Alfred Barrow School, 1888); and Murchie (County Hotel, Barrow, 1894–6). I am grateful to Matthew Hyde for providing details in advance of publication (GB).

106 *BN* 33, 1877, 607. Its '20' entrants is incorrect. There were in fact 23, which are named in *BA* (8, 1877, 299). The *BA* gives details of the entrants on pp 300–1, 313–14.

107 No style had been specified in the instructions (listed in *BA* 12, 1877, 299). The appearance of two Renaissance designs is indicative of the break-up of the Gothic hegemony for major civic buildings that took place at this time.

108 This was J Y McIntosh, who submitted it jointly with a J S Carmichael of Glasgow. The unpremiated entrants are virtually unknown individuals, with only E W Goodwin [*sic*] of London, Austin and Johnson & Hicks entering architectural history books.

109 In Battye & Peascod 1996, 9.

110 Despite correspondence with Furness Railway historians, Michael Andrews, Philip Grosse and Peter Robinson.

111 BE, 145.

112 Much of the following is taken from the duke's diaries held at Chatsworth House. vols 21–3.

113 *BA* 16 (1881), 407.

114 BE, 145.
115 Robinson, J M 'Hoghton Tower, Lancashire – II'. *Country Life*, 30.7. 1992, 50–3 (51–2); BE. An early *Country Life* article (18.2.1905, 238) simply states that Sir Henry began the restoration and that it was sufficiently advanced for Sir Charles to come back to Hoghton in 1880. Sir Bernard de Hoghton kindly allowed me to view the Victorian documentation held at Hoghton Tower.
116 I am grateful to Steven Brindle for discussing the restoration with me.
117 Although pencilled figures suggest the cost rose to £4,640.
118 Robinson 1991, 245.
119 Information here is derived from the Governors' Minute Book, 1874–94.

Chapter 4

1 Anderson was the surname of a family connected to Edmund Paley by two marriages: those of his youngest sister Anne and his granddaughter Catherine, daughter of his daughter Catherine.
2 The only mention of Adams in the BE series is Christ Church, Bournemouth, of 1880, an 'architecturally insignificant' church (later used as a church hall), built with his partner H P Horner (*Hampshire and the Isle of Wight*, 121).
3 RIBA PB 25/43 and PA5/1 respectively.
4 He also gets the credit for the major churches of St Silas, Blackburn; St John, Crawshawbooth; St Mary, Widnes (Me); and St Margaret, Bolton (GM). Secular works in Lancaster are named as Nazareth House, the Storey Institute, and Royal Infirmary (*JRIBA* ser 3, 1946, 422).
5 *LGuar* 26.4.1946.
6 *Huddersfield Daily Chronicle* 14.3.1895; *LMerc* 15.3.1895; *Liverpool Mercury* 14.3.1895; and *Manchester Times* 15.3.1895.
7 This excludes Sharpe's church at Scotforth, which was an entirely independent job.
8 BE, 1969, 190.
9 Quoted in BE. This account says Evelyn Cavendish, who laid the FS, was the daughter of Lady Lucy; in fact, she was a daughter of the marquess of Lansdowne and had married Victor Cavendish in 1892.
10 BE, 1967, 280.
11 ICBS file 10850.
12 I outline the history and some applications of this important feature of church planning in my book on Temple Moore, who made very effective use of it (Brandwood, G K 1997 *Temple Moore: an Architect of the Late Gothic Revival*. Stamford: Paul Watkins, 50–1, 79–83) (GB).
13 It is described fully in Fidler 1973–4, 73–4. He was writing in 1974 and it was clear that the decision to demolish had been taken by then.
14 BE, 1969, 418.
15 BE, 567.
16 The *Hertfordshire Mercury* (2.4.1893), gives a good summary of events up to the confirmation of the appointment of PA&P, and forms the basis of this account unless otherwise noted.
17 Ibid 5.11.1892, advertising the event.
18 The list is given in *BN* (62, 1892, 418), in a notice about the display of the designs at the Shire Hall.
19 BE, 1953, 123.
20 A spin-off from the All Saints' commission was a house designed by HJA for T J Sworder, a Hertford solicitor, under-sheriff for the county, and secretary of the church rebuilding committee. He owned substantial amounts of land on the Queen's Hill Estate nearby the church, which was being parcelled up for sale in the early/mid-1890s.
21 Guildhall Library, London, MS 22549 (register of entrants to Hertford): also MS 12818/15 and MS 12818A/9, 130.
22 The story is told in more detail in Pickford, C J 1987 *The Steeple, Bells, and Ringers of Coventry Cathedral*. Bedford, 34–60 (esp 42–55), although some new information is presented in what follows.
23 Christian wrote on 14.3.1891 (RIBA/V&A, A&P/1/1/5), Shaw two days later: 'taken as a whole I admire it exceedingly. The proportions are charming and it has the general ring of thoroughly good & accomplished work about it. There is an entire absence of any struggle to be original, and thus there are no affectations of any kind about it' (ibid, A&P/1/1/6).
24 It is inscribed 'AMDG E DONO HUBERTI JACOBI AUSTIN HUJUS ECCLESIAE ARCHITECTI MDCCCXCVII'.
25 Unless otherwise stated the information that follows is from Jones 1997.
26 The brewery had been founded in 1835 and was acquired by Smith & Bell in 1850. It was taken over by Stockport brewers Frederic Robinson in 1949, along with its 160 pubs. The building still stands in Hempshaw Lane (Barber, N 2005 *A Century of British Brewers, 1890–2004*. New Ash Green: Brewery History Society, 98).
27 CCALSS, P303/4505/20.
28 He had been Clerk of Works for the building of Middlesbrough Town Hall, 1883–9, designed by G G Hoskins of Darlington.
29 The inscription is 'By Thy Precious Death and by Thy Cross, Deliver us O Lord'.
30 Stewart, C 1956 *The Stones of Manchester*. London: Arnold, 122, 124.
31 BE, 344.
32 This *may* be due to the fact that the nave was extended west in 1909–10, but against this must be set the fact that the S aisle covers the length of the nave.
33 Respectively BE, 1969, 67, and BE, 122. Pevsner referred to the 'Slim piers' but then added 'not very high' – an odd remark, as they are quite lofty.
34 '[O]ne figure stands out above all the others in importance and very likely can be thought of in terms of its [recent English church-building] climax, John Loughborough Pearson.' (Muthesius 1901, 34).
35 Others he considered outstanding (*hervorragenden*) were (his ordering): T G Jackson, G H Fellowes Prynne, John Douglas, W D Caröe, W H Bidlake, Lacy Ridge (why Ridge?) and Charles Nicholson (Muthesius 1901, 48).
36 To some extent the numbers simply reflect the amount and type of material readily available to Muthesius.
37 *BN* 89, 1902, 101.
38 Ibid, 137.
39 1864–*c* 1935. He entered many competitions but, despite his considerable talents, was almost always, as he put it, 'near it – very near it' – as at Liverpool. For details *see* www.scottisharchitects.org.uk (accessed 30.11.2011).
40 *BN* 84, 1903, 647.
41 Apart from his signature on the drawings, *BA* (59, 1903, 402), in its preamble to reproducing watercolour studies for the building, says these were 'made by Mr. H. J. Austin during the preparation of his design'. It then continued this short piece, very properly, but referring to 'Austin & Paley'.
42 *BN* 84, 1903, 741.
43 *Builder's Journal* 17, 1903, 216.
44 *B* 63, 1892, 411: *BN* 66, 1894, 805. It went on: 'Their plan forms an irregular and rather closely-planted set of separate buildings ... which has no symmetrical arrangement of any kind', and criticised the fact that some of the residential houses faced the sun and some did not.
45 One selected entrant withdrew, complaining that the increase from four to six was an infringement of the conditions (*B* 64, 1893, 345).
46 *BN* 66, 1894, 834.
47 Ibid, 805.
48 *B* 66, 1894, 457.
49 She and Hardwicke married in 1878. He was a friend of Hubert Austin (letter, Geoffrey Austin to DM 11.9.1968) and also knew well Fanny's parents Pearson and Emily and her uncle John (ALA).
50 BW, which suggests the link range to the

classroom range to the left must also be by A&P.

51 Chance (1857–1934) was an assistant master at the school 1880–1930, and housemaster 1886–1925. He was a grandson of William (1788–1856), a founding partner of Chance Bros, glassmakers of Smethwick, glaziers of the 1851 Crystal Palace.

52 In an obituary notice of Hubert in family scrapbook in APA. However, there is no record at RIBA.

53 It was his brother Geoffrey who was willed his father's financial and other interests in the firm on his death in 1915 (will of 2.3.1907, just before Geoffrey joined the firm after *his* articles), although *both* sons were the executors. Bernard had two children, Katherine Tate (1901–83) and Basil Brougham (1902–2002), whose distinguished scientific, electronic career involved his being recruited to work on the UK atomic bomb project.

54 Letter by Geoffrey Austin (GLA) to DM, 21.8.1968.

55 Hubbard, E and Shippobottom, M 2009 *A Guide to Port Sunlight Village*. Liverpool, 107, and ex info Unilever Archives & Records Management, Port Sunlight (Aug 2010) (TBA). Unilever was created in 1930 by the merger of Lever Brothers and Margarine Unie. James Lomax-Simpson was on the board; he had been a director of Lever Brothers since 1917. Lord Leverhulme was his godfather.

56 Her father Thomas had been at Richmond Grammar School at the same time as Geoffrey's father, and her great-uncle John Hutton had once shared the same office address in Newcastle as Tom Austin. After their marriage they lived at 4 Hillside, opposite the Castle. He designed a small extension on the south side of the house. Their first four children were born while there: Thomas Martianez (born in Tenerife), John Langshaw, Barbara Bowes and Anthony Rudby (1914–96), father of Tim Austin, collaborator on the present volume.

57 The Shrewsbury School baths extension makes it probable that the original baths of 1887 were by P&A, the Paleys having had a long connection with the school. This link may well explain the firm's work at St Mary's church in 1884, in a town well outside the firm's normal geographic range.

58 Letter GLA to DM, 19.9.1968.

59 In the photograph was the identifiable figure of Geoffrey (in White, A 1993 *A History of Lancaster, 1193–1993*. Keele, 203).

60 Geoffrey's nephew Basil explained to JP that his uncle was told that if he went to the war he need not think of coming back to the firm. Basil was a boy of 12 when his grandfather Hubert died but remembered him as a stern and authoritarian figure (JP).

61 Private, no 3562, 1/5th Battalion of the King's Own Lancaster Regiment (KORL), a Territorial battalion, the regiment whose memorial chapel in the Lancaster Priory church his father had designed in 1903.

62 Geoffrey's second cousin, Kitty Paley (1889–1966), the daughter of Harry Paley, was engaged to Lt Anthony George Attwood Morris, a professional soldier with the 1st Battalion of the KORL. Morris was killed in France on 30.10.1914. She never married.

63 2nd Lieutenant, 2/4th Battalion of the Loyal North Lancashire Regiment (LNLR), a Territorial battalion, based in Preston.

64 Mary Austin lost both her elder brothers in the fighting in the Ypres sector; George on 17.6.1915 and Jack on 7.6.1917.

65 That morning three battalions of the LNLR had casualty rates of one-third, a rate at which it is generally considered that infantry groups cease to function effectively.

66 Building plans for 'Fairlight' for Thomas Bowes-Wilson by HAP, 10.5.1919 (*see* Catalogue, Appendix 5).

67 Letter GLA to DM, 21.1.1968

68 *See* n4.53.

69 The school had been founded in 1877 as the St Andrews School for Girls, later changing its name when it moved its site within the town. Its first headmistress was Louisa Lumsden, one of the five Girton Pioneers, who had been a student when Tom Austin's wife Annie had been the Girton mistress. The school had been attended by Geoffrey's wife Mary, 1897–1901, and would later be attended by his two daughters, Barbara 1921–30, and Ann 1925–38, and one of his granddaughters, Jane 1964–9.

70 The cause was kidney disease: the death certificate cites nephritis and uraemia.

Chapter 5

1 *See* n4.62. In the last year of the war she served in France as a Red Cross orderly.

2 On 4.1.1965, for example, Kitty Paley wrote to Sybil Stewart (née Austin) hoping to arrange a meeting and complaining about the lamentable housing in Caton which 'must have doubled' the population: 'I often wonder what the parents would think. I am sure Father would have a fit if he saw all the ugly houses they are putting up!' she added with some justifiable gloom (ALA).

3 Wilson was Henry Wilson (1864–1934), who went on to a brilliant career as an Arts and Crafts designer. 'Moore' was Leslie Moore (1883–1957), Temple Moore's son-in-law and partner from 1918.

4 LRO, DDSr 10/1–3.

5 Figures extracted by JP are:

	Actual	Possible	Total
Pre-1925	1		1
1925–9	30	5	35
1930–4	57	14	71
1935–9	44	10	54
1940+	6	1	7

Lancashire pre-1974	86
Westmorland, Cumberland pre-1974	20
West Yorkshire	13
Other	14

6 The former, Thomas Ryland, was at Sedbergh 1894–6; the latter, Claude Swanwick (d 1918), in 1891–4 (1930 *Sedbergh School Register 1875 to 1928*. Sedbergh, 119 and 94, respectively).

7 Note from Jackson for Mr Johnson, Hon Secretary of the Parish Church Council, 29.8.1932 (among papers at the church).

8 This was a daughter church of St Mark's. At the time St Mary Magdalene, Coventry, was under construction to Jackson's design.

9 RIBA, JaHT/2, letter 22.5.1933. Jackson designed the rather delightful stalls with their human and animal figures on the ends.

10 BE, 121.

11 CRO(K), WPR P90/40, 46.

12 This was John Brassington of Settle (JP).

13 According to a note in the schedule of parish records for St John, Greenock, apparently prepared by the National Archives of Scotland in the 1960s (item 145).

Appendix 1

1 *LGaz* 3.9.1836.

2 *LGaz* 7.1.1837.

3 *LGaz* 29.4.1837: on this occasion another attendee was George Marton MP, who would shortly provide ES with his major secular commission, the remodelling of Capernwray Hall.

4 *LGaz* 18.4.1840.

5 One of Lancaster's leading citizens for nearly four decades, councillor for 15 years, alderman and mayor twice, he and ES were both involved with sanitary reform, railway building and the development of the Lancaster Asylum.

6 *LGaz* 7.5.1842.

7 *LGaz* 26.1.1842. On 4.1.1840 the *Gazette* reported ES had been given permission 'to erect a wharf, with a stage, etc. for the

shipment of stone, he agreeing to pay a toll of a halfpenny per ton for the stone shipped, and five guineas a year for the land on which the wharf would be established'.

8 *LGaz* 25.9.1840. His son, also Edmund, was an even more skilled archer.

9 Gilchrist, J J 1910 *The Lancaster Cricket Club, 1841–1909*. Lancaster, 4.

10 The following is taken from Betjemann 1982, 20ff.

11 *LGaz* 25.11.1843.

12 From this point the Music Hall was taken over from ES by the Lancaster Athenaeum Co for £2,364, roughly half of it in cash and half in shares. At his death ES still held 180 shares.

13 *LGaz* 4.1.1851 from which further details are taken.

14 Ibid.

15 Reported in the *LGaz* 22.6.1839.

16 *Lancaster and Preston Junction Railway: correspondence between Edmund Sharpe, Architect, Lancaster, and S. Edwd Bolden, Secretary to the Directors of the Company; Letters I to XVIII, with Covering Letter, Address and Appendix, dated 5 March to 17 June 1839*.

17 The last seven miles from Wennington to Bentham opened on 1.6.1850, thus linking the West Riding with the W coast.

18 Baughan, P E 1987 *The Midland Railway: North of Leeds,* 2 edn. Newton Abbot: David & Charles, 91.

19 Ibid, 91–2.

20 Ibid, 93.

21 Ibid, 94.

22 Binns, D 1982 *The 'Little' North Western Railway.* Skipton, 14.

23 These and other details from Jolley 1966, 109–11.

24 Extracts from the Minutes of the Directors' Meetings of the LC&SR, dated: 4, 11, 27.6, 10 & 15.8.1854, and 9.1, 13 & 23.2.1855; National Archives, RAIL 372/3.

25 *LGuar* 18.2.1928.

26 Price, J 1986–7 'The Lune Foundry, Lancaster', *Contrebis* 13, 22–7.

27 *LGaz* 6.11.1847.

28 Such Boards of Health were envisaged under the first Public Health Act of 1848.

29 *A History of the Progress of Sanitary Reform in the Town of Lancaster from 1845 to 1875; and an Account of its Water Supply*. It comprised mainly the reprint of a series of letters written by ES to the *LGuar*.

30 Smith's report was printed in two parts in the *LGuar* for 23 and 30.6.1849.

31 The *LGuar* for 14.7.1849 carried full reports of the three meetings held in quick succession of 'interested parties' opposed to Smith's recommendations on grounds of cost: first the ratepayers, then the Police Commissioners, and finally the Town Council, despite the chairmanship of ES (as mayor) at the first and last.

32 *See* nA1.29, 26–7.

33 Ibid, 28.

34 The tale is told in the *LGuar* 7.5.1881.

35 *LGaz* 24.7.1852, reporting his address to the Local Board of Health on 22.7.1852.

36 1851 *A Letter on Branch Railways addressed to the Right Honourable Lord Stanley of Alderley, President of the Board of Trade, containing Suggestions for the Creation of a System of Secondary Railways for the Agricultural Districts*. London.

37 The engineer was now Birkinshaw of Birkinshaw & Castle, engineers of London.

38 An extension to Betws-y-Coed opened on 6.4.1868, by which time ES was already back in Lancaster, having spent three years abroad. A further extension to Blaenau Ffestiniog opened in July 1879, two years after ES's death.

39 'Sharp rinwedddawl' in the original, the manuscript of which is in the National Library of Wales (ref 9222E): thanks to Rhys Jones for clarifying various aspects of the translation.

40 By this time his two eldest boys, Francis and Edmund, were at Rossall School.

41 This and the subsequent section are edited adaptations from chapter 7 of Jolley's thesis. The information here is derived from a four-page letter to Robert Jolley from *Archives d'État, Hôtel de Ville, Republique et Canton de Genève*, 10.12.1963.

42 The *Indicateur des Adresses pour le commerce et l'industrie de la Ville de Genève, la banlieue, Carouge, Chêne, St Julien et Fernex* for 1866 gives ES's address as 5 Route de la Chêne. More recent research by the State Archives in Geneva (letter to JMH, 18.8.1998) suggests that this was *not* the same as the 'Richemont' named by Burn, but because of two subsequent changes in street names and numbering is now to be identified with 9 Carrefour de Rive, a rebuilt block of flats several storeys high in a relatively built-up area in the centre of town. However, considering that in 1863 Sharpe had *all* his family with him (Mrs Sharpe aged 52; Francis, 18; Edmund, 16; Emily, 14; Catherine, 13; Alfred, 10) plus presumably domestic staff, this seems hard to visualise.

43 Jolley 1966, 153, notes that this was an application of John Howarth's 'patent perambulating principle' registered in 1860 and introduced at Salford in 1861.

44 *Les Chemins de Fer du Midi: étude Historique*, Centre d'Archives, SNCF, 2, avenue de Bretagne, 72100 Le Mans.

45 Ibid.

46 Item 6 from documents obtained by Robert Jolley in June 1965 from the Archives des Pyrénées-Orientales, Perpignan.

47 Information from John Silveyra to JMH, August 1999, quoting material from Mme E Praca of the Pyrénées-Orientales Départment Archives.

Appendix 2

1 Something of an exception relates to Sir Ernest George, 60 of whose pupils signed a 'congratulatory address' to him in 1910 on the occasion of his being elected an Associate of the Royal Academy: they obligingly added (occasionally slightly inaccurately) the dates when they were in his office (*see* Grainger, H J 2011 *The Architecture of Sir Ernest George*. Reading, appendix 1.

2 *See* Hubbard 1991.

3 CS says that Douglas was working on EGP's house commissions at Wennington Hall, 1855–6, and 'The Ridding', Low Bentham (NY), 1857–60.

4 I am most grateful to JMH for these and the following comments (GB).

5 1904 *Lancaster Fifty Years Ago*, vol 2, Jan 1852 to Dec 1853. Lancaster, 401.

6 Obituary of Thomas junior, *BS* 3.8.1859.

7 In all Austin saved five lives, for which he was awarded the Silver Medal of the Royal Humane Society in 1848: reported in *LGaz* 6.1.1849, which noted that the incident took place 'some years ago'.

8 1904 *Lancaster Fifty Years Ago*, vol 2, Jan 1852 to Dec 1853. Lancaster, 401.

9 1855 *Slater's Directory of Lancashire*, 26: *LGaz* 1.12.1855, 29.4.1857.

10 Brodie *et al* 2002, 2, 1051.

11 The minutes of the Lodge of Fortitude 281 in Lancaster for the year 1872 (recorded 3.10.1873) show the address as Barrow (ex info Jack Baxter); however, he did not transfer to the local Hartington Lodge 1021 until 12.1.1874 (membership records of the lodge at the Library and Museum of Freemasonry, London, ex info the librarian, Martin Cherry).

12 This was stated in his obituary in *BH* 11.4.1896. Reports in the *BH* in 1872, however, suggested Noble as being responsible for the base.

13 *BN* 3.4.1896.

14 CRO(B), BBP 2247 for additions at St Mark's church.

15 Visiting his grandmother in Preston at the time.

16 He described himself as an 'Architect, Illuminator, Designer, Lithographic and General Draughtsman'. It seems odd that he paid to advertise in Lancaster when his place of work became Liverpool. No corresponding advertisements were placed in the *Liverpool Mercury* at that time.

17 *Liverpool Mercury* 30.12.1879.
18 Gore's *Directory*: I am grateful to Joseph Sharples for information on the Liverpool directories regarding Johnson (GB).
19 Details thus far from Brodie *et al* 2002, 2, 14, and ex info TBA.
20 Brodie *et al* 2002, 2, 434.
21 Ibid, 1, 16.
22 SSGM, 1898, 1900.
23 Lancaster & Skerton Cooperative store, Skerton (*LGuar* 21.6.1902).
24 LRO, DDSr 10/3, 225.
25 Information from censuses. He was still 'manager' in 1881 but was retired in 1891 and 1901.
26 *LGuar* 15.4.1911.
27 Information from Peter Mason, citing thesis by John Stanley, 'Freemasonry & the Middle Class in Lancaster 1789–1914'.
28 ARIBA nomination papers, British Architectural Library, Av13, 35 (microfiche 59/62).
29 *BN* 67, 1894, 6.
30 Hinge, D G F 1981 *Richard Thomas Beckett, Architect, 1867–1937: a Preliminary Study with a Chronological List of Projects and Executed Work*. Bishop Auckland, from which other details are taken.
31 Brodie *et al* 2002, 1, 821.
32 On census day 1881 he was an 'Architect' lodging in Norwich. By 1901 he was an 'Architectural Draughtsman' living with his family in Preston.
33 Brodie *et al* 2002, 2, 354–5.
34 *LGuar* 19.6.1959.
35 He might well have done but under the A&P banner (LRO MBMO/HE, vol 2, covering 1901–39, 125, 127, 130).
36 *LGuar* 9.3.1929.
37 SSGM, 1874–94, 6.8.1875.
38 Sometimes misattributed to A&P.
39 Ex info CS.
40 Brodie *et al* 2002, 1, 57.
41 Ibid, 1, 122.
42 Ex info TBA.
43 Brodie *et al* 2002, 1, 921.
44 Letter by Geoffrey Austin to DM, 11.9.1968.
45 *Lancaster Observer* 26.3.1915.

Appendix 3

1 This statement, of course, ignores cases where a building contractor erected, say, a war memorial cross, but someone else carved it.
2 I have discussed this with a number of experts on Victorian architecture but with no conclusion (GB).
3 SSGM, 10.8.1877.
4 Governor's Minutes 1874–94, 8.12.1876.
5 *LGaz* 12.9.1885, from which other details are taken.
6 *LGuar* 8.3.1856: Hughes 2010, 3, 379.
7 Hughes 2010, 3, 199–200.
8 Cross Fleury 1891, 352.
9 These and other details are from his lengthy obituary in *LStd* 20.10.1893.
10 1871–2, 1887–8, 1888–9, and 1890–1.
11 *LGaz* 19.1.1878.
12 This and other details from 1990 *Lancaster a Century Ago*. Lancaster, 'a reprint of part of a book first published in 1889' (introduction by JP).
13 For the early history of the firm, *see* Stuart, S 2008 *Gillows of Lancaster and London, 1730–1840*. Woodbridge: Antique Collectors Club.
14 These and other details are from his lengthy obituary in *LStd* 15.2.1895.
15 From obituary of Charles Blades, *see LStd* 20.10.1893.
16 *LGuar* 7.10.1922 (obituary of John Hatch) from which other details here are taken.
17 1894 *A Graphic Description of Lancaster and Morecambe*.
18 This list was formerly in the possession of the late Charles Jackson and is currently in private hands.
19 These 'stray' commissions might be explained, say, by someone in Lancaster memorialising a relative: Hatch's would hardly have been a household name in c 1900 Suffolk or Essex.
20 The Catalogue in this book only names contractors/craftsmen when their involvement is firmly established by documentary evidence (*see* Appendix 5). In addition, there must have been many jobs where Hatch's (and the other men discussed in this appendix) were employed but not named in our sources. The handwritten list quoted in note 6 mentions many places where P&A/A&P were involved but this cannot be taken as sure evidence that Hatch's worked under them on the jobs in the Catalogue of Works (*see* Appendix 5) (especially as the handwritten list contains no dates).
21 *LGuar* 5.9.1986.
22 *LGaz* 21.11.1885.
23 *Liverpool Mercury* 31.12.1897.
24 Catalogue of parish documents, item 124.
25 Ibid.
26 The following draws on Waters 2003.
27 Letter from Geoffrey Austin to DM, 21.8.1968.
28 Waters 2003, 2.
29 Ibid, 29, which unfortunately gives no source.
30 LRO, Order Book 1877–1882, DDSr 5/1.
31 Ibid, 379.
32 This section relies on information from an interview between John Brassington and JP in 1992. The firm had several names during its lifetime: Brassington & Corney, Henry Brassington & Sons, Brassington, Sons, & Co.
33 Much of the following uses obituaries in the *BH* and the *Barrow Times*, both of 9.9.1882. He was born at Lowick, north of Ulverston.
34 Noszlopy, G T & Waterhouse, F 2005 *Public Sculpture in Staffordshire and the Black Country*. Liverpool, 283, say he was in partnership with a Mr Nourse from 1870 but, strangely, and despite Roddis's death in 1887, his name alone appears in Birmingham directories until 1899. The firm is then listed from 1901 until 1923 as 'Roddis & Nourse'. His obituary (*Birmingham Post* 5.8.1887) says that he carried out the carving on the Birmingham Art Gallery (except for the pediment), at Goulbarn Cathedral in South Australia, and at the time of his death was working on a commission for Christchurch Cathedral in New Zealand.
35 *Birmingham Daily Post* 18.10.1871. This article also noted that Roddis was in the course of executing 'a richly wrought alabaster sarcophagus' to the late Earl of Derby at Knowsley church.

BIBLIOGRAPHY

Primary sources

There is no comprehensive archive of the firm's papers, which were destroyed when it closed towards the end of the Second World War. The only substantial body of business papers surviving is the three volumes relating to the post-1918 practice (from the Shrigley & Hunt archive), held at the Lancashire Record Office (LRO) under reference DDsr 10/1–3. Three volumes of mid/late 19th-century sketches and drawings, formerly held at Lancaster Library (LL 1, 2, 3 in the Catalogue), are in the course of transfer to the LRO at the time of writing: the first has a catalogue number of DDX 2743 acc10980; the others do not have numbers assigned at the time of writing.

As to personal information, the situation is rather more fortunate, thanks to an archive first collected by Emily Sharpe, together with her husband James Pearson Langshaw. This collection was preserved and enhanced by their daughter Fanny, with her husband Hubert Austin, and then further enhanced by their daughters Ethel, Sybil and Hilda, until the death of the latter two in 1968. The archive was then dispersed, but has been brought together again for the present work by Tim Austin. Physically, it is now distributed in several places, in particular in photograph albums that remain in family possession (AF); on deposit in the Austin Langshaw Archive, Rare Books & Archives, Lancaster University (ALA; partially catalogued as of 2011); and in the Austin Paley Archive, Lancaster Museum, MS LM 86/129 (APA; partially catalogued as of 2011). Various sketchbooks by E G Paley also survive in private hands. As for Edmund Sharpe, considerable archival material survives, notably in correspondence kept by his cousin, the Revd J W Whittaker of Blackburn, as explained in Chapter 1, note 5. Other material is also referenced in relation to Chapter 1.

Much use has been made of contemporary newspapers, which are a valuable source of information on invitations to tender (as public notices), the laying of foundation stones and the consecration/opening of various buildings. References are provided in the Notes and Catalogue (Appendix 5) as appropriate.

Additional archival material in the form of local authority building plans (for Barrow-in-Furness (CuL) and Lancaster), parish records and other material is referenced in the Notes and Catalogue (Appendix 5).

Writings about the practice

Brandwood, G 2009 'Splendour in the North: The churches of Paley and Austin', *in* Ferry, K (ed) *Powerhouses of Provincial Architecture*. London: Victorian Society

Bullen, J B 2004 'The Romanesque Revival in Britain, 1800–1840: William Gunn, William Whewell and Edmund Sharpe'. *Architectural History* 47, 139–58

Faulkner, T E 1995 'Robert James Johnson, architect and antiquary'. *Durham University Journal* ns, 41:1, 3–10, xii

Fidler, J A 1973–4 'The Ecclesiastical architecture of the firm of E G Paley and H J Austin, 1868–1897 AD', Unpublished BA dissertation, University of Sheffield

Hughes, J M 2010 *Edmund Sharpe, Man of Lancaster: Architect, Engineer and Entrepreneur*, 3 vols. Stockport: J M Hughes

Jolley, R 1966 'Edmund Sharpe (1809–77): A study of a Victorian architect'. Unpublished MA thesis, Liverpool University

Jolley, R 1977 *Edmund Sharpe, 1809–1877*. Lancaster: Visual Arts Centre, University of Lancaster (12pp exhibition guide)

McLaughlin, D 1989 *in (passim)* Howell, P & Sutton, I (eds) *The Faber Guide to Victorian Churches*. London: Faber and Faber

Muthesius, H 1901 *Die neuere kirchliche Baukunst in England.* Berlin

Pearce, M D 2006 'The development of the ecclesiastical architecture of Sharpe, Paley and Austin'. Unpublished Diploma in Conservation of Historic Buildings thesis, Architectural Association

Price, J 1994 *Paley & Austin: Architects of Lancaster,* Local Studies 19. Lancaster: Lancaster City Museums

Price, J 1998 *Sharpe, Paley & Austin: A Lancaster Architectural Practice 1836–1942,* Occasional papers 35. Lancaster: Centre for North-West Regional Studies, University of Lancaster

Price, J 1999 'The architectural works of H A (Harry) Paley, 1923–1939', *Contrebis* 24, 34–7 (published by the Lancaster Archaeological & Historical Society)

Other published sources

Andrews, M 1996 'The development of the Furness Railway' *in* Battye, R & Peascod, M (eds) *Furness Railway 150.* Grange-over-Sands: Cumbrian Railways Association

Anon (Stancliffe Estates) 1996 *Stancliffe Estates Co Ltd, Darley Dale, Derbyshire* (illustrated catalogue for the Darley Dale quarries)

Banks, A G 1984 *H W Schneider of Barrow and Bowness*. Kendal: Titus Wilson

Battye, R & Peascod, M 1996 *Furness Railway 150. A History of the Furness Railway*. Grange-over-Sands: Cumbrian Railways Association

Brodie, A *et al* 2002 *Directory of British Architects 1834–1914*, 2 vols. London: Continuum

Bulmer, J (ed) 1911 *History, Topography and Directory of Furness & Cartmel*. Preston: T Bulmer & Co

Bulmer, J (ed) 1913 *History, Topography and Directory of Lancaster & District*. Preston: T Bulmer & Co

Bulmer, T & Co 1901 *History, Topography and Directory of Cumberland*. Preston: Bulmer & Co

Bulmer, T & Co 1905 *History, Topography and Directory of Westmorland*. Preston: T Bulmer & Co

Fleetwood-Hesketh, P 1955 *Murray's Lancashire*. London: Murray

Grosse, P 1996 'Furness Railway architecture' *in* Battye, R & Peascod, M (eds) *Furness Railway 150*. Grange-over-Sands: Cumbrian Railways Association

Hewitson, A 1900 *Northward: Historic, Topographic, Residential and Scenic Gleanings etc., between Preston and Lancaster* (facsim edn Landy 1993)

Hubbard, E 1991 *The Work of John Douglas*. London: Victorian Society

Norman, K J 2001 *The Furness Railway*, vol 2. Kettering: Silver Link

Port, M H 2006 *Six Hundred New Churches: the Church Building Commission, 1818–1856*. Reading: Spire Books Ltd

Robinson, J M 1991 *A Guide to the Country Houses of the North West*. London: Constable

Slater's Royal National Commercial Directory of Lancashire, 1895. Manchester

Waters, W 2003 *Stained Glass from Shrigley & Hunt of Lancaster and London*. Lancaster: Centre for North-West Regional Studies, University of Lancaster

Works specific to individual places with multiple references in the notes or catalogue (local publication unless otherwise stated)

Abram, W A 1877 *A History of Blackburn, Town and Parish*. Blackburn: Toulmin (facsim ed THCL Books 1990)

Ashworth, E B 1979 *The Church of St Matthew the Apostle, Habergham Eaves, Burnley, 1879–1979*

Barrett, P & Co 1886 *Topography and Directory of Preston, The Fylde, Lancaster and District*. Preston

Bennett, P 1990 *The Chapel of St John the Baptist, Rossall*

Betjemann, A G 1982 *The Grand Theatre, Lancaster: Two Centuries of Entertainment*, Occasional Papers 11. Lancaster: Centre for North-West Regional Studies, University of Lancaster

Bragg, J W 1995 *A Short History of Basford and St Marks Parish Church*

Church of England (Church Congress) 1906 *Guide to the Church Congress and Ecclesiastical Art Exhibition held in Barrow-in-Furness*. London

Cooke, G A 1993 *A History of St. Matthew's Highfield 1867-1993*.

Copeland, B M 1981 *Whittington: The Story of a Country Estate*. Leeds: Maney

Cross Fleury (Rigbye, R G K) 1891 *Time-honoured Lancaster*. Lancaster: Eaton & Bulfield

Fletcher, A M 1923 'The church in Atherton'. *Atherton Parish Magazine*

Hunt, D 1997 *A History of Walton-le-Dale and Bamber Bridge*. Lancaster: Carnegie

Jones, S 1985 *A Guide to Christ Church, Harrogate*

Jones, S 1997 *The History of St George's Church, Stockport 1897–1997*

Kershaw, K 2004 *The History of St Cuthbert's Church Darwen, 1874–2004*. Darwen: St Cuthbert's Church Wardens & PPC

Lambert, S 1991 *Monks, Martyrs and Mayors: The History of Lancaster's Roman Catholic Community and Cathedral 1094–1991*

Leach, F 1872 *Barrow-in-Furness, its Rise and Progress; with Brief Sketches of its Leading Industries*. Barrow-in-Furness: Daily Times Office

Lunn, J 1971 *History of Atherton*. Atherton: Atherton District Council

Mannex & Co, P 1882 *History & Directory of Furness and Cartmel*. Preston

Ockenden, M 2002 *Tower and Steeple: The Story of Ormskirk Parish Church*. Ashby de la Zouch: Ashby de la Zouch Museum

Pollard, J 2000 'Historical outline 1875–2000' *in* Anne Cooper (ed) *St Margaret's, Burnage: Celebration 125*

Pickford, C J 1987 *The Steeple, Bells, and Ringers of Coventry Cathedral*. Bedford: C J Pickford

Richardson, J 1880 *Furness, Past and Present: Its History and Antiquities*, vol 2. Barrow-in-Furness: J Richardson

Richardson, J 1881 *Barrow-in-Furness: Its History, Development, Commerce, Industries and Institutions*. Barrow-in-Furness: J Richardson

Trescatheric, B 1985 *How Barrow was Built*. Barrow-in-Furness: Hougenai

Walmsley, C 1986 'A history of Saint Mark's Church, Witton 1836–1986', illustrated typescript. Blackburn: Blackburn Central Library

Whalley, M & R 1990 *The Parish Church of St Silas, Blackburn*

INDEX

Figures in **bold** refer to illustrations, their captions and diagrams.

Places are all in modern-day Lancashire or are well-known towns and cities unless otherwise specified.

All churches are Anglican unless otherwise indicated.

A

Abberley (Worcs), St Mary 237
Abbeystead
  bridge 38
  school 218
Abbott & Co, stained glass makers 204
Abram (Me), St John the Evangelist 186, **187**, 254
Accrington, St Peter's vicarage 243
Acton (Ch), St Mary 137, 242, 250
Ainslie, Wilfred, pupil 199
Airton (NY), Newfield Hall 217
Alderley (Ch), St Mary 229, 247
Aldford (Ch), St John the Baptist 219
Aldingham (CuL), St Cuthbert 256, 259
Allithwaite (CuL), St Mary and associated buildings 220
Alsager (St), St Mary Magdalene 159, **159**, 235, 241, 254
Altham, St James 259
Altrincham (Ch)
  St Alban 161, **162**, 243
  St George 241–2
Ambleside (CuL), St Mary 241, 250
Appleby (CuW), church 219
Apthorp, Sarah, mother of EGP 49, 50, 51, 81, 207
Arkholme
  St John the Baptist 243
  schools 222
  vicarage 232
Arnside (CuW)
  St James 248, 252
  vicarage 224
Ashford (Kent), Christ Church 86, **87**, 222
Ashton-in-Makerfield (GM), St Thomas 252
Askham (CuL), station **123**, 229
Armstrong, Walter Thomas, pupil, 200–1
Ashton, 1st Baron, (James Williamson), Lancaster industrialist 168
Atherton (GM)
  St Anne, Hindsford 161, 243
  St John the Baptist 111–12, **111–12**, 230, 238, 249
  St Michael & All Angels, Howe Bridge 107, **107**, **108**, 229, 249, 251, 255
Atkinson, John Bownas, architect, York 54
Aughton, St Saviour 220, 248
Austin, Anne (Annie, née Crow), wife of Tom 82, **84**
Austin, Bernard Tate, son of HJA 6, 174
Austin, Fanny, (née Langshaw), wife of HJA 88, **88**, **89**, **91**
Austin, Geoffrey Langshaw, son of HJA 6, 176–7, **177**
Austin, George Brougham, of Australia, brother of HJA 84
Austin, Hubert James **88**, **89**, **136**, **176**
  addresses 85, 88, 89, **89**, **90**, **91**, 177, 231
  attribution of designs to 90, 153, 163, 172, 209, 240, 241
  character 6, 87
  churchmanship 5, 87–8
  competition assessor 230, 240
  competition entrant 90, 101, 104
  death 177
  early influence on the firm's architecture 75–6, 91–2, **92**
  early education 85
  family background 80–1, 85
  interests 87–9, **91**
  joins EGP 76, 87
  John O'Gaunt Sketchbook 86, 90–1
  marriage 88, **88**, **89**, 173
  Paley family, links to 81, 88
  Pugin student 86, 102, 104
  reputation 1
  Scott, G G, assistant to 2, 85
  Sharpe family, links to 88
  Spring Gardens Sketchbook 46, 85–6, **86**, 98
  training 85–6
  travels 102
Austin, Jane, (née Smurthwaite), grandmother of HJA 80
Austin, Jane Eliza, (née Tate), first wife of HJA's father 80, **82**
Austin, Jane Margaret, (née Brougham), mother of HJA 81, 85, **85**
Austin & Paley
  aisles, short **138**, 141, 157
  angular forms 159, **159**, 182–3, **186**
  apsidal east ends to churches 141, **143**
  Art Nouveau details 150, **150**, **156**
  asymmetry in church architecture 143
  canted east ends to churches **167**, **184**, **185**, **186**
  chequerwork, use of 102, **102**, **103**, 167
  churches, numbers of 136
  competition assessors 247
  competition entrants 172, 248
  foundation stone design **160**, **183**
  inscription panels on churches 149, **150**, 167, 183
  mullions, double 112, **112**, 155, 167
  panelled piers/responds 165, 167, **168**
  Perpendicular style 149, **149**, **150**, **151**, **152**, **154**
  polygonal porches, use of 102
  reputation 1, 161–2, 178, 186
  vaulting, use of 155
Austin, Paley & Austin **177**
Austin, Thomas, grandfather of HJA 80
Austin, Revd Thomas, father of HJA 41, 80–1, **81**, **83**, 85, **85**, 207
Austin, Thomas (Tom), half-brother of HJA 31, 41, 44, 81–4, **82**, **83**, **84**, 85, 207, 213

B

Bacup, Christ Church 58, 216
Baines, Thomas, assistant and surveyor 199
Bakewell (Derbys), fountain 238
Balderstone, St Leonard 246
Balterley (St), All Saints' mission church 244
  Bamber Bridge, St Saviour, Cuerden, and schools 19, 21, **22**, 210, 223
Barbon (CuW), St Bartholomew 137, **138**, 239
  war memorial 250
Bardsea (CuL), school 68, 215
Barlow, Luke, pupil and assistant 199–200
Barnacre
  All Saints 143, **145**, 246, 255
  parsonage 248,
Barnton (Ch), Christ Church 25, 35, 256
Barrow, John William, pupil and assistant 201
Barrow-in-Furness 71–3, 119–21
  Abbey Approach, cottages **124**, 125, 226
  'Abbot's Wood' **73**, 73–4, 79, 218, 227, 233, 239
  Adelaide Street, cottages 234
  Barrow Flax & Jute Co 72, 119–20, **120**, 224
  Barrow Haematite Steel Co 102
  Barrow Island, cottage 232
  Barrow Island, hotel 234
  Barrow Shipbuilding Co, entrance and lodge 236
  Butler, Thomas, villa for 237
  cemetery **120**, 227
  Cambridge Street schools 228, 231
  Cavendish Park villas 257
  Central Station 257
  Concle Inn, Ramside 125, 236
  Cumberland Union Bank 226
  'Dale Ghyll', Hawcoat 256
  Devonshire Dock Road, hotels **124**, 234, 235
  Exchange Hall 234
  Ferry Road, hotel 234
  ferry station 232
  Furness Abbey station and hotel

123, 214, 226, 232, 256
Holker Street, hotel 234
Hydraulic engine house 229
Lancaster Banking Co premises **120**, 226, 237
market hall 221
Masonic Hall 234
Michaelson Road, villas 232
Michaelson Road, coffee tavern 233
Millwood House 229
North Lonsdale Hospital 170–1, 224, 233–4, 238, 242, 243, 245
'Oak Lea', house for H W Schneider 73, 227
Piel Castle, restoration 257
Piel Island, cottages 257
Ramsden Dock station etc 257
Ramsden Square 72, 120, 121, 199, 225, 226
Roa Island, house for H W Schneider 73, 257
Roose Road, hotel 234
Royalty Theatre (Star Music Hall) 224–5
St George and associated buildings 59, **59**, 218–19, 222, 232, 234
St George's Square, dwellings and railway offices 256
St James 62, 74–5, **74**, **75**, 90, 222
St James's schools 221, 234
St Mary, Walney Island 164, **165**, 216, 246–7, 252–3
School of Art 234
'shipworks for Ashburner' 257
'shipworks', unspecified 256
Strand, houses etc 234
Strand station 74, 220
temporary churches (St Matthew, St Mark, St Luke, St John and associated buildings) 108, **108**, 229, 233, 234, 236, 237
tenement blocks 121, **121**, 227
Thwaites Flat, cottages 234
Town Hall 121–2, 229
Trinity Presbyterian church 227
Victoria Hall 232
Barthomley (Ch), St Bertoline 251
Barton-on-Irwell (GM), schools 256
Basford (St), St Mark 249, 250, 251
Baynes, Christopher, builder 202, 204, 215, 219, 220, 222, 225, 228, 229, 232
Becconsall (aka Hesketh), All Saints 181, 251, 254
Becket, Richard Thomas, pupil 200
Bective, Earl of, client and governor of Sedbergh School 131, 133, 221, 226, 231, 239
Beetham (CuW), St Michael & All Angels 251, 257
war memorial 249
Bent, Baldwin Harry, client 71, **72**, 218
Bertwistle, James, architect, Blackburn 129
Betws-y-Coed (Caernarvonshire), St Mary 101, **101**, 209, 226, 246
Bickerton (Ch), Holy Trinity 23, 31, 211
Billington, St Leonard 100, **101**, 230, 243
Bilsborrow
St Hilda **182**, 182–3, 251
vicarage 252
Birkdale (Me), St John 117, **118**, 148, 237, 247
Bishopton (D), St Peter 82, 214
Blackburn
Bishop's chapel 253
Holy Trinity 26–7, **29**, **30**, 47, 211, 219
Market Place, new 213
St James 243
St Mark, Witton 20–1, **20**, **21**, 22, 210, 233, 246
St Silas 112, 159–60, **160**, 241, 248, 249
St Thomas 221
schools 216
Blackpool
St John 228
St Stephen-on-the-Cliffs **181**, 181–2, **182**, 251
St Thomas 184, 186, **186**, 253
Blades, Charles, builder, carpentry 202, 203, 214, 216, 219, 220, 221, 222, 223, 224, 225, 231, 236, 237, 238, 239
Blawith (CuL), St John the Baptist 220, 237, 249, 251
Blundellsands (Me), St Nicholas 225
Bodley, George Frederick, architect 83, 162, 163
Boisserée, Sulpiz, architectural scholar 13, 17, 18
Bolton (GM)
All Souls 112–13, **113**, 230–1, 250
Deane, church 248
Evangelical traditions 107
Heaton, church 248
St George 247
St Margaret, Halliwell 164, **166**, 183, 248, 254, 255
St Peter 66, **67**, 68, 215, 222, 229, 236
St Saviour 112–13, **114**, 233, 255
St Stephen & All Martyrs *see* Lever Bridge
St Thomas, Halliwell 66, 106–7, **106**, 227, 253
Bolton-by-Bowland
St Peter & St Paul 235
school 227, 246
Bolton-le-Sands, St Michael/Holy Trinty 214, 215, 232, 242, 255, 257
Boot (CuC), St Catherine 232
Bootle (CuC)
St Michael 136, 238
station 257
village cross 4
Borwick, St Mary 139, 241
Bowness (CuW), St Martin 224
Bowness-on-Solway (CuC), St Michael 257
Bottesford (Leics), St Mary the Virgin 208, 214
Bradford (WY)
Holy Trinity **62**, 63, 221, 225
St Margaret, Thornbury 248
Bradshaw, Jonas James, architect, Bolton 112, 225, 231
Bradshaw (GM), St Maxentius 226
Brassingtons, builders, Settle (NY) 205, 235, 238, 241, 245, 247, 249, 251, 252, 254
Brathay (CuC), Holy Trinity 245
Bretherton, St John the Baptist 25, **27**, 211, 242, 247, 253
Bridgeman, Robert, (& Sons), carvers, Lichfield (St) 151, 205, 206, 237, 239, 240, 241, 242, 243, 239, 250, 253
Bridlington Priory (EY) 37–8, **39**, 214
Briercliffe, St James the Great 24, 25, **25**, **26**, 212
Brindle, St James 259
Brinkburn Priory, Northumberland 83
Broadhurst, Frances, (née Whittaker), wife of Thomas, school in Bath 7
Broadhurst, Revd Thomas, Unitarian minister, uncle of ES 93
Brookhouse *see* Caton
Brooks, James, architect 150, 162, 208
Brougham, Jane Margaret, mother of HJA 81, 85, **85**
Broughton (near Preston), St John the Baptist 246, 253
Broughton-in-Furness (CuL)
'Eccle Riggs' 221
St Mary Magdalene 227, 244
Brown, W Talbot, assistant to ES 46, 91, 198
Brunton, James, benefactor 75
Buccleuch, 5th Duke of **67**, 72, 74, 102, 108, 212, 219, 229, 235, 257
Burlington, 2nd Earl of 72, 74 *see also* Devonshire, 7th Duke of
Burlison & Grylls, stained glass makers 136, 204, 231, 233, 235, 236,
Burney, Dr Charles Parr, headmaster 9, **82**
Burnley
St Andrew 242
St James 223
St Matthew, Habergham Eaves 229, 252, 254
St Peter 217, 256
Burton-in-Kendal (CuW)
Dalton Hall 218
St James 225, 249
Burton-in-Lonsdale (NY)
All Saints 223
parsonage 223
Bury (GM)
All Saints, Elton 219
Holy Trinity, 66, **66**, 220, 258
St Mary 240
St Paul 242
Butler, Samuel, headmaster, Shrewsbury School 49, 81, 207, 208
Butterfield, William, architect 92
Buxton (Derbys), St James 241

C

Calder Bridge (CuC), St Bridget 58, 207, 212
Calvert & Heald, plumbers & glaziers 202, 203, 232, 237, 239, 240, 241, 242, 246
Cambridge Camden Society 32, 49, 56, 57
Cambridge, St John's College 8, 10, **33**, 50, 51
Capel Garmon (Denbighshire), St Garmon 209, 220
Capernwray Hall 38–40, **41**, **42**, 131, 213, 218, 221, 228
chapel 38–9, 212
Carill-Worsley, Thomas, client 36, 214
Carlisle (CuC), Grammar School/ Board School competition(s) 232, 234
Carnforth
regimental HQ 252
station 232
Cartmel (CuL)
Aynsome Agricultural Experimental Station 244
Priory (St Mary) 222, 224, 235,

238, 240, 250, 252
schools 218
Casterton (CuW)
Casterton School 4, 173, 241, 252, 258
Holy Trinity 219, 238, 242
Caton
Co-operative Society shop 244
Crook of Lune, bridge over River Lune 53, **53**, 233
institute 251
Littledale Hall, Brookhouse 41, 256
'Moor Cottage'/'Neville House' 249
'Moorgarth', Brookhouse, house of EGP and HAP 51–2, **52**, 135, 178, 224
St Paul 52, 58, 187, 221, 245
war memorial 250
Cavendish, Evelyn 141
Cavendish, Lord Frederick 73, 108, 133, 229, 235
Cavendish, Lucy 141
Cavendish, Victor 141
Cavendish, William (Burlington, 2nd Earl of) 72
see also Devonshire, 7th Duke of
Chadderton (GM), St Luke 236
Chance, Arthur Frederick, client, master Shrewsbury School 173, 176, 208, 249
Chatburn, Christ Church 23, 210
Chorley
St Laurence 259
town hall 225
Christian, Ewan, as competition assessor 98, 104, 110, 118, 148, 152, 172, 208, 224, 227, 238, 240
Christie-Miller, Wakefield, benefactor of St George, Stockport 153, 239
Christ's Hospital, school
London 49–50, 152, 208
Horsham (W Sussex) 152, 172, **172**, 208, 240
Churchmanship 4–5, 28, 36, 57, 112–13, 155
Churchtown, St Helen 222
Clapham (NY), school 220
Clarke, Somers, architect, Egyptologist, and friend of HJA 85, 88, **88**, 91
Claughton
rectory 218
St Chad 223, 245
Clayton & Bell, stained glass makers/ecclesiastical decorators 222, 231
Clerks of Works, named 210, 213, 220, 221, 222, 223, 225, 227, 228, 230, 231, 232, 233, 235, 237, 239, 241, 244, 247, 259, 251, 253
Cliff & Son, Wortley, Leeds, terracotta manufacturers 38, 228
Clifton, St John the Evangelist 226
Clitheroe
St Mary Magdalene 257
Standen Hall 218
Cloughfold, St John
see Rawtenstall
Cockerham
schools 218
St Michael 247–8, 253
vicarage 41, 212
Cockermouth (CuC), St Michael 259
Collyhurst (GM), church etc 225
Colne, St Bartholomew 136, 238
Colton (CuL), Holy Trinity 259
Commission des Monuments historiques, France 17
Conishead (CuL), station **122**
Coniston (CuL), station 256
Conistone (NY), St Mary 213
contracting, methods of 23, **23**, 202
Corney (CuC), St John the Baptist 233
Cound (Salop), St Peter 238
Coventry
St Barbara, Earlsdon 183, **185**, 208, 253
St Barnabas 184, 208, 253
St Michael 152–3, **152**, 208, 239
St Thomas 209, 215
Cowgill (CuWY), St John the Evangelist 23, **24**, 210
Craven Dunnill, tile manufacturers 231
Crawshawbooth, St John
see Rawtenstall
Crayke (NY), St Cuthbert 220
Crewdson, William Dillworth, memorial church to **xii**, 143, 247
Crewe (Ch), St Barnabas 117, **117**, 235
Crewe Green (Ch), St Michael 255
Crook of Lune, 'The Hermitage' 215
Cross family of Bolton, clients 66, 106, 227–8
Cross family of Lancaster, slaters & plasterers 203, 214, 215, 216, 217, 218, 219, 224, 228, 229, 232, 236, 237, 239, 240, 241, 242, 243, 245, 246, 247, 248
Cross-a-Moor, Swarthmoor, Ulverston (CuL), war memorial 250
Crosscrake (CuW), St Thomas 99, 228

D

Dacre (CuC), 'Ennim Bank' 232
Daisy Hill (GM), St James 114–15, **115**, 231
Dalton-in-Furness (CuL) 71
cemetery 217
Dalton Tower/Castle 69, 217
infants' school 223
National Schools 132
St Mary 102, **103**, 159, 235, 239, 250, 255
Daresbury (Ch), All Saints 96, 97, **97**, **98**, 224
Darwen
mission church 233
St Barnabas 234, 249
St John the Evangelist, Turncroft 66, **66**, 220
Davenham (Ch)
St Wilfrid 31, 212, 256, 257
school 68, 218
Davison, T Raffles, sketches by **97**, **102**, **123**, 125, **132**, 153, **172**, 232, 233, 236
Davyhulme (GM), St Mary 236
Dawson, Pudsey, client 27, 40, 214
De Morgan tiles 231
Dent (CuWY), St Andrew 136, 238
Derby, 12th Earl of 20, 29
Derby, 13th Earl of 19, 20, 29, 32, **34**, **44**, 213, 215
Derby, 14th Earl of, Prime Minister 220, 225
Derby, 15th Earl of 225
Derby, 16th Earl of **132**, 227
Desborough (Co Tipperary)
church 224
Desborough Hall 209, 217
de Vitre, Edward Denis, doctor, Lancaster 75–6, 188
Devonshire, 7th Duke of 72, 74, 90, 102, 108, 125, 133
Dobson, John, architect, Newcastle upon Tyne 83–4
Dodson, Revd John, client 41, 212, 256
Dolphinholme
Wyreside Hall 258–9
St Mark 139–40, **141**, **142**, 242
Douglas (Isle of Man), Christ Church 209, 217
Douglas, John, pupil and assistant, architect, Chester 31, 91, 92, 96–7, 198
Drake, William, links to ES and JWW 216
Duckett, James, builder, Burnley 205, 219, 220, 221
Duckett, Thomas, sculptor and/or builder, Preston 215, 217, 218, 219
Dukinfield (GM), St John the Evangelist 29, 211

E

Early, Thomas, ecclesiastical decorator **61**
Earp, Thomas, sculptor 55
Easingwold (NY) 49, 81, **82**
St John the Baptist 58, 216, 218
East Broughton (CuL)
see Field Broughton
Eaton (Ch), St Thomas 254
Eccles (GM), St Mary the Virgin 241
Ecclesiologist, The 32, 34, 35–6, 37, 44, 47, 57, 198
Ecclesiology 32, 34
Egton-cum-Newland (CuL), St Mary 62, 221
Ellel
'Foxholes' 254
St John 143, 144, 246, 255
schools 218
Eskmeals (CuC), station 232
Euxton, church 227

F

Family tree, Sharpe, Paley and Austin families and connections **x–xi**
Faringdon, St Paul 23, **23**, 211
Farnworth (Me), St Luke 90, 136–7, 235, 241
Fawley (Bucks)
Fawley Court 207, 233, 234
St Mary 207, 233
Fearn, George, patron of St George, Stockport 153, **157**, 239
Feilden family 20, 25, 27, 196
Joseph 10, 20, 21, 26, 210
Mary Haughton, wife of J W Whittaker 8, 10, 20
Fence, 'Hoarstones' 240
Feniscowles, Immanuel 253, 258
Ferguson, Charles James, architect, Carlisle 85, 98, **123**
Field Broughton (aka East Broughton) (CuL) 138–9, **139**, **140**, 240, 245, 248
Finsthwaite (CuL), St Peter 90, 98–9, **99**, 227, 240
Fleetwood 212
bank 246
St Peter 234
Fletcher, Edith, daughter of John, wife of Hardwicke Rawnsley **88**, 173, 240
Fletcher, Elizabeth, wife of ES **10**, 26, 31, **32**, **33**, 37, 47, 66, 107
Fletcher, John, brother-in-law of ES 26, 31, **33**, 34, **35**, 36, 37, 227
Fletcher, Ralph, brother-in-law of

ES **10**, 31, **33**, 107
Flookburgh (CuL), St John the Baptist 103, 141, **143**, **144**, 242
Forsyth, James, sculptor 54–5
Fournessford bridge 38, **41**
Foxfield (CuL), station 231
Fraser, Bishop James, of Manchester 5
Freiburg-im-Breisgau, Germany, Münster 34, **36**
Furness Abbey (CuL) 31
Hotel 40–1, 73
Furness Railway Company 4, 73–4, **74**, 108, 120, 134, 199, 203
buildings for **74**, 122–3, **122–4**, 125

G

Galgate
farmhouse 242
viaduct **190**, 211
Garden, James, builder, Dalton-in-Furness (CuL) 205, 221, 222, 223, 225, 227, 228, 235
Garnett, William, client 219
Garstang,
St Helen 255
St Mary & St Michael (RC), presbytery and schools 4, 56, 58–9, **59**, 218
Gaskell, Mrs Elizabeth, (née Stevenson) 8, 188
Giggleswick (NY)
St Alkelda 136, 238
Giggleswick School 41, 48, 68, 222, 226, 228, 235, 238, 252
Gillow & Co, furniture makers 203, 225, 234, 236, 237
Gillow, Richard Thomas, client 216
Glasson
schools 219, 220
Christ Church 25, 211, 253, 255
Godwin's tiles 54, 221, 224, 225
Goosnargh, St Mary 223, 249
Gosselin, Katharine Margaret, wife of HAP 135
Gradwell, William, builder, Barrow-in-Furness 205–6, 222, 227, 229, 232, 233, 234, 243
Graham family of Netherby (CuC), links with EGP 51
Grappenhall (Ch), St Wilfrid 227
Grange-over-Sands
Grange Hotel 74, 221
parsonage 218
St Paul 234, 253
station 74, **74**, 221
Wesleyan chapel 249
Grasmere (CuW)
'Michael's Fold' 258
St Oswald 231, 247
Great Harwood
St Bartholomew 232
St John 248
Great Ouseburn (NY), St Mary the Virgin 234
Great Salkeld (CuC), St Cuthbert 249
Greenall, Sir Gilbert, client 101, **102**, 131, 222, 224, 233
Greenall, Revd Richard, links to ES 28, 29, 31, 256
Greene, Dawson Cornelius, client 131, 228, 236, 257
Greenhalgh, Nathaniel and Thomas, clients and benefactors, Bolton 112, 113, 230–1, 233
Greenock (Renfrewshire), St John the Evangelist 110, **110**, 209, 230, 242
Greenodd (CuL), station 257
Greenwich Academy, school of ES 9, 10, 49, 82
Grenside, Canon William Bent, friend of HJA 87, 91, 239
Gressingham, St John the Evangelist 219
Grimsargh, St Michael 223
Grindleton, St Ambrose 241, 242
Grüber, Bernhard, German professor of architecture 14, 18
Guizot, François, French Minister of Public Instruction 17

H

Hall, John Compton, assistant 200
Halsall, St Cuthbert 226, 236
Halton
Halton Hall 243
Manor House 242
St Wilfrid 99, 229, 237
war memorial 250
Hampsfield House (CuL) 131, **132**, 167, 232
Hannay, Robert, industrialist, Barrow 73
Harrison, John, manager and architect, P&A's Barrow office 91, 120, **120**, 121, 122, 123, 199, 204, 225, 226, 233, 234, 237
Harrogate (NY)
Christ Church 250
St Andrew, Starbeck **166**, 247
Hatch, James, (& Sons), builders and woodworkers **69**, 127, 146, 151, **152**, **158**, 202, 203–4, 216, 221, 223, 225, 226, 227, 229, 230, 231, 232, 238, 239, 240, 241, 242, 243, 244, 245, 246, 248
Haughton-le-Skerne (D) 81, 85
Haverthwaite (CuL)
station 257
St Anne 247, 255–6
Heidelhoff, Carl Alexander von, architect 14
Hellyer, Thomas, architect, Isle of Wight 31
Henman, William, assistant to ES 198
Hensingham (CuL), vicarage 230
Hertford
All Saints 2, 150–1, **151**, **152**, 208, 240, 245
house for Thomas Joseph Sworder 241
Heversham (CuW)
Heversham House, house of HJA 89, **90**, 243
St Peter 91, **92**, 97, 214, 223, 237, 238, 240, 244
Heysham
'Heysham Tower' 258
rectory 254
shops and houses 248
St Peter 215, 220, 257
Hibbert family, clients **132**, 138, 167, 232, 240
High Bentham (NY), St Margaret 137, 244
Higher Walton (Ch)
St John the Evangelist 101–2, **102**, 233, 236
Walton Hall 131, 224
Hindley (GM)
St Peter 220, 257
schools 219, 226
Hinton, Charles Allen, pupil and assistant 201
Hinton, John Garfield, pupil and assistant 201
Hoddlesden, St Paul and vicarage 219, 229
Hoghton, Sir Henry de, client 127
Hoghton, Sir Charles de, client **128**, 129
Hoghton Tower 127, **127**, **128**, 129, 229, 231
Holcombe (GM), Emmanuel 211
Holker Hall (CuL), 72, **125**, 125–6, **126**, 219, 225
Holland family, links to ES 7–8, 194
Holmrook (CuC), cottages etc 230
Hornby
Castle 40, **43**, 43, 214, 232, 238
court room and police station 228
market cross 217
St Margaret 136, 237
village institute **170**, 171, 249
war memorial 250
Hornby, Revd James John, links to ES 28
Horsham (W Sussex), Christ's Hospital, school 49–50, 152, 172, **172**, 208, 240
Howgill (CuWY), Holy Trinity 23, **24**, 210
Hunt, Arthur William, house for 234
see also Shrigley & Hunt
Hutton Roof (CuW), St John 100, 232

I

Ince-in-Makerfield (GM)
Christ Church **62**, 63, 220
St Mary 148, **148**, 236
Ince Hall (Me) 29, 41, **43**, 214
Ireleth, (CuL), St Mary 66, **67**, 221

J

Jackson, Harold Thomas, architect, Coventry, associate of HAP 184, 253
John O'Gaunt Bowmen 39, 53, 135
Johnson, Richard Wright, pupil of EGP, assistant to ES 199
Johnson, Robert James, partner of Tom Austin 54, 83–4, 85, 91

K

Kearsley (GM), St John the Evangelist 226
Kendal (Cu)
'Heaves' 253
St George 247, 248
Keswick (CuW)
High School 256
School of Industrial Arts 173, 240, 243
Kildwick (WY), St Andrew 216, 226, 231
Kings Worthy Court (Hants), house of HJA 89, **91**
Kirkby (Me), St Chad 92–3, **93**, 224
Kirkby-in-Furness (CuL), vicarage 232
Kirkby Lonsdale (CuW)
fountain 217
house/surgery for Dr Thomas Graham Mathews 246
market cross 258
St Mary the Virgin 221, 250
war memorial 249

Kirkby Malham (NY), St Michael 231
Kirkham
St Michael 34, **34**, 47, 213, 258
vicarage 214
Knowsley
Knowsley Hall 257
St Mary 19, 32, **34**, 213, 219, 225, 239
Knutsford (Ch) 7, 8, 9, **9**, 28, 194
gaol 38, 213
St Cross 116–17, **117**, 232, 236, 237, 246
Kurtz, Charles, benefactor 101, 209, 226

L

Ladyshore Colliery 26, 31, 34, **35**
Lancaster 1, 18, **19**, **50**, **134**, **191**
Alexandra Hotel 259
Athenaeum 53, 189, 217
Blue Coat School (girls') 242
Bowerham, school 242
Brimley, Mgr Canon, administrator St Peter's, garage for 255
Bulk, mission chapel 246
Carriage & Wagon Works 70, **70**, 221
Castle 38, 212, 220, 226
Castle Hill, workshops for Shrigley & Hunt 233
Castle Park 9, 19, 51, 55, **56**, 90, 187
Catholic Apostolic church 228
cemetery buildings/monuments 68, **70**, 217, 218
Centenary Congregational Church 226
Charity School for Girls 215
Christ Church and schools 179, 226, 232, 236, 237, 241, 246, 249, 252
Church Street, bank 248
Church Street, Church House 258
Church Street, E & J L Milner's premises, publishers 243
Church/New Streets, bank and shops 215, 244
Congregational (Independent) Sunday Schools 56, 217
Co-operative Society premises 174, **175**, **176**, 244, 246, 248, 249
Corn Market premises 232
County Hotel 224, 227
County Lunatic Asylum 38, 76, 211, 212, 213, 214, 221
Covell Cross 245
Crimea Memorial 69, **70**, 219
'Croftlands', Westbourne Road, house of HJA 224
'Dallas House', Dallas Road 256
Dallas Place, surgery 245
Damside Street, shop 254
Drill Hall 240, 251
East Road, alterations for the Revd M K Cooper 249
'Fairlight'/'Emmanuel House', Haverbreaks 249
Fenton House, house of ES 19, **88**, 190, 213
fish market **55**, 215
George Street, bank 250
Grammar School 68, **68**, 171, 215–16, 218, 229, 230, 233, 234, 236, 246, 254
Grand, The, (Theatre Royal) 189, **189**
'Greaves House', Greaves Road 213
'The Greaves', Greaves Road, house of EGP 51, 135, 217, 232
Greaves Wesleyan chapel 259
Gregson Memorial, club house etc 237, 245, 248
High Street, Miss Michaelson's cottage 232, 237
Hunt, W, sheds for 238, 241
Independent (Congregational) Sunday Schools 56, 217
Infirmary 168, 170, **170**, 240, 243, 245, 246, 249, 252
King's Arms Hotel 230
'Knoll', 'The', Westbourne Road, house of HJA 88, **89**, 231, 249
Lancaster Banking Co 223
Lancaster Carriage & Wagon Company works 70, **70**, 221
'Longlands', Westbourne Drive, house of Arthur Hunt 234
Lune bridge 211
Lune Road, cricket club pavilion 248
Market Street, bank 248
Market Street/Frances Passage, shop 225
Masonic Hall 256
'Mawdale'/'Rivendell', Westbourne Road 215
Mechanics' Institute 69, 217, 224
Middle Street School 254
militia depot 216
Moor Hospital chapel 222
Music Hall 212, 218
National School (girls) 217
National Schools, St Leonard's Gate 215
Nazareth House 4, **171**, 243
'Netherleigh', Westbourne Road 247
North Road, William Atkinson's premises, 174, **174**, 244
Penny Street, shops and bank 226, 231, 232, 240, 250
Penny's Hospital 252
Phoenix Foundry 192, 216, 221
Phoenix Street, Territorial Army hall 248
Poor Law Union offices 221
practice established in 1, 19
Presbyterian chapel 227
Primrose District mission church 239
Priory Hall (for St Mary's church) 255
Priory Hotel 258
'Quarry Hill'/'Brunton House', Scotforth Road, house of ES 222
Quernmore Road, house 222
Regatta 39, 53
Regent Street, nurses' home 254
Ripley Hospital and chapel 146, **146**, **147**, 235, 236, 238, 240, 242
Royal Albert Asylum 53, 56, 75–7, **76**, **77**, **78**, 79, 87, 90, 222, 232, 237
'Ryelands', Skerton 217, 234
St George 242
St John's National Schools 223
St Leonard's Gate, workshops 234
St Luke, Skerton 241
St Mary, parish church (Priory) 5, 87, 132, 215, 216, 217, 223, 225, 226, 228, 235, 241, 244, 247, 248, 250, 255
St Mary's mission church 246
St Mary's school 231
St Paul, Scotforth *see* Lancaster, Scotforth
St Peter (RC: now Cathedral) and associated work 56, 59, **60**, 61, **61**, 216, 216, 218, 219, 237, 238, 241, 243, 244, 245, 251, 253, 255
St Thomas, and school 212, 216, 241
Scotforth, St Paul, and schools 5, 38, **39**, **40**, 47, 229, 231, 239, 253, 255
Skerton Hotel 239
Skerton, St Luke's schools 252
Skerton, school 244
Springfield Park, lodge 238
Stanmore Drive, house 251
Storey Institute 4, 5, 168–70, **169**, 236–7, 246
Theatre Royal (now The Grand) *see* Lancaster, Grand, The
Town Hall 168, 217, 225
triumphal arches for 1851 royal visit 189, 215
Union Workhouse 212
Upper Church Street, shops 234
Waring & Gillow's showrooms, North Road 257
Wesleyan Chapel and schools 132, 227
'West Bank'/'Parkfield', Greaves Road 256
'Westbourne' 255
White Cross Mills 169, 229
Woodville Street, cottages 234
Workhouse 38
Lancaster & Preston Junction Railway 39, 189–90, 211
Langshaw, Edmund, brother of James Pearson 26
Langshaw, Emily, (née Sharpe), mother of Fanny 8, **10**, **19**, **33**, 88, **88**, **191**
Langshaw, Fanny, wife of HJA 88, **88**, **89**, **91**
Langshaw, George, brother of James Pearson **10**, 26, **29**, 31, **33**, 207
Langshaw, George, brother of Fanny, pupil 88, **88**, 199
Langshaw, James Pearson, father of Fanny 8, **10**, 26, **33**, 51, 88, **88**, 188
Langshaw, John, brother of James Pearson **33**
Langshaw, John, father of James Pearson 26, **67**
Lassaulx, Johann Claudius von Lassaulx, architect and historian 13, 15
Lathom, St James 255
Lawford (Essex), St Mary 207–8, 216
Leck, St Peter 99, 230, 249
Lee, Bishop James Prince, of Manchester 5, 57, 230
Leeds, Grammar School 172–3, **173**, 180, 245, 250, 251
Leigh (GM)
St Mary 95, **95**, **96**, 225, 237, 238, 240, 247
St Peter, Westleigh 115–16, **116**, 231
Leighton Hall 131, **131**, 224
Levens (CuW), St John the Evangelist 254
Lever Bridge, St Stephen & All Martyrs 34–6, **35**, **36**, **37**, 212, 215, 216
Lewis, Neander Gesenius, possible pupil or assistant 173, 201, 209
Leyland, St Andrew 229, 257
Lindale (CuL), Hampsfield House 131, **132**, 167, 232
'Little' North Western Railway 40, 41, 190–2, 214
Littledale Hall *see* Caton
Little Lever (GM), St Matthew

221, 250
Little Ouseburn (NY), Holy Trinity 228
Liverpool
Cathedral 90, 118, 162–4, 163, **163**, **164**, 234–5, 244
Ear & Eye Infirmary 229
St Matthew & St James, Mossley Hill, and vicarage 102, 104, 105, **105**, 224, 227
Livesey, St Andrew 63, **64**, 226
Llandovery College (Carmarthenshire) 173, 209, 244
Llanrwst (Denbighshire) 45, 70, 97, 194, 228, 235
Llansanffraid Glan Conwy (Denbighshire), station 217
Lloyd, Revd Julius, links to EGP's brother Francis Henry 110–11, 209
Lomax-Simpson, James, architect 174, 201, 247
Loyd, Lewis, client 93
Low Bentham (NY), 'The Ridding' 71, **72**, 79, 218
Lowton (Me), St Mary 219
Ludwig I, King of Bavaria 14
Lupton (CuW), All Saints 222
Lutwidge, Charles Robert Fletcher, client 230
Lydiate (Me), St Thomas 248
Lymm (Ch), market cross 242
Lynn, William Henry, architect, Belfast 122
Lytham St Anne's
St Anne 226, 249, 252, 253
St Cuthbert 217, 226, 232, 233, 236, 253
St Thomas 161, **162**, 243, 245
war memorial, St Anne's 250

M

'Malham Tarn House' (NY) 217
Manchester
Cathedral 217
Holy Trinity, Rusholme 36–7, **38**, 47, 213
St John, the Evangelist, Cheetham 93–4, **94**, **95**, 224
St Margaret, Burnage 228, 232, 235, 244, 248, 251
St Mary, Beswick 230
St Wilfrid, Newton Heath, and rectory 68, 165, 247, 248
Manners-Sutton, Archbishop Charles 8, 208
Mansergh (CuW) 100, 231
Marthall (Ch), All Saints 23, 31, 211
Marton, George, MP, client 38, 39, 91
Master, Frances Mary, wife of Joseph Feilden 20
Master, Revd Robert Mosley, links to Feilden family and ES 20, 26
Master, Revd Streynsham, links to Feilden family and ES 26
Mawdesley, St Peter 25, **27**, 211
Mawson, Thomas Hayton, garden designer 247
Meadley, George, biographer of Archdeacon William Paley 81, **82**
medievalism in the 1830s 17
Medlar, Christ Church 256
Melling
'Church Gates' 252
St Wilfrid 220, 239, 242, 253
Mellor, St Mary 137, 242
Melsonby (NY), St James 97, 224
Merimée, Prosper, head of Commission des Monuments historiques, France 17
Merivale, Revd Charles, client, link to ES 207–8, 216
Mickleover (Derbys), house 217
Middleton, John, architect, Darlington 83
Middleton (GM), St Michael 244, 248, 251
Millom (CuC)
Dunningwell Hall 228
St George 103, 228, 238
station 228
Milne, Charles, pupil and assistant 200
Milnthorpe (CuW), St Thomas 248
Mirfield (WY), St Mary 85, 217
Moller, Georg, architectural scholar 13
Morecambe (Poulton-le-Sands)
Co-operative Society premises 174, 249
Holy Trinity 212, 222, 228, 242
Independent chapel 56, **56**, 220
Mission church 237
North Western Hotel 41, 214
rectory 230
St Barnabas 160, **161**, 243, 245, 248
St Christopher, Bare 254
St John the Divine, Sandylands 243
St Lawrence and associated buildings 229, 233, 240, 243
school and house 216
station 227
war memorial 250
Wesleyan chapel 259
Morris, (Marshall, Faulkner) & Co, stained glass makers 55, 204
'mountain chapel' competition 90
Muthesius, Hermann, architectural critic 1, 61, 79, **140**, **149**, **150**, **155**, 157, 161–2

N

Natland (CuW), St Mark **xii**, 143, **145**, 247, 254
Newland, Newland Hall 247, 248
Newton, Newton Hall 232
Newton-le-Willows (Me), St John the Baptist 251, 253
Noble, Matthew, sculptor 72, 225
North Western Railway, ('Little') 40, 41, 190–2, 214
Northwich (Ch)
Holy Trinity 29, **31**, 212
St Helen 234

O

Oldham (GM), St Stephen 254
Ormrod, Peter, client 66, 99–100, **100**, 218, 222, 229, 231
Ormskirk, St Peter & St Paul 218, 230, 231, 232, 233, 236, 238
Orrell (Me)
St Luke 183, **183**, 253, 255
vicarage 261
Osgodby (EY), Osgodby Hall 258
Osmotherley (CuL), St John the Evangelist 99, 227
Over Kellett
farmhouse 223
St Cuthbert 220, 247
Over Peover (Ch), St Laurence 256
Overton
St Helen 244–5
vicarage 237
Over Wyresdale
bridge 214
war memorial, Tarnbrook 250

P

Paley & Austin
addresses 90, 120, 199, 217
aisles, short, use of 138, **138**, **142**
angular design features 102, 103
asymmetry in church architecture 112, 146, **146**, 157
bare walling in churches internally 104
Barrow-in-Furness office 71, 120, 199
bell-turrets, use of **100**, **104**, **115**, **118**
brick, use of for churches 106, **106**, 108, **109**, **110**, **113**, **115**, **116**, **117**, **118**, 119
central towers for churches 92, **93**, **99**, **100**, **102**, **116**, **137**, **138**, **139**, **140**, **141**
chequerwork, use of **102**, **103**
competition entrants 98, **99**, 104, 118, 148, 151, 152, 161, 162, 208, 209, 225, 226, 227, 229, 234–5, 236, 243
flushwork, use of 102, 104
John O'Gaunt Sketchbook 86, 90–1
logo **91**
mountain chapel competition 98, **99**
mullions, detached, use of **112**
muscularity in work of, *c* 1870 91, **92**, **93**, **94**, **101**, 103
office organisation 90
partnership formed 87
Perpendicular revival 57–8, **57**, 94–7, **96**, **97**
polygonal porches, use of 103
range of work 3–4
reputation 1, 119, 134, 135, 161–2
responsibility for/attribution of designs 90, 98, 102, 104
terracotta, use of 108, **109**, **110**, 114, **115**, 117, **117**
Paley, Austin & Paley 135
Paley, Edmund, father of EGP 49, 50, 81, **82**
Paley, Edmund Graham, son of EGP 52, 53, 135
Paley, Edward Graham **48**, **79**, **136**
addresses 19, 51–2, **52**, 55, **56**, **169**, 224, 232
architectural reputation 56, 77, 79
Bridgemaster of the South Lonsdale Hundred 53
character 6, 52
children 52, 53
churchmanship 5, 52, 57
competition assessor 225, 228, 234, 237
continental tours **54**, 54–5, 83
death 54, 135–6, **136**
education 49–50
family background 48–51
first names, choice and use of 51
Freemason 53, 76
interests 52–4
joins ES 19, 31
marriage **33**, 48, 51, **52**, 55
offices 19, 55, **56**
partner of ES 48, 55
pupil of ES 51, 54

range of work 3–4, 68, 79
reputation 1, 77, 79, 162
RIBA, involvement with 54
Sharpe family, links with 50–1
structural polychromy, little use of 62–3
stylistic characteristics 62–3, 66, **75**, 79
town councillor 52
Tate family, links with 81
variety of commissions 68–9
vaulting in churches 107, **107**, 108
Paley family, links with the Buck and Whittaker families 51
Paley, Frances, (née Sharpe), wife of EGP 8, **33**, 48, **52**, 55
Paley, Revd Francis Henry, brother of EGP 111, 209, 225
Paley, Frederick Apthorp, brother of EGP 49, 54, 207, 208
Paley, Henry (Harry) Anderson 6, 48, 80, 89–90, 135, 178–87, **179**
Paley, John Green, industrialist, Bradford 51
Paley, Katherine Margaret (née Gosselin), wife of HAP 135
Paley, Richard, entrepreneur, Leeds 50
Paley, Robert, doctor in Halifax **10**, 51
Paley, Sarah, (née Apthorp), mother of EGP 49, 50, 81, 207
Paley, Thomas, of Halifax, contemporary of ES 10, **10**, 51, 207
Paley, William, headmaster 48–9
Paley, Archdeacon William 49, **49**, 81, **82**, 207
Park, Eliza Jane, (née Yates), daughter of godfather of ES 29, 41
Park, Revd William Waldegrave, husband of Eliza Jane 29
Parker, John Henry, publisher 45
Paxton, Joseph, garden designer and architect 72
Pearson, John Loughborough, architect 93–4, 161
Peel, Sir Robert, Prime Minister, and his father **33**
Pendleton (GM), St James 250
Pennington (CuL), St Michael 251, 254
Penrith (CuC)
'Burbank House', 250
Carleton Hall 254
Penwortham, St Mary 217
Perkin, Joseph Craddock, pupil 200
Perpendicular Revival 57–8, **57**, 94–7, **96**, **97**
Petit, John Louis, architectural writer and critic 32, 45
Pevsner, Sir Nikolaus vi, 1, 29, 34, 66, 75, 79, 93, 104, 106, 113, 114, 115, 125, 126, 137, 144, 149, 151, 157, 159
Pilling
St John the Baptist 137, **137**, **180**, 235, 250
schools 218
vicarage 245
Poole, Henry, & Sons, sculptors 55
Poulton-le-Fylde, St Chad 254, 256, 259
Preesall, St Oswald 143, **145**, 243
Prestolee (GM), Holy Trinity 213–14
Preston
All Saints 217
Christ Church 254, 255
St George 213, 215
St John 250
St John the Divine 217, 218, 251, 252, 253
St John the Evangelist 218
St Mark 62, **63**, 220
St Mary Magdalene, Ribbleton 255
St Matthew 253
St Michael & All Angels, Ashton-on-Ribble 164, **167**, 246, 249, 254
St Thomas **21**
Preston Patrick (CuW), St Patrick 57, **57**, 95, 216, 239
Prestwich (GM)
St Mary 237
church, unnamed [first plan for St Hilda] 242
Pudsey (WY), St James 258
Puttrich, Dr Ludwig, architectural scholar 15

Q

Quernmore, St Peter 62, **62**, 219

R

Ralph, William Chasen, pupil and assistant 199
Ramsden, Sir James, Barrow magnate and client 72, **73**, 91, 108, 120, **120**, 218, 227, 229, 233, 238
Rawnsley, Canon Hardwicke, family connection to ES and HJA 173, 240
Rawtenstall
St John, Cloughfold 148–9, 238
St John, Crawshawbooth 149, **149**, 238, 253
St Paul, Constable Lee 244
Read, St John the Evangelist 258
Redmarshall (D)
rectory 41, 81–2, **84**, 207, 213
St Cuthbert **83**, 207, 213, 258, 259
Rhodes (GM), All Saints 257
Ribby-cum-Wrea, St Nicholas, Wrea Green 215, 235, 253
Rickman, Thomas, architect and architectural historian 11, **11**, 12, 14, 18, 45, 49
Richmond (NY) 80
St Mary, 85
School 81, **81**, **82**, 85
Ringley (GM), St Saviour 215
Rishworth (WY), St John the Divine 250–1
Rochdale (GM), Christ Church 255
Roddis, John, sculptor 104, 205, 206, 224, 225, 229, 231, 233
Romanesque Revival 21–2
Rossall School 68, **69**, 165, 173, 219, 222, 235, 242, 243, 245, 257, 259
Runcorn (Ch), Christ Church, Weston Point 212
Rusholme, Holy Trinity
see Manchester
Ruskin, John, art critic 44, 173
Rylstone (NY), St Peter 58, **58**, 95, 216

S

St Bees School (CuC) 136, 147, 173, 235, 236, 246, 247
St Helens (Me)
All Saints, Sutton 150, 239
St Nicholas, Sutton 214, 257–8
St John's Chapel (D), Town Hall 223
St John in the Vale (CuC), St John 240
Salesbury, orphanage 237
Salford (GM)
St Clement, Ordsall 108, **109**
St James, Broughton 103, 109, **110**, 230
Sandbach (Ch), St Mary 252, 254
Sandside (CuL), station 228
Satterthwaite, Benjamin, uncle of ES 1, 9, 10, 18, 51
Satterthwaite, Esther (née Whittaker), wife of Benjamin 1, 9, 51
Satterthwaite, Thomas, son of Benjamin and Esther 51
Satterthwaite, William, father and son, links to EGP and HJA 224, 256
Saunders, William Allen Francis, client 70
Scarborough (NY)
All Saints' schools 208, 232
St James and associated buildings **104**, 208, 235, 240, 241
Schneider, Henry William, Barrow, industrialist and client 72–3, 98, 102, 108, 122, 131, 196, 225, 227, 229, 235, 257
Schneider, Hannay & Co, Barrow 74, 219
Schweighaeuser, Professor Jean Geoffroy, architectural scholar 15
Scorton
St Peter 99, **100**, 102, 231, 236
schools 232
Wyresdale Hall 66, 100, 218, 231
Scotforth, St Paul
see Lancaster, Scotforth
Scott, Sir George Gilbert, architect 2, 4, 27, 32, 34, 44, 45, 46, 54, 58, 79, 83, 85, 86, 90, 91, 161, 214
Seascale (CuC)
house additions 233
railway buildings 123, **123**, 230, 233
villa 234
Seathwaite (CuC), Holy Trinity 259
seating, church, with doors 58
Sedbergh (CuWY)
St Andrew 136, **136**, 235–6, 237
Sedbergh School 4, 8, 10, **10**, 23, 43, 50, 51, **82**, 133, **133**, 146–7, **147**, 148, 172, **173**, 180, 228, 230, 235, 237, 238, 241, 244, 245, 248, 249, 250, 251, 252, 253, 254
Sedgwick, Adam, geologist 11, 23, 210
Sedgwick House (CuL) 129, **129–30**, 223
Sedgwick, Stephen, benefactor 23, 210
Sefton, 4th Earl of, benefactor 93, 224
Settle (NY), Music Hall 68, **70**, 216
Sharpe, Sir Alfred, son of ES, Governor of Nyasaland (Malawi) 31, 46, 215
Sharpe, Edmund **7**, **20**, **46**, 188–96
addresses 9, 19, 45, 213, 222
Architectural Association, involvement with 45–6
Architectural Parallels 31, 43–4, **44**, 46, 54, 86
Architecture of the Cistercians 46
architectural writer 31, 43–5,

44, 46, 47
Austin family, links to 81
Bridgemaster of the South Lonsdale Hundred 38
Cambridge Camden Society, membership of 32
character/interests 6, 39, 47, 188
churchmanship, Low 5, 38, **40**, 47, 188
continental tour 12–18, **12**, **16**
contracting, methods of 23, **23**
death 46–7
Decorated Windows 31, 44
divided east windows, use of 26–7, **30**
early life 8–9, **9**
early architectural success 19–20, 28, 32
Ecclesiology, and 32, 34, 35–6, 37
education 8–9, 10–12
electoral reformer 196
establishment of practice 19
family background 7–8
Fletcher family, links with 26, 31, **33**
Geneva tramways 194–5, **195**
Gothic architecture, and origins of 17–18
Langshaw family, links with 26, 31, **33**
marriage 31, **32**
memorial book to 45–6, **46**
North Wales, move to 45, 55, 101, 194
Perpignan-Prades railway 195–6, **196**
'pot'churches
see terracotta, use of
railway builder 39, 40, 45, 189–92, **190**, 194–6, **195**, **196**
reputation, architectural 34, 47
retires from architectural practice 48
RIBA Royal Gold Medal, award of 7, 12, 44, 46, 47
Romanesque style, use of **20**, **21**, 21–22, **22**, **23**
sanitary reformer 192–4, **193**
Seven Periods of English Architecture, The 44–5
terracotta, use of 34–8, **35**, **36**, **37**, **38**, **39**, 47
Worts Travelling Bachelorship 11, 12
Sharpe, Edmund, son of ES 45
Sharpe, Elizabeth, (née Fletcher), wife of ES **10**, 26, 31, **32**, **33**, 36, 47, 66, 107
Sharpe, Emily, sister of ES and mother-in-law of HJA 8, **10**, **19**, **33**, 88, **191**
Sharpe, Frances, sister of ES and wife of EGP **33**, 48, **52**, 55, 88
Sharpe, Francis, father of ES 7, 8, 9
Sharpe, Francis, son of ES, son-in-law of EGP 31, 192, 196
Sharpe, Marianne, sister of ES **9**, 28
Sharpe, Martha, (née Whittaker), mother of ES 1, 7, **8**, 9, 10, **10**
Sharpe & Paley 48, 55–6
competition entrants 213
Sharpe, Paley and Austin practices, general
country house work 4
geographical spread of work 2, 3, **3**, 56
non-Anglican church work 4, 56
office, location of, in Lancaster 55, **56**
organisation of office 6
range of architectural work 3–4, 48, 56
records of 5–6
reputation 1, 5, 47
timeline **2**
Shaw, Richard Norman, architect 152, 162, 208, 239, 244
Shrewsbury
St Mary 208, 235
School 49, 81, 173, 176, 207, 208, 248–9, 257
Shrigley & Hunt, stained glass makers 5, **83**, 204–5, 225, 227, 231, 233, 234, 237, 238, 239, 240, 241, 244, 245, 253, 254
Silverdale
St John 241
village institute 246
Singleton
St Anne 219, 249, 254, 255, 258
school 220
Skelmersdale (Me), St Paul 245, 246, 248, 250
Skidmore, Francis, metalworker, Coventry 216
Skipton (NY)
Ermysted's Grammar School 228, 233
Holy Trinity 247, 251
Slaidburn
'central school' 255
villa 69, 218
Slinger, John Bowness, assistant 178, 201
Slyne
'Beaumont Cote' 251
St Luke 140–1, 243
Smith, Thomas Roger, architect 45, 54
Southport (Me), Holy Trinity 251, 254
Spalding (Lincs), St Mary & St Nicholas 239
Spennithorne (NY) 80, **83**
Spring Gardens Sketchbook 46, 85–6, **86**, 98
Stainforth (NY), St Peter 211, 255
Staining, school-chapel 221
Stalmine
cemetery chapels 68–9, **70**, 217
St James 225, 234, 238
vicarage 224
Stalybridge (GM), St George 28, 29, **31**, 211
Standish (GM)
Grammar School 254
St Wilfrid 249, 251, 253, 255
Stanground (Cambs), St John the Baptist 207, 217
Staveley (CuL), St Mary 242
Staveley (CuW)
St James 250, 252
war memorial cross 250
Stockport (GM), St George 90, 112, 153–7, **154**, **155**, **156**, **157**, **158**, 162, **171**, 239, 246, 248, 250
Stockton Heath (Ch), St Thomas 222
Storey family, clients/links to the principals 18, 45, 168–9, 246
Street, George Edmund, architect 54, 88, 111
Sumner, Bishop John Bird, of Chester 21, 28, 29, 36
Sunderland Point mission church 4, 139, **141**, 241

T

Tarney, James, office manager and architect 178, 187, 200, 250, 251, 255
Tate, Jane Eliza, first wife of HJA's father 80, **81**
Tate, Revd James, junior, headmaster Richmond School, brother of Jane Eliza 83, 85
Tate, Revd James, senior, headmaster Richmond School, father of Jane Eliza 80, 81, **81**, **82**
'Tate's Invincibles' 80
Tatham, St James 136, 236
Tatham Fells
Good Shepherd 137, **137**, 237
parsonage 223
Taylor, William, assistant 198
terracotta for church-building 34–8, **35**, **36**, **37** 108, **109**, **110**, 114, **115**, 117, **117**
Thelwall (Ch), All Saints 223
Thompson, John, surveyor and assistant 201
Thoms, Arthur Ogelvie, builder 204, 245, 246, 247, 248, 249, 251, 252, 253, 254, 255, 259
Thornton, Christ Church 249
Thornton-in-Craven (WY), house 235
Thornton-in-Lonsdale (NY)
St Oswald 223, 254
schools 223
Thornton-le-Fylde, Christ Church 254
Thorpe Thewles (D), Holy Trinity 82, 207, 215
Thurland Castle 131
Thwaites (CuC), St Anne 58, **58**
Tonge
church 256
school 215
Tonge, James Humphreys, pupil and/or assistant 200
Torver (CuL), St Luke 100–1, 235
Thwaites (CuL), St Anne 216
Tunstall
church 246
Thurland Castle 131, 231
'Tunstall House' 254

U

Ulverston (CuL)
Holy Trinity 232, 233
Hydraulic engine house 232
St Mary 221, 226, 245, 250
station 228
Underley Hall (CuW) 131, 226
Unsworth (GM), St George 247
Urswick (CuL) 216

V

Vitet, Ludovic, head of Commission des Monuments historiques, France 17

W

Waddington (WY), St Helen 243, 253
Walmsley (GM), Christ Church 26, **28**, 210
Walsh, Thomas Harrison, assistant 198
Walton (CuC), St Mary 92, 207, 223
Walton Hall (Ch) 101, 258
Walton-le-Dale
All Saints, Higher Walton **62**, 63, 219, 221, 225
All Saints' school 257
St Leonard 221
Warbrick, William, builder 202, 203, 204, 236, 237, 239

Waring & Gillow, furniture makers 203, 257
Warton
'Pringle Head' 253, 254
St Oswald 215, 239
Waterhouse, Alfred, architect 118, 122, 152, 208, 239
Waterloo (Me), Christ Church 149–50, **150**, 239
Weaver Navigation (Ch) 29, 256
churches for 29, **31**, 212, 213, 256
Wennington
'Cravens' 253
Wennington Hall 70–1, **71**, 79, 217
Webster, George, architect, Kendal **125**
Wesham, Christ Church 240, 251, 255
Westham (E Sussex), St Mary 208, 229
Westleigh (GM), St Peter 103, 115–16, **116**, 231
Weston Point (Ch), Christ Church 29
Whalley, Abbey 222
St Mary 238
Whewell, William, architectural writer and polymath 8, 10–12, **11**, 13, 14, 15, 17, 18, 19, 21, 23, 27, 32, 256
Whicham (CuC), St Mary 244
Whitefield (probably GM), church 256
Whitehaven (CuC)
colliery schools 257
Bransty station 226, 232
Whittaker, Esther, elder sister of Martha 1, 9, 51
Whittaker, Frances, younger sister of Martha, school in Bath 7
Whittaker, Martha, mother of ES 1, 7, **8**, 9, 10, **10**
Whittaker, Revd Dr John William, cousin of ES 1, 7–8, **8**, 10, **10**, 11, 20, 21, 25, 26, 27, 28, **29**, 51, **82**, 208, 258
Whittaker, Sarah, (née Buck), mother of J W Whittaker 9, 51
Whittington
St Michael 228
'Pearson House' 257
schools 228
Whittington Hall 131, **133**, 235, 236, 238
Widnes (Me), St Mary, West Bank 112, 165–7, **168**, 247
Wigan (GM)
All Saints 56, 94–5, 213, 219
St Catherine, Scholes 23–4, **25**, **35**, 211
St James, Poolstock 63, **64**, **65**, 220
St Matthew, Highfield 157, 179, 240, 247, 249
St Stephen, Whelley 183, **184**, 255
Williams, Thomas Richard & Evan, sculptors, Manchester 75
Williamson, James, 1st Baron Ashton, Lancaster industrialist 168
Willingdon (E Sussex), St Mary 208, 230
Wilmington (E Sussex), St Mary & St Peter 208, 233
Willis, Professor Robert, architectural writer 32, 45
Willock & Co, E P, terracotta manufacturers **33**, 38, **39**
Willock, Edmund Peel, brother of Elizabeth **33**, 37
Willock, Elizabeth, wife of John Fletcher **33**, 37
Wilson-Patten, John, Baron Winmarleigh, client
see Winmarleigh, Baron, John Wilson-Patten
Windermere (CuW)
'Browhead' 223
'Grange', 'The' 235
'Chapel Ridding' 227
St Mary 225, 232–3
Winmarleigh, Baron, John Wilson-Patten, client 99, **100**, 131, 225, 228, 236
Winmarleigh
Winmarleigh Hall 131, 225
St Luke 99, **100**, 228–9, 236
Winnard, William, & Son, builders, Wigan 205, 220, 223, 230
Winsford (Ch)
Christ Church, Over 29, 213
St Chad, Over 242, 246
Winwick (Ch), St Oswald 224, 252, 253, 254
Withers, Robert Jewell, architect 31, 43, 44, **44**, 81, 189, 198
Witherslack (CuL)
St Paul 237
Witherslack Hall (CuL) 131, **132**, 227
Wolverhampton (St), St Bartholomew, Penn 225
Wood, Walter James, assistant to ES 199
Woodland (CuL)
parsonage 223
St John the Evangelist 221
Woodplumpton, St Anne 243
Worksop (Notts), St Anne 248, 252, 253
Worsthorne, St John the Evangelist 245, 259
Worthington, Thomas, architect 54, 180
Wray, Holy Trinity 25, **26**, 211, 231, 245
Wright, Roger Squires, & Sons, builders & joiners 204, 220, 225, 229, 241, 245, 248, 250, 251, 252, 253, 254
Wright, Samuel, pupil, assistant, surveyor, son of William 91, 133, 200, 240, 259
Wright, William, Clerk of Works 200, 221, 223, 227, 235
Wright, William Oswald, pupil and assistant, son of Samuel 200
Wrightington, St James the Great 58, **59**, 216
Wyresdale Hall, Scorton 66, 100, 218, 231

Y

Yarm (NY), St Mary Magdalene 259
Yates, Edmund, godfather of ES 20, 25, 28, 29, **33**, 41
Yealand Conyers
Leighton Hall 131, **131**
St John 219, 233
St Mary (RC) 56, **57**, 216